To Amaury.

Contents at a Glance

Contents

About the Author

Jeff Friesen is a freelance tutor and software developer with an emphasis on Java (and now Android). In addition to writing this book, Jeff has written numerous articles on Java and other technologies for JavaWorld (www.javaworld.com), informIT (www.informit.com), java.net, DevSource (www.devsource.com), SitePoint (www.sitepoint.com), BuildMobile (www.buildmobile.com), and JSPro (www.jspro.com). Jeff can be contacted via his web site at tutortutor.ca.

About the Technical Reviewers

Paul Connolly is the Director of Engineering for Atypon Systems' RightSuite product line. RightSuite is an enterprise access-control and commerce solution used by many of the world's largest publishing and media companies. Paul enjoys designing and implementing high-performance, enterprise-class software systems. He is also an active contributor in the open-source community.

Prior to joining Atypon Systems, Paul worked as a senior software engineer at Standard & Poor's where he designed and developed key communications systems. Paul is a Sun Certified Java Programmer, Sun Certified Business Component Developer, and a Sun Certified Web Component Developer. Paul lives in Rochester, NY, with his wife Marina and daughter Olivia.

Chád Darby is an author, instructor and speaker in the Java development world. As a recognized authority on Java applications and architectures, he has presented technical sessions at software development conferences worldwide. In his 15 years as a professional software architect, he's had the opportunity to work for Blue Cross/Blue Shield, Merck, Boeing, Northrop Grumman, and a handful of startup companies.

Chád is a contributing author to several Java books, including *Professional Java E-Commerce* (Wrox Press), *Beginning Java Networking* (Wrox Press), and *XML and Web Services Unleashed* (Sams Publishing). Chád has Java certifications from Sun Microsystems and IBM. He holds a B.S. in Computer Science from Carnegie Mellon University.

You can read Chád's blog at www.luv2code.com and follow him on Twitter @darbyluvs2code.

Onur Cinar is the author of *Android Apps with Eclipse*, and *Pro Android C++* with the NDK books from Apress. He has over 17 years of experience in design, development, and management of large scale complex software projects, primarily in mobile and telecommunication space. His expertise spans VoIP, video communication, mobile applications, grid computing, and networking technologies on diverse platforms. He has been actively working with the Android platform since its beginning. He has a B.S. degree in Computer Science from Drexel University in Philadelphia, PA. He is currently working at the Skype division of Microsoft as the Sr. Product Engineering Manager for the Skype client on Android platform.

Acknowledgments

I thank Steve Anglin for contacting me to write this book; Katie Sullivan for guiding me through the various aspects of this project; Tom Welsh and Matthew Moodie for helping me with the development of my chapters; and Paul Connolly, Chád Darby, and Onur Cinar for their diligence in catching various flaws that would otherwise have made it into this book.

Introduction

Smartphones and tablets are all the rage these days. Their popularity is largely due to their ability to run apps. Although the iPhone and iPad with their growing collection of Objective-C-based apps had a head start, Android-based smartphones and tablets with their growing collection of Java-based apps are proving to be a strong competitor.

Not only are many iPhone/iPad app developers making money by selling their apps, many Android app developers are also making money by selling similar apps. According to tech web sites such as The Register (www.theregister.co.uk/), some Android app developers are making lots of money (www.theregister.co.uk/2010/03/02/android_app_profit/).

In today's challenging economic climate, perhaps you would like to try your hand at developing Android apps and make some money. If you have good ideas, perseverance, and some artistic talent (or perhaps know some talented individuals), you are already part of the way toward achieving this goal.

> **Tip** A good reason to consider Android app development over iPhone/iPad app development is the lower startup costs that you will incur with Android. For example, you don't need to purchase a Mac on which to develop Android apps (a Mac is required for developing iPhone/iPad apps); your existing Windows, Linux, or Unix machine will do nicely.

Most important, you will need to possess a solid understanding of the Java language and foundational application programming interfaces (APIs) before jumping into Android. After all, Android apps are written in Java and interact with many of the standard Java APIs (e.g., threading and input/output APIs).

I wrote *Learn Java for Android Development* to give you a solid Java foundation that you can later extend with knowledge of Android architecture, API, and tool specifics. This book will give you a strong grasp of the Java language and many important APIs that are fundamental to Android apps and other Java applications. It will also introduce you to key development tools.

Book Organization

The first edition of this book was organized into 10 chapters and one appendix. The second edition is organized into 14 chapters and three appendixes. Each chapter in each edition offers a set of exercises that you should complete to get the most benefit from its content. Their solutions are presented in an appendix.

In Chapter 1 I introduce you to Java by first focusing on Java's dual nature (language and platform). I then briefly introduce you to Oracle's Java SE, Java EE, and Java ME editions of the Java development software, as well as Google's Android edition. You next learn how to download and install the Java SE Development Kit (JDK) and learn some Java basics by developing and playing with a pair of simple Java applications. After a brief introduction to the Eclipse IDE, you receive an overview of the various APIs covered in this book.

In Chapter 2 I start you on an in-depth journey of the Java language by focusing on language fundamentals. You learn about comments, identifiers (and reserved words), types, variables, expressions (and literals), and statements.

In Chapter 3 I continue your journey by focusing on classes and objects. You learn how to declare a class and instantiate objects from the class, how to declare fields within the class and access these fields, how to declare methods within the class and call them, how to initialize classes and objects, and how to get rid of objects when they are no longer needed. You also learn more about arrays, which are first introduced in Chapter 2.

In Chapter 4 I add to Chapter 3's pool of object-based knowledge by introducing you to language features that take you from object-based applications to object-oriented applications. Specifically, you learn about features related to inheritance, polymorphism, and interfaces. While exploring inheritance, you learn about Java's ultimate superclass. Also, while exploring interfaces, you discover why they were included in the Java language; interfaces are not merely a workaround for Java's lack of support for multiple implementation inheritance but serve a higher purpose.

In Chapter 5 I introduce you to four categories of advanced language features: nested types, packages, static imports, and exceptions.

In Chapter 6 I introduce you to four additional advanced language feature categories: assertions, annotations, generics, and enums.

In Chapter 7 I begin a trend that focuses more on APIs than language features. In this chapter I first introduce you to many of Java's math-oriented types (e.g., `Math`, `StrictMath`, `BigDecimal`, and `BigInteger`) and then introduce you to its string-oriented types (e.g., `String`, `StringBuffer`, and `StringBuilder`). Finally, you explore the `Package` class for obtaining package information.

In Chapter 8 I continue to explore Java's basic APIs by focusing on primitive type wrapper classes, threading, and system-oriented APIs.

In Chapter 9 I focus exclusively on Java's Collections Framework, which provides you with a solution for organizing objects in lists, sets, queues, and maps. You also learn about collection-oriented utility classes and review Java's legacy utility types.

In Chapter 10 I continue to explore Java's utility APIs by introducing you to Concurrency Utilities, the `Date` class (for representing time), the `Formatter` class (for formatting data items), the `Random` class (for generating random numbers), the `Timer` and `TimerTask` classes (for occasionally or repeatedly executing tasks), and the APIs for working with ZIP and JAR files.

Chapter 11 is all about classic input/output (I/O), seen largely from a file perspective. In this chapter, you explore classic I/O in terms of the `File` class, `RandomAccessFile` class, various stream classes, and various writer/reader classes. My discussion of stream I/O includes coverage of Java's object serialization and deserialization mechanisms.

In Chapter 12 I continue to explore classic I/O by focusing on networks. You learn about the `Socket`, `ServerSocket`, `DatagramSocket`, and `MulticastSocket` classes along with related types. You also learn about the `URL` class for achieving networked I/O at a higher level. After learning about the low-level `NetworkInterface` and `InterfaceAddress` classes, you explore cookie management in terms of the `CookieHandler` and `CookieManager` classes and the `CookiePolicy` and `CookieStore` interfaces.

In Chapter 13 I introduce you to New I/O. You learn about buffers, channels, and regular expressions in this chapter. I would have loved to cover selectors and charsets as well but could not do so for lack of space. To cover selectors, I would also have had to discuss socket channels, but I could only cover file channels. However, Chapter 11 does give you a small taste of charsets.

In Chapter 14 I wrap up the chapter portion of this book by focusing on databases. You first learn about the Java DB and SQLite database products and then explore JDBC for communicating with databases created via these products.

In Appendix A I present solutions to all exercises in Chapters 1 through 14.

In Appendix B I introduce you to application development in the context of *Four of a Kind*, a console-based card game.

In Appendix C, which is available as a separate PDF file that's bundled with this book's code, I introduce you to advanced APIs (e.g., Reflection and References) as well as APIs that might not be as useful in an Android app context (e.g., Preferences—Android offers its own solution.)

> **Note**   You can download this book's source code by pointing your web browser to `www.apress.com/book/view/1430257226` and clicking the Source Code tab followed by the Download Now link.

First Edition vs. Second Edition

The first edition of this book debuted in September 2010. I'm generally pleased with the first edition, and I thank everyone who purchased it. However, as was pointed out to me on multiple occasions, the first edition is flawed. As well as small technical errors, there are certain organizational and other issues that got by me during that book's development.

For starters, I should not have introduced the *Four of a Kind* card game in Chapter 1. It was too complicated for many readers to encounter at this point. As a result, I've moved the game to Appendix B so as not to overwhelm Java beginners.

Also, I attempted to cover language fundamentals (e.g., statements and expressions) with the basics of classes and objects in the same chapter. Although some people appreciated this approach, it turned out to be too confusing for beginners; I apologize to readers who felt this way. In the second edition I separate these aspects of the Java language to (hopefully) sort out this problem. In Chapter 2 I focus on statements, expressions, and other non-class/non-object fundamentals; in Chapter 3 I focus on classes and objects.

Another issue was the inclusion of complex APIs that are either infrequently used when developing Android apps or are mostly irrelevant to Android developers. Examples include References, Reflection, Preferences, and Internationalization. I moved these APIs to Appendix C so that I could cover simpler (and possibly more useful) APIs such as ZIP and Timer. (I also included additional new content in Appendix C.)

While writing the first edition, I planned to go further by covering Java's support for networking and database access (via JDBC), security, XML, New I/O, and so on. I foolishly presented a plan to write six free chapters, but only managed to complete portions of three chapters.

Unfortunately, my original plan for six free chapters was flawed. For instance, I planned to write a free chapter on networking that would come after a free chapter on New I/O. That wasn't a good organization because New I/O includes socket channels, and so the networking chapter should have preceded a chapter on New I/O.

Also, I've learned (via various blogs about Android and security) that Java's security features aren't as necessary in an Android context. Because this book partly focuses on presenting the most useful Java APIs for subsequent use in an Android context, coverage of Java's security APIs is probably not as important (although I could be wrong).

Note   There are no free chapters to supplement the second edition. However, Appendix C is a freebie. Also, I might eventually offer some additional material (perhaps coverage of socket channels, selectors, and charsets) on my web site (see `http://tutortutor.ca/cgi-bin/makepage.cgi?/books/ljfad`).

What Comes Next?

After you complete this book, I recommend that you obtain a copy of *Beginning Android 4* by Grant Allen (Apress, 2012) and start learning how to develop Android apps. In that book, you learn Android basics and how to create "innovative and salable applications for Android 4 mobile devices." Rather than give a few superficial details of Android development, *Learn Java for Android Development Second Edition* concentrates on teaching you the Java language and APIs such as Collections that you will need to use in your apps. If you don't first understand Java, how can you proceed to understand Android?

Note   I also recommend that you check out the second edition of *Android Recipes* (see `www.apress.com/9781430246145`). Although the content of that book largely contains independent recipes for learning all kinds of things about Android, Chapter 1 contains a summarized and rapid introduction to Android app development. You will learn much about Android basics from reading that chapter.

Thanks for purchasing my book. I hope you find it a helpful preparation for, and I wish you lots of success in achieving, a satisfying and lucrative career as an Android app developer.

Getting Started With Java

Android is Google's software stack for mobile devices. This stack consists of applications (or apps as they are commonly called), a *virtual machine* (software-based processor and associated environment) in which apps run, *middleware* (software that sits on top of the operating system and provides various services to the virtual machine and its apps), and a Linux-based operating system.

Android apps are written in Java and use various Java Application Program Interfaces (APIs). Because you will want to write your own apps but may be unfamiliar with the Java language and these APIs, this book teaches you about Java as a first step into app development. It provides you with the fundamentals of the Java language and Java APIs that are useful when developing apps.

Note   This book illustrates Java concepts via non-Android Java applications. It's easier for beginners to grasp these applications than corresponding Android apps.

An API refers to an interface that an application's code uses to communicate with other code, which is typically stored in some kind of software library. For more information on this term, check out Wikipedia's "Application programming interface" topic (`http://en.wikipedia.org/wiki/Application_ programming_interface`).

This chapter sets the stage for teaching you the essential Java concepts that you need to understand before you embark on your Android app development career. I first answer the "What is Java?" question. I next show you how to install the Java SE Development Kit (JDK), and introduce you to JDK tools for compiling and running Java applications.

After showing you how to install and use the open source Eclipse IDE (Integrated Development Environment) so that you can more easily (and more quickly) develop Java applications (and, eventually, Android apps), I provide you with a high-level overview of various Java APIs that you can access from your Java applications and Android apps. In subsequent chapters, you'll explore these and other useful APIs in greater detail.

> **Note**   Chapter 1 is short but intense, presenting many concepts that you'll encounter in more detail throughout this book. If you are new to Java, you might find yourself a little overwhelmed by these concepts. However, any fog should clear as you progress through remaining chapters. If you still feel somewhat confused, please contact me (jeff@tutortutor.ca) with your questions and I'll do my best to help you.

What Is Java?

Java is a language and a platform originated by Sun Microsystems. In this section, I briefly describe this language and reveal what it means for Java to be a platform. To meet various needs, Sun organized Java into three main editions: Java SE, Java EE, and Java ME. This section also briefly explores each of these editions, along with Android.

> **Note**   Java has an interesting history that dates back to December 1990. At that time, James Gosling, Patrick Naughton, and Mike Sheridan (all employees of Sun Microsystems) were given the task of figuring out the next major trend in computing. They concluded that one trend would involve the convergence of computing devices and intelligent consumer appliances. Thus was born the *Green project.*
>
> The fruits of Green were *Star7*, a handheld wireless device featuring a five-inch color LCD screen, a SPARC processor, a sophisticated graphics capability, and a version of Unix; and *Oak*, a language developed by James Gosling for writing applications to run on Star7, which he named after an oak tree growing outside of his office window at Sun. To avoid a conflict with another language of the same name, Dr. Gosling changed this language's name to Java.
>
> Sun Microsystems subsequently evolved the Java language and platform until Oracle acquired Sun in early 2010. Check out http://oracle.com/technetwork/java/index.html for the latest Java news from Oracle.

Java Is a Language

Java is a language in which developers express *source code* (program text). Java's *syntax* (rules for combining symbols into language features) is partly patterned after the C and C++ languages to shorten the learning curve for C/C++ developers.

The following list identifies a few similarities between Java and C/C++:

- Java and C/C++ share the same single-line and multiline comment styles. Comments let you document source code.

- Many of Java's reserved words are identical to their C/C++ counterparts (for, if, switch, and while are examples) and C++ counterparts (catch, class, public, and try are examples).

- Java supports character, double precision floating-point, floating-point, integer, long integer, and short integer primitive types, and via the same `char`, `double`, `float`, `int`, `long`, and `short` reserved words.

- Java supports many of the same operators, including arithmetic (+, -, *, /, and %) and conditional (?:) operators.

- Java uses brace characters ({ and }) to delimit blocks of statements.

The following list identifies a few differences between Java and C/C++:

- Java supports an additional comment style known as Javadoc. (I briefly introduce Javadoc in Chapter 2.)

- Java provides reserved words not found in C/C++ (`extends`, `strictfp`, `synchronized`, and `transient` are examples).

- Java doesn't require machine-specific knowledge. It supports the byte integer type (see `http://en.wikipedia.org/wiki/Integer_(computer_science)`); doesn't provide a signed version of the character type; and doesn't provide unsigned versions of integer, long integer, and short integer. Furthermore, all of Java's primitive types have guaranteed implementation sizes, which is an important part of achieving portability (discussed later). The same cannot be said of equivalent primitive types in C and C++.

- Java provides operators not found in C/C++. These operators include `instanceof` and `>>>` (unsigned right shift).

- Java provides labeled break and continue statements that you will not find in C/C++.

You will learn about single-line and multiline comments in Chapter 2. Also, you will learn about reserved words, primitive types, operators, blocks, and statements (including labeled break and continue) in that chapter.

Java was designed to be a safer language than C/C++. It achieves safety in part by not letting you overload operators and by omitting C/C++ features such as *pointers* (variables containing addresses—see `http://en.wikipedia.org/wiki/Pointer_(computer_programming)`).

Java also achieves safety by modifying certain C/C++ features. For example, loops must be controlled by Boolean expressions instead of integer expressions where 0 is false and a nonzero value is true. (There is a discussion of loops and expressions in Chapter 2.)

Suppose you must code a C/C++ while loop that repeats no more than 10 times. Being tired, you specify `while (x) x++;` (assume that x is an integer-based variable initialized to 0—I discuss variables in Chapter 2) where x++ adds 1 to x's value. This loop doesn't stop when x reaches 10; you have introduced a bug.

This problem is less likely to occur in Java because it complains when it sees `while (x)`. This complaint requires you to recheck your expression, and you will then most likely specify `while (x != 10)`. Not only is safety improved (you cannot specify just x), meaning is also clarified: `while (x != 10)` is more meaningful than `while (x)`.

These and other fundamental language features support classes, objects, inheritance, polymorphism, and interfaces. Java also provides advanced features related to nested types, packages, static imports, exceptions, assertions, annotations, generics, enums, and more. Subsequent chapters explore most of these language features.

Java Is a Platform

Java is a platform consisting of a virtual machine and an execution environment. The *virtual machine* is a software-based processor that presents an instruction set. The *execution environment* consists of libraries for running programs and interacting with the underlying operating system.

The execution environment includes a huge library of prebuilt classfiles that perform common tasks, such as math operations (e.g., trigonometry) and network communications. This library is commonly referred to as the *standard class library*.

A special Java program known as the *Java compiler* translates source code into instructions (and associated data) that are executed by the virtual machine. These instructions are known as *bytecode*.

The compiler stores a program's bytecode and data in files having the `.class` extension. These files are known as *classfiles* because they typically store the compiled equivalent of classes, a language feature discussed in Chapter 3.

A Java program executes via a tool (e.g., `java`) that loads and starts the virtual machine and passes the program's main classfile to the machine. The virtual machine uses a *classloader* (a virtual machine or execution environment component) to load the classfile.

After the classfile has been loaded, the virtual machine's *bytecode verifier* component makes sure that the classfile's bytecode is valid and doesn't compromise security. The verifier terminates the virtual machine when it finds a problem with the bytecode.

Assuming that all is well with the classfile's bytecode, the virtual machine's *interpreter* interprets the bytecode one instruction at a time. *Interpretation* consists of identifying bytecode instructions and executing equivalent native instructions.

> **Note**   *Native instructions* (also known as *native code*) are the instructions understood by the underlying platform's physical processor.

When the interpreter learns that a sequence of bytecode instructions is executed repeatedly, it informs the virtual machine's *Just in Time (JIT) compiler* to compile these instructions into native code.

JIT compilation is performed only once for a given sequence of bytecode instructions. Because the native instructions execute instead of the associated bytecode instruction sequence, the program executes much faster.

During execution, the interpreter might encounter a request to execute another classfile's bytecode. When that happens, it asks the classloader to load the classfile and the bytecode verifier to verify the bytecode prior to executing that bytecode.

The platform side of Java promotes *portability* by providing an abstraction over the underlying platform. As a result, the same bytecode runs unchanged on Windows-based, Linux-based, Mac OS X-based, and other platforms.

Note Java was introduced with the slogan "write once, run anywhere." Although Java goes to great lengths to enforce portability (e.g., an integer is always 32 binary digits [bits] and a long integer is always 64 bits—see `http://en.wikipedia.org/wiki/Bit` to learn about binary digits), it doesn't always succeed. For example, despite being mostly platform independent, certain parts of Java (e.g., the scheduling of threads, discussed in Chapter 8) vary from underlying platform to underlying platform.

The platform side of Java also promotes *security* by providing a secure environment (e.g., the bytecode verifier) in which code executes. The goal is to prevent malicious code from corrupting the underlying platform (and possibly stealing sensitive information).

Java SE, Java EE, Java ME, and Android

Developers use different editions of the Java platform to create Java programs that run on desktop computers, web browsers, web servers, mobile information devices (e.g., feature phones), and embedded devices (e.g., television set-top boxes):

- *Java Platform, Standard Edition (Java SE)*: The Java platform for developing *applications*, which are stand-alone programs that run on desktops. Java SE is also used to develop *applets*, which are programs that run in web browsers.

- *Java Platform, Enterprise Edition (Java EE)*: The Java platform for developing enterprise-oriented applications and *servlets*, which are server programs that conform to Java EE's Servlet API. Java EE is built on top of Java SE.

- *Java Platform, Micro Edition (Java ME)*: The Java platform for developing *MIDlets*, which are programs that run on mobile information devices, and *Xlets*, which are programs that run on embedded devices.

Developers also use a special Google-created edition of the Java platform (see `http://developer.android.com/index.html`) to create Android apps that run on Android-enabled devices. This edition is known as the *Android platform*.

Google's Android platform presents a *Dalvik virtual machine* that runs on top of a specially modified Linux kernel. An Android app's Java source code is compiled into Java classfiles, which are then translated into a special file for Dalvik to execute.

Note Learn more about the Android OS via Wikipedia's "Android (operating system)" entry (`http://en.wikipedia.org/wiki/Android_(operating_system)`) and about the Dalvik virtual machine via Wikipedia's "Dalvik (software)" entry (`http://en.wikipedia.org/wiki/Dalvik_(software)`).

In this book, I cover the Java language (supported by Java SE and Android) and various Java SE APIs that are also supported by Android. I focus on language features through Java version 5 and on Java APIs through Java 5, with a small amount of Java 6.

> **Note**   Google's Android platform is based on an open source release of Java 5. It doesn't officially recognize language features newer than Java 5, although it's possible to add this support (see www.informit.com/articles/article.aspx?p=1966024). Regarding APIs, this platform supports APIs from Java 6 and previous Java versions. Also, it provides its own unique APIs.

Installing and Exploring the JDK

The *Java Runtime Environment (JRE)* implements the Java SE platform and makes it possible to run Java programs. The public JRE can be downloaded from Oracle's Java SE Downloads page (http://oracle.com/technetwork/java/javase/downloads/index.html).

However, the public JRE doesn't make it possible to develop Java programs. For that task, you need to download and install the *Java SE Development Kit (JDK)*, which contains development tools (including the Java compiler) and a private JRE.

> **Note**   JDK 1.0 was the first JDK to be released (in May 1995). Until JDK 6 arrived, JDK stood for Java Development Kit (SE was not part of the title). Over the years, numerous JDKs have been released, with JDK 7 being current at time of writing.
>
> Each JDK's version number identifies a version of Java. For example, JDK 1.0 identifies Java 1.0, and JDK 5 identifies Java 5.0. JDK 5 was the first JDK to also provide an internal version number: 1.5.0.
>
> Google doesn't provide a JDK. What it does provide is similar to a JRE, but with an Android focus.

The Java SE Downloads page also provides access to the current JDK, which is JDK 7 Update 9 at time of writing. Click the Download JDK link (on the page at http://oracle.com/technetwork/java/javase/downloads/index.html) to download the current JDK's installer program for your platform.

The JDK installer places the JDK in a home directory. (It can also install the public JRE in another directory.) On my Windows 7 platform, the home directory is C:\Program Files\Java\jdk1.7.0_06. (I currently use JDK 7 Update 6.)

> **Tip**   After installing the JDK, you should add the bin subdirectory to your platform's PATH environment variable (see http://java.com/en/download/help/path.xml) so you can execute JDK tools from any directory. Also, you might want to create a projects subdirectory of the JDK's home directory to organize your Java projects and create a separate subdirectory within projects for each of these projects.

The home directory contains various files (e.g., README.html, which provides information about the JDK, and src.zip, which provides the standard class library source code) and subdirectories, including the following three important subdirectories:

- bin: This subdirectory contains assorted JDK tools. You'll use only a few of these tools in this book, mainly javac (Java compiler), java (Java application launcher), jar (Java archive creator, updater, and extractor), and javadoc (Java documentation generator).

- jre: This subdirectory contains the JDK's private copy of the JRE, which lets you run Java programs without having to download and install the public JRE.

- lib: This subdirectory contains library files that are used by JDK tools. For example, tools.jar contains the Java compiler's classfiles—the compiler was written in Java.

> **Note**   javac is not the Java compiler. It is a tool that loads and starts the virtual machine, identifies the compiler's main classfile (located in tools.jar) to the virtual machine, and passes the name of the source file being compiled to the compiler's main classfile.

You execute JDK tools at the *command line*, passing *command-line arguments* to a tool. You can learn about the command line and arguments via Wikipedia's "Command-line interface" entry (http://en.wikipedia.org/wiki/Command-line_interface).

Now that you have installed the JDK and know something about its tools, you're ready to explore a small DumpArgs application that outputs its command-line arguments to the standard output stream.

> **Note**   The standard output stream is part of *Standard I/O* (http://en.wikipedia.org/wiki/Standard_streams), which also consists of standard input and standard error streams, and which originated with the Unix operating system. Standard I/O makes it possible to read text from different sources (keyboard or file) and write text to different destinations (screen or file).
>
> Text is read from the standard input stream, which defaults to the keyboard but can be redirected to a file. Text is written to the standard output stream, which defaults to the screen but can be redirected to a file. Error message text is written to the standard error stream, which defaults to the screen but can be redirected to a file that differs from the standard output file.

Listing 1-1 presents the DumpArgs application source code.

Listing 1-1. Dumping Command-Line Arguments via main()'s args Array to the Standard Output Stream

```java
public class DumpArgs
{
   public static void main(String[] args)
   {
      System.out.println("Passed arguments:");
```

```
        for (int i = 0; i < args.length; i++)
            System.out.println(args[i]);
    }
}
```

Listing 1-1's DumpArgs application consists of a class named DumpArgs and a method within this class named main(), which is the application's entry point and provides the code to execute. (You will learn about classes and methods in Chapter 3.)

The main() method includes a header that identifies this method and a block of code located between an open brace character ({) and a close brace character (}). As well as naming this method, the header provides the following information:

- public: This reserved word makes main() visible to the startup code that calls this method. If public wasn't present, the compiler would output an error message stating that it couldn't find a main() method. (I discuss reserved words in Chapter 2.)

- static: This reserved word causes this method to associate with the class instead of associating with any objects (discussed in Chapter 3) created from this class. Because the startup code that calls main() doesn't create an object from the class to call this method, it requires that the method be declared static. Although the compiler will not report an error when static is missing, it will not be possible to run DumpArgs, which will not be an application when the proper main() method doesn't exist.

- void: This reserved word indicates that the method doesn't return a value. If you change void to a type's reserved word (e.g., int) and then insert a statement that returns a value of this type (e.g., return 0;), the compiler will not report an error. However, you won't be able to run DumpArgs because the proper main() method wouldn't exist. (I discuss types in Chapter 2.)

- (String[] args): This parameter list consists of a single parameter named args of type String[]. Startup code passes a sequence of command-line arguments to args, which makes these arguments available to the code that executes within main(). You'll learn about parameters and arguments in Chapter 3.

main() is called with an array of *strings* (character sequences) that identify the application's command-line arguments. These strings are stored in String-based array variable args. (I discuss method calling, arrays, and variables in Chapters 2 and 3.) Although the array variable is named args, there is nothing special about this name. You could choose another name for this variable.

The block of code first executes System.out.println("Passed arguments:");, which calls System.out's println() method with the "Passed arguments:" string. This string is written to the standard output stream.

From left to write, System identifies a standard class of system utilities; out identifies an object variable located in System whose methods let you output values of various types optionally followed by a newline character to the standard output stream; println identifies a method that prints its argument followed by a newline character to standard output; and "Passed arguments:" is a *string* (a sequence of characters delimited by double quote " characters and treated as a unit) that is passed as the argument to `println` and written to standard output (the starting " and ending " double quote characters are not written; these characters delimit but are not part of the string).

> **Note** `System.out` provides access to a family of `println()` methods and a family of `print()` methods for outputting different kinds of data (e.g., sequences of characters and integers). Unlike the `println()` methods, the `print()` methods don't terminate the current line; subsequent output continues on the current line.
>
> Each `println()` method terminates a line by outputting a line separator string, which is defined by system property `line.separator`, and which is not necessarily a single newline character (identified in source code via character literal `'\n'`). (I discuss system properties in Chapter 8, `line.separator` in Chapter 11, and character literals in Chapter 2.) For example, on Windows platforms, the line separator string is a carriage return character (whose integer code is 13) followed by a line feed character (whose integer code is 10).

The block of code next uses a for loop to repeatedly execute `System.out.println(args[i]);`. The loop executes `args.length` times, or once for each string stored in `args`. (I discuss for loops and `.length` in Chapter 2.)

The `System.out.println(args[i]);` method call reads the string stored in the ith entry of the args array—the first entry is located at *index* (location) 0; the last entry is stored at index `args.length - 1`. This method call then outputs this string to standard output.

Assuming that you're familiar with your platform's command-line interface and are at the command line, make DumpArgs your current directory and copy Listing 1-1 to a file named `DumpArgs.java`. Then compile this source file via the following command line:

```
javac DumpArgs.java
```

Assuming that that you've included the `.java` extension, which is required by `javac`, and that `DumpArgs.java` compiles, you should discover a file named `DumpArgs.class` in the current directory. Run this application via the following command line:

```
java DumpArgs
```

If all goes well, you should see the following line of output on the screen:

```
Passed arguments:
```

For more interesting output, you'll need to pass command-line arguments to DumpArgs. For example, execute the following command line, which specifies `Curly`, `Moe`, and `Larry` as three arguments to pass to DumpArgs:

```
java DumpArgs Curly Moe Larry
```

This time, you should see the following expanded output on the screen:

```
Passed arguments:
Curly
Moe
Larry
```

You can redirect the output destination to a file by specifying the greater than angle bracket (>) followed by a filename. For example, java DumpArgs Curly Moe Larry >out.txt stores the DumpArgs application's output in a file named out.txt.

> **Note** Instead of specifying System.out.println(), you could specify System.err.println() to output characters to the standard error stream. (System.err provides the same families of println() and print() methods as System.out.) However, you should only switch from System.out to System.err when you need to output an error message so that the error messages are displayed on the screen, even when standard output is redirected to a file.

Congratulations on successfully compiling your first application source file and running the application! Listing 1-2 presents the source code to a second application, which echoes text obtained from the standard input stream to the standard output stream.

Listing 1-2. Echoing Text Read from Standard Input to Standard Output

```java
public class EchoText
{
   public static void main(String[] args) throws java.io.IOException
   {
      System.out.println("Please enter some text and press Enter!");
      int ch;
      while ((ch = System.in.read()) != -1)
         System.out.print((char) ch);
      System.out.println();
   }
}
```

After outputting a message that prompts the user to enter some text, main() introduces int variable ch to store each character's integer representation. (You will learn about int and integer in Chapter 2.)

main() now enters a while loop (discussed in Chapter 2) to read and echo characters. The loop first calls System.in.read() to read a character and assign its integer value to ch. The loop ends when this value equals −1 (no more input data is available).

> **Note**   When standard input is redirected to a file, `System.in.read()` reads each character from the file (which is subsequently converted to an integer) until there are no more characters to be read. At that point, this method returns −1. However, when standard input isn't redirected, the loop doesn't end because −1 is never seen. In this case, the end of a line of text is signified (on Windows platforms) by a carriage return character (integer value 13) followed by a line feed character (integer value 10). The exact termination sequence is platform dependent. You must press the Ctrl and C keys simultaneously on Windows (or the equivalent keys on a non-Windows platform) to terminate the loop.

For any other value in `ch`, this value is converted to a character via `(char)`, which is an example of Java's cast operator (discussed in Chapter 2). The character is then output via `System.out.print()`, which doesn't also terminate the current line. The final `System.out.println();` call terminates the current line without outputting any content.

> **Note**   When standard input is redirected to a file and `System.in.read()` is unable to read text from the file (perhaps the file is stored on a removable storage device that has been removed prior to the read operation), `System.in.read()` fails by throwing an object that describes this problem. I acknowledge this possibility by appending `throws java.io.IOException` to the end of the `main()` method header. I discuss `throws` in Chapter 5 and `java.io.IOException` in Chapter 11.

Compile Listing 1-2 via `javac EchoText.java` and run the application via `java EchoText`. You'll be prompted to enter some text. After you input this text and press Enter, the text will be sent to standard output. For example, consider the following output:

```
Please enter some text and press Enter!
Hello Java
Hello Java
```

You can redirect the input source to a file by specifying the less than angle bracket (<) followed by a filename. For example, `java EchoText <EchoText.java` reads its text from `EchoText.java` and outputs this text to the screen.

ANDROID APP ENTRY POINT

The `DumpArgs` and `EchoText` applications demonstrate `public static void main(String[] args)` as a Java application's entry point. This is where the application's execution begins. In contrast, an Android app doesn't require this method for its entry point because the app's architecture is very different.

Android apps are based on a federation of interacting components, which are known as activities, services, broadcast receivers, and content providers. Activities provide user interface screens, services support background processing, broadcast receivers respond to system-wide broadcasts, and content providers offer portable data access.

Consider the activity. This component is implemented as a class that inherits life cycle methods from Android's `android.app.Activity` class and has the opportunity to override them. (I discuss methods in Chapter 3 and inheritance and overriding in Chapter 4.) For example, it could override the `void onCreate(Bundle savedInstanceState)` method to construct a user interface screen when Android calls this method.

In this book, I present Java applications with `public static void main(String[] args)` methods. I do so because the book's focus is on learning Java as a preparatory step to getting into Android app development.

As well as downloading and installing the JDK, you'll need to access the JDK documentation, especially to explore the Java APIs. There are two sets of documentation that you can explore:

- Oracle's JDK 7 documentation
  (`http://docs.oracle.com/javase/7/docs/api/index.html`)
- Google's Java API documentation
  (`https://developer.android.com/reference/packages.html`)

Oracle's JDK 7 documentation presents many APIs that are not supported by Android. Furthermore, it doesn't cover APIs that are specific to Android. This book focuses only on Java APIs that are covered in Google's documentation.

Installing and Exploring the Eclipse IDE

Working with the JDK's tools at the command line is probably okay for small projects. However, this practice is not recommended for large projects, which are hard to manage without the help of an IDE.

An IDE consists of a project manager for managing a project's files, a text editor for entering and editing source code, a debugger for locating bugs, and other features. Eclipse is a popular IDE that Google supports for developing Android apps.

> **Note** For convenience, I use JDK tools throughout this book, except for this section where I discuss and demonstrate the Eclipse IDE.

Eclipse IDE is an open source IDE for developing programs in Java and other languages (e.g., C, COBOL, PHP, Perl, and Python). Eclipse Classic is one distribution of this IDE that is available for download; version 4.2.1 is the current version at time of writing.

You should download and install Eclipse Classic to follow along with this section's Eclipse-oriented example. Begin by pointing your browser to `www.eclipse.org/downloads/` and accomplishing the following tasks:

1. Scroll down the page until you see an Eclipse Classic entry. (It may refer to 4.2.1 or a newer version.)

2. Click one of the platform links (e.g., Windows 32 Bit) to the right of this entry.

3. Select a download mirror from the subsequently displayed page and proceed to download the distribution's archive file.

I downloaded the approximately 183 MB `eclipse-SDK-4.2.1-win32-x86_64.zip` archive file for my Windows 7 platform, unarchived this file, moved the resulting `eclipse` home directory to another location, and created a shortcut to that directory's `eclipse.exe` file.

After installing Eclipse Classic, run this application. You should discover a splash screen identifying this IDE and a dialog box that lets you choose the location of a workspace for storing projects, followed by a main window like that shown in Figure 1-1.

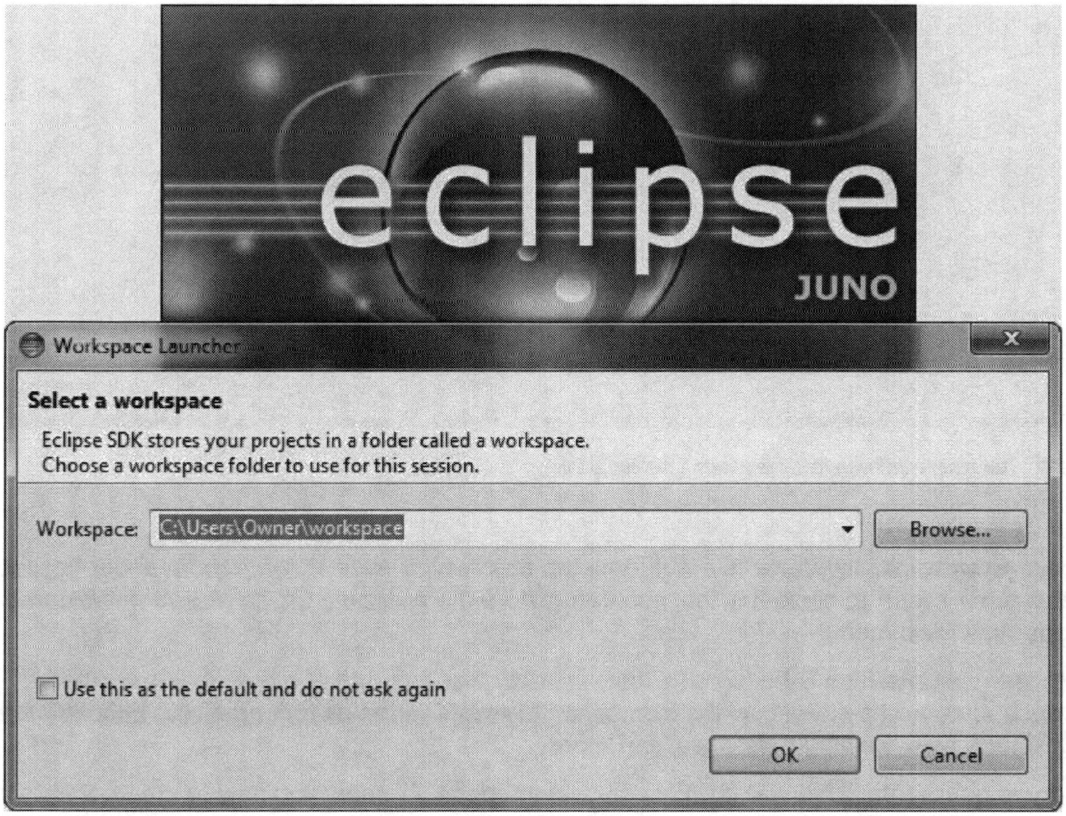

Figure 1-1. Keep the default workspace or choose another workspace

Click the OK button and you're taken to Eclipse's main window. See Figure 1-2.

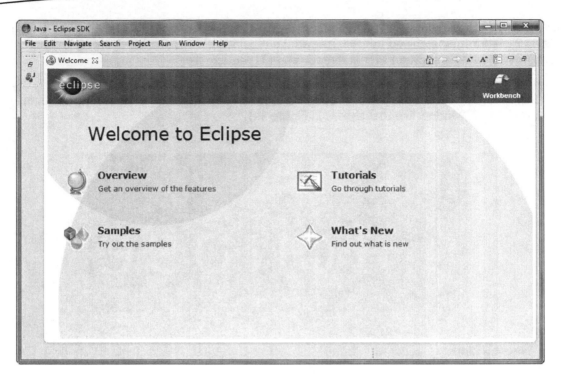

Figure 1-2. The main window initially presents a Welcome tab

The main window initially presents a Welcome tab from which you can learn more about Eclipse. Click this tab's X icon to close this tab; you can restore the Welcome tab by selecting Welcome from the menubar's Help menu.

The Eclipse user interface is based on a main window that consists of a menubar, a toolbar, a workbench area, and a statusbar. The *workbench* presents windows for organizing Eclipse projects, editing source files, viewing messages, and more.

To help you get comfortable with the Eclipse user interface, I'll show you how to create a DumpArgs project containing a single DumpArgs.java source file with Listing 1-1's source code. You'll also learn how to compile and run this application.

Complete the following steps to create the DumpArgs project:

1. Select New from the File menu and Java Project from the resulting pop-up menu.

2. In the resulting New Java Project dialog box, enter **DumpArgs** into the Project name text field. Keep all the other defaults and click the Finish button.

After the second step, you'll see a workbench similar to that shown in Figure 1-3.

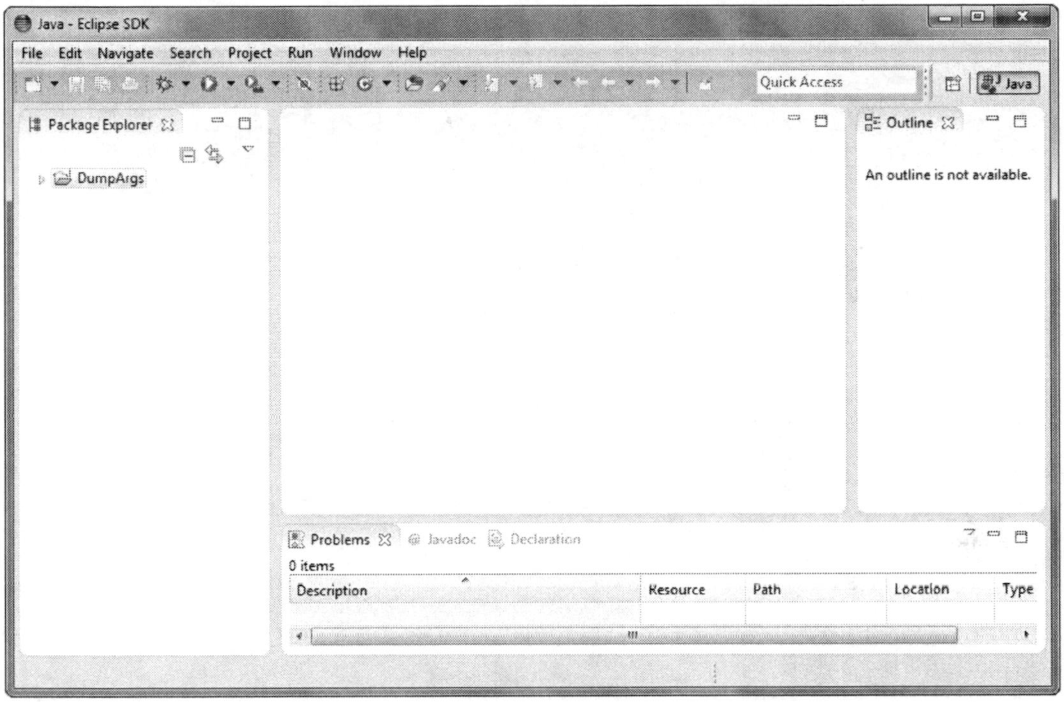

Figure 1-3. A DumpArgs entry appears in the workbench's Package Explorer

On the left side of the workbench, you see a window titled Package Explorer. This window identifies the workspace's projects in terms of packages (discussed in Chapter 5). At the moment, only a single DumpArgs entry appears in this window.

Clicking the triangle icon to the left of DumpArgs expands this entry to reveal src and JRE System Library items. The src item stores the DumpArgs project's source files, and the JRE System Library identifies various JRE files that are used to run this application.

You'll now add a new file named DumpArgs.java to src, as follows:

1. Highlight src and select New from the File menu and File from the resulting pop-up menu.

2. In the resulting New File dialog box, enter **DumpArgs.java** into the File name text field, and click the Finish button.

Eclipse responds by displaying an editor window titled DumpArgs.java. Copy Listing 1-1 content to this window. Then compile and run this application by selecting Run from the Run menu. (If you see a Save and Launch dialog box, click OK to close this dialog box.) Figure 1-4 shows the results.

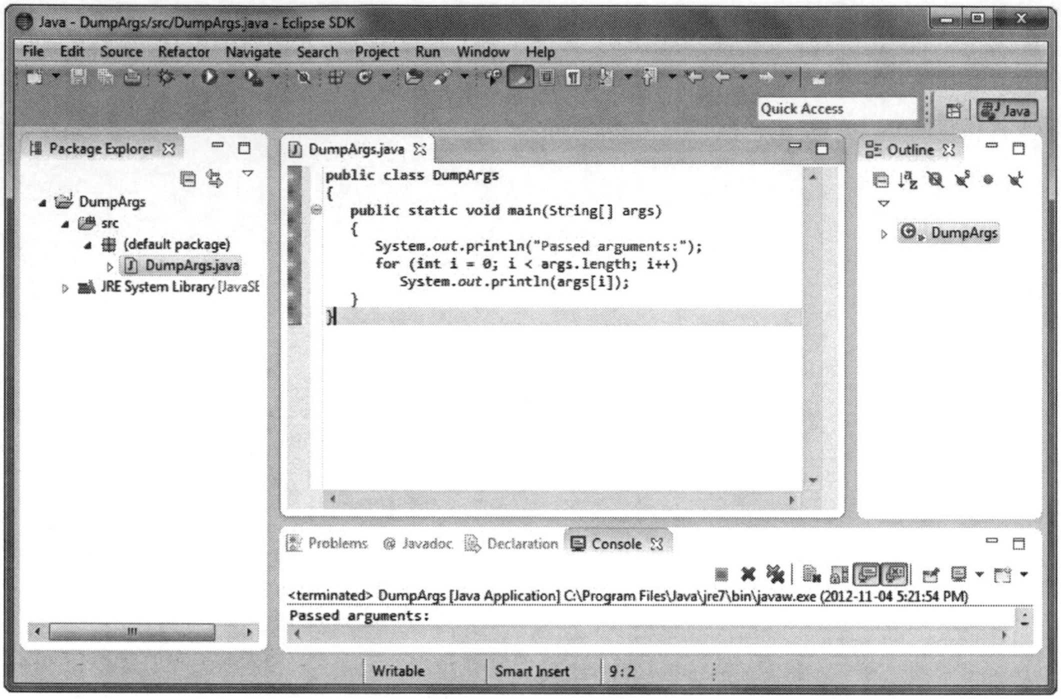

Figure 1-4. The Console tab at the bottom of the workbench presents the DumpArgs application's output

You must pass command-line arguments to DumpArgs to see additional output from this application. Accomplish this task as follows:

1. Select Run Configurations from the Run menu.

2. In the resulting Run Configurations dialog box, select the Arguments tab.

3. Enter **Curly Moe Larry** into the Program arguments text area and click the Close button.

Once again, select Run from the Run menu to run the DumpArgs application. This time, the Console tab reveals Curly, Moe, and Larry on separate lines below "Passed arguments:".

This is all I have to say about the Eclipse IDE. For more information, study the tutorials via the Welcome tab, access IDE help via the Help menu, and explore the Eclipse documentation at www.eclipse.org/documentation/.

Overview of Java APIs

Oracle organizes its standard class library APIs into packages (see Chapter 5), which are analogous to file folders. Similarly, Google organizes its Android-oriented standard class library APIs into packages. In this section, I provide an overview of various Java APIs that are common to Oracle and Google. Furthermore, I discuss (throughout this book) only those APIs that are located in both libraries. By limiting my discussion to common APIs, I avoid discussing Java APIs that cannot be used when creating Android apps.

Language-Support and Other Language-Oriented APIs

Java relies on several APIs to support basic language features, such as strings (see Chapter 7), exceptions (see Chapter 5), and threads (see Chapter 8). For example, the java.lang package offers the String class to support strings, the Throwable class to support exceptions, and the Thread class and Runnable interface to support threads.

Java also provides APIs that fulfill language-oriented tasks. For example, java.lang offers a StringBuffer class (see Chapter 7) for creating changeable strings, a Math class (see Chapter 7) for performing trigonometric and other basic mathematics operations, and a Package class (see Chapter 7) for obtaining package-oriented information.

Collections-Oriented APIs

Java's designers have developed a powerful *Collections Framework* for organizing objects (see Chapter 9). This framework, which is located in the java.util package, is based on interfaces and lets you store objects in lists, queues, sets (sorted or unsorted), and maps (sorted or unsorted). These interfaces are associated with various implementation classes (e.g., ArrayList).

The Collections Framework also offers the Collections and Arrays classes. These *utility classes* (classes consisting of static [class] methods) provide various methods for performing common operations on collections and arrays. For example, Collections lets you conveniently search or sort a collection; and Arrays lets you conveniently search, sort, copy, or fill an array.

Additional Utility APIs

Java's designers have also developed a powerful *Concurrency Utilities* framework that offers a high-level alternative to low-level threads (see Chapter 10). This framework's APIs are organized into java.util.concurrent, java.util.concurrent.atomic, and java.util.concurrent.locks packages. Examples of APIs in the first package include the Executor interface and the CyclicBarrier class.

Additional utility APIs that are located in the java.util package include the Date class for working with dates, the Formatter class for formatting data items (e.g., integers and strings), the Random class for achieving sophisticated random number generation, and the Scanner class for parsing an input stream of characters into integers, strings, and other values. I discuss these APIs in Chapter 10.

Finally, the java.util.zip package offers capabilities for extracting information from existing ZIP archives and creating new ZIP archives (see Chapter 10). Also, the related java.util.jar package extends java.util.zip by offering additional capabilities required by JAR files, specifically, reading attributes from and writing attributes to the JAR file's manifest (see Chapter 10).

Classic I/O APIs

The ability to input and output information has always been important to Java. You've already discovered Standard I/O, but there is much more to explore in Chapter 11. For example, the java.io package offers the File class for performing file-oriented operations (e.g., listing a directory's files), and also offers stream/writer/reader classes for performing I/O (typically involving files).

Networking APIs

Although much I/O takes place in the context of a filesystem, Java also offers the ability to perform I/O over a network via the various types located in its java.net package (see Chapter 12). For example, you can use the Socket and ServerSocket classes to create the client and server ends of a network communication link.

Socket offers a low-level approach to communicating over a network. In some cases, you'll use the higher-level URL class to communicate over the Web, perhaps to obtain a web page. As you interact with the Web, you'll encounter cookies that you can manage via additional java.net interfaces and classes, such as CookiePolicy and CookieManager.

New I/O APIs

Modern operating systems have introduced sophisticated I/O mechanisms such as memory-mapped files and readiness selection. Java supports these new I/O mechanisms via Buffer, Channel, Selector, and related types found in java.nio and related packages. Also, java.util.regex supports new I/O by offering high-performance string operations. See Chapter 13.

Database APIs

Databases store information, and relational databases store this information in tables that can be related to each other via special key columns. Java supports database access via the java.sql and javax.sql packages. The former package includes classes and interfaces such as DriverManager and ResultSet; the latter package offers DataSource, RowSet, and more. See Chapter 14.

EXERCISES

The following exercises are designed to test your understanding of Chapter 1's content:

1. What is Java?

2. What is a virtual machine?

3. What is the purpose of the Java compiler?

4. True or false: A classfile's instructions are commonly referred to as bytecode.

5. What does the virtual machine's interpreter do when it learns that a sequence of bytecode instructions is being executed repeatedly?

6. How does the Java platform promote portability?

7. How does the Java platform promote security?

8. True or false: Java SE is the Java platform for developing servlets.

9. What is the JRE?

10. What is the difference between the public and private JREs?

11. What is the JDK?

12. Which JDK tool is used to compile Java source code?

13. Which JDK tool is used to run Java applications?

14. What is Standard I/O?

15. How do you specify the `main()` method's header?

16. What is an IDE? Identify the IDE that Google supports for developing Android apps.

Summary

Java is a language and a platform. The language is partly patterned after the C and C++ languages to shorten the learning curve for C/C++ developers. The platform consists of a virtual machine and associated execution environment.

Developers use different editions of the Java platform to create Java programs that run on desktop computers, web browsers, web servers, mobile information devices, and embedded devices. These editions are known as Java SE, Java EE, and Java ME.

Developers also use a special Google-created edition of the Java platform to create Android apps that run on Android-enabled devices. This edition, known as the Android platform, presents a Dalvik virtual machine that runs on top of a specially modified Linux kernel.

The public JRE implements the Java SE platform and makes it possible to run Java programs. The JDK provides tools (including the Java compiler) for developing Java programs and also includes a private copy of the JRE.

Working with the JDK's tools at the command line is not recommended for large projects, which are hard to manage without the help of an integrated development environment. Eclipse is a popular IDE that Google supports for developing Android apps.

Oracle organizes its standard class library APIs into packages, which are analogous to file folders. Similarly, Google organizes its Android-oriented standard class library APIs into packages. In this chapter I also presented an overview of some of these packaged APIs.

Chapter 2 starts to introduce you to the Java language by focusing on this language's fundamentals. You'll learn about comments, identifiers, types, variables, expressions, statements, and more.

Learning Language Fundamentals

Aspiring Android app developers need to understand the Java language, which is used to express an app's source code. In Chapter 2, I start to introduce you to this language by focusing on its fundamentals. Specifically, you'll learn about comments, identifiers (and reserved words), types, variables, expressions (and literals), and statements.

> **Note** The American Standard Code for Information Interchange (ASCII) has traditionally been used to encode a program's source code. Because ASCII is limited to the English language, Unicode (http://unicode.org/) was developed as a replacement. *Unicode* is a computing industry standard for consistently encoding, representing, and handling text that's expressed in most of the world's writing systems. Because Java supports Unicode, non-English-oriented symbols can be integrated into or accessed from Java source code. You'll see examples in this chapter.

Learning Comments

Source code needs to be documented so that you (and any others who have to maintain it) can understand it, now and later. Source code should be documented while being written and whenever it's modified. If these modifications impact existing documentation, the documentation must be updated so that it accurately explains the code.

Java provides the *comment* feature for embedding documentation in source code. When the source code is compiled, the Java compiler ignores all comments—no bytecodes are generated. Single-line, multiline, and Javadoc comments are supported.

Single-Line Comments

A *single-line comment* occupies all or part of a single line of source code. This comment begins with the // character sequence and continues with explanatory text. The compiler ignores everything from // to the end of the line in which // appears. The following example presents a single-line comment:

```
System.out.println(Math.sqrt(10 * 10 + 20 * 20)); // Output distance from (0, 0) to (10, 20).
```

This example calculates the distance between the (0, 0) origin and the point (10, 20) in the Cartesian x/y plane. It uses the formula *distance = square root(x*x+y*y)*, where *x* is 10 and *y* is 20, for this task. Java provides a Math class whose sqrt() method returns the square root of its single numeric argument. (I discuss Math in Chapter 7 and arguments in Chapter 3.)

> **Note**   Single-line comments are useful for inserting short but meaningful explanations of source code into this code. Don't use them to insert unhelpful information. For example, when declaring a variable, don't insert a meaningless comment such as // This variable stores integer values.

Multiline Comments

A *multiline comment* occupies one or more lines of source code. This comment begins with the /* character sequence, continues with explanatory text, and ends with the */ character sequence. Everything from /* through */ is ignored by the compiler. The following example demonstrates a multiline comment:

```
/*
   A year is a leap year if it is divisible by 400, or divisible by 4 and
   not also divisible by 100.
*/
return (year % 400 == 0 || (year % 4 == 0 && year % 100 != 0));
```

This example introduces a return statement (discussed in Chapter 3) for determining whether a year (stored in a variable named year; I discuss variables later in this chapter) is a leap year or not. The important part of this code to grasp is the multiline comment, which clarifies the expression (discussed later) that determines whether year's value does or doesn't represent a leap year.

> **Caution**   You cannot place one multiline comment inside another. For example, /*/* Nesting multiline comments is illegal! */*/ is not a valid multiline comment.

Javadoc Comments

A *Javadoc comment* occupies one or more lines of source code. This comment begins with the /** character sequence, continues with explanatory text, and ends with the */ character sequence. Everything from /** through */ is ignored by the compiler. The following example demonstrates a Javadoc comment:

```
/**
 *  Application entry point
 *
 *  @param args array of command-line arguments passed to this method
 */
public static void main(String[] args)
{
   // TODO code application logic here
}
```

This example begins with a Javadoc comment that describes the main() method, which I discussed in Chapter 1. Sandwiched between /** and */ is a description of the method and the @param *Javadoc tag* (an @-prefixed instruction to the javadoc tool).

The following list identifies several commonly used tags:

- @author identifies the source code's author.

- @deprecated identifies a source code entity (such as a method) that should no longer be used.

- @param identifies one of a method's parameters.

- @see provides a see-also reference.

- @since identifies the software release where the entity first originated.

- @return identifies the kind of value that the method returns.

- @throws documents an exception thrown from a method. I discuss exceptions in Chapter 5.

Listing 2-1 presents Chapter 1's DumpArgs application source code with Javadoc comments that describe the DumpArgs class and its main() method.

Listing 2-1. Documenting an Application Class and Its main() Method

```
/**
   Dump all command-line arguments to standard output.

   @author Jeff Friesen
*/

public class DumpArgs
{
   /**
      Application entry point.
```

```
    @param args array of command-line arguments.
 */

 public static void main(String[] args)
 {
    System.out.println("Passed arguments:");
    for (int i = 0; i < args.length; i++)
       System.out.println(args[i]);
 }
}
```

You can extract these documentation comments into a set of HTML files by using the JDK's javadoc tool, as follows:

```
javadoc DumpArgs.java
```

javadoc responds by outputting the following messages:

```
Loading source file DumpArgs.java...
Constructing Javadoc information...
Standard Doclet version 1.7.0_06
Building tree for all the packages and classes...
Generating \DumpArgs.html...
Generating \package-frame.html...
Generating \package-summary.html...
Generating \package-tree.html...
Generating \constant-values.html...
Building index for all the packages and classes...
Generating \overview-tree.html...
Generating \index-all.html...
Generating \deprecated-list.html...
Building index for all classes...
Generating \allclasses-frame.html...
Generating \allclasses-noframe.html...
Generating \index.html...
Generating \help-doc.html...
```

It also generates several files, including the index.html documentation entry-point file. Point your browser to this file and you should see a page similar to that shown in Figure 2-1.

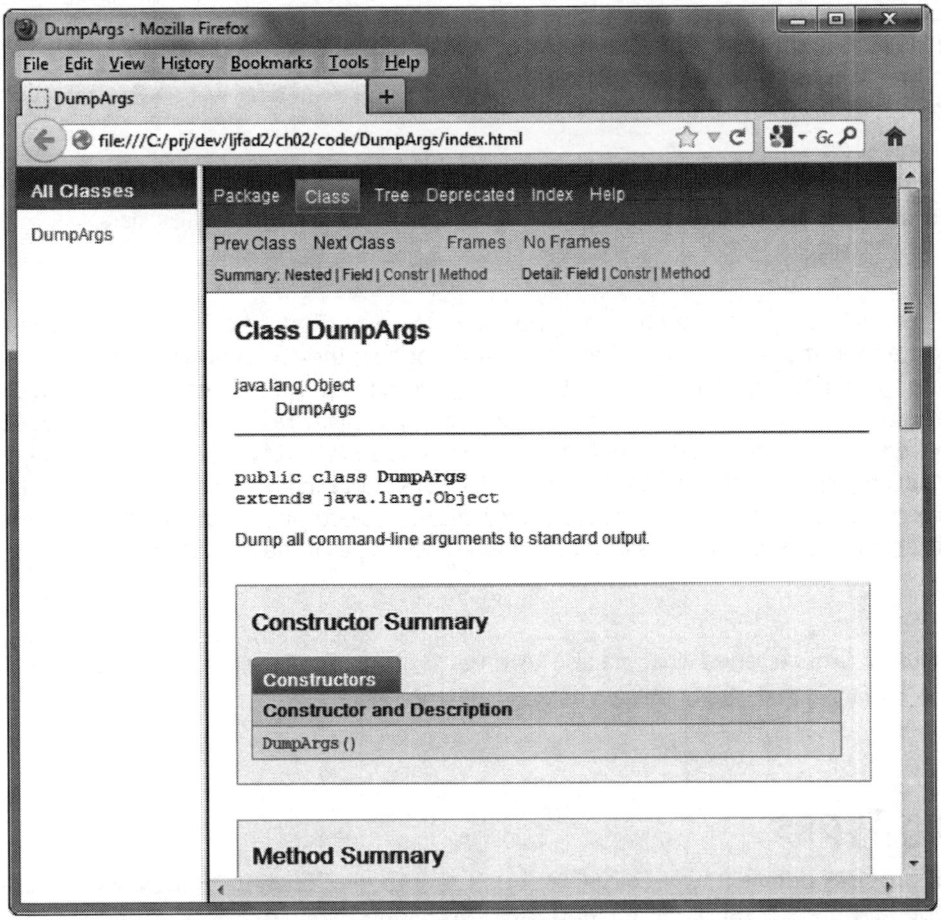

Figure 2-1. The entry-point page into DumpArgs's documentation describes this class

Note   Appendix B provides another (and a more extensive) example involving Javadoc comments and the javadoc tool.

Learning Identifiers

Source code entities such as classes and methods need to be named so that they can be referenced from elsewhere in the code. Java provides the identifiers feature for this purpose.

An *identifier* consists of letters (A–Z, a–z, or equivalent uppercase/lowercase letters in other human alphabets), digits (0–9 or equivalent digits in other human alphabets), connecting punctuation characters (e.g., the underscore), and currency symbols (e.g., the dollar sign $). This name must begin with a letter, a currency symbol, or a connecting punctuation character; and its length cannot exceed the line in which it appears.

Examples of valid identifiers include π (some editors might have problems with such symbols), i, counter, j2, first$name, and _for. Examples of invalid identifiers include 1name (starts with a digit) and first#name (# is not a valid identifier symbol).

> **Note**   Java is a *case-sensitive language*, which means that identifiers differing only in case are considered separate identifiers. For example, temperature and Temperature are separate identifiers.

Almost any valid identifier can be chosen to name a class, method, or other source code entity. However, some identifiers are reserved for special purposes; they are known as *reserved words*. Java reserves the following identifiers: abstract, assert, boolean, break, byte, case, catch, char, class, const, continue, default, do, double, enum, else, extends, false, final, finally, float, for, goto, if, implements, import, instanceof, int, interface, long, native, new, null, package, private, protected, public, return, short, static, strictfp, super, switch, synchronized, this, throw, throws, transient, true, try, void, volatile, and while. The compiler outputs an error message when you attempt to use any of these reserved words outside of their usage contexts.

> **Note**   Most of Java's reserved words are also known as *keywords*. The three exceptions are false, null, and true, which are examples of *literals* (values specified verbatim).

Learning Types

Applications process different types of values such as integers, floating-point values, characters, and strings. A *type* identifies a set of values (and their representation in memory) and a set of operations that transform these values into other values of that set. For example, the integer type identifies numeric values with no fractional parts and integer-oriented math operations, such as adding two integers to yield another integer.

> **Note**   Java is a *strongly typed language*, which means that every expression, variable, and so on has a type known to the compiler. This capability helps the compiler detect type-related errors at compile time rather than having these errors manifest themselves at runtime. Expressions and variables are discussed later in this chapter.

Java classifies types as primitive types, user-defined types, and array types.

Primitive Types

A *primitive type* is a type that's defined by the language and whose values are not objects. Java supports the Boolean, character, byte integer, short integer, integer, long integer, floating-point, and double precision floating-point primitive types. They are described in Table 2-1.

Table 2-1. *Primitive Types*

Primitive Type	Reserved Word	Size	Min Value	Max Value
Boolean	boolean	--	--	--
Character	char	16-bit	Unicode 0	Unicode 65,535
Byte integer	byte	8-bit	−128	+127
Short integer	short	16-bit	−32,768	+32,767
Integer	int	32-bit	−2,147,483,648	+2,147,483,647
Long integer	long	64-bit	−9,223,372,036,854,775,808	+9,223,372,036,854,775,807
Floating-point	float	32-bit	IEEE 754	IEEE 754
Double precision floating-point	double	64-bit	IEEE 754	IEEE 754

Table 2-1 describes each primitive type in terms of its reserved word, size, minimum value, and maximum value. A "--" entry indicates that the column in which it appears is not applicable to the primitive type described in that entry's row.

The size column identifies the size of each primitive type in terms of the number of *bits* (binary digits—each digit is either 0 or 1) that a value of that type occupies in memory. Except for Boolean (whose size is implementation dependent—one Java implementation might store a Boolean value in a single bit, whereas another implementation might require an 8-bit *byte* for performance efficiency), each primitive type's implementation has a specific size.

The minimum value and maximum value columns identify the smallest and largest values that can be represented by each type. Except for Boolean (whose only values are true and false), each primitive type has a minimum value and a maximum value.

The minimum and maximum values of the character type refer to Unicode. **Unicode 0** is shorthand for "the first Unicode code point"—a *code point* is an integer that represents a symbol (such as A) or a control character (such as newline or tab) or that combines with other code points to form a symbol.

> **Note** The character type's limits imply that this type is *unsigned* (all character values are positive). In contrast, each numeric type is *signed* (it supports positive and negative values).

The minimum and maximum values of the byte integer, short integer, integer, and long integer types reveal that there is one more negative value than positive value (0 is typically not regarded as a positive value). The reason for this imbalance has to do with how integers are represented.

Java represents an integer value as a combination of a *sign bit* (the leftmost bit—0 for a positive value and 1 for a negative value) and *magnitude bits* (all remaining bits to the right of the sign bit). When the sign bit is 0, the magnitude is stored directly. However, when the sign bit is 1, the magnitude is stored using *twos-complement representation* in which all 1s are flipped to 0s, all

0s are flipped to 1s, and 1 is added to the number behind the minus sign. Twos-complement is used so that negative integers can naturally coexist with positive integers. For example, adding the representation of –1 to +1 yields 0. Figure 2-2 illustrates byte integer 2's direct representation and byte integer –2's twos-complement representation.

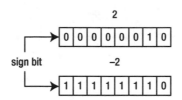

Figure 2-2. The binary representation of two byte-integer values begins with a sign bit

The minimum and maximum values of the floating-point and double precision floating-point types refer to Institute of Electrical and Electronics Engineers (*IEEE) 754*, which is a standard for representing floating-point values in memory. Check out Wikipedia's "IEEE 754-2008" entry (http://en.wikipedia.org/wiki/IEEE_754) to learn more about this standard.

> **Note**   Developers who argue that Java should support objects only are not happy about the inclusion of primitive types in the language. However, Java was designed to include primitive types to overcome the speed and memory limitations of early 1990s-era devices, to which Java was originally targeted.

User-Defined Types

A *user-defined type* is a type that's often used to model a real-world concept (e.g., a color or a bank account). It's defined by the developer using a class, an interface, an enum, or an annotation type; and its values are objects. (I discuss classes in Chapter 3, interfaces in Chapter 4, and enums and annotation types in Chapter 6.)

For example, you could create a `Color` class to model colors; its values could describe colors as red/green/blue component values. Also, Java's `String` class defines the string user-defined type; its values describe strings of characters, and its methods perform various string operations such as concatenating two strings together. (I discuss methods in Chapter 3.)

User-defined types are also known as *reference types* because a variable of that type stores a *reference* (a memory address or some other identifier) to a region of memory that stores an object of that type. In contrast, variables of primitive types store the values directly; they don't store references to these values.

Array Types

An *array type* is a special reference type that signifies an *array*, a region of memory that stores values in equal-size and contiguous slots, which are commonly referred to as *elements*.

This type consists of the *element type* (a primitive type or a user-defined type) and one or more pairs of square brackets that indicate the number of *dimensions* (extents). A single pair of brackets signifies a *one-dimensional array* (a vector), two pairs of brackets signify a *two-dimensional array* (a table), three pairs of brackets signify a one-dimensional array of two-dimensional arrays (a vector of tables), and so on. For example, `int[]` signifies a one-dimensional array (with `int` as the element type), and `double[][]` signifies a two-dimensional array (with `double` as the element type).

Learning Variables

Applications manipulate values that are stored in memory, which is symbolically represented in source code through the use of the variables feature. A *variable* is a named memory location that stores some type of value. A variable that stores a reference is often referred to as *reference variable*.

Variables must be declared before they are used. A declaration minimally consists of a type name, optionally followed by a sequence of square bracket pairs, followed by a name, optionally followed by a sequence of square bracket pairs, and terminated with a semicolon character (;). Consider the following examples:

```
int counter;
double temperature;
String firstName;
int[] ages;
char gradeLetters[];
float[][] matrix;
double π;
```

The first example declares an integer variable named `counter`, the second example declares a variable (of double precision floating-point type) named `temperature`, the third example declares a string variable named `firstName`, the fourth example declares a one-dimensional integer array variable named `ages`, the fifth example declares a one-dimensional character array variable named `gradeLetters`, the sixth example declares a two-dimensional floating-point array variable named `matrix`, and the seventh example declares a double precision floating-point variable named π. No string is yet associated with `firstName`, and no arrays are yet associated with `ages`, `gradeLetters`, and `matrix`.

> **Note**   Square brackets can appear after the type name or after the variable name, but not in both places. For example, the compiler reports an error when it encounters `int[] x[];`. It is common practice to place the square brackets after the type name (as in `int[] ages;`) instead of after the variable name (as in `char gradeLetters[];`), unless the array is being declared in a context such as `int x, y[], z;`.

You can declare multiple variables on one line by separating each variable from its predecessor with a comma, as demonstrated by the following example:

```
int x, y[], z;
```

This example declares three variables named x, y, and z. Each variable shares the same type, which happens to be integer. Unlike x and z, which store single integer values, y[ ] signifies a one-dimensional array whose element type is integer—each element stores an integer value. No array is yet associated with y.

The square brackets must appear after the variable name when the array is declared on the same line as the other variables. If you place the square brackets before the variable name, as in int x, []y, z;, the compiler reports an error. If you place the square brackets after the type name, as in int[] x, y, z;, all three variables signify one-dimensional arrays of integers.

Learning Expressions

The previously declared variables were not explicitly initialized to any values. As a result, they are either initialized to default values (such as 0 for int and 0.0 for double) or remain uninitialized, depending on the contexts in which they appear (declared within classes or declared within methods). In Chapter 3 I discuss variable contexts in terms of fields, local variables, and parameters.

Java provides the expressions feature for initializing variables and for other purposes. An *expression* is a combination of literals, variable names, method calls, and operators. At runtime, it evaluates to a value whose type is referred to as the expression's type. If the expression is being assigned to a variable, the expression's type must agree with the variable's type; otherwise, the compiler reports an error.

Java classifies expressions as simple expressions and compound expressions.

Simple Expressions

A *simple expression* is a *literal* (a value expressed verbatim), the name of a variable (containing a value), or a method call (returning a value). Java supports several kinds of literals: string, Boolean true and false, character, integer, floating-point, and null.

Note   A method call that doesn't return a value—the called method is known as a *void method*—is a special kind of simple expression; for example, System.out.println("Hello, World!");. This standalone expression cannot be assigned to a variable. Attempting to do so (as in int i = System.out.println("X");) causes the compiler to report an error.

A *string literal* consists of a sequence of Unicode characters surrounded by a pair of double quotes; for example, "The quick brown fox jumps over the lazy dog." It might also contain *escape sequences*, which are special syntax for representing certain printable and nonprintable characters that cannot otherwise appear in the literal. For example, "The quick brown \"fox\" jumps over the lazy dog." uses the \" escape sequence to surround fox with double quotes.

Table 2-2 describes all supported escape sequences.

Table 2-2. Escape Sequences

Escape Syntax	Description
\\	Backslash
\"	Double quote
\'	Single quote
\b	Backspace
\f	Form feed
\n	Newline (also referred to as line feed)
\r	Carriage return
\t	Horizontal tab

Finally, a string literal might contain *Unicode escape sequences*, which are special syntax for representing Unicode characters. A Unicode escape sequence begins with \u and continues with four hexadecimal digits (0–9, A–F, a–f) with no intervening space. For example, \u0041 represents capital letter A, and \u20ac represents the European Union's euro currency symbol.

A *Boolean literal* consists of reserved word true or reserved word false.

A *character literal* consists of a single Unicode character surrounded by a pair of single quotes ('A' is an example). You can also represent, as a character literal, an escape sequence (e.g., '\'') or a Unicode escape sequence (e.g., '\u0041').

An *integer literal* consists of a sequence of digits. If the literal is to represent a long integer value, it must be suffixed with an uppercase L or lowercase l (L is easier to read). If there is no suffix, the literal represents a 32-bit integer (an int).

Integer literals can be specified in the decimal, hexadecimal, and octal formats:

- The decimal format is the default format; for example, 127.

- The hexadecimal format requires that the literal begin with 0x or 0X and continue with hexadecimal digits (0–9, A–F, a–f); for example, 0x7F.

- The octal format requires that the literal be prefixed with 0 and continue with octal digits (0–7); for example, 0177.

A *floating-point literal* consists of an integer part, a decimal point (represented by the period character [.]), a fractional part, an exponent (starting with letter E or e), and a type suffix (letter D, d, F, or f). Most parts are optional, but enough information must be present to differentiate the floating-point literal from an integer literal. Examples include 0.1 (double precision floating-point), 89F (floating-point), 600D (double precision floating-point), and 13.08E+23 (double precision floating-point).

Finally, the null literal is assigned to a reference variable to indicate that the variable doesn't refer to an object.

The following examples use literals to initialize the previously presented variables:

```
int counter = 10;
double temperature = 98.6; // Assume Fahrenheit scale.
String firstName = "Mark";
int[] ages = { 52, 28, 93, 16 };
char gradeLetters[] = { 'A', 'B', 'C', 'D', 'F' };
float[][] matrix = { { 1.0F, 2.0F, 3.0F }, { 4.0F, 5.0F, 6.0F }};
int x = 1, y[] = { 1, 2, 3 }, z = 3;
double π = 3.14159;
```

The fourth through seventh examples use array initializers to initialize the ages, gradeLetters, matrix, and y arrays. An *array initializer* consists of a brace-and-comma-delimited list of expressions, which (as the matrix example shows) may themselves be array initializers. The matrix example results in a table that looks like the following:

```
1.0F 2.0F 3.0F
4.0F 5.0F 6.0F
```

ORGANIZING VARIABLES IN MEMORY

Perhaps you're curious about how variables are organized in memory. Figure 2-3 presents one possible high-level organization for the counter, ages, and matrix variables, along with the arrays assigned to ages and matrix.

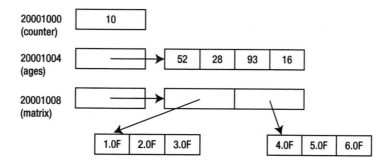

Figure 2-3. *The* counter *variable stores a 4-byte integer value, whereas* ages *and* matrix *store 4-byte references to their respective arrays*

Figure 2-3 reveals that each of counter, ages, and matrix is stored at a memory address (starting at a fictitious 20001000 value in this example) and divisible by 4 (each variable stores a 4-byte value); that counter's 4-byte value is stored at this address; and that each of the ages and matrix 4-byte memory locations stores the 32-bit address of its respective array (64-bit addresses would most likely be used on 64-bit virtual machines). Also, a one-dimensional array is stored as a list of values, whereas a two-dimensional array is stored as a one-dimensional row array of addresses, where each address identifies a one-dimensional column array of values for that row.

Although Figure 2-3 implies that array addresses are stored in ages and matrix, which equates references with addresses, a Java implementation might equate references with *handles* (integer values that identify slots in a list). This alternative is presented in Figure 2-4 for ages and its referenced array.

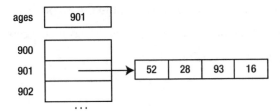

Figure 2-4. A handle is stored in ages, and the list entry identified by this handle stores the address of the associated array

Handles make it easy to move around regions of memory during garbage collection (discussed in Chapter 3). If multiple variables referenced the same array via the same address, each variable's address value would have to be updated when the array was moved. However, if multiple variables referenced the array via the same handle, only the handle's list entry would need to be updated. A downside to using handles is that accessing memory via these handles can be slower than directly accessing this memory via an address. Regardless of how references are implemented, this implementation detail is hidden from the Java developer to promote portability.

The following example shows a simple expression where a literal is assigned to a variable, followed by a simple expression where one variable is assigned the value of another variable:

```
int counter1 = 1;
int counter2 = counter1;
```

Finally, the following example shows a simple expression that assigns the result of a method call to a variable named isLeap:

```
boolean isLeap = isLeapYear(2012);
```

The previous examples have assumed that only those expressions whose types are the same as the types of the variables that they are initializing can be assigned to those variables. However, under certain circumstances, it's possible to assign an expression having a different type. For example, Java permits you to assign certain integer literals to short integer variables, as in short s = 20;, and assign a short integer expression to an integer variable, as in int i = s;.

Java permits the former assignment because 20 can be represented as a short integer (no information is lost). In contrast, Java would complain about short s = 40000; because integer literal 40000 cannot be represented as a short integer (32767 is the maximum positive integer that can be stored in a short integer variable). Java permits the latter assignment because no information is lost when Java converts from a type with a smaller set of values to a type with a wider set of values.

Java supports the following primitive-type conversions via widening conversion rules:

- Byte integer to short integer, integer, long integer, floating-point, or double precision floating-point
- Short integer to integer, long integer, floating-point, or double precision floating-point
- Character to integer, long integer, floating-point, or double precision floating-point

- Integer to long integer, floating-point, or double precision floating-point
- Long integer to floating-point or double precision floating-point
- Floating-point to double precision floating-point

Note   When converting from a smaller integer to a larger integer, Java copies the smaller integer's sign bit into the extra bits of the larger integer.

In Chapter 4, I discuss the widening conversion rules for performing type conversions in the contexts of user-defined and array types.

Compound Expressions

A *compound expression* is a sequence of simple expressions and operators, where an *operator* (a sequence of instructions symbolically represented in source code) transforms its operand expression value(s) into another value. For example, -6 is a compound expression consisting of operator - and integer literal 6 as its operand. This expression transforms 6 into its negative equivalent. Similarly, x + 5 is a compound expression consisting of variable name x, integer literal 5, and operator + sandwiched between these operands. Variable x's value is fetched and added to 5 when this expression is evaluated. The sum becomes the value of the expression.

Note   When x's type is byte integer or short integer, this variable's value is widened to an integer. However, when x's type is long integer, floating-point, or double precision floating-point, 5 is widened to the appropriate type. The addition operation is performed after the widening conversion takes place.

Java supplies many operators, which are classified by the number of operands that they take. A *unary operator* takes only one operand (unary minus [–] is an example), a *binary operator* takes two operands (addition [+] is an example), and Java's single *ternary operator* (conditional [?:]) takes three operands.

Operators are also classified as prefix, postfix, and infix. A *prefix operator* is a unary operator that precedes its operand (as in –6), a *postfix operator* is a unary operator that trails its operand (as in x++), and an *infix operator* is a binary or ternary operator that is sandwiched between the binary operator's two or the ternary operator's three operands (as in x + 5).

Table 2-3 presents all supported operators in terms of their symbols, descriptions, and precedence levels—I discuss the concept of precedence at the end of this section. Various operator descriptions refer to "integer type," which is shorthand for specifying any of byte integer, short integer, integer, or long integer unless "integer type" is qualified as a 32-bit integer. Also, "numeric type" refers to any of these integer types along with floating-point and double precision floating-point.

Table 2-3. *Operators*

Operator	Symbol	Description	Precedence
Addition	+	Given *operand1* + *operand2*, where each operand must be of character or numeric type, add *operand2* to *operand1* and return the sum.	10
Array index	[ ]	Given *variable*[*index*], where *index* must be of integer type, read value from or store value into *variable*'s storage element at location *index*.	13
Assignment	=	Given *variable* = *operand*, which must be *assignment-compatible* (their types must agree), store *operand* in *variable*.	0
Bitwise AND	&	Given *operand1* & *operand2*, where each operand must be of character or integer type, bitwise AND their corresponding bits and return the result. A result bit is set to 1 when each operand's corresponding bit is 1. Otherwise, the result bit is set to 0.	6
Bitwise complement	~	Given ~*operand*, where *operand* must be of character or integer type, flip *operand*'s bits (1s to 0s and 0s to 1s) and return the result.	12
Bitwise exclusive OR	^	Given *operand1* ^ *operand2*, where each operand must be of character or integer type, bitwise exclusive OR their corresponding bits and return the result. A result bit is set to 1 when one operand's corresponding bit is 1 and the other operand's corresponding bit is 0. Otherwise, the result bit is set to 0.	5
Bitwise inclusive OR	|	Given *operand1* | *operand2*, which must be of character or integer type, bitwise inclusive OR their corresponding bits and return the result. A result bit is set to 1 when either (or both) of the operands' corresponding bits is 1. Otherwise, the result bit is set to 0.	4
Cast	(type)	Given (*type*) *operand*, convert *operand* to an equivalent value that can be represented by *type*. For example, you could use this operator to convert a floating-point value to a 32-bit integer value.	12

(continued)

Table 2-3. (*continued*)

Operator	Symbol	Description	Precedence
Compound assignment	+=, −=, *=, /=, %=, &=, |=, ^=, <<=, >>=, >>>=	Given *variable operator operand*, where *operator* is one of the listed compound operator symbols and where *operand* is assignment compatible with *variable*, perform the indicated operation using *variable*'s value as *operator*'s left operand value and store the resulting value in *variable*.	0
Conditional	?:	Given *operand1* ? *operand2* : *operand3*, where *operand1* must be of Boolean type, return *operand2* when *operand1* is true or *operand3* when *operand1* is false. The types of *operand2* and *operand3* must agree.	1
Conditional AND	&&	Given *operand1* && *operand2*, where each operand must be of Boolean type, return true when both operands are true. Otherwise, return false. When *operand1* is false, *operand2* is not examined. This is known as *short-circuiting*.	3
Conditional OR	||	Given *operand1* || *operand2*, where each operand must be of Boolean type, return true when at least one operand is true. Otherwise, return false. When *operand1* is true, *operand2* is not examined. This is known as *short-circuiting*.	2
Division	/	Given *operand1* / *operand2*, where each operand must be of character or numeric type, divide *operand1* by *operand2* and return the quotient.	11
Equality	==	Given *operand1* == *operand2*, where both operands must be comparable (you cannot compare an integer with a string literal, for example), compare both operands for equality. Return true when these operands are equal. Otherwise, return false.	7
Inequality	!=	Given *operand1* != *operand2*, where both operands must be comparable (you cannot compare an integer with a string literal, for example), compare both operands for inequality. Return true when these operands are not equal. Otherwise, return false.	7

(*continued*)

Table 2-3. (*continued*)

Operator	Symbol	Description	Precedence
Left shift	<<	Given *operand1* << *operand2*, where each operand must be of character or integer type, shift *operand1*'s binary representation left by the number of bits that *operand2* specifies. For each shift, a 0 is shifted into the rightmost bit and the leftmost bit is discarded. Only the 5 low-order bits of *operand2* are used when shifting a 32–bit integer (to prevent shifting more than the number of bits in a 32–bit integer). Only the 6 low-order bits of *operand2* are used when shifting a 64-bit integer (to prevent shifting more than the number of bits in a 64-bit integer). The shift preserves negative values. Furthermore, it is equivalent to (but faster than) multiplying by a multiple of 2.	9
Logical AND	&	Given *operand1* & *operand2*, where each operand must be of Boolean type, return true when both operands are true. Otherwise, return false. In contrast to conditional AND, logical AND doesn't perform short-circuiting.	6
Logical complement	!	Given !*operand*, where *operand* must be of Boolean type, flip *operand*'s value (true to false or false to true) and return the result.	12
Logical exclusive OR	^	Given *operand1* ^ *operand2*, where each operand must be of Boolean type, return true when one operand is true and the other operand is false. Otherwise, return false.	5
Logical inclusive OR	|	Given *operand1* | *operand2*, where each operand must be of Boolean type, return true when at least one operand is true. Otherwise, return false. In contrast to conditional OR, logical inclusive OR doesn't perform short-circuiting.	4
Member access	.	Given *identifier1*.*identifier2*, access the *identifier2* member of *identifier1*. You will learn about this operator in Chapter 3.	13
Method call	()	Given *identifier(argument list)*, call the method identified by *identifier* and matching parameter list. You will learn about method calling in Chapter 3.	13

(*continued*)

Table 2-3. (*continued*)

Operator	Symbol	Description	Precedence
Multiplication	*	Given *operand1* * *operand2*, where each operand must be of character or numeric type, multiply *operand1* by *operand2* and return the product.	11
Object creation	new	Given new *identifier*(*argument list*), allocate memory for object and call constructor (discussed in Chapter 3) specified as *identifier*(*argument list*). Given new *identifier*[*integer size*], allocate a one-dimensional array of values.	12
Postdecrement	--	Given *variable*--, where *variable* must be of character or numeric type, subtract 1 from *variable*'s value (storing the result in *variable*) and return the original value.	13
Postincrement	++	Given *variable*++, where *variable* must be of character or numeric type, add 1 to *variable*'s value (storing the result in *variable*) and return the original value.	13
Predecrement	--	Given --*variable*, where *variable* must be of character or numeric type, subtract 1 from its value, store the result in *variable*, and return the new decremented value.	12
Preincrement	++	Given ++*variable*, where *variable* must be of character or numeric type, add 1 to its value, store the result in *variable*, and return the new incremented value.	12
Relational greater than	>	Given *operand1* > *operand2*, where each operand must be of character or numeric type, return true when *operand1* is greater than *operand2*. Otherwise, return false.	8
Relational greater than or equal to	>=	Given *operand1* >= *operand2*, where each operand must be of character or numeric type, return true when *operand1* is greater than or equal to *operand2*. Otherwise, return false.	8
Relational less than	<	Given *operand1* < *operand2*, where each operand must be of character or numeric type, return true when *operand1* is less than *operand2*. Otherwise, return false.	8

(*continued*)

Table 2-3. (*continued*)

Operator	Symbol	Description	Precedence
Relational less than or equal to	<=	Given *operand1* <= *operand2*, where each operand must be of character or numeric type, return true when *operand1* is less than or equal to *operand2*. Otherwise, return false.	8
Relational type checking	instanceof	Given *operand1* instanceof *operand2*, where *operand1* is an object and *operand2* is a class (or other user-defined type), return true when *operand1* is an instance of *operand2*. Otherwise, return false.	8
Remainder	%	Given *operand1* % *operand2*, where each operand must be of character or numeric type, divide *operand1* by *operand2* and return the remainder. Also known as the modulus operator.	11
Signed right shift	>>	Given *operand1* >> *operand2*, where each operand must be of character or integer type, shift *operand1*'s binary representation right by the number of bits that *operand2* specifies. For each shift, a copy of the sign bit (the leftmost bit) is shifted to the right and the rightmost bit is discarded. Only the 5 low-order bits of *operand2* are used when shifting a 32-bit integer (to prevent shifting more than the number of bits in a 32-bit integer). Only the 6 low-order bits of *operand2* are used when shifting a 64-bit integer (to prevent shifting more than the number of bits in a 64-bit integer). The shift preserves negative values. Furthermore, it is equivalent to (but faster than) dividing by a multiple of 2.	9
String concatenation	+	Given *operand1* + *operand2*, where at least one operand is of String type, append *operand2*'s string representation to *operand1*'s string representation and return the concatenated result.	10
Subtraction	-	Given *operand1* - *operand2*, where each operand must be of character or numeric type, subtract *operand2* from *operand1* and return the difference.	10
Unary minus	-	Given -*operand*, where *operand* must be of character or numeric type, return *operand*'s arithmetic negative.	12

(*continued*)

Table 2-3. (continued)

Operator	Symbol	Description	Precedence
Unary plus	+	Like its predecessor, but return *operand*. Rarely used.	12
Unsigned right shift	>>>	Given *operand1* >>> *operand2*, where each operand must be of character or integer type, shift *operand1*'s binary representation right by the number of bits that *operand2* specifies. For each shift, a zero is shifted into the leftmost bit and the rightmost bit is discarded. Only the 5 low-order bits of *operand2* are used when shifting a 32–bit integer (to prevent shifting more than the number of bits in a 32–bit integer). Only the 6 low-order bits of *operand2* are used when shifting a 64-bit integer (to prevent shifting more than the number of bits in a 64-bit integer). The shift does not preserve negative values. Furthermore, it is equivalent to (but faster than) dividing by a multiple of 2.	9

Table 2-3's operators can be classified as additive, array index, assignment, bitwise, cast, conditional, equality, logical, member access, method call, multiplicative, object creation, relational, shift, and unary minus/plus.

Additive Operators

The additive operators consist of addition (+), subtraction (-), postdecrement (--), postincrement (++), predecrement (--), preincrement (++), and string concatenation (+). Addition returns the sum of its operands (e.g., 6 + 4 returns 10), subtraction returns the difference between its operands (e.g., 6 - 4 returns 2 and 4 - 6 returns -2), postdecrement subtracts one from its variable operand and returns the variable's prior value (e.g., x--), postincrement adds one to its variable operand and returns the variable's prior value (e.g., x++), predecrement subtracts one from its variable operand and returns the variable's new value (e.g., --x), preincrement adds one to its variable operand and returns the variable's new value (e.g., ++x), and string concatenation merges its string operands and returns the merged string (e.g., "A" + "B" returns "AB").

The addition, subtraction, postdecrement, postincrement, predecrement, and preincrement operators can yield values that overflow or underflow the limits of the resulting value's type. For example, adding two large positive 32-bit integer values can produce a value that cannot be represented as a 32-bit integer value. The result is said to overflow. Java doesn't detect overflows and underflows.

Java provides a special widening conversion rule for use with string operands and the string concatenation operator. When either operand is not a string, the operand is first converted to a string prior to string concatenation. For example, when presented with "A" + 5, the compiler generates code that first converts 5 to "5" and then performs the string concatenation operation, resulting in "A5".

Array Index Operator

The array index operator ([ ]) accesses an array element by presenting the location of that element as an integer index. This operator is specified after an array variable's name, for example, ages[0].

Indexes are relative to 0, which implies that ages[0] accesses the first element, whereas ages[6] accesses the seventh element. The index must be greater than or equal to 0 and less than the length of the array; otherwise, the virtual machine throws ArrayIndexOutOfBoundsException (consult Chapter 5 to learn about exceptions).

An array's length is returned by appending ".length" to the array variable. For example, ages.length returns the length of (the number of elements in) the array that ages references. Similarly, matrix.length returns the number of row elements in the matrix two-dimensional array, whereas matrix[0].length returns the number of column elements assigned to the first row element of this array.

Assignment Operators

The assignment operator (=) assigns an expression's result to a variable (as in int x = 4;). The types of the variable and expression must agree; otherwise, the compiler reports an error.

Java also supports several compound assignment operators that perform a specific operation and assign its result to a variable. For example, the += operator evaluates the numeric expression on its right and adds the result to the contents of the variable on its left. The other compound assignment operators behave in a similar way.

Bitwise Operators

The bitwise operators consist of bitwise AND (&), bitwise complement (~), bitwise exclusive OR (^), and bitwise inclusive OR (|). These operators are designed to work on the binary representations of their character or integral operands. Because this concept can be hard to understand if you haven't previously worked with these operators in another language, the following output from a hypothetical application demonstrates these operators:

```
~00000000000000000000000010110101 results in 11111111111111111111111101001010
00011010 & 10110111 results in 00000000000000000000000000010010
00011010 ^ 10110111 results in 00000000000000000000000010101101
00011010 | 10110111 results in 00000000000000000000000010111111
```

The &, ^, and | operators in the last three lines first convert their byte integer operands to 32-bit integer values (through sign bit extension, copying the sign bit's value into the extra bits) before performing their operations.

Cast Operator

The cast operator—(*type*)—attempts to convert the type of its operand to *type*. This operator exists because the compiler will not allow you to convert a value from one type to another in which information will be lost without specifying your intention do so (via the cast operator). For example, when presented with short s = 1.65 + 3;, the compiler reports an error because attempting to convert a double precision floating-point value to a short integer results in the loss of the fraction .65—s would contain 4 instead of 4.65.

Recognizing that information loss might not always be a problem, Java permits you to explicitly state your intention by casting to the target type. For example, `short s = (short) 1.65 + 3;` tells the compiler that you want `1.65 + 3` to be converted to a short integer and that you realize that the fraction will disappear.

The following example provides another demonstration of the need for a cast operator:

```
char c = 'A';
byte b = c;
```

The compiler reports an error about loss of precision when it encounters `byte b = c;`. The reason is that c can represent any unsigned integer value from 0 through 65535, whereas b can only represent a signed integer value from −128 through +127. Even though 'A' equates to +65, which can fit within b's range, c could just have easily been initialized to '\u0323', which would not fit.

The solution to this problem is to introduce a (byte) cast, as follows, which causes the compiler to generate code to cast c's character type to byte integer:

```
byte b = (byte) c;
```

Java supports the following primitive-type conversions via cast operators:

- Byte integer to character
- Short integer to byte integer or character
- Character to byte integer or short integer
- Integer to byte integer, short integer, or character
- Long integer to byte integer, short integer, character, or integer
- Floating-point to byte integer, short integer, character, integer, or long integer
- Double precision floating-point to byte integer, short integer, character, integer, long integer, or floating-point

A cast operator is not always required when converting from more to fewer bits and where no data loss occurs. For example, when it encounters `byte b = 100;`, the compiler generates code that assigns integer 100 to byte integer variable b because 100 can easily fit into the 8-bit storage location assigned to this variable.

Conditional Operators

The conditional operators consist of conditional AND (&&), conditional OR (||), and conditional (?:). The first two operators always evaluate their left operand (a Boolean expression that evaluates to true or false) and conditionally evaluate their right operand (another Boolean expression). The third operator evaluates one of two operands based on a third Boolean operand.

Conditional AND always evaluates its left operand and evaluates its right operand only when its left operand evaluates to true. For example, `age > 64 && stillWorking` first evaluates `age > 64`. If this subexpression is true, `stillWorking` is evaluated, and its true or false value (`stillWorking` is a Boolean variable) serves as the value of the overall expression. If `age > 64` is false, `stillWorking` is not evaluated.

Conditional OR always evaluates its left operand and evaluates its right operand only when its left operand evaluates to false. For example, value < 20 || value > 40 first evaluates value < 20. If this subexpression is false, value > 40 is evaluated, and its true or false value serves as the overall expression's value. If value < 20 is true, value > 40 is not evaluated.

Conditional AND and conditional OR boost performance by preventing the unnecessary evaluation of subexpressions, which is known as *short-circuiting*. For example, if its left operand is false, there is no way that conditional AND's right operand can change the fact that the overall expression will evaluate to false.

If you aren't careful, short-circuiting can prevent *side effects* (the results of subexpressions that persist after the subexpressions have been evaluated) from executing. For example, age > 64 && ++numEmployees > 5 increments numEmployees for only those employees whose ages are greater than 64. Incrementing numEmployees is an example of a side effect because the value in numEmployees persists after the subexpression ++numEmployees > 5 has evaluated.

The conditional operator is useful for making a decision by evaluating and returning one of two operands based on the value of a third operand. The following example converts a Boolean value to its integer equivalent (1 for true and 0 for false):

```
boolean b = true;
int i = b ? 1 : 0; // 1 assigns to i
```

Equality Operators

The equality operators consist of equality (==) and inequality (!=). These operators compare their operands to determine whether they are equal or unequal. The former operator returns true when equal; the latter operator returns true when unequal. For example, each of 2 == 2 and 2 != 3 evaluates to true, whereas each of 2 == 4 and 4 != 4 evaluates to false.

When it comes to object operands (discussed in Chapter 3), these operators do not compare their contents. For example, "abc" == "xyz" doesn't compare a with x. Instead, because string literals are really String objects (in Chapter 7 I discuss this concept further), == compares the references to these objects.

Logical Operators

The logical operators consist of logical AND (&), logical complement (!), logical exclusive OR (^), and logical inclusive OR (|). Although these operators are similar to their bitwise counterparts, whose operands must be integer/character, the operands passed to the logical operators must be Boolean. For example, !false returns true. Also, when confronted with age > 64 & stillWorking, logical AND evaluates both subexpressions. This same pattern holds for logical exclusive OR and logical inclusive OR.

Member Access Operator

The member access operator (.) is used to access a class's members or an object's members. For example, String s = "Hello"; int len = s.length(); returns the length of the string assigned to variable s. It does so by calling the length() method member of the String class. In Chapter 3 I discuss member access in more detail.

Arrays are special objects that have a single `length` member. When you specify an array variable followed by the member access operator, followed by `length`, the resulting expression returns the number of elements in the array as a 32-bit integer. For example, `ages.length` returns the length of (the number of elements in) the array that `ages` references.

Method Call Operator

The method call operator—`()`—is used to signify that a method (discussed in Chapter 3) is being called. Furthermore, it identifies the number, order, and types of arguments that are passed to the method to be picked up by the method's parameters. `System.out.println("Hello");` is an example.

Multiplicative Operators

The multiplicative operators consist of multiplication (*), division (/), and remainder (%). Multiplication returns the product of its operands (e.g., 6*4 returns 24), division returns the quotient of dividing its left operand by its right operand (e.g., 6/4 returns 1), and remainder returns the remainder of dividing its left operand by its right operand (e.g., 6%4 returns 2).

The multiplication, division, and remainder operators can yield values that overflow or underflow the limits of the resulting value's type. For example, multiplying two large positive 32-bit integer values can produce a value that cannot be represented as a 32-bit integer value. The result is said to overflow. Java doesn't detect overflows and underflows.

Dividing a numeric value by 0 (via the division or remainder operator) also results in interesting behavior. Dividing an integer value by integer 0 causes the operator to throw an `ArithmeticException` object (I cover exceptions in Chapter 5). Dividing a floating-point/double precision floating-point value by 0 causes the operator to return +infinity or -infinity, depending on whether the dividend is positive or negative. Finally, dividing floating-point 0 by 0 causes the operator to return NaN (Not a Number).

Object Creation Operator

The object creation operator (new) creates an object from a class and also creates an array from an initializer. I discuss these topics in Chapter 3.

Relational Operators

The relational operators consist of greater than (>), greater than or equal to (>=), less than (<), less than or equal to (<=), and type checking (`instanceof`). The former four operators compare their operands and return true when the left operand is (respectively) greater than, greater than or equal to, less than, or less than or equal to the right operand. For example, each of 5.0 > 3, 2 >= 2, 16.1 < 303.3, and 54.0 <= 54.0 evaluates to true.

The type-checking operator is used to determine if an object belongs to a specific type. I discuss this topic in Chapter 4.

Shift Operators

The shift operators consist of left shift (<<), signed right shift (>>), and unsigned right shift (>>>). Left shift shifts the binary representation of its left operand leftward by the number of positions specified by its right operand. Each shift is equivalent to multiplying by 2. For example, 2 << 3 shifts 2's binary representation left by 3 positions; the result is equivalent to multiplying 2 by 8.

Each of signed and unsigned right shift shifts the binary representation of its left operand rightward by the number of positions specified by its right operand. Each shift is equivalent to dividing by 2. For example, 16 >> 3 shifts 16's binary representation right by 3 positions; the result is equivalent to dividing 16 by 8.

The difference between signed and unsigned right shift is what happens to the sign bit during the shift. Signed right shift includes the sign bit in the shift, whereas unsigned right shift ignores the sign bit. As a result, signed right shift preserves negative numbers, but unsigned right shift doesn't. For example, –4 >> 1 (the equivalent of –4 / 2) evaluates to –2, whereas –4 >>> 1 evaluates to 2147483646.

> **Tip**   The shift operators are faster than multiplying or dividing by powers of 2.

Unary Minus/Plus Operators

Unary minus (–) and unary plus (+) are the simplest of all operators. Unary minus returns the negative of its operand (such as –5 returns –5 and --5 returns 5), whereas unary plus returns its operand verbatim (such as +5 returns 5 and +–5 returns –5). Unary plus is not commonly used but is present for completeness.

Precedence and Associativity

When evaluating a compound expression, Java takes each operator's *precedence* (level of importance) into account to ensure that the expression evaluates as expected. For example, when presented with the expression 60 + 3 * 6, you expect multiplication to be performed before addition (multiplication has higher precedence than addition), and the final result to be 78. You don't expect addition to occur first, yielding a result of 378.

> **Note**   Table 2-3's rightmost column presents a value that indicates an operator's precedence: the higher the number, the higher the precedence. For example, addition's precedence level is 10 and multiplication's precedence level is 11, which means that multiplication is performed before addition.

Precedence can be circumvented by introducing open and close parentheses, (and), into the expression, where the innermost pair of nested parentheses is evaluated first. For example, evaluating 2 * ((60 + 3) * 6) results in (60 + 3) being evaluated first, (60 + 3) * 6 being evaluated next, and the overall expression being evaluated last. Similarly, in the expression 60 / (3–6), subtraction is performed before division.

During evaluation, operators with the same precedence level (such as addition and subtraction, which both have level 10) are processed according to their *associativity* (a property that determines how operators having the same precedence are grouped when parentheses are missing).

For example, expression 9 * 4 / 3 is evaluated as if it was (9 * 4) / 3 because * and / are left-to-right associative operators. In contrast, expression x = y = z = 100 is evaluated as if it was x = (y = (z = 100))—100 is assigned to z, z's new value (100) is assigned to y, and y's new value (100) is assigned to x—because = is a right-to-left associative operator.

Most of Java's operators are left-to-right associative. Right-to-left associative operators include assignment, bitwise complement, cast, compound assignment, conditional, logical complement, object creation, predecrement, preincrement, unary minus, and unary plus.

Note   Unlike languages such as C++, Java doesn't let you overload operators. However, Java overloads the +, ++, and -- operator symbols.

Learning Statements

Statements are the workhorses of a program. They assign values to variables, control a program's flow by making decisions and/or repeatedly executing other statements, and perform other tasks. A statement can be expressed as a simple statement or as a compound statement:

- A *simple statement* is a single, stand-alone source code instruction for performing some task; it's terminated with a semicolon.

- A *compound statement* is a (possibly empty) sequence of simple and other compound statements sandwiched between open and close brace delimiters—a *delimiter* is a character that marks the beginning or end of some section. A method body (such as the main() method's body) is an example. Compound statements can appear wherever simple statements appear and are alternatively referred to as *blocks*.

In this section I introduce you to many of Java's statements. Additional statements are covered in later chapters. For example, in Chapter 3 I discuss the return statement.

Assignment Statements

The *assignment statement* is an expression that assigns a value to a variable. This statement begins with a variable name, continues with the assignment operator (=) or a compound assignment operator (such as +=), and concludes with an assignment-compatible expression and a semicolon. Following are three examples:

```
x = 10;
ages[0] = 25;
counter += 10;
```

The first example assigns integer 10 to variable x, which is presumably of type integer as well. The second example assigns integer 25 to the first element of the ages array. The third example adds 10 to the value stored in `counter` and stores the sum in `counter`.

> **Note** Initializing a variable in the variable's declaration (such as int counter = 1;) can be thought of as a special form of the assignment statement.

Decision Statements

The previously described conditional operator (?:) is useful for choosing between two expressions to evaluate and cannot be used to choose between two statements. For this purpose, Java supplies three decision statements: if, if-else, and switch.

If Statement

The *if statement* evaluates a Boolean expression and executes another statement when this expression evaluates to true. This statement has the following syntax:

```
if (Boolean expression)
   statement
```

If consists of reserved word `if`, followed by a *Boolean expression* in parentheses, followed by a *statement* to execute when *Boolean expression* evaluates to true.

The following example demonstrates this statement:

```
if (numMonthlySales > 100)
   wage += bonus;
```

If the number of monthly sales exceeds 100, numMonthlySales > 100 evaluates to true and the wage += bonus; assignment statement executes. Otherwise, this assignment statement doesn't execute.

> **Note** Some people prefer to wrap a single statement in brace characters to prevent the possibility of error. As a result, they would write the previous example as follows:
>
> ```
> if (numMonthlySales > 100){
>    wage += bonus;
> }
> ```
>
> I don't do this for single statements because I view the extra braces as unnecessary clutter. However, you may feel differently. Use whatever approach makes you the most comfortable.

If-Else Statement

The *if-else statement* evaluates a Boolean expression and executes one of two statements depending on whether this expression evaluates to true or false. This statement has the following syntax:

```
if (Boolean expression)
   statement1
else
   statement2
```

If-else consists of reserved word if, followed by a *Boolean expression* in parentheses, followed by a *statement1* to execute when *Boolean expression* evaluates to true, followed by a *statement2* to execute when *Boolean expression* evaluates to false.

The following example demonstrates this statement:

```
if ((n & 1) == 1)
   System.out.println("odd");
else
   System.out.println("even");
```

This example assumes the existence of an int variable named n that has been initialized to an integer. It then proceeds to determine if the integer is odd (not divisible by 2) or even (divisible by 2).

The Boolean expression first evaluates n & 1, which bitwise ANDs n's value with 1. It then compares the result to 1. If they are equal, a message stating that n's value is odd outputs; otherwise, a message stating that n's value is even outputs.

The parentheses are required because == has higher precedence than &. Without these parentheses, the expression's evaluation order would change to first evaluating 1 == 1 and then trying to bitwise AND the Boolean result with n's integer value. This order results in a compiler error message because of a type mismatch: you cannot bitwise AND an integer with a Boolean value.

You could rewrite this if-else statement example to use the conditional operator, as follows: System.out.println((n & 1) == 1 ? "odd" : "even");. However, you cannot do so with the following example:

```
if ((n & 1) == 1)
   odd();
else
   even();
```

This example assumes the existence of odd() and even() methods that don't return anything. Because the conditional operator requires that each of its second and third operands evaluates to a value, the compiler reports an error when attempting to compile (n & 1) == 1 ? odd() : even().

You can chain multiple if-else statements together, resulting in the following syntax:

```
if (Boolean expression1)
   statement1
else
if (Boolean expression2)
   statement2
```

```
else
   ...
else
   statementN
```

If *Boolean expression1* evaluates to true, *statement1* executes. Otherwise, if *Boolean expression2* evaluates to true, *statement2* executes. This pattern continues until one of these expressions evaluates to true and its corresponding statement executes, or the final else is reached and *statementN* (the default statement) executes.

The following example demonstrates this chaining:

```
if (testMark >= 90)
{
   gradeLetter = 'A';
   System.out.println("You aced the test.");
}
else
if (testMark >= 80)
{
   gradeLetter = 'B';
   System.out.println("You did very well on this test.");
}
else
if (testMark >= 70)
{
   gradeLetter = 'C';
   System.out.println("Not bad, but you need to study more for future tests.");
}
else
if (testMark >= 60)
{
   gradeLetter = 'D';
   System.out.println("Your test result suggests that you need a tutor.");
}
else
{
   gradeLetter = 'F';
   System.out.println("Your test result is pathetic; you need summer school.");
}
```

DANGLING-ELSE PROBLEM

When if and if-else are used together, and the source code is not properly indented, it can be difficult to determine which if associates with the else. See the following, for example:

```
if (car.door.isOpen())
   if (car.key.isPresent())
      car.start();
else car.door.open();
```

Did the developer intend for the else to match the inner if, but improperly formatted the code to make it appear otherwise? See the following, for example:

```
if (car.door.isOpen())
    if (car.key.isPresent())
        car.start();
    else
        car.door.open();
```

If `car.door.isOpen()` and `car.key.isPresent()` each return true, `car.start()` executes. If `car.door.isOpen()` returns true and `car.key.isPresent()` returns false, `car.door.open();` executes. Attempting to open an open door makes no sense.

The developer must have wanted the else to match the outer if but forgot that else matches the nearest if. This problem can be fixed by surrounding the inner if with braces, as follows:

```
if (car.door.isOpen())
{
    if (car.key.isPresent())
        car.start();
}
else
    car.door.open();
```

When `car.door.isOpen()` returns true, the compound statement executes. When this method returns false, `car.door.open();` executes, which makes sense.

Forgetting that else matches the nearest if and using poor indentation to obscure this fact is known as the *dangling-else problem*.

Switch Statement

The *switch statement* lets you choose from among several execution paths in a more efficient manner than with equivalent chained if-else statements. This statement has the following syntax:

```
switch (selector expression)
{
    case value1: statement1 [break;]
    case value2: statement2 [break;]
    ...
    case valueN: statementN [break;]
    [default: statement]
}
```

Switch consists of reserved word `switch`, followed by a *selector expression* in parentheses, followed by a body of cases. The *selector expression* is any expression that evaluates to an integer or character value. For example, it might evaluate to a 32-bit integer or to a 16-bit character.

Each case begins with reserved word case; continues with a literal value and a colon character (:); continues with a statement to execute; and optionally concludes with a break statement, which causes execution to continue after the switch statement.

After evaluating the *selector expression*, switch compares this value with each case's value until it finds a match. When there is a match, the case's statement is executed. For example, when the *selector expression*'s value matches *value1*, *statement1* executes.

The optional break statement (anything placed in square brackets is optional), which consists of reserved word break followed by a semicolon, prevents the flow of execution from continuing with the next case's statement. Instead, execution continues with the first statement following switch.

> **Note**   You will usually place a break statement after a case's statement. Forgetting to include break can lead to a hard-to-find bug. However, there are situations where you want to group several cases together and have them execute common code. In such a situation, you would omit the break statement from the participating cases.

If none of the cases' values match the *selector expression*'s value, and if a default case (signified by the default reserved word followed by a colon) is present, the default case's statement is executed.

The following example demonstrates this statement:

```
switch (direction)
{
   case  0: System.out.println("You are travelling north."); break;
   case  1: System.out.println("You are travelling east."); break;
   case  2: System.out.println("You are travelling south."); break;
   case  3: System.out.println("You are travelling west."); break;
   default: System.out.println("You are lost.");
}
```

This example assumes that direction stores an integer value. When this value is in the range 0–3, an appropriate direction message is output; otherwise, a message about being lost is output.

> **Strong**   This example hardcodes values 0, 1, 2, and 3, which is not a good idea in practice. Instead, constants should be used. In Chapter 3 I introduce you to constants.

Loop Statements

It's often necessary to repeatedly execute a statement, and this repeated execution is called a *loop*. Java provides three kinds of loop statements: for, while, and do-while. In this section, I first discuss these statements. I then examine the topic of looping over the empty statement. Finally, I discuss the break, labeled break, continue, and labeled continue statements for prematurely ending all or part of a loop.

For Statement

The *for statement* lets you loop over a statement a specific number of times or even indefinitely. This statement has the following syntax:

```
for ([initialize]; [test]; [update])
   statement
```

For consists of reserved word `for`, followed by a header in parentheses, followed by a *statement* to execute. The header consists of an optional *initialize* section, followed by an optional *test* section, followed by an optional *update* section. A nonoptional semicolon separates each of the first two sections from the next section.

The *initialize* section consists of a comma-separated list of variable declarations or variable assignments. Some or all of these variables are typically used to control the loop's duration and are known as *loop-control variables*.

The *test* section consists of a Boolean expression that determines how long the loop executes. Execution continues as long as this expression evaluates to true.

Finally, the *update* section consists of a comma-separated list of expressions that typically modify the loop-control variables.

For is perfect for *iterating* (looping) over an array. Each *iteration* (loop execution) accesses one of the array's elements via an *array[index]* expression, where *array* is the array whose element is being accessed and *index* is the zero-based location of the element being accessed.

The following example uses the for statement to iterate over the array of command-line arguments that is passed to the `main()` method:

```
public static void main(String[] args)
{
   for (int i = 0; i < args.length; i++)
      System.out.println(args[i]);
}
```

For's initialization section declares variable i for controlling the loop, its test section compares i's current value to the length of the `args` array to ensure that this value is less than the array's length, and its update section increments i by 1. The loop continues until i's value equals the array's length.

Each iteration accesses one of the array's values via the `args[i]` expression. This expression returns this array's ith value (which happens to be a `String` object in this example). The first value is stored in `args[0]`.

Note   Although I've named the array containing command-line arguments `args`, this name isn't mandatory. I could as easily have named it `arguments` (or even `some_other_name`).

The following example uses for to output the contents of the previously declared `matrix` array, which is redeclared here for convenience:

```
float[][] matrix = { { 1.0F, 2.0F, 3.0F }, { 4.0F, 5.0F, 6.0F }};
for (int row = 0; row < matrix.length; row++)
{
    for (int col = 0; col < matrix[row].length; col++)
        System.out.print(matrix[row][col] + " ");
    System.out.print("\n");
}
```

Expression `matrix.length` returns the number of rows in this tabular array. For each row, expression `matrix[row].length` returns the number of columns for that row. This latter expression suggests that each row can have a different number of columns, although each row has the same number of columns in the example.

`System.out.print()` is closely related to `System.out.println()`. Unlike the latter method, `System.out.print()` outputs its argument without a trailing newline.

This example generates the following output:

```
1.0 2.0 3.0
4.0 5.0 6.0
```

While Statement

The *while statement* repeatedly executes another statement while its Boolean expression evaluates to true. This statement has the following syntax:

```
while (Boolean expression)
    statement
```

While consists of reserved word while, followed by a parenthesized *Boolean expression*, followed by a *statement* to repeatedly execute.

The while statement first evaluates the *Boolean expression*. If it is true, while executes the other *statement*. Once again, the *Boolean expression* is evaluated. If it is still true, while re-executes the *statement*. This cyclic pattern continues.

Prompting the user to enter a specific character is one situation in which while is useful. For example, suppose that you want to prompt the user to enter a specific uppercase letter or its lowercase equivalent. The following example provides a demonstration:

```
int ch = 0;
while (ch != 'C' && ch != 'c')
{
    System.out.println("Press C or c to continue.");
    ch = System.in.read();
}
```

This example begins by initializing variable ch. This variable must be initialized; otherwise, the compiler will report an uninitialized variable when it tries to read ch's value in the while statement's Boolean expression.

This expression uses the conditional AND operator (&&) to test ch's value. This operator first evaluates its left operand, which happens to be expression ch != 'C'. (The != operator converts 'C' from 16-bit unsigned char type to 32-bit signed int type prior to the comparison.)

If ch doesn't contain C (it doesn't at this point—0 was just assigned to ch), this expression evaluates to true.

The && operator next evaluates its right operand, which happens to be expression ch != 'c'. Because this expression also evaluates to true, conditional AND returns true and while executes the compound statement.

The compound statement first outputs, via the System.out.println() method call, a message that prompts the user to press the C key with or without the Shift key. It next reads the entered keystroke via System.in.read(), saving its integer value in ch.

From left to write, System identifies a standard class of system utilities, in identifies an object located in System that provides methods for inputting 1 or more bytes from the standard input device, and read() returns the next byte (or –1 when there are no more bytes).

Following this assignment, the compound statement ends and while re-evaluates its Boolean expression.

Suppose ch contains C's integer value. Conditional AND evaluates ch != 'C', which evaluates to false. Seeing that the expression is already false, conditional AND short-circuits its evaluation by not evaluating its right operand and returns false. The while statement subsequently detects this value and terminates.

Suppose ch contains c's integer value. Conditional AND evaluates ch != 'C', which evaluates to true. Seeing that the expression is true, conditional AND evaluates ch != 'c', which evaluates to false. Once again, the while statement terminates.

Note   A for statement can be coded as a while statement. For example,

```
for (int i = 0; i < 10; i++)
   System.out.println(i);
```

is equivalent to

```
int i = 0;
while (i < 10)
{
   System.out.println(i);
   i++;
}
```

Do-While Statement

The *do-while statement* repeatedly executes a statement while its Boolean expression evaluates to true. Unlike the while statement, which evaluates the Boolean expression at the top of the loop, do-while evaluates the Boolean expression at the bottom of the loop. This statement has the following syntax:

```
do
    statement
while (Boolean expression);
```

Do-while consists of the do reserved word, followed by a *statement* to repeatedly execute, followed by the while reserved word, followed by a parenthesized *Boolean expression*, followed by a semicolon.

The do-while statement first executes the other *statement*. It then evaluates the *Boolean expression*. If it is true, do-while executes the other *statement*. Once again, the *Boolean expression* is evaluated. If it is still true, do-while re-executes the *statement*. This cyclic pattern continues.

The following example demonstrates do-while prompting the user to enter a specific uppercase letter or its lowercase equivalent:

```
int ch;
do
{
   System.out.println("Press C or c to continue.");
   ch = System.in.read();
}
while (ch != 'C' && ch != 'c');
```

This example is similar to its predecessor. Because the compound statement is no longer executed prior to the test, it's no longer necessary to initialize ch—ch is assigned System.in.read()'s return value prior to the Boolean expression's evaluation.

Looping Over the Empty Statement

Java refers to a semicolon character appearing by itself as the *empty statement*. It's sometimes convenient for a loop statement to execute the empty statement repeatedly. The actual work performed by the loop statement takes place in the statement header. Consider the following example:

```
for (String line; (line = readLine()) != null; System.out.println(line));
```

This example uses for to present a programming idiom for copying lines of text that are read from some source, via the fictitious readLine() method in this example, to some destination, via System.out.println() in this example. Copying continues until readLine() returns null. Note the semicolon (empty statement) at the end of the line.

Caution   Be careful with the empty statement because it can introduce subtle bugs into your code. For example, the following loop is supposed to output the string Hello on 10 lines. Instead, only one instance of this string is output because it is the empty statement and not System.out.println() that's executed 10 times:

```
for (int i = 0; i < 10; i++); // this ; represents the empty statement
   System.out.println("Hello");
```

Break and Labeled Break Statements

What do for (;;);, while (true); and do;while (true); have in common? Each of these loop statements presents an extreme example of an *infinite loop* (a loop that never ends). An infinite loop is something that you should avoid because its unending execution causes your application to hang, which is not desirable from the point of view of your application's users.

Caution   An infinite loop can also arise from a loop's Boolean expression comparing a floating-point value against a nonzero value via the equality or inequality operator because many floating-point values have inexact internal representations. For example, the following example never ends because 0.1 doesn't have an exact internal representation:

```
for (double d = 0.0; d != 1.0; d += 0.1)
   System.out.println(d);
```

However, there are times when it is handy to code a loop as if it were infinite by using one of the aforementioned programming idioms. For example, you might code a while (true) loop that repeatedly prompts for a specific keystroke until the correct key is pressed. When the correct key is pressed, the loop must end. Java provides the break statement for this purpose.

The *break statement* transfers execution to the first statement following a switch statement (as discussed earlier) or a loop. In either scenario, this statement consists of reserved word break followed by a semicolon.

The following example uses break with an if decision statement to exit a while (true)-based infinite loop when the user presses the C or c key:

```
int ch;
while (true)
{
   System.out.println("Press C or c to continue.");
   ch = System.in.read();
   if (ch == 'C' || ch == 'c')
      break;
}
```

The break statement is also useful in the context of a finite loop. For example, consider a scenario where an array of values is searched for a specific value, and you want to exit the loop when this value is found. The following example reveals this scenario:

```java
int[] employeeIDs = { 123, 854, 567, 912, 224 };
int employeeSearchID = 912;
boolean found = false;
for (int i = 0; i < employeeIDs.length; i++)
   if (employeeSearchID == employeeIDs[i])
   {
      found = true;
      break;
   }
System.out.println((found) ? "employee " + employeeSearchID + " exists"
                           : "no employee ID matches " + employeeSearchID);
```

The example uses for and if to search an array of employee IDs to determine if a specific employee ID exists. If this ID is found, if's compound statement assigns true to found. Because there is no point in continuing the search, it then uses break to quit the loop.

The *labeled break statement* transfers execution to the first statement following the loop that's prefixed by a label (an identifier followed by a colon). It consists of reserved word break, followed by an identifier for which the matching label must exist. Furthermore, the label must immediately precede a loop statement.

Labeled break is useful for breaking out of *nested loops* (loops within loops). The following example reveals the labeled break statement transferring execution to the first statement that follows the outer for loop:

```java
outer:
for (int i = 0; i < 3; i++)
   for (int j = 0; j < 3; j++)
      if (i == 1 && j == 1)
         break outer;
      else
         System.out.println("i=" + i + ", j=" + j);
System.out.println("Both loops terminated.");
```

When i's value is 1 and j's value is 1, break outer; is executed to terminate both for loops. This statement transfers execution to the first statement after the outer for loop, which happens to be System.out.println("Both loops terminated.");.

The following output is generated:

```
i=0, j=0
i=0, j=1
i=0, j=2
i=1, j=0
Both loops terminated.
```

Continue and Labeled Continue Statements

The *continue statement* skips the remainder of the current loop iteration, re-evaluates the loop's Boolean expression, and performs another iteration (if true) or terminates the loop (if false). Continue consists of reserved word `continue` followed by a semicolon.

Consider a while loop that reads lines from a source and processes nonblank lines in some manner. Because it should not process blank lines, while skips the current iteration when a blank line is detected, as demonstrated in the following example:

```
String line;
while ((line = readLine()) != null)
{
   if (isBlank(line))
      continue;
   processLine(line);
}
```

This example employs a fictitious `isBlank()` method to determine if the currently read line is blank. If this method returns true, if executes the continue statement to skip the rest of the current iteration and read the next line whenever a blank line is detected. Otherwise, the fictitious `processLine()` method is called to process the line's contents.

Look carefully at this example and you should realize that the continue statement is not needed. Instead, this listing can be shortened via *refactoring* (rewriting source code to improve its readability, organization, or reusability), as demonstrated in the following example:

```
String line;
while ((line = readLine()) != null)
{
   if (!isBlank(line))
      processLine(line);
}
```

This example's refactoring modifies if's Boolean expression to use the logical complement operator (!). Whenever `isBlank()` returns false, this operator flips this value to true and if executes `processLine()`. Although continue isn't necessary in this example, you'll find it convenient to use this statement in more complex code where refactoring isn't as easy to perform.

The *labeled continue statement* skips the remaining iterations of one or more nested loops and transfers execution to the labeled loop. It consists of reserved word `continue` followed by an identifier for which a matching label must exist. Furthermore, the label must immediately precede a loop statement.

Labeled continue is useful for breaking out of nested loops while still continuing to execute the labeled loop. The following example reveals the labeled continue statement terminating the inner for loop's iterations:

```
outer:
for (int i = 0; i < 3; i++)
   for (int j = 0; j < 3; j++)
```

```
      if (i == 1 && j == 1)
         continue outer;
      else
         System.out.println("i=" + i + ", j=" + j);
System.out.println("Both loops terminated.");
```

When i's value is 1 and j's value is 1, continue outer; is executed to terminate the inner for loop and continue with the outer for loop at its next value of i. Both loops continue until they finish.

The following output is generated:

```
i=0, j=0
i=0, j=1
i=0, j=2
i=1, j=0
i=2, j=0
i=2, j=1
i=2, j=2
Both loops terminated.
```

EXERCISES

The following exercises are designed to test your understanding of Chapter 2's content:

1. What is Unicode?

2. What is a comment?

3. Identify the three kinds of comments that Java supports.

4. What is an identifier?

5. True or false: Java is a case-insensitive language.

6. What is a type?

7. Define primitive type.

8. Identify all of Java's primitive types.

9. Define user-defined type.

10. Define array type.

11. What is a variable?

12. What is an expression?

13. Identify the two expression categories.

14. What is a literal?

15. Is string literal "The quick brown fox \jumps\ over the lazy dog." legal or illegal? Why?

16. What is an operator?

17. Identify the difference between a prefix operator and a postfix operator.

18.   What is the purpose of the cast operator?

19.   What is precedence?

20.   True or false: Most of Java's operators are left-to-right associative.

21.   What is a statement?

22.   What is the difference between the while and do-while statements?

23.   What is the difference between the break and continue statements?

24.   Write an OutputGradeLetter application (the class is named OutputGradeLetter) whose main() method executes the grade letter code sequence presented earlier while discussing the if-else statement. Use the DumpArgs application presented in Listing 2-1 as the basis for this application. (You don't need to include Javadoc comments, but you can if you want.)

25.   Create a Triangle application whose Triangle class's main() method uses a pair of nested for statements along with System.out.print() to output a 10-row triangle of asterisks, where each row contains an odd number of asterisks (1, 3, 5, 7, and so on), as shown following:

```
        *
       ***
      *****
     *******
    *********
   ***********
  *************
 ***************
*****************
*******************
```

Compile and run this application.

Summary

Source code needs to be documented so that you (and any others who have to maintain it) can understand it, now and later. Java provides the comment feature for embedding documentation in source code. Single-line, multiline, and documentation comments are supported.

A single-line comment occupies all or part of a single line of source code. This comment begins with the // character sequence and continues with explanatory text. The compiler ignores everything from // to the end of the line in which // appears.

A multiline comment occupies one or more lines of source code. This comment begins with the /* character sequence, continues with explanatory text, and ends with the */ character sequence. Everything from /* through */ is ignored by the compiler.

A Javadoc comment occupies one or more lines of source code. This comment begins with the /** character sequence, continues with explanatory text, and ends with the */ character sequence. Everything from /** through */ is ignored by the compiler.

Identifiers are used to name classes, methods, and other source code entities. An identifier consists of letters (A–Z, a–z, or equivalent uppercase/lowercase letters in other human alphabets), digits (0–9 or equivalent digits in other human alphabets), connecting punctuation characters (e.g., the underscore), and currency symbols (e.g., the dollar sign $). This name must begin with a letter, a currency symbol, or a connecting punctuation character; and its length cannot exceed the line in which it appears. Some identifiers are reserved by Java. Examples include `abstract` and `case`.

Applications process different types of values such as integers, floating-point values, characters, and strings. A type identifies a set of values (and their representation in memory) and a set of operations that transform these values into other values of that set.

A primitive type is a type that's defined by the language and whose values are not objects. Java supports the Boolean, character, byte integer, short integer, integer, long integer, floating-point, and double precision floating-point primitive types.

A user-defined type is a type that's defined by the developer using a class, an interface, an enum, or an annotation type and whose values are objects. User-defined types are also known as reference types.

An array type is a reference type that signifies an array, a region of memory that stores values in equal-size and contiguous slots, which are commonly referred to as elements. This type consists of the element type and one or more pairs of square brackets that indicate the number of dimensions.

Applications manipulate values that are stored in memory, which is symbolically represented in source code through the use of the variables feature. A variable is a named memory location that stores some type of value.

Java provides the expressions feature for initializing variables and for other purposes. An expression combines some arrangement of literals, variable names, method calls, and operators. At runtime, it evaluates to a value whose type is referred to as the expression's type.

A simple expression is a literal (a value specified verbatim), a variable name (containing a value), or a method call (returning a value). Java supports several kinds of literals: string, Boolean `true` and `false`, character, integer, floating-point, and `null`.

A compound expression is a sequence of simple expressions and operators, where an operator (a sequence of instructions symbolically represented in source code) transforms its operand expression value(s) into another value.

Java supplies many operators, which are classified by the number of operands that they take. A unary operator takes only one operand, a binary operator takes two operands, and Java's single ternary operator takes three operands.

Operators are also classified as prefix, postfix, and infix. A prefix operator is a unary operator that precedes its operand, a postfix operator is a unary operator that trails its operand, and an infix operator is a binary or ternary operator that is sandwiched between its operands.

Statements are the workhorses of a program. They assign values to variables, control a program's flow by making decisions and/or repeatedly executing other statements, and perform other tasks. A statement can be expressed as a simple statement or as a compound statement.

In Chapter 3 I continue to explore the Java language by examining its support for classes and objects. You also learn more about arrays.

Chapter 3

Discovering Classes and Objects

In Chapter 2 I introduced you to the fundamentals of the Java language. You now know how to write simple applications by inserting statements into a class's main() method. However, when you try to develop complex applications in this manner, you're bound to find development tedious, slow, and prone to error. Classes and objects address these problems by simplifying application architecture.

In Chapter 3 I introduce you to Java's support for classes and objects. You learn how to declare a class and instantiate objects from the class, how to declare fields within the class and access these fields, how to declare methods within the class and call them, how to initialize classes and objects, and how to get rid of objects when they are no longer needed.

While discussing variables in Chapter 2, I introduced you to arrays. You learned about array variables and discovered a simple way to create an array. However, Java also provides a more powerful and more flexible way to create arrays, which is somewhat similar to the manner in which objects are created. This chapter also extends Chapter 2's array coverage by introducing you to this capability.

Declaring Classes and Instantiating Objects

Before the modern approach to programming that involves classes and objects, applications adhered to *structured programming* in which *data structures* were created to organize and store data items, and *functions* (named code sequences that return values) and *procedures* (named code sequences that don't return values) were used to manipulate data structure content. This separation of data from code made it difficult to model *real-world entities* (such as a bank accounts and employees) and often led to maintenance headaches for complex applications.

Computer scientists such as Bjarne Stroustrup (the creator of the C++ programming language) found that this complexity could be simplified by merging data structures with functions and procedures into discrete units known as classes. These classes could describe real-world entities and be instantiated. The resulting objects proved to be an effective way to model these entities.

You first learn how to declare a class and then learn how to create objects from this class with the help of the new operator and a constructor. Last, you learn about constructor parameters and how to specify them for initializing objects and about local variables and how to specify them for helping to control the flow of code within a constructor.

Declaring Classes

A *class* is a template for manufacturing *objects* (named groupings of code and data), which are also known as *class instances*, or *instances* for short. Classes generalize real-world entities, and objects are specific manifestations of these entities at the application level. You might think of classes as cookie cutters and objects as the cookies that cookie cutters create.

Because you cannot instantiate objects from a class that doesn't exist, you must first declare the class. The declaration consists of a header followed by a body. At minimum, the header consists of reserved word class followed by a name that identifies the class (so that it can be referred to from elsewhere in the source code). The body starts with an open brace character ({) and ends with a close brace (}). Sandwiched between these delimiters are various kinds of declarations. Consider Listing 3-1.

Listing 3-1. Declaring a Skeletal Image Class

```
class Image
{
   // various member declarations
}
```

Listing 3-1 declares a class named Image, which presumably describes some kind of image for displaying on the screen. By convention, a class's name begins with an uppercase letter. Furthermore, the first letter of each subsequent word in a multiword class name is capitalized. This is known as *camelcasing*.

Instantiating Objects with the New Operator and a Constructor

Image is an example of a user-defined type from which objects can be created. You create these objects by using the new operator with a constructor, as follows:

```
Image image = new Image();
```

The new operator allocates memory to store the object whose type is specified by new's solitary operand, which happens to be Image() in this example. The object is stored in a region of memory known as the *heap*.

The parentheses (round brackets) that follow Image signify a *constructor*, which is a block of code for constructing an object by initializing it in some manner. The new operator *invokes* (calls) the constructor immediately after allocating memory to store the object.

When the constructor ends, new returns a *reference* (a memory address or other identifier) to the object so that it can be accessed elsewhere in the application. Regarding the newly created Image object, its reference is stored in a variable named image whose type is specified as Image. (It's common to refer to the variable as an object, as in the image object, although it stores only an object's reference and not the object itself.)

> **Note**   new's returned reference is represented in source code by keyword `this`. Wherever `this` appears, it represents the current object. Also, variables that store references are called *reference variables*.

Image doesn't explicitly declare a constructor. When a class doesn't declare a constructor, Java implicitly creates a constructor for that class. The created constructor is known as the *default noargument constructor* because no arguments (discussed shortly) appear between its (and) characters when the constructor is invoked.

> **Note**   Java doesn't create a default noargument constructor when at least one constructor is declared.

Specifying Constructor Parameters and Local Variables

You explicitly declare a constructor within a class's body by specifying the name of the class followed by a *parameter list*, which is a round bracket-delimited and comma-separated list of zero or more parameter declarations. A *parameter* is a constructor or method variable that receives an expression value passed to the constructor or method when it is called. This expression value is known as an *argument*.

Listing 3-2 enhances Listing 3-1's `Image` class by declaring three constructors with parameter lists that declare zero, one, or two parameters and a `main()` method for testing this class.

Listing 3-2. Declaring an `Image` Class with Three Constructors and a `main()` Method

```
public class Image
{
   Image()
   {
      System.out.println("Image() called");
   }

   Image(String filename)
   {
      this(filename, null);
      System.out.println("Image(String filename) called");
   }

   Image(String filename, String imageType)
   {
      System.out.println("Image(String filename, String imageType) called");
      if (filename != null)
      {
         System.out.println("reading " + filename);
         if (imageType != null)
            System.out.println("interpreting " + filename + " as storing a " +
                               imageType + " image");
      }
```

```
        // Perform other initialization here.
    }

    public static void main(String[] args)
    {
        Image image = new Image();
        System.out.println();
        image = new Image("image.png");
        System.out.println();
        image = new Image("image.png", "PNG");
    }
}
```

Listing 3-2's Image class first declares a noargument constructor for initializing an Image object to default values (whatever they may be). This constructor simulates default initialization. It does so by invoking System.out.println() to output a message signifying that it's been called.

Image next declares an Image(String filename) constructor whose parameter list consists of a single *parameter declaration*—a variable's type followed by the variable's name. The java.lang.String parameter is named filename, signifying that this constructor obtains image content from a file.

> **Note**   Throughout this chapter and remaining chapters, I typically prefix the first use of a predefined type (such as String) with the package hierarchy in which the type is stored. For example, String is stored in the lang subpackage of the java package. I do so to help you learn where types are stored so that you can more easily specify import statements for importing these types (without having to first search for a type's package) into your source code—you don't have to import types that are stored in the java.lang package, but I still prefix the java.lang package to the type name for completeness. I will have more to say about packages and the import statement in Chapter 5.

Some constructors rely on other constructors to help them initialize their objects. This is done to avoid redundant code, which increases the size of an object and unnecessarily takes memory away from the heap that could be used for other purposes. For example, Image(String filename) relies on Image(String filename, String imageType) to read the file's image content into memory.

Although it appears otherwise, constructors don't have names (however, it is common to refer to a constructor by specifying the class name and parameter list). A constructor calls another constructor by using keyword this and a round bracket-delimited and comma-separated list of arguments. For example, Image(String filename) executes this(filename, null); to execute Image(String filename, String imageType).

> **Caution**   You must use keyword this to call another constructor—you cannot use the class's name, as in Image(). The this() constructor call (when present) must be the first code that is executed within the constructor—this rule prevents you from specifying multiple this() constructor calls in the same constructor. Finally, you cannot specify this() in a method—constructors can be called only by other constructors and during object creation. (I discuss methods later in this chapter.)

When present, the constructor call must be the first code that is specified within a constructor; otherwise, the compiler reports an error. For this reason, a constructor that calls another constructor can perform additional work only after the other constructor has finished. For example, Image(String filename) executes System.out.println("Image(String filename) called"); after the invoked Image(String filename, String imageType) constructor finishes.

The Image(String filename, String imageType) constructor declares an imageType parameter that signifies the kind of image stored in the file—a Portable Network Graphics (PNG) image, for example. Presumably, the constructor uses imageType to speed up processing by not examining the file's contents to learn the image format. When null is passed to imageType, as happens with the Image(String filename) constructor, Image(String filename, String imageType) examines file contents to learn the format. If null was also passed to filename, Image(String filename, String imageType) wouldn't read the file but would presumably notify the code attempting to create the Image object of an error condition.

After declaring the constructors, Listing 3-2 declares a main() method that lets you create Image objects and view output messages. main() creates three Image objects, calling the first constructor with no arguments, the second constructor with argument "image.png", and the third constructor with arguments "image.png" and "PNG".

> **Note**   The number of arguments passed to a constructor or method, or the number of operator operands, is known as the constructor's, method's, or operator's *arity*.

Each object's reference is assigned to a reference variable named image, replacing the previously stored reference for the second and third object assignments. (Each occurrence of System.out.println(); outputs a blank line to make the output easier to read.)

The presence of main() changes Image from only a class to an application. You typically place main() in classes that are used to create objects to test such classes. When constructing an application for use by others, you usually declare main() in a class where the intent is to run an application and not to create an object from that class—the application is then run from only that class. See Chapter 1's DumpArgs and EchoText classes for examples.

After saving Listing 3-2 to Image.java, compile this file by executing javac Image.java at the command line. Assuming that there are no error messages, execute the application by specifying java Image. You should observe the following output:

```
Image() called

Image(String filename, String imageType) called
reading image.png
Image(String filename) called

Image(String filename, String imageType) called
reading image.png
interpreting image.png as storing a PNG image
```

The first output line indicates that the noargument constructor has been called. Subsequent output lines indicate that the second and third constructors have been called.

As well as declaring parameters, a constructor can declare variables within its body to help it perform various tasks. For example, the previously presented Image(String filename, String imageType) constructor might create an object from a (hypothetical) File class that provides the means to read a file's contents. At some point, the constructor instantiates this class and assigns the instance's reference to a variable, as demonstrated by the following code:

```java
Image(String filename, String imageType)
{
   System.out.println("Image(String filename, String imageType) called");
   if (filename != null)
   {
      System.out.println("reading " + filename);
      File file = new File(filename);
      // Read file contents into object.
      if (imageType != null)
         System.out.println("interpreting " + filename + " as storing a " +
                            imageType + " image");
      else
         // Inspect image contents to learn image type.
         ; // Empty statement is used to make if-else syntactically valid.
   }
   // Perform other initialization here.
}
```

As with the filename and imageType parameters, file is a variable that is local to the constructor and is known as a *local variable* to distinguish it from a parameter. Although all three variables are local to the constructor, there are two key differences between parameters and local variables:

- The filename and imageType parameters come into existence at the point where the constructor begins to execute and exist until execution leaves the constructor. In contrast, file comes into existence at its point of declaration and continues to exist until the block in which it is declared is terminated (via a closing brace character). This property of a parameter or a local variable is known as *lifetime*.

- The filename and imageType parameters can be accessed from anywhere in the constructor. In contrast, file can be accessed only from its point of declaration to the end of the block in which it is declared. It cannot be accessed before its declaration or after its declaring block, but nested subblocks can access the local variable. This property of a parameter or a local variable is known as *scope*.

> **Note**   The lifetime and scope (also known as *visibility*) properties also apply to classes, objects, and fields (discussed later). Classes come into existence when loaded into memory and cease to exist when unloaded from memory, typically when an application exits. Also, loaded classes are typically visible to other classes.
>
> An object's lifetime ranges from its creation via the new operator until the moment when it is removed from memory by the garbage collector (discussed later in this chapter). Its scope depends on various factors, such as when its reference is assigned to a local variable or to a field. I discuss fields later in this chapter.
>
> The lifetime of a field depends on whether it is an instance field or a class field. When the field belongs to an object (an instance field), it comes into existence when the object is created and dies when the object disappears from memory. When the field belongs to a class (a class field), the field begins its existence when the class is loaded and disappears when the class is removed from memory. As with an object, a field's scope depends on various factors, such as whether the field is declared to have private access or not—you'll learn about private access later in this chapter.

A local variable cannot have the same name as a parameter because a parameter always has the same scope as the local variable. However, a local variable can have the same name as another local variable provided that both variables are located within different scopes (that is, within different blocks). For example, you could specify int x = 1; within an if-else statement's if block and specify double x = 2.0; within the statement's corresponding else block, and each local variable would be distinct.

> **Note**   The discussion of constructor parameters, arguments, and local variables also applies to method parameters, arguments, and local variables—I discuss methods later in this chapter.

Encapsulating State and Behaviors

Classes model real-world entities from a template perspective, for example, car and savings account. Objects represent specific entities, for example, John's red Toyota Camry (a car instance) and Cuifen's savings account with a balance of twenty thousand dollars (a savings account instance).

Entities have *attributes*, such as color red, make Toyota, model Camry, and balance twenty thousand dollars. An entity's collection of attributes is referred to as its *state*. Entities also have *behaviors*, such as open car door, drive car, display fuel consumption, deposit, withdraw, and show account balance.

A class and its objects model an entity by combining state with behaviors into a single unit—the class abstracts state, whereas its objects provide concrete state values. This bringing together of state and behaviors is known as *encapsulation*. Unlike in structured programming, where the developer focuses on separately modeling behaviors through structured code and modeling state through data structures that store data items for the structured code to manipulate, the developer working with classes and objects focuses on templating entities by declaring classes that encapsulate state and behaviors, instantiating objects with specific state values from these classes to represent specific entities and interacting with objects through their behaviors.

In this section, I first introduce you to Java's language features for representing state, and then I introduce you to its language features for representing behaviors. Because some state and behaviors support the class's internal architecture and should not be visible to those wanting to use the class, I conclude this section by presenting the important concept of information hiding.

Representing State via Fields

Java lets you represent state via *fields*, which are variables declared within a class's body. Entity attributes are described via *instance fields*. Because Java also supports state that's associated with a class and not with an object, Java provides *class fields* to describe this class state.

You first learn how to declare and access instance fields and then learn how to declare and access class fields. After discovering how to declare read-only instance and class fields, you review the rules for accessing fields from different contexts.

Declaring and Accessing Instance Fields

You can declare an instance field by minimally specifying a type name, followed by an identifier that names the field, followed by a semicolon character (;). Listing 3-3 presents a Car class with three instance field declarations.

Listing 3-3. Declaring a Car Class with make, model, and numDoors Instance Fields

```
class Car
{
   String make;
   String model;
   int numDoors;
}
```

Listing 3-3 declares two String instance fields named make and model. It also declares an int instance field named numDoors. By convention, a field's name begins with a lowercase letter, and the first letter of each subsequent word in a multiword field name is capitalized.

When an object is created, instance fields are initialized to default zero values, which you interpret at the source code level as literal value false, '\u0000', 0, 0L, 0.0, 0.0F, or null (depending on element type). For example, if you were to execute Car car = new Car();, make and model would be initialized to null and numDoors would be initialized to 0.

You can assign values to or read values from an object's instance fields by using the member access operator (.); the left operand specifies the object's reference and the right operand specifies the instance field to be accessed. Listing 3-4 uses this operator to initialize a Car object's make, model, and numDoors instance fields.

Listing 3-4. Initializing a Car Object's Instance Fields

```
public class Car
{
   String make;
   String model;
   int numDoors;

   public static void main(String[] args)
   {
      Car car = new Car();
      car.make = "Toyota";
      car.model = "Camry";
      car.numDoors = 4;
   }
}
```

Listing 3-4 presents a `main()` method that instantiates `Car`. The `car` instance's `make` instance field is assigned the "Toyota" string, its `model` instance field is assigned the "Camry" string, and its `numDoors` instance field is assigned integer literal 4. (A string's double quotes delimit a string's sequence of characters but are not part of the string.)

You can explicitly initialize an instance field when declaring that field to provide a nonzero default value, which overrides the default zero value. Listing 3-5 demonstrates this point.

Listing 3-5. Initializing Car's numDoors Instance Field to a Default Nonzero Value

```
public class Car
{
   String make;
   String model;
   int numDoors = 4;

   Car()
   {
   }

   public static void main(String[] args)
   {
      Car johnDoeCar = new Car();
      johnDoeCar.make = "Chevrolet";
      johnDoeCar.model = "Volt";
   }
}
```

Listing 3-5 explicitly initializes numDoors to 4 because the developer has assumed that most cars being modeled by this class have four doors. When `Car` is initialized via the `Car()` constructor, the developer only needs to initialize the `make` and `model` instance fields for those cars that have four doors.

It is usually not a good idea to directly initialize an object's instance fields, and you will learn why when I discuss information hiding (later in this chapter). Instead, you should perform this initialization in the class's constructor(s)—see Listing 3-6.

Listing 3-6. Initializing Car's Instance Fields via Constructors

```
public class Car
{
   String make;
   String model;
   int numDoors;

   Car(String make, String model)
   {
      this(make, model, 4);
   }

   Car(String make, String model, int nDoors)
   {
      this.make = make;
      this.model = model;
      numDoors = nDoors;
   }

   public static void main(String[] args)
   {
      Car myCar = new Car("Toyota", "Camry");
      Car yourCar = new Car("Mazda", "RX-8", 2);
   }
}
```

Listing 3-6's Car class declares Car(String make, String model) and Car(String make, String model, int nDoors) constructors. The first constructor lets you specify the make and model, whereas the second constructor lets you specify values for the three instance fields.

The first constructor executes this(make, model, 4); to pass the values of its make and model parameters along with a default value of 4 to the second constructor. Doing so demonstrates an alternative to explicitly initializing an instance field and is preferable from a code maintenance perspective.

The Car(String make, String model, int numDoors) constructor demonstrates another use for keyword this. Specifically, it demonstrates a scenario where constructor parameters have the same names as the class's instance fields. Prefixing a variable name with "this." causes the Java compiler to create bytecode that accesses the instance field. For example, this.make = make; assigns the make parameter's String object reference to this (the current) Car object's make instance field. If make = make; was specified instead, it would accomplish nothing by assigning make's value to itself; a Java compiler might not generate code to perform the unnecessary assignment. In contrast, "this." isn't necessary for the numDoors = nDoors; assignment, which initializes the numDoors field from the nDoors parameter value.

Note To minimize error (by forgetting to prefix a field name with "this."), it's preferable to keep field names and parameter names distinct (e.g., numDoors and nDoors). Alternatively, you might prefix a field name with an underscore (e.g., _nDoors). Either way, you wouldn't have to worry about the "this." prefix (and forgetting to specify it).

Declaring and Accessing Class Fields

In many situations, instance fields are all that you need. However, you might encounter a situation where you need a single copy of a field no matter how many objects are created.

For example, suppose you want to track the number of Car objects that have been created and introduce a counter instance field (initialized to 0) into this class. You also place code in the class's constructor that increases counter's value by 1 when an object is created. However, because each object has its own copy of the counter instance field, this field's value never advances past 1. Listing 3-7 solves this problem by declaring counter to be a class field by prefixing the field declaration with the static keyword.

Listing 3-7. Adding a counter Class Field to Car

```
public class Car
{
   String make;
   String model;
   int numDoors;
   static int counter;

   Car(String make, String model)
   {
      this(make, model, 4);
   }

   Car(String make, String model, int numDoors)
   {
      this.make = make;
      this.model = model;
      this.numDoors = numDoors;
      counter++; // This code is unsafe because counter can be accessed directly.
   }

   public static void main(String[] args)
   {
      Car myCar = new Car("Toyota", "Camry");
      Car yourCar = new Car("Mazda", "RX-8", 2);
      System.out.println(Car.counter);
   }
}
```

Listing 3-7's static prefix implies that there is only one copy of the counter field and not one copy per object. When a class is loaded into memory, class fields are initialized to default zero values. For example, counter is initialized to 0. (As with an instance field, you can alternatively assign a value to a class field in its declaration.) Each time an object is created, counter will increase by 1 thanks to the counter++ expression in the Car(String make, String model, int numDoors) constructor.

Unlike instance fields, class fields are normally accessed directly via the member access operator. Although you could access a class field via an object reference (as in myCar.counter), it is conventional to access a class field by using the class's name, as in Car.counter. (It is also easier to tell that the code is accessing a class field.)

> **Note**   Because the `main()` method is a member of Listing 3-7's `Car` class, you could access
> `counter` directly, as in `System.out.println(counter);`. To access `counter` in the context of
> another class's `main()` method, however, you would have to specify `Car.counter`.

If you run Listing 3-7, you'll notice that it outputs 2, because two `Car` objects have been created.

Declaring Read-Only Instance and Class Fields

The previously declared fields can be written to as well as read from. However, you might want to declare a field that is read-only, for example, a field that names a constant value such as pi (3.14159…). Java lets you accomplish this task by providing reserved word `final`.

Each object receives its own copy of a read-only instance field. This field must be initialized as part of the field's declaration or in the class's constructor. When initialized in the constructor, the read-only instance field is known as a *blank final* because it doesn't have a value until one is assigned to it in the constructor. Because a constructor can potentially assign a different value to each object's blank final, these read-only variables are not truly constants.

If you want a true *constant*, which is a single read-only value that is available to all objects, you need to create a read-only class field. You can accomplish this task by including the reserved word `static` with `final` in that field's declaration.

Listing 3-8 shows how to declare a read-only class field.

Listing 3-8. Declaring a True Constant in the Employee Class

```
class Employee
{
   final static int RETIREMENT_AGE = 65;
}
```

Listing 3-8's `RETIREMENT_AGE` declaration is an example of a *compile-time constant*. Because there is only one copy of its value (thanks to the `static` keyword), and because this value will never change (thanks to the `final` keyword), the compiler is free to optimize the compiled code by inserting the constant value into all calculations where it is used. The code runs faster because it doesn't have to access a read-only class field.

Reviewing Field-Access Rules

The previous examples of field access may seem confusing because you can sometimes specify the field's name directly, whereas you need to prefix a field name with an object reference or a class name and the member access operator at other times. The following rules dispel this confusion by giving you guidance on how to access fields from the various contexts:

- Specify the name of a class field as is from anywhere within the same class as the class field declaration. Example: `counter`

- Specify the name of a class field's class, followed by the member access operator, followed by the name of the class field from outside the class. Example: `Car.counter`

- Specify the name of an instance field as is from any instance method, constructor, or instance initializer (discussed later) in the same class as the instance field declaration. Example: numDoors

- Specify an object reference, followed by the member access operator, followed by the name of the instance field from any class method or class initializer (discussed later) within the same class as the instance field declaration or from outside the class. Example: Car car = new Car(); car.numDoors = 2;

Although the final rule might seem to imply that you can access an instance field from a class context, this is not the case. Instead, you are accessing the field from an object context.

The previous access rules are not exhaustive because there are two more field-access scenarios to consider: declaring a local variable (or even a parameter) with the same name as an instance field or as a class field. In either scenario, the local variable/parameter is said to *shadow* (hide or mask) the field.

If you find that you have declared a local variable or a parameter that shadows a field, you can rename the local variable/parameter, or you can use the member access operator with reserved word this (instance field) or class name (class field) to explicitly identify the field. For example, Listing 3-6's Car(String make, String model, int nDoors) constructor demonstrated this latter solution by specifying statements such as this.make = make; to distinguish an instance field from a same-named parameter.

Representing Behaviors via Methods

Java lets you represent behaviors via *methods*, which are named blocks of code declared within a class's body. Entity behaviors are described via *instance methods*. Because Java also supports behaviors that are associated with a class and not with an object, Java provides *class methods* to describe these class behaviors.

You first learn how to declare and invoke instance methods, and then learn how to create instance method call chains. Next, you discover how to declare and invoke class methods, encounter additional details about passing arguments to methods, and explore Java's return statement. After learning how to invoke methods recursively as an alternative to iteration, and how to overload methods, you review the rules for invoking methods from different contexts.

Declaring and Invoking Instance Methods

You can declare an instance method by minimally specifying a return type name, followed by an identifier that names the method, followed by a parameter list, followed by a brace-delimited body. Listing 3-9 presents a Car class with a printDetails() instance method.

Listing 3-9. Declaring a printDetails() Instance Method in the Car Class

```
public class Car
{
   String make;
   String model;
   int numDoors;
```

```java
Car(String make, String model)
{
   this(make, model, 4);
}

Car(String make, String model, int numDoors)
{
   this.make = make;
   this.model = model;
   this.numDoors = numDoors;
}

void printDetails()
{
   System.out.println("Make = " + make);
   System.out.println("Model = " + model);
   System.out.println("Number of doors = " + numDoors);
   System.out.println();
}

public static void main(String[] args)
{
   Car myCar = new Car("Toyota", "Camry");
   myCar.printDetails();
   Car yourCar = new Car("Mazda", "RX-8", 2);
   yourCar.printDetails();
}
}
```

Listing 3-9 declares an instance method named printDetails(). By convention, a method's name begins with a lowercase letter, and the first letter of each subsequent word in a multiword method name is capitalized.

Methods are like constructors in that they have parameter lists. You pass arguments to these parameters when you call the method. Because printDetails() doesn't take arguments, its parameter list is empty.

Note   A method's name and the number, types, and order of its parameters are known as its *signature*.

When a method is invoked, the code within its body is executed. In the case of printDetails(), this method's body executes a sequence of System.out.println() method calls to output the values of its make, model, and numDoors instance fields.

Unlike constructors, methods are declared to have return types. A return type identifies the kind of values returned by the method (e.g., int count() returns 32-bit integers). When a method doesn't return a value (and printDetails() doesn't), its return type is replaced with keyword void, as in void printDetails().

> **Note**   Constructors don't have return types because they cannot return values. If a constructor could return an arbitrary value, how would Java return that value? After all, the new operator returns a reference to an object; how could new also return a constructor value?

A method is invoked by using the member access operator: the left operand specifies the object's reference and the right operand specifies the method to be called. For example, the myCar.printDetails() and yourCar.printDetails() expressions invoke the printDetails() instance method on the myCar and yourCar objects.

Compile Listing 3-9 (javac Car.java) and run this application (java Car). You should observe the following output, whose different instance field values prove that printDetails() associates with an object:

```
Make = Toyota
Model = Camry
Number of doors = 4

Make = Mazda
Model = RX-8
Number of doors = 2
```

When an instance method is invoked, Java passes a hidden argument to the method (as the leftmost argument in a list of arguments). This argument is the reference to the object on which the method is invoked. It is represented at the source code level via reserved word this. You don't need to prefix an instance field name with "this." from within the method whenever you attempt to access an instance field name that isn't also the name of a parameter because the Java compiler ensures that the hidden argument is used to access the instance field.

METHOD-CALL STACK

Method invocations require a *method-call stack* (also known as a *method-invocation stack*) to keep track of the statements to which execution must return. Think of the method-call stack as a simulation of a pile of clean trays in a cafeteria—you *pop* (remove) the clean tray from the top of the pile and the dishwasher will *push* (insert) the next clean tray onto the top of the pile.

When a method is invoked, the virtual machine pushes its arguments and the address of the first statement to execute following the invoked method onto the method-call stack. The virtual machine also allocates stack space for the method's local variables. When the method returns, the virtual machine removes local variable space, pops the address and arguments off of the stack, and transfers execution to the statement at this address.

Chaining Together Instance Method Calls

Two or more instance method calls can be chained together via the member access operator, which results in more compact code. To accomplish instance method call chaining, you need to rearchitect your instance methods somewhat differently, which Listing 3-10 reveals.

Listing 3-10. Implementing Instance Methods so That Calls to These Methods Can Be Chained Together

```java
public class SavingsAccount
{
   int balance;

   SavingsAccount deposit(int amount)
   {
      balance += amount;
      return this;
   }

   SavingsAccount printBalance()
   {
      System.out.println(balance);
      return this;
   }

   public static void main(String[] args)
   {
      new SavingsAccount().deposit(1000).printBalance();
   }
}
```

Listing 3-10 shows that you must specify the class's name as the instance method's return type. Each of deposit() and printBalance() must specify SavingsAccount as the return type. Also, you must specify return this; (return current object's reference) as the last statement—I discuss the return statement later.

For example, new SavingsAccount().deposit(1000).printBalance(); creates a SavingsAccount object, uses the returned SavingsAccount reference to invoke SavingsAccount's deposit() instance method, to add one thousand dollars to the savings account (I'm ignoring cents for convenience), and finally uses deposit()'s returned SavingsAccount reference (which is the same SavingsAccount instance) to invoke SavingsAccount's printBalance() instance method to output the account balance.

Declaring and Invoking Class Methods

In many situations, instance methods are all that you need. However, you might encounter a situation where you need to describe a behavior that is independent of any object.

For example, suppose you would like to introduce a *utility class* (a class consisting of static [class] methods) whose class methods perform various kinds of conversions (such as converting from degrees Celsius to degrees Fahrenheit). You don't want to create an object from this class to perform a conversion. Instead, you simply want to call a method and obtain its result. Listing 3-11 addresses this requirement by presenting a Conversions class with a pair of class methods. These methods can be called without having to create a Conversions object.

Listing 3-11. A Conversions Utility Class with a Pair of Class Methods

```
class Conversions
{
   static double c2f(double degrees)
   {
      return degrees * 9.0 / 5.0 + 32;
   }

   static double f2c(double degrees)
   {
      return (degrees - 32) * 5.0 / 9.0;
   }
}
```

Listing 3-11's Conversions class declares c2f() and f2c() methods for converting from degrees Celsius to degrees Fahrenheit and vice-versa and returning the results of these conversions. Each *method header* (method signature and other information) is prefixed with keyword static to turn the method into a class method.

To execute a class method, you typically prefix its name with the class name. For example, you can execute Conversions.c2f(100.0); to find out the Fahrenheit equivalent of 100 degrees Celsius, and Conversions.f2c(98.6); to discover the Celsius equivalent of the normal body temperature. You don't need to instantiate Conversions and then call these methods via that instance, although you could do so (but that isn't good form).

> **Note**   Every application has at least one class method. Specifically, an application must specify public static void main(String[] args) to serve as the application's entry point. The static reserved word makes this method a class method. (I will explain reserved word public later in this chapter.)

Because class methods are not called with a hidden argument that refers to the current object, c2f(), f2c(), and main() cannot access an object's instance fields or call its instance methods. These class methods can only access class fields and call class methods.

Passing Arguments to Methods

A method call includes a list of (zero or more) arguments being passed to the method. Java passes arguments to methods via a style of argument passing called *pass-by-value*, which the following example demonstrates:

```
Employee emp = new Employee("John ");
int recommendedAnnualSalaryIncrease = 1000;
printReport(emp, recommendAnnualSalaryIncrease);
printReport(new Employee("Cuifen"), 1500);
```

Pass-by-value passes the value of a variable (the reference value stored in emp or the 1000 value stored in recommendedAnnualSalaryIncrease, for example) or the value of some other expression (such as new Employee("Cuifen") or 1500) to the method.

Because of pass-by-value, you cannot assign a different Employee object's reference to emp from inside printReport() via the printReport() parameter for this argument. After all, you have only passed a copy of emp's value to the method.

Many methods and constructors require you to pass a fixed number of arguments when they are called. However, Java also provides the ability to pass a variable number of arguments—such methods/constructors are often referred to as *varargs methods/constructors*. To declare a method or constructor that takes a variable number of arguments, specify three consecutive periods after the type name of the method's/constructor's rightmost parameter. The following example presents a sum() method that accepts a variable number of arguments:

```java
double sum(double... values)
{
   int total = 0;
   for (int i = 0; i < values.length; i++)
      total += values[i];
   return total;
}
```

sum()'s implementation totals the number of arguments passed to this method, for example, sum(10.0, 20.0) or sum(30.0, 40.0, 50.0). (Behind the scenes, these arguments are stored in a one-dimensional array, as evidenced by values.length and values[i].) After these values have been totaled, this total is returned via the return statement.

Returning from a Method via the Return Statement

The execution of statements within a method that doesn't return a value (its return type is set to void) flows from the first statement to the last statement. However, Java's return statement lets a method or a constructor exit before reaching the last statement. As Listing 3-12 shows, this form of the return statement consists of reserved word return followed by a semicolon.

Listing 3-12. Using the Return Statement to Return Prematurely from a Method

```java
public class Employee
{
   String name;

   Employee(String name)
   {
      setName(name);
   }

   void setName(String name)
   {
      if (name == null)
      {
         System.out.println("name cannot be null");
```

```
            return;
        }
        else
            this.name = name;
    }

    public static void main(String[] args)
    {
        Employee john = new Employee(null);
    }
}
```

Listing 3-12's `Employee(String name)` constructor invokes the `setName()` instance method to initialize the name instance field. Providing a separate method for this purpose is a good idea because it lets you initialize the instance field at construction time and also at a later time. (Perhaps the employee changes his or her name.)

> **Note**   When you invoke a class's instance or class method from a constructor or method within the same class, you specify only the method's name. You don't prefix the method invocation with the member access operator and an object reference or class name.

`setName()` uses an if statement to detect an attempt to assign the null reference to the name field. When such an attempt is detected, it outputs the "name cannot be null" error message and returns prematurely from the method so that the null value cannot be assigned (and replace a previously assigned name).

> **Caution**   When using the return statement, you might run into a situation where the compiler reports an "unreachable code" error message. It does so when it detects code that will never be executed and occupies memory unnecessarily. One area where you might encounter this problem is the switch statement. For example, suppose you specify `case 2: printUsageInstructions(); return; break;` as part of this statement. The compiler reports an error when it detects the break statement following the return statement because the break statement is unreachable; it never can be executed.

The previous form of the return statement is not legal in a method that returns a value. For such methods, Java provides an alternate version of return that lets the method return a value (whose type must match the method's return type). The following example demonstrates this version:

```
double divide(double dividend, double divisor)
{
    if (divisor == 0.0)
    {
        System.out.println("cannot divide by zero");
        return 0.0;
    }
    return dividend / divisor;
}
```

`divide()` uses an if statement to detect an attempt to divide its first argument by 0.0 and outputs an error message when this attempt is detected. Furthermore, it returns `0.0` to signify this attempt. If there is no problem, the division is performed and the result is returned.

> **Caution**   You cannot use this form of the return statement in a constructor because constructors don't have return types.

Invoking Methods Recursively

A method normally executes statements that may include calls to other methods, such as `printDetails()` invoking `System.out.println()`. However, it is occasionally convenient to have a method call itself. This scenario is known as *recursion*.

For example, suppose you need to write a method that returns a *factorial* (the product of all the positive integers up to and including a specific integer). For example, 3! (the ! is the mathematical symbol for factorial) equals 3×2×1 or 6.

Your first approach to writing this method might consist of the code presented in the following example:

```
int factorial(int n)
{
   int product = 1;
   for (int i = 2; i <= n; i++)
      product *= i;
   return product;
}
```

Although this code accomplishes its task (via iteration), `factorial()` could also be written according to the following example's recursive style:

```
int factorial(int n)
{
   if (n == 1)
      return 1; // base problem
   else
      return n * factorial(n - 1);
}
```

The recursive approach takes advantage of being able to express a problem in simpler terms of itself. According to this example, the simplest problem, which is also known as the *base problem*, is 1! (1).

When an argument greater than 1 is passed to `factorial()`, this method breaks the problem into a simpler problem by calling itself with the next smaller argument value. Eventually, the base problem will be reached.

For example, calling `factorial(4)` results in the following stack of expressions:

```
4 * factorial(3)
3 * factorial(2)
2 * factorial(1)
```

This last expression is at the top of the stack. When `factorial(1)` returns 1, these expressions are evaluated as the stack begins to unwind:

- 2 * `factorial(1)` now becomes 2*1 (2)

- 3 * `factorial(2)` now becomes 3*2 (6)

- 4 * `factorial(3)` now becomes 4*6 (24)

Recursion provides an elegant way to express many problems. Additional examples include searching tree-based data structures for specific values and, in a hierarchical file system, finding and outputting the names of all files that contain specific text.

> **Caution**   Recursion consumes stack space, so make sure that your recursion eventually ends in a base problem; otherwise, you will run out of stack space and your application will be forced to terminate.

Overloading Methods

Java lets you introduce methods with the same name but different parameter lists into the same class. This feature is known as *method overloading*. When the compiler encounters a method invocation expression, it compares the called method's arguments list with each overloaded method's parameter list as it looks for the correct method to invoke.

Two same-named methods are overloaded when their parameter lists differ in number or order of parameters. For example, Java's `String` class provides overloaded `int indexOf(int ch)` and `int indexOf(int ch, int fromIndex)` methods. These methods differ in parameter counts. (I explore `String` in Chapter 7.)

Two same-named methods are overloaded when at least one parameter differs in type. For example, Java's `java.lang.Math` class provides overloaded `static double abs(double a)` and `static int abs(int a)` methods. One method's parameter is a `double`; the other method's parameter is an `int`. (I explore `Math` in Chapter 7.)

You cannot overload a method by changing only the return type. For example, `double sum(double... values)` and `int sum(double... values)` are not overloaded. These methods are not overloaded because the compiler doesn't have enough information to choose which method to call when it encounters `sum(1.0, 2.0)` in source code.

Reviewing Method-Invocation Rules

The previous examples of method invocation may seem confusing because you can sometimes specify the method's name directly, whereas you need to prefix a method name with an object reference or a class name and the member access operator at other times. The following rules dispel this confusion by giving you guidance on how to invoke methods from the various contexts:

- Specify the name of a class method as is from anywhere within the same class as the class method. Example: `c2f(37.0);`

- Specify the name of the class method's class, followed by the member access operator, followed by the name of the class method from outside the class. Example: `Conversions.c2f(37.0);` (You can also invoke a class method via an object instance, but that is considered bad form because it hides from casual observation the fact that a class method is being invoked.)

- Specify the name of an instance method as is from any instance method, constructor, or instance initializer in the same class as the instance method. Example: `setName(name);`

- Specify an object reference, followed by the member access operator, followed by the name of the instance method from any class method or class initializer within the same class as the instance method or from outside the class. Example: `Car car = new Car("Toyota", "Camry"); car.printDetails();`

Although the latter rule might seem to imply that you can call an instance method from a class context, this is not the case. Instead, you call the method from an object context.

Also, don't forget to make sure that the number of arguments passed to a method, along with the order in which these arguments are passed, and the types of these arguments agree with their parameter counterparts in the method being invoked.

Note   Field access and method call rules are combined in expression `System.out.println();`, where the leftmost member access operator accesses the `out` class field (of type `java.io.PrintStream`) in the `java.lang.System` class, and where the rightmost member access operator calls this field's `println()` method. You'll learn about `PrintStream` in Chapter 11 and `System` in Chapter 8.

Hiding Information

Every class **X** exposes an *interface* (a protocol consisting of constructors, methods, and [possibly] fields that are made available to objects created from other classes for use in creating and communicating with **X**'s objects).

An interface serves as a one-way contract between a class and its *clients*, which are the external constructors, methods, and other (initialization-oriented) class entities (discussed later in this chapter) that communicate with the class's instances by calling constructors and methods and by accessing fields (typically `public static final` fields, or constants). The contract is such that the class promises to not change its interface, which would break clients that depend on the interface.

X also provides an *implementation* (the code within exposed methods along with optional helper methods and optional supporting fields that should not be exposed) that codifies the interface. *Helper methods* are methods that assist exposed methods and should not be exposed.

When designing a class, your goal is to expose a useful interface while hiding details of that interface's implementation. You hide the implementation to prevent developers from accidentally accessing parts of your class that don't belong to the class's interface so that you are free to change the implementation without breaking client code. Hiding the implementation is often referred to as *information hiding*. Furthermore, many developers consider implementation hiding to be part of encapsulation.

Java supports implementation hiding by providing four levels of access control, where three of these levels are indicated via a reserved word. You can use the following access control levels to control access to fields, methods, and constructors and two of these levels to control access to classes:

- *Public*: A field, method, or constructor that is declared `public` is accessible from anywhere. Classes can be declared `public` as well.

- *Protected*: A field, method, or constructor that is declared `protected` is accessible from all classes in the same package as the member's class as well as subclasses of that class regardless of package. (I discuss packages in Chapter 5.)

- *Private*: A field, method, or constructor that is declared `private` cannot be accessed from beyond the class in which it is declared.

- *Package-private*: In the absence of an access-control reserved word, a field, method, or constructor is only accessible to classes within the same package as the member's class. The same is true for non-`public` classes. The absence of `public`, `protected`, or `private` implies package-private.

> **Note** A class that is declared `public` must be stored in a file with the same name. For example, a `public` Image class must be stored in `Image.java`. A source file can declare one `public` top-level class only. (It's also possible to declare nested classes that are `public`, and you will learn how to do so in Chapter 5.)

You will often declare your class's instance fields to be `private` and provide special `public` instance methods for setting and getting their values. By convention, methods that set field values have names starting with `set` and are known as *setters*. Similarly, methods that get field values have names with `get` (or `is`, for Boolean fields) prefixes and are known as *getters*. Listing 3-13 demonstrates this pattern in the context of an Employee class declaration.

Listing 3-13. Separation of Interface from Implementation

```
public class Employee
{
   private String name;
```

```
   public Employee(String name)
   {
      setName(name);
   }

   public void setName(String empName)
   {
      name = empName; // Assign the empName argument to the name field.
   }

   public String getName()
   {
      return name;
   }
}
```

Listing 3-13 presents an interface consisting of the public Employee class, its public constructor, and its public setter/getter methods. This class and these members can be accessed from anywhere. The implementation consists of the private name field and constructor/method code, which is only accessible within the Employee class.

It might seem pointless to go to all this bother when you could simply omit private and access the name field directly. However, suppose you are told to introduce a new constructor that takes separate first and last name arguments and new methods that set/get the employee's first and last names into this class. Furthermore, suppose that it has been determined that the first and last names will be accessed more often than the entire name. Listing 3-14 reveals these changes.

Listing 3-14. Revising Implementation Without Affecting Existing Interface

```
public class Employee
{
   private String firstName;
   private String lastName;

   public Employee(String name)
   {
      setName(name);
   }

   public Employee(String firstName, String lastName)
   {
      setName(firstName + " " + lastName);
   }

   public void setName(String name)
   {
      // Assume that the first and last names are separated by a
      // single space character. indexOf() locates a character in a
      // string; substring() returns a portion of a string.
      setFirstName(name.substring(0, name.indexOf(' ')));
      setLastName(name.substring(name.indexOf(' ') + 1));
   }
```

```
    public String getName()
    {
        return getFirstName() + " " + getLastName();
    }

    public void setFirstName(String empFirstName)
    {
        firstName = empFirstName;
    }

    public String getFirstName()
    {
        return firstName;
    }

    public void setLastName(String empLastName)
    {
        lastName = empLastName;
    }

    public String getLastName()
    {
        return lastName;
    }
}
```

Listing 3-14 reveals that the name field has been removed in favor of new firstName and lastName fields, which were added to improve performance. Because setFirstName() and setLastName() will be called more frequently than setName(), and because getFirstName() and getLastName() will be called more frequently than getName(), it is more performant (in each case) to have the first two methods set/get firstName's and lastName's values rather than merging either value into/extracting this value from name's value.

Listing 3-14 also reveals setName() calling setFirstName() and setLastName(), and getName() calling getFirstName() and getLastName(), rather than directly accessing the firstName and lastName fields. Although avoiding direct access to these fields is not necessary in this example, imagine another implementation change that adds more code to setFirstName(), setLastName(), getFirstName(), and getLastName(); not calling these methods will result in the new code not executing.

Client code (code that instantiates and uses a class, such as Employee) will not break when Employee's implementation changes from that shown in Listing 3-13 to that shown in Listing 3-14, because the original interface remains intact, although the interface has been extended. This lack of breakage results from hiding Listing 3-13's implementation, especially the name field.

Note setName() invokes the String class's indexOf() and substring() methods. You'll learn about these and other String methods in Chapter 7.

Java provides a little known information hiding-related language feature that lets one object (or class method/initializer) access another object's `private` fields or invoke its `private` methods. Listing 3-15 provides a demonstration.

Listing 3-15. One Object Accessing Another Object's `private` Field

```java
public class PrivateAccess
{
   private int x;

   PrivateAccess(int x)
   {
      this.x = x;
   }

   boolean equalTo(PrivateAccess pa)
   {
      return pa.x == x;
   }

   public static void main(String[] args)
   {
      PrivateAccess pa1 = new PrivateAccess(10);
      PrivateAccess pa2 = new PrivateAccess(20);
      PrivateAccess pa3 = new PrivateAccess(10);
      System.out.println("pa1 equal to pa2: " + pa1.equalTo(pa2));
      System.out.println("pa2 equal to pa3: " + pa2.equalTo(pa3));
      System.out.println("pa1 equal to pa3: " + pa1.equalTo(pa3));
      System.out.println(pa2.x);
   }
}
```

Listing 3-15's `PrivateAccess` class declares a `private int` field named x. It also declares an `equalTo()` method that takes a `PrivateAccess` argument. The idea is to compare the argument object with the current object to determine if they are equal.

The equality determination is made by using the `==` operator to compare the value of the argument object's x instance field with the value of the current object's x instance field, returning Boolean true when they are the same. What may seem baffling is that Java lets you specify `pa.x` to access the argument object's `private` instance field. Also, `main()` is able to directly access x via the pa2 object.

I previously presented Java's four access-control levels and presented the following statement regarding the private access-control level: "A field, method, or constructor that is declared `private` cannot be accessed from beyond the class in which it is declared." When you carefully consider this statement and examine Listing 3-15, you will realize that x is not being accessed from beyond the `PrivateAccess` class in which it is declared. Therefore, the private access-control level is not being violated.

The only code that can access this `private` instance field is code located within the `PrivateAccess` class. If you attempted to access x via a `PrivateAccess` object that was created in the context of another class, the compiler would report an error.

Being able to directly access x from within `PrivateAccess` is a performance enhancement; it is faster to directly access this implementation detail than to call a method that returns its value.

Compile `PrivateAccess.java` (`javac PrivateAccess.java`) and run the application
(`java PrivateAccess`). You should observe the following output:

```
pa1 equal to pa2: false
pa2 equal to pa3: false
pa1 equal to pa3: true
20
```

> **Tip**   Get into the habit of developing useful interfaces while hiding implementations because it will
> save you much trouble when maintaining your classes.

Initializing Classes and Objects

Classes and objects need to be properly initialized before they are used. You've already learned
that class fields are initialized to default zero values after a class loads and can be subsequently
initialized by assigning values to them in their declarations via *class field initializers*, for example,
`static int counter = 1;`. Similarly, instance fields are initialized to default values when an object's
memory is allocated via `new` and can be subsequently initialized by assigning values to them in their
declarations via *instance field initializers*; for example, `int numDoors = 4;`.

Another aspect of initialization that's already been discussed is the constructor, which is used to
initialize an object, typically by assigning values to various instance fields, but is also capable of
executing arbitrary code such as code that opens a file and reads the file's contents.

Java provides two additional initialization features: class initializers and instance initializers. After
introducing you to these features in this section, I discuss the order in which all of Java's initializers
perform their work.

Class Initializers

Constructors perform initialization tasks for objects. Their counterpart from a class initialization
perspective is the class initializer.

A *class initializer* is a `static`-prefixed block that is introduced into a class body. It is used to initialize
a loaded class via a sequence of statements. For example, I once used a class initializer to load a
custom database driver class. Listing 3-16 shows the loading details.

Listing 3-16. Loading a Database Driver via a Class Initializer

```
class JDBCFilterDriver implements Driver
{
   static private Driver d;

   static
   {
      // Attempt to load JDBC-ODBC Bridge Driver and register that
      // driver.
```

```
      try
      {
         Class c = Class.forName("sun.jdbc.odbc.JdbcOdbcDriver");
         d = (Driver) c.newInstance();
         DriverManager.registerDriver(new JDBCFilterDriver());
      }
      catch (Exception e)
      {
         System.out.println(e);
      }
   }
   //...
}
```

Listing 3-16's JDBCFilterDriver class uses its class initializer to load and instantiate the class that describes Java's JDBC-ODBC Bridge Driver and to register a JDBCFilterDriver instance with Java's database driver. Although this listing's JDBC-oriented code is probably meaningless to you right now, the listing illustrates the usefulness of class initializers. (I discuss JDBC in Chapter 14.)

A class can declare a mix of class initializers and class field initializers as demonstrated in Listing 3-17.

Listing 3-17. Mixing Class Initializers with Class Field Initializers

```
class C
{
   static
   {
      System.out.println("class initializer 1");
   }

   static int counter = 1;

   static
   {
      System.out.println("class initializer 2");
      System.out.println("counter = " + counter);
   }
}
```

Listing 3-17 declares a class named C that specifies two class initializers and one class field initializer. When the Java compiler compiles into a classfile a class that declares at least one class initializer or class field initializer, it creates a special void <clinit>() class method that stores the bytecode equivalent of all class initializers and class field initializers in the order they occur (from top to bottom).

> **Note**   <clinit> is not a valid Java method name but is a valid name from the runtime perspective. The angle brackets were chosen as part of the name to prevent a name conflict with any clinit() methods that you might declare in the class.

For class C, `<clinit>()` would first contain the bytecode equivalent of `System.out.println("class initializer 1");`, it would next contain the bytecode equivalent of `static int counter = 1;`, and it would finally contain the bytecode equivalent of `System.out.println("class initializer 2"); System.out.println("counter = " + counter);`.

When class C is loaded into memory, `<clinit>()` executes immediately and generates the following output:

```
class initializer 1
class initializer 2
counter = 1
```

Instance Initializers

Not all classes can have constructors, as you will discover in Chapter 5 when I present anonymous classes. For these classes, Java supplies the instance initializer to take care of instance initialization tasks.

An *instance initializer* is a block that is introduced into a class body as opposed to being introduced as the body of a method or a constructor. The instance initializer is used to initialize an object via a sequence of statements as demonstrated in Listing 3-18.

Listing 3-18. Initializing a Pair of Arrays via an Instance Initializer

```
class Graphics
{
   double[] sines;
   double[] cosines;

   {
      sines = new double[360];
      cosines = new double[sines.length];
      for (int degree = 0; degree < sines.length; degree++)
      {
         sines[degree] = Math.sin(Math.toRadians(degree));
         cosines[degree] = Math.cos(Math.toRadians(degree));
      }
   }
}
```

Listing 3-18's `Graphics` class uses an instance initializer to create an object's `sines` and `cosines` arrays and to initialize these arrays' elements to the sines and cosines of angles ranging from 0 through 359 degrees. It does so because it's faster to read array elements than to repeatedly call `Math.sin()` and `Math.cos()` elsewhere; performance matters. (In Chapter 7 I introduce `Math.sin()` and `Math.cos()`.)

A class can declare a mix of instance initializers and instance field initializers as shown in Listing 3-19.

Listing 3-19. Mixing Instance Initializers with Instance Field Initializers

```
class C
{
   {
      System.out.println("instance initializer 1");
   }

   int counter = 1;

   {
      System.out.println("instance initializer 2");
      System.out.println("counter = " + counter);
   }
}
```

Listing 3-19 declares a class named C that specifies two instance initializers and one instance field initializer. When the Java compiler compiles a class into a classfile, it creates a special void <init>() method representing the default noargument constructor when no constructor is explicitly declared; otherwise, it creates an <init>() method for each encountered constructor. Furthermore, it stores in each <init>() method the bytecode equivalent of all instance initializers and instance field initializers in the order they occur (from top to bottom) and before the constructor code.

> **Note** <init> is not a valid Java method name but is a valid name from the runtime perspective. The angle brackets were chosen as part of the name to prevent a name conflict with any init() methods that you might declare in the class.

For class C, <init>() would first contain the bytecode equivalent of System.out.println("instance initializer 1");, it would next contain the bytecode equivalent of int counter = 1;, and it would finally contain the bytecode equivalent of System.out.println("instance initializer 2"); System.out.println("counter = " + counter);.

When new C() executes, <init>() executes immediately and generates the following output:

```
instance initializer 1
instance initializer 2
counter = 1
```

> **Note** You should rarely need to use the instance initializer, which is not commonly used in industry. Other developers would likely miss the instance initializer while scanning the source code and might find it confusing.

Initialization Order

A class's body can contain a mixture of class field initializers, class initializers, instance field initializers, instance initializers, and constructors. (You should prefer constructors to instance field initializers, although I am guilty of not doing so consistently, and restrict your use of instance initializers to anonymous classes, discussed in Chapter 5.) Furthermore, class fields and instance fields initialize to default values. Understanding the order in which all of this initialization occurs is necessary to preventing confusion, so check out Listing 3-20.

Listing 3-20. A Complete Initialization Demo

```java
public class InitDemo
{
   static double double1;
   double double2;
   static int int1;
   int int2;
   static String string1;
   String string2;

   static
   {
      System.out.println("[class] double1 = " + double1);
      System.out.println("[class] int1 = " + int1);
      System.out.println("[class] string1 = " + string1);
      System.out.println();
   }

   {
      System.out.println("[instance] double2 = " + double2);
      System.out.println("[instance] int2 = " + int2);
      System.out.println("[instance] string2 = " + string2);
      System.out.println();
   }

   static
   {
      double1 = 1.0;
      int1 = 1000000000;
      string1 = "abc";
   }

   {
      double2 = 1.0;
      int2 = 1000000000;
      string2 = "abc";
   }

   InitDemo()
   {
      System.out.println("InitDemo() called");
```

```
      System.out.println();
   }

   static double double3 = 10.0;
   double double4 = 10.0;

   static
   {
      System.out.println("[class] double3 = " + double3);
      System.out.println();
   }


   {
      System.out.println("[instance] double4 = " + double3);
      System.out.println();
   }

   public static void main(String[] args)
   {
      System.out.println ("main() started");
      System.out.println();
      System.out.println("[class] double1 = " + double1);
      System.out.println("[class] double3 = " + double3);
      System.out.println("[class] int1 = " + int1);
      System.out.println("[class] string1 = " + string1);
      System.out.println();
      for (int i = 0; i < 2; i++)
      {
         System.out.println("About to create InitDemo object");
         System.out.println();
         InitDemo id = new InitDemo();
         System.out.println("id created");
         System.out.println();
         System.out.println("[instance] id.double2 = " + id.double2);
         System.out.println("[instance] id.double4 = " + id.double4);
         System.out.println("[instance] id.int2 = " + id.int2);
         System.out.println("[instance] id.string2 = " + id.string2);
         System.out.println();
      }
   }
}
```

Listing 3-20's InitDemo class declares two class fields and two instance fields for the double precision floating-point primitive type, one class field and one instance field for the integer primitive type, and one class field and one instance field for the String reference type. It also introduces one explicitly initialized class field, one explicitly initialized instance field, three class initializers, three instance initializers, and one constructor. If you compile and run this code, you will observe the following output:

```
[class] double1 = 0.0
[class] int1 = 0
[class] string1 = null
```

```
[class] double3 = 10.0

main() started

[class] double1 = 1.0
[class] double3 = 10.0
[class] int1 = 1000000000
[class] string1 = abc

About to create InitDemo object

[instance] double2 = 0.0
[instance] int2 = 0
[instance] string2 = null

[instance] double4 = 10.0

InitDemo() called

id created

[instance] id.double2 - 1.0
[instance] id.double4 = 10.0
[instance] id.int2 = 1000000000
[instance] id.string2 = abc

About to create InitDemo object

[instance] double2 = 0.0
[instance] int2 = 0
[instance] string2 = null

[instance] double4 = 10.0

InitDemo() called

id created

[instance] id.double2 = 1.0
[instance] id.double4 = 10.0
[instance] id.int2 = 1000000000
[instance] id.string2 = abc
```

As you study this output in conjunction with the aforementioned discussion of class initializers and instance initializers, you'll discover some interesting facts about initialization:

- Class fields initialize to default or explicit values just after a class is loaded. Immediately after a class loads, all class fields are zeroed to default values. Code within the `<clinit>()` method performs explicit initialization.

- All class initialization occurs prior to the `<clinit>()` method returning.

- Instance fields initialize to default or explicit values during object creation. When new allocates memory for an object, it zeros all instance fields to default values. Code within an `<init>()` method performs explicit initialization.

- All instance initialization occurs prior to the `<init>()` method returning.

Additionally, because initialization occurs in a top-down manner, attempting to access the contents of a class field before that field is declared or attempting to access the contents of an instance field before that field is declared causes the compiler to report an *illegal forward reference*.

Collecting Garbage

Objects are created via reserved word new, but how are they destroyed? Without some way to destroy objects, they will eventually fill up the heap's available space and the application will not be able to continue. Java doesn't provide the developer with the ability to remove them from memory. Instead, Java handles this task by providing a *garbage collector*, which is code that runs in the background and occasionally checks for unreferenced objects. When the garbage collector discovers an unreferenced object (or multiple objects that reference each other and where there are no other references to each other—only A references B and only B references A, for example), it removes the object from the heap, making more heap space available.

An *unreferenced object* is an object that cannot be accessed from anywhere within an application. For example, new Employee("John", "Doe"); is an unreferenced object because the Employee reference returned by new is thrown away. In contrast, a *referenced object* is an object where the application stores at least one reference. For example, Employee emp = new Employee("John", "Doe"); is a referenced object because variable emp contains a reference to the Employee object.

A referenced object becomes unreferenced when the application removes its last stored reference. For example, if emp is a local variable that contains the only reference to an Employee object, this object becomes unreferenced when the method in which emp is declared returns. An application can also remove a stored reference by assigning null to its reference variable. For example, emp = null; removes the reference to the Employee object that was previously stored in emp.

Java's garbage collector eliminates a form of memory leakage in C++ implementations that do not rely on a garbage collector. In these C++ implementations, the developer must destroy dynamically created objects before they go out of scope. If they vanish before destruction, they remain in the heap. Eventually, the heap fills and the application halts.

Although this form of memory leakage is not a problem in Java, a related form of leakage is problematic: continually creating objects and forgetting to remove even one reference to each object causes the heap to fill up and the application to eventually come to a halt. This form of memory leakage typically occurs in the context of *collections* (object-based data structures that store objects) and is a major problem for applications that run for lengthy periods of time—a web server is one example. For shorter-lived applications, you will normally not notice this form of memory leakage.

Consider Listing 3-21.

Listing 3-21. A Memory-Leaking Stack

```java
public class Stack
{
   private Object[] elements;
   private int top;

   public Stack(int size)
   {
      elements = new Object[size];
      top = -1; // indicate that stack is empty
   }

   public void push(Object o)
   {
      if (top + 1 == elements.length)
      {
         System.out.println("stack is full");
         return;
      }
      elements[++top] = o;
   }

   public Object pop()
   {
      if (top == -1)
      {
         System.out.println("stack is empty");
         return null;
      }
      Object element = elements[top--];
//       elements[top + 1] = null;
      return element;
   }

   public static void main(String[] args)
   {
      Stack stack = new Stack(2);
      stack.push("A");
      stack.push("B");
      stack.push("C");
      System.out.println(stack.pop());
      System.out.println(stack.pop());
      System.out.println(stack.pop());
   }
}
```

Listing 3-21 describes a collection known as a *stack*, a data structure that stores elements in last-in, first-out order. Stacks are useful for remembering things, such as the instruction to return to when a method stops executing and must return to its caller.

Stack provides a push() method for pushing arbitrary objects onto the *top* of the stack and a pop() method for popping objects off of the stack's top in the reverse order to which they were pushed.

After creating a Stack object that can store a maximum of two objects, main() invokes push() three times to push three String objects onto the stack. Because the stack's internal array can store two objects only, push() outputs an error message when main() tries to push "C".

At this point, main() attempts to pop three Objects off of the stack, outputting each object to the standard output device. The first two pop() method calls succeed, but the final method call fails and outputs an error message because the stack is empty when it is called.

When you run this application, it generates the following output:

```
stack is full
B
A
stack is empty
null
```

There is a problem with the Stack class: it leaks memory. When you push an object onto the stack, its reference is stored in the internal elements array. When you pop an object off of the stack, the object's reference is obtained and top is decremented, but the reference remains in the array (until you invoke push()).

Imagine a scenario where the Stack object's reference is assigned to a class field, which means that the Stack object hangs around for the life of the application. Furthermore, suppose that you have pushed three 50-megabyte Image objects onto the stack and then subsequently popped them off of the stack. After using these objects, you assign null to their reference variables, thinking that they will be garbage collected the next time the garbage collector runs. However, this won't happen because the Stack object still maintains its references to these objects, and so 150 megabytes of heap space will not be available to the application, and maybe the application will run out of memory.

The solution to this problem is for pop() to explicitly assign null to the elements entry prior to returning the reference. Simply uncomment the elements[top + 1] = null; line in Listing 3-21 to make this happen.

You might think that you should always assign null to reference variables when their referenced objects are no longer required. However, doing so often doesn't improve performance or free up significant amounts of heap space and can lead to thrown instances of the java.lang. NullPointerException class when you're not careful. (I discuss NullPointerException in the context of Chapter 5's coverage of Java's exceptions-oriented language features). You typically nullify reference variables in classes that manage their own memory, such as the aforementioned Stack class.

Note To learn more about garbage collection in a Java 5 context, check out Oracle's "Memory Management in the Java HotSpot Virtual Machine" whitepaper (www.oracle.com/technetwork/java/javase/tech/memorymanagement-whitepaper-1-150020.pdf).

Revisiting Arrays

In Chapter 2 I introduced you to *arrays*, which are regions of memory (specifically, the heap) that store values in equal-size and contiguous slots, known as *elements*. I also presented several examples, including the following example:

```
char gradeLetters[] = { 'A', 'B', 'C', 'D', 'F' };
```

Here you have an array variable named gradeLetters that stores a reference to a five-element region of memory, which stores the characters A, B, C, D, and F in contiguous and equal-size (16-bit) memory locations.

> **Note**   I've placed the [ ] brackets after gradeLetters. Although this is legal, it's conventional to place these brackets after the type name, as in char[] gradeLetters = { 'A', 'B', 'C', 'D', 'F' };. I demonstrate both approaches in this section.

You access an element by specifying gradeLetters[*x*], where *x* is an integer that identifies an array element and is known as an *index*; the first array element is always located at index 0. The following example shows you how to output and change the first element's value:

```
System.out.println(gradeLetters[0]); // Output the first grade letter.
gradeLetters[0] = 'a'; // Perhaps you prefer lowercase grade letters.
```

The { 'A', 'B', 'C', 'D', 'F' } array-creation syntax is an example of *syntactic sugar* (syntax that simplifies a language, making it "sweeter" to use). Behind the scenes, the array is created with the new operator and initializes to these values, as follows:

```
char gradeLetters[] = new char[] { 'A', 'B', 'C', 'D', 'F' };
```

First, a five-character region of memory is allocated. Next, the region's five character elements are initialized to A, B, C, D, and F. Finally, a reference to these elements is stored in array variable gradeLetters.

> **Caution**   It's an error to place an integer value between the square brackets following char. For example, the compiler reports an error when it encounters the 5 in new char[5] { 'A', 'B', 'C', 'D', 'F' };.

You can think of an array as a special kind of object, although it's not an object in the same sense that a class instance is an object. This pseudo-object has a solitary and read-only length field that contains the array's size (the number of elements). For example, gradeLetters.length returns the number of elements (5) in the gradeLetters array.

Although you can use either of the previous two approaches to create an array, you will often specify a third approach that doesn't involve explicit element initialization and subsequently initialize the array. This approach is demonstrated by the following code:

```
char gradeLetters[] = new char[5];
```

You specify the number of elements as a positive integer between the square brackets. Operator new zeros the bits in each array element's storage location, which you interpret at the source code level as literal value false, '\u0000', 0, 0L, 0.0, 0.0F, or null (depending on element type).

You can then initialize the array, as follows:

```
gradeLetters[0] = 'A';
gradeLetters[1] = 'B';
gradeLetters[2] = 'C';
gradeLetters[3] = 'D';
gradeLetters[4] = 'F';
```

However, you will probably find it more convenient to use a loop for this task, as follows:

```
for (int i = 0; i < gradeLetters.length; i++)
   gradeLetters[i] = 'A' + i;
```

The previous examples focused on creating an array whose values share a common primitive type (character, represented by the char keyword). You can also create an array of object references. For example, you can create an array to store three Image object references, as follows:

```
Image[] imArray = { new Image("image0.png"), new Image("image1.png"), new Image("image2.png") };
```

Here you have an array variable named imArray that stores a reference to a three-element region of memory, where each element stores a reference to an Image object. The Image object is located elsewhere in memory.

You access an Image element by specifying imArray[x]. The following example assumes the existence of a getLength() method that returns the image's length (in bytes) and calls this method on the first Image object to return the first image's length, which is subsequently output:

```
System.out.println(imArray[0].getLength());
```

As with the previous gradeLetters example, you can combine the new operator with the syntactic sugar initializer, as follows:

```
Image[] imArray = new Image[] { new Image("image0.png"), new Image("image1.png"),
                                new Image("image2.png") };
```

Finally, you can use the third approach, which initializes each object reference to the null reference by setting all of the bits in each element to 0. This approach is demonstrated following:

```
Image[] imArray = new Image[3];
```

Because new initializes each element to the null reference, you must explicitly initialize this array, and you can conveniently do so as follows:

```
for (int i = 0; i < imArray.length; i++)
   imArray[i] = new Image("image" + i + ".png"); // image0.png, image1.png, and so on
```

The `"image" + i + ".png"` expression uses the string concatenation operator (+) to combine image with the string equivalent of the integer value stored in variable i with `.png`. The resulting string is passed to Image's `Image(String filename)` constructor, and the resulting reference is stored in one of the array elements.

> **Note**   Use of the string concatenation operator in a loop context can result in a lot of unnecessary `String` object creation, depending on the length of the loop. I will discuss this topic in Chapter 7 when I introduce you to the `String` class.

The previous examples have focused on creating *one-dimensional arrays*. However, you can also create *multidimensional arrays* (that is, arrays with two or more dimensions). For example, consider a two-dimensional array of temperature values.

Although you can use any of the three approaches to create the `temperatures` array, the third approach is preferable when the values vary greatly. The following example creates this array as a three-row-by-two-column table of double precision floating-point temperature values:

```
double[][] temperatures = new double[3][2];
```

Notice the two sets of square brackets between `double` and `temperatures`. These two sets of brackets signify the array as two-dimensional (a table). Also notice the two sets of square brackets following `new` and `double`. Each set contains a positive integer value signifying the number of rows (3) or the number of columns (2) for each row.

> **Note**   When creating a multidimensional array, the number of square bracket pairs that are associated with the array variable and the number of square bracket pairs that follow new and the type name must be the same.

After creating the array, you can populate its elements with suitable values. The following example initializes each `temperatures` element, which is accessed as `temperatures[row][col]`, to a randomly generated temperature value via `Math.random()`, which I'll explain in Chapter 7:

```
for (int row = 0; row < temperatures.length; row++)
   for (int col = 0; col < temperatures[row].length; col++)
      temperatures[row][col] = Math.random() * 100;
```

The outer for loop selects each row from row 0 to the length of the array (which identifies the number of rows in the array). The inner for loop selects each column from 0 to the length of the current row array (which identifies the number of columns represented by that array). In essence, you are looking at a one-dimensional row array where each element references a one-dimensional column array.

You can subsequently output these values in a tabular format by using another for loop as demonstrated by the following example—the code makes no attempt to align the temperature values in perfect columns:

```
for (int row = 0; row < temperatures.length; row++)
{
   for (int col = 0; col < temperatures[row].length; col++)
      System.out.print(temperatures[row][col] + " ");
   System.out.println();
}
```

Java provides an alternative for creating a multidimensional array in which you create each dimension separately. For example, to create the previous two-dimensional temperatures array via new in this manner, first create a one-dimensional row array (the outer array), and then create a one-dimensional column array (the inner array), as demonstrated by the following code:

```
// Create the row array.
double[][] temperatures = new double[3][]; // Note the extra empty pair of brackets.
// Create a column array for each row.
for (int row = 0; row < temperatures.length; row++)
   temperatures[row] = new double[2]; // 2 columns per row
```

This kind of an array is known as a *ragged array* because each row can have a different number of columns; the array is not rectangular, but is ragged.

> **Note**   When creating the row array, you must specify an extra pair of empty brackets as part of the expression following new. (For a three-dimensional array—a one-dimensional array of tables, where this array's elements reference row arrays—you must specify two pairs of empty brackets as part of the expression following new.)

EXERCISES

The following exercises are designed to test your understanding of Chapter 3's content:

1. What is a class?
2. How do you declare a class?
3. What is an object?
4. How do you instantiate an object?

5. What is a constructor?

6. True or false: Java creates a default noargument constructor when a class declares no constructors.

7. What is a parameter list and what is a parameter?

8. What is an argument list and what is an argument?

9. True or false: You invoke another constructor by specifying the name of the class followed by an argument list.

10. Define arity.

11. What is a local variable?

12. Define lifetime.

13. Define scope.

14. What is encapsulation?

15. Define field.

16. What is the difference between an instance field and a class field?

17. What is a blank final and how does it differ from a true constant?

18. How do you prevent a field from being shadowed?

19. Define method.

20. What is the difference between an instance method and a class method?

21. Define recursion.

22. How do you overload a method?

23. What is a class initializer, and what is an instance initializer?

24. Define garbage collector.

25. True or false: `String[] letters = new String[2] { "A", "B" };` is correct syntax.

26. What is a ragged array?

27. The `factorial()` method provides an example of *tail recursion*, a special case of recursion in which the method's last statement contains a recursive call, which is known as a *tail call*. Provide another example of tail recursion.

28. Create a Book class with name, author, and International Standard Book Number (ISBN) fields. Provide a suitable constructor and getter methods that return field values. Introduce a `main()` method into this class that creates an array of Book objects and iterates over this array outputting each book's name, author, and ISBN.

Summary

A class is a template for manufacturing objects, which are named aggregates of code and data. Classes generalize real-world entities, and objects are specific manifestations of these entities at the application level.

The new operator allocates memory to store the object whose type is specified by new's solitary operand. This operator is followed by a constructor, which is a block of code for initializing an object. new calls the constructor immediately after allocating memory to store the object.

Java lets you represent an entity's state via fields, which are variables declared within a class's body. Entity attributes are described via instance fields. Because Java also supports state that's associated with a class and not with an object, Java provides class fields to describe this class state.

Java lets you represent an entity's behaviors via methods, which are named blocks of code declared within a class's body. Entity behaviors are described via instance methods. Because Java also supports behaviors that are associated with classes and not with objects, Java provides class methods to describe these class behaviors.

Classes and objects need to be properly initialized before they are used. You've already learned that class fields are initialized to default zero values after a class loads and can be subsequently initialized by assigning values to them in their declarations via class field initializers. Similarly, instance fields are initialized to default values when an object's memory is allocated via new and can be subsequently initialized by assigning values to them in their declarations via instance field initializers or via constructors.

Java also supports class initializers and instance initializers for this task. A class initializer is a static-prefixed block that is introduced into a class body. It is used to initialize a loaded class via a sequence of statements. An instance initializer is a block that is introduced into a class body, as opposed to being introduced as the body of a method or a constructor. The instance initializer is used to initialize an object via a sequence of statements.

Objects are created via reserved word new, but how are they destroyed? Without some way to destroy objects, they will eventually fill up the heap's available space and the application will not be able to continue. Java doesn't provide the developer with the ability to remove them from memory. Instead, Java handles this task by providing a garbage collector, which is code that runs in the background and occasionally checks for unreferenced objects.

You can think of an array as a special kind of object, although it's not an object in the same sense that a class instance is an object. This pseudo-object has a solitary and read-only length field that contains the array's size (the number of elements).

As well as using the syntactic sugar first presented in Chapter 2 for creating an array, you can also create an array using the new operator, with or without the syntactic sugar.

In Chapter 4 I continue to explore the Java language by examining its support for inheritance, polymorphism, and interfaces.

Chapter 4

Discovering Inheritance, Polymorphism, and Interfaces

An *object-based language* is a language that encapsulates state and behaviors in objects. Java's support for encapsulation (discussed in Chapter 3) qualifies it as an object-based language. However, Java is also an *object-oriented language* because it supports inheritance and polymorphism (as well as encapsulation). (Object-oriented languages are a subset of object-based languages.) In Chapter 4 I introduce you to Java's language features that support inheritance and polymorphism. Also, I introduce you to interfaces, Java's ultimate abstract type mechanism.

Building Class Hierarchies

We tend to categorize stuff by saying things like "cars are vehicles" or "savings accounts are bank accounts." By making these statements, we really are saying (from a software development perspective) that cars inherit vehicular state (e.g., make and color) and behaviors (e.g., park and display mileage) and that savings accounts inherit bank account state (e.g., balance) and behaviors (e.g., deposit and withdraw). Car, vehicle, savings account, and bank account are examples of real-world entity categories, and *inheritance* is a hierarchical relationship between similar entity categories in which one category inherits state and behaviors from at least one other entity category. Inheriting from a single category is *single inheritance*, and inheriting from at least two categories is *multiple inheritance*.

Java supports single inheritance and multiple inheritance to facilitate code reuse—why reinvent the wheel? Java supports single inheritance in a class context in which a class inherits state and behaviors from another class through class extension. Because classes are involved, Java refers to this kind of inheritance as *implementation inheritance*.

Java also supports single inheritance and multiple inheritance in an interface context in which a class inherits behavior templates from one or more interfaces through interface implementation or in which an interface inherits behavior templates from one or more interfaces through interface extension.

Because interfaces are involved, Java refers to this kind of inheritance as *interface inheritance*. (I discuss interfaces later in this chapter.)

> **Note**   You reuse code by carefully extending classes, implementing interfaces, and extending interfaces. You start with something that is close to what you want and extend it to meet your goal. You don't reuse code by simply copying and pasting it. Copying and pasting often results in redundant (i.e., nonreusable) and buggy code.

In this section I introduce you to Java's support for implementation inheritance by first focusing on class extension. I then introduce you to a special class that sits at the top of Java's class hierarchy. After introducing you to composition, which is an alternative to implementation inheritance for reusing code, I show you how composition can be used to overcome problems with implementation inheritance.

Extending Classes

Java provides the reserved word extends for specifying a hierarchical relationship between two classes. For example, suppose you have a Vehicle class and want to introduce a Car class as a kind of Vehicle. Listing 4-1 uses extends to cement this relationship.

Listing 4-1. Relating Two Classes via extends

```
class Vehicle
{
   // member declarations
}

class Car extends Vehicle
{
   // member declarations
}
```

Listing 4-1 codifies a relationship that is known as an "is-a" relationship: a car is a kind of vehicle. In this relationship, Vehicle is known as the *base class*, *parent class*, or *superclass*; and Car is known as the *derived class*, *child class*, or *subclass*.

> **Caution**   You cannot extend a final class. For example, if you declared Vehicle as final class Vehicle, the compiler would report an error on encountering class Car extends Vehicle. Developers declare their classes final when they don't want these classes to be extended (for security or other reasons).

As well as being capable of providing its own member declarations, Car is capable of inheriting member declarations from its Vehicle superclass. As Listing 4-2 shows, non-private inherited members become accessible to members of the Car class.

Listing 4-2. Inheriting Members

```java
class Vehicle
{
   private String make;
   private String model;
   private int year;

   Vehicle(String make, String model, int year)
   {
      this.make = make;
      this.model = model;
      this.year = year;
   }

   String getMake()
   {
      return make;
   }

   String getModel()
   {
      return model;
   }

   int getYear()
   {
      return year;
   }
}

public class Car extends Vehicle
{
   private int numWheels;

   Car(String make, String model, int year, int numWheels)
   {
      super(make, model, year);
      this.numWheels = numWheels;
   }

   public static void main(String[] args)
   {
      Car car = new Car("Ford", "Fiesta", 2009, 4);
      System.out.println("Make = " + car.getMake());
      System.out.println("Model = " + car.getModel());
      System.out.println("Year = " + car.getYear());
```

```
        // Normally, you cannot access a private field via an object
        // reference. However, numWheels is being accessed from
        // within a method (main()) that is part of the Car class.
        System.out.println("Number of wheels = " + car.numWheels);
    }
}
```

Listing 4-2's Vehicle class declares private fields that store a vehicle's make, model, and year; a constructor that initializes these fields to passed arguments; and getter methods that retrieve these fields' values.

The Car subclass provides a private numWheels field, a constructor that initializes a Car object's Vehicle and Car layers, and a main() class method for testing this class.

Car's constructor uses reserved word super to call Vehicle's constructor with Vehicle-oriented arguments and then initializes Car's numWheels instance field. The super() call is analogous to specifying this() to call another constructor in the same class, but invokes a superclass constructor instead.

Caution   The super() call can only appear in a constructor. Furthermore, it must be the first code that is specified in the constructor. If super() is not specified, and if the superclass does not have a noargument constructor, the compiler will report an error because the subclass constructor must call a noargument superclass constructor when super() is not present.

Car's main() method creates a Car object, initializing this object to a specific make, model, year, and number of wheels. Four System.out.println() method calls subsequently output this information.

The first three System.out.println() method calls retrieve their pieces of information by calling the Car instance's inherited getMake(), getModel(), and getYear() methods. The final System.out.println() method call accesses the instance's numWheels field directly. Although it is generally not a good idea to access an instance field directly (doing so violates information hiding), Car's main() method, which provides this access, is present only to test this class and would not exist in a real application that uses this class.

Because Car is declared to be a public class, Listing 4-2 would be stored in a file named Car.java. Therefore, execute javac Car.java to compile this source code into Vehicle.class and Car.class. Then execute java Car to test the Car class. This execution results in the following output:

```
Make = Ford
Model = Fiesta
Year = 2009
Number of wheels = 4
```

> **Note**   A class whose instances cannot be modified is known as an *immutable class*. Vehicle is an
> example. If Car's main() method, which can directly read or write numWheels, was not present, Car
> would also be an example of an immutable class. Also, a class cannot inherit constructors, nor can it
> inherit private fields and methods. For example, Car doesn't inherit Vehicle's constructor, nor does
> it inherit Vehicle's private make, model, and year fields.

A subclass can *override* (replace) an inherited method so that the subclass's version of the method
is called instead. Listing 4-3 shows you that the overriding method must specify the same name,
parameter list, and return type as the method being overridden.

Listing 4-3. Overriding a Method

```
class Vehicle
{
    private String make;
    private String model;
    private int year;

    Vehicle(String make, String model, int year)
    {
        this.make = make;
        this.model = model;
        this.year = year;
    }

    void describe()
    {
        System.out.println(year + " " + make + " " + model);
    }
}

public class Car extends Vehicle
{
    private int numWheels;

    Car(String make, String model, int year, int numWheels)
    {
        super(make, model, year);
    }

    void describe()
    {
        System.out.print("This car is a "); // Print without newline - see Chapter 1.
        super.describe();
    }

    public static void main(String[] args)
```

```
    {
        Car car = new Car("Ford", "Fiesta", 2009, 4);
        car.describe();
    }
}
```

Listing 4-3's Car class declares a describe() method that overrides Vehicle's describe() method to output a car-oriented description. This method uses reserved word super to call Vehicle's describe() method via super.describe();.

> **Note**   Call a superclass method from the overriding subclass method by prefixing the method's name with reserved word super and the member access operator. If you don't do this, you end up recursively calling the subclass's overriding method. Use super and the member access operator to access non-private superclass fields from subclasses that mask these fields by declaring same-named fields.

If you were to compile Listing 4-3 (javac Car.java) and run the Car application (java Car), you would discover that Car's overriding describe() method executes instead of Vehicle's overridden describe() method and outputs This car is a 2009 Ford Fiesta.

> **Caution**   You cannot override a final method. For example, if Vehicle's describe() method was declared as final void describe(), the compiler would report an error on encountering an attempt to override this method in the Car class. Developers declare their methods final when they don't want these methods to be overridden (for security or other reasons). Also, you cannot make an overriding method less accessible than the method it overrides. For example, if Car's describe() method was declared as private void describe(), the compiler would report an error because private access is less accessible than the default package access. However, describe() could be made more accessible by declaring it public, as in public void describe().

Suppose you happened to replace Listing 4-3's describe() method with the method shown here:

```
void describe(String owner)
{
    System.out.print("This car, which is owned by " + owner + ", is a ");
    super.describe();
}
```

The modified Car class now has two describe() methods, the preceding explicitly declared method and the method inherited from Vehicle. The void describe(String owner) method doesn't override Vehicle's describe() method. Instead, it overloads this method.

The Java compiler helps you detect an attempt to overload instead of override a method at compile time by letting you prefix a subclass's method header with the @Override annotation as shown in the following code (I will discuss annotations in Chapter 6):

```
@Override
void describe()
{
   System.out.print("This car is a ");
   super.describe();
}
```

Specifying @Override tells the compiler that the method overrides another method. If you overload the method instead, the compiler reports an error. Without this annotation, the compiler would not report an error because method overloading is a valid feature.

> **Tip**   Get into the habit of prefixing overriding methods with the @Override annotation. This habit will help you detect overloading mistakes much sooner.

In Chapter 3 I discussed the initialization order of classes and objects, where you learned that class members are always initialized first and in a top-down order (the same order applies to instance members). Implementation inheritance adds a couple more details:

- A superclass's class initializers always execute before a subclass's class initializers.

- A subclass's constructor always calls the superclass constructor to initialize an object's superclass layer and then initializes the subclass layer.

Java's support for implementation inheritance only permits you to extend a single class. You cannot extend multiple classes because doing so can lead to problems. For example, suppose Java supported multiple implementation inheritance, and you decided to model a flying horse (from Greek mythology) via the class structure shown in Listing 4-4.

Listing 4-4. A Fictional Demonstration of Multiple Implementation Inheritance

```
class Bird
{
   void describe()
   {
      // code that outputs a description of a bird's appearance and behaviors
   }
}

class Horse
{
   void describe()
   {
      // code that outputs a description of a horse's appearance and behaviors
   }
}
```

```
public class FlyingHorse extends Bird, Horse
{
   public static void main(String[] args)
   {
      FlyingHorse pegasus = new FlyingHorse();
      pegasus.describe();
   }
}
```

Listing 4-4's class structure reveals an ambiguity resulting from each of `Bird` and `Horse` declaring a `describe()` method. Which of these methods does `FlyingHorse` inherit? A related ambiguity arises from same-named fields, possibly of different types. Which field is inherited?

The Ultimate Superclass

A class that doesn't explicitly extend another class implicitly extends Java's `Object` class (located in the `java.lang` package—I will discuss packages in the next chapter). For example, Listing 4-1's `Vehicle` class extends `Object`, whereas `Car` extends `Vehicle`.

`Object` is Java's ultimate superclass because it serves as the ancestor of every other class but doesn't itself extend any other class. `Object` provides a common set of methods that other classes inherit. Table 4-1 describes these methods.

Table 4-1. Object's Methods

Method	Description
`Object clone()`	Create and return a copy of the current object.
`boolean equals(Object obj)`	Determine if the current object is equal to the object identified by `obj`.
`void finalize()`	Finalize the current object.
`Class<?> getClass()`	Return the current object's `Class` object.
`int hashCode()`	Return the current object's hash code.
`void notify()`	Wake up one of the threads that are waiting on the current object's monitor.
`void notifyAll()`	Wake up all threads that are waiting on the current object's monitor.
`String toString()`	Return a string representation of the current object.
`void wait()`	Cause the current thread to wait on the current object's monitor until it is woken up via `notify()` or `notifyAll()`.
`void wait(long timeout)`	Cause the current thread to wait on the current object's monitor until it is woken up via `notify()` or `notifyAll()` or until the specified `timeout` value (in milliseconds) has elapsed, whichever comes first.
`void wait(long timeout, int nanos)`	Cause the current thread to wait on the current object's monitor until it is woken up via `notify()` or `notifyAll()` or until the specified `timeout` value (in milliseconds) plus nanos value (in nanoseconds) has elapsed, whichever comes first.

I will discuss the clone(), equals(), finalize(), hashCode(), and toString() methods shortly, but defer a discussion of notify(), notifyAll(), and the wait() methods to Chapter 8.

Cloning

The clone() method *clones* (duplicates) an object without calling a constructor. It copies each primitive or reference field's value to its counterpart in the clone, a task known as *shallow copying* or *shallow cloning*. Listing 4-5 demonstrates this behavior.

Listing 4-5. Shallowly Cloning an Employee Object

```
public class Employee implements Cloneable
{
   String name;
   int age;

   Employee(String name, int age)
   {
      this.name = name;
      this.age = age;
   }

   public static void main(String[] args) throws CloneNotSupportedException
   {
      Employee e1 = new Employee("John Doe", 46);
      Employee e2 = (Employee) e1.clone();
      System.out.println(e1 == e2); // Output: false
      System.out.println(e1.name == e2.name); // Output: true
   }
}
```

Listing 4-5 declares an Employee class with name and age instance fields and a constructor for initializing these fields. The main() method uses this constructor to initialize a new Employee object's copies of these fields to John Doe and 46.

> **Note** A class must implement the java.lang.Cloneable interface or its instances cannot be shallowly cloned via Object's clone() method—this method performs a runtime check to see if the class implements Cloneable. (I will discuss interfaces later in this chapter.) If a class doesn't implement Cloneable, clone() throws java.lang.CloneNotSupportedException. (Because CloneNotSupportedException is a checked exception, it's necessary for Listing 4-5 to satisfy the compiler by appending throws CloneNotSupportedException to the main() method's header. I will discuss exceptions in the next chapter.) The java.lang.String class is an example of a class that doesn't implement Cloneable; hence, String objects cannot be shallowly cloned.

After assigning the Employee object's reference to local variable e1, main() calls the clone() method on this variable to duplicate the object and then assigns the resulting reference to variable e2. The (Employee) cast is needed because clone() returns Object.

To prove that the objects whose references were assigned to e1 and e2 are different, main() next compares these references via == and outputs the Boolean result, which happens to be false. To prove that the Employee object was shallowly cloned, main() next compares the references in both Employee objects' name fields via == and outputs the Boolean result, which happens to be true.

> **Note**   Object's clone() method was originally specified as a public method, which meant that any object could be cloned from anywhere. For security reasons, this access was later changed to protected, which means that only code within the same package as the class whose clone() method is to be called, or code within a subclass of this class (regardless of package), can call clone().

Shallow cloning is not always desirable because the original object and its clone refer to the same object via their equivalent reference fields. For example, each of Listing 4-5's two Employee objects refers to the same String object via its name field.

Although not a problem for String, whose instances are immutable, changing a mutable object via the clone's reference field causes the original (noncloned) object to see the same change via its reference field. For example, suppose you add a reference field named hireDate to Employee. This field is of type Date with year, month, and day instance fields. Because Date is intended to be mutable, you can change the contents of these fields in the Date instance assigned to hireDate.

Now suppose you plan to change the clone's date but want to preserve the original Employee object's date. You cannot do this with shallow cloning because the change is also visible to the original Employee object. To solve this problem, you must modify the cloning operation so that it assigns a new Date reference to the Employee clone's hireDate field. This task, which is known as *deep copying* or *deep cloning*, is demonstrated in Listing 4-6.

Listing 4-6. Deeply Cloning an Employee Object

```java
class Date
{
   int year, month, day;

   Date(int year, int month, int day)
   {
      this.year = year;
      this.month = month;
      this.day = day;
   }
}

public class Employee implements Cloneable
{
   String name;
   int age;
   Date hireDate;
```

```
Employee(String name, int age, Date hireDate)
{
   this.name = name;
   this.age = age;
   this.hireDate = hireDate;
}

@Override
protected Object clone() throws CloneNotSupportedException
{
   Employee emp = (Employee) super.clone();
   if (hireDate != null) // no point cloning a null object (one that doesn't exist)
      emp.hireDate = new Date(hireDate.year, hireDate.month, hireDate.day);
   return emp;
}

public static void main(String[] args) throws CloneNotSupportedException
{
   Employee e1 = new Employee("John Doe", 46, new Date(2000, 1, 20));
   Employee e2 = (Employee) e1.clone();
   System.out.println(e1 == e2); // Output: false
   System.out.println(e1.name == e2.name); // Output: true
   System.out.println(e1.hireDate == e2.hireDate); // Output: false
   System.out.println(e2.hireDate.year + " " + e2.hireDate.month + " " +
                     e2.hireDate.day); // Output: 2000 1 20
}
}
```

Listing 4-6 declares Date and Employee classes. The Date class declares year, month, and day fields and a constructor. (You can declare a comma-separated list of variables on one line provided that these variables all share the same type, which is int in this case.)

Employee overrides the clone() method to deeply clone the hireDate field. This method first calls Object's clone() method to shallowly clone the current Employee object's instance fields and then stores the new object's reference in emp. Assuming that hireDate doesn't contain the null reference, it next assigns a new Date object's reference to emp's hireDate field; this object's fields are initialized to the same values as those in the original Employee object's hireDate instance.

At this point, you have an Employee clone with shallowly cloned name and age fields and a deeply cloned hireDate field. The clone() method finishes by returning this Employee clone.

> **Note** If you're not calling Object's clone() method from an overridden clone() method (because you prefer to deeply clone reference fields and do your own shallow copying of nonreference fields), it isn't necessary for the class containing the overriding clone() method to implement Cloneable, but it should implement this interface for consistency. String doesn't override clone(), so String objects cannot be deeply cloned.

Equality

The == and != operators compare two primitive values (such as integers) for equality (==) or inequality (!=). These operators also compare two references to see whether they refer to the same object or not. This latter comparison is known as an *identity check*.

You cannot use == and != to determine whether two objects are logically the same (or not). For example, two Car objects with the same field values are logically equivalent. However, == reports them as unequal because of their different references.

> **Note**   Because == and != perform the fastest possible comparisons and because string comparisons need to be performed quickly (especially when sorting a huge number of strings), the String class contains special support that allows literal strings and string-valued constant expressions to be compared via == and !=. (I will discuss this support when I present String in Chapter 7.) The following statements demonstrate these comparisons:
>
> ```
> System.out.println("abc" == "abc"); // Output: true
> System.out.println("abc" == "a" + "bc"); // Output: true
> System.out.println("abc" == "Abc"); // Output: false
> System.out.println("abc" != "def"); // Output: true
> System.out.println("abc" == new String("abc")); // Output: false
> ```

Recognizing the need to support logical equality in addition to reference equality, Java provides an equals() method in the Object class. Because this method defaults to comparing references, you need to override equals() to compare object contents.

Before overriding equals(), make sure that this is necessary. For example, Java's java.lang. StringBuffer class doesn't override equals(). Perhaps this class's designers didn't think it necessary to determine whether two StringBuffer objects are logically equivalent or not.

You cannot override equals() with arbitrary code. Doing so will probably prove disastrous to your applications. Instead, you need to adhere to the contract that is specified in the Java documentation for this method, which I present next.

The equals() method implements an equivalence relation on nonnull object references:

- *It is reflexive*: For any nonnull reference value x, x.equals(x) returns true.

- *It is symmetric*: For any nonnull reference values x and y, x.equals(y) returns true if and only if y.equals(x) returns true.

- *It is transitive*: For any nonnull reference values x, y, and z, if x.equals(y) returns true and y.equals(z) returns true, then x.equals(z) returns true.

- *It is consistent*: For any nonnull reference values x and y, multiple invocations of x.equals(y) consistently return true or consistently return false, provided no information used in equals() comparisons on the objects is modified.

- For any nonnull reference value x, x.equals(null) returns false.

Although this contract probably looks somewhat intimidating, it isn't that difficult to satisfy. For proof, take a look at the implementation of the equals() method in Listing 4-7's Point class.

Listing 4-7. Logically Comparing Point Objects

```java
public class Point
{
   private int x, y;

   Point(int x, int y)
   {
      this.x = x;
      this.y = y;
   }

   int getX()
   {
      return x;
   }

   int getY()
   {
      return y;
   }

   @Override
   public boolean equals(Object o)
   {
      if (!(o instanceof Point))
         return false;
      Point p = (Point) o;
      return p.x == x && p.y == y;
   }

   public static void main(String[] args)
   {
      Point p1 = new Point(10, 20);
      Point p2 = new Point(20, 30);
      Point p3 = new Point(10, 20);
      // Test reflexivity
      System.out.println(p1.equals(p1)); // Output: true
      // Test symmetry
      System.out.println(p1.equals(p2)); // Output: false
      System.out.println(p2.equals(p1)); // Output: false
      // Test transitivity
      System.out.println(p2.equals(p3)); // Output: false
      System.out.println(p1.equals(p3)); // Output: true
      // Test nullability
      System.out.println(p1.equals(null)); // Output: false
```

```
    // Extra test to further prove the instanceof operator's usefulness.
    System.out.println(p1.equals("abc")); // Output: false
  }
}
```

Listing 4-7's overriding `equals()` method begins with an if statement that uses the `instanceof` operator to determine whether the argument passed to parameter o is an instance of the `Point` class. If not, the if statement executes `return false;`.

The `o instanceof Point` expression satisfies the last portion of the contract: for any nonnull reference value x, x.`equals(null)` returns false. Because the null reference is not an instance of any class, passing this value to `equals()` causes the expression to evaluate to false.

The `o instanceof Point` expression also prevents a `java.lang.ClassCastException` instance from being thrown via expression `(Point) o` in the event that you pass an object other than a `Point` object to `equals()`. (I will discuss exceptions in the next chapter.)

Following the cast, the contract's reflexivity, symmetry, and transitivity requirements are met by only allowing `Points` to be compared with other `Points` via expression `p.x == x && p.y == y`.

The final contract requirement, consistency, is met by making sure that the `equals()` method is deterministic. In other words, this method doesn't rely on any field value that could change from method call to method call.

> **Tip**   You can optimize the performance of a time-consuming `equals()` method by first using `==` to determine if o's reference identifies the current object. Simply specify `if (o == this) return true;` as the `equals()` method's first statement. This optimization isn't necessary in Listing 4-7's `equals()` method, which has satisfactory performance.

It's important to always override the `hashCode()` method when overriding `equals()`. I didn't do so in Listing 4-7 because I have yet to formally introduce `hashCode()`.

Finalization

Finalization refers to cleanup via the `finalize()` method, which is known as a *finalizer*. The `finalize()` method's Java documentation states that `finalize()` is "called by the garbage collector on an object when garbage collection determines that there are no more references to the object. A subclass overrides the `finalize()` method to dispose of system resources or to perform other cleanup."

`Object`'s version of `finalize()` does nothing; you must override this method with any needed cleanup code. Because the virtual machine might never call `finalize()` before an application terminates, you should provide an explicit cleanup method and have `finalize()` call this method as a safety net in case the method isn't otherwise called.

> **Caution**   Never depend on `finalize()` for releasing limited resources such as file descriptors.
> For example, if an application object opens files, expecting that its `finalize()` method will close
> them, the application might find itself unable to open additional files when a tardy virtual machine is
> slow to call `finalize()`. What makes this problem worse is that `finalize()` might be called more
> frequently on another virtual machine, resulting in this too-many-open-files problem not revealing itself.
> The developer might falsely believe that the application behaves consistently across different virtual
> machines.

If you decide to override `finalize()`, your object's subclass layer must give its superclass layer an
opportunity to perform finalization. You can accomplish this task by specifying `super.finalize();`
as the last statement in your method, which the following example demonstrates:

```
protected void finalize() throws Throwable
{
   try
   {
      // Perform subclass cleanup.
   }
   finally
   {
      super.finalize();
   }
}
```

The example's `finalize()` declaration appends `throws Throwable` to the method header because
the cleanup code might throw an exception. If an exception is thrown, execution leaves the method
and, in the absence of try-finally, `super.finalize();` never executes. (I will discuss exceptions and
try-finally in Chapter 5.)

To guard against this possibility, the subclass's cleanup code executes in a block that follows
reserved word `try`. If an exception is thrown, Java's exception-handling logic executes the block
following the `finally` reserved word, and `super.finalize();` executes the superclass's `finalize()`
method.

> **Note** The `finalize()` method has often been used to perform *resurrection* (making an unreferenced object referenced) to implement *object pools* that recycle the same objects when these objects are expensive (time wise) to create (database connection objects are an example).
>
> Resurrection occurs when you assign `this` (a reference to the current object) to a class or instance field (or to another long-lived variable). For example, you might specify `r = this;` within `finalize()` to assign the unreferenced object identified as `this` to a class field named `r`.
>
> Because of the possibility for resurrection, there is a severe performance penalty imposed on the garbage collection of an object that overrides `finalize()`.
>
> A resurrected object's finalizer cannot be called again.

Hash Codes

The `hashCode()` method returns a 32-bit integer that identifies the current object's *hash code*, a small value that results from applying a mathematical function to a potentially large amount of data. The calculation of this value is known as *hashing*.

You must override `hashCode()` when overriding `equals()` and in accordance with the following contract, which is specified in `hashCode()`'s Java documentation:

- Whenever it is invoked on the same object more than once during an execution of a Java application, the `hashCode()` method must consistently return the same integer, provided no information used in `equals(Object)` comparisons on the object is modified. This integer need not remain consistent from one execution of an application to another execution of the same application.

- If two objects are equal according to the `equals(Object)` method, then calling the `hashCode()` method on each of the two objects must produce the same integer result.

- It is not required that if two objects are unequal according to the `equals(Object)` method, then calling the `hashCode()` method on each of the two objects must produce distinct integer results. However, the programmer should be aware that producing distinct integer results for unequal objects might improve the performance of hash tables.

Fail to obey this contract and your class's instances will not work properly with Java's hash-based Collections Framework classes, such as `java.util.HashMap`. (I will discuss `HashMap` and other Collections Framework classes in Chapter 9.)

If you override `equals()` but not `hashCode()`, you most importantly violate the second item in the contract: the hash codes of equal objects must also be equal. This violation can lead to serious consequences, as demonstrated in the following example:

```
java.util.Map<Point, String> map = new java.util.HashMap<Point, String>();
map.put(p1, "first point");
```

```
System.out.println(map.get(p1)); // Output: first point
System.out.println(map.get(new Point(10, 20))); // Output: null
```

Assume that the example's statements are appended to Listing 4-7's `main()` method—the `java.util.` prefix and `<Point, String>` have to do with packages and generics, which I discuss in Chapters 5 and 6.

After `main()` creates its `Point` objects and calls its `System.out.println()` methods, it executes the example's statements, which perform the following tasks:

- The first statement instantiates `HashMap`, which is in the `java.util` package.

- The second statement calls `HashMap`'s `put()` method to store Listing 4-7's `p1` object key and the `"first point"` value in the hashmap.

- The third statement retrieves the value of the hashmap entry whose `Point` key is logically equal to `p1` via `HashMap`'s `get()` method.

- The fourth statement is equivalent to the third statement but returns the null reference instead of `"first point"`.

Although objects `p1` and `Point(10, 20)` are logically equivalent, these objects have different hash codes, resulting in each object referring to a different entry in the hashmap. If an object is not stored (via `put()`) in that entry, `get()` returns null.

Correcting this problem requires that `hashCode()` be overridden to return the same integer value for logically equivalent objects. I will show you how to accomplish this task when I discuss `HashMap` in Chapter 9.

String Representation

The `toString()` method returns a string-based representation of the current object. This representation defaults to the object's class name, followed by the @ symbol, followed by a hexadecimal representation of the object's hash code.

For example, if you were to execute `System.out.println(p1);` to output Listing 4-7's `p1` object, you would see a line of output similar to `Point@3e25a5`. (`System.out.println()` calls `p1`'s inherited `toString()` method behind the scenes.)

You should strive to override `toString()` so that it returns a concise but meaningful description of the object. For example, you might declare, in Listing 4-7's `Point` class, a `toString()` method that is similar to the following:

```
@Override
public String toString()
{
    return "(" + x + ", " + y + ")";
}
```

This time, executing `System.out.println(p1);` results in more meaningful output, such as `(10, 20)`.

Composition

Implementation inheritance and composition offer two different approaches to reusing code. As you have learned, implementation inheritance is concerned with extending a class with a new class, which is based on an "is-a" relationship between them: a Car is a Vehicle, for example.

On the other hand, *composition* is concerned with composing classes out of other classes, which is based on a "has-a" relationship between them. For example, a Car has an Engine, Wheels, and a SteeringWheel.

You have already seen examples of composition in this chapter. For example, Listing 4-2's Car class includes String make and String model fields. Listing 4-8's Car class provides another example of composition.

Listing 4-8. A Car Class Whose Instances Are Composed of Other Objects

```
class Car extends Vehicle
{
   private Engine engine; // bicycles don't have engines
   private Wheel[] wheels; // boats don't have wheels
   private SteeringWheel steeringWheel; // hang gliders don't have steering wheels
}
```

Listing 4-8 demonstrates that composition and implementation inheritance are not mutually exclusive. Although not shown, Car inherits various members from its Vehicle superclass, in addition to providing its own engine, wheels, and steeringWheel fields.

The Trouble with Implementation Inheritance

Implementation inheritance is potentially dangerous, especially when the developer doesn't have complete control over the superclass or when the superclass isn't designed and documented with extension in mind.

The problem is that implementation inheritance breaks encapsulation. The subclass relies on implementation details in the superclass. If these details change in a new version of the superclass, the subclass might break, even when the subclass isn't touched.

For example, suppose you have purchased a library of Java classes, and one of these classes describes an appointment calendar. Although you don't have access to this class's source code, assume that Listing 4-9 describes part of its code.

Listing 4-9. An Appointment Calendar Class

```
public class ApptCalendar
{
   private final static int MAX_APPT = 1000;
   private Appt[] appts;
   private int size;

   public ApptCalendar()
   {
      appts = new Appt[MAX_APPT];
```

```
      size = 0; // redundant because field automatically initialized to 0
               // adds clarity, however
   }

   public void addAppt(Appt appt)
   {
      if (size == appts.length)
         return; // array is full
      appts[size++] = appt;
   }

   public void addAppts(Appt[] appts)
   {
      for (int i = 0; i < appts.length; i++)
         addAppt(appts[i]);
   }
}
```

Listing 4-9's ApptCalendar class stores an array of appointments, with each appointment described by an Appt instance. For this discussion, the details of Appt are irrelevant. It could be as trivial as class Appt {}.

Suppose you want to log each appointment in a file. Because a logging capability isn't provided, you extend ApptCalendar with Listing 4-10's LoggingApptCalendar class, which adds logging behavior in overriding addAppt() and addAppts() methods.

Listing 4-10. Extending the Appointment Calendar Class

```
public class LoggingApptCalendar extends ApptCalendar
{
   // A constructor is not necessary because the Java compiler will add a
   // noargument constructor that calls the superclass's noargument
   // constructor by default.

   @Override
   public void addAppt(Appt appt)
   {
      Logger.log(appt.toString());
      super.addAppt(appt);
   }

   @Override
   public void addAppts(Appt[] appts)
   {
      for (int i = 0; i < appts.length; i++)
         Logger.log(appts[i].toString());
      super.addAppts(appts);
   }
}
```

Listing 4-10's `LoggingApptCalendar` class relies on a `Logger` class whose void `log(String msg)` class method logs a string to a file (the details are unimportant). Notice the use of `toString()` to convert an `Appt` object to a `String` object, which is then passed to `log()`.

Although this class looks okay, it doesn't work as you might expect. Suppose you instantiate this class and add a few `Appt` instances to this instance via `addAppts()`, as demonstrated in the following manner:

```
LoggingApptCalendar lapptc = new LoggingApptCalendar();
lapptc.addAppts(new Appt[] { new Appt(), new Appt(), new Appt() });
```

If you also add a `System.out.println(msg);` method call to Logger's `log(String msg)` method, to output this method's argument, you will discover that `log()` outputs a total of six messages; each of the expected three messages (one per `Appt` object) is duplicated.

When `LoggingApptCalendar`'s `addAppts()` method is called, it first calls `Logger.log()` for each `Appt` instance in the `appts` array that is passed to `addAppts()`. This method then calls `ApptCalendar`'s `addAppts()` method via `super.addAppts(appts);`.

`ApptCalendar`'s `addAppts()` method calls `LoggingApptCalendar`'s overriding `addAppt()` method for each `Appt` instance in its `appts` array argument. `addAppt()` executes `Logger.log(appt.toString());` to log its `appt` argument's string representation, and you end up with three additional logged messages.

If you didn't override the `addAppts()` method, this problem would go away. However, the subclass would be tied to an implementation detail: `ApptCalendar`'s `addAppts()` method calls `addAppt()`.

It isn't a good idea to rely on an implementation detail when the detail isn't documented. (I previously stated that you don't have access to `ApptCalendar`'s source code.) When a detail isn't documented, it can change in a new version of the class.

Because a base class change can break a subclass, this problem is known as the *fragile base class problem*. A related cause of fragility that also has to do with overriding methods occurs when new methods are added to a superclass in a subsequent release.

For example, suppose a new version of the library introduces a new `public void addAppt(Appt appt, boolean unique)` method into the `ApptCalendar` class. This method adds the `appt` instance to the calendar when `unique` is false; and, when `unique` is true, it adds the `appt` instance only if it has not previously been added.

Because this method has been added after the `LoggingApptCalendar` class was created, `LoggingApptCalendar` doesn't override the new `addAppt()` method with a call to `Logger.log()`. As a result, `Appt` instances passed to the new `addAppt()` method are not logged.

Here is another problem: you introduce a method into the subclass that is not also in the superclass. A new version of the superclass presents a new method that matches the subclass method signature and return type. Your subclass method now overrides the superclass method and probably doesn't fulfill the superclass method's contract.

There is a way to make these problems disappear. Instead of extending the superclass, create a private field in a new class, and have this field reference an instance of the superclass. This task demonstrates composition because you are forming a "has-a" relationship between the new class and the superclass.

Additionally, have each of the new class's instance methods call the corresponding superclass method via the superclass instance that was saved in the private field, and also return the called method's return value. This task is known as *forwarding*, and the new methods are known as *forwarding methods*.

Listing 4-11 presents an improved LoggingApptCalendar class that uses composition and forwarding to forever eliminate the fragile base class problem and the additional problem of unanticipated method overriding.

Listing 4-11. A Composed Logging Appointment Calendar Class

```java
public class LoggingApptCalendar
{
   private ApptCalendar apptCal;

   public LoggingApptCalendar(ApptCalendar apptCal)
   {
      this.apptCal = apptCal;
   }

   public void addAppt(Appt appt)
   {
      Logger.log(appt.toString());
      apptCal.addAppt(appt);
   }

   public void addAppts(Appt[] appts)
   {
      for (int i = 0; i < appts.length; i++)
         Logger.log(appts[i].toString());
      apptCal.addAppts(appts);
   }
}
```

Listing 4-11's LoggingApptCalendar class doesn't depend on implementation details of the ApptCalendar class. You can add new methods to ApptCalendar and they will not break LoggingApptCalendar.

Note LoggingApptCalendar is an example of a *wrapper class*, a class whose instances wrap other instances. Each LoggingApptCalendar instance wraps an ApptCalendar instance. LoggingApptCalendar is also an example of the *Decorator design pattern*, which is presented on page 175 of *Design Patterns: Elements of Reusable Object-Oriented Software* by Erich Gamma, Richard Helm, Ralph Johnson, and John Vlissides (Addison-Wesley, 1995; ISBN: 0201633612).

When should you extend a class and when should you use a wrapper class? Extend a class when an "is-a" relationship exists between the superclass and the subclass, and either you have control over the superclass or the superclass has been designed and documented for class extension. Otherwise, use a wrapper class.

What does "design and document for class extension" mean? Design means provide `protected` methods that hook into the class's inner workings (to support writing efficient subclasses) and ensure that constructors and the `clone()` method never call overridable methods. Document means clearly state the impact of overriding methods.

> **Caution**   Wrapper classes shouldn't be used in a *callback framework*, an object framework in which an object passes its own reference to another object (via `this`) so that the latter object can call the former object's methods at a later time. This "calling back to the former object's method" is known as a *callback*. Because the wrapped object doesn't know of its wrapper class, it passes only its reference (via `this`), and resulting callbacks don't involve the wrapper class's methods.

Changing Form

Some real-world entities can change their forms. For example, water (on Earth as opposed to interstellar space) is naturally a liquid, but it changes to a solid when frozen, and it changes to a gas when heated to its boiling point. Insects such as butterflies that undergo metamorphosis are another example.

The ability to change form is known as *polymorphism* and is useful to model in a programming language. For example, code that draws arbitrary shapes can be expressed more concisely by introducing a single Shape class and its `draw()` method and by invoking that method for each Circle instance, Rectangle instance, and other Shape instance stored in an array. When Shape's `draw()` method is called for an array instance, it is the Circle's, Rectangle's or other Shape instance's `draw()` method that gets called. There are many forms of Shape's `draw()` method. In other words, this method is polymorphic.

Java supports four kinds of polymorphism:

- *Coercion*: An operation serves multiple types through implicit type conversion. For example, division lets you divide an integer by another integer or divide a floating-point value by another floating-point value. If one operand is an integer and the other operand is a floating-point value, the compiler *coerces* (implicitly converts) the integer to a floating-point value to prevent a type error. (There is no division operation that supports an integer operand and a floating-point operand.) Passing a subclass object reference to a method's superclass parameter is another example of coercion polymorphism. The compiler coerces the subclass type to the superclass type to restrict operations to those of the superclass.

- ■ *Overloading*: The same operator symbol or method name can be used in different contexts. For example, + can be used to perform integer addition, floating-point addition, or string concatenation, depending on the types of its operands. Also, multiple methods having the same name can appear in a class (through declaration and/or inheritance).

- ■ *Parametric*: Within a class declaration, a field name can associate with different types and a method name can associate with different parameter and return types. The field and method can then take on different types in each class instance. For example, a field might be of type java.lang.Integer and a method might return an Integer in one class instance, and the same field might be of type String and the same method might return a String in another class instance. Java supports parametric polymorphism via generics, which I will discuss in Chapter 6.

- ■ *Subtype*: A type can serve as another type's subtype. When a subtype instance appears in a supertype context, executing a supertype operation on the subtype instance results in the subtype's version of that operation executing. For example, suppose that Circle is a subclass of Point and that both classes contain a draw() method. Assigning a Circle instance to a variable of type Point, and then calling the draw() method via this variable, results in Circle's draw() method being called.

Many developers don't regard coercion and overloading as valid kinds of polymorphism. They see coercion and overloading as nothing more than type conversions and syntactic sugar. In contrast, parametric and subtype are regarded as valid kinds of polymorphism.

In this section I focus on subtype polymorphism by first examining upcasting and late binding. I then introduce you to abstract classes and abstract methods, downcasting and runtime type identification, and covariant return types.

Upcasting and Late Binding

Listing 4-7's Point class represents a point as an x-y pair. Because a circle (in this example) is an x-y pair denoting its center, and has a radius denoting its extent, you can extend Point with a Circle class that introduces a radius field. Check out Listing 4-12.

Listing 4-12. A Circle Class Extending the Point Class

```
class Circle extends Point
{
   private int radius;

   Circle(int x, int y, int radius)
   {
      super(x, y);
      this.radius = radius;
   }

   int getRadius()
```

```
   {
      return radius;
   }

   @Override
   public String toString()
   {
      return "" + radius;
   }
}
```

Listing 4-12's `Circle` class describes a `Circle` as a `Point` with a `radius`, which implies that you can treat a `Circle` instance as if it was a `Point` instance. Accomplish this task by assigning the `Circle` instance to a `Point` variable, as demonstrated here:

```
Circle c = new Circle(10, 20, 30);
Point p = c;
```

The cast operator isn't needed to convert from `Circle` to `Point` because access to a `Circle` instance via `Point`'s interface is legal. After all, a `Circle` is at least a `Point`. This assignment is known as *upcasting* because you are implicitly casting up the type hierarchy (from the `Circle` subclass to the `Point` superclass). It's also an example of *covariance* in that a type with a wider range of values (`Circle`) is being converted to a type with a narrower range of values (`Point`).

After upcasting `Circle` to `Point`, you cannot call `Circle`'s `getRadius()` method because this method is not part of `Point`'s interface. Losing access to subtype features after narrowing it to a superclass seems useless but is necessary for achieving subtype polymorphism.

In addition to upcasting the subclass instance to a variable of the superclass type, subtype polymorphism involves declaring a method in the superclass and overriding this method in the subclass. For example, suppose `Point` and `Circle` are to be part of a graphics application, and you need to introduce a `draw()` method into each class to draw a point and a circle, respectively. You end with the class structure shown in Listing 4-13.

Listing 4-13. Declaring a Graphics Application's `Point` and `Circle` Classes

```
class Point
{
   private int x, y;

   Point(int x, int y)
   {
      this.x = x;
      this.y = y;
   }

   int getX()
   {
      return x;
   }
```

```java
    int getY()
    {
        return y;
    }

    @Override
    public String toString()
    {
        return "(" + x + ", " + y + ")";
    }

    void draw()
    {
        System.out.println("Point drawn at " + toString());
    }
}

class Circle extends Point
{
    private int radius;

    Circle(int x, int y, int radius)
    {
        super(x, y);
        this.radius = radius;
    }

    int getRadius()
    {
        return radius;
    }

    @Override
    public String toString()
    {
        return "" + radius;
    }

    @Override
    void draw()
    {
        System.out.println("Circle drawn at " + super.toString() +
                        " with radius " + toString());
    }
}
```

Listing 4-13's draw() methods will ultimately draw graphics shapes, but simulating their behaviors via System.out.println() method calls is sufficient during the early testing phase of the graphics application.

Now that you have temporarily finished with Point and Circle, you will want to test their draw() methods in a simulated version of the graphics application. To achieve this objective, you write Listing 4-14's Graphics class.

Listing 4-14. A Graphics Class for Testing Point's and Circle's draw() Methods

```java
public class Graphics
{
   public static void main(String[] args)
   {
      Point[] points = new Point[] { new Point(10, 20), new Circle(10, 20, 30) };
      for (int i = 0; i < points.length; i++)
         points[i].draw();
   }
}
```

Listing 4-14's main() method first declares an array of Points. Upcasting is demonstrated by first having the array's initializer instantiate the Circle class and then by assigning this instance's reference to the second element in the points array.

Moving on, main() uses a for loop to call each Point element's draw() method. Because the first iteration calls Point's draw() method, whereas the second iteration calls Circle's draw() method, you observe the following output:

```
Point drawn at (10, 20)
Circle drawn at (10, 20) with radius 30
```

How does Java "know" that it must call Circle's draw() method on the second loop iteration? Should it not call Point's draw() method because Circle is being treated as a Point thanks to the upcast?

At compile time, the compiler doesn't know which method to call. All it can do is verify that a method exists in the superclass and verify that the method call's arguments list and return type match the superclass's method declaration.

In lieu of knowing which method to call, the compiler inserts an instruction into the compiled code that, at runtime, fetches and uses whatever reference is in points[i] to call the correct draw() method. This task is known as *late binding*.

Late binding is used for calls to non-final instance methods. For all other method calls, the compiler knows which method to call and inserts an instruction into the compiled code that calls the method associated with the variable's type (not its value). This task is known as *early binding*.

You can also upcast from one array to another provided that the array being upcast is a subtype of the other array. Consider Listing 4-15.

Listing 4-15. Demonstrating Array Upcasting

```java
class Point
{
   private int x, y;

   Point(int x, int y)
```

```
   {
      this.x = x;
      this.y = y;
   }

   int getX() { return x; }
   int getY() { return y; }
}

class ColoredPoint extends Point
{
   private int color;

   ColoredPoint(int x, int y, int color)
   {
      super(x, y);
      this.color = color;
   }

   int getColor() { return color; }
}

public class UpcastArrayDemo
{
   public static void main(String[] args)
   {
      ColoredPoint[] cptArray = new ColoredPoint[1];
      cptArray[0] = new ColoredPoint(10, 20, 5);
      Point[] ptArray = cptArray;
      System.out.println(ptArray[0].getX()); // Output: 10
      System.out.println(ptArray[0].getY()); // Output: 20
      //      System.out.println(ptArray[0].getColor()); // Illegal
   }
}
```

Listing 4-15's main() method first creates a ColoredPoint array consisting of one element. It then instantiates this class and assigns the object's reference to this element. Because ColoredPoint[] is a subtype of Point[], main() is able to upcast cptArray's ColoredPoint[] type to Point[] and assign its reference to ptArray.

main() then invokes the ColoredPoint instance's getX() and getY() methods via ptArray[0]. It cannot invoke getColor() because ptArray has narrower scope than cptArray. In other words, getColor() is not part of Point's interface.

Abstract Classes and Abstract Methods

Suppose new requirements dictate that your graphics application must include a Rectangle class. Furthermore, this class must include a draw() method, and this method must be tested in a manner similar to that shown in Listing 4-14's Graphics application class.

In contrast to Circle, which is a Point with a radius, it doesn't make sense to think of a Rectangle as being a Point with a width and height. Rather, a Rectangle instance would probably be composed of a Point instance indicating its origin and a Point instance indicating its width and height extents.

Because circles, points, and rectangles are examples of shapes, it makes more sense to declare a Shape class with its own draw() method than to specify class Rectangle extends Point. Listing 4-16 presents Shape's declaration.

Listing 4-16. Declaring a Shape Class

```
class Shape
{
   void draw()
   {
   }
}
```

Listing 4-16's Shape class declares an empty draw() method that only exists to be overridden and to demonstrate subtype polymorphism.

You can now refactor Listing 4-13's Point class to extend Listing 4-16's Shape class, leave Circle as is, and introduce a Rectangle class that extends Shape. You can then refactor Listing 4-14's Graphics class's main() method to take Shape into account. Listing 4-17 presents the resulting Graphics class.

Listing 4-17. A Graphics Class with a New main() Method That Takes Shape into Account

```
public class Graphics
{
   public static void main(String[] args)
   {
      Shape[] shapes = new Shape[] { new Point(10, 20), new Circle(10, 20, 30),
                              new Rectangle(20, 30, 15, 25) };
      for (int i = 0; i < shapes.length; i++)
         shapes[i].draw();
   }
}
```

Because Point and Rectangle directly extend Shape, and because Circle indirectly extends Shape by extending Point, Listing 4-17's main() method will call the appropriate subclass's draw() method in response to shapes[i].draw();.

Although Shape makes the code more flexible, there is a problem. What is to stop the developer from instantiating Shape and adding this meaningless instance to the shapes array, as follows?

```
Shape[] shapes = new Shape[] { new Point(10, 20), new Circle(10, 20, 30),
                        new Rectangle(20, 30, 15, 25), new Shape() };
```

What does it mean to instantiate Shape? Because this class describes an abstract concept, what does it mean to draw a generic shape? Fortunately, Java provides a solution to this problem, which is demonstrated in Listing 4-18.

Listing 4-18. Abstracting the Shape Class

```
abstract class Shape
{
   abstract void draw(); // semicolon is required
}
```

Listing 4-18 uses Java's `abstract` reserved word to declare a class that cannot be instantiated. The compiler reports an error when you try to instantiate this class.

> **Tip**   Get into the habit of declaring classes that describe generic categories (such as shape, animal, vehicle, and account) `abstract`. This way, you will not inadvertently instantiate them.

The `abstract` reserved word is also used to declare a method without a body. The `draw()` method doesn't need a body because it cannot draw an abstract shape.

> **Caution**   The compiler reports an error when you attempt to declare a class that is both abstract and final. For example, `abstract final class Shape` is an error because an abstract class cannot be instantiated and a final class cannot be extended. The compiler also reports an error when you declare a method to be abstract but do not declare its class to be abstract. For example, removing `abstract` from the Shape class's header in Listing 4-18 results in an error. This removal is an error because a non-abstract (concrete) class cannot be instantiated when it contains an abstract method. Finally, when you extend an abstract class, the extending class must override all of the abstract class's abstract methods, or else the extending class must itself be declared to be abstract; otherwise, the compiler will report an error.

An abstract class can contain non-`abstract` methods in addition to or instead of `abstract` methods. For example, Listing 4-2's `Vehicle` class could have been declared `abstract`. The constructor would still be present, to initialize private fields, even though you could not instantiate the resulting class.

Downcasting and Runtime Type Identification

Moving up the type hierarchy, via upcasting, causes loss of access to subtype features. For example, assigning a `Circle` instance to `Point` variable p means that you cannot use p to call `Circle`'s `getRadius()` method.

However, it is possible to once again access the `Circle` instance's `getRadius()` method by performing an explicit cast operation, for example, `Circle c = (Circle) p;`. This assignment is known as *downcasting* because you are explicitly moving down the type hierarchy (from the `Point` superclass to the `Circle` subclass). It is also an example of *contravariance* in that a type with a narrower range of values (`Point`) is being converted to a type with a wider range of values (`Circle`).

Although an upcast is always safe (the superclass's interface is a subset of the subclass's interface), the same cannot be said of a downcast. Listing 4-19 shows you what kind of trouble you can get into when downcasting is used incorrectly.

Listing 4-19. The Trouble with Downcasting

```
class A
{
}

class B extends A
{
   void m()
   {
   }
}

public class DowncastDemo
{
   public static void main(String[] args)
   {
      A a = new A();
      B b = (B) a;
      b.m();
   }
}
```

Listing 4-19 presents a class hierarchy consisting of a superclass named A and a subclass named B. Although A doesn't declare any members, B declares a single m() method.

A third class named DowncastDemo provides a main() method that first instantiates A and then tries to downcast this instance to B and assign the result to variable b. The compiler will not complain because downcasting from a superclass to a subclass in the same type hierarchy is legal.

However, if the assignment is allowed, the application will undoubtedly crash when it tries to execute b.m();. The crash happens because the virtual machine will attempt to call a method that doesn't exist—class A doesn't have an m() method.

Fortunately, this scenario will never happen because the virtual machine verifies that the cast is legal. Because it detects that A doesn't have an m() method, it doesn't permit the cast by throwing an instance of the ClassCastException class.

The virtual machine's cast verification illustrates *runtime type identification* (or *RTTI*, for short). Cast verification performs RTTI by examining the type of the cast operator's operand to see whether the cast should be allowed or not. Clearly, the cast should not be allowed.

A second form of RTTI involves the `instanceof` operator. This operator checks the left operand to see whether or not it is an instance of the right operand and returns true if this is the case. The following example introduces `instanceof` to Listing 4-19 to prevent the `ClassCastException`:

```
if(a instanceof B)
{
   B b = (B) a;
   b.m();
}
```

The `instanceof` operator detects that variable a's instance was not created from B and returns false to indicate this fact. As a result, the code that performs the illegal cast will not execute. (Overuse of `instanceof` probably indicates poor software design.)

Because a subtype is a kind of supertype, `instanceof` will return true when its left operand is a subtype instance or a supertype instance of its right operand supertype. The following example demonstrates:

```
A a = new A();
B b = new B();
System.out.println(b instanceof A); // Output: true
System.out.println(a instanceof A); // Output: true
```

This example assumes the class structure shown in Listing 4-19 and instantiates superclass A and subclass B. The first `System.out.println()` method call outputs true because b's reference identifies an instance of B, a subclass of A; the second `System.out.println()` method call outputs true because a's reference identifies an instance of superclass A.

You can also downcast from one array to another provided that the array being downcast is a supertype of the other array, and its elements types are those of the subtype. Consider Listing 4-20.

Listing 4-20. Demonstrating Array Downcasting

```
class Point
{
   private int x, y;

   Point(int x, int y)
   {
      this.x = x;
      this.y = y;
   }

   int getX() { return x; }
   int getY() { return y; }
}

class ColoredPoint extends Point
{
   private int color;

   ColoredPoint(int x, int y, int color)
```

```
   {
      super(x, y);
      this.color = color;
   }

   int getColor() { return color; }
}

public class DowncastArrayDemo
{
   public static void main(String[] args)
   {
      ColoredPoint[] cptArray = new ColoredPoint[1];
      cptArray[0] = new ColoredPoint(10, 20, 5);
      Point[] ptArray = cptArray;
      System.out.println(ptArray[0].getX()); // Output: 10
      System.out.println(ptArray[0].getY()); // Output: 20
      //       System.out.println(ptArray[0].getColor()); // Illegal
      if (ptArray instanceof ColoredPoint[])
      {
         ColoredPoint cp = (ColoredPoint) ptArray[0];
         System.out.println(cp.getColor());
      }
   }
}
```

Listing 4-20 is similar to Listing 4-15 except that it also demonstrates downcasting. Notice its use of instanceof to verify that ptArray's referenced object is of type ColoredPoint[]. If this operator returns true, it is safe to downcast ptArray[0] from Point to ColoredPoint and assign the reference to ColoredPoint.

Covariant Return Types

A *covariant return type* is a method return type that, in the superclass's method declaration, is the supertype of the return type in the subclass's overriding method declaration. Listing 4-21 provides a demonstration of this language feature.

Listing 4-21. A Demonstration of Covariant Return Types

```
class SuperReturnType
{
   @Override
   public String toString()
   {
      return "superclass return type";
   }
}

class SubReturnType extends SuperReturnType
{
   @Override
```

```java
   public String toString()
   {
      return "subclass return type";
   }
}

class Superclass
{
   SuperReturnType createReturnType()
   {
      return new SuperReturnType();
   }
}

class Subclass extends Superclass
{
   @Override
   SubReturnType createReturnType()
   {
      return new SubReturnType();
   }
}

public class CovarDemo
{
   public static void main(String[] args)
   {
      SuperReturnType suprt = new Superclass().createReturnType();
      System.out.println(suprt); // Output: superclass return type
      SubReturnType subrt = new Subclass().createReturnType();
      System.out.println(subrt); // Output: subclass return type
   }
}
```

Listing 4-21 declares SuperReturnType and Superclass superclasses and SubReturnType and Subclass subclasses; each of Superclass and Subclass declares a createReturnType() method. Superclass's method has its return type set to SuperReturnType, whereas Subclass's overriding method has its return type set to SubReturnType, a subclass of SuperReturnType.

Covariant return types minimize upcasting and downcasting. For example, Subclass's createReturnType() method doesn't need to upcast its SubReturnType instance to its SubReturnType return type. Furthermore, this instance doesn't need to be downcast to SubReturnType when assigning to variable subrt.

In the absence of covariant return types, you would end up with Listing 4-22.

Listing 4-22. Upcasting and Downcasting in the Absence of Covariant Return Types

```java
class SuperReturnType
{
    @Override
    public String toString()
    {
        return "superclass return type";
    }
}

class SubReturnType extends SuperReturnType
{
    @Override
    public String toString()
    {
        return "subclass return type";
    }
}

class Superclass
{
    SuperReturnType createReturnType()
    {
        return new SuperReturnType();
    }
}

class Subclass extends Superclass
{
    @Override
    SuperReturnType createReturnType()
    {
        return new SubReturnType();
    }
}

public class CovarDemo
{
    public static void main(String[] args)
    {
        SuperReturnType suprt = new Superclass().createReturnType();
        System.out.println(suprt); // Output: superclass return type
        SubReturnType subrt = (SubReturnType) new Subclass().createReturnType();
        System.out.println(subrt); // Output: subclass return type
    }
}
```

In Listing 4-22, the first bolded code reveals an upcast from SubReturnType to SuperReturnType, and the second bolded code uses the required (SubReturnType) cast operator to downcast from SuperReturnType to SubReturnType, prior to the assignment to subrt.

Formalizing Class Interfaces

In my introduction to information hiding (see Chapter 3), I stated that every class *X* exposes an interface (a protocol consisting of constructors, methods, and [possibly] fields that are made available to objects created from other classes for use in creating and communicating with *X*'s objects).

Java formalizes the interface concept by providing reserved word `interface`, which is used to introduce a type without implementation. Java also provides language features to declare, implement, and extend interfaces. After looking at interface declaration, implementation, and extension in this section, I explain the rationale for using interfaces.

Declaring Interfaces

An interface declaration consists of a header followed by a body. At minimum, the header consists of reserved word `interface` followed by a name that identifies the interface. The body starts with an open brace character and ends with a close brace. Sandwiched between these delimiters are constant and method header declarations. Consider Listing 4-23.

Listing 4-23. Declaring a Drawable Interface

```
interface Drawable
{
   int RED = 1;    // For simplicity, integer constants are used. These constants are
   int GREEN = 2; // not that descriptive, as you will see.
   int BLUE = 3;
   int BLACK = 4;
   void draw(int color);
}
```

Listing 4-23 declares an interface named Drawable. By convention, an interface's name begins with an uppercase letter. Furthermore, the first letter of each subsequent word in a multiword interface name is capitalized.

> **Note** Many interface names end with the `able` suffix. For example, the standard class library includes interfaces named `Callable`, `Comparable`, `Cloneable`, `Iterable`, `Runnable`, and `Serializable`. It is not mandatory to use this suffix; the standard class library also provides interfaces named `CharSequence`, `Collection`, `Executor`, `Future`, `Iterator`, `List`, `Map`, and `Set`.

Drawable declares four fields that identify color constants. Drawable also declares a `draw()` method that must be called with one of these constants to specify the color used to draw something.

> **Note**   You can precede `interface` with `public` to make your interface accessible to code outside of its package. (I will discuss packages in the next chapter). Otherwise, the interface is only accessible to other types in its package. You can also precede `interface` with `abstract` to emphasize that an interface is abstract. Because an interface is already abstract, it is redundant to specify `abstract` in the interface's declaration. An interface's fields are implicitly declared `public`, `static`, and `final`. It is therefore redundant to declare them with these reserved words. Because these fields are constants, they must be explicitly initialized; otherwise, the compiler reports an error. Finally, an interface's methods are implicitly declared `public` and `abstract`. Therefore, it is redundant to declare them with these reserved words. Because these methods must be instance methods, don't declare them `static` or the compiler will report errors.

Drawable identifies a type that specifies what to do (draw something) but not how to do it. It leaves implementation details to classes that implement this interface. Instances of such classes are known as *drawables* because they know how to draw themselves.

> **Note**   An interface that declares no members is known as a *marker interface* or a *tagging interface*. It associates metadata with a class. For example, the presence of the `Cloneable` marker/tagging interface implies that instances of its implementing class can be shallowly cloned. RTTI is used to detect that an object's class implements a marker/tagging interface. For example, when `Object`'s `clone()` method detects, via RTTI, that the calling instance's class implements `Cloneable`, it shallowly clones the object.

Implementing Interfaces

By itself, an interface is useless. To be of any benefit to an application, the interface needs to be implemented by a class. Java provides the `implements` reserved word for this task. This reserved word is demonstrated in Listing 4-24.

Listing 4-24. Implementing the Drawable Interface

```
class Point implements Drawable
{
   private int x, y;

   Point(int x, int y)
   {
      this.x = x;
      this.y = y;
   }
```

```java
    int getX()
    {
        return x;
    }

    int getY()
    {
        return y;
    }

    @Override
    public String toString()
    {
        return "(" + x + ", " + y + ")";
    }

    @Override
    public void draw(int color)
    {
        System.out.println("Point drawn at " + toString() + " in color " + color);
    }
}

class Circle extends Point implements Drawable
{
    private int radius;

    Circle(int x, int y, int radius)
    {
        super(x, y);
        this.radius = radius;
    }

    int getRadius()
    {
        return radius;
    }

    @Override
    public String toString()
    {
        return "" + radius;
    }

    @Override
    public void draw(int color)
    {
        System.out.println("Circle drawn at " + super.toString() +
                        " with radius " + toString() + " in color " + color);
    }
}
```

Listing 4-24 retrofits Listing 4-13's class hierarchy to take advantage of Listing 4-23's Drawable interface. You will notice that each of classes Point and Circle implements this interface by attaching the implements Drawable clause to its class header.

To implement an interface, the class must specify, for each interface method header, a method whose header has the same signature and return type as the interface's method header and a code body to go with the method header.

> **Caution**   When implementing a method, don't forget that the interface's methods are implicitly declared public. If you forget to include public in the implemented method's declaration, the compiler will report an error because you are attempting to assign weaker access to the implemented method.

When a class implements an interface, the class inherits the interface's constants and method headers and overrides the method headers by providing implementations (hence the @Override annotation). This is known as *interface inheritance.*

It turns out that Circle's header doesn't need the implements Drawable clause. If this clause is not present, Circle inherits Point's draw() method and is still considered to be a Drawable, whether it overrides this method or not.

An interface specifies a type whose data values are the objects whose classes implement the interface and whose behaviors are those specified by the interface. This fact implies that you can assign an object's reference to a variable of the interface type, provided that the object's class implements the interface. The following example provides a demonstration:

```
public static void main(String[] args)
{
   Drawable[] drawables = new Drawable[] { new Point(10, 20), new Circle(10, 20, 30) };
   for (int i = 0; i < drawables.length; i++)
      drawables[i].draw(Drawable.RED);
}
```

Because Point and Circle instances are drawables by virtue of these classes implementing the Drawable interface, it is legal to assign Point and Circle instance references to variables (including array elements) of type Drawable.

When you run this method, it generates the following output:

```
Point drawn at (10, 20) in color 1
Circle drawn at (10, 20) with radius 30 in color 1
```

Listing 4-23's Drawable interface is useful for drawing a shape's outline. Suppose you also need to fill a shape's interior. You might attempt to satisfy this requirement by declaring Listing 4-25's Fillable interface.

Listing 4-25. Declaring a `Fillable` Interface

```
interface Fillable
{
   int RED = 1;
   int GREEN = 2;
   int BLUE = 3;
   int BLACK = 4;
   void fill(int color);
}
```

Given Listings 4-23 and 4-25, you can declare that the `Point` and `Circle` classes implement both interfaces by specifying `class Point implements Drawable, Fillable` and `class Circle implements Drawable, Fillable`. You can then modify the `main()` method to also treat the drawables as *fillables* so that you can fill these shapes, as follows:

```
public static void main(String[] args)
{
   Drawable[] drawables = new Drawable[] { new Point(10, 20),
                                           new Circle(10, 20, 30) };
   for (int i = 0; i < drawables.length; i++)
      drawables[i].draw(Drawable.RED);
   Fillable[] fillables = new Fillable[drawables.length];
   for (int i = 0; i < drawables.length; i++)
   {
      fillables[i] = (Fillable) drawables[i];
      fillables[i].fill(Fillable.GREEN);
   }
}
```

After invoking each drawable's `draw()` method, `main()` creates a `Fillable` array of the same length as the `Drawable` array. It then proceeds to copy each `Drawable` array element to a `Fillable` array element and then invoke the fillable's `fill()` method. The `(Fillable)` cast is necessary because a drawable is not a fillable. This cast operation will succeed because the `Point` and `Circle` instances being copied implement `Fillable` as well as `Drawable`.

> **Tip**   You can list as many interfaces as you need to implement by specifying a comma-separated list of interface names after `implements`.

Implementing multiple interfaces can lead to name collisions, and the compiler will report errors. For example, suppose that you attempt to compile Listing 4-26's interface and class declarations.

Listing 4-26. Colliding Interfaces

```
interface A
{
   int X = 1;
   void foo();
}
```

```
interface B
{
   int X = 1;
   int foo();
}

class Collision implements A, B
{
   @Override
   public void foo();

   @Override
   public int foo() { return X; }
}
```

Each of Listing 4-26's A and B interfaces declares a constant named X. Despite each constant having the same type and value, the compiler will report an error when it encounters X in Collision's second foo() method because it doesn't know which X is being inherited.

Speaking of foo(), the compiler reports an error when it encounters Collision's second foo() declaration because foo() has already been declared. You cannot overload a method by changing only its return type.

The compiler will probably report additional errors. For example, the Java 7 compiler has this to say when told to compile Listing 4-26:

```
Collision.java:19: error: method foo() is already defined in class Collision
   public int foo() { return X; }
             ^
Collision.java:13: error: Collision is not abstract and does not override abstract method foo()
in B class Collision implements A, B
^
Collision.java:16: error: foo() in Collision cannot implement foo() in B
   public void foo();
             ^
   return type void is not compatible with int
Collision.java:19: error: reference to X is ambiguous, both variable X in A and variable X
in B match
   public int foo() { return X; }
                            ^
4 errors
```

Extending Interfaces

Just as a subclass can extend a superclass via reserved word extends, you can use this reserved word to have a *subinterface* extend a *superinterface*. This, too, is known as *interface inheritance*.

For example, the duplicate color constants in Drawable and Fillable lead to name collisions when you specify their names by themselves in an implementing class. To avoid these name collisions, prefix a name with its interface name and the member access operator, or place these constants in their own interface, and have Drawable and Fillable extend this interface, as demonstrated in Listing 4-27.

Listing 4-27. Extending the Colors Interface

```
interface Colors
{
    int RED = 1;
    int GREEN = 2;
    int BLUE = 3;
    int BLACK = 4;
}

interface Drawable extends Colors
{
    void draw(int color);
}

interface Fillable extends Colors
{
    void fill(int color);
}
```

The fact that Drawable and Fillable both inherit constants from Colors is not a problem for the compiler. There is only a single copy of these constants (in Colors) and no possibility of a name collision, and so the compiler is satisfied.

If a class can implement multiple interfaces by declaring a comma-separated list of interface names after implements, it seems that an interface should be able to extend multiple interfaces in a similar way. This feature is demonstrated in Listing 4-28.

Listing 4-28. Extending a Pair of Interfaces

```
interface A
{
    int X = 1;
}

interface B
{
    double X = 2.0;
}

interface C extends A, B
{
}
```

Listing 4-28 will compile even though C inherits two same-named constants X with different types and initializers. However, if you implement C and then try to access X, as in Listing 4-29, you will run into a name collision.

Listing 4-29. Discovering a Name Collision

```
class Collision implements C
{
   public void output()
   {
      System.out.println(X); // Which X is accessed?
   }
}
```

Suppose you introduce a void foo(); method header declaration into interface A and an int foo(); method header declaration into interface B. This time, the compiler will report an error when you attempt to compile the modified Listing 4-28.

Why Use Interfaces?

Now that the mechanics of declaring, implementing, and extending interfaces are out of the way, you can focus on the rationale for using them. Unfortunately, newcomers to Java's interfaces feature are often told that this feature was created as a workaround to Java's lack of support for multiple implementation inheritance. While interfaces are useful in this capacity, this is not their reason for existence. Instead, *Java's interfaces feature was created to give developers the utmost flexibility in designing their applications by decoupling interface from implementation. You should always code to the interface (supplied by an interface type or an abstract class).*

Those who are adherents to *agile software development* (a group of software development methodologies based on iterative development that emphasizes keeping code simple, testing frequently, and delivering functional pieces of the application as soon as they are deliverable) know the importance of flexible coding. They cannot afford to tie their code to a specific implementation because a change in requirements for the next iteration could result in a new implementation, and they might find themselves rewriting significant amounts of code, which wastes time and slows development.

Interfaces help you achieve flexibility by decoupling interface from implementation. For example, the main() method in Listing 4-17's Graphics class creates an array of objects from classes that subclass the Shape class and then iterates over these objects, calling each object's draw() method. The only objects that can be drawn are those that subclass Shape.

Suppose you also have a hierarchy of classes that model resistors, transistors, and other electronic components. Each component has its own symbol that allows the component to be shown in a schematic diagram of an electronic circuit. Perhaps you want to add a drawing capability to each class that draws that component's symbol.

You might consider specifying Shape as the superclass of the electronic component class hierarchy. However, electronic components are not shapes (although they have shapes), so it makes no sense to place these classes in a class hierarchy rooted in Shape.

However, you can make each component class implement the Drawable interface, which lets you add expressions that instantiate these classes to the drawables array in the main() method appearing prior to Listing 4-25 (so you can draw their symbols). This is legal because these instances are drawables.

Wherever possible, you should strive to specify interfaces instead of classes in your code to keep your code adaptable to change. This is especially true when working with Java's Collections Framework, which I will discuss at length in Chapter 9.

For now, consider a simple example that consists of the Collections Framework's java.util.List interface and its java.util.ArrayList and java.util.LinkedList implementation classes. The following example presents inflexible code based on the ArrayList class:

```
ArrayList<String> arrayList = new ArrayList<String>();
void dump(ArrayList<String> arrayList)
{
   // suitable code to dump out the arrayList
}
```

This example uses the generics-based parameterized type language feature (which I will discuss in Chapter 6) to identify the kind of objects stored in an ArrayList instance. In this example, String objects are stored.

The example is inflexible because it hardwires the ArrayList class into multiple locations. This hardwiring focuses the developer into thinking specifically about array lists instead of generically about lists.

Lack of focus is problematic when a requirements change, or perhaps a performance issue brought about by *profiling* (analyzing a running application to check its performance), suggests that the developer should have used LinkedList.

The example only requires a minimal number of changes to satisfy the new requirement. In contrast, a larger code base might need many more changes. Although you only need to change ArrayList to LinkedList, to satisfy the compiler, consider changing arrayList to linkedList to keep *semantics* (meaning) clear—you might have to change multiple occurrences of names that refer to an ArrayList instance throughout the source code.

The developer is bound to lose time while refactoring the code to adapt to LinkedList. Instead, time could have been saved by writing this example to use the equivalent of constants. In other words, the example could have been written to rely on interfaces and to only specify ArrayList in one place. The following example shows you what the resulting code would look like:

```
List<String> list = new ArrayList<String>();
void dump(List<String> list)
{
   // suitable code to dump out the list
}
```

This example is much more flexible than the previous example. If a requirements or profiling change suggests that LinkedList should be used instead of ArrayList, simply replace Array with Linked and you are done. You don't even have to change the parameter name.

> **Note**   Java provides interfaces and abstract classes for describing *abstract types* (types that cannot be instantiated). Abstract types represent abstract concepts (drawable and shape, for example), and instances of such types would be meaningless.
>
> Interfaces promote flexibility through lack of implementation—Drawable and List illustrate this flexibility. They are not tied to any single class hierarchy but can be implemented by any class in any hierarchy. In contrast, abstract classes support implementation but can be genuinely abstract (Listing 4-18's abstract Shape class, for example). However, they are limited to appearing in the upper levels of class hierarchies.
>
> Interfaces and abstract classes can be used together. For example, the Collections Framework's java.util package provides List, Map, and Set interfaces and AbstractList, AbstractMap, and AbstractSet abstract classes that provide skeletal implementations of these interfaces.
>
> By implementing many interface methods, the skeletal implementations make it easy for you to create your own interface implementations to address your unique requirements. If they don't meet your needs, you can optionally have your class directly implement the appropriate interface.

EXERCISES

The following exercises are designed to test your understanding of Chapter 4's content:

1. What is implementation inheritance?

2. How does Java support implementation inheritance?

3. Can a subclass have two or more superclasses?

4. How do you prevent a class from being subclassed?

5. True or false: The super() call can appear in any method.

6. If a superclass declares a constructor with one or more parameters, and if a subclass constructor doesn't use super() to call that constructor, why does the compiler report an error?

7. What is an immutable class?

8. True or false: A class can inherit constructors.

9. What does it mean to override a method?

10. What is required to call a superclass method from its overriding subclass method?

11. How do you prevent a method from being overridden?

12. Why can you not make an overriding subclass method less accessible than the superclass method it is overriding?

13. How do you tell the compiler that a method overrides another method?

14. Why does Java not support multiple implementation inheritance?

15. What is the name of Java's ultimate superclass?

16. What is the purpose of the `clone()` method?

17. When does `Object`'s `clone()` method throw `CloneNotSupportedException`?

18. Explain the difference between shallow copying and deep copying.

19. Can the `==` operator be used to determine if two objects are logically equivalent? Why or why not?

20. What does `Object`'s `equals()` method accomplish?

21. Does expression `"abc" == "a" + "bc"` return true or false?

22. How can you optimize a time-consuming `equals()` method?

23. What is the purpose of the `finalize()` method?

24. Should you rely on `finalize()` for closing open files? Why or why not?

25. What is a hash code?

26. True or false: You should override the `hashCode()` method whenever your override the `equals()` method.

27. What does `Object`'s `toString()` method return?

28. Why should you override `toString()`?

29. Define composition.

30. True or false: Composition is used to describe "is-a" relationships and implementation inheritance is used to describe "has-a" relationships.

31. Identify the fundamental problem of implementation inheritance. How do you fix this problem?

32. Define subtype polymorphism.

33. How is subtype polymorphism accomplished?

34. Why would you use abstract classes and abstract methods?

35. Can an abstract class contain concrete methods?

36. What is the purpose of downcasting?

37. List two forms of RTTI.

38. What is a covariant return type?

39. How do you formally declare an interface?

40. True or false: You can precede an interface declaration with the `abstract` reserved word.

41. Define marker interface.

42. What is interface inheritance?

43. How do you implement an interface?

44. What problem might you encounter when you implement multiple interfaces?

45. How do you form a hierarchy of interfaces?

46. Why is Java's interfaces feature so important?

47. What do interfaces and abstract classes accomplish?

48. How do interfaces and abstract classes differ?

49. Model part of an animal hierarchy by declaring Animal, Bird, Fish, AmericanRobin, DomesticCanary, RainbowTrout, and SockeyeSalmon classes:

   - Animal is public and abstract, declares private String-based kind and appearance fields, declares a public constructor that initializes these fields to passed-in arguments, declares public and abstract eat() and move() methods that take no arguments and whose return type is void, and overrides the toString() method to output the contents of kind and appearance.

   - Bird is public and abstract, extends Animal, declares a public constructor that passes its kind and appearance parameter values to its superclass constructor, overrides its eat() method to output eats seeds and insects (via System.out.println()), and overrides its move() method to output flies through the air.

   - Fish is public and abstract; extends Animal; declares a public constructor that passes its kind and appearance parameter values to its superclass constructor; overrides its eat() method to output eats krill, algae, and insects; and overrides its move() method to output swims through the water.

   - AmericanRobin is public, extends Bird, and declares a public noargument constructor that passes "americanrobin" and "red breast" to its superclass constructor.

   - DomesticCanary is public, extends Bird, and declares a public noargument constructor that passes "domesticcanary" and "yellow, orange, black, brown, white, red" to its superclass constructor.

   - RainbowTrout is public, extends Fish, and declares a public noargument constructor that passes "rainbowtrout" and "bands of brilliant speckled multicolored stripes running nearly the whole length of its body" to its superclass constructor.

   - SockeyeSalmon is public, extends Fish, and declares a public noargument constructor that passes "sockeyesalmon" and "bright red with a green head" to its superclass constructor.

Note For brevity, I have omitted from the Animal hierarchy abstract Robin, Canary, Trout, and Salmon classes that generalize robins, canaries, trout, and salmon. Perhaps you might want to include these classes in the hierarchy.

Although this exercise illustrates the accurate modeling of a natural scenario using inheritance, it also reveals the potential for *class explosion*—too many classes may be introduced to model a scenario, and it might be difficult to maintain all of these classes. Keep this in mind when modeling with inheritance.

50. Continuing from the previous exercise, declare an Animals class with a main() method. This
     method first declares an animals array that is initialized to AmericanRobin, RainbowTrout,
     DomesticCanary, and SockeyeSalmon objects. The method then iterates over this array, first
     outputting animals[i] (which causes toString() to be called) and then calling each object's
     eat() and move() methods (demonstrating subtype polymorphism).

51. Continuing from the previous exercise, declare a public Countable interface with a String
     getID() method. Modify Animal to implement Countable and have this method return kind's
     value. Modify Animals to initialize the animals array to AmericanRobin, RainbowTrout,
     DomesticCanary, SockeyeSalmon, RainbowTrout, and AmericanRobin objects. Also,
     introduce code that computes a census of each kind of animal. This code will use the Census class
     that is declared in Listing 4-30.

Listing 4-30. The Census Class Stores Census Data on Four Kinds of Animals

```
public class Census
{
   public final static int SIZE = 4;
   private String[] IDs;
   private int[] counts;

   public Census()
   {
      IDs = new String[SIZE];
      counts = new int[SIZE];
   }

   public String get(int index)
   {
      return IDs[index] + " " + counts[index];
   }

   public void update(String ID)
   {
      for (int i = 0; i < IDs.length; i++)
      {
         // If ID not already stored in the IDs array (which is indicated by
         // the first null entry that is found), store ID in this array, and
         // also assign 1 to the associated element in the counts array, to
         // initialize the census for that ID.
         if (IDs[i] == null)
         {
            IDs[i] = ID;
            counts[i] = 1;
            return;
         }
```

```
                  // If a matching ID is found, increment the associated element in
                  // the counts array to update the census for that ID.
                  if (IDs[i].equals(ID))
                  {
                     counts[i]++;
                     return;
                  }
               }
            }
         }
      }
```

Summary

Inheritance is a hierarchical relationship between similar entity categories in which one category inherits state and behaviors from at least one other entity category. Inheriting from a single category is called single inheritance, and inheriting from at least two categories is called multiple inheritance.

Java supports single inheritance and multiple inheritance to facilitate code reuse—why reinvent the wheel? Java supports single inheritance in a class context (via reserved word extends) in which a class inherits fields and methods from another class through class extension. Because classes are involved, Java refers to this kind of inheritance as implementation inheritance. Java supports multiple inheritance only in an interface context in which a class inherits method templates from one or more interfaces through interface implementation (via reserved word implements) or in which an interface inherits method templates from one or more interfaces through interface extension (via reserved word extends). Because interfaces are involved, Java refers to this kind of inheritance as interface inheritance.

Some real-world entities have the ability to change their forms. The ability to change form is known as polymorphism and is useful to model in a programming language. Although Java supports the coercion, overloading, parametric, and subtype kinds of polymorphism, in this chapter I only focused on subtype polymorphism, which is achieved through upcasting and method overriding.

Every class X exposes an interface (a protocol consisting of constructors, methods, and [possibly] fields that are made available to objects created from other classes for use in creating and communicating with X's objects). Java formalizes the interface concept by providing reserved word interface, which is used to introduce a type without implementation.

Although many believe that the interfaces language feature was created as a workaround to Java's lack of support for multiple implementation inheritance, this is not the real reason for its existence. Instead, Java's interfaces feature was created to give developers the utmost flexibility in designing their applications by decoupling interface from implementation. You should always code to the interface.

In Chapter 5 I continue to explore the Java language by focusing on nested types, packages, static imports, and exceptions.

Chapter 5

Mastering Advanced Language Features Part 1

In Chapters 2 through 4 I laid a foundation for learning the Java language. In Chapter 5 I build onto this foundation by introducing you to some of Java's more advanced language features, specifically, those features related to nested types, packages, static imports, and exceptions. Additional advanced language features are covered in Chapter 6.

Mastering Nested Types

Classes that are declared outside of any class are known as *top-level classes*. Java also supports *nested classes*, which are classes that are declared as members of other classes or scopes. Nested classes help you implement top-level class architecture.

There are four kinds of nested classes: static member classes, nonstatic member classes, anonymous classes, and local classes. The latter three categories are known as *inner classes*.

In this section I introduce you to static member classes and inner classes. For each kind of nested class, I provide you with a brief introduction, an abstract example, and a more practical example. I then briefly examine the topic of nesting interfaces within classes.

Static Member Classes

A *static member class* is a static member of an enclosing class. Although enclosed, it doesn't have an enclosing instance of that class and cannot access the enclosing class's instance fields and invoke its instance methods. However, it can access the enclosing class's static fields and invoke its static methods, even those members that are declared private. Listing 5-1 presents a static member class declaration.

Listing 5-1. Declaring a Static Member Class

```java
class EnclosingClass
{
   private static int i;

   private static void m1()
   {
      System.out.println(i);
   }

   static void m2()
   {
      EnclosedClass.accessEnclosingClass();
   }

   static class EnclosedClass
   {
      static void accessEnclosingClass()
      {
         i = 1;
         m1();
      }

      void accessEnclosingClass2()
      {
         m2();
      }
   }
}
```

Listing 5-1 declares a top-level class named EnclosingClass with class field i, class methods m1() and m2(), and static member class EnclosedClass. Also, EnclosedClass declares class method accessEnclosingClass() and instance method accessEnclosingClass2().

Because accessEnclosingClass() is declared static, m2() must be prefixed with EnclosedClass and the member access operator to call this method.

Listing 5-2 presents the source code to an application class that demonstrates how to invoke EnclosedClass's accessEnclosingClass() class method and instantiate EnclosedClass and invoke its accessEnclosingClass2() instance method.

Listing 5-2. Invoking a Static Member Class's Class and Instance Methods

```java
public class SMCDemo
{
   public static void main(String[] args)
   {
      EnclosingClass.EnclosedClass.accessEnclosingClass(); // Output: 1
      EnclosingClass.EnclosedClass ec = new EnclosingClass.EnclosedClass();
      ec.accessEnclosingClass2(); // Output: 1
   }
}
```

Listing 5-2's `main()` method reveals that you must prefix the name of an enclosed class with the name of its enclosing class to invoke a class method, for example, `EnclosingClass.EnclosedClass.accessEnclosingClass();`.

This listing also reveals that you must prefix the name of the enclosed class with the name of its enclosing class when instantiating the enclosed class, for example, `EnclosingClass.EnclosedClass ec = new EnclosingClass.EnclosedClass();`. You can then invoke the instance method in the normal manner, for example, `ec.accessEnclosingClass2();`.

Static member classes have their uses. For example, Listing 5-3's `Double` and `Float` static member classes provide different implementations of their enclosing `Rectangle` class. The `Float` version occupies less memory because of its 32-bit `float` fields, and the `Double` version provides greater accuracy because of its 64-bit `double` fields.

Listing 5-3. Using Static Member Classes to Declare Multiple Implementations of Their Enclosing Class

```
abstract class Rectangle
{
    abstract double getX();
    abstract double getY();
    abstract double getWidth();
    abstract double getHeight();

    static class Double extends Rectangle
    {
        private double x, y, width, height;

        Double(double x, double y, double width, double height)
        {
            this.x = x;
            this.y = y;
            this.width = width;
            this.height = height;
        }

        double getX() { return x; }
        double getY() { return y; }
        double getWidth() { return width; }
        double getHeight() { return height; }
    }

    static class Float extends Rectangle
    {
        private float x, y, width, height;

        Float(float x, float y, float width, float height)
        {
            this.x = x;
            this.y = y;
            this.width = width;
            this.height = height;
        }
```

```
    double getX() { return x; }
    double getY() { return y; }
    double getWidth() { return width; }
    double getHeight() { return height; }
  }

  // Prevent subclassing. Use the type-specific Double and Float
  // implementation subclass classes to instantiate.
  private Rectangle() {}

  boolean contains(double x, double y)
  {
    return (x >= getX() && x < getX() + getWidth()) &&
           (y >= getY() && y < getY() + getHeight());
  }
}
```

Listing 5-3's Rectangle class demonstrates nested subclasses. Each of the Double and Float static member classes subclass the abstract Rectangle class, providing private floating-point or double precision floating-point fields and overriding Rectangle's abstract methods to return these fields' values as doubles.

Rectangle is abstract because it makes no sense to instantiate this class. Because it also makes no sense to directly extend Rectangle with new implementations (the Double and Float nested subclasses should be sufficient), its default constructor is declared private. Instead, you must instantiate Rectangle.Float (to save memory) or Rectangle.Double (when accuracy is required), as demonstrated by Listing 5-4.

Listing 5-4. Creating and Using Different Rectangle Implementations

```
public class SMCDemo
{
  public static void main(String[] args)
  {
    Rectangle r = new Rectangle.Double(10.0, 10.0, 20.0, 30.0);
    System.out.println("x = " + r.getX());
    System.out.println("y = " + r.getY());
    System.out.println("width = " + r.getWidth());
    System.out.println("height = " + r.getHeight());
    System.out.println("contains(15.0, 15.0) = " + r.contains(15.0, 15.0));
    System.out.println("contains(0.0, 0.0) = " + r.contains(0.0, 0.0));
    System.out.println();
    r = new Rectangle.Float(10.0f, 10.0f, 20.0f, 30.0f);
    System.out.println("x = " + r.getX());
    System.out.println("y = " + r.getY());
    System.out.println("width = " + r.getWidth());
    System.out.println("height = " + r.getHeight());
    System.out.println("contains(15.0, 15.0) = " + r.contains(15.0, 15.0));
    System.out.println("contains(0.0, 0.0) = " + r.contains(0.0, 0.0));
  }
}
```

Listing 5-4 first instantiates Rectangle's Double subclass via new Rectangle.Double(10.0, 10.0, 20.0, 30.0) and then invokes its various methods. Continuing, Listing 5-4 instantiates Rectangle's Float subclass via new Rectangle.Float(10.0f, 10.0f, 20.0f, 30.0f) before invoking Rectangle methods on this instance.

Compile both listings (javac SMCDemo.java or javac *.java) and run the application (java SMCDemo). You will then observe the following output:

```
x = 10.0
y = 10.0
width = 20.0
height = 30.0
contains(15.0, 15.0) = true
contains(0.0, 0.0) = false

x = 10.0
y = 10.0
width = 20.0
height = 30.0
contains(15.0, 15.0) = true
contains(0.0, 0.0) = false
```

Java's class library contains many static member classes. For example, the java.lang.Character class encloses a static member class named Subset whose instances represent subsets of the Unicode character set. Additional examples include java.util.AbstractMap.SimpleEntry and java.io.ObjectInputStream.GetField.

> **Note** When you compile an enclosing class that contains a static member class, the compiler creates a classfile for the static member class whose name consists of its enclosing class's name, a dollar-sign character, and the static member class's name. For example, compile Listing 5-1 and you will discover EnclosingClass$EnclosedClass.class in addition to EnclosingClass.class. This format also applies to nonstatic member classes.

Nonstatic Member Classes

A *nonstatic member class* is a non-static member of an enclosing class. Each instance of the nonstatic member class implicitly associates with an instance of the enclosing class. The nonstatic member class's instance methods can call instance methods in the enclosing class and access the enclosing class instance's nonstatic fields. Listing 5-5 presents a nonstatic member class declaration.

Listing 5-5. Declaring a Nonstatic Member Class

```
class EnclosingClass
{
   private int i;

   private void m()
   {
      System.out.println(i);
   }

   class EnclosedClass
   {
      void accessEnclosingClass()
      {
         i = 1;
         m();
      }
   }
}
```

Listing 5-5 declares a top-level class named EnclosingClass with instance field i, instance method m1(), and nonstatic member class EnclosedClass. Furthermore, EnclosedClass declares instance method accessEnclosingClass().

Because accessEnclosingClass() is nonstatic, EnclosedClass must be instantiated before this method can be called. This instantiation must take place via an instance of EnclosingClass. Listing 5-6 accomplishes these tasks.

Listing 5-6. Calling a Nonstatic Member Class's Instance Method

```
public class NSMCDemo
{
   public static void main(String[] args)
   {
      EnclosingClass ec = new EnclosingClass();
      ec.new EnclosedClass().accessEnclosingClass(); // Output: 1
   }
}
```

Listing 5-6's main() method first instantiates EnclosingClass and saves its reference in local variable ec. Then, main() uses this reference as a prefix to the new operator to instantiate EnclosedClass, whose reference is then used to call accessEnclosingClass(), which outputs 1.

> **Note** Prefixing new with a reference to the enclosing class is rare. Instead, you will typically call an enclosed class's constructor from within a constructor or an instance method of its enclosing class.

Suppose you need to maintain a to-do list of items, where each item consists of a name and a description. After some thought, you create Listing 5-7's ToDo class to implement these items.

Listing 5-7. Implementing To-Do Items as Name-Description Pairs

```java
class ToDo
{
    private String name;
    private String desc;

    ToDo(String name, String desc)
    {
        this.name = name;
        this.desc = desc;
    }

    String getName()
    {
        return name;
    }

    String getDesc()
    {
        return desc;
    }

    @Override
    public String toString()
    {
        return "Name = " + getName() + ", Desc = " + getDesc();
    }
}
```

You next create a ToDoList class to store ToDo instances. ToDoList uses its ToDoArray nonstatic member class to store ToDo instances in a growable array—you don't know how many instances will be stored, and Java arrays have fixed lengths. See Listing 5-8.

Listing 5-8. Storing a Maximum of Two ToDo Instances in a ToDoArray Instance

```java
class ToDoList
{
    private ToDoArray toDoArray;
    private int index = 0;

    ToDoList()
    {
        toDoArray = new ToDoArray(2);
    }

    boolean hasMoreElements()
    {
        return index < toDoArray.size();
    }
```

```
ToDo nextElement()
{
   return toDoArray.get(index++);
}

void add(ToDo item)
{
   toDoArray.add(item);
}

private class ToDoArray
{
   private ToDo[] toDoArray;
   private int index = 0;

   ToDoArray(int initSize)
   {
      toDoArray = new ToDo[initSize];
   }

   void add(ToDo item)
   {
      if (index >= toDoArray.length)
      {
         ToDo[] temp = new ToDo[toDoArray.length*2];
         for (int i = 0; i < toDoArray.length; i++)
            temp[i] = toDoArray[i];
         toDoArray = temp;
      }
      toDoArray[index++] = item;
   }

   ToDo get(int i)
   {
      return toDoArray[i];
   }

   int size()
   {
      return index;
   }
}
}
```

As well as providing an add() method to store ToDo instances in the ToDoArray instance, ToDoList provides hasMoreElements() and nextElement() methods to iterate over and return the stored instances. Listing 5-9 demonstrates these methods.

Listing 5-9. Creating and Iterating Over a ToDoList of ToDo Instances

```java
public class NSMCDemo
{
   public static void main(String[] args)
   {
      ToDoList toDoList = new ToDoList();
      toDoList.add(new ToDo("#1", "Do laundry."));
      toDoList.add(new ToDo("#2", "Buy groceries."));
      toDoList.add(new ToDo("#3", "Vacuum apartment."));
      toDoList.add(new ToDo("#4", "Write report."));
      toDoList.add(new ToDo("#5", "Wash car."));
      while (toDoList.hasMoreElements())
         System.out.println(toDoList.nextElement());
   }
}
```

Compile all three listings (javac NSMCDemo.java or javac *.java) and run the application (java NSMCDemo). You will then observe the following output:

```
Name = #1, Desc = Do laundry.
Name = #2, Desc = Buy groceries.
Name = #3, Desc = Vacuum apartment.
Name = #4, Desc = Write report.
Name = #5, Desc = Wash car.
```

Java's class library presents many examples of nonstatic member classes. For example, the java.util package's HashMap class declares private HashIterator, ValueIterator, KeyIterator, and EntryIterator classes for iterating over a hashmap's values, keys, and entries. (I will discuss HashMap in Chapter 9.)

> **Note** Code within an enclosed class can obtain a reference to its enclosing class instance by qualifying reserved word this with the enclosing class's name and the member access operator. For example, if code within accessEnclosingClass() needed to obtain a reference to its EnclosingClass instance, it would specify EnclosingClass.this.

Anonymous Classes

An *anonymous class* is a class without a name. Furthermore, it is not a member of its enclosing class. Instead, an anonymous class is simultaneously declared (as an anonymous extension of a class or as an anonymous implementation of an interface) and instantiated any place where it is legal to specify an expression. Listing 5-10 demonstrates an anonymous class declaration and instantiation.

Listing 5-10. Declaring and Instantiating an Anonymous Class That Extends a Class

```
abstract class Speaker
{
   abstract void speak();
}

public class ACDemo
{
   public static void main(final String[] args)
   {
      new Speaker()
      {
         String msg = (args.length == 1) ? args[0] : "nothing to say";

         @Override
         void speak()
         {
            System.out.println(msg);
         }
      }
      .speak();
   }
}
```

Listing 5-10 introduces an abstract class named Speaker and a concrete class named ACDemo. The latter class's main() method declares an anonymous class that extends Speaker and overrides its speak() method. When this method is called, it outputs main()'s first command-line argument or a default message when there are no arguments.

An anonymous class doesn't have a constructor (because the anonymous class doesn't have a name). However, its classfile does contain an <init>() method that performs instance initialization. This method calls the superclass's noargument constructor (prior to any other initialization), which is the reason for specifying Speaker() after new.

Anonymous class instances should be able to access the surrounding scope's local variables and parameters. However, an instance might outlive the method in which it was conceived (as a result of storing the instance's reference in a field) and try to access local variables and parameters that no longer exist after the method returns.

Because Java cannot allow this illegal access, which would most likely crash the virtual machine, it lets an anonymous class instance only access local variables and parameters that are declared final (see Listing 5-10). On encountering a final local variable/parameter name in an anonymous class instance, the compiler does one of two things:

- If the variable's type is primitive (int or double, for example), the compiler replaces its name with the variable's read-only value.

- If the variable's type is reference (String, for example), the compiler introduces, into the classfile, a *synthetic variable* (a manufactured variable) and code that stores the local variable's/parameter's reference in the synthetic variable.

Listing 5-11 demonstrates an alternative anonymous class declaration and instantiation.

Listing 5-11. Declaring and Instantiating an Anonymous Class That Implements an Interface

```java
interface Speakable
{
   void speak();
}

public class ACDemo
{
   public static void main(final String[] args)
   {
      new Speakable()
      {
         String msg = (args.length == 1) ? args[0] : "nothing to say";

         @Override
         public void speak()
         {
            System.out.println(msg);
         }
      }
      .speak();
   }
}
```

Listing 5-11 is very similar to Listing 5-10. However, instead of subclassing a Speaker class, this listing's anonymous class implements an interface named Speakable. Apart from the <init>() method calling java.lang.Object() (interfaces have no constructors), Listing 5-11 behaves like Listing 5-10.

Although an anonymous class doesn't have a constructor, you can provide an instance initializer to handle complex initialization. For example, new Office() {{addEmployee(new Employee ("John Doe"));}}; instantiates an anonymous subclass of Office and adds one Employee object to this instance by calling Office's addEmployee() method.

You will often find yourself creating and instantiating anonymous classes for their convenience. For example, suppose you need to return a list of all filenames having the .java suffix. The following example shows you how an anonymous class simplifies using the java.io package's File and FilenameFilter classes to achieve this objective:

```java
String[] list = new File(directory).list(new FilenameFilter()
                {
                   @Override
                   public boolean accept(File f, String s)
                   {
                      return s.endsWith(".java");
                   }
                });
```

Local Classes

A *local class* is a class that is declared anywhere that a local variable is declared. Furthermore, it has the same scope as a local variable. Unlike an anonymous class, a local class has a name and can be reused. Like anonymous classes, local classes only have enclosing instances when used in nonstatic contexts.

A local class instance can access the surrounding scope's local variables and parameters. However, the local variables and parameters that are accessed must be declared final. For example, Listing 5-12's local class declaration accesses a final parameter and a final local variable.

Listing 5-12. Declaring a Local Class

```
class EnclosingClass
{
   void m(final int x)
   {
      final int y = x * 2;
      class LocalClass
      {
         int a = x;
         int b = y;
      }
      LocalClass lc = new LocalClass();
      System.out.println(lc.a);
      System.out.println(lc.b);
   }
}
```

Listing 5-12 declares EnclosingClass with its instance method m() declaring a local class named LocalClass. This local class declares a pair of instance fields (a and b) that are initialized to the values of final parameter x and final local variable y when LocalClass is instantiated: new EnclosingClass().m(10);, for example.

Listing 5-13 demonstrates this local class.

Listing 5-13. Demonstrating a Local Class

```
public class LCDemo
{
   public static void main(String[] args)
   {
      EnclosingClass ec = new EnclosingClass();
      ec.m(10);
   }
}
```

After instantiating EnclosingClass, Listing 5-13's main() method invokes m(10). The called m() method multiplies this argument by 2; instantiates LocalClass, whose <init>() method assigns the argument and the doubled value to its pair of instance fields (in lieu of using a constructor to perform this task); and outputs the LocalClass instance fields. The following output results:

```
10
20
```

Local classes help improve code clarity because they can be moved closer to where they are needed. For example, Listing 5-14 declares an Iterator interface and a ToDoList class whose iterator() method returns an instance of its local Iter class as an Iterator instance (because Iter implements Iterator).

Listing 5-14. The Iterator Interface and the ToDoList Class

```java
interface Iterator
{
   boolean hasMoreElements();
   Object nextElement();
}

class ToDoList
{
   private ToDo[] toDoList;
   private int index = 0;

   ToDoList(int size)
   {
      toDoList = new ToDo[size];
   }

   Iterator iterator()
   {
      class Iter implements Iterator
      {
         int index = 0;

         @Override
         public boolean hasMoreElements()
         {
            return index < toDoList.length;
         }

         @Override
         public Object nextElement()
         {
            return toDoList[index++];
         }
      }
      return new Iter();
   }
```

```
    void add(ToDo item)
    {
       toDoList[index++] = item;
    }
}
```

Listing 5-15 demonstrates Iterator, the refactored ToDoList class, and Listing 5-7's ToDo class.

Listing 5-15. Creating and Iterating Over a ToDoList of ToDo Instances with a Reusable Iterator

```
public class LCDemo
{
   public static void main(String[] args)
   {
      ToDoList toDoList = new ToDoList(5);
      toDoList.add(new ToDo("#1", "Do laundry."));
      toDoList.add(new ToDo("#2", "Buy groceries."));
      toDoList.add(new ToDo("#3", "Vacuum apartment."));
      toDoList.add(new ToDo("#4", "Write report."));
      toDoList.add(new ToDo("#5", "Wash car."));
      Iterator iter = toDoList.iterator();
      while (iter.hasMoreElements())
         System.out.println(iter.nextElement());
   }
}
```

The Iterator instance that is returned from iterator() returns ToDo items in the same order as when they were added to the list. Although you can only use the returned Iterator object once, you can call iterator() whenever you need a new Iterator object. This capability is a big improvement over the one-shot iterator presented in Listing 5-9.

Interfaces within Classes

Interfaces can be nested within classes. Once declared, an interface is considered to be static even when it is not declared static. For example, Listing 5-16 declares an enclosing class named X along with two nested static interfaces named A and B.

Listing 5-16. Declaring a Pair of Interfaces Within a Class

```
class X
{
   interface A
   {
   }

   static interface B
   {
   }
}
```

You would access Listing 5-16's interfaces in the same way. For example, you would specify `class C implements X.A {}` or `class D implements X.B {}`.

As with nested classes, nested interfaces help to implement top-level class architecture by being implemented by nested classes. Collectively, these types are nested because they cannot (as in Listing 5-14's `Iter` local class) or need not appear at the same level as a top-level class and pollute its package namespace.

> **Note**   In Chapter 4's introduction to interfaces, I showed you how to declare constants and method headers in the body of an interface. You can also declare interfaces and classes in an interface's body. Because there are few good reasons to do this (`java.util.Map.Entry` is one exception), it is probably best to avoid nesting interfaces and/or classes within interfaces.

Mastering Packages

Hierarchical structures organize items in terms of hierarchical relationships that exist between those items. For example, a filesystem might contain a `taxes` directory with multiple year subdirectories, where each subdirectory contains tax information pertinent to that year. Also, an enclosing class might contain multiple nested classes that only make sense in the context of the enclosing class.

Hierarchical structures also help to avoid name conflicts. For example, two files cannot have the same name in a nonhierarchical filesystem (which consists of a single directory). In contrast, a hierarchical filesystem lets same-named files exist in different directories. Similarly, two enclosing classes can contain same-named nested classes. Name conflicts don't exist because items are partitioned into different *namespaces*.

Java also supports the partitioning of top-level user-defined types into multiple namespaces to better organize these types and to also prevent name conflicts. Java uses packages to accomplish these tasks.

In this section I introduce you to packages. After defining this term and explaining why package names must be unique, I present the package and import statements. I next explain how the virtual machine searches for packages and types and then present an example that shows you how to work with packages. I close this section by showing you how to encapsulate a package of classfiles into JAR files.

> **Tip**   Except for the most trivial of top-level types and (typically) those classes that serve as application entry points (they have `main()` methods), you should consider storing your types (especially when they are reusable) in packages. Get into the habit now because you'll use packages extensively when developing Android apps. Each Android app must be stored in its own unique package.

What Are Packages?

A *package* is a unique namespace that can contain a combination of top-level classes, other top-level types, and subpackages. Only types that are declared `public` can be accessed from outside the package. Furthermore, the constants, constructors, methods, and nested types that describe a class's interface must be declared `public` to be accessible from beyond the package.

Every package has a name, which must be a nonreserved identifier. The member access operator separates a package name from a subpackage name and separates a package or subpackage name from a type name. For example, the two member access operators in `graphics.shapes.Circle` separate package name `graphics` from the `shapes` subpackage name and separate subpackage name `shapes` from the `Circle` type name.

> **Note**   Each of Oracle's and Google Android's standard class libraries organizes its many classes and other top-level types into multiple packages. Many of these packages are subpackages of the standard `java` package. Examples include `java.io` (types related to input/output operations), `java.lang` (language-oriented types), `java.net` (network-oriented types), and `java.util` (utility types).

Package Names Must Be Unique

Suppose you have two different `graphics.shapes` packages, and suppose that each `shapes` subpackage contains a `Circle` class with a different interface. When the compiler encounters `System.out.println(new Circle(10.0, 20.0, 30.0).area());` in the source code, it needs to verify that the `area()` method exists.

The compiler will search all accessible packages until it finds a `graphics.shapes` package that contains a `Circle` class. If the found package contains the appropriate `Circle` class with an `area()` method, everything is fine. Otherwise, if the `Circle` class doesn't have an `area()` method, the compiler will report an error.

This scenario illustrates the importance of choosing unique package names. Specifically, the top-level package name must be unique. The convention in choosing this name is to take your Internet domain name and reverse it. For example, I would choose `ca.tutortutor` as my top-level package name because `tutortutor.ca` is my domain name. I would then specify `ca.tutortutor.graphics.shapes.Circle` to access `Circle`.

> **Note**   Reversed Internet domain names are not always valid package names. One or more of its component names might start with a digit (`6.com`), contain a hyphen (–) or other illegal character (`aq-x.com`), or be one of Java's reserved words (`int.com`). Convention dictates that you prefix the digit with an underscore (`com._6`), replace the illegal character with an underscore (`com.aq_x`), and suffix the reserved word with an underscore (`com.int_`).

The Package Statement

The package statement identifies the package in which a source file's types are located. This statement consists of reserved word package, followed by a member access operator-separated list of package and subpackage names, followed by a semicolon.

For example, `package graphics;` specifies that the source file's types locate in a package named `graphics`, and `package graphics.shapes;` specifies that the source file's types locate in the `graphics` package's `shapes` subpackage.

By convention, a package name is expressed in lowercase. When the name consists of multiple words, each word except for the first word is capitalized.

Only one package statement can appear in a source file. When it is present, nothing apart from comments must precede this statement.

> **Caution**   Specifying multiple package statements in a source file or placing anything apart from comments above a package statement causes the compiler to report an error.

Java implementations map package and subpackage names to same-named directories. For example, an implementation would map `graphics` to a directory named `graphics` and would map `graphics.shapes` to a `shapes` subdirectory of `graphics`. The Java compiler stores the classfiles that implement the package's types in the corresponding directory.

> **Note**   When a source file doesn't contain a package statement, the source file's types are said to belong to the *unnamed package*. This package corresponds to the current directory.

The Import Statement

Imagine having to repeatedly specify `ca.tutortutor.graphics.shapes.Circle` or some other lengthy package-qualified type name for each occurrence of that type in source code. Java provides an alternative that lets you avoid having to specify package details. This alternative is the import statement.

The import statement imports types from a package by telling the compiler where to look for unqualified type names during compilation. This statement consists of reserved word `import`, followed by a member access operator-separated list of package and subpackage names, followed by a type name or * (asterisk), followed by a semicolon.

The * symbol is a wildcard that represents all unqualified type names. It tells the compiler to look for such names in the import statement's specified package, unless the type name is found in a previously searched package. (Using the wildcard doesn't have a performance penalty or lead to code bloat but can lead to name conflicts, as you will see.)

For example, `import ca.tutortutor.graphics.shapes.Circle;` tells the compiler that an unqualified `Circle` class exists in the `ca.tutortutor.graphics.shapes` package. Similarly, `import ca.tutortutor.graphics.shapes.*;` tells the compiler to look in this package when it encounters a `Rectangle` class, a `Triangle` class, or even an `Employee` class (if `Employee` hasn't already been found).

> **Tip**   You should avoid using the * wildcard so that other developers can easily see which types are used in source code.

Because Java is case sensitive, package and subpackage names specified in an import statement must be expressed in the same case as that used in the package statement.

When import statements are present in source code, only a package statement and comments can precede them.

> **Caution**   Placing anything other than a package statement, import statements, static import statements (discussed shortly), and comments above an import statement causes the compiler to report an error.

You can run into name conflicts when using the wildcard version of the import statement because any unqualified type name matches the wildcard. For example, you have `graphics.shapes` and `geometry` packages that each contain a `Circle` class, the source code begins with `import geometry.*;` and `import graphics.shape.*;` statements, and it also contains an unqualified occurrence of `Circle`. Because the compiler doesn't know if `Circle` refers to geometry's `Circle` class or `graphics.shape`'s `Circle` class, it reports an error. You can fix this problem by qualifying `Circle` with the correct package name.

> **Note**   The compiler automatically imports the `String` class and other types from the `java.lang` package, which is why it's not necessary to qualify `String` with `java.lang`.

Searching for Packages and Types

Newcomers to Java who first start to work with packages often become frustrated by "no class definition found" and other errors. This frustration can be partly avoided by understanding how the virtual machine searches for packages and types.

In this section I explain how the search process works. To understand this process, you need to realize that the compiler is a special Java application that runs under the control of the virtual machine. Furthermore, there are two different forms of search.

Compile-Time Search

When the compiler encounters a type expression (such as a method call) in source code, it must locate that type's declaration to verify that the expression is legal (a method exists in the type's class whose parameter types match the types of the arguments passed in the method call, for example).

The compiler first searches the Java platform packages (which contain class library types). It then searches extension packages (for extension types). When the -sourcepath command-line option is specified when starting the virtual machine (via javac), the compiler searches the indicated path's source files.

> **Note** Java platform packages are stored in rt.jar and a few other important JAR files. Extension packages are stored in a special extensions directory named ext.

Otherwise, the compiler searches the user classpath (in left-to-right order) for the first user classfile or source file containing the type. If no user classpath is present, the current directory is searched. If no package matches or the type still cannot be found, the compiler reports an error. Otherwise, the compiler records the package information in the classfile.

> **Note** The user classpath is specified via the -classpath option used to start the virtual machine or, when not present, the CLASSPATH environment variable.

Runtime Search

When the compiler or any other Java application runs, the virtual machine will encounter types and must load their associated classfiles via special code known as a *classloader*. The virtual machine will use the previously stored package information that is associated with the encountered type in a search for that type's classfile.

The virtual machine searches the Java platform packages, followed by extension packages, followed by the user classpath (in left-to-right order) for the first classfile that contains the type. If no user classpath is present, the current directory is searched. If no package matches or the type cannot be found, a "no class definition found" error is reported. Otherwise, the classfile is loaded into memory.

> **Note** Whether you use the -classpath option or the CLASSPATH environment variable to specify a user classpath, there is a specific format that must be followed. Under Windows, this format is expressed as path1;path2;..., where path1, path2, and so on are the locations of package directories. Under Unix and Linux, this format changes to path1:path2:....

Playing with Packages

Suppose your application needs to log messages to the console, to a file, or to another destination. It can accomplish this task with the help of a logging library. My implementation of this library consists of an interface named `Logger`, an abstract class named `LoggerFactory`, and a pair of package-private classes named `Console` and `File`.

> **Note** The logging library that I present is an example of the *Abstract Factory design pattern*, which is presented on page 87 of *Design Patterns: Elements of Reusable Object-Oriented Software* by Erich Gamma, Richard Helm, Ralph Johnson, and John Vlissides (Addison-Wesley, 1995; ISBN: 0201633612).

Listing 5-17 presents the `Logger` interface, which describes objects that log messages.

Listing 5-17. Describing Objects That Log Messages via the Logger Interface

```
package logging;

public interface Logger
{
   boolean connect();
   boolean disconnect();
   boolean log(String msg);
}
```

Each of the `connect()`, `disconnect()`, and `log()` methods returns true on success and false on failure. (Later in this chapter you will discover a better technique for dealing with failure.) These methods are not declared `public` explicitly because an interface's methods are implicitly `public`.

Listing 5-18 presents the `LoggerFactory` abstract class.

Listing 5-18. Obtaining a Logger for Logging Messages to a Specific Destination

```
package logging;

public abstract class LoggerFactory
{
   public final static int CONSOLE = 0;
   public final static int FILE = 1;

   public static Logger newLogger(int dstType, String... dstName)
   {
      switch (dstType)
      {
         case CONSOLE: return new Console(dstName.length == 0 ? null
                                                  : dstName[0]);
```

```
            case FILE   : return new File(dstName.length == 0 ? null
                                                              : dstName[0]);
            default     : return null;
        }
    }
}
```

newLogger() returns a Logger object for logging messages to an appropriate destination. It uses the varargs (variable arguments) feature (see Chapter 3) to optionally accept an extra String argument for those destination types that require the argument. For example, FILE requires a filename.

Listing 5-19 presents the package-private Console class—this class is not accessible beyond the classes in the logging package because reserved word class is not preceded by reserved word public.

Listing 5-19. Logging Messages to the Console

```
package logging;

class Console implements Logger
{
    private String dstName;

    Console(String dstName)
    {
        this.dstName = dstName;
    }

    @Override
    public boolean connect()
    {
        return true;
    }

    @Override
    public boolean disconnect()
    {
        return true;
    }

    @Override
    public boolean log(String msg)
    {
        System.out.println(msg);
        return true;
    }
}
```

Console's package-private constructor saves its argument, which most likely will be null because there is no need for a String argument. Perhaps a future version of Console will use this argument to identify one of multiple console windows.

Listing 5-20 presents the package-private File class.

Listing 5-20. Logging Messages to a File (Eventually)

```
package logging;

class File implements Logger
{
   private String dstName;

   File(String dstName)
   {
      this.dstName = dstName;
   }

   @Override
   public boolean connect()
   {
      if (dstName == null)
         return false;
      System.out.println("opening file " + dstName);
      return true;
   }

   @Override
   public boolean disconnect()
   {
      if (dstName == null)
         return false;
      System.out.println("closing file " + dstName);
      return true;
   }

   @Override
   public boolean log(String msg)
   {
      if (dstName == null)
         return false;
      System.out.println("writing "+msg+" to file " + dstName);
      return true;
   }
}
```

Unlike Console, File requires a nonnull argument. Each method first verifies that this argument is not null. If the argument is null, the method returns false to signify failure. (In Chapter 11, I refactor File to incorporate appropriate file-writing code.)

The logging library allows us to introduce portable logging code into an application. Apart from a call to newLogger(), this code will remain the same regardless of the logging destination. Listing 5-21 presents an application that tests this library.

Listing 5-21. Testing the Logging Library

```java
import logging.Logger;
import logging.LoggerFactory;

public class TestLogger
{
   public static void main(String[] args)
   {
      Logger logger = LoggerFactory.newLogger(LoggerFactory.CONSOLE);
      if (logger.connect())
      {
         logger.log("test message #1");
         logger.disconnect();
      }
      else
         System.out.println("cannot connect to console-based logger");
      logger = LoggerFactory.newLogger(LoggerFactory.FILE, "x.txt");
      if (logger.connect())
      {
         logger.log("test message #2");
         logger.disconnect();
      }
      else
         System.out.println("cannot connect to file-based logger");
      logger = LoggerFactory.newLogger(LoggerFactory.FILE);
      if (logger.connect())
      {
         logger.log("test message #3");
         logger.disconnect();
      }
      else
         System.out.println("cannot connect to file-based logger");
   }
}
```

Follow the steps (which assume that the JDK has been installed) to create the `logging` package and `TestLogger` application, and to run this application:

1. Create a new directory and make this directory current.

2. Create a `logging` directory in the current directory.

3. Copy Listing 5-17 to a file named `Logger.java` in the `logging` directory.

4. Copy Listing 5-18 to a file named `LoggerFactory.java` in the `logging` directory.

5. Copy Listing 5-19 to a file named `Console.java` in the `logging` directory.

6.   Copy Listing 5-20 to a file named `File.java` in the `logging` directory.

7.   Copy Listing 5-21 to a file named `TestLogger.java` in the current directory.

8.   Execute `javac TestLogger.java`, which also compiles `logger`'s source files.

9.   Execute `java TestLogger`.

After completing the previous step, you should observe the following output from the `TestLogger` application:

```
test message #1
opening file x.txt
writing test message #2 to file x.txt
closing file x.txt
cannot connect to file-based logger
```

What happens when `logging` is moved to another location? For example, move `logging` to the root directory and run `TestLogger`. You will now observe an error message about the virtual machine not finding the `logging` package and its `LoggerFactory` classfile.

You can solve this problem by specifying `-classpath` when running the `java` tool or by adding the location of the `logging` package to the CLASSPATH environment variable. For example, I chose to use `-classpath` (which I find more convenient) in the following Windows-specific command line:

```
java -classpath \;. TestLogger
```

The backslash represents the root directory in Windows. (I could have specified a forward slash as an alternative.) Also, the period represents the current directory. If it is missing, the virtual machine complains about not finding the `TestLogger` classfile.

> **Tip**   If you discover an error message where the virtual machine reports that it cannot find an application classfile, try appending a period character to the classpath. Doing so will probably fix the problem.

Packages and JAR Files

The JDK provides a `jar` tool that is used to archive classfiles in *JAR* (Java ARchive) files and is also used to extract a JAR file's classfiles. It probably comes as no surprise that you can store packages in JAR files, which greatly simplify the distribution of your package-based class libraries.

To show you how easy it is to store a package in a JAR file, you will create a `logger.jar` file that contains the `logging` package's four classfiles (`Logger.class`, `LoggerFactory.class`, `Console.class`, and `File.class`). Complete the following steps to accomplish this task:

1.   Make sure that the current directory contains the previously created `logging` directory with its four classfiles.

2.   Execute `jar cf logger.jar logging\*.class`. You could alternatively execute `jar cf logger.jar logging/*.class`. (The `c` option stands for "create new archive" and the `f` option stands for "specify archive filename".)

You should now find a `logger.jar` file in the current directory. To prove to yourself that this file contains the four classfiles, execute `jar tf logger.jar`. (The t option stands for "list table of contents".)

You can run `TestLogger.class` by adding `logger.jar` to the classpath. For example, you can run `TestLogger` under Windows via `java -classpath logger.jar;. TestLogger`.

> **Note** If you need a logging capability, you can either create your own logging framework as previously demonstrated or leverage the `java.util.logging` package that's included in the standard class library.

Mastering Static Imports

An interface should only be used to declare a type. However, some developers violate this principle by using interfaces to only export constants. Such interfaces are known as *constant interfaces*, and Listing 5-22 presents an example.

Listing 5-22. Declaring a Constant Interface

```
interface Directions
{
   int NORTH = 0;
   int SOUTH = 1;
   int EAST = 2;
   int WEST = 3;
}
```

Developers who resort to constant interfaces do so to avoid having to prefix a constant's name with the name of its class (as in `Math.PI`, where PI is a constant in the `java.lang.Math` class). They do this by implementing the interface—see Listing 5-23.

Listing 5-23. Implementing a Constant Interface

```
public class TrafficFlow implements Directions
{
   public static void main(String[] args)
   {
      showDirection((int) (Math.random()* 4));
   }

   static void showDirection(int dir)
   {
      switch (dir)
      {
         case NORTH: System.out.println("Moving north"); break;
         case SOUTH: System.out.println("Moving south"); break;
```

```
        case EAST : System.out.println("Moving east"); break;
        case WEST : System.out.println("Moving west");
      }
   }
}
```

Listing 5-23's TrafficFlow class implements Directions for the sole purpose of not having to specify Directions.NORTH, Directions.SOUTH, Directions.EAST, and Directions.WEST.

This is an appalling misuse of an interface. These constants are nothing more than an implementation detail that should not be allowed to leak into the class's exported *interface* because they might confuse the class's users (what is the purpose of these constants?). Also, they represent a future commitment: even when the class no longer uses these constants, the interface must remain to ensure binary compatibility.

Java 5 introduced an alternative that satisfies the desire for constant interfaces while avoiding their problems. This static imports feature lets you import a class's static members so that you don't have to qualify them with their class names. It's implemented via a small modification to the import statement as follows:

```
import static packagespec . classname . ( staticmembername | * );
```

The static import statement specifies static after import. It then specifies a member access operator-separated list of package and subpackage names, which is followed by the member access operator and a class's name. Once again, the member access operator is specified, followed by a single static member name or the asterisk wildcard.

Caution   Placing anything apart from a package statement, import/static import statements, and comments above a static import statement causes the compiler to report an error.

You specify a single static member name to import only that name:

```
import static java.lang.Math.PI;  // Import the PI static field only.
import static java.lang.Math.cos; // Import the cos() static method only.
```

In contrast, you specify the wildcard to import all static member names:

```
import static java.lang.Math.*;   // Import all static members from Math.
```

You can now refer to the static member(s) without having to specify the class name:

```
System.out.println(cos(PI));
```

Using multiple static import statements can result in name conflicts, which causes the compiler to report errors. For example, suppose your geom package contains a Circle class with a static member named PI. Now suppose you specify import static java.lang.Math.*; and import static geom.Circle.*; at the top of your source file. Finally, suppose you specify System.out.println(PI); somewhere in that file's code. The compiler reports an error because it doesn't know whether PI belongs to Math or to Circle.

Mastering Exceptions

In an ideal world, nothing bad ever happens when an application runs. For example, a file always exists when the application needs to open the file, the application is always able to connect to a remote computer, and the virtual machine never runs out of memory when the application needs to instantiate objects.

In contrast, real-world applications occasionally attempt to open files that don't exist, attempt to connect to remote computers that are unable to communicate with them, and require more memory than the virtual machine can provide. Your goal is to write code that properly responds to these and other exceptional situations (exceptions).

In this section I introduce you to exceptions. After defining this term, I look at representing exceptions in source code. I then examine the topics of throwing and handling exceptions and conclude by discussing how to perform cleanup tasks before a method returns, whether or not an exception has been thrown.

What Are Exceptions?

An *exception* is a divergence from an application's normal behavior. For example, the application attempts to open a nonexistent file for reading. The normal behavior is to successfully open the file and begin reading its contents. However, the file cannot be read when the file doesn't exist.

This example illustrates an exception that cannot be prevented. However, a workaround is possible. For example, the application can detect that the file doesn't exist and take an alternate course of action, which might include telling the user about the problem. Unpreventable exceptions where workarounds are possible must not be ignored.

Exceptions can occur because of poorly written code. For example, an application might contain code that accesses each element in an array. Because of careless oversight, the array-access code might attempt to access a nonexistent array element, which leads to an exception. This kind of exception is preventable by writing correct code.

Finally, an exception might occur that cannot be prevented and for which there is no workaround. For example, the virtual machine might run out of memory, or perhaps it cannot find a classfile. This kind of exception, known as an *error*, is so serious that it's impossible (or at least inadvisable) to work around; the application must terminate, presenting a message to the user that explains why it's terminating.

Representing Exceptions in Source Code

An exception can be represented via error codes or objects. After discussing each kind of representation and explaining why objects are superior, I introduce you to Java's exception and error class hierarchy, emphasizing the difference between checked and runtime exceptions. I close my discussion on representing exceptions in source code by discussing custom exception classes.

Error Codes vs. Objects

One way to represent exceptions in source code is to use error codes. For example, a method might return true on success and false when an exception occurs. Alternatively, a method might return 0 on success and a nonzero integer value that identifies a specific kind of exception.

Developers traditionally designed methods to return error codes; I demonstrated this tradition in each of the three methods in Listing 5-17's Logger interface. Each method returns true on success or returns false to represent an exception (unable to connect to the logger, for example).

Although a method's return value must be examined to see if it represents an exception, error codes are all too easy to ignore. For example, a lazy developer might ignore the return code from Logger's connect() method and attempt to call log(). Ignoring error codes is one reason why a new approach to dealing with exceptions has been invented.

This new approach is based on objects. When an exception occurs, an object representing the exception is created by the code that was running when the exception occurred. Details describing the exception's surrounding context are stored in the object. These details are later examined to work around the exception.

The object is then *thrown* or handed off to the virtual machine to search for a *handler*, code that can handle the exception. (If the exception is an error, the application should not provide a handler because errors are so serious [e.g., the virtual machine has run out of memory] that there's practically nothing that can be done about them.) When a handler is located, its code is executed to provide a workaround. Otherwise, the virtual machine terminates the application.

> **Caution**   Code that handles exceptions can be a source of bugs because it's often not thoroughly tested. Always make sure to test any code that handles exceptions.

Apart from being too easy to ignore, an error code's Boolean or integer value is less meaningful than an object name. For example, fileNotFound is self-evident, but what does false mean? Also, an object can contain information about what led to the exception. These details can be helpful to a suitable workaround.

The Throwable Class Hierarchy

Java provides a hierarchy of classes that represent different kinds of exceptions. These classes are rooted in java.lang.Throwable, the ultimate superclass for all *throwables* (exception and error objects—exceptions and errors, for short—that can be thrown). Table 5-1 identifies and describes most of Throwable's constructors and methods.

Table 5-1. Throwable's Constructors and Methods

Method	Description
Throwable()	Create a throwable with a null detail message and cause.
Throwable(String message)	Create a throwable with the specified detail message and a null cause.
Throwable(String message, Throwable cause)	Create a throwable with the specified detail message and cause.
Throwable(Throwable cause)	Create a throwable whose detail message is the string representation of a nonnull cause or null.
Throwable fillInStackTrace()	Fill in the execution stack trace. This method records information about the current state of the stack frames for the current thread within this throwable. (I discuss threads in Chapter 8.)
Throwable getCause()	Return the cause of this throwable. When there is no cause, null is returned.
String getMessage()	Return this throwable's detail message, which might be null.
StackTraceElement[] getStackTrace()	Provide programmatic access to the stack trace information printed by printStackTrace() as an array of stack trace elements, each representing one stack frame.
Throwable initCause(Throwable cause)	Initialize the cause of this throwable to the specified value.
void printStackTrace()	Print this throwable and its backtrace of stack frames to the standard error stream.
void setStackTrace(StackTraceElement[] stackTrace)	Set the stack trace elements that will be returned by getStackTrace() and printed by printStackTrace() and related methods.

It's not uncommon for a class's public methods to call helper methods that throw various exceptions. A public method will probably not document exceptions thrown from a helper method because they are implementation details that often should not be visible to the public method's caller.

However, because this exception might be helpful in diagnosing the problem, the public method can wrap the lower-level exception in a higher-level exception that is documented in the public method's contract interface. The wrapped exception is known as a *cause* because its existence causes the higher-level exception to be thrown.

A cause is created by invoking the Throwable(Throwable cause) or Throwable(String message, Throwable cause) constructor, which invoke the initCause() method to store the cause. If you don't call either constructor, you can alternatively call initCause() directly, but you must do so immediately after creating the throwable. Call the getCause() method to return the cause.

When an exception is thrown, it leaves behind a stack of unfinished method calls. Throwable's constructors call fillInStackTrace() to record this stack trace information, which is output by calling printStackTrace().

The getStackTrace() method provides programmatic access to the stack trace by returning this information as an array of java.lang.StackTraceElement instances—each instance represents one entry. StackTraceElement provides methods to return stack trace information. For example, String getMethodName() returns the name of an unfinished method.

The setStackTrace() method is designed for use by Remote Procedure Call (RPC) frameworks (see http://en.wikipedia.org/wiki/Remote_procedure_call) and other advanced systems, allowing the client to override the default stack trace that is generated by fillInStackTrace() when a throwable is constructed or deserialized when a throwable is read from a serialization stream. (I will discuss serialization in Chapter 11.)

Moving down the throwable hierarchy, you encounter the java.lang.Exception and java.lang.Error classes, which respectively represent exceptions and errors. Each class offers four constructors that pass their arguments to their Throwable counterparts but provides no methods apart from those that are inherited from Throwable.

Exception is itself subclassed by java.lang.CloneNotSupportedException (discussed in Chapter 4), java.lang.IOException (discussed in Chapter 11), and other classes. Similarly, Error is itself subclassed by java.lang.AssertionError (discussed in Chapter 6), java.lang.OutOfMemoryError, and other classes.

Caution   Never instantiate Throwable, Exception, or Error. The resulting objects are meaningless because they are too generic.

Checked Exceptions vs. Runtime Exceptions

A *checked exception* is an exception that represents a problem with the possibility of recovery and for which the developer must provide a workaround. The developer should *check* (examine) the code to ensure that the exception is handled in the method where it is thrown or is explicitly identified as being handled elsewhere.

Exception and all subclasses except for java.lang.RuntimeException (and its subclasses) describe checked exceptions. For example, the CloneNotSupportedException and IOException classes describe checked exceptions. (CloneNotSupportedException should not be checked because there is no runtime workaround for this kind of exception.)

A *runtime exception* is an exception that represents a coding mistake. This kind of exception is also known as an *unchecked exception* because it doesn't need to be handled or explicitly identified—the mistake must be fixed. Because these exceptions can occur in many places, it would be burdensome to be forced to handle them.

RuntimeException and its subclasses describe unchecked exceptions. For example, java.lang.ArithmeticException describes arithmetic problems such as integer division by zero. Another example is java.lang.ArrayIndexOutOfBoundsException, which is thrown when you attempt to access an array element with a negative index or an index that is greater than or equal to the length of the array. (In hindsight, RuntimeException should have been named UncheckedException because all exceptions occur at runtime.)

Note   Many developers are unhappy with checked exceptions because of the work involved in having to handle them. This problem is made worse by libraries providing methods that throw checked exceptions when they should throw unchecked exceptions. As a result, many modern languages support only unchecked exceptions.

Custom Exception Classes

You can declare your own exception classes. Before doing so, ask yourself if an existing exception class in the standard class library meets your needs. If you find a suitable class, you should reuse it. (Why reinvent the wheel?) Other developers will already be familiar with the existing class, and this knowledge will make your code easier to learn. When no existing class meets your needs, think about whether to subclass `Exception` or `RuntimeException`. In other words, will your exception class be checked or unchecked? As a rule of thumb, your class should subclass `RuntimeException` if you think that it will describe a coding mistake.

Tip   When you name your class, follow the convention of providing an `Exception` suffix. This suffix clarifies that your class describes an exception.

Suppose you are creating a `Media` class whose static methods are to perform media-oriented utility tasks. For example, one method converts sound files in non-MP3 media formats to MP3 format. This method will be passed source file and destination file arguments and will convert the source file to the format implied by the destination file's extension.

Before performing the conversion, the method needs to verify that the source file's format agrees with the format implied by its file extension. If there is no agreement, an exception must be thrown. Furthermore, this exception must store the expected and existing media formats so that a handler can identify them when presenting a message to the user.

Because Java's class library doesn't provide a suitable exception class, you decide to introduce a class named `InvalidMediaFormatException`. Detecting an invalid media format is not the result of a coding mistake, and so you also decide to extend `Exception` to indicate that the exception is checked. Listing 5-24 presents this class's declaration.

Listing 5-24. Declaring a Custom Exception Class

```
package media;

public class InvalidMediaFormatException extends Exception
{
   private String expectedFormat;
   private String existingFormat;
```

```
    public InvalidMediaFormatException(String expectedFormat,
                                       String existingFormat)
    {
       super("Expected format: " + expectedFormat + ", Existing format: " +
             existingFormat);
       this.expectedFormat = expectedFormat;
       this.existingFormat = existingFormat;
    }

    public String getExpectedFormat()
    {
       return expectedFormat;
    }

    public String getExistingFormat()
    {
       return existingFormat;
    }
}
```

InvalidMediaFormatException provides a constructor that calls Exception's public
Exception(String message) constructor with a detail message that includes the expected and
existing formats. It is wise to capture such details in the detail message because the problem that
led to the exception might be hard to reproduce.

InvalidMediaFormatException also provides getExpectedFormat() and getExistingFormat()
methods that return these formats. Perhaps a handler will present this information in a message
to the user. Unlike the detail message, this message might be *localized*, expressed in the user's
language (French, German, English, etc.).

Throwing Exceptions

Now that you have created an InvalidMediaFormatException class, you can declare the Media class
and begin to code its convert() method. The initial version of this method validates its arguments
and then verifies that the source file's media format agrees with the format implied by its file
extension. Check out Listing 5-25.

Listing 5-25. Throwing Exceptions from the convert() Method

```
package media;

import java.io.IOException;

public final class Media
{
    public static void convert(String srcName, String dstName)
       throws InvalidMediaFormatException, IOException
```

```
   {
      if (srcName == null)
         throw new NullPointerException(srcName + " is null");
      if (dstName == null)
         throw new NullPointerException(dstName + " is null");
      // Code to access source file and verify that its format matches the
      // format implied by its file extension.
      //
      // Assume that the source file's extension is RM (for Real Media) and
      // that the file's internal signature suggests that its format is
      // Microsoft WAVE.
      String expectedFormat = "RM";
      String existingFormat = "WAVE";
      throw new InvalidMediaFormatException(expectedFormat, existingFormat);
   }
}
```

Listing 5-25 declares the Media class to be final because this utility class will only consist of class methods and there's no reason to extend it.

Media's convert() method appends throws InvalidMediaFormatException, IOException to its header. A *throws clause* identifies all checked exceptions that are thrown out of the method and must be handled by some other method. It consists of reserved word throws followed by a comma-separated list of checked exception class names and is always appended to a method header. The convert() method's throws clause indicates that this method is capable of throwing an InvalidMediaException or IOException instance to the virtual machine.

convert() also demonstrates the throw statement, which consists of reserved word throw followed by an instance of Throwable or a subclass. (You will typically instantiate an Exception subclass.) This statement throws the instance to the virtual machine, which then searches for a suitable handler to handle the exception.

The first use of the throw statement is to throw a java.lang.NullPointerException instance when a null reference is passed as the source or destination filename. This unchecked exception is commonly thrown to indicate that a contract has been violated via a passed null reference. For example, you cannot pass null filenames to convert().

The second use of the throw statement is to throw a media.InvalidMediaFormatException instance when the expected media format doesn't match the existing format. In the contrived example, the exception is thrown because the expected format is RM and the existing format is WAVE.

Unlike InvalidMediaFormatException, NullPointerException is not listed in convert()'s throws clause because NullPointerException instances are unchecked. They can occur so frequently that it is too big a burden to force the developer to properly handle these exceptions. Instead, the developer should write code that minimizes their occurrences.

Although not thrown from convert(), IOException is listed in this method's throws clause in preparation for refactoring this method to perform the conversion with the help of file-handling code.

`NullPointerException` is one kind of exception that is thrown when an argument proves to be invalid. The `java.lang.IllegalArgumentException` class generalizes the illegal argument scenario to include other kinds of illegal arguments. For example, the following method throws an `IllegalArgumentException` instance when a numeric argument is negative:

```
public static double sqrt(double x)
{
   if (x < 0)
      throw new IllegalArgumentException(x + " is negative");
   // Calculate the square root of x.
}
```

There are a few additional items to keep in mind when working with throws clauses and throw statements:

- You can append a throws clause to a constructor and throw an exception from the constructor when something goes wrong while the constructor is executing. The resulting object will not be created.

- When an exception is thrown out of an application's `main()` method, the virtual machine terminates the application and calls the exception's `printStackTrace()` method to print, to the console, the sequence of nested method calls that was awaiting completion when the exception was thrown.

- If a superclass method declares a throws clause, the overriding subclass method doesn't have to declare a throws clause. However, if the subclass method does declare a throws clause, the clause must not include the names of checked exception classes that are not also included in the superclass method's throws clause, unless they are the names of exception subclasses. For example, given superclass method `void foo() throws IOException {}`, the overriding subclass method could be declared as `void foo() {}`, `void foo() throws IOException {}`, or `void foo() throws FileNotFoundException {}`—the `java.io.FileNotFoundException` class subclasses `IOException`.

- A checked exception class name doesn't need to appear in a throws clause when the name of its superclass appears.

- The compiler reports an error when a method throws a checked exception and doesn't also handle the exception or list the exception in its throws clause.

- Don't include the names of unchecked exception classes in a throws clause. These names are not required because such exceptions should never occur. Furthermore, they only clutter source code and possibly confuse someone who is trying to understand that code.

- You can declare a checked exception class name in a method's throws clause without throwing an instance of this class from the method. (Perhaps the method has yet to be fully coded.) However, Java requires that you provide code to handle this exception, even though it is not thrown.

Handling Exceptions

A method indicates its intention to handle one or more exceptions by specifying a try statement that includes one or more appropriate catch blocks. The try statement consists of reserved word `try` followed by a brace-delimited body. You place code that throws exceptions into this block.

A catch block consists of reserved word `catch`, followed by a round bracket-delimited single-parameter list that specifies an exception class name, followed by a brace-delimited body. You place code that handles exceptions whose types match the type of the catch block's parameter list's exception class parameter in this block.

A catch block is specified immediately after a try block. When an exception is thrown, the virtual machine will search for a handler. It first examines the catch block to see whether its parameter type matches or is the superclass type of the exception that has been thrown.

If the catch block is found, its body executes and the exception is handled. Otherwise, the virtual machine proceeds up the method-call stack, looking for the first method whose try statement contains an appropriate catch block. This process continues unless a catch block is found or execution leaves the `main()` method.

The following example illustrates try and catch:

```
try
{
   int x = 1 / 0;
}
catch (ArithmeticException ae)
{
   System.out.println("attempt to divide by zero");
}
```

When execution enters the try block, an attempt is made to divide integer 1 by integer 0. The virtual machine responds by instantiating `ArithmeticException` and throwing this exception. It then detects the catch block, which is capable of handling thrown `ArithmeticException` objects, and transfers execution to this block, which invokes `System.out.println()` to output a suitable message—the exception is handled.

Because `ArithmeticException` is an example of an unchecked exception type, and because unchecked exceptions represent coding mistakes that must be fixed, you typically don't catch them, as demonstrated previously. Instead, you would fix the problem that led to the thrown exception.

> **Tip**   You might want to name your catch block parameters using the abbreviated style shown in the preceding section. Not only does this convention result in more meaningful exception-oriented parameter names (ae indicates that an `ArithmeticException` has been thrown), it can help reduce compiler errors. For example, it is common practice to name a catch block's parameter e, for convenience. (Why type a long name?) However, the compiler will report an error when a previously declared local variable or parameter also uses e as its name—multiple same-named local variables and parameters cannot exist in the same scope.

Handling Multiple Exception Types

You can specify multiple catch blocks after a try block. For example, Listing 5-25's convert() method specifies a throws clause indicating that convert() can throw InvalidMediaFormatException, which is currently thrown, and IOException, which will be thrown when convert() is refactored. This refactoring will result in convert() throwing IOException when it cannot read from the source file or write to the destination file and throwing FileNotFoundException (a subclass of IOException) when it cannot open the source file or create the destination file. All these exceptions must be handled, as demonstrated in Listing 5-26.

Listing 5-26. Handling Different Kinds of Exceptions

```
import java.io.FileNotFoundException;
import java.io.IOException;

import media.InvalidMediaFormatException;
import media.Media;

public class Converter
{
   public static void main(String[] args)
   {
      if (args.length != 2)
      {
         System.err.println("usage: java Converter srcfile dstfile");
         return;
      }
      try
      {
         Media.convert(args[0], args[1]);
      }
      catch (InvalidMediaFormatException imfe)
      {
         System.out.println("Unable to convert " + args[0] + " to " + args[1]);
         System.out.println("Expecting " + args[0] + " to conform to " +
                            imfe.getExpectedFormat() + " format.");
         System.out.println("However, " + args[0] + " conformed to " +
                            imfe.getExistingFormat() + " format.");
      }
      catch (FileNotFoundException fnfe)
      {
      }
      catch (IOException ioe)
      {
      }
   }
}
```

The call to Media's convert() method in Listing 5-26 is placed in a try block because this method is capable of throwing an instance of the checked InvalidMediaFormatException, IOException, or FileNotFoundException class—checked exceptions must be handled or be declared to be thrown via a throws clause that is appended to the method.

The catch (InvalidMediaFormatException imfe) block's statements are designed to provide a descriptive error message to the user. A more sophisticated application would localize these names so that the user could read the message in the user's language. The developer-oriented detail message is not output because it is not necessary in this trivial application.

> **Note**   A developer-oriented detail message is typically not localized. Instead, it is expressed in the developer's language. Users should never see detail messages.

Although not thrown, a catch block for IOException is required because this checked exception type appears in convert()'s throws clause. Because the catch (IOException ioe) block can also handle thrown FileNotFoundException instances (because FileNotFoundException subclasses IOException), the catch (FileNotFoundException fnfe) block isn't necessary at this point but is present to separate out the handling of a situation where a file cannot be opened for reading or created for writing (which will be addressed once convert() is refactored to include file code).

Assuming that the current directory contains Listing 5-26 and a media subdirectory containing InvalidMediaFormatException.java and Media.java, compile this listing (javac Converter.java), which also compiles media's source files, and run the application, as in java Converter A B. Converter responds by presenting the following output:

```
Unable to convert A to B
Expecting A to conform to RM format.
However, A conformed to WAVE format.
```

Listing 5-26's empty FileNotFoundException and IOException catch blocks illustrate the often-seen problem of leaving catch blocks empty because they are inconvenient to code. Unless you have a good reason, don't create an empty catch block. It swallows exceptions and you don't know that the exceptions were thrown. (For brevity, I don't always code catch blocks in this book's examples.)

> **Caution**   The compiler reports an error when you specify two or more catch blocks with the same parameter type after a try body. Example: try {} catch (IOException ioe1) {} catch (IOException ioe2) {}. You must merge these catch blocks into one block.

Although you can write catch blocks in any order, the compiler restricts this order when one catch block's parameter is a supertype of another catch block's parameter. The subtype parameter catch block must precede the supertype parameter catch block; otherwise, the subtype parameter catch block will never be executed.

For example, the FileNotFoundException catch block must precede the IOException catch block. If the compiler allowed the IOException catch block to be specified first, the FileNotFoundException catch block would never execute because a FileNotFoundException instance is also an instance of its IOException superclass.

Rethrowing Exceptions

While discussing the Throwable class, I discussed wrapping lower-level exceptions in higher-level exceptions. This activity will typically take place in a catch block and is illustrated in the following example:

```
catch (IOException ioe)
{
   throw new ReportCreationException(ioe);
}
```

This example assumes that a helper method has just thrown a generic IOException instance as the result of trying to create a report. The public method's contract states that ReportCreationException is thrown in this case. To satisfy the contract, the latter exception is thrown. To satisfy the developer who is responsible for debugging a faulty application, the IOException instance is wrapped inside the ReportCreationException instance that is thrown to the public method's caller.

Sometimes, a catch block might not be able to fully handle an exception. Perhaps it needs access to information provided by some ancestor method in the method-call stack. However, the catch block might be able to partly handle the exception. In this case, it should partly handle the exception and then rethrow the exception so that a handler in an ancestor method can finish handling it. Another possibility is to log the exception (for later analysis), which is demonstrated in the following example:

```
catch (FileNotFoundException fnfe)
{
   logger.log(fnfe);
   throw fnfe; // Rethrow the exception here.
}
```

Performing Cleanup

In some situations, you might want to execute cleanup code before execution leaves a method following a thrown exception. For example, you might want to close a file that was opened, but could not be written, possibly because of insufficient disk space. Java provides the finally block for this situation.

The finally block consists of reserved word finally followed by a body, which provides the cleanup code. A finally block follows either a catch block or a try block. In the former case, the exception may be handled (and possibly rethrown) before finally executes. In the latter case, the exception is handled (and possibly rethrown) after finally executes.

Listing 5-27 demonstrates the first scenario in the context of a simulated file-copying application's main() method.

Listing 5-27. Cleaning Up by Closing Files After Handling a Thrown Exception

```java
import java.io.IOException;

public class Copy
{
   public static void main(String[] args)
   {
      if (args.length != 2)
      {
         System.err.println("usage: java Copy srcFile dstFile");
         return;
      }

      int fileHandleSrc = 0;
      int fileHandleDst = 1;
      try
      {
         fileHandleSrc = open(args[0]);
         fileHandleDst = create(args[1]);
         copy(fileHandleSrc, fileHandleDst);
      }
      catch (IOException ioe)
      {
         System.err.println("I/O error: " + ioe.getMessage());
         return;
      }
      finally
      {
         close(fileHandleSrc);
         close(fileHandleDst);
      }
   }

   static int open(String filename)
   {
      return 1; // Assume that filename is mapped to integer.
   }

   static int create(String filename)
   {
      return 2; // Assume that filename is mapped to integer.
   }

   static void close(int fileHandle)
   {
      System.out.println("closing file: " + fileHandle);
   }

   static void copy(int fileHandleSrc, int fileHandleDst) throws IOException
   {
      System.out.println("copying file " + fileHandleSrc + " to file " +
                          fileHandleDst);
```

```
      if (Math.random() < 0.5)
          throw new IOException("unable to copy file");
   }
}
```

Listing 5-27 presents a Copy application class that simulates the copying of bytes from a source file to a destination file. The try block invokes the open() method to open the source file and the create() method to create the destination file. Each method returns an integer-based *file handle* that uniquely identifies the file.

Next, this block calls the copy() method to perform the copy. After outputting a suitable message, copy() invokes the Math class's random() method (officially discussed in Chapter 7) to return a random number between 0 and 1. When this method returns a value less than 0.5, which simulates a problem (perhaps the disk is full), the IOException class is instantiated and this instance is thrown.

The virtual machine locates the catch block that follows the try block and causes its handler to execute, which outputs a message. Then, the code in the finally block that follows the catch block is allowed to execute. Its purpose is to close both files by invoking the close() method on the passed file handle.

Compile this source code (javac Copy.java) and run the application with two arbitrary arguments (java Copy x.txt x.bak). You should observe the following output when there is no problem:

```
copying file 1 to file 2
closing file: 1
closing file: 2
```

When something goes wrong, you should observe the following output:

```
copying file 1 to file 2
I/O error: unable to copy file
closing file: 1
closing file: 2
```

Whether or not an I/O error occurs, notice that the finally block is the final code to execute. The finally block executes even though the catch block ends with a return statement.

This example illustrates finally block execution after a thrown exception is handled. However, you might want to perform cleanup before the exception is handled. Listing 5-28 presents a variation of the Copy application that demonstrates this alternative.

Listing 5-28. Cleaning Up by Closing Files Before Handling a Thrown Exception

```
import java.io.IOException;

public class Copy
{
   public static void main(String[] args) throws IOException
   {
      if (args.length != 2)
      {
         System.err.println("usage: java Copy srcFile dstFile");
         return;
      }
```

```java
      int fileHandleSrc = 0;
      int fileHandleDst = 1;
      try
      {
         fileHandleSrc = open(args[0]);
         fileHandleDst = create(args[1]);
         copy(fileHandleSrc, fileHandleDst);
      }
      finally
      {
         close(fileHandleSrc);
         close(fileHandleDst);
      }
   }

   static int open(String filename)
   {
      return 1; // Assume that filename is mapped to integer.
   }

   static int create(String filename)
   {
      return 2; // Assume that filename is mapped to integer.
   }

   static void close(int fileHandle)
   {
      System.out.println("closing file: " + fileHandle);
   }

   static void copy(int fileHandleSrc, int fileHandleDst) throws IOException
   {
      System.out.println("copying file " + fileHandleSrc + " to file " +
                          fileHandleDst);
      if (Math.random() < 0.5)
         throw new IOException("unable to copy file");
   }
}
```

Listing 5-28 is nearly identical to Listing 5-27. The only difference is the throws clause appended to the main() method header and the removal of the catch block. When IOException is thrown, the finally block executes before execution leaves the main() method. This time, Java's default exception handler executes printStackTrace() and you observe output similar to the following:

```
copying file 1 to file 2
closing file: 1
closing file: 2
Exception in thread "main" java.io.IOException: unable to copy file
            at Copy.copy(Copy.java:48)
            at Copy.main(Copy.java:19)
```

EXERCISES

The following exercises are designed to test your understanding of Chapter 5's content:

1.   What is a nested class?

2.   Identify the four kinds of nested classes.

3.   Which nested classes are also known as inner classes?

4.   True or false: A static member class has an enclosing instance.

5.   How do you instantiate a nonstatic member class from beyond its enclosing class?

6.   When is it necessary to declare local variables and parameters final?

7.   True or false: An interface can be declared within a class or within another interface.

8.   Define package.

9.   How do you ensure that package names are unique?

10.   What is a package statement?

11.   True or false: You can specify multiple package statements in a source file.

12.   What is an import statement?

13.   How do you indicate that you want to import multiple types via a single import statement?

14.   During a runtime search, what happens when the virtual machine cannot find a classfile?

15.   How do you specify the user classpath to the virtual machine?

16.   Define constant interface.

17.   Why are constant interfaces used?

18.   Why are constant interfaces bad?

19.   What is a static import statement?

20.   How do you specify a static import statement?

21.   What is an exception?

22.   In what ways are objects superior to error codes for representing exceptions?

23.   What is a throwable?

24.   What does the `getCause()` method return?

25.   What is the difference between `Exception` and `Error`?

26.   What is a checked exception?

27.   What is a runtime exception?

28.   Under what circumstance would you introduce your own exception class?

29. True or false: You use a throw statement to identify exceptions that are thrown from a method by appending this statement to a method's header.

30. What is the purpose of a try statement, and what is the purpose of a catch block?

31. What is the purpose of a finally block?

32. A 2D graphics package supports two-dimensional drawing and transformations (rotation, scaling, translation, etc.). These transformations require a 3-by-3 *matrix* (a table). Declare a G2D class that encloses a private Matrix nonstatic member class. Instantiate Matrix within G2D's no argument constructor, and initialize the Matrix instance to the *identity matrix* (a matrix where all entries are 0 except for those on the upper-left to lower-right diagonal, which are 1).

33. Extend the logging package to support a null device in which messages are thrown away.

34. Modify the logging package so that Logger's connect() method throws CannotConnectException when it cannot connect to its logging destination, and the other two methods each throw NotConnectedException when connect() was not called or when it threw CannotConnectException.

35. Modify TestLogger to respond appropriately to thrown CannotConnectException and NotConnectedException objects.

Summary

Classes that are declared outside of any class are known as top-level classes. Java also supports nested classes, which are classes that are declared as members of other classes or scopes.

There are four kinds of nested classes: static member classes, nonstatic member classes, anonymous classes, and local classes. The latter three categories are known as inner classes.

Java supports the partitioning of top-level types into multiple namespaces, to better organize these types and to also prevent name conflicts. Java uses packages to accomplish these tasks.

The package statement identifies the package in which a source file's types are located. The import statement imports types from a package by telling the compiler where to look for unqualified type names during compilation.

An exception is a divergence from an application's normal behavior. Although it can be represented by an error code or object, Java uses objects because error codes are meaningless and cannot contain information about what led to the exception.

Java provides a hierarchy of classes that represent different kinds of exceptions. These classes are rooted in Throwable. Moving down the throwable hierarchy, you encounter the Exception and Error classes, which represent nonerror exceptions and errors.

Exception and its subclasses, except for RuntimeException (and its subclasses), describe checked exceptions. They are checked because you must check the code to ensure that an exception is handled where thrown or identified as being handled elsewhere.

RuntimeException and its subclasses describe unchecked exceptions. You don't have to handle these exceptions because they represent coding mistakes (fix the mistakes). Although the names of their classes can appear in throws clauses, doing so adds clutter.

The throw statement throws an exception to the virtual machine, which searches for an appropriate handler. When the exception is checked, its name must appear in the method's throws clause, unless the name of the exception's superclass is listed in this clause.

A method handles one or more exceptions by specifying a try statement and appropriate catch blocks. A finally block can be included to execute cleanup code whether an exception is thrown or not and before a thrown exception leaves the method.

Chapter 6 continues to explore the Java language by focusing on assertions, annotations, generics, and enums.

Mastering Advanced Language Features Part 2

In Chapters 2 through 4 I laid a foundation for learning the Java language and in Chapter 5 built onto this foundation by introducing some of Java's more advanced language features. In Chapter 6 I continue to cover advanced language features by focusing on those features related to assertions, annotations, generics, and enums.

Mastering Assertions

Writing source code is not an easy task. All too often, bugs are introduced into the code. When a bug is not discovered before compiling the source code, it makes it into runtime code, which will probably fail unexpectedly (or show no sign of failure but give wrong output). At this point, the cause of failure can be very difficult to determine.

Developers often make assumptions about application correctness, and some developers think that specifying comments that state their beliefs about what they think is true at the comment locations is sufficient for determining correctness. However, comments are useless for preventing bugs because the compiler ignores them.

Many languages address this problem by providing a language feature called *assertions* that lets the developer codify assumptions about application correctness. When the application runs, and if an assertion fails, the application terminates with a message that helps the developer diagnose the failure's cause. (You might think of assertions as comments that the compiler understands.)

> **Note**   In his "Assert Statements Shine Light Into Dark Corners" blog post
> (www.drdobbs.com/cpp/assert-statements-shine-light-into-dark/240012746), computer
> scientist Andrew Koenig mentions that assertions are used to detect invariant failures, where an *invariant* is
> something in your code that should not change. For example, you might want to verify the expectation that a list
> of data items is sorted (an invariant) before attempting to search that list via the Binary Search algorithm, which
> requires that the list be sorted. You would use an assertion to learn whether the invariant holds or not.

In this section I introduce you to Java's assertions language feature. After defining this term, showing you how to declare assertions, and providing examples, I look at using and avoiding assertions. Finally, you learn how to selectively enable and disable assertions via the `javac` compiler tool's command-line arguments.

Declaring Assertions

An *assertion* is a statement that lets you express an assumption of program correctness via a Boolean expression. If this expression evaluates to true, execution continues with the next statement. Otherwise, an error that identifies the cause of failure is thrown.

There are two forms of the assertion statement, with each form beginning with reserved word assert:

```
assert expression1 ;
assert expression1 : expression2 ;
```

In both forms of this statement, `expression1` is the Boolean expression. In the second form, `expression2` is any expression that returns a value. It cannot be a call to a method whose return type is void.

When `expression1` evaluates to false, this statement instantiates class `java.lang.AssertionError`. The first statement form calls this class's noargument constructor, which doesn't associate a message identifying failure details with the `AssertionError` instance. The second form calls an `AssertionError` constructor whose type matches the type of `expression2`'s value. This value is passed to the constructor and its string representation is used as the error's detail message.

When the error is thrown, the name of the source file and the number of the line from where the error was thrown are output to the console as part of the thrown error's stack trace. In many situations, this information is sufficient for identifying what led to the failure, and the first form of the assertion statement should be used.

Listing 6-1 demonstrates the first form of the assertion statement.

Listing 6-1. Throwing an Assertion Error Without a Detail Message

```
public class AssertionDemo
{
   public static void main(String[] args)
   {
      int x = 1;
      assert x == 0;
   }
}
```

When assertions are enabled (I discuss this task later), running the previous application results in the following output:

```
Exception in thread "main" java.lang.AssertionError
        at AssertionDemo.main(AssertionDemo.java:6)
```

In other situations, more information is needed to help diagnose the cause of failure. For example, suppose expression1 compares variables x and y and throws an error when x's value exceeds y's value. Because this should never happen, you would probably use the second statement form to output these values so you could diagnose the problem.

Listing 6-2 demonstrates the second form of the assertion statement.

Listing 6-2. Throwing an Assertion Error with a Detail Message

```
public class AssertionDemo
{
   public static void main(String[] args)
   {
      int x = 1;
      assert x == 0: x;
   }
}
```

Once again, it is assumed that assertions are enabled. Running the previous application results in the following output:

```
Exception in thread "main" java.lang.AssertionError: 1
        at AssertionDemo.main(AssertionDemo.java:6)
```

The value in x is appended to the end of the first output line, which is somewhat cryptic. To make this output more meaningful, you might want to specify an expression that also includes the variable's name: assert x == 0: "x = " + x;, for example.

Using Assertions

There are many situations where assertions should be used. These situations organize into internal invariant, control-flow invariant, and design-by-contract categories. An *invariant* is something in your code that should not change.

Internal Invariants

An *internal invariant* is expression-oriented behavior that is not expected to change. For example, Listing 6-3 introduces an internal invariant by way of chained if-else statements that output the state of water based on its temperature.

Listing 6-3. Discovering That an Internal Invariant Can Vary

```java
public class IIDemo
{
   public static void main(String[] args)
   {
      double temperature = 50.0; // Celsius
      if (temperature < 0.0)
         System.out.println("water has solidified");
      else
      if (temperature >= 100.0)
         System.out.println("water is boiling into a gas");
      else
      {
         // temperature > 0.0 and temperature < 100.0
         assert(temperature > 0.0 && temperature < 100.0): temperature;
         System.out.println("water is remaining in its liquid state");
      }
   }
}
```

A developer might specify only a comment stating an assumption as to what expression causes the final else to be reached. Because the comment might not be enough to detect the lurking < 0.0 expression bug (water is also solid at zero degrees), an assertion statement is necessary.

Another example of an internal invariant concerns a switch statement with no default case. The default case is avoided because the developer believes that all paths have been covered. However, this is not always true, as Listing 6-4 demonstrates.

Listing 6-4. Another Buggy Internal Invariant

```java
public class IIDemo
{
   final static int NORTH = 0;
   final static int SOUTH = 1;
   final static int EAST = 2;
   final static int WEST = 3;

   public static void main(String[] args)
   {
      int direction = (int) (Math.random() * 5);
      switch (direction)
      {
         case NORTH: System.out.println("travelling north"); break;
         case SOUTH: System.out.println("travelling south"); break;
         case EAST : System.out.println("travelling east"); break;
```

```
         case WEST : System.out.println("travelling west"); break;
         default   : assert false;
      }
   }
}
```

Listing 6-4 assumes that the expression tested by switch will only evaluate to one of four integer constants. However, (int) (Math.random() * 5) can also return 4, causing the default case to execute assert false;, which always throws AssertionError. (You might have to run this application a few times to see the assertion error, but first you need to learn how to enable assertions, which I discuss later in this chapter.)

> **Tip**   When assertions are disabled, assert false; doesn't execute and the bug goes undetected. To always detect this bug, replace assert false; with throw new AssertionError(direction);.

Control-Flow Invariants

A *control-flow invariant* is a flow of control that is not expected to change. For example, Listing 6-4 uses an assertion to test an assumption that switch's default case will not execute. Listing 6-5, which fixes Listing 6-4's bug, provides another example.

Listing 6-5. A Buggy Control-Flow Invariant

```
public class CFDemo
{
   final static int NORTH = 0;
   final static int SOUTH = 1;
   final static int EAST = 2;
   final static int WEST = 3;

   public static void main(String[] args)
   {
      int direction = (int) (Math.random() * 4);
      switch (direction)
      {
         case NORTH: System.out.println("travelling north"); break;
         case SOUTH: System.out.println("travelling south"); break;
         case EAST : System.out.println("travelling east"); break;
         case WEST : System.out.println("travelling west");
         default   : assert false;
      }
   }
}
```

Because the original bug has been fixed, the default case should never be reached. However, the omission of a break statement that terminates case WEST causes execution to reach the default case. This control-flow invariant has been broken. (Again, you might have to run this application a few times to see the assertion error, but first you need to learn how to enable assertions, which I discuss later in this chapter.)

> **Caution**   Be careful when using an assertion statement to detect code that should never be executed. If the assertion statement cannot be reached according to the rules set forth in *The Java Language Specification, Third Edition*, by James Gosling, Bill Joy, Guy Steele, and Gilad Bracha (Addison-Wesley, 2005; ISBN: 0321246780; also available at http://docs.oracle.com/javase/specs/), the compiler will report an error. For example, for (;;); assert false; causes the compiler to report an error because the infinite for loop prevents the assertion statement from executing.

Design-by-Contract

Design-by-Contract (http://en.wikipedia.org/wiki/Design_by_contract) is a way to design software based on preconditions, postconditions, and class invariants. Assertion statements support an informal design-by-contract style of development.

Preconditions

A *precondition* is something that must be true when a method is called. Assertion statements are often used to satisfy a helper method's preconditions by checking that its arguments are legal. Listing 6-6 provides an example.

Listing 6-6. Verifying a Precondition

```
public class Lotto649
{
   public static void main(String[] args)
   {
      // Lotto 649 requires that six unique numbers be chosen.
      int[] selectedNumbers = new int[6];
      // Assign a unique random number from 1 to 49 (inclusive) to each slot
      // in the selectedNumbers array.
      for (int slot = 0; slot < selectedNumbers.length; slot++)
      {
         int num;
         // Obtain a random number from 1 to 49. That number becomes the
         // selected number if it has not previously been chosen.
         try_again:
         do
         {
            num = rnd(49) + 1;
            for (int i = 0; i < slot; i++)
               if (selectedNumbers[i] == num)
                  continue try_again;
            break;
         }
         while (true);
         // Assign selected number to appropriate slot.
         selectedNumbers[slot] = num;
      }
```

```
        // Sort all selected numbers into ascending order and then print these
        // numbers.
        sort(selectedNumbers);
        for (int i = 0; i < selectedNumbers.length; i++)
            System.out.print(selectedNumbers[i] + " ");
    }

    static int rnd(int limit)
    {
        // This method returns a random number (actually, a pseudorandom number)
        // ranging from 0 through limit - 1 (inclusive).
        assert limit > 1: "limit = " + limit;
        return (int) (Math.random() * limit);
    }

    static void sort(int[] x)
    {
        // This method sorts the integers in the passed array into ascending
        // order.
        for (int pass = 0; pass < x.length - 1; pass++)
            for (int i = x.length - 1; i > pass; i--)
                if (x[i] < x[pass])
                {
                    int temp = x[i];
                    x[i] = x[pass];
                    x[pass] = temp;
                }
    }
}
```

Listing 6-6's application simulates Lotto 6/49, one of Canada's national lottery games. The rnd() helper method returns a randomly chosen integer between 0 and limit - 1. An assertion statement verifies the precondition that limit's value must be 2 or higher.

Note   The sort() helper method *sorts* (orders) the selectedNumbers array's integers into ascending order by implementing an *algorithm* (a recipe for accomplishing some task) called Bubble Sort.

Bubble Sort works by making multiple passes over the array. During each pass, various comparisons and swaps ensure that the next smallest element value "bubbles" toward the top of the array, which would be the element at index 0.

Bubble Sort is not efficient but is more than adequate for sorting a six-element array. Although I could have used one of the efficient sort() methods located in the java.util package's Arrays class (e.g., Arrays.sort(selectedNumbers); accomplishes the same objective as Listing 6-6's sort(selectedNumbers); method call, but does so more efficiently), I chose to use Bubble Sort because I prefer to wait until Chapter 9 before getting into the Arrays class.

Postconditions

A *postcondition* is something that must be true after a method successfully completes. Assertion statements are often used to satisfy a helper method's postconditions by checking that its result is legal. Listing 6-7 provides an example.

Listing 6-7. Verifying a Postcondition in Addition to Preconditions

```java
public class MergeArrays
{
   public static void main(String[] args)
   {
      int[] x = { 1, 2, 3, 4, 5 };
      int[] y = { 1, 2, 7, 9 };
      int[] result = merge(x, y);
      for (int i = 0; i < result.length; i++)
         System.out.println(result[i]);
   }

   static int[] merge(int[] a, int[] b)
   {
      if (a == null)
         throw new NullPointerException("a is null");
      if (b == null)
         throw new NullPointerException("b is null");
      int[] result = new int[a.length + b.length];
      // Precondition
      assert result.length == a.length + b.length: "length mismatch";
      for (int i = 0; i < a.length; i++)
         result[i] = a[i];
      for (int i = 0; i < b.length; i++)
         result[a.length + i - 1] = b[i];
      // Postcondition
      assert containsAll(result, a, b): "value missing from array";
      return result;
   }

   static boolean containsAll(int[] result, int[] a, int[] b)
   {
      for (int i = 0; i < a.length; i++)
         if (!contains(result, a[i]))
            return false;
      for (int i = 0; i < b.length; i++)
         if (!contains(result, b[i]))
            return false;
      return true;
   }
```

```
   static boolean contains(int[] a, int val)
   {
      for (int i = 0; i < a.length; i++)
         if (a[i] == val)
            return true;
      return false;
   }
}
```

Listing 6-7 uses an assertion statement to verify the postcondition that all of the values in the two arrays being merged are present in the merged array. The postcondition is not satisfied, however, because this listing contains a bug.

Listing 6-7 also shows preconditions and postconditions being used together. The solitary precondition verifies that the merged array length equals the lengths of the arrays being merged prior to the merge logic.

Class Invariants

A *class invariant* is a kind of internal invariant that applies to every instance of a class at all times, except when an instance is transitioning from one consistent state to another.

For example, suppose instances of a class contain arrays whose values are sorted in ascending order. You might want to include an isSorted() method in the class that returns true when the array is still sorted and verify that each constructor and method that modifies the array specifies assert isSorted(); prior to exit, to satisfy the assumption that the array is still sorted when the constructor or method exits.

Avoiding Assertions

Although there are many situations where assertions should be used, there also are situations where they should be avoided. For example, you should not use assertions to check the arguments that are passed to public methods for the following reasons:

- Checking a public method's arguments is part of the contract that exists between the method and its caller. If you use assertions to check these arguments, and if assertions are disabled, this contract is violated because the arguments will not be checked.

- Assertions also prevent appropriate exceptions from being thrown. For example, when an illegal argument is passed to a public method, it is common to throw java.lang.IllegalArgumentException or java.lang.NullPointerException. However, AssertionError is thrown instead.

You should also avoid using assertions to perform work required by the application to function correctly. This work is often performed as a side effect of the assertion's Boolean expression. When assertions are disabled, the work is not performed.

For example, suppose you have a list of Employee objects and a few null references that are also stored in this list and you want to remove all of the null references. It would not be correct to remove these references via the following assertion statement:

```
assert employees.removeAll(null);
```

Although the assertion statement will not throw AssertionError because there is at least one null reference in the employees list, the application that depends on this statement executing will fail when assertions are disabled.

Instead of depending on the former code to remove the null references, you would be better off using code similar to the following:

```
boolean allNullsRemoved = employees.removeAll(null);
assert allNullsRemoved;
```

This time, all null references are removed regardless of whether assertions are enabled or disabled and you can still specify an assertion to verify that nulls were removed.

Enabling and Disabling Assertions

The compiler records assertions in the classfile. However, assertions are disabled at runtime because they can affect performance. An assertion might call a method that takes awhile to complete, and this would impact the running application's performance.

You must enable the classfile's assertions before you can test assumptions about the behaviors of your classes. Accomplish this task by specifying the -enableassertions or -ea command-line option when running the java application launcher tool.

The -enableassertions and -ea command-line options let you enable assertions at various granularities based on one of the following arguments (except for the noargument scenario, you must use a colon to separate the option from its argument):

- *No argument*: Assertions are enabled in all classes except system classes.

- *PackageName*. . . : Assertions are enabled in the specified package and its subpackages by specifying the package name followed by. . . .

- . . . : Assertions are enabled in the unnamed package, which happens to be whatever directory is current.

- *ClassName*: Assertions are enabled in the named class by specifying the class name.

For example, you can enable all assertions except system assertions when running the MergeArrays application via java –ea MergeArrays. Also, you could enable any assertions that you might add to Chapter 5's logging package by specifying java -ea:logging TestLogger.

Assertions can be disabled, and also at various granularities, by specifying either of the -disableassertions or –da command-line options. These options take the same arguments as -enableassertions and -ea. For example, java -ea –da:loneclass mainclass enables all assertions except for those in loneclass. (Think of loneclass and mainclass as placeholders for the actual classes that you specify.)

The previous options apply to all classloaders. Except when taking no arguments, they also apply to system classes. This exception simplifies the enabling of assertion statements in all classes except for system classes, which is often desirable.

To enable system assertions, specify either -enablesystemassertions or -esa, for example, java -esa –ea:logging TestLogger. Specify either -disablesystemassertions or -dsa to disable system assertions.

Mastering Annotations

While developing a Java application, you might want to *annotate* (associate *metadata* [data that describes other data] with) various application elements. For example, you might want to identify methods that are not fully implemented so that you will not forget to implement them. Java's annotations language feature lets you accomplish this task.

In this section I introduce you to annotations. After defining this term and presenting three kinds of compiler-supported annotations as examples, I show you how to declare your own annotation types and use these types to annotate source code. Finally, you discover how to process your own annotations to accomplish useful tasks.

> **Note**   Java has always supported ad hoc annotation mechanisms. For example, the java.lang.Cloneable interface identifies classes whose instances can be shallowly cloned via java.lang.Object's clone() method; the transient reserved word marks fields that are to be ignored during serialization, and the @deprecated Javadoc tag documents methods that are no longer supported. In contrast, the annotations feature is a standard for annotating code.

Discovering Annotations

An *annotation* is an instance of an annotation type and associates metadata with an application element. It is expressed in source code by prefixing the type name with the @ symbol. For example, @Readonly is an annotation and Readonly is its type.

> **Note**   You can use annotations to associate metadata with constructors, fields, local variables, methods, packages, parameters, and types (annotation, class, enum, and interface).

The compiler supports the Override, Deprecated, and SuppressWarnings annotation types. These types are located in the java.lang package.

@Override annotations are useful for expressing that a subclass method overrides a method in the superclass and doesn't overload that method instead. The following example reveals this annotation being used to prefix the overriding method:

```
@Override
public void draw(int color)
{
   // drawing code
}
```

@Deprecated annotations are useful for indicating that the marked application element is *deprecated* (phased out) and should no longer be used. The compiler warns you when a deprecated application element is accessed by nondeprecated code.

In contrast, the @deprecated javadoc tag and associated text warns you against using the deprecated item and tells you what to use instead. The following example demonstrates that @Deprecated and @deprecated can be used together:

```
/**
 * Allocates a <code>Date</code> object and initializes it so that
 * it represents midnight, local time, at the beginning of the day
 * specified by the <code>year</code>, <code>month</code>, and
 * <code>date</code> arguments.
 *
 * @param    year     the year minus 1900.
 * @param    month    the month between 0-11.
 * @param    date     the day of the month between 1-31.
 * @see      java.util.Calendar
 * @deprecated As of JDK version 1.1,
 * replaced by <code>Calendar.set(year + 1900, month, date)</code>
 * or <code>GregorianCalendar(year + 1900, month, date)</code>.
 */
@Deprecated
public Date(int year, int month, int date)
{
    this(year, month, date, 0, 0, 0);
}
```

This example excerpts one of the constructors in Java's Date class (located in the java.util package). Its Javadoc comment reveals that Date(int year, int month, int date) has been deprecated in favor of using the set() method in the Calendar class (also located in the java.util package. I explore Date in Chapter 10.)

The compiler suppresses warnings when a compilation unit (typically a class or interface) refers to a deprecated class, method, or field. This feature lets you modify legacy APIs without generating deprecation warnings and is demonstrated in Listing 6-8.

Listing 6-8. Referencing a Deprecated Field from Within the Same Class Declaration

```
public class Employee
{
   /**
    * Employee's name
    * @deprecated New version uses firstName and lastName fields.
    */
   @Deprecated
   String name;
   String firstName;
   String lastName;

   public static void main(String[] args)
   {
      Employee emp = new Employee();
      emp.name = "John Doe";
   }
}
```

Listing 6-8 declares an Employee class with a name field that has been deprecated. Although Employee's main() method refers to name, the compiler will suppress a deprecation warning because the deprecation and reference occur in the same class.

Suppose you refactor this listing by introducing a new UseEmployee class and moving Employee's main() method to this class. Listing 6-9 presents the resulting class structure.

Listing 6-9. Referencing a Deprecated Field from Within Another Class Declaration

```
class Employee
{
   /**
    * Employee's name
    * @deprecated New version uses firstName and lastName fields.
    */
   @Deprecated
   String name;
   String firstName;
   String lastName;
}

public class UseEmployee
{
   public static void main(String[] args)
   {
      Employee emp = new Employee();
      emp.name = "John Doe";
   }
}
```

If you attempt to compile this source code via the javac compiler tool, you will discover the following messages:

```
Note: UseEmployee.java uses or overrides a deprecated API.
Note: Recompile with -Xlint:deprecation for details.
```

You will need to specify -Xlint:deprecation as one of javac's command-line arguments (as in javac -Xlint:deprecation UseEmployee.java) to discover the deprecated item and the code that refers to this item:

```
Employee.java:18: warning: [deprecation] name in Employee has been deprecated
      emp.name = "John Doe";
         ^
1 warning
```

@SuppressWarnings annotations are useful for suppressing deprecation or unchecked warnings via a "deprecation" or an "unchecked" argument. (Unchecked warnings occur when mixing code that uses generics with pre-generics legacy code. I discuss generics and unchecked warnings later in this chapter.)

For example, Listing 6-10 uses @SuppressWarnings with a "deprecation" argument to suppress the compiler's deprecation warnings when code within the UseEmployee class's main() method accesses the Employee class's name field.

Listing 6-10. Suppressing the Previous Deprecation Warning

```
public class UseEmployee
{
   @SuppressWarnings("deprecation")
   public static void main(String[] args)
   {
      Employee emp = new Employee();
      emp.name = "John Doe";
   }
}
```

> **Note**   As a matter of style, you should always specify @SuppressWarnings on the most deeply nested element where it is effective. For example, if you want to suppress a warning in a particular method, you should annotate that method rather than its class.

Declaring Annotation Types and Annotating Source Code

Before you can annotate source code, you need annotation types that can be instantiated. Java supplies many annotation types in addition to Override, Deprecated, and SuppressWarnings. Java also lets you declare your own types.

You declare an annotation type by specifying the @ symbol, immediately followed by reserved word interface, followed by the type's name, followed by a body. For example, Listing 6-11 uses @interface to declare an annotation type named Stub.

Listing 6-11. Declaring the Stub Annotation Type

```
public @interface Stub
{
}
```

Instances of annotation types that supply no data apart from a name—their bodies are empty—are known as *marker annotations* because they mark application elements for some purpose. As Listing 6-12 reveals, @Stub is used to mark empty methods (stubs).

Listing 6-12. Annotating a Stubbed-Out Method

```
public class Deck // Describes a deck of cards.
{
   @Stub
   public void shuffle()
   {
      // This method is empty and will presumably be filled in with appropriate
      // code at some later date.
   }
}
```

Listing 6-12's Deck class declares an empty shuffle() method. This fact is indicated by instantiating Stub and prefixing shuffle()'s method header with the resulting @Stub annotation.

> **Note**   Although marker interfaces (introduced in Chapter 4) appear to have been replaced by marker annotations, this is not the case because marker interfaces have advantages over marker annotations. One advantage is that a marker interface specifies a type that is implemented by a marked class, which lets you catch problems at compile time. For example, when a class doesn't implement the Cloneable interface, its instances cannot be shallowly cloned via Object's clone() method. If Cloneable had been implemented as a marker annotation, this problem would not be detected until runtime.

Although marker annotations are useful (@Override and @Deprecated are good examples), you will typically want to enhance an annotation type so that you can store metadata via its instances. You accomplish this task by adding elements to the type.

An *element* is a method header that appears in the annotation type's body. It cannot have parameters or a throws clause, and its return type must be a primitive type (such as int), java.lang.String, java.lang.Class, an enum, an annotation type, or an array of the preceding types. However, it can have a default value.

Listing 6-13 adds three elements to Stub.

Listing 6-13. Adding Three Elements to the Stub Annotation Type

```
public @interface Stub
{
    int id(); // A semicolon must terminate an element declaration.
    String dueDate();
    String developer() default "unassigned";
}
```

The id() element specifies a 32-bit integer that identifies the stub. The dueDate() element specifies a String-based date that identifies when the method stub is to be implemented. Finally, developer() specifies the String-based name of the developer responsible for coding the method stub.

Unlike id() and dueDate(), developer() is declared with a default value, "unassigned". When you instantiate Stub and don't assign a value to developer() in that instance, as is the case with Listing 6-14, this default value is assigned to developer().

Listing 6-14. Initializing a Stub Instance's Elements

```
public class Deck
{
    @Stub
    (
        id = 1,
        dueDate = "12/21/2012"
    )
    public void shuffle()
    {
    }
}
```

Listing 6-14 reveals one @Stub annotation that initializes its id() element to 1 and its dueDate() element to "12/21/2012". Each element name doesn't have a trailing (), and the comma-separated list of two element initializers appears between (and).

Suppose you decide to replace Stub's id(), dueDate(), and developer() elements with a single String value() element whose string specifies comma-separated ID, due date, and developer name values. Listing 6-15 shows you two ways to initialize value.

Listing 6-15. Initializing Each Stub Instance's value() Element

```
public class Deck
{
    @Stub(value = "1,12/21/2012,unassigned")
    public void shuffle()
    {
    }

    @Stub("2,12/21/2012,unassigned")
    public Card[] deal(int ncards)
    {
        return null;
    }
}
```

Listing 6-15 reveals special treatment for the value() element. When it's an annotation type's only element, you can omit value()'s name and = from the initializer. I used this fact to specify @SuppressWarnings("deprecation") in Listing 6-10.

Using Meta-Annotations in Annotation Type Declarations

Each of the Override, Deprecated, and SuppressWarnings annotation types is itself annotated with *meta-annotations* (annotations that annotate annotation types). For example, Listing 6-16 shows you that the SuppressWarnings annotation type is annotated with two meta-annotations.

Listing 6-16. The Annotated SuppressWarnings Type Declaration

```
@Target(value={TYPE,FIELD,METHOD,PARAMETER,CONSTRUCTOR,LOCAL_VARIABLE})
@Retention(value=SOURCE)
public @interface SuppressWarnings
```

The Target annotation type, which is located in the java.lang.annotation package, identifies the kinds of application elements to which an annotation type applies. @Target indicates that @SuppressWarnings annotations can be used to annotate types, fields, methods, parameters, constructors, and local variables.

Each of TYPE, FIELD, METHOD, PARAMETER, CONSTRUCTOR, and LOCAL_VARIABLE is a member of the ElementType enum, which is also located in the java.lang.annotation package. (I discuss enums later in this chapter.)

The { and } characters surrounding the comma-separated list of values assigned to Target's value() element signify an array—value()'s return type is String[]. Although these braces are necessary (unless the array consists of one item), value= could be omitted when initializing @Target because Target declares only a value() element.

The Retention annotation type, which is located in the java.lang.annotation package, identifies the retention (also known as lifetime) of an annotation type's annotations. @Retention indicates that @SuppressWarnings annotations have a lifetime that is limited to source code—they don't exist after compilation.

SOURCE is one of the members of the RetentionPolicy enum (located in the java.lang.annotation package). The other members are CLASS and RUNTIME. These three members specify the following retention policies:

- CLASS: The compiler records annotations in the classfile, but the virtual machine doesn't retain them (to save memory space). This policy is the default.

- RUNTIME: The compiler records annotations in the classfile, and the virtual machine retains them so that they can be read via the Reflection API at runtime.

- SOURCE: The compiler discards annotations after using them.

There are two problems with the Stub annotation type shown in Listings 6-11 and 6-13. First, the lack of an @Target meta-annotation means that you can annotate any application element @Stub. However, this annotation only makes sense when applied to methods and constructors. Check out Listing 6-17.

Listing 6-17. Annotating Undesirable Application Elements

```
@Stub("1,12/21/2012,unassigned")
public class Deck
{
   @Stub("2,12/21/2012,unassigned")
   private Card[] cardsRemaining = new Card[52];

   @Stub("3,12/21/2012,unassigned")
   public Deck()
   {
   }

   @Stub("4,12/21/2012,unassigned")
   public void shuffle()
   {
   }

   @Stub("5,12/21/2012,unassigned")
   public Card[] deal(@Stub("5,12/21/2012,unassigned") int ncards)
   {
      return null;
   }
}
```

Listing 6-17 uses @Stub to annotate the Deck class, the cardsRemaining field, and the ncards parameter as well as annotating the constructor and the two methods. The first three application elements are inappropriate to annotate because they are not stubs.

You can fix this problem by prefixing the Stub annotation type declaration with @Target({ElementType.METHOD, ElementType.CONSTRUCTOR}) so that Stub only applies to methods and constructors. After doing this, the javac compiler tool will output the following error messages when you attempt to compile Listing 6-17:

```
Deck.java:1: error: annotation type not applicable to this kind of declaration
@Stub("1,12/21/2012,unassigned")
^
Deck.java:4: error: annotation type not applicable to this kind of declaration
   @Stub("2,12/21/2012,unassigned")
   ^
Deck.java:18: error: annotation type not applicable to this kind of declaration
   public Card[] deal(@Stub("5,12/21/2012,unassigned") int ncards)
                      ^
3 errors
```

The second problem is that the default CLASS retention policy makes it impossible to process @Stub annotations at runtime. You can fix this problem by prefixing the Stub type declaration with @Retention(RetentionPolicy.RUNTIME).

Listing 6-18 presents the Stub annotation type with the desired @Target and @Retention meta-annotations.

Listing 6-18. A Revamped Stub Annotation Type

```java
import java.lang.annotation.ElementType;
import java.lang.annotation.Retention;
import java.lang.annotation.RetentionPolicy;
import java.lang.annotation.Target;

@Target({ElementType.METHOD, ElementType.CONSTRUCTOR})
@Retention(RetentionPolicy.RUNTIME)
public @interface Stub
{
   String value();
}
```

> **Note**   Java also provides Documented and Inherited meta-annotation types in the `java.lang.annotation` package. Instances of @Documented-annotated annotation types are to be documented by `javadoc` and similar tools, whereas instances of `@Inherited`-annotated annotation types are automatically inherited. According to `Inherited`'s Java documentation, if "the user queries the annotation type on a class declaration, and the class declaration has no annotation for this type, then the class's superclass will automatically be queried for the annotation type. This process will be repeated until an annotation for this type is found, or the top of the class hierarchy (`Object`) is reached. If no superclass has an annotation for this type, then the query will indicate that the class in question has no such annotation."

Processing Annotations

It's not enough to declare an annotation type and use that type to annotate source code. Unless you do something specific with those annotations, they remain dormant. One way to accomplish something specific is to write an application that processes the annotations. Listing 6-19's StubFinder application does just that.

Listing 6-19. The StubFinder Application

```java
import java.lang.reflect.Method;

public class StubFinder
{
   public static void main(String[] args) throws Exception
   {
      if (args.length != 1)
      {
         System.err.println("usage: java StubFinder classfile");
         return;
      }
      Method[] methods = Class.forName(args[0]).getMethods();
      for (int i = 0; i < methods.length; i++)
```

```
        if (methods[i].isAnnotationPresent(Stub.class))
        {
            Stub stub = methods[i].getAnnotation(Stub.class);
            String[] components = stub.value().split(",");
            System.out.println("Stub ID = " + components[0]);
            System.out.println("Stub Date = " + components[1]);
            System.out.println("Stub Developer = " + components[2]);
            System.out.println();
        }
    }
}
```

StubFinder loads a classfile whose name is specified as a command-line argument and outputs the metadata associated with each @Stub annotation that precedes each public method header. These annotations are instances of Listing 6-18's Stub annotation type.

StubFinder next uses a special class named Class and its forName() class method to load a classfile. Class also provides a getMethods() method that returns an array of java.lang.reflect.Method objects describing the loaded class's public methods.

For each loop iteration, a Method object's isAnnotationPresent() method is called to determine if the method is annotated with the annotation described by the Stub class (referred to as Stub.class).

If isAnnotationPresent() returns true, Method's getAnnotation() method is called to return the annotation Stub instance. This instance's value() method is called to retrieve the string stored in the annotation.

Next, String's split() method is called to split the string's comma-separated list of ID, date, and developer values into an array of String objects. Each object is then output along with descriptive text. (You will be formally introduced to split() in Chapter 7.)

Class's forName() method is capable of throwing various exceptions that must be handled or explicitly declared as part of a method's header. For simplicity, I chose to append a throws Exception clause to the main() method's header.

> **Caution**   There are two problems with throws Exception. First, it is often better to handle the exception and present a suitable error message than to "pass the buck" by throwing it out of main(). Second, Exception is generic—it hides the names of the kinds of exceptions that are thrown. However, I find it convenient to specify throws Exception in a throwaway utility.

After compiling StubFinder (javac StubFinder.java), Stub (javac Stub.java), and Listing 6-15's Deck class (javac Deck.java), run StubFinder with Deck as its single command-line argument (java StubFinder Deck). You will observe the following output:

```
Stub ID = 1
Stub Date = 12/21/2012
Stub Developer = unassigned
```

```
Stub ID = 2
Stub Date = 12/21/2012
Stub Developer = unassigned
```

Mastering Generics

Java 5 introduced *generics*, language features for declaring and using type-agnostic classes and interfaces. While working with Java's Collections Framework (which I introduce in Chapter 9), these features help you avoid `java.lang.ClassCastExceptions`.

> **Note**   Although the main use for generics is the Collections Framework, the standard class library also contains *generified* (retrofitted to make use of generics) classes that have nothing to do with this framework: `java.lang.Class`, `java.lang.ThreadLocal`, and `java.lang.ref.WeakReference` are three examples.

In this section I introduce you to generics. You first learn how generics promote type safety in the context of the Collections Framework classes, and then you explore generics in the contexts of generic types and generic methods. Finally, you learn about generics in the context of arrays.

Collections and the Need for Type Safety

Java's Collections Framework makes it possible to store objects in various kinds of containers (known as collections) and later retrieve those objects. For example, you can store objects in a list, a set, or a map. You can then retrieve a single object, or iterate over the collection and retrieve all objects.

Before Java 5 overhauled the Collections Framework to take advantage of generics, there was no way to prevent a collection from containing objects of mixed types. The compiler didn't check an object's type to see if it was suitable before it was added to a collection, and this lack of static type checking led to `ClassCastExceptions`.

Listing 6-20 demonstrates how easy it is to generate a `ClassCastException`.

Listing 6-20. Lack of Type Safety Leading to a ClassCastException at Runtime

```java
import java.util.ArrayList;
import java.util.Iterator;
import java.util.List;

class Employee
{
   private String name;

   Employee(String name)
   {
      this.name = name;
   }
}
```

```
    String getName()
    {
        return name;
    }
}

public class TypeSafety
{
    public static void main(String[] args)
    {
        List employees = new ArrayList();
        employees.add(new Employee("John Doe"));
        employees.add(new Employee("Jane Smith"));
        employees.add("Jack Frost");
        Iterator iter = employees.iterator();
        while (iter.hasNext())
        {
            Employee emp = (Employee) iter.next();
            System.out.println(emp.getName());
        }
    }
}
```

Listing 6-20's main() method first instantiates java.util.ArrayList and then uses this list collection object's reference to add a pair of Employee objects to the list. It then adds a String object, which violates the implied contract that ArrayList is supposed to store only Employee objects.

main() next obtains a java.util.Iterator instance for iterating over the list of Employees. As long as Iterator's hasNext() method returns true, its next() method is called to return an object stored in the array list.

The Object that next() returns must be downcast to Employee so that the Employee object's getName() method can be called to return the employee's name. The string that this method returns is then output to the standard output device via System.out.println().

The (Employee) cast checks the type of each object returned by next() to make sure that it is an Employee. Although this is true of the first two objects, it's not true of the third object. The attempt to cast "Jack Frost" to Employee results in a ClassCastException.

The ClassCastException occurs because of an assumption that a list is *homogenous*. In other words, a list stores only objects of a single type or a family of related types. In reality, the list is *heterogeneous* in that it can store any Object.

Listing 6-21's generics-based homogenous list avoids ClassCastException.

Listing 6-21. Lack of Type Safety Leading to a Compiler Error

```
import java.util.ArrayList;
import java.util.Iterator;
import java.util.List;

class Employee
{
    private String name;
```

```
    Employee(String name)
    {
        this.name = name;
    }

    String getName()
    {
        return name;
    }
}

public class TypeSafety
{
    public static void main(String[] args)
    {
        List<Employee> employees = new ArrayList<Employee>();
        employees.add(new Employee("John Doe"));
        employees.add(new Employee("Jane Smith"));
        employees.add("Jack Frost");
        Iterator<Employee> iter = employees.iterator();
        while (iter.hasNext())
        {
            Employee emp = iter.next();
            System.out.println(emp.getName());
        }
    }
}
```

Listing 6-21's refactored `main()` method illustrates the central feature of generics, which is the *parameterized type* (a class or interface name followed by an angle-bracket delimited type list identifying what kinds of objects are legal in that context).

For example, `java.util.List<Employee>` indicates only `Employee` objects can be stored in the `List`. As shown, the `<Employee>` designation must be repeated with `ArrayList`, as in `ArrayList<Employee>`, which is the collection implementation that stores the `Employee`s.

Also, `Iterator<Employee>` indicates that `iterator()` returns an `Iterator` whose `next()` method returns only `Employee` objects. It's not necessary to cast `iter.next()`'s returned value to `Employee` because the compiler inserts the cast on your behalf.

If you attempt to compile this listing, the compiler will report an error when it encounters `employees.add("Jack Frost");`. The error message will tell you that the compiler cannot find an `add(java.lang.String)` method in the `java.util.List<Employee>` interface.

Unlike in the pre-generics `List` interface, which declares an `add(Object)` method, the generified `List` interface's `add()` method parameter reflects the interface's parameterized type name. For example, `List<Employee>` implies `add(Employee)`.

Listing 6-20 reveals that the unsafe code causing the `ClassCastException` (`employees.add("Jack Frost");`) and the code that triggers the exception (`(Employee) iter.next()`) are quite close. However, they are often farther apart in larger applications.

Rather than having to deal with angry clients while hunting down the unsafe code that ultimately led to the ClassCastException, you can rely on the compiler saving you this frustration and effort by reporting an error when it detects this code during compilation. *Detecting type safety violations at compile time is the main benefit of using generics.*

Generic Types

A *generic type* is a class or interface that introduces a family of parameterized types by declaring a *formal type parameter list* (a comma-separated list of *type parameter* names between angle brackets). This syntax is expressed as follows:

```
class identifier<formal_type_parameter_list> {}
interface identifier<formal_type_parameter_list> {}
```

For example, List<E> is a generic type, where List is an interface and type parameter E identifies the list's element type. Similarly, Map<K, V> is a generic type, where Map is an interface and type parameters K and V identify the map's key and value types.

> **Note** When declaring a generic type, it's conventional to specify single uppercase letters as type parameter names. Furthermore, these names should be meaningful. For example, E indicates element, T indicates type, K indicates key, and V indicates value. If possible, you should avoid choosing a type parameter name that is meaningless where it is used. For example, List<E> means list of elements, but what does List<S> mean?

Parameterized types are instances of generic types. Each parameterized type replaces the generic type's type parameters with type names. For example, List<Employee> (List of Employee) and List<String> (List of String) are examples of parameterized types based on List<E>. Similarly, Map<String, Employee> is an example of a parameterized type based on Map<K, V>.

The type name that replaces a type parameter is known as an *actual type argument*. Five kinds of actual type arguments are supported by generics:

- *Concrete type*: The name of a class or interface is passed to the type parameter. For example, List<Employee> employees; specifies that the list elements are Employee instances.

- *Concrete parameterized type*: The name of a parameterized type is passed to the type parameter. For example, List<List<String>> nameLists; specifies that the list elements are lists of strings.

- *Array type*: An array is passed to the type parameter. For example, List<String[]> countries; specifies that the list elements are arrays of Strings, possibly city names.

- *Type parameter*: A type parameter is passed to the type parameter. For example, given class declaration class X<E> { List<E> queue; }, X's type parameter E is passed to List's type parameter E.

- *Wildcard*: The ? is passed to the type parameter. For example, List<?> list; specifies that the list elements are unknown. You will learn about wildcards later in this chapter.

A generic type also identifies a *raw type*, which is a generic type without its type parameters. For example, List<Employee>'s raw type is List. Raw types are nongeneric and can hold any Object.

> **Note**   Java allows raw types to be intermixed with generic types to support the vast amount of legacy code that was written prior to the arrival of generics. However, the compiler outputs a warning message whenever it encounters a raw type in source code.

Declaring and Using Your Own Generic Types

It's not difficult to declare your own generic types. In addition to specifying a formal type parameter list, your generic type specifies its type parameter(s) throughout its implementation. For example, Listing 6-22 declares a Queue<E> generic type.

Listing 6-22. Declaring and Using a Queue<E> Generic Type

```
public class Queue<E>
{
   private E[] elements;
   private int head, tail;

   @SuppressWarnings("unchecked")
   Queue(int size)
   {
      if (size < 2)
         throw new IllegalArgumentException("" + size);
      elements = (E[]) new Object[size];
      head = 0;
      tail = 0;
   }

   void insert(E element) throws QueueFullException
   {
      if (isFull())
         throw new QueueFullException();
      elements[tail] = element;
      tail = (tail + 1) % elements.length;
   }

   E remove() throws QueueEmptyException
   {
      if (isEmpty())
         throw new QueueEmptyException();
```

```java
        E element = elements[head];
        head = (head + 1) % elements.length;
        return element;
    }

    boolean isEmpty()
    {
        return head == tail;
    }

    boolean isFull()
    {
        return (tail + 1) % elements.length == head;
    }

    public static void main(String[] args)
        throws QueueFullException, QueueEmptyException
    {
        Queue<String> queue = new Queue<String>(6);
        System.out.println("Empty: " + queue.isEmpty());
        System.out.println("Full: " + queue.isFull());
        System.out.println("Adding A");
        queue.insert("A");
        System.out.println("Adding B");
        queue.insert("B");
        System.out.println("Adding C");
        queue.insert("C");
        System.out.println("Adding D");
        queue.insert("D");
        System.out.println("Adding E");
        queue.insert("E");
        System.out.println("Empty: " + queue.isEmpty());
        System.out.println("Full: " + queue.isFull());
        System.out.println("Removing " + queue.remove());
        System.out.println("Empty: " + queue.isEmpty());
        System.out.println("Full: " + queue.isFull());
        System.out.println("Adding F");
        queue.insert("F");
        while (!queue.isEmpty())
            System.out.println("Removing " + queue.remove());
        System.out.println("Empty: " + queue.isEmpty());
        System.out.println("Full: " + queue.isFull());
    }
}

class QueueEmptyException extends Exception
{
}

class QueueFullException extends Exception
{
}
```

Listing 6-22 declares Queue, QueueEmptyException, and QueueFullException classes. The latter two classes describe checked exceptions that are thrown from methods of the former class.

Queue implements a *queue*, a data structure that stores elements in first-in, first-out order. An element is inserted at the *tail* and removed at the *head*. The queue is empty when the head equals the tail and full when the tail is one less than the head. As a result, a queue of size *n* can store a maximum of *n* - 1 elements.

Notice that Queue<E>'s E type parameter appears throughout the source code. For example, E appears in the elements array declaration to denote the array's element type. E is also specified as the type of insert()'s parameter and as remove()'s return type.

E also appears in elements = (E[]) new Object[size];. (I will explain later why I specified this expression instead of specifying the more compact elements = new E[size]; expression.)

The E[] cast results in the compiler warning about this cast being unchecked. The compiler is concerned that downcasting from Object[] to E[] might result in a violation of type safety because any kind of object can be stored in Object[].

The compiler's concern isn't justified in this example. There is no way that a non-E object can appear in the E[] array. Because the warning is meaningless in this context, it is suppressed by prefixing the constructor with @SuppressWarnings("unchecked").

Caution Be careful when suppressing an unchecked warning. You must first prove that a ClassCastException cannot occur, and then you can suppress the warning.

When you run this application, it generates the following output:

```
Empty: true
Full: false
Adding A
Adding B
Adding C
Adding D
Adding E
Empty: false
Full: true
Removing A
Empty: false
Full: false
Adding F
Removing B
Removing C
Removing D
Removing E
Removing F
Empty: true
Full: false
```

Type Parameter Bounds

List<E>'s E type parameter and Map<K, V>'s K and V type parameters are examples of *unbounded type parameters*. You can pass any actual type argument to an unbounded type parameter.

It is sometimes necessary to restrict the kinds of actual type arguments that can be passed to a type parameter. For example, you might want to declare a class whose instances can only store instances of classes that subclass an abstract Shape class (such as Circle and Rectangle).

To restrict actual type arguments, you can specify an *upper bound*, a type that serves as an upper limit on the types that can be chosen as actual type arguments. The upper bound is specified via reserved word extends followed by a type name.

For example, ShapesList<E extends Shape> identifies Shape as an upper bound. You can specify ShapesList<Circle>, ShapesList<Rectangle>, and even ShapesList<Shape>, but not ShapesList<String> because String is not a subclass of Shape.

You can assign more than one upper bound to a type parameter, where the first bound is a class or interface and where each additional upper bound is an interface, by using the ampersand character (&) to separate bound names. Consider Listing 6-23.

Listing 6-23. Assigning Multiple Upper Bounds to a Type Parameter

```
abstract class Shape
{
}

class Circle extends Shape implements Comparable<Circle>
{
   private double x, y, radius;

   Circle(double x, double y, double radius)
   {
      this.x = x;
      this.y = y;
      this.radius = radius;
   }

   @Override
   public int compareTo(Circle circle)
   {
      if (radius < circle.radius)
         return -1;
      else
      if (radius > circle.radius)
         return 1;
      else
         return 0;
   }
}
```

```java
    @Override
    public String toString()
    {
        return "(" + x + ", " + y + ", " + radius + ")";
    }
}

class SortedShapesList<S extends Shape & Comparable<S>>
{
    @SuppressWarnings("unchecked")
    private S[] shapes = (S[]) new Shape[2];
    private int index = 0;

    void add(S shape)
    {
        shapes[index++] = shape;
        if (index < 2)
            return;
        System.out.println("Before sort: " + this);
        sort();
        System.out.println("After sort: " + this);
    }

    private void sort()
    {
        if (index == 1)
            return;
        if (shapes[0].compareTo(shapes[1]) > 0)
        {
            S shape = (S) shapes[0];
            shapes[0] = shapes[1];
            shapes[1] = shape;
        }
    }

    @Override
    public String toString()
    {
        return shapes[0].toString() + " " + shapes[1].toString();
    }
}

public class SortedShapesListDemo
{
    public static void main(String[] args)
    {
        SortedShapesList<Circle> ssl = new SortedShapesList<Circle>();
        ssl.add(new Circle(100, 200, 300));
        ssl.add(new Circle(10, 20, 30));
    }
}
```

Listing 6-23's Circle class extends Shape and implements the java.lang.Comparable interface, which is used to specify the *natural ordering* of Circle objects. The interface's compareTo() method implements this ordering by returning a value to reflect the order:

- A negative value is returned when the current object should precede the object passed to compareTo() in some fashion.

- A zero value is returned when the current and argument objects are the same.

- A positive value is returned when the current object should succeed the argument object.

Circle's overriding compareTo() method compares two Circle objects based on their radii. This method orders a Circle instance with the smaller radius before a Circle instance with a larger radius.

The SortedShapesList class specifies <S extends Shape & Comparable<S>> as its parameter list. The actual type argument passed to the S parameter must subclass Shape, and it must also implement the Comparable interface.

> **Note**   A type parameter bound that includes the type parameter is known as a *recursive type bound*. For example, Comparable<S> in S extends Shape & Comparable<S> is a recursive type bound. Recursive type bounds are rare and typically show up in conjunction with the Comparable interface for specifying a type's natural ordering.

Circle satisfies both criteria: it subclasses Shape and implements Comparable. As a result, the compiler doesn't report an error when it encounters the main() method's SortedShapesList<Circle> ssl = new SortedShapesList<Circle>(); statement.

An upper bound offers extra static type checking that guarantees that a parameterized type adheres to its bounds. This assurance means that the upper bound's methods can be called safely. For example, sort() can call Comparable's compareTo() method.

If you run this application, you will discover the following output, which shows that the two Circle objects are sorted in ascending order of radius:

```
Before sort: (100.0, 200.0, 300.0) (10.0, 20.0, 30.0)
After sort: (10.0, 20.0, 30.0) (100.0, 200.0, 300.0)
```

> **Note**   Type parameters cannot have lower bounds. Angelika Langer explains the rationale for this restriction in her "Java Generics FAQs" at www.angelikalanger.com/GenericsFAQ/FAQSections/ TypeParameters.html#FAQ107.

Type Parameter Scope

A type parameter's *scope* (visibility) is its generic type except where *masked* (hidden). This scope includes the formal type parameter list of which the type parameter is a member. For example, the scope of S in SortedShapesList<S extends Shape & Comparable<S>> is all of SortedShapesList and the formal type parameter list.

It is possible to mask a type parameter by declaring a same-named type parameter in a nested type's formal type parameter list. For example, Listing 6-24 masks an enclosing class's T type parameter.

Listing 6-24. Masking a Type Variable

```
class EnclosingClass<T>
{
   static class EnclosedClass<T extends Comparable<T>>
   {
   }
}
```

EnclosingClass's T type parameter is masked by EnclosedClass's T type parameter, which specifies an upper bound where only those types that implement the Comparable interface can be passed to EnclosedClass. Referencing T from within EnclosedClass refers to the bounded T and not the unbounded T passed to EnclosingClass.

If masking is undesirable, it is best to choose a different name for the type parameter. For example, you might specify EnclosedClass<U extends Comparable<U>>. Although U is not as meaningful a name as T, this situation justifies this choice.

The Need for Wildcards

Suppose that you have created a List of String and want to output this list. Because you might create a List of Employee and other kinds of lists, you want this method to output an arbitrary List of Object. You end up creating Listing 6-25.

Listing 6-25. Attempting to Output a List of Object

```
import java.util.ArrayList;
import java.util.List;

public class OutputList
{
   public static void main(String[] args)
   {
      List<String> ls = new ArrayList<String>();
      ls.add("first");
      ls.add("second");
      ls.add("third");
      outputList(ls);
   }
```

```
    static void outputList(List<Object> list)
    {
        for (int i = 0; i < list.size(); i++)
            System.out.println(list.get(i));
    }
}
```

Now that you've accomplished your objective (or so you think), you compile Listing 6-25 via javac OutputList.java. Much to your surprise, you receive the following error message:

```
OutputList.java:12: error: method outputList in class OutputList cannot be applied to given types;
        outputList(ls);
        ^
  required: List<Object>
  found: List<String>
  reason: actual argument List<String> cannot be converted to List<Object> by method invocation
conversion
1 error
```

This error message results from being unaware of the fundamental rule of generic types: *for a given subtype x of type y, and given G as a raw type declaration, G<x> is not a subtype of G<y>*.

To understand this rule, you must refresh your understanding of subtype polymorphism (see Chapter 4). Basically, a subtype is a specialized kind of its supertype. For example, Circle is a specialized kind of Shape and String is a specialized kind of Object. This polymorphic behavior also applies to related parameterized types with the same type parameters (e.g., List<Object> is a specialized kind of java.util.Collection<Object>).

However, this polymorphic behavior doesn't apply to multiple parameterized types that differ only in regard to one type parameter being a subtype of another type parameter. For example, List<String> is not a specialized kind of List<Object>. The following example reveals why parameterized types differing only in type parameters are not polymorphic:

```
List<String> ls = new ArrayList<String>();
List<Object> lo = ls;
Lo.add(new Employee());
String s = ls.get(0);
```

This example will not compile because it violates type safety. If it compiled, a ClassCastException instance would be thrown at runtime because of the implicit cast to String on the final line.

The first line instantiates a List of String and the second line upcasts its reference to a List of Object. The third line adds a new Employee object to the List of Object. The fourth line obtains the Employee object via get() and attempts to assign it to the List of String reference variable. However, ClassCastException is thrown because of the implicit cast to String—an Employee is not a String.

Note   Although you cannot upcast List<String> to List<Object>, you can upcast List<String> to the raw type List to interoperate with legacy code.

The aforementioned error message reveals that List of String is not also List of Object. To call Listing 6-25's outputList() method without violating type safety, you can only pass an argument of List<Object> type, which limits the usefulness of this method.

However, generics offer a solution: the wildcard argument (?), which stands for any type. By changing outputList()'s parameter type from List<Object> to List<?>, you can call outputList() with a List of String, a List of Employee, and so on.

Generic Methods

Suppose you need a method to copy a List of any kind of object to another List. Although you might consider coding a void copyList(List<Object> src, List<Object> dest) method, this method would have limited usefulness because it could only copy lists whose element type is Object. You couldn't copy a List<Employee>, for example.

If you want to pass source and destination lists whose elements are of arbitrary type (but their element types agree), you need to specify the wildcard character as a placeholder for that type. For example, you might consider writing the following copyList() class method that accepts collections of arbitrary-typed objects as its arguments:

```
static void copyList(List<?> src, List<?> dest)
{
   for (int i = 0; i < src.size(); i++)
      dest.add(src.get(i));
}
```

This method's parameter list is correct, but there is another problem: the compiler outputs the following error message when it encounters dest.add(src.get(i));.

```
CopyList.java:19: error: no suitable method found for add(Object)
         dest.add(src.get(i));
             ^  *
   method List.add(int,CAP#1) is not applicable
     (actual and formal argument lists differ in length)
   method List.add(CAP#1) is not applicable
     (actual argument Object cannot be converted to CAP#1 by method invocation conversion)
  where CAP#1 is a fresh type-variable:
   CAP#1 extends Object from capture of ?
1 error
```

This error message assumes that copyList() is part of a class named CopyList. Although it appears to be incomprehensible, the message basically means that the dest.add(src.get(i)) method call violates type safety. Because ? implies that any type of object can serve as a list's element type, it's possible that the destination list's element type is incompatible with the source list's element type.

For example, suppose you create a List of String as the source list and a List of Employee as the destination list. Attempting to add the source list's elements to the destination list, which expects Employees, violates type safety. If this copy operation were allowed, a ClassCastException instance would be thrown when trying to obtain the destination list's elements.

You could solve this problem in a limited way as follows:

```
static void copyList(List<? extends String> src,
                     List<? super String> dest)
{
   for (int i = 0; i < src.size(); i++)
      dest.add(src.get(i));
}
```

This method demonstrates a wildcard argument feature in which you can supply an upper bound or (unlike with a type parameter) a lower bound to limit the types that can be passed as actual type arguments to the generic type. Specifically, it shows an upper bound via extends followed by the upper bound type after the ?, and a lower bound via super followed by the lower bound type after the ?.

You interpret ? extends String to mean that any actual type argument that is String or a subclass of this type can be passed, and you interpret ? super String to imply that any actual type argument that is String or a superclass of this type can be passed. Because String cannot be subclassed, this means that you can only pass source lists of String and destination lists of String or Object.

The problem of copying lists of arbitrary element types to other lists can be solved through the use of a *generic method* (a class or instance method with a type-generalized implementation). Generic methods are syntactically expressed as follows:

<formal_type_parameter_list> return_type identifier(parameter_list)

The *formal_type_parameter_list* is the same as when specifying a generic type: it consists of type parameters with optional bounds. A type parameter can appear as the method's *return_type*, and type parameters can appear in the *parameter_list*. The compiler infers the actual type arguments from the context in which the method is invoked.

You'll discover many examples of generic methods in the Collections Framework. For example, its java.util.Collections class provides a public static <T extends Object & Comparable<? super T>> T min(Collection<? extends T> coll) method for returning the minimum element in the given collection according to the natural ordering of its elements.

You can easily convert copyList() into a generic method by prefixing the return type with <T> and replacing each wildcard with T. The resulting method header is <T> void copyList(List<T> src, List<T> dest), and Listing 6-26 presents its source code as part of an application that copies a List of Circle to another List of Circle.

Listing 6-26. Declaring and Using a copyList() Generic Method

```
import java.util.ArrayList;
import java.util.List;

class Circle
{
   private double x, y, radius;

   Circle(double x, double y, double radius)
   {
      this.x = x;
      this.y = y;
      this.radius = radius;
   }
```

```java
   @Override
   public String toString()
   {
      return "(" + x + ", " + y + ", " + radius + ")";
   }
}

public class CopyList
{
   public static void main(String[] args)
   {
      List<String> ls = new ArrayList<String>();
      ls.add("A");
      ls.add("B");
      ls.add("C");
      outputList(ls);
      List<String> lsCopy = new ArrayList<String>();
      copyList(ls, lsCopy);
      outputList(lsCopy);
      List<Circle> lc = new ArrayList<Circle>();
      lc.add(new Circle(10.0, 20.0, 30.0));
      lc.add(new Circle (5.0, 4.0, 16.0));
      outputList(lc);
      List<Circle> lcCopy = new ArrayList<Circle>();
      copyList(lc, lcCopy);
      outputList(lcCopy);
   }

   static <T> void copyList(List<T> src, List<T> dest)
   {
      for (int i = 0; i < src.size(); i++)
         dest.add(src.get(i));
   }

   static void outputList(List<?> list)
   {
      for (int i = 0; i < list.size(); i++)
         System.out.println(list.get(i));
      System.out.println();
   }
}
```

The generic method's type parameters are inferred from the context in which the method was invoked. For example, the compiler determines that copyList(ls, lsCopy); copies a List of String to another List of String. Similarly, it determines that copyList(lc, lcCopy); copies a List of Circle to another List of Circle.

When you run this application, it generates the following output:

```
A
B
C
```

```
A
B
C

(10.0, 20.0, 30.0)
(5.0, 4.0, 16.0)

(10.0, 20.0, 30.0)
(5.0, 4.0, 16.0)
```

Arrays and Generics

After presenting Listing 6-22's Queue<E> generic type, I mentioned that I would explain why I specified elements = (E[]) new Object[size]; instead of the more compact elements = new E[size]; expression. Because of Java's generics implementation, it isn't possible to specify array-creation expressions that involve type parameters (e.g., new E[size] or new List<E>[50]) or actual type arguments (e.g., new Queue<String>[15]). If you attempt to do so, the compiler will report a generic array creation error message.

Before I present an example that demonstrates why allowing array-creation expressions that involve type parameters or actual type arguments is dangerous, you need to understand reification and covariance in the context of arrays, and erasure, which is at the heart of how generics are implemented.

Reification is representing the abstract as if it was concrete—for example, making a memory address available for direct manipulation by other language constructs. Java arrays are reified in that they're aware of their element types (an element type is stored internally) and can enforce these types at runtime. Attempting to store an invalid element in an array causes the virtual machine to throw an instance of the java.lang.ArrayStoreException class.

Listing 6-27 teaches you how array manipulation can lead to an ArrayStoreException.

Listing 6-27. How an ArrayStoreException Arises

```java
class Point
{
   int x, y;
}

class ColoredPoint extends Point
{
   int color;
}

public class ReificationDemo
{
   public static void main(String[] args)
   {
      ColoredPoint[] cptArray = new ColoredPoint[1];
      Point[] ptArray = cptArray;
      ptArray[0] = new Point();
   }
}
```

Listing 6-27's `main()` method first instantiates a `ColoredPoint` array that can store one element. In contrast to this legal assignment (the types are compatible), specifying `ColoredPoint[] cptArray = new Point[1];` is illegal (and won't compile) because it would result in a `ClassCastException` at runtime—the array knows that the assignment is illegal.

> **Note** If it's not obvious, `ColoredPoint[] cptArray = new Point[1];` is illegal because `Point` instances have fewer members (only x and y) than `ColoredPoint` instances (x, y, and color). Attempting to access a `Point` instance's nonexistent `color` field from its entry in the `ColoredPoint` array would result in a memory violation (because no memory has been assigned to color) and ultimately crash the virtual machine.

The second line (`Point[] ptArray = cptArray;`) is legal because of *covariance* (an array of supertype references is a supertype of an array of subtype references). In this case, an array of `Point` references is a supertype of an array of `ColoredPoint` references. The nonarray analogy is that a subtype is also a supertype. For example, a `java.lang.Throwable` instance is a kind of `Object` instance.

Covariance is dangerous when abused. For example, the third line (`ptArray[0] = new Point();`) results in `ArrayStoreException` at runtime because a `Point` instance is not a `ColoredPoint` instance. Without this exception, an attempt to access the nonexistent member `color` crashes the virtual machine.

Unlike with arrays, a generic type's type parameters are not reified. They're not available at runtime because they're thrown away after the source code is compiled. This "throwing away of type parameters" is a result of *erasure*, which also involves inserting casts to appropriate types when the code isn't type correct and replacing type parameters by their upper bounds (such as `Object`).

> **Note** The compiler performs erasure to let generic code interoperate with legacy (nongeneric) code. It transforms generic source code into nongeneric runtime code. One consequence of erasure is that you cannot use the `instanceof` operator with parameterized types apart from unbounded wildcard types. For example, it's illegal to specify `List<Employee> le = null; if (le instanceof ArrayList<Employee>) {}`. Instead, you must change the `instanceof` expression to `le instanceof ArrayList<?>` (unbounded wildcard) or `le instanceof ArrayList` (raw type, which is the preferred use).

Suppose you could specify an array-creation expression involving a type parameter or an actual type argument. Why would this be bad? For an answer, consider the following example, which should generate an `ArrayStoreException` instead of a `ClassCastException` but doesn't do so:

```
List<Employee>[] empListArray = new List<Employee>[1];
List<String> strList = new ArrayList<String>();
strList.add("string");
Object[] objArray = empListArray;
objArray[0] = strList;
Employee e = empListArray[0].get(0);
```

Assume that the first line, which creates a one-element array where this element stores a List of Employee, is legal. The second line creates a List of String, and the third line stores a single String object in this list.

The fourth line assigns empListArray to objArray. This assignment is legal because arrays are covariant and erasure converts List<Employee>[] to the List runtime type and List subtypes Object.

Because of erasure, the virtual machine doesn't throw ArrayStoreException when it encounters objArray[0] = strList;. After all, you're assigning a List reference to a List[] array at runtime. However, this exception would be thrown if generic types were reified because you'd then be assigning a List<String> reference to a List<Employee>[] array.

However, there is a problem. A List<String> instance has been stored in an array that can only hold List<Employee> instances. When the compiler-inserted cast operator attempts to cast empListArray[0].get(0)'s return value ("string") to Employee, the cast operator throws a ClassCastException object.

Mastering Enums

An *enumerated type* is a type that specifies a named sequence of related constants as its legal values. The months in a calendar, the coins in a currency, and the days of the week are examples of enumerated types.

Java developers have traditionally used sets of named integer constants to represent enumerated types. Because this form of representation has proven to be problematic, Java 5 introduced the enum alternative.

In this section I introduce you to enums. After discussing the problems with traditional enumerated types, I present the enum alternative. I then introduce you to the Enum class, from which enums originate.

The Trouble with Traditional Enumerated Types

Listing 6-28 declares a Coin enumerated type whose set of constants identifies different kinds of coins in a currency.

Listing 6-28. An Enumerated Type Identifying Coins

```
class Coin
{
   final static int PENNY = 0;
   final static int NICKEL = 1;
   final static int DIME = 2;
   final static int QUARTER = 3;
}
```

Listing 6-29 declares a Weekday enumerated type whose constants identify the days of the week.

Listing 6-29. An Enumerated Type Identifying Weekdays

```
class Weekday
{
   final static int SUNDAY = 0;
   final static int MONDAY = 1;
   final static int TUESDAY = 2;
   final static int WEDNESDAY = 3;
   final static int THURSDAY = 4;
   final static int FRIDAY = 5;
   final static int SATURDAY = 6;
}
```

Listing 6-28's and 6-29's approach to representing an enumerated type is problematic, where the biggest problem is the lack of compile-time type safety. For example, you can pass a coin to a method that requires a weekday and the compiler will not complain.

You can also compare coins to weekdays, as in `Coin.NICKEL == Weekday.MONDAY`, and specify even more meaningless expressions, such as `Coin.DIME + Weekday.FRIDAY - 1 / Coin.QUARTER`. The compiler doesn't complain because it only sees `int`s.

Applications that depend on enumerated types are brittle. Because the type's constants are compiled into an application's classfiles, changing a constant's `int` value requires you to recompile dependent applications or risk them behaving erratically.

Another problem with enumerated types is that `int` constants cannot be translated into meaningful string descriptions. For example, what does the number 4 mean when debugging a faulty application? Being able to see THURSDAY instead of 4 would be more helpful.

Note   You could circumvent the previous problem by using `String` constants. For example, you might specify `public final static String THURSDAY = "THURSDAY";`. Although the constant value is more meaningful, `String`-based constants can impact performance because you cannot use `==` to efficiently compare just any old strings (as you will discover in Chapter 7). Other problems related to `String`-based constants include hard-coding the constant's value ("THURSDAY") instead of the constant's name (THURSDAY) into source code, which makes it very difficult to change the constant's value at a later time; and misspelling a hard-coded constant ("THURZDAY"), which compiles correctly but is problematic at runtime.

The Enum Alternative

Java 5 introduced enums as a better alternative to traditional enumerated types. An *enum* is an enumerated type that is expressed via reserved word enum. The following example uses enum to declare Listing 6-28's and 6-29's enumerated types:

```
enum Coin { PENNY, NICKEL, DIME, QUARTER }
enum Weekday { SUNDAY, MONDAY, TUESDAY, WEDNESDAY, THURSDAY, FRIDAY, SATURDAY }
```

Despite their similarity to the int-based enumerated types found in C++ and other languages, this example's enums are classes. Each constant is a `public static final` field that represents an instance of its enum class.

Because constants are final and because you cannot call an enum's constructors to create more constants, you can use == to compare constants efficiently and (unlike string constant comparisons) safely. For example, you can specify c == Coin.NICKEL.

Enums promote compile-time type safety by preventing you from comparing constants in different enums. For example, the compiler will report an error when it encounters Coin.PENNY == Weekday.SUNDAY.

The compiler also frowns on passing a constant of the wrong enum kind to a method. For example, you cannot pass Weekday.FRIDAY to a method whose parameter type is Coin.

Applications depending on enums are not brittle because the enum's constants are not compiled into an application's classfiles. Also, the enum provides a toString() method for returning a more useful description of a constant's value.

Because enums are so useful, Java 5 enhanced the switch statement to support them. Listing 6-30 demonstrates this statement switching on one of the constants in the previous example's Coin enum.

Listing 6-30. Using the Switch Statement with an Enum

```java
public class EnhancedSwitch
{
   enum Coin { PENNY, NICKEL, DIME, QUARTER }

   public static void main(String[] args)
   {
      Coin coin = Coin.NICKEL;
      switch (coin)
      {
         case PENNY  : System.out.println("1 cent"); break;
         case NICKEL : System.out.println("5 cents"); break;
         case DIME   : System.out.println("10 cents"); break;
         case QUARTER: System.out.println("25 cents"); break;
         default     : assert false;
      }
   }
}
```

Listing 6-30 demonstrates switching on an enum's constants. This enhanced statement only allows you to specify the name of a constant as a case label. If you prefix the name with the enum, as in case Coin.DIME, the compiler reports an error.

Enhancing an Enum

You can add fields, constructors, and methods to an enum—you can even have the enum implement interfaces. For example, Listing 6-31 adds a field, a constructor and two methods to Coin to associate a denomination value with a Coin constant (such as 1 for penny and 5 for nickel) and convert pennies to the denomination.

Listing 6-31. Enhancing the Coin Enum

```
enum Coin
{
   PENNY(1),
   NICKEL(5),
   DIME(10),
   QUARTER(25);

   private final int denomValue;

   Coin(int denomValue)
   {
      this.denomValue = denomValue;
   }

   int denomValue()
   {
      return denomValue;
   }

   int toDenomination(int numPennies)
   {
      return numPennies / denomValue;
   }
}
```

Listing 6-31's constructor accepts a denomination value, which it assigns to a `private` blank final field named denomValue—all fields should be declared `final` because constants are immutable. Notice that this value is passed to each constant during its creation (PENNY(1), for example).

Caution   When the comma-separated list of constants is followed by anything other than an enum's closing brace, you must terminate the list with a semicolon or the compiler will report an error.

Furthermore, this listing's denomValue() method returns denomValue, and its toDenomination() method returns the number of coins of that denomination that are contained within the number of pennies passed to this method as its argument. For example, 3 nickels are contained in 16 pennies.

Listing 6-32 shows how to use the enhanced Coin enum.

Listing 6-32. Exercising the Enhanced Coin Enum

```
public class Coins
{
   public static void main(String[] args)
   {
      if (args.length == 1)
      {
         int numPennies = Integer.parseInt(args[0]);
         System.out.println(numPennies + " pennies is equivalent to:");
```

```
            int numQuarters = Coin.QUARTER.toDenomination(numPennies);
            System.out.println(numQuarters + " " + Coin.QUARTER.toString() +
                               (numQuarters != 1 ? "s," : ","));
            numPennies -= numQuarters * Coin.QUARTER.denomValue();
            int numDimes = Coin.DIME.toDenomination(numPennies);
            System.out.println(numDimes + " " + Coin.DIME.toString() +
                               (numDimes != 1 ? "s, " : ","));
            numPennies -= numDimes * Coin.DIME.denomValue();
            int numNickels = Coin.NICKEL.toDenomination(numPennies);
            System.out.println(numNickels + " " + Coin.NICKEL.toString() +
                               (numNickels != 1 ? "s, " : ", and"));
            numPennies -= numNickels*Coin.NICKEL.denomValue();
            System.out.println(numPennies + " " + Coin.PENNY.toString() +
                               (numPennies != 1 ? "s" : ""));
        }
      System.out.println();
      System.out.println("Denomination values:");
      for (int i = 0; i < Coin.values().length; i++)
          System.out.println(Coin.values()[i].denomValue());
   }
}
```

Listing 6-32 describes an application that converts its solitary "pennies" command-line argument to an equivalent amount expressed in quarters, dimes, nickels, and pennies. In addition to calling a Coin constant's denomValue() and toDenomValue() methods, the application calls toString() to output a string representation of the coin.

Another called enum method is values(). This method returns an array of all Coin constants that are declared in the Coin enum (value()'s return type, in this example, is Coin[ ]). This array is useful when you need to iterate over these constants. For example, Listing 6-32 calls this method to output each coin's denomination.

When you run this application with 119 as its command-line argument (java Coins 119), it generates the following output:

```
119 pennies is equivalent to:
4 QUARTERs,
1 DIME,
1 NICKEL, and
4 PENNYs

Denomination values:
1
5
10
25
```

The output shows that toString() returns a constant's name. It is sometimes useful to override this method to return a more meaningful value. For example, a method that extracts *tokens* (named character sequences) from a string might use a Token enum to list token names and, via an overriding toString() method, values—see Listing 6-33.

Listing 6-33. Overriding toString() to Return a Token Constant's Value

```
public enum Token
{
   IDENTIFIER("ID"),
   INTEGER("INT"),
   LPAREN("("),
   RPAREN(")"),
   COMMA(",");

   private final String tokValue;

   Token(String tokValue)
   {
      this.tokValue = tokValue;
   }

   @Override
   public String toString()
   {
      return tokValue;
   }

   public static void main(String[] args)
   {
      System.out.println("Token values:");
      for (int i = 0; i < Token.values().length; i++)
         System.out.println(Token.values()[i].name() + " = " +
                            Token.values()[i]);
   }
}
```

Listing 6-33's main() method calls values() to return the array of Token constants. For each constant, it calls the constant's name() method to return the constant's name and implicitly calls toString() to return the constant's value. If you were to run this application, you would observe the following output:

```
Token values:
IDENTIFIER = ID
INTEGER = INT
LPAREN = (
RPAREN = )
COMMA = ,
```

Another way to enhance an enum is to assign a different behavior to each constant. You can accomplish this task by introducing an abstract method into the enum and overriding this method in an anonymous subclass of the constant. Listing 6-34's TempConversion enum demonstrates this technique.

Listing 6-34. Using Anonymous Subclasses to Vary the Behaviors of Enum Constants

```
public enum TempConversion
{
   C2F("Celsius to Fahrenheit")
   {
      @Override
      double convert(double value)
      {
         return value * 9.0 / 5.0 + 32.0;
      }
   },

   F2C("Fahrenheit to Celsius")
   {
      @Override
      double convert(double value)
      {
         return (value - 32.0) * 5.0 / 9.0;
      }
   };

   TempConversion(String desc)
   {
      this.desc = desc;
   }

   private String desc;

   @Override
   public String toString()
   {
      return desc;
   }

   abstract double convert(double value);

   public static void main(String[] args)
   {
      System.out.println(C2F + " for 100.0 degrees = " + C2F.convert(100.0));
      System.out.println(F2C + " for 98.6 degrees = " + F2C.convert(98.6));
   }
}
```

When you run this application, it generates the following output:

```
Celsius to Fahrenheit for 100.0 degrees = 212.0
Fahrenheit to Celsius for 98.6 degrees = 37.0
```

The Enum Class

The compiler regards enum as syntactic sugar. When it encounters an enum type declaration (enum Coin {}), it generates a class whose name (Coin) is specified by the declaration, which also subclasses the abstract Enum class (in the java.lang package), the common base class of all Java language-based enumeration types.

If you examine Enum's Java documentation, you will discover that it overrides Object's clone(), equals(), finalize(), hashCode(), and toString() methods:

- clone() is overridden to prevent constants from being cloned so that there is never more than one copy of a constant; otherwise, constants could not be compared via ==.

- equals() is overridden to compare constants via their references—constants with the same identities (==) must have the same contents (equals()), and different identities imply different contents.

- finalize() is overridden to ensure that constants cannot be finalized.

- hashCode() is overridden because equals() is overridden.

- toString() is overridden to return the constant's name.

Except for toString(), all of the overriding methods are declared final so that they cannot be overridden in a subclass.

Enum also provides its own methods. These methods include the final compareTo() (Enum implements Comparable), getDeclaringClass(), name(), and ordinal() methods:

- compareTo() compares the current constant with the constant passed as an argument to see which constant precedes the other constant in the enum and returns a value indicating their order. This method makes it possible to sort an array of unsorted constants.

- getDeclaringClass() returns the Class object corresponding to the current constant's enum. For example, the Class object for Coin is returned when calling Coin.PENNY.getDeclaringClass() for enum Coin { PENNY, NICKEL, DIME, QUARTER}. Also, TempConversion is returned when calling TempConversion.C2F. getDeclaringClass() for Listing 6-34's TempConversion enum. The compareTo() method uses Class's getClass() method and Enum's getDeclaringClass() method to ensure that only constants belonging to the same enum are compared. Otherwise, a ClassCastException is thrown.

- name() returns the constant's name. Unless overridden to return something more descriptive, toString() also returns the constant's name.

- ordinal() returns a zero-based *ordinal*, an integer that identifies the position of the constant within the enum type. compareTo() compares ordinals.

Enum also provides the public static <T extends Enum<T>> T valueOf(Class<T> enumType, String name) method for returning the enum constant from the specified enum with the specified name:

- enumType identifies the Class object of the enum from which to return a constant.

- name identifies the name of the constant to return.

For example, `Coin penny = Enum.valueOf(Coin.class, "PENNY");` assigns the Coin constant whose name is PENNY to penny.

You will not discover a `values()` method in Enum's Java documentation because the compiler *synthesizes* (manufactures) this method while generating the class.

Extending the Enum Class

Enum's generic type is `Enum<E extends Enum<E>>`. Although the formal type parameter list looks ghastly, it's not that hard to understand. But first, take a look at Listing 6-35.

Listing 6-35. The Coin Class As It Appears from the Perspective of Its Classfile

```
public final class Coin extends Enum<Coin>
{
   public static final Coin PENNY = new Coin("PENNY", 0);
   public static final Coin NICKEL = new Coin("NICKEL", 1);
   public static final Coin DIME = new Coin("DIME", 2);
   public static final Coin QUARTER = new Coin("QUARTER", 3);
   private static final Coin[] $VALUES = { PENNY, NICKEL, DIME, QUARTER };

   public static Coin[] values()
   {
      return Coin.$VALUES.clone();
   }

   public static Coin valueOf(String name)
   {
      return Enum.valueOf(Coin.class, "Coin");
   }

   private Coin(String name, int ordinal)
   {
      super(name, ordinal);
   }
}
```

Behind the scenes, the compiler converts `enum Coin { PENNY, NICKEL, DIME, QUARTER}` into a class declaration that is similar to Listing 6-35.

The following rules show you how to interpret `Enum<E extends Enum<E>>` in the context of `Coin extends Enum<Coin>`:

- Any subclass of Enum must supply an actual type argument to Enum. For example, Coin's header specifies `Enum<Coin>`.

- The actual type argument must be a subclass of Enum. For example, Coin is a subclass of Enum.

- A subclass of Enum (such as Coin) must follow the idiom that it supplies its own name (Coin) as an actual type argument.

The third rule allows Enum to declare methods—compareTo(), getDeclaringClass(), and valueOf()— whose parameter and/or return types are specified in terms of the subclass (Coin) and not in terms of Enum. The rationale for doing this is to avoid having to specify casts. For example, you don't need to cast valueOf()'s return value to Coin in Coin penny = Enum.valueOf(Coin.class, "PENNY");.

> **Note**   You cannot compile Listing 6-35 because the compiler will not compile any class that extends Enum. It will also complain about super(name, ordinal);.

EXERCISES

The following exercises are designed to test your understanding of Chapter 6's content:

1.   What is an assertion?

2.   When would you use assertions?

3.   True or false: Specifying the -ea command-line option with no argument enables all assertions, including system assertions.

4.   Define annotation.

5.   What kinds of application elements can be annotated?

6.   Identify the three compiler-supported annotation types.

7.   How do you declare an annotation type?

8.   What is a marker annotation?

9.   What is an element?

10.   How do you assign a default value to an element?

11.   What is a meta-annotation?

12.   Identify Java's four meta-annotation types.

13.   Define generics.

14.   Why would you use generics?

15.   What is the difference between a generic type and a parameterized type?

16.   Which one of the nonstatic member class, local class, and anonymous class inner class categories cannot be generic?

17.   Identify the five kinds of actual type arguments.

18.   True or false: You cannot specify the name of a primitive type (such as double or int) as an actual type argument.

19.   What is a raw type?

20.   When does the compiler report an unchecked warning message and why?

21. How do you suppress an unchecked warning message?

22. True or false: `List<E>`'s E type parameter is unbounded.

23. How do you specify a single upper bound?

24. What is a recursive type bound?

25. Why are wildcard type arguments necessary?

26. What is a generic method?

27. In Listing 6-36, which overloaded method does the `methodCaller()` generic method call?

Listing 6-36. Which someOverloadedMethod() Is Called?

```
import java.util.Date;

public class CallOverloadedNGMethodFromGMethod
{
   public static void someOverloadedMethod(Object o)
   {
      System.out.println("call to someOverloadedMethod(Object o)");
   }
   public static void someOverloadedMethod(Date d)
   {
      System.out.println("call to someOverloadedMethod(Date d)");
   }
   public static <T> void methodCaller(T t)
   {
      someOverloadedMethod(t);
   }
   public static void main(String[] args)
   {
      methodCaller(new Date());
   }
}
```

28. What is reification?

29. True or false: Type parameters are reified.

30. What is erasure?

31. Define enumerated type.

32. Identify three problems that can arise when you use enumerated types whose constants are `int` based.

33. What is an enum?

34. How do you use the switch statement with an enum?

35. In what ways can you enhance an enum?

36. What is the purpose of the abstract Enum class?

37.   What is the difference between Enum's name() and toString() methods?

38.   True or false: Enum's generic type is Enum<E extends Enum<E>>.

39.   Declare a ToDo marker annotation type that annotates only type elements and that also uses the default retention policy.

40.   Rewrite the StubFinder application to work with Listing 6-13's Stub annotation type (with appropriate @Target and @Retention annotations) and Listing 6-14's Deck class.

41.   Implement a Stack<E> generic type in a manner that is similar to Listing 6-22's Queue class. Stack must declare push(), pop(), and isEmpty() methods (it could also declare an isFull() method, but that method is not necessary in this exercise); push() must throw a StackFullException instance when the stack is full; and pop() must throw a StackEmptyException instance when the stack is empty. (You must create your own StackFullException and StackEmptyException helper classes because they are not provided for you in the standard class library.) Declare a similar main() method and insert two assertions into this method that validate your assumptions about the stack being empty immediately after being created and immediately after popping the last element.

42.   Declare a Compass enum with NORTH, SOUTH, EAST, and WEST members. Declare a UseCompass class whose main() method randomly selects one of these constants and then switches on that constant. Each of the switch statement's cases should output a message such as heading north.

Summary

An assertion is a statement that lets you express an assumption of application correctness via a Boolean expression. If this expression evaluates to true, execution continues with the next statement. Otherwise, an error that identifies the cause of failure is thrown.

There are many situations where assertions should be used. These situations organize into internal invariant, control-flow invariant, and design-by-contract categories. An invariant is something that doesn't change.

Although there are many situations where assertions should be used, there also are situations where they should be avoided. For example, you should not use assertions to check the arguments that are passed to public methods.

The compiler records assertions in the classfile. However, assertions are disabled at runtime because they can affect performance. You must enable the classfile's assertions before you can test assumptions about the behaviors of your classes.

Annotations are instances of annotation types and associate metadata with application elements. They are expressed in source code by prefixing their type names with @ symbols. For example, @Readonly is an annotation and Readonly is its type.

Java supplies a wide variety of annotation types, including the compiler-oriented Override, Deprecated, and SuppressWarnings types. However, you can also declare your own annotation types by using the @interface syntax.

Annotation types can be annotated with meta-annotations that identify the application elements they can target (such as constructors, methods, or fields), their retention policies, and other characteristics.

Annotations whose types are assigned a runtime retention policy via @Retention annotations can be processed at runtime using custom applications. (Java 5 introduced an apt tool for this purpose, but its functionality was largely integrated into the compiler starting with Java 6.)

Java 5 introduced generics, language features for declaring and using type-agnostic classes and interfaces. While working with Java's Collections Framework, these features help you avoid ClassCastExceptions.

A generic type is a class or interface that introduces a family of parameterized types by declaring a formal type parameter list. The type name that replaces a type parameter is known as an actual type argument.

There are five kinds of actual type arguments: concrete type, concrete parameterized type, array type, type parameter, and wildcard. Furthermore, a generic type also identifies a raw type, which is a generic type without its type parameters.

A generic method is a class or instance method with a type-generalized implementation, for example, <T> void copyList(List<T> src, List<T> dest). The compiler infers the actual type argument from the context in which the method is invoked.

An enumerated type is a type that specifies a named sequence of related constants as its legal values. Java developers have traditionally used sets of named integer constants to represent enumerated types.

Because sets of named integer constants have proven to be problematic, Java 5 introduced the enum alternative. An enum is an enumerated type that is expressed in source code via reserved word enum.

You can add fields, constructors, and methods to an enum—you can even have the enum implement interfaces. Also, you can override toString() to provide a more useful description of a constant's value and subclass constants to assign different behaviors.

The compiler regards enum as syntactic sugar for a class that subclasses Enum. This abstract class overrides various Object methods to provide default behaviors (usually for safety reasons) and provides additional methods for various purposes.

This chapter largely completes a tour of the Java language. In Chapter 7 I begin to emphasize Java APIs by focusing on those APIs related to mathematics, string management, and packages.

Chapter **7**

Exploring the Basic APIs Part 1

The standard class library's java.lang and java.math packages provide many basic APIs, which are designed to support language features. You have already encountered a few of these APIs, such as the Object and String classes and the Throwable class hierarchy. In this chapter I introduce you to those basic library APIs that pertain to mathematics, string management, and packages.

Exploring the Math APIs

In Chapter 2 I presented Java's +, -, *, /, and % operators for performing basic arithmetic on primitive-type values. Java also provides classes for performing trigonometry and other advanced math operations, representing monetary values accurately, and supporting extremely long integers for use in RSA encryption (http://en.wikipedia.org/wiki/RSA_(algorithm)) and other contexts.

Math and StrictMath

The java.lang.Math class declares double constants E and PI that represent the natural logarithm base value (2.71828...) and the ratio of a circle's circumference to its diameter (3.14159...). E is initialized to 2.718281828459045 and PI is initialized to 3.141592653589793. Math also declares assorted class methods to perform various math operations. Table 7-1 describes many of these methods.

Table 7-1. Math Methods

Method	Description
double abs(double d)	Return the absolute value of d. There are four special cases: abs(−0.0) = +0.0, abs(+infinity) = +infinity, abs(−infinity) = +infinity, and abs(NaN) = NaN.
float abs(float f)	Return the absolute value of f. There are four special cases: abs(−0.0) = +0.0, abs(+infinity) = +infinity, abs(−infinity) = +infinity, and abs(NaN) = NaN.
int abs(int i)	Return the absolute value of i. There is one special case: the absolute value of Integer.MIN_VALUE is Integer.MIN_VALUE.
long abs(long l)	Return the absolute value of l. There is one special case: the absolute value of Long.MIN_VALUE is Long.MIN_VALUE.
double acos(double d)	Return angle d's arc cosine within the range 0 through PI. There are three special cases: acos(anything > 1) = NaN, acos(anything < −1) = NaN, and acos(NaN) = NaN.
double asin(double d)	Return angle d's arc sine within the range -PI/2 through PI/2. There are three special cases: asin(anything > 1) = NaN, asin(anything < −1) = NaN, and asin(NaN) = NaN.
double atan(double d)	Return angle d's arc tangent within the range -PI/2 through PI/2. There are five special cases: atan(+0.0) = +0.0, atan(−0.0) = −0.0, atan(+infinity) = +PI/2, atan(−infinity) = −PI/2, and atan(NaN) = NaN.
double ceil(double d)	Return the smallest value (closest to negative infinity) that is not less than d and is equal to an integer. There are six special cases: ceil(+0.0) = +0.0, ceil(−0.0) = −0.0, ceil(anything > −1.0 and < 0.0) = −0.0, ceil(+infinity) = +infinity, ceil(−infinity) = −infinity, and ceil(NaN) = NaN.
double cos(double d)	Return the cosine of angle d (expressed in radians). There are three special cases: cos(+infinity) = NaN, cos(−infinity) = NaN, and cos(NaN) = NaN.
double exp(double d)	Return Euler's number e to the power d. There are three special cases: exp(+infinity) = +infinity, exp(−infinity) = +0.0, and exp(NaN) = NaN.
double floor(double d)	Return the largest value (closest to positive infinity) that is not greater than d and is equal to an integer. There are five special cases: floor(+0.0) = +0.0, floor(−0.0) = −0.0, floor(+infinity) = +infinity, floor(−infinity) = −infinity, and floor(NaN) = NaN.
double log(double d)	Return the natural logarithm (base e) of d. There are six special cases: log(+0.0) = −infinity, log(−0.0) = −infinity, log(anything < 0) = NaN, log(+infinity) = +infinity, log(−infinity) = NaN, and log(NaN) = NaN.
double log10(double d)	Return the base 10 logarithm of d. There are six special cases: log10(+0.0) = −infinity, log10(−0.0) = −infinity, log10(anything < 0) = NaN, log10(+infinity) = +infinity, log10(−infinity) = NaN, and log10(NaN) = NaN.

(continued)

Table 7-1. *(continued)*

Method	Description
double max(double d1, double d2)	Return the most positive (closest to positive infinity) of d1 and d2. There are four special cases: max(NaN, anything) = NaN, max(anything, NaN) = NaN, max(+0.0, -0.0) = +0.0, and max(-0.0, +0.0) = +0.0.
float max(float f1, float f2)	Return the most positive (closest to positive infinity) of f1 and f2. There are four special cases: max(NaN, anything) = NaN, max(anything, NaN) = NaN, max(+0.0, -0.0) = +0.0, and max(-0.0, +0.0) = +0.0.
int max(int i1, int i2)	Return the most positive (closest to positive infinity) of i1 and i2.
long max(long l1, long l2)	Return the most positive (closest to positive infinity) of l1 and l2.
double min(double d1, double d2)	Return the most negative (closest to negative infinity) of d1 and d2. There are four special cases: min(NaN, anything) = NaN, min(anything, NaN) = NaN, min(+0.0, -0.0) = −0.0, and min(-0.0, +0.0) = −0.0.
float min(float f1, float f2)	Return the most negative (closest to negative infinity) of f1 and f2. There are four special cases: min(NaN, anything) = NaN, min(anything, NaN) = NaN, min(+0.0, -0.0) = −0.0, and min(-0.0, +0.0) = −0.0.
int min(int i1, int i2)	Return the most negative (closest to negative infinity) of i1 and i2.
long min(long l1, long l2)	Return the most negative (closest to negative infinity) of l1 and l2.
double random()	Return a pseudorandom number between 0.0 (inclusive) and 1.0 (exclusive).
long round(double d)	Return the result of rounding d to a long integer. The result is equivalent to (long) Math.floor(d + 0.5). There are seven special cases: round(+0.0) = +0.0, round(−0.0) = +0.0, round(anything > Long.MAX_VALUE) = Long.MAX_VALUE, round(anything < Long.MIN_VALUE) = Long.MIN_VALUE, round(+infinity) = Long.MAX_VALUE, round(−infinity) = Long.MIN_VALUE, and round(NaN) = +0.0.
int round(float f)	Return the result of rounding f to an integer. The result is equivalent to (int) Math.floor(f + 0.5). There are seven special cases: round(+0.0) = +0.0, round(−0.0) = +0.0, round(anything > Integer.MAX_VALUE) = Integer.MAX_VALUE, round(anything < Integer.MIN_VALUE) = Integer.MIN_VALUE, round(+infinity) = Integer.MAX_VALUE, round(−infinity) = Integer.MIN_VALUE, and round(NaN) = +0.0.
double signum(double d)	Return the sign of d as −1.0 (d less than 0.0), 0.0 (d equals 0.0), and 1.0 (d greater than 0.0). There are five special cases: signum(+0.0) = +0.0, signum(−0.0) = −0.0, signum(+infinity) = +1.0, signum(−infinity) = −1.0, and signum(NaN) = NaN.
float signum(float f)	Return the sign of f as −1.0 (f less than 0.0), 0.0 (f equals 0.0), and 1.0 (f greater than 0.0). There are five special cases: signum(+0.0) = +0.0, signum(−0.0) = −0.0, signum(+infinity) = +1.0, signum(−infinity) = −1.0, and signum(NaN) = NaN.

(continued)

Table 7-1. (continued)

Method	Description
double sin(double d)	Return the sine of angle d (expressed in radians). There are five special cases: sin(+0.0) = +0.0, sin(−0.0) = −0.0, sin(+infinity) = NaN, sin(−infinity) = NaN, and sin(NaN) = NaN.
double sqrt(double d)	Return the square root of d. There are five special cases: sqrt(+0.0) = +0.0, sqrt(−0.0) = −0.0, sqrt(anything < 0) = NaN, sqrt(+infinity) = +infinity, and sqrt(NaN) = NaN.
double tan(double d)	Return the tangent of angle d (expressed in radians). There are five special cases: tan(+0.0) = +0.0, tan(−0.0) = −0.0, tan(+infinity) = NaN, tan(−infinity) = NaN, and tan(NaN) = NaN.
double toDegrees(double angrad)	Convert angle angrad from radians to degrees via expression angrad * 180 / PI. There are five special cases: toDegrees(+0.0) = +0.0, toDegrees(−0.0) = −0.0, toDegrees(+infinity) = +infinity, toDegrees(−infinity) = −infinity, and toDegrees(NaN) = NaN.
double toRadians(double angdeg)	Convert angle angdeg from degrees to radians via expression angdeg / 180 * PI. There are five special cases: toRadians(+0.0) = +0.0, toRadians(−0.0) = −0.0, toRadians(+infinity) = +infinity, toRadians(−infinity) = −infinity, and toRadians(NaN) = NaN.

Table 7-1 reveals a wide variety of useful math-oriented methods. For example, each abs() method returns its argument's *absolute value* (number without regard for sign).

abs(double) and abs(float) are useful for comparing double precision floating-point and floating-point values safely. For example, 0.3 == 0.1 + 0.1 + 0.1 evaluates to false because 0.1 has no exact representation. However, you can compare these expressions with abs() and a tolerance value, which indicates an acceptable range of error. For example, Math.abs(0.3 - (0.1 + 0.1 + 0.1)) < 0.1 returns true because the absolute difference between 0.3 and 0.1 + 0.1 + 0.1 is less than a 0.1 tolerance value.

In previous chapters I demonstrated other Math methods. For example, in Chapter 3 I demonstrated Math's sin(), toRadians(), cos(), and random() methods.

As Chapter 6's Lotto649 application revealed, random() (which returns a number that appears to be randomly chosen but is actually chosen by a predictable math calculation and hence is *pseudorandom*) is useful in simulations (as well as in games and wherever an element of chance is needed). However, its double precision floating-point range of 0.0 through (almost) 1.0 isn't practical. To make random() more useful, its return value must be transformed into a more useful range, perhaps integer values 0 through 49, or maybe -100 through 100. You will find the following rnd() method useful for making these transformations:

```
static int rnd(int limit)
{
   return (int) (Math.random() * limit);
}
```

rnd() transforms random()'s 0.0 to (almost) 1.0 double precision floating-point range to a 0 through limit - 1 integer range. For example, rnd(50) returns an integer ranging from 0 through 49. Also, -100 + rnd(201) transforms 0.0 to (almost) 1.0 into –100 through 100 by adding a suitable offset and passing an appropriate limit value.

> **Caution** Don't specify (int) Math.random() * limit because this expression always evaluates to 0. The expression first casts random()'s double precision floating-point fractional value (0.0 through 0.99999…) to integer 0 by truncating the fractional part and then multiplies 0 by limit, which results in 0.

The sin() and cos() methods implement the sine and cosine trigonometric functions—see http://en.wikipedia.org/wiki/Trigonometric_functions. These functions have uses ranging from the study of triangles to modeling periodic phenomena (such as simple harmonic motion—see http://en.wikipedia.org/wiki/Simple_harmonic_motion).

You can use sin() and cos() to generate and display sine and cosine waves. Listing 7-1 presents the source code to an application that does just this.

Listing 7-1. Graphing Sine and Cosine Waves

```java
public class Graph
{
   final static int ROWS = 11; // Must be odd
   final static int COLS = 23;

   public static void main(String[] args)
   {
      char[][] screen = new char[ROWS][COLS];
      double scaleX = COLS / 360.0;
      for (int degree = 0; degree < 360; degree++)
      {
         int row = ROWS / 2 +
                   (int) Math.round(ROWS / 2 * Math.sin(Math.toRadians(degree)));
         int col = (int) (degree * scaleX);
         screen[row][col] = 'S';
         row = ROWS / 2 +
               (int) Math.round(ROWS / 2 * Math.cos(Math.toRadians(degree)));
         screen[row][col] = (screen[row][col] == 'S') ? '*' : 'C';
      }
      for (int row = ROWS - 1; row >= 0; row--)
      {
         for (int col = 0; col < COLS; col++)
            System.out.print(screen[row][col]);
         System.out.println();
      }
   }
}
```

Listing 7-1 introduces a Graph class that first declares a pair of constants: ROWS and COLS. These constants specify the dimensions of an array on which the graphs are generated. ROWS must be assigned an odd integer; otherwise, an instance of the java.lang.ArrayIndexOutOfBoundsException class is thrown.

> **Tip**   It's a good idea to use constants wherever possible. The source code is easier to maintain because you only need to change the constant's value in one place instead of having to change each corresponding value throughout the source code.

Graph next declares its main() method, which first creates a two-dimensional screen array of characters. This array is used to simulate an old-style character-based screen for viewing the graphs.

main() next calculates a horizontal scale value for scaling each graph horizontally so that 360 horizontal (degree) positions fit into the number of columns specified by COLS.

Continuing, main() enters a for loop that, for each of the sine and cosine graphs, creates (row, column) coordinates for each degree value, and assigns a character to the screen array at those coordinates. The character is S for the sine graph, C for the cosine graph, and * when the cosine graph intersects the sine graph.

The row calculation invokes toRadians() to convert its degree argument to radians, which is required by the sin() and cos() methods. The value returned from sin() or cos() (–1 to 1) is then multiplied by ROWS / 2 to scale this value to half the number of rows in the screen array. After rounding the result to the nearest long integer via the long round(double d) method, a cast is used to convert from long integer to integer, and this integer is added to ROW / 2 to offset the row coordinate so that it's relative to the array's middle row. The column calculation is simpler, multiplying the degree value by the horizontal scale factor.

The screen array is dumped to the standard output device via a pair of nested for loops. The outer for loop reverses the array output so that it appears right side up—row number 0 should output last.

Compile Listing 7-1 (javac Graph.java) and run the application (java Graph). You will observe the following output:

```
CC  SSSS                CC
 CSSS  SS               CC
  S*C     SS           CC
  S CC     SS         CC
 SS  CC     SS       CC
 S      CC     S    CC     S
        C     SS  C     SS
       CC     SS CC     S
       CC      SCC     SS
      CC     CSS  SSS
     CCCCC  SSSS
```

Table 7-1 also reveals some curiosities beginning with +infinity, –infinity, +0.0, –0.0, and NaN (Not a Number).

Java's floating-point calculations are capable of returning +infinity, –infinity, +0.0, –0.0, and NaN because Java largely conforms to IEEE 754 (http://en.wikipedia.org/wiki/IEEE_754), a standard for floating-point calculations. The following are the circumstances under which these special values arise:

- +infinity returns from attempting to divide a positive number by 0.0. For example, System.out.println(1.0 / 0.0); outputs Infinity.

- –infinity returns from attempting to divide a negative number by 0.0. For example, System.out.println(–1.0 / 0.0); outputs -Infinity.

- NaN returns from attempting to divide 0.0 by 0.0, attempting to calculate the square root of a negative number, and attempting other strange operations. For example, System.out.println(0.0 / 0.0); and System.out.println(Math.sqrt(–1.0)); each output NaN.

- +0.0 results from attempting to divide a positive number by +infinity. For example, System.out.println(1.0 / (1.0 / 0.0)); outputs 0.0 (+0.0 without the + sign).

- –0.0 results from attempting to divide a negative number by +infinity. For example, System.out.println(–1.0 / (1.0 / 0.0)); outputs –0.0.

After an operation yields +infinity, -infinity, or NaN, the rest of the expression usually equals that special value. For example, System.out.println(1.0 / 0.0 * 20.0); outputs Infinity. Also, an expression that first yields +infinity or -infinity might devolve into NaN. For example, expression 1.0 / 0.0 * 0.0 first yields +infinity (1.0 / 0.0) and then yields NaN (+infinity * 0.0).

Another curiosity is Integer.MAX_VALUE, Integer.MIN_VALUE, Long.MAX_VALUE, and Long.MIN_VALUE. Each of these items is a primitive wrapper class constant that identifies the maximum or minimum value that can be represented by the class's associated primitive type. (I discuss the primitive type wrapper classes in Chapter 8.)

Finally, you might wonder why the abs(), max(), and min() overloaded methods don't include byte and short versions, as in byte abs(byte b) and short abs(short s). There is no need for these methods because the limited ranges of bytes and short integers make them unsuitable in calculations. If you need such a method, check out Listing 7-2.

Listing 7-2. Obtaining Absolute Values for Byte Integers and Short Integers

```
public class AbsByteShort
{
   static byte abs(byte b)
   {
      return (b < 0) ? (byte) -b : b;
   }

   static short abs(short s)
   {
      return (s < 0) ? (short) -s : s;
   }
```

```
public static void main(String[] args)
{
    byte b = -2;
    System.out.println(abs(b)); // Output: 2
    short s = -3;
    System.out.println(abs(s)); // Output: 3
}
}
```

Listing 7-2's (byte) and (short) casts are necessary because -b converts b's value from a byte to an int, and -s converts s's value from a short to an int. In contrast, these casts are not needed with (b < 0) and (s < 0), which automatically cast b's and s's values to an int before comparing them with int-based 0.

> **Tip** Their absence from Math suggests that byte and short are not very useful in method declarations. However, these types are useful when declaring arrays whose elements store small values (such as a binary file's byte values). If you declared an array of int or long to store such values, you would end up wasting heap space (and might even run out of memory).

While searching through the java.lang package documentation, you will probably encounter a class named StrictMath. Apart from a longer name, this class appears to be identical to Math. The differences between these classes can be summed up as follows:

- StrictMath's methods return exactly the same results on all platforms. In contrast, some of Math's methods might return values that vary ever so slightly from platform to platform.

- Because StrictMath cannot utilize platform-specific features such as an extended-precision math coprocessor, an implementation of StrictMath might be less efficient than an implementation of Math.

For the most part, Math's methods call their StrictMath counterparts. Two exceptions are toDegrees() and toRadians(). Although these methods have identical code bodies in both classes, StrictMath's implementations include reserved word strictfp in the method headers:

```
public static strictfp double toDegrees(double angrad)
public static strictfp double toRadians(double angdeg)
```

Wikipedia's "strictfp" entry (http://en.wikipedia.org/wiki/Strictfp) mentions that strictfp restricts floating-point calculations to ensure portability. This reserved word accomplishes portability in the context of intermediate floating-point representations and overflows/underflows (generating a value too large or small to fit a representation).

Without strictfp, an intermediate calculation is not limited to the IEEE 754 32-bit and 64-bit floating-point representations that Java supports. Instead, the calculation can take advantage of a larger representation (perhaps 128 bits) on a platform that supports this representation.

An intermediate calculation that overflows or underflows when its value is represented in 32/64 bits might not overflow/underflow when its value is represented in more bits. Because of this discrepancy, portability is compromised. strictfp levels the playing field by requiring all platforms to use 32/64 bits for intermediate calculations.

When applied to a method, strictfp ensures that all floating-point calculations performed in that method are in strict compliance. However, strictfp can be used in a class header declaration (as in public strictfp class FourierTransform) to ensure that all floating-point calculations performed in that class are strict.

> **Note**   Math and StrictMath are declared final so that they cannot be extended. Also, they declare private empty noargument constructors so that they cannot be instantiated. Finally, Math and StrictMath are examples of utility classes because they exist as placeholders for utility constants and utility (static) methods.

BigDecimal

In Chapter 3 I introduced a SavingsAccount class with a balance field of type int. This field records the number of dollars in this account. Alternatively, it could represent the number of pennies that the account contains.

Perhaps you are wondering why I didn't declare balance to be of type double or float. That way, balance could store values such as 18.26 (18 dollars in the whole number part and 26 pennies in the fraction part). I didn't declare balance to be a double or float for the following reasons:

- Not all floating-point values that can represent monetary amounts (dollars and cents) can be stored exactly in memory. For example, 0.1 (which you might use to represent 10 cents), has no exact storage representation. If you executed double total = 0.1; for (int i = 0; i < 50; i++) total += 0.1; System.out.println(total);, you would observe 5.099999999999998 instead of the correct 5.1 as the output.

- The result of each floating-point calculation needs to be rounded to the nearest cent. Failure to do so introduces tiny errors that can cause the final result to differ from the correct result. Although Math supplies a pair of round() methods that you might consider using to round a calculation to the nearest cent, these methods round to the nearest integer (dollar).

Listing 7-3's InvoiceCalc application demonstrates both problems. However, the first problem isn't serious because it contributes very little to the inaccuracy. The more serious problem occurs from failing to round to the nearest cent after performing a calculation.

Listing 7-3. Floating-Point-Based Invoice Calculations Leading to Confusing Results

```java
import java.text.NumberFormat;

public class InvoiceCalc
{
   final static double DISCOUNT_PERCENT = 0.1; // 10%
   final static double TAX_PERCENT = 0.05; // 5%

   public static void main(String[] args)
   {
      double invoiceSubtotal = 285.36;
      double discount = invoiceSubtotal * DISCOUNT_PERCENT;
      double subtotalBeforeTax = invoiceSubtotal - discount;
      double salesTax = subtotalBeforeTax * TAX_PERCENT;
      double invoiceTotal = subtotalBeforeTax + salesTax;
      NumberFormat currencyFormat = NumberFormat.getCurrencyInstance();
      System.out.println("Subtotal: " + currencyFormat.format(invoiceSubtotal));
      System.out.println("Discount: " + currencyFormat.format(discount));
      System.out.println("SubTotal after discount: " +
                         currencyFormat.format(subtotalBeforeTax));
      System.out.println("Sales Tax: " + currencyFormat.format(salesTax));
      System.out.println("Total: " + currencyFormat.format(invoiceTotal));
   }
}
```

Listing 7-3 performs several invoice-related calculations that result in an incorrect final total. After performing these calculations, it obtains a currency-based formatter for formatting double precision floating-point values into string-based monetary amounts with a currency symbol (such as the dollar sign [$]). The formatter is obtained by calling the java.text.NumberFormat class's NumberFormat getCurrencyInstance() method. A value is then formatted into a currency string by passing this value as an argument to NumberFormat's String format(double value) method.

When you run InvoiceCalc, you will discover the following output:

```
Subtotal: $285.36
Discount: $28.54
SubTotal after discount: $256.82
Sales Tax: $12.84
Total: $269.67
```

This output reveals the correct subtotal, discount, subtotal after discount, and sales tax. In contrast, it incorrectly reveals 269.67 instead of 269.66 as the final total. The customer will probably not appreciate paying an extra penny, even though 269.67 is the correct value according to the floating-point calculations:

```
Subtotal: 285.36
Discount: 28.536
SubTotal after discount: 256.824
Sales Tax: 12.8412
Total: 269.6652
```

The problem arises from not rounding the result of each calculation to the nearest cent before performing the next calculation. As a result, the 0.024 in 256.824 and 0.0012 in 12.84 contribute to the final value, causing NumberFormat's format() method to round this value to 269.67.

> **Caution**   Never use float or double to represent monetary values.

Java provides a solution to both problems in the form of a java.math.BigDecimal class. This immutable class (a BigDecimal instance cannot be modified) represents a signed decimal number (such as 23.653) of arbitrary *precision* (number of digits) with an associated *scale* (an integer that specifies the number of digits after the decimal point).

BigDecimal declares three convenience constants: ONE, TEN, and ZERO. Each constant is the BigDecimal equivalent of 1, 10, and 0 with a zero scale.

> **Caution**   BigDecimal declares several ROUND_-prefixed constants. These constants are largely obsolete and should be avoided, along with the public BigDecimal divide(BigDecimal divisor, int scale, int roundingMode) and public BigDecimal setScale(int newScale, int roundingMode) methods, which are still present so that dependent legacy code continues to compile.

BigDecimal also declares a variety of useful constructors and methods. A few of these constructors and methods are described in Table 7-2.

Table 7-2. BigDecimal Constructors and Methods

Method	Description
BigDecimal(int val)	Initialize the BigDecimal instance to val's digits. Set the scale to 0.
BigDecimal(String val)	Initialize the BigDecimal instance to the decimal equivalent of val. Set the scale to the number of digits after the decimal point or 0 when no decimal point is specified. This constructor throws java.lang.NullPointerException when val is null and java.lang.NumberFormatException when val's string representation is invalid (contains letters, for example).
BigDecimal abs()	Return a new BigDecimal instance that contains the absolute value of the current instance's value. The resulting scale is the same as the current instance's scale.
BigDecimal add(BigDecimal augend)	Return a new BigDecimal instance that contains the sum of the current value and the argument value. The resulting scale is the maximum of the current and argument scales. This method throws NullPointerException when augend is null.

(continued)

Table 7-2. (*continued*)

Method	Description
BigDecimal divide(BigDecimal divisor)	Return a new BigDecimal instance that contains the quotient of the current value divided by the argument value. The resulting scale is the difference of the current and argument scales. It might be adjusted when the result requires more digits. This method throws NullPointerException when divisor is null or java.lang.ArithmeticException when divisor represents 0 or the result cannot be represented exactly.
BigDecimal max(BigDecimal val)	Return either this or val, whichever BigDecimal instance contains the larger value. This method throws NullPointerException when val is null.
BigDecimal min(BigDecimal val)	Return either this or val, whichever BigDecimal instance contains the smaller value. This method throws NullPointerException when val is null.
BigDecimal multiply(BigDecimal multiplicand)	Return a new BigDecimal instance that contains the product of the current value and the argument value. The resulting scale is the sum of the current and argument scales. This method throws NullPointerException when multiplicand is null.
BigDecimal negate()	Return a new BigDecimal instance that contains the negative of the current value. The resulting scale is the same as the current scale.
int precision()	Return the precision of the current BigDecimal instance.
BigDecimal remainder(BigDecimal divisor)	Return a new BigDecimal instance that contains the remainder of the current value divided by the argument value. The resulting scale is the difference of the current scale and the argument scale. It might be adjusted when the result requires more digits. This method throws NullPointerException when divisor is null or ArithmeticException when divisor represents 0.
int scale()	Return the scale of the current BigDecimal instance.
BigDecimal setScale(int newScale, RoundingMode roundingMode)	Return a new BigDecimal instance with the specified scale and rounding mode. If the new scale is greater than the old scale, additional zeros are added to the unscaled value. In this case no rounding is necessary. If the new scale is smaller than the old scale, trailing digits are removed. If these trailing digits are not zero, the remaining unscaled value has to be rounded. For this rounding operation, the specified rounding mode is used. This method throws NullPointerException when roundingMode is null and ArithmeticException when roundingMode is set to RoundingMode.ROUND_UNNECESSARY, but rounding is necessary based on the current scale.
BigDecimal subtract(BigDecimal subtrahend)	Return a new BigDecimal instance that contains the current value minus the argument value. The resulting scale is the maximum of the current and argument scales. This method throws NullPointerException when subtrahend is null.
String toString()	Return a string representation of this BigDecimal instance. Scientific notation is used when necessary.

Table 7-2 refers to java.math.RoundingMode, which is an enum containing various rounding mode constants. These constants are described in Table 7-3.

Table 7-3. RoundingMode Constants

Constant	Description
CEILING	Round toward positive infinity.
DOWN	Round toward zero.
FLOOR	Round toward negative infinity.
HALF_DOWN	Round toward the "nearest neighbor" unless both neighbors are equidistant, in which case round down.
HALF_EVEN	Round toward the "nearest neighbor" unless both neighbors are equidistant, in which case round toward the even neighbor.
HALF_UP	Round toward "nearest neighbor" unless both neighbors are equidistant, in which case round up. (This is the rounding mode commonly taught at school.)
UNNECESSARY	Rounding isn't necessary because the requested operation produces the exact result.
UP	Positive values are rounded toward positive infinity and negative values are rounded toward negative infinity.

The best way to get comfortable with BigDecimal is to try it out. Listing 7-4 uses this class to correctly perform the invoice calculations that were presented in Listing 7-3.

Listing 7-4. BigDecimal-Based Invoice Calculations Not Leading to Confusing Results

```java
import java.math.BigDecimal;
import java.math.RoundingMode;

public class InvoiceCalc
{
   public static void main(String[] args)
   {
      BigDecimal invoiceSubtotal = new BigDecimal("285.36");
      BigDecimal discountPercent = new BigDecimal("0.10");
      BigDecimal discount = invoiceSubtotal.multiply(discountPercent);
      discount = discount.setScale(2, RoundingMode.HALF_UP);
      BigDecimal subtotalBeforeTax = invoiceSubtotal.subtract(discount);
      subtotalBeforeTax = subtotalBeforeTax.setScale(2, RoundingMode.HALF_UP);
      BigDecimal salesTaxPercent = new BigDecimal("0.05");
      BigDecimal salesTax = subtotalBeforeTax.multiply(salesTaxPercent);
      salesTax = salesTax.setScale(2, RoundingMode.HALF_UP);
      BigDecimal invoiceTotal = subtotalBeforeTax.add(salesTax);
      invoiceTotal = invoiceTotal.setScale(2, RoundingMode.HALF_UP);
      System.out.println("Subtotal: " + invoiceSubtotal);
      System.out.println("Discount: " + discount);
      System.out.println("SubTotal after discount: " + subtotalBeforeTax);
```

```
        System.out.println("Sales Tax: " + salesTax);
        System.out.println("Total: " + invoiceTotal);
    }
}
```

Listing 7-4's main() method first creates BigDecimal objects invoiceSubtotal and discountPercent that are initialized to 285.36 and 0.10, respectively. It multiplies invoiceSubtotal by discountPercent and assigns the BigDecimal result to discount.

At this point, discount contains 28.5360. Apart from the trailing zero, this value is the same as that generated by invoiceSubtotal * DISCOUNT_PERCENT in Listing 7–3. The value that should be stored in discount is 28.54. To correct this problem before performing another calculation, main() calls discount's setScale() method with these arguments:

- 2: Two digits after the decimal point
- RoundingMode.HALF_UP: The conventional approach to rounding

After setting the scale and proper rounding mode, main() subtracts discount from invoiceSubtotal and assigns the resulting BigDecimal instance to subtotalBeforeTax. main() calls setScale() on subtotalBeforeTax to properly round its value before moving on to the next calculation.

main() next creates a BigDecimal object named salesTaxPercent that is initialized to 0.05. It then multiplies subtotalBeforeTax by salesTaxPercent, assigning the result to salesTax, and calls setScale() on this BigDecimal object to properly round its value.

Moving on, main() adds salesTax to subtotalBeforeTax, saving the result in invoiceTotal, and rounds the result via setScale(). The values in these objects are sent to the standard output device via System.out.println(), which calls their toString() methods to return string representations of the BigDecimal values.

When you run this new version of InvoiceCalc, you will discover the following output:

```
Subtotal: 285.36
Discount: 28.54
SubTotal after discount: 256.82
Sales Tax: 12.84
Total: 269.66
```

> **Caution**   BigDecimal declares a BigDecimal(double val) constructor that you should avoid using if at all possible. This constructor initializes the BigDecimal instance to the value stored in val, making it possible for this instance to reflect an invalid representation when the double cannot be stored exactly. For example, BigDecimal(0.1) results in 0.1000000000000000055511151231257827021181583404541 015625 being stored in the instance. In contrast, BigDecimal("0.1") stores 0.1 exactly.

BigInteger

BigDecimal stores a signed decimal number as an unscaled value with a 32-bit integer scale. The unscaled value is stored in an instance of the java.math.BigInteger class.

BigInteger is an immutable class that represents a signed integer of arbitrary precision. It stores its value in *two's complement format* (all bits are flipped—1s to 0s and 0s to 1s—and 1 is added to the result to be compatible with the two's complement format used by Java's byte integer, short integer, integer, and long integer types).

> **Note**   Check out Wikipedia's "Two's complement" entry (http://en.wikipedia.org/wiki/Two's_complement) to learn more about two's complement.

BigInteger declares three convenience constants: ONE, TEN, and ZERO. Each constant is the BigInteger equivalent of 1, 10, and 0.

BigInteger also declares a variety of useful constructors and methods. A few of these constructors and methods are described in Table 7-4.

Table 7-4. BigInteger Constructors and Methods

Method	Description
BigInteger(byte[] val)	Initialize the BigInteger instance to the integer that is stored in the val array, with val[0] storing the integer's most significant (leftmost) 8 bits. This constructor throws NullPointerException when val is null and NumberFormatException when val.length equals 0.
BigInteger(String val)	Initialize the BigInteger instance to the integer equivalent of val. This constructor throws NullPointerException when val is null and NumberFormatException when val's string representation is invalid (contains letters, for example).
BigInteger abs()	Return a new BigInteger instance that contains the absolute value of the current instance's value.
BigInteger add(BigInteger augend)	Return a new BigInteger instance that contains the sum of the current value and the argument value. This method throws NullPointerException when augend is null.
BigInteger divide(BigInteger divisor)	Return a new BigInteger instance that contains the quotient of the current value divided by the argument value. This method throws NullPointerException when divisor is null and ArithmeticException when divisor represents 0 or the result cannot be represented exactly.
BigInteger max(BigInteger val)	Return either this or val, whichever BigInteger instance contains the larger value. This method throws NullPointerException when val is null.
BigInteger min(BigInteger val)	Return either this or val, whichever BigInteger instance contains the smaller value. This method throws NullPointerException when val is null.

(continued)

Table 7-4. (continued)

Method	Description
BigInteger multiply(BigInteger multiplicand)	Return a new BigInteger instance that contains the product of the current value and the argument value. This method throws NullPointerException when multiplicand is null.
BigInteger negate()	Return a new BigInteger instance that contains the negative of the current value.
BigInteger remainder(BigInteger divisor)	Return a new BigInteger instance that contains the remainder of the current value divided by the argument value. This method throws NullPointerException when divisor is null and ArithmeticException when divisor represents 0.
BigInteger subtract(BigInteger subtrahend)	Return a new BigInteger instance that contains the current value minus the argument value. This method throws NullPointerException when subtrahend is null.
String toString()	Return a string representation of this BigInteger instance.

> **Note**   BigInteger also declares several bit-oriented methods, such as BigInteger and(BigInteger val), BigInteger flipBit(int n), and BigInteger shiftLeft(int n). These methods are useful for when you need to perform low-level bit manipulation.

The best way to get comfortable with BigInteger is to try it out. Listing 7-5 uses this class in a factorial() method comparison context.

Listing 7-5. Comparing factorial() Methods

```java
import java.math.BigInteger;

public class FactComp
{
   public static void main(String[] args)
   {
      System.out.println(factorial(12));
      System.out.println();
      System.out.println(factorial(20L));
      System.out.println();
      System.out.println(factorial(170.0));
      System.out.println();
      System.out.println(factorial(new BigInteger("170")));
      System.out.println();
      System.out.println(factorial(25.0));
      System.out.println();
      System.out.println(factorial(new BigInteger("25")));
   }
```

```
static int factorial(int n)
{
   if (n == 0)
      return 1;
   else
      return n * factorial(n - 1);
}

static long factorial(long n)
{
   if (n == 0)
      return 1;
   else
      return n * factorial(n - 1);
}

static double factorial(double n)
{
   if (n == 1.0)
      return 1.0;
   else
      return n * factorial(n - 1);
}

static BigInteger factorial(BigInteger n)
{
   if (n.equals(BigInteger.ZERO))
      return BigInteger.ONE;
   else
      return n.multiply(factorial(n.subtract(BigInteger.ONE)));
}
}
```

Listing 7-5 compares four versions of the recursive factorial() method. This comparison reveals the largest argument that can be passed to each of the first three methods before the returned factorial value becomes meaningless because of limits on the range of values that can be accurately represented by the numeric type.

The first version is based on int and has a useful argument range of 0 through 12. Passing any argument greater than 12 results in a factorial that cannot be represented accurately as an int.

You can increase the useful range of factorial(), but not by much, by changing the parameter and return types to long. After making these changes, you will discover that the upper limit of the useful range is 20.

To further increase the useful range, you might create a version of factorial() whose parameter and return types are double. This is possible because whole numbers can be represented exactly as doubles. However, the largest useful argument that can be passed is 170.0. Anything higher than this value results in factorial() returning +infinity.

It's possible that you might need to calculate a higher factorial value, perhaps in the context of calculating a statistics problem involving combinations or permutations. The only way to accurately calculate this value is to use a version of factorial() based on BigInteger.

When you run the previous application, it generates the following output:

479001600

2432902008176640000

7.257415615307994E306

7257415615307998967396728211129263114716991681296451376543577798900561843401706157852350749242617459511490991237838520776666022565442753025328900773207510902400430280058295603966612599658257104398558294257568966313439612262571094946806711205568880457193340212661452800000000000000000000000000000000000000000000

1.5511210043330986E25

15511210043330985984000000

The first three values represent the highest factorials that can be returned by the int-based, long-based, and double-based factorial() methods. The fourth value represents the BigInteger equivalent of the highest double factorial.

Notice that the double method fails to accurately represent 170! (! is the math symbol for factorial). Its precision is simply too small. Although the method attempts to round the smallest digit, rounding doesn't always work—the number ends in 7994 instead of 7998. Rounding is only accurate up to argument 25.0, as the last two output lines reveal.

Exploring String Management

Many computer languages implement the concept of a *string*, a sequence of characters treated as a single unit (and not as individual characters). For example, the C language implements a string as an array of characters terminated by the null character ('\0'). In contrast, Java implements a string via the java.lang.String class.

String objects are immutable: you cannot modify a String object's string. The various String methods that appear to modify the String object actually return a new String object with modified string content instead. Because returning new String objects is often wasteful, Java provides the java.lang.StringBuffer and equivalent java.lang.StringBuilder classes as a workaround.

In this section I introduce you to String and StringBuffer/StringBuilder.

String

String represents a string as a sequence of characters. In contrast to C strings, this sequence is not terminated by a null character. Instead, its length is stored separately. Unlike other reference types, the Java language treats the String class specially by providing syntactic sugar that simplifies working with strings. For example, Java recognizes String favLanguage = "Java"; as the assignment of string literal "Java" to String variable favLanguage. Without this sugar, you would have to specify String favLanguage = new String("Java");. The Java language also overloads the + and += operators to perform string concatenation.

Table 7-5 describes some of `String`'s constructors and methods for initializing `String` objects and working with strings.

Table 7-5. *String Constructors and Methods*

Method	Description
String(char[] data)	Initialize this `String` object to the characters in the data array. Modifying data after initializing this `String` object has no effect on the object.
String(String s)	Initialize this `String` object to s's string.
char charAt(int index)	Return the character located at the zero-based index in this `String` object's string. This method throws `java.lang.StringIndexOutOfBoundsException` when index is less than 0 or greater than or equal to the length of the string.
String concat(String s)	Return a new `String` object containing this `String` object's string followed by the s argument's string.
boolean endsWith(String suffix)	Return true when this `String` object's string ends with the characters in the suffix argument, when suffix is empty (contains no characters), or when suffix contains the same character sequence as this `String` object's string. This method performs a case-sensitive comparison (a is not equal to A, for example) and throws `NullPointerException` when suffix is null.
boolean equals(Object object)	Return true when object is of type `String` and this argument's string contains the same characters (and in the same order) as this `String` object's string.
boolean equalsIgnoreCase(String s)	Return true when s and this `String` object contain the same characters (ignoring case). This method returns false when the character sequences differ or when null is passed to s.
int indexOf(int c)	Return the zero-based index of the first occurrence (from the start of the string to the end of the string) of the character represented by c in this `String` object's string. Return −1 when this character is not present.
int indexOf(String s)	Return the zero-based index of the first occurrence (from the start of the string to the end of the string) of s's character sequence in this `String` object's string. Return −1 when s is not present. This method throws `NullPointerException` when s is null.
String intern()	Search an internal table of `String` objects for an object whose string is equal to this `String` object's string. This `String` object's string is added to the table when not present. Return the object contained in the table whose string is equal to this `String` object's string. The same `String` object is always returned for strings that are equal.
int lastIndexOf(int c)	Return the zero-based index of the last occurrence (from the start of the string to the end of the string) of the character represented by c in this `String` object's string. Return −1 when this character is not present.

(continued)

Table 7-5. (*continued*)

Method	Description
`int lastIndexOf(String s)`	Return the zero-based index of the last occurrence (from the start of the string to the end of the string) of s's character sequence in this `String` object's string. Return -1 when s is not present. This method throws `NullPointerException` when s is null.
`int length()`	Return the number of characters in this `String` object's string.
`String replace(char oldChar, char newChar)`	Return a new `String` object whose string matches this `String` object's string except that all occurrences of oldChar have been replaced by newChar.
`String[] split(String expr)`	Split this `String` object's string into an array of `String` objects using the *regular expression* (a string whose *pattern* [template] is used to search a string for substrings that match the pattern) specified by expr as the basis for the split. This method throws `NullPointerException` when expr is null and `java.util.regex.PatternSyntaxException` when expr's syntax is invalid.
`boolean startsWith(String prefix)`	Return true when this `String` object's string starts with the characters in the prefix argument, when prefix is empty (contains no characters), or when prefix contains the same character sequence as this `String` object's string. This method performs a case-sensitive comparison (a is not equal to A, for example) and throws `NullPointerException` when prefix is null.
`String substring(int start)`	Return a new `String` object whose string contains this `String` object's characters beginning with the character located at start. This method throws `StringIndexOutOfBoundsException` when start is negative or greater than the length of this `String` object's string.
`char[] toCharArray()`	Return a character array that contains the characters in this `String` object's string.
`String toLowerCase()`	Return a new `String` object whose string contains this `String` object's characters where uppercase letters have been converted to lowercase. This `String` object is returned when it contains no uppercase letters to convert.
`String toUpperCase()`	Return a new `String` object whose string contains this `String` object's characters where lowercase letters have been converted to uppercase. This `String` object is returned when it contains no lowercase letters to convert.
`String trim()`	Return a new `String` object that contains this `String` object's string with *whitespace characters* (characters whose Unicode values are 32 or less) removed from the start and end of the string or this `String` object when there is no leading/trailing whitespace.

Table 7-5 reveals a couple of interesting items about String. First, this class's String(String s) constructor doesn't initialize a String object to a string literal. Instead, it behaves similarly to the C++ copy constructor by initializing the String object to the contents of another String object. This behavior suggests that a string literal is more than it appears to be.

In reality, a string literal is a String object. You can prove this to yourself by executing System.out.println("abc".length()); and System.out.println("abc" instanceof String);. The first method call outputs 3, which is the length of the "abc" String object's string, and the second method call outputs true ("abc" is a String object).

> **Note** String literals are stored in a classfile data structure known as the *constant pool*. When a class is loaded, a String object is created for each literal and is stored in an internal table of String objects.

The second interesting item is the intern() method, which *interns* (stores a unique copy of) a String object in an internal table of String objects. intern() makes it possible to compare strings via their references and == or !=. These operators are the fastest way to compare strings, which is especially valuable when sorting a huge number of strings.

By default, String objects denoted by literal strings ("abc") and string-valued constant expressions ("a" + "bc") are interned in this table, which is why System.out.println("abc" == "a" + "bc"); outputs true. However, String objects created via String constructors are not interned, which is why System.out.println("abc" == new String("abc")); outputs false. In contrast, System.out.println("abc" == new String("abc").intern()); outputs true.

> **Caution** Be careful with this string comparison technique (which only compares references) because you can easily introduce a bug when one of the strings being compared has not been interned. When in doubt, use the equals() or equalsIgnoreCase() method. For example, each of "abc".equals(new String("abc")) and "abc".equalsIgnoreCase(new String("ABC")) returns true.

Table 7-5 also reveals the charAt() and length() methods, which are useful for iterating over a string's characters. For example, String s = "abc"; for (int i = 0; i < s.length(); i++) System.out.println(s.charAt(i)); returns each of s's a, b, and c characters and outputs each character on a separate line.

Finally, Table 7-5 presents split(), a method that I employed in Chapter 6's StubFinder application to split a string's comma-separated list of values into an array of String objects. This method uses a regular expression that identifies a sequence of characters around which the string is split. (I will discuss regular expressions in Chapter 13.)

> **Note** StringIndexOutOfBoundsException and ArrayIndexOutOfBoundsException are sibling classes that share a common java.lang.IndexOutOfBoundsException superclass.

StringBuffer and StringBuilder

String objects are immutable: you cannot modify a String object's string. The String methods that appear to modify the String object (such as replace()) actually return a new String object with modified string content instead. Because returning new String objects is often wasteful, Java provides the java.lang.StringBuffer and java.lang.StringBuilder classes as a workaround.

StringBuffer and StringBuilder are identical apart from the fact that StringBuilder offers better performance than StringBuffer but cannot be used in the context of multiple threads without explicit thread synchronization (discussed in Chapter 8).

Tip   Use StringBuffer in a multithreaded context (for safety) and StringBuilder in a single-threaded context (for performance).

StringBuffer and StringBuilder provide an internal character array for building a string efficiently. After creating a StringBuffer/StringBuilder object, you call various methods to append, delete, and insert the character representations of various values to, from, and into the array. You then call toString() to convert the array's content to a String object and return this object.

Table 7-6 describes some of StringBuffer's constructors and methods for initializing StringBuffer objects and working with string buffers. StringBuilder's constructors and methods are identical and won't be discussed.

Table 7-6. StringBuffer Constructors and Methods

Method	Description
StringBuffer()	Initialize this StringBuffer object to an empty array with an initial capacity of 16 characters.
StringBuffer(int capacity)	Initialize this StringBuffer object to an empty array with an initial capacity of capacity characters. This constructor throws java.lang.NegativeArraySizeException when capacity is negative.
StringBuffer(String s)	Initialize this StringBuffer object to an array containing s's characters. This object's initial capacity is 16 plus the length of s. This constructor throws NullPointerException when s is null.
StringBuffer append(boolean b)	Append "true" to this StringBuffer object's array when b is true and "false" to the array when b is false, and return this StringBuffer object.
StringBuffer append(char ch)	Append ch's character to this StringBuffer object's array, and return this StringBuffer object.
StringBuffer append(char[] chars)	Append the characters in the chars array to this StringBuffer object's array, and return this StringBuffer object. This method throws NullPointerException when chars is null.

(continued)

Table 7-6. (continued)

Method	Description
StringBuffer append(double d)	Append the string representation of d's double precision floating-point value to this StringBuffer object's array, and return this StringBuffer object.
StringBuffer append(float f)	Append the string representation of f's floating-point value to this StringBuffer object's array, and return this StringBuffer object.
StringBuffer append(int i)	Append the string representation of i's integer value to this StringBuffer object's array, and return this StringBuffer object.
StringBuffer append(long l)	Append the string representation of l's long integer value to this StringBuffer object's array, and return this StringBuffer object.
StringBuffer append(Object obj)	Call obj's toString() method and append the returned string's characters to this StringBuffer object's array. Append "null" to the array when null is passed to obj. Return this StringBuffer object.
StringBuffer append(String s)	Append s's string to this StringBuffer object's array. Append "null" to the array when null is passed to s. Return this StringBuffer object.
int capacity()	Return the current capacity of this StringBuffer object's array.
char charAt(int index)	Return the character located at index in this StringBuffer object's array. This method throws StringIndexOutOfBoundsException when index is negative or greater than or equal to this StringBuffer object's length.
void ensureCapacity(int min)	Ensure that this StringBuffer object's capacity is at least that specified by min. If the current capacity is less than min, a new internal array is created with greater capacity. The new capacity is set to the larger of min and the current capacity multiplied by 2, with 2 added to the result. No action is taken when min is negative or zero.
int length()	Return the number of characters stored in this StringBuffer object's array.
StringBuffer reverse()	Return this StringBuffer object with its array contents reversed.
void setCharAt(int index, char ch)	Replace the character at index with ch. This method throws StringIndexOutOfBoundsException when index is negative or greater than or equal to the length of this StringBuffer object's array.
void setLength(int length)	Set the length of this StringBuffer object's array to length. If the length argument is less than the current length, the array's contents are truncated. If the length argument is greater than or equal to the current length, sufficient null characters ('\u0000') are appended to the array. This method throws StringIndexOutOfBoundsException when length is negative.
String substring(int start)	Return a new String object that contains all characters in this StringBuffer object's array starting with the character located at start. This method throws StringIndexOutOfBoundsException when start is less than 0 or greater than or equal to the length of this StringBuffer object's array.
String toString()	Return a new String object whose string equals the contents of this StringBuffer object's array.

A StringBuffer or StringBuilder object's internal array is associated with the concepts of capacity and length. *Capacity* refers to the maximum number of characters that can be stored in the array before the array grows to accommodate additional characters. *Length* refers to the number of characters that are already stored in the array.

Consider a scenario where you've written code to format an integer value into a string. As part of the formatter, you need to prepend a specific number of leading spaces to the integer. You decide to use the following initialization code and loop to build a spacesPrefix string with 3 leading spaces:

```
int numLeadingSpaces = 3; // default value
String spacesPrefix = "";
for (int j = 0; j < numLeadingSpaces; j++)
   spacesPrefix += "0";
```

This loop is inefficient because each of the iterations creates a StringBuilder object and a String object. The compiler transforms this code fragment into the following fragment:

```
int numLeadingSpaces = 3; // default value
String spacesPrefix = "";
for (int j = 0; j < numLeadingSpaces; j++)
   spacesPrefix = new StringBuffer().append(spacesPrefix).append("0").toString();
```

A more efficient way to code the previous loop involves creating a StringBuffer/StringBuilder object prior to entering the loop, calling the appropriate append() method in the loop, and calling toString() after the loop. The following code fragment demonstrates this more efficient scenario:

```
int numLeadingSpaces = 3; // default value
StringBuffer sb = new StringBuffer();
for (int j = 0; j < numLeadingSpaces; j++)
   sb.append('0');
String spacesPrefix = sb.toString();
```

> **Caution**   Avoid using the string concatenation operator in a lengthy loop because it results in the creation of many unnecessary StringBuilder and String objects.

Obtaining Package Information

The java.lang.Package class provides access to information about a package (see Chapter 5 for an introduction to packages). This information includes version details about the implementation and specification of a Java package, the name of the package, and an indication of whether or not the package has been *sealed* (all classes that are part of the package are archived in the same JAR file).

Table 7-7 describes some of Package's methods.

Table 7-7. Package Methods

Method	Description
`String getImplementationTitle()`	Return the title of this package's implementation, which might be null. The format of the title is unspecified.
`String getImplementationVendor()`	Return the name of the vendor or organization that provides this package's implementation. This name might be null. The format of the name is unspecified.
`String getImplementationVersion()`	Return the version number of this package's implementation, which might be null. This version string must be a sequence of positive decimal integers separated by periods and might have leading zeros.
`String getName()`	Return the name of this package in standard dot notation, for example, `java.lang`.
`static Package getPackage(String packageName)`	Return the `Package` object that is associated with the package identified as packageName or null when the package identified as packageName cannot be found. This method throws `NullPointerException` when packageName is null.
`static Package[] getPackages()`	Return an array of all `Package` objects that are accessible to this method's caller.
`String getSpecificationTitle()`	Return the title of this package's specification, which might be null. The format of the title is unspecified.
`String getSpecificationVendor()`	Return the name of the vendor or organization that provides the specification that is implemented by this package. This name might be null. The format of the name is unspecified.
`String getSpecificationVersion()`	Return the version number of the specification of this package's implementation, which might be null. This version string must be a sequence of positive decimal integers separated by periods and might have leading zeros.
`boolean isCompatibleWith(String desired)`	Check this package to determine if it is compatible with the specified version string by comparing this package's specification version with the desired version. Return true when this package's specification version number is greater than or equal to the desired version number (this package is compatible); otherwise, return false. This method throws `NullPointerException` when desired is null and `NumberFormatException` when this package's version number or the desired version number is not in dotted form.
`boolean isSealed()`	Return true when this package has been sealed; otherwise, return false.

I have created a `PackageInfo` application that demonstrates most of Table 7-7's `Package` methods. Listing 7-6 presents this application's source code.

Listing 7-6. Obtaining Information About a Package

```java
public class PackageInfo
{
   public static void main(String[] args)
   {
      if (args.length == 0)
      {
         System.err.println("usage: java PackageInfo packageName [version]");
         return;
      }
      Package pkg = Package.getPackage(args[0]);
      if (pkg == null)
      {
         System.err.println(args[0] + " not found");
         return;
      }
      System.out.println("Name: " + pkg.getName());
      System.out.println("Implementation title: " +
                         pkg.getImplementationTitle());
      System.out.println("Implementation vendor: " +
                         pkg.getImplementationVendor());
      System.out.println("Implementation version: " +
                         pkg.getImplementationVersion());
      System.out.println("Specification title: " +
                         pkg.getSpecificationTitle());
      System.out.println("Specification vendor: " +
                         pkg.getSpecificationVendor());
      System.out.println("Specification version: " +
                         pkg.getSpecificationVersion());
      System.out.println("Sealed: " + pkg.isSealed());
      if (args.length > 1)
         System.out.println("Compatible with " + args[1] + ": " +
                            pkg.isCompatibleWith(args[1]));
   }
}
```

After compiling Listing 7-6 (javac PackageInfo.java), specify at least a package name on the command line. For example, java PackageInfo java.lang returns the following output under Java 7:

```
Name: java.lang
Implementation title: Java Runtime Environment
Implementation vendor: Oracle Corporation
Implementation version: 1.7.0_06
Specification title: Java Platform API Specification
Specification vendor: Oracle Corporation
Specification version: 1.7
Sealed: false
```

PackageInfo also lets you determine if the package's specification is compatible with a specific version number. A package is compatible with its predecessors.

For example, java PackageInfo java.lang 1.6 outputs Compatible with 1.6: true, whereas java PackageInfo java.lang 1.8 outputs Compatible with 1.8: false.

You can also use PackageInfo with your own packages, which you learned to create in Chapter 5. For example, that chapter presented a logging package.

Copy PackageInfo.class into the directory containing the logging package directory (which contains the compiled classfiles), and execute java PackageInfo logging.

PackageInfo responds by displaying the following output:

```
logging not found
```

This error message is presented because getPackage() requires at least one classfile to be loaded from the package before it returns a Package object describing that package.

The only way to eliminate the previous error message is to load a class from the package. Accomplish this task by merging the following code fragment into Listing 7–6.

```
if (args.length == 3)
try
{
    Class.forName(args[2]);
}
catch (ClassNotFoundException cnfe)
{
    System.err.println("cannot load " + args[2]);
    return;
}
```

This code fragment, which must precede Package pkg = Package.getPackage(args[0]);, loads the classfile named by the revised PackageInfo application's third command-line argument.

Run the new PackageInfo application via java PackageInfo logging 1.5 logging.File and you will observe the following output, provided that File.class exists (you need to compile this package before specifying this command line)—this command line identifies logging's File class as the class to load:

```
Name: logging
Implementation title: null
Implementation vendor: null
Implementation version: null
Specification title: null
Specification vendor: null
Specification version: null
Sealed: false
Exception in thread "main" java.lang.NumberFormatException: Empty version string
                at java.lang.Package.isCompatibleWith(Unknown Source)
                at PackageInfo.main(PackageInfo.java:41)
```

It's not surprising to see all of these null values because no package information has been added to the logging package. Also, NumberFormatException is thrown from isCompatibleWith() because the logging package doesn't contain a specification version number in dotted form (it is null).

Perhaps the simplest way to place package information into the logging package is to create a logging.jar file in a similar manner to the example shown in Chapter 5. But first, you must create a small text file that contains the package information. You can choose any name for the file. Listing 7-7 reveals my choice of manifest.mf.

Listing 7-7. manifest.mf Containing the Package Information

```
Implementation-Title: Logging Implementation
Implementation-Vendor: Jeff Friesen
Implementation-Version: 1.0a
Specification-Title: Logging Specification
Specification-Vendor: Jeff "JavaJeff" Friesen
Specification-Version: 1.0
Sealed: true
```

> **Note** Make sure to press the Return/Enter key at the end of the final line (Sealed: true). Otherwise, you will probably observe Sealed: false in the output because this entry will not be stored in the logging package by the JDK's jar tool—jar is a bit quirky.

Execute the following command line to create a JAR file that includes logging and its files and whose *manifest*, a special file named MANIFEST.MF that stores information about the contents of a JAR file, contains the contents of Listing 7-7:

```
jar cfm logging.jar manifest.mf logging
```

Alternatively, you can specify one of the following slightly longer command lines, which are equivalent to the former command line:

```
jar cfm logging.jar manifest.mf logging\*.class
jar cfm logging.jar manifest.mf logging/*.class
```

Either command line creates a JAR file named logging.jar (via the c [create] and f [file] options). It also merges the contents of manifest.mf (via the m [manifest] option) into MANIFEST.MF, which is stored in the package's/JAR file's META-INF directory.

> **Note** To learn more about a JAR file's manifest, read the "JAR Manifest" section of the JDK documentation's "JAR File Specification" page (http://docs.oracle.com/javase/7/docs/technotes/guides/jar/jar.html#JAR_Manifest).

Assuming that the jar tool presents no error messages, execute the following Windows-oriented command line (or a command line suitable for your platform) to run PackageInfo and extract the package information from the logging package:

```
java -cp logging.jar;. PackageInfo logging 1.0 logging.File
```

The -cp command-line option lets you specify the classpath, which consists of logging.jar and the current directory (represented by the dot (.) character). Fail to specify the dot and java outputs an error message complaining that it cannot locate PackageInfo.class.

This time, you should see the following output:

```
Name: logging
Implementation title: Logging Implementation
Implementation vendor: Jeff Friesen (IV)
Implementation version: 1.0a
Specification title: Logging Specification
Specification vendor: Jeff Friesen (SV)
Specification version: 1.0
Sealed: true
Compatible with 1.0: true
```

EXERCISES

The following exercises are designed to test your understanding of Chapter 7's content:

1. What constants does Math declare?

2. Why is Math.abs(Integer.MIN_VALUE) equal to Integer.MIN_VALUE?

3. What does Math's random() method accomplish? Why is expression (int) Math.random() * limit incorrect?

4. Identify the five special values that can arise during floating-point calculations.

5. How do Math and StrictMath differ?

6. What is the purpose of strictfp?

7. What is BigDecimal and why might you use this class?

8. Which RoundingMode constant describes the form of rounding commonly taught at school?

9. What is BigInteger?

10. True or false: A string literal is a String object.

11. What is the purpose of String's intern() method?

12. How do String and StringBuffer differ?

13. How do StringBuffer and StringBuilder differ?

14. What is the purpose of Package's isSealed() method?

15. True or false: getPackage() requires at least one classfile to be loaded from the package before it returns a Package object describing that package.

16. A *prime number* is a positive integer greater than 1 that is evenly divisible only by 1 and itself. Create a PrimeNumberTest application that determines if its solitary integer argument is prime or not prime and outputs a suitable message. For example, java PrimeNumberTest 289 should output the message 289 is not prime. A simple way to check for primality is to loop from 2 through the square root of the integer argument and use the remainder operator in the loop to determine if the argument is divided evenly by the loop index. For example, because 6 % 2 yields a remainder of 0 (2 divides evenly into 6), integer 6 is not a prime number.

17. Rewrite the following inefficient loop to use StringBuffer. The resulting loop should minimize object creation:

```
String[] imageNames = new String[NUM_IMAGES];
for (int i = 0; i < imageNames.length; i++)
    imageNames[i] = new String("image" + i + ".png");
```

18. Create a DigitsToWords application that accepts a single integer-based command-line argument. This application converts this argument to an int value (via Integer.parseInt(args[0])) and then passes the result to a String convertDigitsToWords(int integer) class method that returns a string containing a textual representation of that number. For example, 1 converts to one, 16 converts to sixteen, 69 converts to sixty-nine, 123 converts to one hundred and twenty-three, and 2938 converts to two thousand nine hundred and thirty-eight. Throw java.lang.IllegalArgumentException when the value passed to integer is less than 0 or greater than 9999. Use the StringBuffer class to serve as a repository for the generated text. Usage example: java DigitsToWords 2938.

Summary

The standard class library offers many basic APIs via its java.lang and java.math packages. These APIs include the Math, StrictMath, BigDecimal, BigInteger, String, StringBuffer, StringBuilder, and Package classes and the RoundingMode enum.

Math supplements the basic math operations (+, -, *, /, and %) with advanced operations (such as trigonometry). The companion StrictMath class ensures that all of these operations yield the same values on all platforms.

Money must never be represented by floating-point and double precision floating-point variables because not all monetary values can be represented exactly. In contrast, the BigDecimal class lets you accurately represent and manipulate these values.

BigDecimal relies on the BigInteger class for representing its unscaled value. A BigInteger instance describes an integer value that can be of arbitrary length (subject to the limits of the virtual machine's memory).

String represents a string as a sequence of characters. Because String instances are immutable, Java provides StringBuffer and StringBuilder for building strings more efficiently. The former class is used in multithreaded contexts; the latter (and more performant) class is for single-threaded use.

The Package class provides access to package information. This information includes version information about the implementation and specification of a Java package, the package's name, and an indication of whether the package is sealed or not.

In Chapter 8 I continue to explore the basic APIs by focusing on the primitive type wrapper classes, threads, and system capabilities.

Exploring the Basic APIs Part 2

The standard class library's java.lang package provides many basic APIs, which are designed to support language features. You encountered APIs for mathematics, string management, and packages in the previous chapter. In this chapter I introduce you to those basic library APIs that pertain to the primitive type wrapper classes, threads, and system capabilities.

Exploring the Primitive Type Wrapper Classes

The java.lang package includes Boolean, Byte, Character, Double, Float, Integer, Long, and Short. These classes are known as *primitive type wrapper classes* because their instances wrap themselves around values of primitive types.

> **Note** The primitive type wrapper classes are also known as *value classes*.

Java provides these eight primitive type wrapper classes for two reasons:

- The Collections Framework (discussed in Chapter 9) provides lists, sets, and maps that can only store objects; they cannot store primitive-type values. You store a primitive-type value in a primitive type wrapper class instance and store the instance in the collection.

- These classes provide a good place to associate useful constants (such as MAX_VALUE and MIN_VALUE) and class methods (such as Integer's parseInt() methods and Character's isDigit(), isLetter(), and toUpperCase() methods) with the primitive types.

In this section I introduce you to each of these primitive type wrapper classes and a java.lang class named Number.

Boolean

Boolean is the smallest of the primitive type wrapper classes. This class declares three constants, including TRUE and FALSE, which denote precreated Boolean objects. It also declares a pair of constructors for initializing a Boolean object:

- Boolean(boolean value) initializes the Boolean object to value.

- Boolean(String s) converts s's text to a true or false value and stores this value in the Boolean object.

The second constructor compares s's value with true. Because the comparison is case insensitive, any uppercase/lowercase combination of these four letters (such as true, TRUE, or tRue) results in true being stored in the object. Otherwise, the constructor stores false in the object.

> **Note**   Boolean's constructors are complemented by boolean booleanValue(), which returns the wrapped Boolean value.

Boolean also declares or overrides the following methods:

- int compareTo(Boolean b) compares the current Boolean object with b to determine their relative order. The method returns 0 when the current object contains the same Boolean value as b, a positive value when the current object contains true and b contains false, and a negative value when the current object contains false and b contains true.

- boolean equals(Object o) compares the current Boolean object with o and returns true when o is not null, o is of type Boolean, and both objects contain the same Boolean value.

- static boolean getBoolean(String name) returns true when a system property (discussed later in this chapter) identified by name exists and is equal to true.

- int hashCode() returns a suitable hash code that allows Boolean objects to be used with hash-based collections (discussed in Chapter 9).

- static boolean parseBoolean(String s) parses s, returning true when s equals "true", "TRUE", "True", or any other uppercase/lowercase combination. Otherwise, this method returns false. (*Parsing* breaks a sequence of characters into meaningful components, known as *tokens*.)

- String toString() returns "true" when the current Boolean instance contains true; otherwise, this method returns "false".

- static String toString(boolean b) returns "true" when b contains true; otherwise, this method returns "false".

- static Boolean valueOf(boolean b) returns TRUE when b contains true or FALSE when b contains false.

- static Boolean valueOf(String s) returns TRUE when s equals "true", "TRUE", "True", or any other uppercase/lowercase combination. Otherwise, this method returns FALSE.

> **Caution**   Newcomers to the Boolean class often think that getBoolean() returns a Boolean object's true/false value. However, getBoolean() returns the value of a Boolean-based system property—I discuss system properties later in this chapter. If you need to return a Boolean object's true/false value, use the booleanValue() method instead.

It's often better to use TRUE and FALSE than to create Boolean objects. For example, suppose you need a method that returns a Boolean object containing true when the method's double argument is negative, or false when this argument is zero or positive. You might declare your method like the following isNegative() method:

```
Boolean isNegative(double d)
{
    return new Boolean(d < 0);
}
```

Although this method is concise, it unnecessarily creates a Boolean object. When the method is called frequently, many Boolean objects are created that consume heap space. When heap space runs low, the garbage collector runs and slows down the application, which impacts performance.

The following example reveals a better way to code isNegative():

```
Boolean isNegative(double d)
{
    return (d < 0) ? Boolean.TRUE : Boolean.FALSE;
}
```

This method avoids creating Boolean objects by returning either the precreated TRUE or FALSE object.

> **Tip**   You should strive to create as few objects as possible. Not only will your applications have smaller memory footprints, they'll perform better because the garbage collector will not run as often.

Character

Character is the largest of the primitive type wrapper classes, containing many constants, a constructor, many methods, and a pair of nested classes (Subset and UnicodeBlock).

> **Note**   Character's complexity derives from Java's support for Unicode (http://en.wikipedia.org/wiki/Unicode). For brevity, I ignore much of Character's Unicode-related complexity, which is beyond the scope of this chapter.

Character declares a single Character(char value) constructor, which you use to initialize a Character object to value. This constructor is complemented by char charValue(), which returns the wrapped character value.

When you start writing applications, you might codify expressions such as ch >= '0' && ch <= '9' (test ch to see if it contains a digit) and ch >= 'A' && ch <= 'Z' (test ch to see if it contains an uppercase letter). You should avoid doing so for three reasons:

- It's too easy to introduce a bug into the expression. For example, ch > '0' && ch <= '9' introduces a subtle bug that doesn't include '0' in the comparison.

- The expressions are not very descriptive of what they are testing.

- The expressions are biased toward Latin digits (0–9) and letters (A–Z and a–z). They don't take into account digits and letters that are valid in other languages. For example, '\u0beb' is a character literal representing one of the digits in the Tamil language.

Character declares several comparison and conversion class methods that address these concerns. These methods include the following:

- static boolean isDigit(char ch) returns true when ch contains a digit (typically 0 through 9 but also digits in other alphabets).

- static boolean isLetter(char ch) returns true when ch contains a letter (typically A–Z or a–z but also letters in other alphabets).

- static boolean isLetterOrDigit(char ch) returns true when ch contains a letter or digit (typically A–Z, a–z, or 0–9 but also letters or digits in other alphabets).

- static boolean isLowerCase(char ch) returns true when ch contains a lowercase letter.

- static boolean isUpperCase(char ch) returns true when ch contains an uppercase letter.

- static boolean isWhitespace(char ch) returns true when ch contains a whitespace character (typically a space, a horizontal tab, a carriage return, or a line feed).

- static char toLowerCase(char ch) returns the lowercase equivalent of ch's uppercase letter; otherwise, this method returns ch's value.

- static char toUpperCase(char ch) returns the uppercase equivalent of ch's lowercase letter; otherwise, this method returns ch's value.

For example, isDigit(ch) is preferable to ch >= '0' && ch <= '9' because it avoids a source of bugs, is more readable, and returns true for non-Latin digits (e.g., '\u0beb') as well as Latin digits.

Float and Double

Float and Double store floating-point and double precision floating-point values in Float and Double objects, respectively. These classes declare the following constants:

- MAX_VALUE identifies the maximum value that can be represented as a float or double.

- MIN_VALUE identifies the minimum value that can be represented as a float or double.

- NaN represents 0.0F/0.0F as a `float` and 0.0/0.0 as a `double`.
- `NEGATIVE_INFINITY` represents -infinity as a `float` or `double`.
- `POSITIVE_INFINITY` represents +infinity as a `float` or `double`.

`Float` and `Double` also declare the following constructors for initializing their objects:

- `Float(float value)` initializes the `Float` object to `value`.
- `Float(double value)` initializes the `Float` object to the `float` equivalent of `value`.
- `Float(String s)` converts `s`'s text to a floating-point value and stores this value in the `Float` object.
- `Double(double value)` initializes the `Double` object to `value`.
- `Double(String s)` converts `s`'s text to a double precision floating-point value and stores this value in the `Double` object.

`Float`'s constructors are complemented by `float floatValue()`, which returns the wrapped floating-point value. Similarly, `Double`'s constructors are complemented by `double doubleValue()`, which returns the wrapped double precision floating-point value.

`Float` declares several utility methods in addition to `floatValue()`. These methods include the following:

- `static int floatToIntBits(float value)` converts `value` to a 32-bit integer.
- `static boolean isInfinite(float f)` returns true when `f`'s value is +infinity or −infinity. A related `boolean isInfinite()` method returns true when the current `Float` object's value is +infinity or −infinity.
- `static boolean isNaN(float f)` returns true when `f`'s value is NaN. A related `boolean isNaN()` method returns true when the current `Float` object's value is NaN.
- `static float parseFloat(String s)` parses `s`, returning the floating-point equivalent of `s`'s textual representation of a floating-point value or throwing `java.lang.NumberFormatException` when this representation is invalid (contains letters, for example).

`Double` declares several utility methods as well as `doubleValue()`. These methods include the following:

- `static long doubleToLongBits(double value)` converts `value` to a long integer.
- `static boolean isInfinite(double d)` returns true when `d`'s value is +infinity or −infinity. A related `boolean isInfinite()` method returns true when the current `Double` object's value is +infinity or −infinity.
- `static boolean isNaN(double d)` returns true when `d`'s value is NaN. A related `public boolean isNaN()` method returns true when the current `Double` object's value is NaN.
- `static double parseDouble(String s)` parses `s`, returning the double precision floating-point equivalent of `s`'s textual representation of a double precision floating-point value or throwing `NumberFormatException` when this representation is invalid.

The floatToIntBits() and doubleToIntBits() methods are used in implementations of the equals() and hashCode() methods that must take float and double fields into account. floatToIntBits() and doubleToIntBits() allow equals() and hashCode() to respond properly to the following situations:

- equals() must return true when f1 and f2 contain Float.NaN (or d1 and d2 contain Double.NaN). If equals() was implemented in a manner similar to f1.floatValue() == f2.floatValue() (or d1.doubleValue() == d2.doubleValue()), this method would return false because NaN is not equal to anything, including itself.

- equals() must return false when f1 contains +0.0 and f2 contains –0.0 (or vice versa), or d1 contains +0.0 and d2 contains -0.0 (or vice versa). If equals() was implemented in a manner similar to f1.floatValue() == f2.floatValue() (or d1.doubleValue() == d2.doubleValue()), this method would return true because +0.0 == –0.0 returns true.

These requirements are needed for hash-based collections (discussed in Chapter 9) to work properly. Listing 8-1 shows how they impact Float's and Double's equals() methods.

Listing 8-1. Demonstrating Float's equals() Method in a NaN Context and Double's equals() Method in a +/-0.0 Context

```java
public class FloatDoubleDemo
{
   public static void main(String[] args)
   {
      Float f1 = new Float(Float.NaN);
      System.out.println(f1.floatValue());
      Float f2 = new Float(Float.NaN);
      System.out.println(f2.floatValue());
      System.out.println(f1.equals(f2));
      System.out.println(Float.NaN == Float.NaN);
      System.out.println();
      Double d1 = new Double(+0.0);
      System.out.println(d1.doubleValue());
      Double d2 = new Double(-0.0);
      System.out.println(d2.doubleValue());
      System.out.println(d1.equals(d2));
      System.out.println(+0.0 == -0.0);
   }
}
```

Compile Listing 8-1 (javac FloatDoubleDemo.java) and run this application (java FloatDoubleDemo). The following output proves that Float's equals() method properly handles NaN and Double's equals() method properly handles +/-0.0:

```
NaN
NaN
true
false
```

```
0.0
-0.0
false
true
```

> **Tip**　When you want to test a `float` or `double` value for equality with +infinity or −infinity (but not both), don't use `isInfinite()`. Instead, compare the value with `NEGATIVE_INFINITY` or `POSITIVE_INFINITY` via `==`. For example, `f == Float.NEGATIVE_INFINITY`.

You will find `parseFloat()` and `parseDouble()` useful in many contexts. For example, Listing 8-2 uses `parseDouble()` to parse command-line arguments into doubles.

Listing 8-2. Parsing Command-Line Arguments into Double Precision Floating-Point Values

```java
public class Calc
{
   public static void main(String[] args)
   {
      if (args.length != 3)
      {
         System.err.println("usage: java Calc value1 op value2");
         System.err.println("op is one of +, -, x, or /");
         return;
      }
      try
      {
         double value1 = Double.parseDouble(args[0]);
         double value2 = Double.parseDouble(args[2]);
         if (args[1].equals("+"))
            System.out.println(value1 + value2);
         else
         if (args[1].equals("-"))
            System.out.println(value1 - value2);
         else
         if (args[1].equals("x"))
            System.out.println(value1 * value2);
         else
         if (args[1].equals("/"))
            System.out.println(value1 / value2);
         else
            System.err.println("invalid operator: " + args[1]);
      }
      catch (NumberFormatException nfe)
      {
         System.err.println("Bad number format: " + nfe.getMessage());
      }
   }
}
```

Specify java Calc 10E+3 + 66.0 to try out the Calc application. This application responds by outputting 10066.0. If you specified java Calc 10E+3 + A instead, you would observe Bad number format: For input string: "A" as the output, which is in response to the second parseDouble() method call's throwing of a NumberFormatException object.

Although NumberFormatException describes an unchecked exception, and although unchecked exceptions are often not handled because they represent coding mistakes, NumberFormatException doesn't fit this pattern in this example. The exception doesn't arise from a coding mistake; it arises from someone passing an illegal numeric argument to the application, which cannot be avoided through proper coding. Perhaps NumberFormatException should have been implemented as a checked exception.

Integer, Long, Short, and Byte

Integer, Long, Short, and Byte store 32-bit, 64-bit, 16-bit, and 8-bit integer values in Integer, Long, Short, and Byte objects, respectively.

Each class declares MAX_VALUE and MIN_VALUE constants that identify the maximum and minimum values that can be represented by its associated primitive type. These classes also declare the following constructors for initializing their objects:

- Integer(int value) initializes the Integer object to value.

- Integer(String s) converts s's text to a 32-bit integer value and stores this value in the Integer object.

- Long(long value) initializes the Long object to value.

- Long(String s) converts s's text to a 64-bit integer value and stores this value in the Long object.

- Short(short value) initializes the Short object to value.

- Short(String s) converts s's text to a 16-bit integer value and stores this value in the Short object.

- Byte(byte value) initializes the Byte object to value.

- Byte(String s) converts s's text to an 8-bit integer value and stores this value in the Byte object.

Integer's constructors are complemented by int intValue(), Long's constructors are complemented by long longValue(), Short's constructors are complemented by short shortValue(), and Byte's constructors are complemented by byte byteValue(). These methods return wrapped integers.

These classes declare various useful integer-oriented methods. For example, Integer declares the following class methods for converting a 32-bit integer to a String according to a specific representation (binary, hexadecimal, octal, and decimal):

- static String toBinaryString(int i) returns a String object containing i's binary representation. For example, Integer.toBinaryString(255) returns a String object containing 11111111.

- ▨ `static String toHexString(int i)` returns a `String` object containing i's hexadecimal representation. For example, `Integer.toHexString(255)` returns a `String` object containing ff.

- ▨ `static String toOctalString(int i)` returns a `String` object containing i's octal representation. For example, `toOctalString(64)` returns a `String` object containing 100.

- ▨ `static String toString(int i)` returns a `String` object containing i's decimal representation. For example, `toString(255)` returns a `String` object containing 255.

It's often convenient to prepend zeros to a binary string so that you can align multiple binary strings in columns. For example, you might want to create an application that displays the following aligned output:

```
11110001
+
00000111
--------
11111000
```

Unfortunately, `toBinaryString()` doesn't let you accomplish this task. For example, `Integer.toBinaryString(7)` returns a `String` object containing 111 instead of 00000111. Listing 8-3's `toAlignedBinaryString()` method addresses this oversight.

Listing 8-3. Aligning Binary Strings

```
public class AlignBinaryString
{
   public static void main(String[] args)
   {
      System.out.println(toAlignedBinaryString(7, 8));
      System.out.println(toAlignedBinaryString(255, 16));
      System.out.println(toAlignedBinaryString(255, 7));
   }

   static String toAlignedBinaryString(int i, int numBits)
   {
      String result = Integer.toBinaryString(i);
      if (result.length() > numBits)
         return null; // cannot fit result into numBits columns
      int numLeadingZeros = numBits - result.length();
      StringBuilder sb = new StringBuilder();
      for (int j = 0; j < numLeadingZeros; j++)
         sb.append('0');
      return sb.toString() + result;
   }
}
```

The `toAlignedBinaryString()` method takes two arguments: the first argument specifies the 32-bit integer that is to be converted into a binary string, and the second argument specifies the number of bit columns in which to fit the string.

After calling toBinaryString() to return i's equivalent binary string without leading zeros, toAlignedBinaryString() verifies that the string's digits can fit into the number of bit columns specified by numBits. If they don't fit, this method returns null.

Moving on, toAlignedBinaryString() calculates the number of leading "0"s to prepend to result and then uses a for loop to create a string of leading zeros. This method ends by returning the leading zeros string prepended to the result string.

When you run this application, it generates the following output:

```
00000111
0000000011111111
null
```

Number

Each of Float, Double, Integer, Long, Short, and Byte provides the other classes' *x*Value() methods in addition to its own *x*Value() method. For example, Float provides doubleValue(), intValue(), longValue(), shortValue(), and byteValue() as well as floatValue().

All six methods are members of Number, which is the abstract superclass of Float, Double, Integer, Long, Short, and Byte—Number's floatValue(), doubleValue(), intValue(), and longValue() methods are abstract. Number is also the superclass of java.math.BigDecimal and java.math. BigInteger (and some concurrency-related classes; see Chapter 10).

Number exists to simplify iterating over a collection of Number subclass objects. For example, you can declare a variable of java.util.List<Number> type and initialize it to an instance of java.util.ArrayList<Number>. You can then store a mixture of Number subclass objects in the collection, and iterate over this collection by calling a subclass method polymorphically.

Exploring Threads

Applications execute via *threads*, which are independent paths of execution through an application's code. When multiple threads are executing, each thread's path can differ from other thread paths. For example, a thread might execute one of a switch statement's cases, and another thread might execute another of this statement's cases.

> **Note**   Applications use threads to improve performance. Some applications can get by with only the *default main thread* (the thread that executes the main() method) to carry out their tasks, but other applications need additional threads to perform time-intensive tasks in the background so that they remain responsive to their users.

The virtual machine gives each thread its own method-call stack to prevent threads from interfering with each other. Separate stacks let threads keep track of their next instructions to execute, which can differ from thread to thread. The stack also provides a thread with its own copy of method parameters, local variables, and return value.

Java supports threads via its Threads API. This API consists of one interface (Runnable) and four classes (Thread, ThreadGroup, ThreadLocal, and InheritableThreadLocal) in the java.lang package. After exploring Runnable and Thread (and mentioning ThreadGroup during this exploration), in this section I explore thread synchronization, ThreadLocal, and InheritableThreadLocal.

> **Note**   Java 5 introduced the java.util.concurrent package as a high-level alternative to the low-level Threads API. (I will discuss this package in Chapter 10.) Although java.util.concurrent is the preferred API for working with threads, you should also be somewhat familiar with Threads because it's helpful in simple threading scenarios. Also, you might have to analyze someone else's source code that depends on Threads.

Runnable and Thread

Java provides the Runnable interface to identify those objects that supply code for threads to execute via this interface's solitary void run() method—a thread receives no arguments and returns no value. Classes implement Runnable to supply this code, and one of these classes is Thread.

Thread provides a consistent interface to the underlying operating system's threading architecture. (The operating system is typically responsible for creating and managing threads.) Thread makes it possible to associate code with threads as well as start and manage those threads. Each Thread instance associates with a single thread.

Thread declares several constructors for initializing Thread objects. Some of these constructors take Runnable arguments: you can supply code to run without having to extend Thread. Other constructors don't take Runnable arguments: you must extend Thread and override its run() method to supply the code to run.

For example, Thread(Runnable runnable) initializes a new Thread object to the specified runnable whose code is to be executed. In contrast, Thread() doesn't initialize Thread to a Runnable argument. Instead, your Thread subclass provides a constructor that calls Thread(), and the subclass also overrides Thread's run() method.

In the absence of an explicit name argument, each constructor assigns a unique default name (starting with Thread-) to the Thread object. Names make it possible to differentiate threads. In contrast to the previous two constructors, which choose default names, Thread(String threadName) lets you specify your own thread name.

Thread also declares methods for starting and managing threads. Table 8-1 describes many of the more useful methods.

Table 8-1. Thread Methods

Method	Description
static Thread currentThread()	Return the Thread object associated with the thread that calls this method.
String getName()	Return the name associated with this Thread object.
Thread.State getState()	Return the state of the thread associated with this Thread object. The state is identified by the Thread.State enum as one of BLOCKED (waiting to acquire a lock, discussed later), NEW (created but not started), RUNNABLE (executing), TERMINATED (the thread has died), TIMED_WAITING (waiting for a specified amount of time to elapse), or WAITING (waiting indefinitely).
void interrupt()	Set the interrupt status flag in this Thread object. If the associated thread is blocked or is waiting, clear this flag and wake up the thread by throwing an instance of the java.lang.InterruptedException class.
static boolean interrupted()	Return true when the thread associated with this Thread object has a pending interrupt request. Clear the interrupt status flag.
boolean isAlive()	Return true to indicate that this Thread object's associated thread is alive and not dead. A thread's life span ranges from just before it is actually started within the start() method to just after it leaves the run() method, at which point it dies.
boolean isDaemon()	Return true when the thread associated with this Thread object is a *daemon thread*, a thread that acts as a helper to a *user thread* (nondaemon thread) and dies automatically when the application's last nondaemon thread dies so the application can exit.
boolean isInterrupted()	Return true when the thread associated with this Thread object has a pending interrupt request.
void join()	The thread that calls this method on this Thread object waits for the thread associated with this object to die. This method throws InterruptedException when this Thread object's interrupt() method is called.
void join(long millis)	The thread that calls this method on this Thread object waits for the thread associated with this object to die, or until millis milliseconds have elapsed, whichever happens first. This method throws InterruptedException when this Thread object's interrupt() method is called.
void setDaemon(boolean isDaemon)	Mark this Thread object's associated thread as a daemon thread when isDaemon is true. This method throws java.lang.IllegalThreadStateException when the thread has not yet been created and started.
void setName(String threadName)	Assign threadName's value to this Thread object as the name of its associated thread.
static void sleep(long time)	Pause the thread associated with this Thread object for time milliseconds. This method throws InterruptedException when this Thread object's interrupt() method is called while the thread is sleeping.
void start()	Create and start this Thread object's associated thread. This method throws IllegalThreadStateException when the thread was previously started and is running or has died.

Listing 8-4 introduces you to the Threads API via a main() method that demonstrates Runnable, Thread(Runnable runnable), currentThread(), getName(), and start().

Listing 8-4. A Pair of Counting Threads

```java
public class CountingThreads
{
   public static void main(String[] args)
   {
      Runnable r = new Runnable()
                   {
                      @Override
                      public void run()
                      {
                         String name = Thread.currentThread().getName();
                         int count = 0;
                         while (true)
                            System.out.println(name + ": " + count++);
                      }
                   };
      Thread thdA = new Thread(r);
      Thread thdB = new Thread(r);
      thdA.start();
      thdB.start();
   }
}
```

According to Listing 8-4, the default main thread that executes main() first instantiates an anonymous class that implements Runnable. It then creates two Thread objects, initializing each object to the runnable, and calls Thread's start() method to create and start both threads. After completing these tasks, the main thread exits main() and dies.

Each of the two started threads executes the runnable's run() method. It calls Thread's currentThread() method to obtain its associated Thread instance, uses this instance to call Thread's getName() method to return its name, initializes count to 0, and enters an infinite loop where it outputs name and count and increments count on each iteration.

> **Tip** To stop an application that doesn't end, press the Ctrl and C keys simultaneously on a Windows platform or do the equivalent on a non-Windows platform.

I observe both threads alternating in their execution when I run this application on the 64-bit Windows 7 platform. Partial output from one run appears here:

```
Thread-0: 0
Thread-0: 1
Thread-1: 0
Thread-0: 2
Thread-1: 1
Thread-0: 3
```

```
Thread-1: 2
Thread-0: 4
Thread-1: 3
Thread-0: 5
Thread-1: 4
Thread-0: 6
Thread-1: 5
Thread-0: 7
Thread-1: 6
Thread-1: 7
Thread-1: 8
Thread-1: 9
Thread-1: 10
Thread-1: 11
Thread-1: 12
```

Note I executed `java CountThreads >output.txt` to capture the output to `output.txt` and then presented part of this file's content previously. Capturing output to a file may significantly affect the output that would otherwise be observed if output wasn't captured. Because I present captured thread output throughout this section, bear this in mind when executing the application on your platform. Also, note that your platform's threading architecture may impact the observable results. I've tested each example in this section on the 64-bit Windows 7 platform.

When a computer has enough processors and/or processor cores, the computer's operating system assigns a separate thread to each processor or core so the threads execute *concurrently* (at the same time). When a computer doesn't have enough processors and/or cores, a thread must wait its turn to use the shared processor/core.

The operating system uses a scheduler (`http://en.wikipedia.org/wiki/Scheduling_(computing)`) to determine when a waiting thread executes. The following list identifies three different schedulers:

- Linux 2.6 through 2.6.22 uses the O(1) scheduler (`http://en.wikipedia.org/wiki/O(1)_scheduler`).

- Linux 2.6.23 uses the Completely Fair Scheduler (`http://en.wikipedia.org/wiki/Completely_Fair_Scheduler`).

- Windows NT-based operating systems (NT, XP, Vista, and 7) use a multilevel feedback queue scheduler (`http://en.wikipedia.org/wiki/Multilevel_feedback_queue`). This scheduler has been adjusted in Windows Vista and Windows 7 to optimize performance.

Caution Although the previous output indicates that the first thread (Thread-0) starts executing, never assume that the thread associated with the `Thread` object whose `start()` method is called first is the first thread to execute. Although this might be true of some schedulers, it might not be true of others.

A multilevel feedback queue and many other thread schedulers take the concept of *priority* (thread relative importance) into account. They often combine *preemptive scheduling* (higher priority threads preempt—interrupt and run instead of—lower priority threads) with *round robin scheduling* (equal priority threads are given equal slices of time, which are known as *time slices*, and take turns executing).

Thread supports priority via its `void setPriority(int priority)` method (set the priority of this Thread object's thread to priority, which ranges from `Thread.MIN_PRIORITY` to `Thread.MAX_PRIORITY`—`Thread.NORMAL_PRIORITY` identifies the default priority) and `int getPriority()` method (return the current priority).

> **Caution**   Using the `setPriority()` method can impact an application's portability across platforms because different schedulers can handle a priority change in different ways. For example, one platform's scheduler might delay lower priority threads from executing until higher priority threads finish. This delaying can lead to *indefinite postponement* or *starvation* because lower priority threads "starve" while waiting indefinitely for their turn to execute, and this can seriously hurt the application's performance. Another platform's scheduler might not indefinitely delay lower priority threads, improving application performance.

Listing 8-5 refactors Listing 8-4's `main()` method to give each thread a nondefault name and to put each thread to sleep after outputting name and count.

Listing 8-5. A Pair of Counting Threads Revisited

```
public class CountingThreads
{
   public static void main(String[] args)
   {
      Runnable r = new Runnable()
                   {
                      @Override
                      public void run()
                      {
                         String name = Thread.currentThread().getName();
                         int count = 0;
                         while (true)
                         {
                            System.out.println(name + ": " + count++);
                            try
                            {
                               Thread.sleep(100);
                            }
                            catch (InterruptedException ie)
                            {
                            }
                         }
                      }
                   };
```

```
        Thread thdA = new Thread(r);
        thdA.setName("A");
        Thread thdB = new Thread(r);
        thdB.setName("B");
        thdA.start();
        thdB.start();
    }
}
```

Listing 8-5 reveals that threads A and B execute Thread.sleep(100); to sleep for 100 milliseconds. This sleep results in each thread executing more frequently, as the following partial output reveals:

```
A: 0
B: 0
A: 1
B: 1
B: 2
A: 2
B: 3
A: 3
B: 4
A: 4
B: 5
A: 5
B: 6
A: 6
B: 7
A: 7
```

A thread will occasionally start another thread to perform a lengthy calculation, download a large file, or perform some other time-consuming activity. After finishing its other tasks, the thread that started the *worker thread* is ready to process the results of the worker thread and waits for the worker thread to finish and die.

It's possible to wait for the worker thread to die by using a while loop that repeatedly calls Thread's isAlive() method on the worker thread's Thread object and sleeps for a certain length of time when this method returns true. However, Listing 8-6 demonstrates a less verbose alternative: the join() method.

Listing 8-6. Joining the Default Main Thread with a Background Thread

```java
public class JoinDemo
{
    public static void main(String[] args)
    {
        Runnable r = new Runnable()
                     {
                         @Override
                         public void run()
                         {
                             System.out.println("Worker thread is simulating " +
                                         "work by sleeping for 5 seconds.");
```

```
                    try
                    {
                        Thread.sleep(5000);
                    }
                    catch (InterruptedException ie)
                    {
                    }
                    System.out.println("Worker thread is dying.");
                }
            };
    Thread thd = new Thread(r);
    thd.start();
    System.out.println("Default main thread is doing work.");
    try
    {
        Thread.sleep(2000);
    }
    catch (InterruptedException ie)
    {
    }
    System.out.println("Default main thread has finished its work.");
    System.out.println("Default main thread is waiting for worker thread " +
                       "to die.");
    try
    {
        thd.join();
    }
    catch (InterruptedException ie)
    {
    }
    System.out.println("Main thread is dying.");
    }
}
```

Listing 8-6 demonstrates the default main thread starting a worker thread, performing some work, and then waiting for the worker thread to die by calling join() via the worker thread's thd object. When you run this application, you will discover output similar to the following (message order might differ somewhat):

```
Default main thread is doing work.
Worker thread is simulating work by sleeping for 5 seconds.
Default main thread has finished its work.
Default main thread is waiting for worker thread to die.
Worker thread is dying.
Main thread is dying.
```

Every Thread object belongs to some ThreadGroup object; Thread declares a ThreadGroup getThreadGroup() method that returns this object. You should ignore thread groups because they are not that useful. If you need to logically group Thread objects, you should use an array or collection instead.

> **Caution**   Various ThreadGroup methods are flawed. For example, int enumerate(Thread[]
> threads) will not include all active threads in its enumeration when its threads array argument is too
> small to store their Thread objects. Although you might think that you could use the return value from
> the int activeCount() method to properly size this array, there is no guarantee that the array will be
> large enough because activeCount()'s return value fluctuates with the creation and death of threads.

However, you should still know about ThreadGroup because of its contribution in handling exceptions that are thrown while a thread is executing. Listing 8-7 sets the stage for learning about exception handling by presenting a run() method that attempts to divide an integer by 0, which results in a thrown java.lang.ArithmeticException instance.

Listing 8-7. Throwing an Exception from the run() Method

```
public class ExceptionThread
{
   public static void main(String[] args)
   {
      Runnable r = new Runnable()
                  {
                     @Override
                     public void run()
                     {
                        int x = 1 / 0; // Line 10
                     }
                  };
      Thread thd = new Thread(r);
      thd.start();
   }
}
```

Run this application and you will see an exception trace that identifies the thrown ArithmeticException:

```
Exception in thread "Thread-0" java.lang.ArithmeticException: / by zero
            at ExceptionThread$1.run(ExceptionThread.java:10)
            at java.lang.Thread.run(Unknown Source)
```

When an exception is thrown out of the run() method, the thread terminates and the following activities take place:

- The virtual machine looks for an instance of Thread.UncaughtExceptionHandler installed via Thread's void setUncaughtExceptionHandler(Thread.UncaughtExceptionHandler eh) method. When this handler is found, it passes execution to the instance's void uncaughtException(Thread t, Throwable e) method, where t identifies the Thread object of the thread that threw the exception, and e identifies the thrown exception or error—perhaps a java.lang.OutOfMemoryError instance was thrown. If this method throws an exception/error, the exception/error is ignored by the virtual machine.

■ Assuming that setUncaughtExceptionHandler() was not called to install a
   handler, the virtual machine passes control to the associated ThreadGroup
   object's uncaughtException(Thread t, Throwable e) method. Assuming that
   ThreadGroup was not extended and that its uncaughtException() method was
   not overridden to handle the exception, uncaughtException() passes control
   to the parent ThreadGroup object's uncaughtException() method when a
   parent ThreadGroup is present. Otherwise, it checks to see if a default uncaught
   exception handler has been installed (via Thread's static void
   setDefaultUncaughtExceptionHandler(Thread.UncaughtExceptionHandler
   handler) method). If a default uncaught exception handler has been installed, its
   uncaughtException() method is called with the same two arguments. Otherwise,
   uncaughtException() checks its Throwable argument to determine if it is an instance
   of java.lang.ThreadDeath. If so, nothing special is done. Otherwise, as Listing 8-7's
   exception message shows, a message containing the thread's name, as returned
   from the thread's getName() method, and a stack backtrace, using the Throwable
   argument's printStackTrace() method, is printed to the standard error stream.

Listing 8-8 demonstrates Thread's setUncaughtExceptionHandler() and
setDefaultUncaughtExceptionHandler() methods.

Listing 8-8. Demonstrating Uncaught Exception Handlers

```
public class ExceptionThread
{
   public static void main(String[] args)
   {
      Runnable r = new Runnable()
                   {
                      @Override
                      public void run()
                      {
                         int x = 1 / 0;
                      }
                   };
      Thread thd = new Thread(r);
      Thread.UncaughtExceptionHandler uceh;
      uceh = new Thread.UncaughtExceptionHandler()
             {
                @Override
                public void uncaughtException(Thread t, Throwable e)
                {
                   System.out.println("Caught throwable " + e + " for thread "
                                      + t);
                }
             };
      thd.setUncaughtExceptionHandler(uceh);
      uceh = new Thread.UncaughtExceptionHandler()
             {
                @Override
                public void uncaughtException(Thread t, Throwable e)
                {
```

```
                    System.out.println("Default uncaught exception handler");
                    System.out.println("Caught throwable " + e + " for thread "
                                       + t);
                }
            };
        thd.setDefaultUncaughtExceptionHandler(uceh);
        thd.start();
    }
}
```

When you run this application, you will observe the following output:

```
Caught throwable java.lang.ArithmeticException: / by zero for thread Thread[Thread-0,5,main]
```

You will not also see the default uncaught exception handler's output because the default handler is not called. To see that output, you must comment out `thd.setUncaughtExceptionHandler(uceh);`. If you also comment out `thd.setDefaultUncaughtExceptionHandler(uceh);`, you will see Listing 8-7's output.

> **Caution**   Thread declares several deprecated methods, including `stop()` (stop an executing thread).
> These methods have been deprecated because they are unsafe. Do *not* use these deprecated methods.
> (I will show you how to safely stop a thread later in this chapter.) Also, you should avoid the `static void`
> `yield()` method, which is intended to switch execution from the current thread to another thread, because
> it can affect portability and hurt application performance. Although `yield()` might switch to another thread
> on some platforms (which can improve performance), `yield()` might only return to the current thread on
> other platforms (which hurts performance because the `yield()` call has only wasted time).

Thread Synchronization

Throughout its execution, each thread is isolated from other threads because it has been given its own method-call stack. However, threads can still interfere with each other when they access and manipulate shared data. This interference can corrupt the shared data, and this corruption can cause an application to fail.

For example, consider a checking account in which a husband and wife have joint access. Suppose that the husband and wife decide to empty this account at the same time without knowing that the other is doing the same thing. Listing 8-9 demonstrates this scenario.

Listing 8-9. A Problematic Checking Account

```
public class CheckingAccount
{
    private int balance;

    public CheckingAccount(int initialBalance)
    {
        balance = initialBalance;
    }
```

```
public boolean withdraw(int amount)
{
   if (amount <= balance)
   {
      try
      {
         Thread.sleep((int) (Math.random() * 200));
      }
      catch (InterruptedException ie)
      {
      }
      balance -= amount;
      return true;
   }
   return false;
}

public static void main(String[] args)
{
   final CheckingAccount ca = new CheckingAccount(100);
   Runnable r = new Runnable()
               {
                  public void run()
                  {
                     String name = Thread.currentThread().getName();
                     for (int i = 0; i < 10; i++)
                        System.out.println (name + " withdraws $10: " +
                                            ca.withdraw(10));
                  }
               };
   Thread thdHusband = new Thread(r);
   thdHusband.setName("Husband");
   Thread thdWife = new Thread(r);
   thdWife.setName("Wife");
   thdHusband.start();
   thdWife.start();
}
}
```

This application lets more money be withdrawn than is available in the account. For example, the following output reveals $110 being withdrawn when only $100 is available:

```
Wife withdraws $10: true
Husband withdraws $10: true
Husband withdraws $10: true
Wife withdraws $10: true
Wife withdraws $10: true
Husband withdraws $10: true
Wife withdraws $10: true
Wife withdraws $10: true
Wife withdraws $10: true
Husband withdraws $10: true
```

```
Husband withdraws $10: false
Husband withdraws $10: false
Husband withdraws $10: false
Husband withdraws $10: false
Husband withdraws $10: false
Husband withdraws $10: false
Wife withdraws $10: true
Wife withdraws $10: false
Wife withdraws $10: false
Wife withdraws $10: false
```

The reason why more money is withdrawn than is available for withdrawal is that a race condition exists between the husband and wife threads.

> **Note**   A *race condition* is a scenario in which multiple threads update the same object at the same time or nearly at the same time. Part of the object stores values written to it by one thread, and another part of the object stores values written to it by another thread.

The race condition exists because the actions of checking the amount for withdrawal to ensure that it is less than what appears in the balance and deducting the amount from the balance are not *atomic* (indivisible) operations. (Although atoms are divisible, atomic is commonly used to refer to something being indivisible.)

> **Note**   The `Thread.sleep()` method call that sleeps for a variable amount of time (up to a maximum of 199 milliseconds) is present so that you can observe more money being withdrawn than is available for withdrawal. Without this method call, you might have to execute the application hundreds of times (or more) to witness this problem because the scheduler might rarely pause a thread between the `amount <= balance` expression and the `balance -= amount;` expression statement—the code executes rapidly.

Consider the following scenario:

- The Husband thread executes `withdraw()`'s amount <= balance expression, which returns true. The scheduler pauses the Husband thread and lets the Wife thread execute.

- The Wife thread executes `withdraw()`'s amount <= balance expression, which returns true.

- The Wife thread performs the withdrawal. The scheduler pauses the Wife thread and lets the Husband thread execute.

- The Husband thread performs the withdrawal.

This problem can be corrected by synchronizing access to `withdraw()` so that only one thread at a time can execute inside this method. You synchronize access at the method level by adding reserved word `synchronized` to the method header prior to the method's return type, for example, `synchronized boolean withdraw(int amount)`.

As I demonstrate later, you can also synchronize access to a block of statements by specifying `synchronized(`*object*`) { /* synchronized statements */ }`, where *object* is an arbitrary object reference. No thread can enter a synchronized method or block until execution leaves the method/block; this is known as *mutual exclusion*.

Synchronization is implemented in terms of monitors and locks. A *monitor* is a concurrency construct for controlling access to a *critical section*, a region of code that must execute atomically. It is identified at the source code level as a synchronized method or a synchronized block.

A *lock* is a token that a thread must acquire before a monitor allows that thread to execute inside a monitor's critical section. The token is released automatically when the thread exits the monitor to give another thread an opportunity to acquire the token and enter the monitor.

> **Note**   A thread that has acquired a lock doesn't release this lock when it calls one of `Thread`'s `sleep()` methods.

A thread entering a synchronized instance method acquires the lock associated with the object on which the method is called. A thread entering a synchronized class method acquires the lock associated with the class's `java.lang.Class` object. Finally, a thread entering a synchronized block acquires the lock associated with the block's controlling object.

> **Tip**   `Thread` declares a `static boolean holdsLock(Object o)` method that returns true when the calling thread holds the monitor lock on object o. You will find this method handy in assertion statements, such as `assert Thread.holdsLock(o);`.

The need for synchronization is often subtle. For example, Listing 8-10's ID utility class declares a `getNextID()` method that returns a unique `long`-based ID, perhaps to be used when generating unique filenames. Although you might not think so, this method can cause data corruption and return duplicate values.

Listing 8-10. A Utility Class for Returning Unique IDs

```
class ID
{
   private static long nextID = 0;
   static long getNextID()
   {
      return nextID++;
   }
}
```

There are two lack-of-synchronization problems with `getNextID()`. Because 32-bit virtual machine implementations require two steps to update a 64-bit long integer, adding 1 to `nextID` is not atomic: the scheduler could interrupt a thread that has only updated half of nextID, which corrupts the contents of this variable.

> **Note**   Variables of type long and double are subject to corruption when being written to in an unsynchronized context on 32-bit virtual machines. This problem doesn't occur with variables of type boolean, byte, char, float, int, or short; each type occupies 32 bits or less.

Assume that multiple threads call getNextID(). Because postincrement (++) reads and writes the nextID field in two steps, multiple threads might retrieve the same value. For example, thread A executes ++, reading nextID but not incrementing its value before being interrupted by the scheduler. Thread B now executes and reads the same value.

Both problems can be corrected by synchronizing access to nextID so that only one thread can execute this method's code. All that is required is to add synchronized to the method header prior to the method's return type, for example, static synchronized int getNextID().

Synchronization is also used to communicate between threads. For example, you might design your own mechanism for stopping a thread (because you cannot use Thread's unsafe stop() methods for this task). Listing 8-11 shows how you might accomplish this task.

Listing 8-11. Attempting to Stop a Thread

```java
public class ThreadStopping
{
   public static void main(String[] args)
   {
      class StoppableThread extends Thread
      {
         private boolean stopped = false;

         @Override
         public void run()
         {
            while(!stopped)
               System.out.println("running");
         }

         void stopThread()
         {
            stopped = true;
         }
      }
      StoppableThread thd = new StoppableThread();
      thd.start();
      try
      {
         Thread.sleep(1000); // sleep for 1 second
      }
```

```
         catch (InterruptedException ie)
         {
         }
         thd.stopThread();
      }
}
```

Listing 8-11 introduces a main() method with a local class named StoppableThread that subclasses Thread. StoppableThread declares a stopped field initialized to false, a stopThread() method that sets this field to true, and a run() method whose infinite loop checks stopped on each loop iteration to see if its value has changed to true.

After instantiating StoppableThread, the default main thread starts the thread associated with this Thread object. It then sleeps for one second and calls StoppableThread's stop() method before dying. When you run this application on a single-processor/single-core machine, you will probably observe the application stopping. You might not see this stoppage when the application runs on a multiprocessor machine or a uniprocessor machine with multiple cores. For performance reasons, each processor or core probably has its own *cache* (localized high-speed memory) with its own copy of stopped. When one thread modifies its copy of this field, the other thread's copy of stopped isn't changed.

Listing 8-12 refactors Listing 8-11 to guarantee that the application will run correctly on all kinds of machines.

Listing 8-12. Guaranteed Stoppage on a Multiprocessor/Multicore Machine

```
public class ThreadStopping
{
   public static void main(String[] args)
   {
      class StoppableThread extends Thread
      {
         private boolean stopped = false;

         @Override
         public void run()
         {
            while(!isStopped())
              System.out.println("running");
         }

         synchronized void stopThread()
         {
            stopped = true;
         }

         private synchronized boolean isStopped()
         {
            return stopped;
         }
      }
```

```
        StoppableThread thd = new StoppableThread();
        thd.start();
        try
        {
            Thread.sleep(1000); // sleep for 1 second
        }
        catch (InterruptedException ie)
        {
        }
        thd.stopThread();
    }
}
```

Listing 8-12's stopThread() and isStopped() methods are synchronized to support thread communication (between the default main thread that calls stopThread() and the started thread that executes inside run()). When a thread enters one of these methods, it's guaranteed to access a single shared copy of the stopped field (not a cached copy).

Synchronization is necessary to support mutual exclusion or mutual exclusion combined with thread communication. However, there exists an alternative to synchronization when the only purpose is to communicate between threads. This alternative is reserved word volatile, which Listing 8-13 demonstrates.

Listing 8-13. The volatile Alternative to Synchronization for Thread Communication

```
public class ThreadStopping
{
    public static void main(String[] args)
    {
        class StoppableThread extends Thread
        {
            private volatile boolean stopped = false;

            @Override
            public void run()
            {
                while(!stopped)
                    System.out.println("running");
            }

            void stopThread()
            {
                stopped = true;
            }
        }
        StoppableThread thd = new StoppableThread();
        thd.start();
        try
        {
            Thread.sleep(1000); // sleep for 1 second
        }
```

```
        catch (InterruptedException ie)
        {
        }
        thd.stopThread();
    }
}
```

Listing 8-13 declares `stopped` to be `volatile`; threads that access this field will always access a single shared copy (not cached copies on multiprocessor/multicore machines). In addition to generating code that is less verbose, `volatile` might offer improved performance over synchronization.

When a field is declared `volatile`, it cannot also be declared `final`. If you're depending on the *semantics* (meaning) of volatility, you still get those from a `final` field. For more information, check out Brian Goetz's "Java Theory and Practice: Fixing the Java Memory Model, Part 2" article (`www.ibm.com/developerworks/library/j-jtp03304/`).

> **Caution**   Use `volatile` only in a thread communication context. Also, you can only use this reserved word in the context of field declarations. Although you can declare `double` and `long` fields `volatile`, you should avoid doing so on 32-bit virtual machines because it takes two operations to access a `double` or `long` variable's value, and mutual exclusion via synchronization is required to access their values safely.

`java.lang.Object`'s `wait()`, `notify()`, and `notifyAll()` methods support a form of thread communication where a thread voluntarily waits for some *condition* (a prerequisite for continued execution) to arise, at which time another thread notifies the waiting thread that it can continue. `wait()` causes its calling thread to wait on an object's monitor, and `notify()` and `notifyAll()` wake up one or all threads waiting on the monitor.

> **Caution**   Because the `wait()`, `notify()`, and `notifyAll()` methods depend on a lock, they cannot be called from outside of a synchronized method or synchronized block. If you fail to heed this warning, you will encounter a thrown instance of the `java.lang.IllegalMonitorStateException` class. Also, a thread that has acquired a lock releases this lock when it calls one of `Object`'s `wait()` methods.

A classic example of thread communication involving conditions is the relationship between a producer thread and a consumer thread. The producer thread produces data items to be consumed by the consumer thread. Each produced data item is stored in a shared variable.

Imagine that the threads are not communicating and are running at different speeds. The producer might produce a new data item and record it in the shared variable before the consumer retrieves the previous data item for processing. Also, the consumer might retrieve the contents of the shared variable before a new data item is produced.

To overcome those problems, the producer thread must wait until it is notified that the previously produced data item has been consumed, and the consumer thread must wait until it is notified that a new data item has been produced. Listing 8-14 shows you how to accomplish this task via wait() and notify().

Listing 8-14. The Producer-Consumer Relationship

```java
public class PC
{
   public static void main(String[] args)
   {
      Shared s = new Shared();
      new Producer(s).start();
      new Consumer(s).start();
   }
}

class Shared
{
   private char c = '\u0000';
   private boolean writeable = true;

   synchronized void setSharedChar(char c)
   {
      while (!writeable)
         try
         {
            wait();
         }
         catch (InterruptedException e) {}
      this.c = c;
      writeable = false;
      notify();
   }

   synchronized char getSharedChar()
   {
      while (writeable)
         try
         {
            wait();
         }
         catch (InterruptedException e) {}
      writeable = true;
      notify();
      return c;
   }
}
```

```
class Producer extends Thread
{
    private Shared s;

    Producer(Shared s)
    {
        this.s = s;
    }

    @Override
    public void run()
    {
        for (char ch = 'A'; ch <= 'Z'; ch++)
        {
            synchronized(s)
            {
                s.setSharedChar(ch);
                System.out.println(ch + " produced by producer.");
            }
        }
    }
}
class Consumer extends Thread
{
    private Shared s;

    Consumer(Shared s)
    {
        this.s = s;
    }

    @Override
    public void run()
    {
        char ch;
        do
        {
            synchronized(s)
            {
                ch = s.getSharedChar();
                System.out.println(ch + " consumed by consumer.");
            }
        }
        while (ch != 'Z');
    }
}
```

This application creates a Shared object and two threads that get a copy of the object's reference. The producer calls the object's setSharedChar() method to save each of 26 uppercase letters; the consumer calls the object's getSharedChar() method to acquire each letter.

The writeable instance field tracks two conditions: the producer waiting on the consumer to consume a data item and the consumer waiting on the producer to produce a new data item. It helps coordinate execution of the producer and consumer. The following scenario, where the consumer executes first, illustrates this coordination:

1. The consumer executes s.getSharedChar() to retrieve a letter.

2. Inside of that synchronized method, the consumer calls wait() because writeable contains true. The consumer now waits until it receives notification from the producer.

3. The producer eventually executes s.setSharedChar(ch);.

4. When the producer enters that synchronized method (which is possible because the consumer released the lock inside of the wait() method prior to waiting), the producer discovers writeable's value to be true and doesn't call wait().

5. The producer saves the character, sets writeable to false (which will cause the producer to wait on the next setSharedChar() call when the consumer has not consumed the character by that time), and calls notify() to awaken the consumer (assuming the consumer is waiting).

6. The producer exits setSharedChar(char c).

7. The consumer wakes up (and reacquires the lock), sets writeable to true (which will cause the consumer to wait on the next getSharedChar() call when the producer has not produced a character by that time), notifies the producer to awaken that thread (assuming the producer is waiting), and returns the shared character.

Although the synchronization works correctly, you might observe output (on some platforms) that shows multiple producing messages before a consuming message. For example, you might see A produced by producer., followed by B produced by producer., followed by A consumed by consumer. at the beginning of the application's output.

This strange output order is caused by the call to setSharedChar() followed by its companion System.out.println() method call not being atomic and by the call to getSharedChar() followed by its companion System.out.println() method call not being atomic. The output order is corrected by wrapping each of these method call pairs in a synchronized block that synchronizes on the Shared object referenced by s.

When you run this application, its output should always appear in the same alternating order as shown next (only the first few lines are shown for brevity):

```
A produced by producer.
A consumed by consumer.
B produced by producer.
B consumed by consumer.
C produced by producer.
C consumed by consumer.
D produced by producer.
D consumed by consumer.
```

> **Caution**   Never call `wait()` outside of a loop. The loop tests the condition (`!writeable` or `writeable` in the previous example) before and after the `wait()` call. Testing the condition before calling `wait()` ensures *liveness*. If this test was not present, and if the condition held and `notify()` had been called prior to `wait()` being called, it is unlikely that the waiting thread would ever wake up. Retesting the condition after calling `wait()` ensures *safety*. If retesting didn't occur, and if the condition didn't hold after the thread had awakened from the `wait()` call (perhaps another thread called `notify()` accidentally when the condition didn't hold), the thread would proceed to destroy the lock's protected invariants.

Too much synchronization can be problematic. If you are not careful, you might encounter a situation where locks are acquired by multiple threads, neither thread holds its own lock but holds the lock needed by some other thread, and neither thread can enter and later exit its critical section to release its held lock because some other thread holds the lock to that critical section. Listing 8-15's atypical example demonstrates this scenario, which is known as *deadlock*.

Listing 8-15. A Pathological Case of Deadlock

```
public class DeadlockDemo
{
   private Object lock1 = new Object();
   private Object lock2 = new Object();

   public void instanceMethod1()
   {
      synchronized(lock1)
      {
         synchronized(lock2)
         {
            System.out.println("first thread in instanceMethod1");
            // critical section guarded first by
            // lock1 and then by lock2
         }
      }
   }

   public void instanceMethod2()
   {
      synchronized(lock2)
      {
         synchronized(lock1)
         {
            System.out.println("second thread in instanceMethod2");
            // critical section guarded first by
            // lock2 and then by lock1
         }
      }
   }
```

```java
    public static void main(String[] args)
    {
        final DeadlockDemo dld = new DeadlockDemo();
        Runnable r1 = new Runnable()
                    {
                        @Override
                        public void run()
                        {
                            while(true)
                            {
                                dld.instanceMethod1();
                                try
                                {
                                    Thread.sleep(50);
                                }
                                catch (InterruptedException ie)
                                {
                                }
                            }
                        }
                    };
        Thread thdA = new Thread(r1);
        Runnable r2 = new Runnable()
                    {
                        @Override
                        public void run()
                        {
                            while(true)
                            {
                                dld.instanceMethod2();
                                try
                                {
                                    Thread.sleep(50);
                                }
                                catch (InterruptedException ie)
                                {
                                }
                            }
                        }
                    };
        Thread thdB = new Thread(r2);
        thdA.start();
        thdB.start();
    }
}
```

Listing 8-15's thread A and thread B call instanceMethod1() and instanceMethod2(), respectively, at different times. Consider the following execution sequence:

1. Thread A calls instanceMethod1(), obtains the lock assigned to the lock1-referenced object, and enters its outer critical section (but has not yet acquired the lock assigned to the lock2-referenced object).

2. Thread B calls instanceMethod2(), obtains the lock assigned to the lock2-referenced object, and enters its outer critical section (but has not yet acquired the lock assigned to the lock1-referenced object).

3. Thread A attempts to acquire the lock associated with lock2. The virtual machine forces the thread to wait outside of the inner critical section because thread B holds that lock.

4. Thread B attempts to acquire the lock associated with lock1. The virtual machine forces the thread to wait outside of the inner critical section because thread A holds that lock.

5. Neither thread can proceed because the other thread holds the needed lock. You have a deadlock situation and the program (at least in the context of the two threads) freezes up.

Although the previous example clearly identifies a deadlock state, it's often not that easy to detect deadlock. For example, your code might contain the following circular relationship among various classes (in several source files):

- Class A's synchronized method calls class B's synchronized method.

- Class B's synchronized method calls class C's synchronized method.

- Class C's synchronized method calls class A's synchronized method.

If thread A calls class A's synchronized method and thread B calls class C's synchronized method, thread B will block when it attempts to call class A's synchronized method and thread A is still inside of that method. Thread A will continue to execute until it calls class C's synchronized method and then block. Deadlock results.

Note   Neither the Java language nor the virtual machine provides a way to prevent deadlock, and so the burden falls on you. The simplest way to prevent deadlock from happening is to avoid having either a synchronized method or a synchronized block call another synchronized method/block. Although this advice prevents deadlock from happening, it is impractical because one of your synchronized methods/ blocks might need to call a synchronized method in a Java API, and the advice is overkill because the synchronized method/block being called might not call any other synchronized method/block, so deadlock would not occur.

You will sometimes want to associate per-thread data (such as a user ID) with a thread. Although you can accomplish this task with a local variable, you can only do so while the local variable exists. You could use an instance field to keep this data around longer, but then you would have to deal with synchronization. Thankfully, Java supplies ThreadLocal as a simple (and very handy) alternative.

Each instance of the ThreadLocal class describes a *thread-local variable*, which is a variable that provides a separate storage slot to each thread that accesses the variable. You can think of a thread-local variable as a multislot variable in which each thread can store a different value in the same variable. Each thread sees only its value and is unaware of other threads having their own values in this variable.

ThreadLocal is generically declared as ThreadLocal<T>, where T identifies the type of value that is stored in the variable. This class declares the following constructor and methods:

- ThreadLocal() creates a new thread-local variable.

- T get() returns the value in the calling thread's storage slot. If an entry doesn't exist when the thread calls this method, get() calls initialValue().

- T initialValue() creates the calling thread's storage slot and stores an initial (default) value in this slot. The initial value defaults to null. You must subclass ThreadLocal and override this protected method to provide a more suitable initial value.

- void remove() removes the calling thread's storage slot. If this method is followed by get() with no intervening set(), get() calls initialValue().

- void set(T value) sets the value of the calling thread's storage slot to value.

Listing 8-16 shows how to use ThreadLocal to associate different user IDs with two threads.

Listing 8-16. Different User IDs for Different Threads

```
public class ThreadLocalDemo
{
   private static volatile ThreadLocal<String> userID =
      new ThreadLocal<String>();

   public static void main(String[] args)
   {
      Runnable r = new Runnable()
                   {
                      @Override
                      public void run()
                      {
                         String name = Thread.currentThread().getName();
                         if (name.equals("A"))
                            userID.set("foxtrot");
                         else
                            userID.set("charlie");
                         System.out.println(name + " " + userID.get());
                      }
                   };
```

```
        Thread thdA = new Thread(r);
        thdA.setName("A");
        Thread thdB = new Thread(r);
        thdB.setName("B");
        thdA.start();
        thdB.start();
    }
}
```

After instantiating ThreadLocal and assigning the reference to a volatile class field named userID (the field is volatile because it is accessed by different threads, which might execute on a multiprocessor/multicore machine), the default main thread creates two more threads that store different String objects in userID and output their objects.

When you run this application, you will observe the following output (possibly not in this order):

```
A foxtrot
B charlie
```

Values stored in thread-local variables are not related. When a new thread is created, it gets a new storage slot containing initialValue()'s value. Perhaps you would prefer to pass a value from a *parent thread*, a thread that creates another thread, to a *child thread*, the created thread. You accomplish this task with InheritableThreadLocal.

InheritableThreadLocal is a subclass of ThreadLocal. As well as declaring an InheritableThreadLocal() constructor, this class declares the following protected method:

- ▪ T childValue(T parentValue) calculates the child's initial value as a function of the parent's value at the time the child thread is created. This method is called from the parent thread before the child thread is started. The method returns the argument passed to parentValue and should be overridden when another value is desired.

Listing 8-17 shows how to use InheritableThreadLocal to pass a parent thread's Integer object to a child thread.

Listing 8-17. Passing an Object from Parent Thread to Child Thread

```
public class InheritableThreadLocalDemo
{
    private static volatile InheritableThreadLocal<Integer> intVal =
        new InheritableThreadLocal<Integer>();

    public static void main(String[] args)
    {
        Runnable rP = new Runnable()
                      {
                          @Override
                          public void run()
                          {
                              intVal.set(new Integer(10));
                              Runnable rC = new Runnable()
                                            {
```

```
                                        @Override
                                        public void run()
                                        {
                                           Thread thd;
                                           thd = Thread.currentThread();
                                           String name = thd.getName();
                                           System.out.println(name + " " +
                                                              intVal.get());
                                        }
                                     };
                        Thread thdChild = new Thread(rC);
                        thdChild.setName("Child");
                        thdChild.start();
                     }
                  };
         new Thread(rP).start();
      }
}
```

After instantiating InheritableThreadLocal and assigning it to a volatile class field named intVal, the default main thread creates a parent thread, which stores an Integer object containing 10 in intVal. The parent thread creates a child thread, which accesses intVal and retrieves its parent thread's Integer object.

When you run this application, you will observe the following output:

```
Child 10
```

Exploring System Capabilities

The java.lang package includes four system-oriented classes: System, Runtime, Process, and ProcessBuilder. These classes let you obtain information about the system on which the application is running (such as environment variable values) and perform various system tasks (such as execute another application). For brevity, in this section I introduce you to the first three classes only.

> **Note** ProcessBuilder is a convenient alternative to Runtime for creating application *processes* and managing their attributes. To learn more about this class, check out "Getting Started with Java's ProcessBuilder: A Simple Utility Class to Interact with Linux from Java Program" (http://singztechmusings.wordpress.com/2011/06/21/getting-started-with-javas-processbuilder-a-sample-utility-class-to-interact-with-linux-from-java-program/).

System

System is a utility class that declares in, out, and err class fields, which refer to the current standard input, standard output, and standard error streams, respectively. The first field is of type java. io.InputStream, and the last two fields are of type java.io.PrintStream. (I will formally introduce these classes in Chapter 11.)

System also declares class methods that provide access to the current time (in milliseconds), system property values, environment variable values, and other kinds of system information. Furthermore, it declares class methods that support the system tasks of copying one array to another array, requesting garbage collection, and so on.

Table 8-2 describes some of System's methods.

Table 8-2. System Methods

Method	Description
`void arraycopy(Object src, int srcPos, Object dest, int destPos, int length)`	Copy the number of elements specified by `length` from the `src` array starting at zero-based offset `srcPos` into the `dest` array starting at zero-based offset `destPos`. This method throws `java.lang.NullPointerException` when `src` or `dest` is null, `java.lang.IndexOutOfBoundsException` when copying causes access to data outside array bounds, and `java.lang.ArrayStoreException` when an element in the `src` array could not be stored into the `dest` array because of a type mismatch.
`long currentTimeMillis()`	Return the current system time in milliseconds since January 1, 1970 00:00:00 UTC (Coordinated Universal Time—see `http://en.wikipedia.org/wiki/Coordinated_Universal_Time`).
`void gc()`	Inform the virtual machine that now would be a good time to run the garbage collector. This is only a hint; there is no guarantee that the garbage collector will run.
`String getEnv(String name)`	Return the value of the environment variable identified by name.
`String getProperty(String name)`	Return the value of the *system property* (platform-specific attribute, such as a version number) identified by name or return null when such a property doesn't exist. Examples of system properties that are useful in an Android context include `file.separator`, `java.class.path`, `java.home`, `java.io.tmpdir`, `java.library.path`, `line.separator`, `os.arch`, `os.name`, `path.separator`, and `user.dir`.
`void runFinalization()`	Inform the virtual machine that now would be a good time to perform any outstanding object finalizations. This is only a hint; there is no guarantee that outstanding object finalizations will be performed.
`void setErr(PrintStream err)`	Set the standard error device to point to err.
`void setIn(InputStream in)`	Set the standard input device to point to in.
`void setOut(PrintStream out)`	Set the standard output device to point to out.

> **Note**   System declares SecurityManager getSecurityManager() and void
> setSecurityManager(SecurityManager sm) methods that are not supported by Android.
> On an Android device, the former method always returns null, and the latter method always throws
> an instance of the java.lang.SecurityException class. Regarding the latter method, its
> documentation states that "security managers do not provide a secure environment for executing
> untrusted code and are unsupported on Android. Untrusted code cannot be safely isolated within a
> single virtual machine on Android."

Listing 8-18 demonstrates the arraycopy(), currentTimeMillis(), and getProperty() methods.

Listing 8-18. Experimenting with System Methods

```
public class SystemDemo
{
   public static void main(String[] args)
   {
      int[] grades = { 86, 92, 78, 65, 52, 43, 72, 98, 81 };
      int[] gradesBackup = new int[grades.length];
      System.arraycopy(grades, 0, gradesBackup, 0, grades.length);
      for (int i = 0; i < gradesBackup.length; i++)
         System.out.println(gradesBackup[i]);
      System.out.println("Current time: " + System.currentTimeMillis());
      String[] propNames =
      {
         "file.separator",
         "java.class.path",
         "java.home",
         "java.io.tmpdir",
         "java.library.path",
         "line.separator",
         "os.arch",
         "os.name",
         "path.separator",
         "user.dir"
      };
      for (int i = 0; i < propNames.length; i++)
         System.out.println(propNames[i] + ": " +
                           System.getProperty(propNames[i]));
   }
}
```

Listing 8-18's main() method begins by demonstrating arraycopy(). It uses this method to copy the
contents of a grades array to a gradesBackup array.

> **Tip** The `arraycopy()` method is the fastest portable way to copy one array to another. Also, when you write a class whose methods return a reference to an internal array, you should use `arraycopy()` to create a copy of the array and then return the copy's reference. That way, you prevent clients from directly manipulating (and possibly screwing up) the internal array.

`main()` next calls `currentTimeMillis()` to return the current time as a milliseconds value. Because this value is not human readable, you might want to use the `java.util.Date` class (discussed in Chapter 10). The `Date()` constructor calls `currentTimeMillis()` and its `toString()` method converts this value to a readable date and time.

`main()` concludes by demonstrating `getProperty()` in a for loop. This loop iterates over all of Table 8-2's property names, outputting each name and value.

Compile Listing 8-18: `javac SystemDemo.java`. Then execute the following command line:

`java SystemDemo`

When I run this application on my platform, it generates the following output:

```
86
92
78
65
52
43
72
98
81
Current time: 1353115138889
file.separator: \
java.class.path: .;C:\Program Files (x86)\QuickTime\QTSystem\QTJava.zip
java.home: C:\Program Files\Java\jre7
java.io.tmpdir: C:\Users\Owner\AppData\Local\Temp\
java.library.path: C:\Windows\system32;C:\Windows\Sun\Java\bin;C:\Windows\system32;C:\Windows;
c:\Program Files (x86)\AMD APP\bin\x86_64;c:\Program Files (x86)\AMD APP\bin\x86;C:\Program
Files\Common Files\Microsoft Shared\Windows Live;C:\Program Files (x86)\Common Files\Microsoft
Shared\Windows Live;C:\Windows\system32;C:\Windows;C:\Windows\System32\Wbem;C:\Windows\System32\
WindowsPowerShell\v1.0\;C:\Program Files (x86)\ATI Technologies\ATI.ACE\Core-Static;
C:\Program Files (x86)\Windows Live\Shared;C:\Program Files\java\jdk1.7.0_06\bin;
C:\Program Files (x86)\Borland\BCC55\bin;C:\android;C:\android\tools;C:\android\platform-tools;
C:\Program Files (x86)\apache-ant-1.8.2\bin;C:\Program Files (x86)\QuickTime\QTSystem\;.
line.separator:

os.arch: amd64
os.name: Windows 7
path.separator: ;
user.dir: C:\prj\dev\ljfad2\ch08\code\SystemDemo
```

> **Note**   line.separator stores the actual line separator character/characters, not its/their representation (such as \r\n), which is why a blank line appears after line.separator:.

When you invoke System.in.read(), the input is originating from the source identified by the InputStream instance assigned to in. Similarly, when you invoke System.out.print() or System.err.println(), the output is being sent to the destination identified by the PrintStream instance assigned to out or err, respectively.

> **Tip**   On an Android device, you can view content sent to standard output and standard error by first executing adb logcat at the command line. adb is one of the tools included in the Android SDK.

Java initializes in to refer to the keyboard or a file when the standard input device is redirected to the file. Similarly, Java initializes out/err to refer to the screen or a file when the standard output/error device is redirected to the file. You can specify the input source, output destination, and error destination by calling setIn(), setOut(), and setErr()—see Listing 8-19.

Listing 8-19. Programmatically Specifying the Standard Input Device Source and Standard Output/Error Device Destinations

```
import java.io.FileInputStream;
import java.io.IOException;
import java.io.PrintStream;

public class RedirectIO
{
   public static void main(String[] args) throws IOException
   {
      if (args.length != 3)
      {
         System.err.println("usage: java RedirectIO stdinfile stdoutfile stderrfile");
         return;
      }

      System.setIn(new FileInputStream(args[0]));
      System.setOut(new PrintStream(args[1]));
      System.setErr(new PrintStream(args[2]));

      int ch;
      while ((ch = System.in.read()) != -1)
         System.out.print((char) ch);

      System.err.println("Redirected error output");
   }
}
```

Listing 8-19 presents a RedirectIO application that lets you specify (via command-line arguments) the name of a file from which System.in.read() obtains its content as well as the names of files to which System.out.print() and System.err.println() send their content. It then proceeds to copy standard input to standard output and then demonstrates outputting content to standard error.

> **Note** FileInputStream provides access to the input sequence of bytes that is stored in the file identified, in this example, by args[0]. Similarly, the PrintStream provides access to the files identified by args[1] and args[2], which will store the output and error sequences of bytes.

Compile Listing 8-19: javac RedirectIO.java. Then execute the following command line:

java RedirectIO RedirectIO.java out.txt err.txt

This command line produces no visual output on the screen. Instead, it copies the contents of RedirectIO.java to out.txt. It also stores Redirected error output in err.txt.

Runtime and Process

Runtime provides Java applications with access to the environment in which they are running. An instance of this class is obtained by invoking its Runtime getRuntime() class method.

> **Note** There is only one instance of the Runtime class.

Runtime declares several methods that are also declared in System. For example, Runtime declares a void gc() method. Behind the scenes, System defers to its Runtime counterpart by first obtaining the Runtime instance and then invoking this method via that instance. For example, System's static void gc() method executes Runtime.getRuntime().gc();.

Runtime also declares methods with no System counterparts. The following list describes a few of these methods:

- int availableProcessors() returns the number of processors that are available to the virtual machine. The minimum value returned by this method is 1.

- long freeMemory() returns the amount of free memory (measured in bytes) that the virtual machine makes available to the application.

- long maxMemory() returns the maximum amount of memory (measured in bytes) that the virtual machine may use (or Long.MAX_VALUE when there is no limit).

- long totalMemory() returns the total amount of memory (measured in bytes) that is available to the virtual machine. This amount may vary over time depending on the environment that is hosting the virtual machine.

Listing 8-20 demonstrates these methods.

Listing 8-20. Experimenting with Runtime Methods

```java
public class RuntimeDemo
{
   public static void main(String[] args)
   {
      Runtime rt = Runtime.getRuntime();
      System.out.println("Available processors: " + rt.availableProcessors());
      System.out.println("Free memory: "+ rt.freeMemory());
      System.out.println("Maximum memory: " + rt.maxMemory());
      System.out.println("Total memory: " + rt.totalMemory());
   }
}
```

Compile Listing 8-20: `javac RuntimeDemo.java`. Then execute the following command line:

```
java RuntimeDemo
```

When I run this application on my platform, I observe the following results:

```
Available processors: 2
Free memory: 123997936
Maximum memory: 1849229312
Total memory: 124649472
```

Some of `Runtime`'s methods are dedicated to executing other applications. For example, `Process exec(String program)` executes the program named `program` in a separate native *process*. The new process inherits the environment of the method's caller, and a `Process` object is returned to allow communication with the new process. `IOException` is thrown when an I/O error occurs.

> **Tip**   `ProcessBuilder` is a convenient alternative for configuring process attributes and running a process. For example, `Process p = new ProcessBuilder("myCommand", "myArg").start();`.

Table 8-3 describes `Process` methods.

Table 8-3. Process Methods

Method	Description
`void destroy()`	Terminate the calling process and close any associated streams.
`int exitValue()`	Return the exit value of the native process represented by this `Process` object (the new process). `IllegalThreadStateException` is thrown when the native process has not yet terminated.
`InputStream getErrorStream()`	Return an input stream that is connected to the standard error stream of the native process represented by this `Process` object. The stream obtains data piped from the error output of the process represented by this `Process` object.

(continued)

Table 8-3. (*continued*)

Method	Description
InputStream getInputStream()	Return an input stream that is connected to the standard output stream of the native process represented by this Process object. The stream obtains data piped from the standard output of the process represented by this Process object.
OutputStream getOutputStream()	Return an output stream that is connected to the standard input stream of the native process represented by this Process object. Output to the stream is piped into the standard input of the process represented by this Process object.
int waitFor()	Cause the calling thread to wait for the native process associated with this Process object to terminate. The process's exit value is returned. By convention, 0 indicates normal termination. This method throws InterruptedException when the current thread is interrupted by another thread while it is waiting.

Listing 8-21 demonstrates exec(String program) and three of Process's methods.

Listing 8-21. Executing Another Application and Displaying Its Standard Output/Error Content

```java
import java.io.InputStream;
import java.io.IOException;

public class Exec
{
   public static void main(String[] args)
   {
      if (args.length != 1)
      {
         System.err.println("usage: java Exec program");
         return;
      }
      try
      {
         Process p = Runtime.getRuntime().exec(args[0]);
         // Obtaining process standard output.
         InputStream is = p.getInputStream();
         int _byte;
         while ((_byte = is.read()) != -1)
            System.out.print((char) _byte);
         // Obtaining process standard error.
         is = p.getErrorStream();
         while ((_byte = is.read()) != -1)
            System.out.print((char) _byte);
         System.out.println("Exit status: " + p.waitFor());
      }
      catch (InterruptedException ie)
      {
         assert false; // should never happen
      }
```

```
        catch (IOException ioe)
        {
            System.err.println("I/O error: " + ioe.getMessage());
        }
    }
}
```

After verifying that exactly one command-line argument has been specified, Listing 8-21's main() method attempts to run the application identified by this argument. IOException is thrown when the application cannot be located or when some other I/O error occurs.

Assuming that everything is fine, getInputStream() is called to obtain a reference to an input stream that is used to input the bytes that the newly invoked application writes to its standard output stream, if any. These bytes are subsequently output.

Next, main() calls getErrorStream() to obtain a reference to an input stream that is used to input the bytes that the newly invoked application writes to its standard error stream, if any. These bytes are subsequently output.

> **Note**   To guard against confusion, remember that Process's getInputStream() method is used to read bytes that the new process writes to its output stream, whereas Process's getErrorStream() method is used to read bytes that the new process writes to its error stream.

Finally, main() calls waitFor() to block until the new process exits. If the new process is a GUI-based application, this method will not return until you explicitly terminate the new process. For simple command-line-based applications, Exec should terminate immediately.

Compile Listing 8-21: javac Exec.java. Then execute a command line that identifies an application, such as the java application launcher:

java Exec java

You should observe java's usage information followed by the following line:

Exit status: 1

> **Caution**   Because some native platforms provide limited buffer size for standard input and output streams, failure to promptly write the new process's input stream or read its output stream may cause the new process to block or even deadlock.

EXERCISES

The following exercises are designed to test your understanding of Chapter 8's content:

1. What is a primitive type wrapper class?

2. Identify Java's primitive type wrapper classes.

3. Why does Java provide primitive type wrapper classes?

4. True or false: `Byte` is the smallest of the primitive type wrapper classes.

5. Why should you use `Character` class methods instead of expressions such as `ch >= '0' && ch <= '9'` to determine whether or not a character is a digit, a letter, and so on?

6. How do you determine whether or not `double` variable d contains +infinity or -infinity?

7. Identify the class that is the superclass of `Byte`, `Character`, and the other primitive type wrapper classes.

8. Define thread.

9. What is the purpose of the `Runnable` interface?

10. What is the purpose of the `Thread` class?

11. True or false: A `Thread` object associates with multiple threads.

12. Define race condition.

13. What is thread synchronization?

14. How is synchronization implemented?

15. How does synchronization work?

16. True or false: Variables of type `long` or `double` are not atomic on 32-bit virtual machines.

17. What is the purpose of reserved word `volatile`?

18. True or false: `Object`'s `wait()` methods can be called from outside of a synchronized method or block.

19. Define deadlock.

20. What is the purpose of the `ThreadLocal` class?

21. How does `InheritableThreadLocal` differ from `ThreadLocal`?

22. Identify the four `java.lang` package system classes discussed earlier in this chapter.

23. What system method do you invoke to copy an array to another array?

24. What does the `exec(String program)` method accomplish?

25. What does `Process`'s `getInputStream()` method accomplish?

26. Create a `MultiPrint` application that takes two arguments: text and an integer value that represents a count. This application should print count copies of the text, one copy per line.

27. Modify Listing 8-4's CountingThreads application by marking the two started threads as daemon threads. What happens when you run the resulting application?

28. Modify Listing 8-4's CountingThreads application by adding logic to stop both counting threads when the user presses the Return/Enter key. The default main thread of the new StopCountingThreads application should call System.in.read() before terminating and assign true to a variable named stopped after this method call returns. At each loop iteration start, each counting thread should test this variable to see if it contains true and only continue the loop when the variable contains false.

29. Create an EVDump application that dumps all environment variables (not system properties) to the standard output.

Summary

The java.lang package includes Boolean, Byte, Character, Double, Float, Integer, Long, and Short. These classes are known as primitive type wrapper classes because their instances wrap themselves around values of primitive types.

Java provides these eight primitive type wrapper classes so that primitive-type values can be stored in collections, such as lists, sets, and maps. Furthermore, these classes provide a good place to associate useful constants and class methods with the primitive types.

Applications execute via threads, which are independent paths of execution through an application's code. The virtual machine gives each thread its own method-call stack to prevent threads from interfering with each other.

Java supports threads via its Threads API. This API consists of one interface (Runnable) and four classes (Thread, ThreadGroup, ThreadLocal, and InheritableThreadLocal) in the java.lang package. ThreadGroup is not as useful as these other types.

Throughout its execution, each thread is isolated from other threads because it has been given its own method-call stack. However, threads can still interfere with each other when they access and manipulate shared data. This interference can corrupt the shared data, causing an application to fail.

Corruption can be avoided by using thread synchronization so that only one thread at a time can execute inside a critical section, a region of code that must execute atomically. It is identified at the source code level as a synchronized method or a synchronized block.

You synchronize access at the method level by adding reserved word synchronized to the method header prior to the method's return type. You can also synchronize access to a block of statements by specifying synchronized(*object*) { /* synchronized statements */ }.

Synchronization is implemented in terms of monitors and locks. A monitor is a concurrency construct for controlling access to a critical section. A lock is a token that a thread must acquire before a monitor allows that thread to execute inside a monitor's critical section.

Synchronization is necessary to support mutual exclusion or mutual exclusion combined with thread communication. However, there exists an alternative to synchronization when the only purpose is to communicate between threads. This alternative is reserved word volatile.

Object's `wait()`, `notify()`, and `notifyAll()` methods support a form of thread communication where a thread voluntarily waits for some condition (a prerequisite for continued execution) to arise, at which time another thread notifies the waiting thread that it can continue. `wait()` causes its calling thread to wait on an object's monitor, and `notify()` and `notifyAll()` wake up one or all threads waiting on the monitor.

Too much synchronization can be problematic. If you are not careful, you might encounter a situation where locks are acquired by multiple threads, neither thread holds its own lock but holds the lock needed by some other thread, and neither thread can enter and later exit its critical section to release its held lock because some other thread holds the lock to that critical section. This scenario is known as deadlock.

You will sometimes want to associate per-thread data with a thread. Although you can accomplish this task with a local variable, you can only do so while the local variable exists. You could use an instance field to keep this data around longer, but then you would have to deal with synchronization. Java supplies the `ThreadLocal` class as a simple (and very handy) alternative.

Each `ThreadLocal` instance describes a thread-local variable, which is a variable that provides a separate storage slot to each thread that accesses the variable. Think of a thread-local variable as a multislot variable in which each thread can store a different value in the same variable. Each thread sees only its value and is unaware of other threads having their own values in this variable.

Values stored in thread-local variables are not related. When a new thread is created, it gets a new storage slot containing `initialValue()`'s value. However, you can pass a value from a parent thread, a thread that creates another thread, to a child thread, the created thread, by working with the `InheritableThreadLocal` class.

The `java.lang` package includes four system-oriented classes: `System`, `Runtime`, `Process`, and `ProcessBuilder`. These classes let you obtain information about the system on which the application is running and perform various system tasks.

`System` is a utility class that declares `in`, `out`, and `err` class fields, which refer to the current standard input, standard output, and standard error streams, respectively. The first field is of type `InputStream` and the last two fields are of type `PrintStream`.

`System` also declares class methods that provide access to the current time (in milliseconds), system property values, environment variable values, and other kinds of system information. Furthermore, it declares class methods that support system tasks such as copying one array to another array.

`Runtime` provides Java applications with access to the environment in which they are running. An instance of this class is obtained by invoking its `Runtime getRuntime()` class method. You can then call various environment-access methods, including methods that are also declared in `System`.

Some of `Runtime`'s methods execute other applications. For example, `Process exec(String program)` executes `program` in a separate native process. The new process inherits the environment of the method's caller; a `Process` object is returned to allow communication with the new process.

This chapter completes my tour of Java's basic APIs. In Chapter 9 I begin to explore Java's utility APIs by focusing on the Collections Framework and classic collections APIs.

9

Exploring the Collections Framework

Applications often must manage collections of objects. Although you can use arrays for this purpose, they are not always a good choice. For example, arrays have fixed sizes, making it tricky to determine an optimal size when you need to store a variable number of objects. Also, arrays can be indexed by integers only, making them unsuitable for mapping arbitrary objects to other objects.

The standard class library provides the Collections Framework and legacy utility APIs to manage collections on behalf of applications. In Chapter 9 I first present this framework and then introduce you to these legacy APIs (in case you encounter them in legacy code). As you will discover, some of the legacy APIs are still useful.

> **Note** Java's Concurrency Utilities API suite (discussed in Chapter 10) extends the Collections Framework.

Exploring Collections Framework Fundamentals

The *Collections Framework* is a group of types (mainly located in the `java.util` package) that offers a standard architecture for representing and manipulating *collections*, which are groups of objects stored in instances of classes designed for this purpose. This framework's architecture is divided into three sections:

- *Core interfaces*: The framework provides core interfaces for manipulating collections independently of their implementations.

- *Implementation classes*: The framework provides classes that provide different core interface implementations to address performance and other requirements.

- *Utility classes*: The framework provides utility classes with methods for sorting arrays, obtaining synchronized collections, and more.

The core interfaces include java.lang.Iterable, Collection, List, Set, SortedSet, NavigableSet, Queue, Deque, Map, SortedMap, and NavigableMap. Collection extends Iterable; List, Set, and Queue each extend Collection; SortedSet extends Set; NavigableSet extends SortedSet; Deque extends Queue; SortedMap extends Map; and NavigableMap extends SortedMap.

Figure 9-1 illustrates the core interfaces hierarchy (arrows point to parent interfaces).

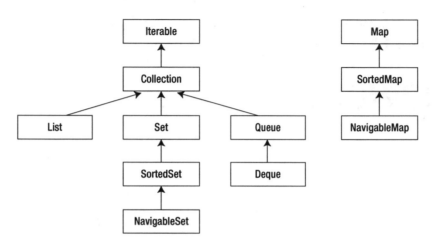

Figure 9-1. *The Collections Framework is based on a hierarchy of core interfaces*

The framework's implementation classes include ArrayList, LinkedList, TreeSet, HashSet, LinkedHashSet, EnumSet, PriorityQueue, ArrayDeque, TreeMap, HashMap, LinkedHashMap, IdentityHashMap, WeakHashMap, and EnumMap. The name of each concrete class ends in a core interface name, identifying the core interface on which it is based.

> **Note**   Additional implementation classes are part of the concurrency utilities.

The framework's implementation classes also include the abstract AbstractCollection, AbstractList, AbstractSequentialList, AbstractSet, AbstractQueue, and AbstractMap classes. These classes offer skeletal implementations of the core interfaces to facilitate the creation of concrete implementation classes.

Finally, the framework provides two utility classes: Arrays and Collections.

Comparable Versus Comparator

A collection implementation stores its elements in some *order* (arrangement). This order may be unsorted, or it may be sorted according to some criterion (such as alphabetical, numerical, or chronological).

A sorted collection implementation defaults to storing its elements according to their *natural ordering*. For example, the natural ordering of java.lang.String objects is *lexicographic* or *dictionary* (also known as alphabetical) order.

A collection cannot rely on equals() to dictate natural ordering because this method can only determine if two elements are equivalent. Instead, element classes must implement the java.lang.Comparable<T> interface and its int compareTo(T o) method.

> **Note** According to Comparable's Oracle-based Java documentation, this interface is considered to be part of the Collections Framework even though it is a member of the java.lang package.

A sorted collection uses compareTo() to determine the natural ordering of this method's element argument o in a collection. compareTo() compares argument o with the current element (which is the element on which compareTo() was called) and does the following:

- It returns a negative value when the current element should precede o.

- It returns a zero value when the current element and o are the same.

- It returns a positive value when the current element should succeed o.

When you need to implement Comparable's compareTo() method, there are some rules that you must follow. These rules, listed next, are similar to those shown in Chapter 4 for implementing the equals() method:

- compareTo() *must be reflexive*: For any nonnull reference value x, x.compareTo(x) must return 0.

- compareTo() *must be symmetric*: For any nonnull reference values x and y, x.compareTo(y) == -y.compareTo(x) must hold.

- compareTo() *must be transitive*: For any nonnull reference values x, y, and z, if x.compareTo(y) > 0 is true, and if y.compareTo(z) > 0 is true, then x.compareTo(z) > 0 must also be true.

Also, compareTo() should throw java.lang.NullPointerException when the null reference is passed to this method. However, you don't need to check for null because this method throws NullPointerException when it attempts to access a null reference's nonexistent members.

> **Note** Before Java 5 and its introduction of generics, compareTo()'s argument was of type java.lang.Object and had to be cast to the appropriate type before the comparison could be made. The cast operator would throw a java.lang.ClassCastException instance when the argument's type was not compatible with the cast.

You might occasionally need to store in a collection objects that are sorted in some order that differs from their natural ordering. In this case, you would supply a comparator to provide that ordering.

A *comparator* is an object whose class implements the Comparator interface. This interface, whose generic type is Comparator<T>, provides the following pair of methods:

- int compare(T o1, T o2) compares both arguments for order. This method returns 0 when o1 equals o2, a negative value when o1 is less than o2, and a positive value when o1 is greater than o2.

- boolean equals(Object o) returns true when o "equals" this Comparator in that o is also a Comparator and imposes the same ordering. Otherwise, this method returns false.

> **Note** Comparator declares equals() because this interface places an extra condition on this method's contract. *Additionally, this method can return true only if the specified object is also a comparator and it imposes the same ordering as this comparator. You don't have to override* equals(), *but doing so may improve performance by allowing programs to determine that two distinct comparators impose the same order.*

Chapter 6 provided an example that illustrated implementing Comparable, and you will discover another example later in this chapter. Also, in this chapter I will present examples of implementing Comparator.

Iterable and Collection

Most of the core interfaces are rooted in Iterable and its Collection subinterface. Their generic types are Iterable<T> and Collection<E>.

Iterable describes any object that can return its contained objects in some sequence. This interface declares an Iterator<T> iterator() method that returns an Iterator instance for iterating over all of the contained objects.

Collection represents a collection of objects that are known as *elements*. This interface provides methods that are common to the Collection subinterfaces on which many collections are based. Table 9-1 describes these methods.

Table 9-1. Collection Methods

Method	Description
boolean add(E e)	Add element e to this collection. Return true if this collection was modified as a result; otherwise, return false. (Attempting to add e to a collection that doesn't permit duplicates and already contains a same-valued element results in e not being added.) This method throws java.lang.UnsupportedOperationException when add() is not supported, ClassCastException when e's class is not appropriate for this collection, java.lang.IllegalArgumentException when some property of e prevents it from being added to this collection, NullPointerException when e contains the null reference and this collection doesn't support null elements, and java.lang.IllegalStateException when the element cannot be added at this time because of insertion restrictions. IllegalStateException signals that a method has been invoked at an illegal or inappropriate time. In other words, the Java/Android environment or application is not in an appropriate state for the requested operation. It is often thrown when you try to add an element to a *bounded queue* (a queue with a maximum length) and the queue is full.
boolean addAll (Collection<? extends E> c)	Add all elements of collection c to this collection. Return true if this collection was modified as a result; otherwise, return false. This method throws UnsupportedOperationException when this collection doesn't support addAll(), ClassCastException when the class of one of c's elements is inappropriate for this collection, IllegalArgumentException when some property of an element prevents it from being added to this collection, NullPointerException when c contains the null reference or when one of its elements is null and this collection doesn't support null elements, and IllegalStateException when not all the elements can be added at this time because of insertion restrictions.
void clear()	Remove all elements from this collection. This method throws UnsupportedOperationException when this collection doesn't support clear().
boolean contains(Object o)	Return true when this collection contains o; otherwise, return false. This method throws ClassCastException when the class of o is inappropriate for this collection and NullPointerException when o contains the null reference and this collection doesn't support null elements.
boolean containsAll (Collection<?> c)	Return true when this collection contains all of the elements that are contained in the collection specified by c; otherwise, return false. This method throws ClassCastException when the class of one of c's elements is inappropriate for this collection and NullPointerException when c contains the null reference or when one of its elements is null and this collection doesn't support null elements.
boolean equals(Object o)	Compare o with this collection and return true when o equals this collection; otherwise, return false.

(continued)

Table 9-1. (*continued*)

Method	Description
int hashCode()	Return this collection's hash code. Equal collections have equal hash codes.
boolean isEmpty()	Return true when this collection contains no elements; otherwise, return false.
Iterator<E> iterator()	Return an Iterator instance for iterating over all of the elements contained in this collection. There are no guarantees concerning the order in which the elements are returned (unless this collection is an instance of some class that provides a guarantee). This Iterable method is redeclared in Collection for convenience.
boolean remove(Object o)	Remove the element identified as o from this collection. Return true when the element is removed; otherwise, return false. This method throws UnsupportedOperationException when this collection doesn't support remove(), ClassCastException when the class of o is inappropriate for this collection, and NullPointerException when o contains the null reference and this collection doesn't support null elements.
boolean removeAll (Collection<?> c)	Remove all of the elements from this collection that are also contained in collection c. Return true when this collection is modified by this operation; otherwise, return false. This method throws UnsupportedOperationException when this collection doesn't support removeAll(), ClassCastException when the class of one of c's elements is inappropriate for this collection, and NullPointerException when c contains the null reference or when one of its elements is null and this collection doesn't support null elements.
boolean retainAll (Collection<?> c)	Retain all of the elements in this collection that are also contained in collection c. Return true when this collection is modified by this operation; otherwise, return false. This method throws UnsupportedOperationException when this collection doesn't support retainAll(), ClassCastException when the class of one of c's elements is inappropriate for this collection, and NullPointerException when c contains the null reference or when one of its elements is null and this collection doesn't support null elements.
int size()	Return the number of elements contained in this collection or java.lang.Integer.MAX_VALUE when there are more than Integer.MAX_VALUE elements contained in the collection.
Object[] toArray()	Return an array containing all of the elements stored in this collection. If this collection makes any guarantees as to what order its elements are returned in by its iterator, this method returns the elements in the same order.
	The returned array is "safe" in that no references to it are maintained by this collection. (In other words, this method allocates a new array even when this collection is backed by an array.) The caller can safely modify the returned array.

(*continued*)

Table 9-1. (*continued*)

Method	Description
`<T> T[] toArray(T[] a)`	Return an array containing all of the elements in this collection; the runtime type of the returned array is that of the specified array. If the collection fits in the specified array, it's returned in the array. Otherwise, a new array is allocated with the runtime type of the specified array and the size of this collection. This method throws `NullPointerException` when `null` is passed to a and `java.lang.ArrayStoreException` when a's runtime type is not a supertype of the runtime type of every element in this collection.

Table 9-1 reveals three exceptional things about various `Collection` methods. First, some methods can throw instances of the `UnsupportedOperationException` class. For example, `add()` throws `UnsupportedOperationException` when you attempt to add an object to an *immutable* (unmodifiable) collection (discussed later in this chapter).

Second, some of `Collection`'s methods can throw instances of the `ClassCastException` class. For example, `remove()` throws `ClassCastException` when you attempt to remove an entry (also known as mapping) from a tree-based map whose keys are `String`s but specify a non-`String` key instead.

Finally, `Collection`'s `add()` and `addAll()` methods throw `IllegalArgumentException` instances when some *property* (attribute) of the element to be added prevents it from being added to this collection. For example, a third-party collection class's `add()` and `addAll()` methods might throw this exception when they detect negative `Integer` values.

Note   Perhaps you're wondering why `remove()` is declared to accept any `Object` argument instead of accepting only objects whose types are those of the collection. In other words, why is `remove()` not declared as `boolean remove(E e)`? Also, why are `containsAll()`, `removeAll()`, and `retainAll()` not declared with an argument of type `Collection<? extends E>` to ensure that the collection argument only contains elements of the same type as the collection on which these methods are called? The answer to these questions is the need to maintain backward compatibility. The Collections Framework was introduced before Java 5 and its introduction of generics. To let legacy code written before version 5 continue to compile, these four methods were declared with weaker type constraints.

Iterator and the Enhanced For Loop Statement

By extending `Iterable`, `Collection` inherits that interface's `iterator()` method, which makes it possible to iterate over a collection. `iterator()` returns an instance of a class that implements the Iterator interface, whose generic type is expressed as Iterator<E> and which declares the following three methods:

- boolean hasNext() returns true when this Iterator instance has more elements to return; otherwise, this method returns false.

- E next() returns the next element from the collection associated with this Iterator instance, or throws NoSuchElementException when there are no more elements to return.

- void remove() removes the last element returned by next() from the collection associated with this Iterator instance. This method can be called only once per next() call. The behavior of an Iterator instance is unspecified when the underlying collection is modified while iteration is in progress in any way other than by calling remove(). This method throws UnsupportedOperationException when it is not supported by this Iterator, and IllegalStateException when remove() has been called without a previous call to next() or when multiple remove() calls occur with no intervening next() calls.

The following example shows you how to iterate over a collection after calling iterator() to return an Iterator instance:

```
Collection<String> col = ... // This code doesn't compile because of the ...
// Add elements to col.
Iterator iter = col.iterator();
while (iter.hasNext())
   System.out.println(iter.next());
```

The while loop repeatedly calls the iterator's hasNext() method to determine whether or not iteration should continue and (if it should continue) the next() method to return the next element from the associated collection.

Because this idiom is commonly used, Java 5 introduced syntactic sugar to the for loop statement to simplify iteration in terms of the idiom. This sugar makes this statement appear like the foreach statement found in languages such as Perl and is revealed in the following simplified equivalent of the previous example:

```
Collection<String> col = ... // This code doesn't compile because of the ...
// Add elements to col.
for (String s: col)
   System.out.println(s);
```

This sugar hides col.iterator(), a method call that returns an Iterator instance for iterating over col's elements. It also hides calls to Iterator's hasNext() and next() methods on this instance. You interpret this sugar to read as follows: "for each String object in col, assign this object to s at the start of the loop iteration."

> **Note**   The enhanced for loop statement is also useful in an arrays context in which it hides the array index variable. Consider the following example:
>
> ```
> String[] verbs = { "run", "walk", "jump" };
> for (String verb: verbs)
>     System.out.println (verb);
> ```
>
> This example, which reads as "for each `String` object in the `verbs` array, assign that object to `verb` at the start of the loop iteration," is equivalent to the following example:
>
> ```
> String[] verbs = { "run", "walk", "jump" };
> for (int i = 0; i < verbs.length; i++)
>     System.out.println (verbs[i]);
> ```

The enhanced for loop statement is limited in that you cannot use this statement where access to the iterator is required to remove an element from a collection. Also, it's not usable where you must replace elements in a collection/array during a traversal; and it cannot be used where you must iterate over multiple collections or arrays in parallel.

Autoboxing and Unboxing

Developers who believe that Java should support only reference types have complained about Java's support for primitive types. One area where the dichotomy of Java's type system is clearly seen is the Collections Framework: you can store objects but not primitive-type-based values in collections.

Although you cannot directly store a primitive-type-based value in a collection, you can indirectly store this value by first wrapping it in an object created from a primitive type wrapper class such as `Integer` and then storing this primitive type wrapper class instance in the collection—see the following example:

```
Collection<Integer> col = ...; // This code doesn't compile because of the ...
int x = 27;
col.add(new Integer(x)); // Indirectly store int value 27 via an Integer object.
```

The reverse situation is also tedious. When you want to retrieve the `int` from `col`, you must invoke `Integer`'s `intValue()` method (which, if you recall, is inherited from `Integer`'s `java.lang.Number` superclass). Continuing on from this example, you would specify `int y = col.iterator().next().intValue();` to assign the stored 32-bit integer to y.

To alleviate this tedium, Java 5 introduced autoboxing and unboxing, which are a pair of complementary syntactic sugar-based language features that make primitive-type values appear more like objects. (This "sleight of hand" isn't complete because you cannot specify expressions such as `27.doubleValue()`.)

Autoboxing automatically *boxes* (wraps) a primitive-type value in an object of the appropriate primitive type wrapper class whenever a primitive-type value is specified but a reference is required. For example, you could change the example's third line to col.add(x); and have the compiler box x into an Integer object.

Unboxing automatically *unboxes* (unwraps) a primitive-type value from its wrapper object whenever a reference is specified but a primitive-type value is required. For example, you could specify int y = col.iterator().next(); and have the compiler unbox the returned Integer object to int value 27 prior to the assignment.

Although autoboxing and unboxing were introduced to simplify working with primitive type values in a collections context, these language features can be used in other contexts; and this arbitrary use can lead to a problem that is difficult to understand without knowledge of what is happening behind the scenes. Consider the following example:

```
Integer i1 = 127;
Integer i2 = 127;
System.out.println(i1 == i2); // Output: true
System.out.println(i1 < i2); // Output: false
System.out.println(i1 > i2); // Output: false
System.out.println(i1 + i2); // Output: 254
i1 = 30000;
i2 = 30000;
System.out.println(i1 == i2); // Output: false
System.out.println(i1 < i2); // Output: false
System.out.println(i1 > i2); // Output: false
i2 = 30001;
System.out.println(i1 < i2); // Output: true
System.out.println(i1 + i2); // Output: 60001
```

With one exception, this example's output is as expected. The exception is the i1 == i2 comparison where each of i1 and i2 contains 30000. Instead of returning true, as is the case where each of i1 and i2 contains 127, i1 == i2 returns false. What is causing this problem?

Examine the generated code and you will discover that Integer i1 = 127; is converted to Integer i1 = Integer.valueOf(127); and Integer i2 = 127; is converted to Integer i2 = Integer.valueOf(127);. According to valueOf()'s Java documentation, this method takes advantage of caching to improve performance.

> **Note**   valueOf() is also used when adding a primitive-type value to a collection. For example, col.add(27) is converted to col.add(Integer.valueOf(27)).

Integer maintains an internal cache of unique Integer objects over a small range of values. The low bound of this range is -128, and the high bound defaults to 127. However, you can change the high bound by assigning a different value to system property java.lang.Integer.IntegerCache.high (via the java.lang.System class's String setProperty(String name, String value) method—I demonstrated this method's String getProperty(String name) counterpart in Chapter 8).

> **Note**   Each of `java.lang.Byte`, `java.lang.Long`, and `java.lang.Short` also maintains an internal cache of unique `Byte`, `Long`, and `Short` objects, respectively.

Because of the cache, each `Integer.valueOf(127)` call returns the same `Integer` object reference, which is why `i1 == i2` (which compares references) evaluates to true. Because 30000 lies outside of the default range, each `Integer.valueOf(30000)` call returns a reference to a new `Integer` object, which is why `i1 == i2` evaluates to false.

In contrast to `==` and `!=`, which don't unbox the boxed values prior to the comparison, operators such as `<`, `>`, and `+` unbox these values before performing their operations. As a result, `i1 < i2` is converted to `i1.intValue() < i2.intValue()` and `i1 + i2` is converted to `i1.intValue() + i2.intValue()`.

> **Caution**   Don't assume that autoboxing and unboxing are used in the context of the `==` and `!=` operators.

Exploring Lists

A *list* is an ordered collection, which is also known as a *sequence*. Elements can be stored in and accessed from specific locations via integer indexes. Some of these elements may be duplicates or null (when the list's implementation allows null elements). Lists are described by the `List` interface, whose generic type is `List<E>`.

`List` extends `Collection` and redeclares its inherited methods, partly for convenience. It also redeclares `iterator()`, `add()`, `remove()`, `equals()`, and `hashCode()` to place extra conditions on their contracts. For example, `List`'s contract for `add()` specifies that it appends an element to the end of the list rather than adding the element to the collection.

`List` also declares Table 9-2's list-specific methods.

Table 9-2. List-Specific Methods

Method	Description
`void add(int index, E e)`	Insert element e into this list at position index. Shift the element currently at this position (if any) and any subsequent elements to the right. This method throws `UnsupportedOperationException` when this list doesn't support `add()`, `ClassCastException` when e's class is inappropriate for this list, `IllegalArgumentException` when some property of e prevents it from being added to this list, `NullPointerException` when e contains the null reference and this list doesn't support null elements, and `java.lang.IndexOutOfBoundsException` when index is less than 0 or index is greater than `size()`.

(continued)

Table 9-2. (continued)

Method	Description
`boolean addAll (int index, Collection<? extends E> c)`	Insert all of c's elements into this list starting at position index and in the order that they are returned by c's iterator. Shift the element currently at this position (if any) and any subsequent elements to the right. This method throws `UnsupportedOperationException` when this list doesn't support `addAll()`, `ClassCastException` when the class of one of c's elements is inappropriate for this list, `IllegalArgumentException` when some property of an element prevents it from being added to this list, `NullPointerException` when c contains the null reference or when one of its elements is null and this list doesn't support null elements, and `IndexOutOfBoundsException` when index is less than 0 or index is greater than `size()`.
`E get(int index)`	Return the element stored in this list at position index. This method throws `IndexOutOfBoundsException` when index is less than 0 or index is greater than or equal to `size()`.
`int indexOf (Object o)`	Return the index of the first occurrence of element o in this list or -1 when this list doesn't contain the element. This method throws `ClassCastException` when o's class is inappropriate for this list and `NullPointerException` when o contains the null reference and this list doesn't support null elements.
`int lastIndexOf (Object o)`	Return the index of the last occurrence of element o in this list or -1 when this list doesn't contain the element. This method throws `ClassCastException` when o's class is inappropriate for this list and `NullPointerException` when o contains the null reference and this list doesn't support null elements.
`ListIterator<E> listIterator()`	Return a list iterator over the elements in this list. The elements are returned in the same order as they appear in the list.
`ListIterator<E> listIterator(int index)`	Return a list iterator over the elements in this list starting with the element located at index. The elements are returned in the same order as they appear in the list. This method throws `IndexOutOfBoundsException` when index is less than 0 or index is greater than `size()`.
`E remove(int index)`	Remove the element at position index from this list, shift any subsequent elements to the left, and return this element. This method throws `UnsupportedOperationException` when this list doesn't support `remove()` and `IndexOutOfBoundsException` when index is less than 0 or index is greater than or equal to `size()`.
`E set(int index, E e)`	Replace the element at position index in this list with element e and return the element previously stored at this position. This method throws `UnsupportedOperationException` when this list doesn't support `set()`, `ClassCastException` when e's class is inappropriate for this list, `IllegalArgumentException` when some property of e prevents it from being added to this list, `NullPointerException` when e contains the null reference and this list doesn't support null elements, and `IndexOutOfBoundsException` when index is less than 0 or index is greater than or equal to `size()`.

(continued)

Table 9-2. (*continued*)

Method	Description
List<E> subList(int fromIndex, int toIndex)	Return a view (discussed later) of the portion of this list between fromIndex (inclusive) and toIndex (exclusive). (If fromIndex and toIndex are equal, the returned list is empty.) The returned list is backed by this list, so nonstructural changes in the returned list are reflected in this list and vice versa. The returned list supports all of the optional list methods (those methods that can throw UnsupportedOperationException) supported by this list. This method throws IndexOutOfBoundsException when fromIndex is less than 0, toIndex is greater than size(), or fromIndex is greater than toIndex.

Table 9-2 refers to the ListIterator interface, which is more flexible than its Iterator superinterface in that ListIterator provides methods for iterating over a list in either direction, modifying the list during iteration, and obtaining the iterator's current position in the list.

> **Note**   The Iterator and ListIterator instances that are returned by the iterator() and listIterator() methods in the ArrayList and LinkedList List implementation classes are *fail-fast*: when a list is structurally modified (by calling the implementation's add() method to add a new element, for example) after the iterator is created, in any way except through the iterator's own add() and remove() methods, the iterator throws ConcurrentModificationException. Therefore, in the face of concurrent modification, the iterator fails quickly and cleanly rather than risking arbitrary, nondeterministic behavior at an undetermined time in the future.

ListIterator declares the following methods:

- void add(E e) inserts e into the list being iterated over. This element is inserted immediately before the next element that would be returned by next(), if any, and after the next element that would be returned by previous(), if any. This method throws UnsupportedOperationException when this list iterator doesn't support add(), ClassCastException when e's class is inappropriate for the list, and IllegalArgumentException when some property of e prevents it from being added to the list.

- boolean hasNext() returns true when this list iterator has more elements when traversing the list in the forward direction.

- boolean hasPrevious() returns true when this list iterator has more elements when traversing the list in the reverse direction.

- E next() returns the next element in the list and advances the cursor position. This method throws NoSuchElementException when there is no next element.

- int nextIndex() returns the index of the element that would be returned by a subsequent call to next() or the size of the list when at the end of the list.

- ▪ E previous() returns the previous element in the list and moves the cursor position backward. This method throws NoSuchElementException when there is no previous element.

- ▪ int previousIndex() returns the index of the element that would be returned by a subsequent call to previous() or -1 when at the beginning of the list.

- ▪ void remove() removes from the list the last element that was returned by next() or previous(). This call can be made only once per call to next() or previous(). Furthermore, it can be made only when add() has not been called after the last call to next() or previous(). This method throws UnsupportedOperationException when this list iterator doesn't support remove() and IllegalStateException when neither next() nor previous() has been called or remove() or add() has already been called after the last call to next() or previous().

- ▪ void set(E e) replaces the last element returned by next() or previous() with element e. This call can be made only when neither remove() nor add() has been called after the last call to next() or previous(). This method throws UnsupportedOperationException when this list iterator doesn't support set(), ClassCastException when e's class is inappropriate for the list, IllegalArgumentException when some property of e prevents it from being added to the list, and IllegalStateException when neither next() nor previous() has been called or remove() or add() has already been called after the last call to next() or previous().

A ListIterator instance doesn't have the concept of a current element. Instead, it has the concept of a *cursor* for navigating through a list. The nextIndex() and previousIndex() methods return the *cursor position*, which always lies between the element that would be returned by a call to previous() and the element that would be returned by a call to next(). A list iterator for a list of length *n* has *n*+1 possible cursor positions as illustrated by each caret (^) in the following:

```
                   Element(0)   Element(1)   Element(2)   ... Element(n-1)
cursor positions:  ^            ^            ^            ^            ^
```

> **Note**   You can mix calls to next() and previous() as long as you are careful. Keep in mind that the first call to previous() returns the same element as the last call to next(). Furthermore, the first call to next() following a sequence of calls to previous() returns the same element as the last call to previous().

Table 9-2's description of the subList() method refers to the concept of a *view*, which is a list that is backed by another list. Changes that are made to the view are reflected in this backing list. The view can cover the entire list or, as subList()'s name implies, only part of the list.

The subList() method is useful for performing *range-view* operations over a list in a compact manner. For example, list.subList(fromIndex, toIndex).clear(); removes a range of elements from list where the first element is at fromIndex and the last element is at toIndex - 1.

> **Caution**   A view's meaning becomes undefined when changes are made to the backing list. Therefore, you should only use subList() temporarily whenever you need to perform a sequence of range operations on the backing list.

ArrayList

The ArrayList class provides a list implementation that is based on an internal array. As a result, access to the list's elements is fast. However, because elements must be moved to open a space for insertion or to close a space after deletion, insertions and deletions of elements is slow.

ArrayList supplies three constructors:

- ArrayList() creates an empty array list with an initial *capacity* (storage space) of 10 elements. Once this capacity is reached, a larger array is allocated, elements from the current array are copied into the larger array, and the larger array becomes the new current array. This process repeats as additional elements are added to the array list.

- ArrayList(Collection<? extends E> c) creates an array list containing c's elements in the order in which they are returned by c's iterator. NullPointerException is thrown when c contains the null reference.

- ArrayList(int initialCapacity) creates an empty array list with an initial capacity of initialCapacity elements. IllegalArgumentException is thrown when initialCapacity is negative.

Listing 9-1 demonstrates an array list.

Listing 9-1. A Demonstration of an Array-Based List

```
import java.util.ArrayList;
import java.util.List;

public class ArrayListDemo
{
   public static void main(String[] args)
   {
      List<String> ls = new ArrayList<String>();
      String[] weekDays = {"Sun", "Mon", "Tue", "Wed", "Thu", "Fri", "Sat"};
      for (String weekDay: weekDays)
         ls.add(weekDay);
      dump("ls:", ls);
      ls.set(ls.indexOf("Wed"), "Wednesday");
      dump("ls:", ls);
```

```
        ls.remove(ls.lastIndexOf("Fri"));
        dump("ls:", ls);
    }

    static void dump(String title, List<String> ls)
    {
        System.out.print(title + " ");
        for (String s: ls)
            System.out.print(s + " ");
        System.out.println();
    }
}
```

ArrayListDemo creates an array list and an array of short weekday names. It then populates this list with these names, dumps the list to standard output, changes one of the list entries, dumps the list again, removes a list entry, and dumps the list one last time. The dump() method's enhanced for loop statement uses iterator(), hasNext(), and next() behind the scenes.

When you run this application, it generates the following output:

```
ls: Sun Mon Tue Wed Thu Fri Sat
ls: Sun Mon Tue Wednesday Thu Fri Sat
ls: Sun Mon Tue Wednesday Thu Sat
```

LinkedList

The LinkedList class provides a list implementation that is based on linked nodes. Because links must be traversed, access to the list's elements is slow. However, because only node references need to be changed, insertions and deletions of elements are fast.

WHAT IS A NODE?

A *node* is a fixed sequence of value and link memory locations. Unlike an array, where each slot stores a single value of the same primitive type or reference supertype, a node can store multiple values of different types. It can also store *links* (references to other nodes).

Consider the following simple Node class:

```
class Node
{
   String name; // value field
   Node next;   // link field
}
```

Node describes simple nodes where each node consists of a single name value field and a single next link field. Notice that next is of the same type as the class in which it is declared. This arrangement lets a node instance store a reference to another node instance (which is the next node) in this field. The resulting nodes are linked together.

The following code fragment creates two Node objects and links the second Node object to the first Node object. This fragment also demonstrates how to traverse this linked list by following each Node object's next field. Node traversal stops when the traversal code discovers that next contains the null reference, which signifies the end of the list:

```
Node first = new Node();
first.name = "First node"; // You would normally provide getter and setter methods.
Node last = new Node();
last.name = "Last node";
last.next = null;
first.next = last;
Node temp = first;
while (temp != null)
{
   System.out.println(temp.name);
   temp = temp.next;
}
```

The code first builds a linked list of two Nodes and then assigns first to local variable temp to traverse the list without losing the reference to the first node that is stored in first. While temp is not null, the loop outputs the name field. It also navigates to the next Node object in the list via the temp = temp.next; statement.

If you convert this code into an application and run the application, you will discover the following output:

```
First node
Last node
```

LinkedList supplies two constructors:

- LinkedList() creates an empty linked list.

- LinkedList(Collection<? extends E> c) creates a linked list containing c's elements in the order in which they are returned by c's iterator. NullPointerException is thrown when c contains the null reference.

Listing 9-2 demonstrates a linked list.

Listing 9-2. A Demonstration of a List of Linked Nodes

```
import java.util.LinkedList;
import java.util.List;
import java.util.ListIterator;

public class LinkedListDemo
{
   public static void main(String[] args)
   {
      List<String> ls = new LinkedList<String>();
      String[] weekDays = {"Sun", "Mon", "Tue", "Wed", "Thu", "Fri", "Sat"};
      for (String weekDay: weekDays)
         ls.add(weekDay);
      dump("ls:", ls);
```

```
        ls.add(1,  "Sunday");
        ls.add(3,  "Monday");
        ls.add(5,  "Tuesday");
        ls.add(7,  "Wednesday");
        ls.add(9,  "Thursday");
        ls.add(11, "Friday");
        ls.add(13, "Saturday");
        dump("ls:", ls);
        ListIterator<String> li = ls.listIterator(ls.size());
        while (li.hasPrevious())
            System.out.print(li.previous() + " ");
        System.out.println();
    }

    static void dump(String title, List<String> ls)
    {
        System.out.print(title + " ");
        for (String s: ls)
            System.out.print(s + " ");
        System.out.println();
    }
}
```

LinkedListDemo creates a linked list and an array of short weekday names. It then populates this list with these names, dumps the list to standard output, inserts longer weekday names after their shorter name counterparts, dumps the list again, and outputs the list in reverse order by using a list iterator with its cursor initialized past the list's end and repeatedly calling its previous() method.

When you run this application, it generates the following output:

```
ls: Sun Mon Tue Wed Thu Fri Sat
ls: Sun Sunday Mon Monday Tue Tuesday Wed Wednesday Thu Thursday Fri Friday Sat Saturday
Saturday Sat Friday Fri Thursday Thu Wednesday Wed Tuesday Tue Monday Mon Sunday Sun
```

Exploring Sets

A *set* is a collection that contains no duplicate elements. In other words, a set contains no pair of elements *e1* and *e2* such that *e1*.equals(*e2*) returns true. Furthermore, a set can contain at most one null element. Sets are described by the Set interface whose generic type is Set<E>.

Set extends Collection and redeclares its inherited methods, for convenience and also to add stipulations to the contracts for add(), equals(), and hashCode() to address how they behave in a set context. Also, Set's documentation states that all constructors of implementation classes must create sets that contain no duplicate elements.

Set doesn't introduce new methods.

TreeSet

The TreeSet class provides a set implementation that is based on a tree data structure. As a result, elements are stored in sorted order. However, accessing these elements is somewhat slower than with the other Set implementations (which are not sorted) because links must be traversed.

> **Note** Check out Wikipedia's "Tree (data structure)" entry (`http://en.wikipedia.org/wiki/Tree_(data_structure)`) to learn about trees.

TreeSet supplies four constructors:

- `TreeSet()` creates a new, empty tree set that is sorted according to the natural ordering of its elements. All elements inserted into the set must implement the `Comparable` interface.

- `TreeSet(Collection<? extends E> c)` creates a new tree set containing c's elements sorted according to the natural ordering of its elements. All elements inserted into the new set must implement the `Comparable` interface. This constructor throws `ClassCastException` when c's elements don't implement `Comparable` or are not mutually comparable and `NullPointerException` when c contains the null reference.

- `TreeSet(Comparator<? super E> comparator)` creates a new, empty tree set that is sorted according to the specified `comparator`. Passing `null` to comparator implies that natural ordering will be used.

- `TreeSet(SortedSet<E> ss)` creates a new tree set containing the same elements and using the same ordering as ss. (I discuss sorted sets later in this chapter.) This constructor throws `NullPointerException` when ss contains the null reference.

Listing 9-3 demonstrates a tree set.

Listing 9-3. A Demonstration of a Tree Set with `String` Elements Sorted According to Their Natural Ordering

```java
import java.util.Set;
import java.util.TreeSet;

public class TreeSetDemo
{
   public static void main(String[] args)
   {
      Set<String> ss = new TreeSet<String>();
      String[] fruits = {"apples", "pears", "grapes", "bananas", "kiwis"};
      for (String fruit: fruits)
         ss.add(fruit);
      dump("ss:", ss);
   }

   static void dump(String title, Set<String> ss)
   {
      System.out.print(title + " ");
      for (String s: ss)
         System.out.print(s + " ");
      System.out.println();
   }
}
```

TreeSetDemo creates a tree set and an array of fruit names. It then populates this set with these names and dumps the set to standard output. Because String implements Comparable, it's legal for this application to insert the contents of the fruits array into a tree set that was created via the TreeSet() constructor.

When you run this application, it generates the following output:

```
ss: apples bananas grapes kiwis pears
```

HashSet

The HashSet class provides a set implementation that is backed by a hashtable data structure (implemented as a HashMap instance, discussed later, which provides a quick way to determine if an element has already been stored in this structure). Although this class provides no ordering guarantees for its elements, HashSet is much faster than TreeSet. Furthermore, HashSet permits the null reference to be stored in its instances.

Note   Check out Wikipedia's "Hash table" entry (http://en.wikipedia.org/wiki/Hash_table) to learn about hashtables.

HashSet supplies four constructors:

- HashSet() creates a new, empty hashset where the backing HashMap instance has an initial capacity of 16 and a load factor of 0.75. You will learn what these items mean when I discuss HashMap later in this chapter.

- HashSet(Collection<? extends E> c) creates a new hashset containing c's elements. The backing HashMap has an initial capacity sufficient to contain c's elements and a load factor of 0.75. This constructor throws NullPointerException when c contains the null reference.

- HashSet(int initialCapacity) creates a new, empty hashset where the backing HashMap instance has the capacity specified by initialCapacity and a load factor of 0.75. This constructor throws IllegalArgumentException when initialCapacity's value is less than 0.

- HashSet(int initialCapacity, float loadFactor) creates a new, empty hashset where the backing HashMap instance has the capacity specified by initialCapacity and the load factor specified by loadFactor. This constructor throws IllegalArgumentException when initialCapacity is less than 0 or when loadFactor is less than or equal to 0.

Listing 9-4 demonstrates a hashset.

Listing 9-4. A Demonstration of a Hashset with String Elements Unordered

```java
import java.util.HashSet;
import java.util.Set;

public class HashSetDemo
{
   public static void main(String[] args)
   {
      Set<String> ss = new HashSet<String>();
      String[] fruits = {"apples", "pears", "grapes", "bananas", "kiwis",
                         "pears", null};
      for (String fruit: fruits)
         ss.add(fruit);
      dump("ss:", ss);
   }

   static void dump(String title, Set<String> ss)
   {
      System.out.print(title + " ");
      for (String s: ss)
         System.out.print(s + " ");
      System.out.println();
   }
}
```

HashSetDemo creates a hashset and an array of fruit names. It then populates this set with these names and dumps the set to standard output. Unlike with TreeSet, HashSet permits null to be added (NullPointerException isn't thrown), which is why Listing 9-4 includes null in HashSetDemo's fruits array.

When you run this application, it generates unordered output such as the following:

```
ss: null grapes bananas kiwis pears apples
```

Suppose you want to add instances of your classes to a hashset. As with String, your classes must override equals() and hashCode(); otherwise, duplicate class instances can be stored in the hashset. For example, Listing 9-5 presents the source code to an application whose Planet class overrides equals() but fails to also override hashCode().

Listing 9-5. A Custom Planet Class Not Overriding hashCode()

```java
import java.util.HashSet;
import java.util.Set;

public class CustomClassAndHashSet
{
   public static void main(String[] args)
   {
      Set<Planet> sp = new HashSet<Planet>();
      sp.add(new Planet("Mercury"));
      sp.add(new Planet("Venus"));
```

```
        sp.add(new Planet("Earth"));
        sp.add(new Planet("Mars"));
        sp.add(new Planet("Jupiter"));
        sp.add(new Planet("Saturn"));
        sp.add(new Planet("Uranus"));
        sp.add(new Planet("Neptune"));
        sp.add(new Planet("Fomalhaut b"));
        Planet p1 = new Planet("51 Pegasi b");
        sp.add(p1);
        Planet p2 = new Planet("51 Pegasi b");
        sp.add(p2);
        System.out.println(p1.equals(p2));
        System.out.println(sp);
    }
}

class Planet
{
    private String name;

    Planet(String name)
    {
        this.name = name;
    }

    @Override
    public boolean equals(Object o)
    {
        if (!(o instanceof Planet))
            return false;
        Planet p = (Planet) o;
        return p.name.equals(name);
    }

    String getName()
    {
        return name;
    }

    @Override
    public String toString()
    {
        return name;
    }
}
```

Listing 9-5's Planet class declares a single name field of type String. Although it might seem pointless to declare Planet with a single String field because I could refactor this listing to remove Planet and work with String, I might want to introduce additional fields to Planet (perhaps to store a planet's mass and other characteristics) in the future.

When you run this application, it generates unordered output such as the following:

```
true
[Neptune, Mars, Mercury, Fomalhaut b, Venus, 51 Pegasi b, 51 Pegasi b, Jupiter, Saturn, Earth,
Uranus]
```

This output reveals two 51 Pegasi b elements in the hashset. Although these elements are equal from the perspective of the overriding equals() method (the first output line, true, proves this point), overriding equals() isn't enough to avoid duplicate elements being stored in a hashset: you must also override hashCode().

The easiest way to override hashCode() in Listing 9-5's Planet class is to have the overriding method call the name field's hashCode() method and return its value. (This technique only works with a class whose single reference field's class provides a valid hashCode() method.) Listing 9-6 presents this overriding hashCode() method.

Listing 9-6. A Custom Planet Class Overriding hashCode()

```java
import java.util.HashSet;
import java.util.Set;

public class CustomClassAndHashSet
{
    public static void main(String[] args)
    {
        Set<Planet> sp = new HashSet<Planet>();
        sp.add(new Planet("Mercury"));
        sp.add(new Planet("Venus"));
        sp.add(new Planet("Earth"));
        sp.add(new Planet("Mars"));
        sp.add(new Planet("Jupiter"));
        sp.add(new Planet("Saturn"));
        sp.add(new Planet("Uranus"));
        sp.add(new Planet("Neptune"));
        sp.add(new Planet("Fomalhaut b"));
        Planet p1 = new Planet("51 Pegasi b");
        sp.add(p1);
        Planet p2 = new Planet("51 Pegasi b");
        sp.add(p2);
        System.out.println(p1.equals(p2));
        System.out.println(sp);
    }
}

class Planet
{
    private String name;

    Planet(String name)
    {
        this.name = name;
    }
```

```java
    @Override
    public boolean equals(Object o)
    {
        if (!(o instanceof Planet))
            return false;
        Planet p = (Planet) o;
        return p.name.equals(name);
    }

    String getName()
    {
        return name;
    }

    @Override
    public int hashCode()
    {
        return name.hashCode();
    }

    @Override
    public String toString()
    {
        return name;
    }
}
```

Compile Listing 9-6 (javac `CustomClassAndHashSet.java`) and run the application (java `CustomClassAndHashSet`). You will observe output (similar to that shown following) that reveals no duplicate elements:

```
true
[Saturn, Earth, Uranus, Fomalhaut b, 51 Pegasi b, Venus, Jupiter, Mercury, Mars, Neptune]
```

> **Note**   LinkedHashSet is a subclass of HashSet that uses a linked list to store its elements. As a result, LinkedHashSet's iterator returns elements in the order in which they were inserted. For example, if Listing 9-4 had specified Set<String> ss = new LinkedHashSet<String>();, the application's output would have been ss: apples pears grapes bananas kiwis null. Also, LinkedHashSet offers slower performance than HashSet and faster performance than TreeSet.

EnumSet

In Chapter 6 I introduced you to traditional enumerated types and their enum replacement. (An *enum* is an enumerated type that is expressed via reserved word enum.) The following example demonstrates the traditional enumerated type:

```java
static final int SUNDAY = 1;
static final int MONDAY = 2;
```

```
static final int TUESDAY = 4;
static final int WEDNESDAY = 8;
static final int THURSDAY = 16;
static final int FRIDAY = 32;
static final int SATURDAY = 64;
```

Although the enum has many advantages over the traditional enumerated type, the traditional enumerated type is less awkward to use when combining constants into a set, for example, `static final int DAYS_OFF = SUNDAY | MONDAY;`.

DAYS_OFF is an example of an integer-based, fixed-length *bitset*, which is a set of bits where each bit indicates that its associated member belongs to the set when the bit is set to 1 and is absent from the set when the bit is set to 0.

> **Note** An `int`-based bitset cannot contain more than 32 members because `int` has a size of 32 bits. Similarly, a `long`-based bitset cannot contain more than 64 members because `long` has a size of 64 bits.

This bitset is formed by bitwise inclusive ORing the traditional enumerated type's integer constants together via the bitwise inclusive OR operator (|): you could also use +. Each constant must be a unique power of two (starting with one) because otherwise it's impossible to distinguish between the members of this bitset.

To determine if a constant belongs to the bitset, create an expression that involves the bitwise AND operator (&). For example, ((DAYS_OFF & MONDAY) == MONDAY) bitwise ANDs DAYS_OFF (3) with MONDAY (2), which results in 2. This value is compared via == with MONDAY (2), and the result of the expression is true: MONDAY is a member of the DAYS_OFF bitset.

You can accomplish the same task with an enum by instantiating an appropriate Set implementation class and calling the add() method multiple times to store the constants in the set. Listing 9-7 illustrates this more awkward alternative.

Listing 9-7. Creating the Set Equivalent of DAYS_OFF

```
import java.util.Set;
import java.util.TreeSet;

enum Weekday
{
    SUNDAY, MONDAY, TUESDAY, WEDNESDAY, THURSDAY, FRIDAY, SATURDAY
}

public class DaysOff
{
    public static void main(String[] args)
    {
        Set<Weekday> daysOff = new TreeSet<Weekday>();
        daysOff.add(Weekday.SUNDAY);
```

```
        daysOff.add(Weekday.MONDAY);
        System.out.println(daysOff);
    }
}
```

When you run this application, it generates the following output:

```
[SUNDAY, MONDAY]
```

> **Note**   The constants' ordinals and not their names are stored in the tree set, which is why the names
> appear unordered (S before M) even though the constants are stored in sorted order of their ordinals.

As well as being more awkward to use (and verbose) than the bitset, the Set alternative requires
more memory to store each constant and isn't as fast. Because of these problems, EnumSet was
introduced.

The EnumSet class provides a Set implementation that is based on a bitset. Its elements are
constants that must come from the same enum, which is specified when the enum set is
created. Null elements are not permitted; any attempt to store a null element results in a thrown
NullPointerException.

Listing 9-8 demonstrates EnumSet.

Listing 9-8. Creating the EnumSet Equivalent of DAYS_OFF

```
import java.util.EnumSet;
import java.util.Iterator;
import java.util.Set;

enum Weekday
{
    SUNDAY, MONDAY, TUESDAY, WEDNESDAY, THURSDAY, FRIDAY, SATURDAY
}

public class EnumSetDemo
{
    public static void main(String[] args)
    {
        Set<Weekday> daysOff = EnumSet.of(Weekday.SUNDAY, Weekday.MONDAY);
        Iterator<Weekday> iter = daysOff.iterator();
        while (iter.hasNext())
            System.out.println(iter.next());
    }
}
```

EnumSetDemo takes advantage of the fact that EnumSet, whose generic type is EnumSet<E extends
Enum<E>>, provides various class methods for conveniently constructing enum sets. For example,
<E extends Enum<E>> EnumSet<E> of(E e1, E e2) returns an EnumSet instance consisting of
elements e1 and e2. In this example, those elements are Weekday.SUNDAY and Weekday.MONDAY.

When you run this application, it generates the following output:

```
SUNDAY
MONDAY
```

> **Note** As well as providing several overloaded of() methods, EnumSet provides other methods for conveniently creating enum sets. For example, allOf() returns an EnumSet instance that contains all of an enum's constants, where this method's solitary argument is a *class literal* (an expression consisting of a class's name followed by a dot followed by reserved word class) that identifies the enum:
>
> ```
> Set<Weekday> allWeekDays = EnumSet.allOf(Weekday.class);
> ```
>
> Similarly, range() returns an EnumSet instance containing a range of an enum's elements (with the range's limits as specified by this method's two arguments):
>
> ```
> for (WeekDay wd: EnumSet.range(WeekDay.MONDAY, WeekDay.FRIDAY))
>     System.out.println(wd);
> ```

Exploring Sorted Sets

TreeSet is an example of a *sorted set*, which is a set that maintains its elements in ascending order, sorted according to their natural ordering or according to a comparator that is supplied when the sorted set is created. Sorted sets are described by the SortedSet interface.

SortedSet, whose generic type is SortedSet<E>, extends Set. With two exceptions, the methods it inherits from Set behave identically on sorted sets as on other sets:

- The Iterator instance returned from iterator() traverses the sorted set in ascending element order.
- The array returned by toArray() contains the sorted set's elements in order.

> **Note** Although not guaranteed, the toString() methods of SortedSet implementations in the Collections Framework (e.g., TreeSet) return a string containing all of the sorted set's elements in order.

SortedSet's documentation requires that an implementation provide the four standard constructors that I presented in my discussion of TreeSet. Furthermore, implementations of this interface must implement the methods that are described in Table 9-3.

Table 9-3. *SortedSet-Specific Methods*

Method	Description
Comparator<? super E> comparator()	Return the comparator used to order the elements in this set or null when this set uses the natural ordering of its elements.
E first()	Return the first (lowest) element currently in this set, or throw a NoSuchElementException instance when this set is empty.
SortedSet<E> headSet(E toElement)	Return a view of that portion of this set whose elements are strictly less than toElement. The returned set is backed by this set, so changes in the returned set are reflected in this set and vice versa. The returned set supports all optional set operations that this set supports. This method throws ClassCastException when toElement is not compatible with this set's comparator (or, when the set has no comparator, when toElement doesn't implement Comparable), NullPointerException when toElement is null and this set doesn't permit null elements, and IllegalArgumentException when this set has a restricted range and toElement lies outside of this range's bounds.
E last()	Return the last (highest) element currently in this set or throw a NoSuchElementException instance when this set is empty.
SortedSet<E> subSet(E fromElement, E toElement)	Return a view of the portion of this set whose elements range from fromElement, inclusive, to toElement, exclusive. (When fromElement and toElement are equal, the returned set is empty.) The returned set is backed by this set, so changes in the returned set are reflected in this set and vice versa. The returned set supports all optional set operations that this set supports. This method throws ClassCastException when fromElement and toElement cannot be compared to one another using this set's comparator (or, when the set has no comparator, using natural ordering), NullPointerException when fromElement or toElement is null and this set doesn't permit null elements, and IllegalArgumentException when fromElement is greater than toElement or when this set has a restricted range and fromElement or toElement lies outside of this range's bounds.
SortedSet<E> tailSet(E fromElement)	Return a view of that portion of this set whose elements are greater than or equal to fromElement. The returned set is backed by this set, so changes in the returned set are reflected in this set and vice versa. The returned set supports all optional set operations that this set supports. This method throws ClassCastException when fromElement is not compatible with this set's comparator (or, when the set has no comparator, when fromElement doesn't implement Comparable), NullPointerException when fromElement is null and this set doesn't permit null elements, and IllegalArgumentException when this set has a restricted range and fromElement lies outside of the range's bounds.

The set-based range views returned from headSet(), subSet(), and tailSet() are analogous to the list-based range view returned from List's subList() method except that a set-based range view remains valid even when the backing sorted set is modified. As a result, a set-based range view can be used for a lengthy period of time.

> **Note** Unlike a list-based range view whose endpoints are elements in the backing list, the endpoints of a set-based range view are absolute points in element space, allowing a set-based range view to serve as a window onto a portion of the set's element space. Any changes made to the set-based range view are written back to the backing sorted set and vice versa.

Each range view returned by headSet(), subSet(), or tailSet() is *half open* because it doesn't include its high endpoint (headSet() and subSet()) or its low endpoint (tailSet()). For the first two methods, the high endpoint is specified by argument toElement; for the last method, the low endpoint is specified by argument fromElement.

> **Note** You could also regard the returned range view as being *half closed* because it includes only one of its endpoints.

Listing 9-9 demonstrates a sorted set based on a tree set.

Listing 9-9. A Sorted Set of Fruit and Vegetable Names

```java
import java.util.SortedSet;
import java.util.TreeSet;

public class SortedSetDemo
{
   public static void main(String[] args)
   {
      SortedSet<String> sss = new TreeSet<String>();
      String[] fruitAndVeg =
      {
         "apple", "potato", "turnip", "banana", "corn", "carrot", "cherry",
         "pear", "mango", "strawberry", "cucumber", "grape", "banana",
         "kiwi", "radish", "blueberry", "tomato", "onion", "raspberry",
         "lemon", "pepper", "squash", "melon", "zucchini", "peach", "plum",
         "turnip", "onion", "nectarine"
      };
      System.out.println("Array size = " + fruitAndVeg.length);
      for (String fruitVeg: fruitAndVeg)
         sss.add(fruitVeg);
      dump("sss:", sss);
      System.out.println("Sorted set size = " + sss.size());
      System.out.println("First element = " + sss.first());
      System.out.println("Last element = " + sss.last());
      System.out.println("Comparator = " + sss.comparator());
      dump("hs:", sss.headSet("n"));
      dump("ts:", sss.tailSet("n"));
      System.out.println("Count of p-named fruits & vegetables = " +
                          sss.subSet("p", "q").size());
```

```
        System.out.println("Incorrect count of c-named fruits & vegetables = " +
                           sss.subSet("carrot", "cucumber").size());
        System.out.println("Correct count of c-named fruits & vegetables = " +
                           sss.subSet("carrot", "cucumber\0").size());
    }

    static void dump(String title, SortedSet<String> sss)
    {
        System.out.print(title + " ");
        for (String s: sss)
            System.out.print(s + " ");
        System.out.println();
    }
}
```

SortedSetDemo creates a sorted set and an array of fruit and vegetable names and then proceeds to populate the set from this array. After dumping out the set's contents, it outputs information about the set, including head and tail views of portions of the set.

When you run this application, it generates the following output:

```
Array size = 29
sss: apple banana blueberry carrot cherry corn cucumber grape kiwi lemon mango melon nectarine onion
peach pear pepper plum potato radish raspberry squash strawberry tomato turnip zucchini
Sorted set size = 26
First element = apple
Last element = zucchini
Comparator = null
hs: apple banana blueberry carrot cherry corn cucumber grape kiwi lemon mango melon
ts: nectarine onion peach pear pepper plum potato radish raspberry squash strawberry tomato turnip
zucchini
Count of p-named fruits & vegetables = 5
Incorrect count of c-named fruits & vegetables = 3
Correct count of c-named fruits & vegetables = 4
```

This output reveals that the sorted set's size is less than the array's size because a set cannot contain duplicate elements: the duplicate banana, turnip, and onion elements are not stored in the sorted set.

The comparator() method returns null because the sorted set was not created with a comparator. Instead, the sorted set relies on the natural ordering of String elements to store them in sorted order.

The headSet() and tailSet() methods are called with argument "n" to return, respectively, a set of elements whose names begin with a letter that is strictly less than n and a letter that is greater than or equal to n.

Finally, the output shows you that you must be careful when passing an upper limit to subSet(). As you can see, ss.subSet("carrot", "cucumber") doesn't include cucumber in the returned range view because cucumber is subSet()'s high endpoint.

To include cucumber in the range view, you need to form a *closed range* or *closed interval* (both endpoints are included). With String objects, you accomplish this task by appending \0 to the string. For example, ss.subSet("carrot", "cucumber\0") includes cucumber because it is less than cucumber\0.

This same technique can be applied wherever you need to form an *open range* or *open interval* (neither endpoint is included). For example, ss.subSet("carrot\0", "cucumber") doesn't include carrot because it is less than carrot\0. Furthermore, it doesn't include high endpoint cucumber.

> **Note** When you want to create closed and open ranges for elements created from your own classes, you need to provide some form of predecessor() and successor() methods that return an element's predecessor and successor.

You need to be careful when designing classes that work with sorted sets. For example, the class must implement Comparable when you plan to store the class's instances in a sorted set where these elements are sorted according to their natural ordering. Consider Listing 9-10.

Listing 9-10. A Custom Employee Class Not Implementing Comparable

```
import java.util.SortedSet;
import java.util.TreeSet;

public class CustomClassAndSortedSet
{
   public static void main(String[] args)
   {
      SortedSet<Employee> sse = new TreeSet<Employee>();
      sse.add(new Employee("Sally Doe"));
      sse.add(new Employee("Bob Doe")); // ClassCastException thrown here
      sse.add(new Employee("John Doe"));
      System.out.println(sse);
   }
}

class Employee
{
   private String name;

   Employee(String name)
   {
      this.name = name;
   }

   @Override
   public String toString()
   {
      return name;
   }
}
```

When you run this application, it generates the following output:

```
Exception in thread "main" java.lang.ClassCastException: Employee cannot be cast to
java.lang.Comparable
        at java.util.TreeMap.compare(Unknown Source)
        at java.util.TreeMap.put(Unknown Source)
        at java.util.TreeSet.add(Unknown Source)
        at CustomClassAndSortedSet.main(CustomClassAndSortedSet.java:9)
```

The ClassCastException instance is thrown during the second add() method call because the sorted set implementation, an instance of TreeSet, is unable to call the second Employee element's compareTo() method, because Employee doesn't implement Comparable.

The solution to this problem is to have the class implement Comparable, which is exactly what is revealed in Listing 9-11.

Listing 9-11. Making Employee Elements Comparable

```
import java.util.SortedSet;
import java.util.TreeSet;

public class CustomClassAndSortedSet
{
   public static void main(String[] args)
   {
      SortedSet<Employee> sse = new TreeSet<Employee>();
      sse.add(new Employee("Sally Doe"));
      sse.add(new Employee("Bob Doe"));
      Employee e1 = new Employee("John Doe");
      Employee e2 = new Employee("John Doe");
      sse.add(e1);
      sse.add(e2);
      System.out.println(sse);
      System.out.println(e1.equals(e2));
   }
}

class Employee implements Comparable<Employee>
{
   private String name;

   Employee(String name)
   {
      this.name = name;
   }

   @Override
   public int compareTo(Employee e)
   {
      return name.compareTo(e.name);
   }
```

```
    @Override
    public String toString()
    {
        return name;
    }
}
```

Listing 9-11's `main()` method differs from Listing 9-10 in that it also creates two `Employee` objects initialized to "John Doe", adds these objects to the sorted set, and compares these objects for equality via `equals()`. Furthermore, Listing 9-11 declares `Employee` to implement `Comparable`, introducing a `compareTo()` method into `Employee`.

When you run this application, it generates the following output:

```
[Bob Doe, John Doe, Sally Doe]
false
```

This output shows that only one "John Doe" `Employee` object is stored in the sorted set. After all, a set cannot contain duplicate elements. However, the `false` value (resulting from the `equals()` comparison) also shows that the sorted set's natural ordering is inconsistent with `equals()`, which violates `SortedSet`'s contract:

The ordering maintained by a sorted set (whether or not an explicit comparator is provided) must be consistent with `equals()` *if the sorted set is to correctly implement the* Set *interface. This is so because the* Set *interface is defined in terms of the* `equals()` *operation, but a sorted set performs all element comparisons using its* `compareTo()` *(or* `compare()`*) method, so two elements that are deemed equal by this method are, from the standpoint of the sorted set, equal.*

Because the application works correctly, why should `SortedSet`'s contract matter? Although the contract doesn't appear to matter with respect to the `TreeSet` implementation of `SortedSet`, perhaps it will matter in the context of a third-party class that implements this interface.

Listing 9-12 shows you how to correct this problem and make `Employee` instances work with any implementation of a sorted set.

Listing 9-12. A Contract-Compliant Employee Class

```
import java.util.SortedSet;
import java.util.TreeSet;

public class CustomClassAndSortedSet
{
    public static void main(String[] args)
    {
        SortedSet<Employee> sse = new TreeSet<Employee>();
        sse.add(new Employee("Sally Doe"));
        sse.add(new Employee("Bob Doe"));
        Employee e1 = new Employee("John Doe");
        Employee e2 = new Employee("John Doe");
        sse.add(e1);
        sse.add(e2);
```

```
        System.out.println(sse);
        System.out.println(e1.equals(e2));
    }
}

class Employee implements Comparable<Employee>
{
    private String name;

    Employee(String name)
    {
        this.name = name;
    }

    @Override
    public int compareTo(Employee e)
    {
        return name.compareTo(e.name);
    }

    @Override
    public boolean equals(Object o)
    {
        if (!(o instanceof Employee))
            return false;
        Employee e = (Employee) o;
        return e.name.equals(name);
    }

    @Override
    public String toString()
    {
        return name;
    }
}
```

Listing 9-12 corrects the SortedSet contract violation by overriding equals(). Run the resulting application and you will observe [Bob Doe, John Doe, Sally Doe] as the first line of output and true as the second line: the sorted set's natural ordering is now consistent with equals().

> **Note**   Although it's important to override hashCode() whenever you override equals(), I didn't override hashCode() (although I overrode equals()) in Listing 9-12's Employee class to emphasize that tree-based sorted sets ignore hashCode().

Exploring Navigable Sets

TreeSet is an example of a *navigable set*, which is a sorted set that can be iterated over in descending order as well as ascending order and which can report closest matches for given search targets. Navigable sets are described by the NavigableSet interface, whose generic type is NavigableSet<E>, which extends SortedSet and which is described in Table 9-4.

Table 9-4. *NavigableSet-Specific Methods*

Method	Description
E ceiling(E e)	Return the least element in this set greater than or equal to e, or null when there is no such element. This method throws ClassCastException when e cannot be compared with the elements currently in the set and NullPointerException when e is null and this set doesn't permit null elements.
Iterator<E> descendingIterator()	Return an iterator over the elements in this set, in descending order. Equivalent in effect to descendingSet().iterator().
NavigableSet<E> descendingSet()	Return a reverse order view of the elements contained in this set. The descending set is backed by this set, so changes to the set are reflected in the descending set and vice versa. If either set is modified (except through the iterator's own remove() operation) while iterating over the set, the results of the iteration are undefined.
E floor(E e)	Return the greatest element in this set less than or equal to e or null when there is no such element. This method throws ClassCastException when e cannot be compared with the elements currently in the set and NullPointerException when e is null and this set doesn't permit null elements.
NavigableSet<E> headSet (E toElement, boolean inclusive)	Return a view of the portion of this set whose elements are less than (or equal to, when inclusive is true) toElement. The returned set is backed by this set, so changes in the returned set are reflected in this set and vice versa. The returned set supports all optional set operations that this set supports. This method throws ClassCastException when toElement is not compatible with this set's comparator (or, when the set has no comparator, when toElement doesn't implement Comparable), NullPointerException when toElement is null and this set doesn't permit null elements, and IllegalArgumentException when this set has a restricted range and toElement lies outside of this range's bounds.
E higher(E e)	Return the least element in this set strictly greater than the given element or null when there is no such element. This method throws ClassCastException when e cannot be compared with the elements currently in the set and NullPointerException when e is null and this set doesn't permit null elements.
E lower(E e)	Return the greatest element in this set strictly less than the given element or null when there is no such element. This method throws ClassCastException when e cannot be compared with the elements currently in the set and NullPointerException when e is null and this set doesn't permit null elements.
E pollFirst()	Return and remove the first (lowest) element from this set or return null when this set is empty.

(continued)

Table 9-4. (continued)

Method	Description
E pollLast()	Return and remove the last (highest) element from this set or return null when this set is empty.
NavigableSet<E> subSet (E fromElement, boolean fromInclusive, E toElement, boolean toInclusive)	Return a view of the portion of this set whose elements range from fromElement to toElement. (When fromElement and toElement are equal, the returned set is empty unless fromInclusive and toInclusive are both true.) The returned set is backed by this set, so changes in the returned set are reflected in this set and vice versa. The returned set supports all optional set operations that this set supports. This method throws ClassCastException when fromElement and toElement cannot be compared to one another using this set's comparator (or, when the set has no comparator, using natural ordering), NullPointerException when fromElement or toElement is null and this set doesn't permit null elements, and IllegalArgumentException when fromElement is greater than toElement or when this set has a restricted range and fromElement or toElement lies outside of this range's bounds.
NavigableSet<E> tailSet(E fromElement, boolean inclusive)	Return a view of the portion of this set whose elements are greater than (or equal to, when inclusive is true) fromElement. The returned set is backed by this set, so changes in the returned set are reflected in this set and vice versa. The returned set supports all optional set operations that this set supports. This method throws ClassCastException when fromElement is not compatible with this set's comparator (or, when the set has no comparator, when fromElement doesn't implement Comparable), NullPointerException when fromElement is null and this set doesn't permit null elements, and IllegalArgumentException when this set has a restricted range and fromElement lies outside of this range's bounds.

Listing 9-13 demonstrates a navigable set based on a tree set.

Listing 9-13. Navigating a Set of Integers

```java
import java.util.Iterator;
import java.util.NavigableSet;
import java.util.TreeSet;

public class NavigableSetDemo
{
   public static void main(String[] args)
   {
      NavigableSet<Integer> ns = new TreeSet<Integer>();
      int[] ints = { 82, -13, 4, 0, 11, -6, 9 };
      for (int i: ints)
         ns.add(i);
      System.out.print("Ascending order: ");
      Iterator iter = ns.iterator();
      while (iter.hasNext())
         System.out.print(iter.next() + " ");
      System.out.println();
```

```
        System.out.print("Descending order: ");
        iter = ns.descendingIterator();
        while (iter.hasNext())
            System.out.print(iter.next() + " ");
        System.out.println("\n");
        outputClosestMatches(ns, 4);
        outputClosestMatches(ns.descendingSet(), 12);
    }

    static void outputClosestMatches(NavigableSet<Integer> ns, int i)
    {
        System.out.println("Element < " + i + " is " + ns.lower(i));
        System.out.println("Element <= " + i + " is " + ns.floor(i));
        System.out.println("Element > " + i + " is " + ns.higher(i));
        System.out.println("Element >= " + i +" is " + ns.ceiling(i));
        System.out.println();
    }
}
```

Listing 9-13 creates a navigable set of Integer elements. It takes advantage of autoboxing to ensure that ints are converted to Integers.

When you run this application, it generates the following output:

```
Ascending order: -13 -6 0 4 9 11 82
Descending order: 82 11 9 4 0 -6 -13

Element < 4 is 0
Element <= 4 is 4
Element > 4 is 9
Element >= 4 is 4

Element < 12 is 82
Element <= 12 is 82
Element > 12 is 11
Element >= 12 is 11
```

The first four output lines beginning with Element pertain to an ascending-order set where the element being matched (4) is a member of the set. The second four Element-prefixed lines pertain to a descending-order set where the element being matched (12) is not a member.

As well as letting you conveniently locate set elements via its closest-match methods (ceiling(), floor(), higher(), and lower()), NavigableSet lets you return set views containing all elements within certain ranges as demonstrated by the following examples:

- ns.subSet(-13, true, 9, true): Return all elements from -13 through 9.

- ns.tailSet(-6, false): Return all elements greater than -6.

- ns.headSet(4, true): Return all elements less than or equal to 4.

Finally, you can return and remove from the set the first (lowest) element by calling pollFirst() and the last (highest) element by calling pollLast(). For example, ns.pollFirst() removes and returns -13, and ns.pollLast() removes and returns 82.

Exploring Queues

A *queue* is a collection in which elements are stored and retrieved in a specific order. Most queues are categorized as one of the following:

- *First-In, First-Out (FIFO) queue*: Elements are inserted at the queue's *tail* and removed at the queue's *head*.

- *Last-In, First-Out (LIFO) queue*: Elements are inserted and removed at one end of the queue such that the last element inserted is the first element retrieved. This kind of queue behaves as a *stack*.

- *Priority queue*: Elements are inserted according to their natural ordering or according to a comparator that is supplied to the queue implementation.

Queue, whose generic type is Queue<E>, extends Collection, redeclaring add() to adjust its contract (insert the specified element into this queue if it's possible to do so immediately without violating capacity restrictions), and inheriting the other methods from Collection. Table 9-5 describes add() and the other Queue-specific methods.

Table 9-5. Queue-Specific Methods

Method	Description
boolean add(E e)	Insert element e into this queue if it is possible to do so immediately without violating capacity restrictions. Return true on success; otherwise, throw IllegalStateException when the element cannot be added at this time because no space is currently available. This method also throws ClassCastException when e's class prevents e from being added to this queue, NullPointerException when e contains the null reference and this queue doesn't permit null elements to be added, and IllegalArgumentException when some property of e prevents it from being added to this queue.
E element()	Return but don't also remove the element at the head of this queue. This method throws NoSuchElementException when this queue is empty.
boolean offer(E e)	Insert element e into this queue if it is possible to do so immediately without violating capacity restrictions. Return true on success; otherwise, return false when the element cannot be added at this time because no space is currently available. This method throws ClassCastException when e's class prevents e from being added to this queue, NullPointerException when e contains the null reference and this queue doesn't permit null elements to be added, and IllegalArgumentException when some property of e prevents it from being added to this queue.
E peek()	Return but don't also remove the element at the head of this queue. This method returns null when this queue is empty.
E poll()	Return and also remove the element at the head of this queue. This method returns null when this queue is empty.
E remove()	Return and also remove the element at the head of this queue. This method throws NoSuchElementException when this queue is empty. This is the only difference between remove() and poll().

Table 9-5 reveals two sets of methods: in one set, a method (e.g., add()) throws an exception when an operation fails; in the other set, a method (e.g., offer()) returns a special value (false or null) in the presence of failure. The methods that return a special value are useful in the context of capacity-restricted Queue implementations where failure is a normal occurrence.

> **Note**   The offer() method is generally preferable to add() when using a capacity-restricted queue because offer() doesn't throw IllegalStateException.

Java supplies many Queue implementation classes, where most of these classes are members of the java.util.concurrent package: LinkedBlockingQueue and SynchronousQueue are examples. In contrast, the java.util package provides LinkedList and PriorityQueue as its Queue implementation classes.

> **Caution**   Many Queue implementation classes don't allow null elements to be added. However, some classes (e.g., LinkedList) permit null elements. You should avoid adding a null element because null is used as a special return value by the peek() and poll() methods to indicate that a queue is empty.

PriorityQueue

The PriorityQueue class provides an implementation of a *priority queue*, which is a queue that orders its elements according to their natural ordering or by a comparator provided when the queue is instantiated. Priority queues don't permit null elements and don't permit insertion of non-Comparable objects when relying on natural ordering.

The element at the head of the priority queue is the least element with respect to the specified ordering. When multiple elements are tied for least element, one of those elements is arbitrarily chosen as the least element. Similarly, the element at the tail of the priority queue is the greatest element, which is arbitrarily chosen when there is a tie.

Priority queues are unbounded but have a capacity that governs the size of the internal array that is used to store the priority queue's elements. The capacity value is at least as large as the queue's length and grows automatically as elements are added to the priority queue.

PriorityQueue (whose generic type is PriorityQueue<E>) supplies six constructors:

- PriorityQueue() creates a PriorityQueue instance with an initial capacity of 11 elements and which orders its elements according to their natural ordering.

- PriorityQueue(Collection<? extends E> c) creates a PriorityQueue instance containing c's elements. If c is a SortedSet or PriorityQueue instance, this priority queue will be ordered according to the same ordering. Otherwise, this priority queue will be ordered according to the natural ordering of its elements. This constructor throws ClassCastException when c's elements cannot be compared to one another according to the priority queue's ordering and NullPointerException when c or any of its elements contain the null reference.

- PriorityQueue(int initialCapacity) creates a PriorityQueue instance with the specified initialCapacity and which orders its elements according to their natural ordering. This constructor throws IllegalArgumentException when initialCapacity is less than 1.

- PriorityQueue(int initialCapacity, Comparator<? super E> comparator) creates a PriorityQueue instance with the specified initialCapacity and which orders its elements according to the specified comparator. Natural ordering is used when comparator contains the null reference. This constructor throws IllegalArgumentException when initialCapacity is less than 1.

- PriorityQueue(PriorityQueue<? extends E> pq) creates a PriorityQueue instance containing pq's elements. This priority queue will be ordered according to the same ordering as pq. This constructor throws ClassCastException when pq's elements cannot be compared to one another according to pq's ordering and NullPointerException when pq or any of its elements contains the null reference.

- PriorityQueue(SortedSet<? extends E> ss) creates a PriorityQueue instance containing ss's elements. This priority queue will be ordered according to the same ordering as ss. This constructor throws ClassCastException when ss's elements cannot be compared to one another according to ss's ordering and NullPointerException when ss or any of its elements contains the null reference.

Listing 9-14 demonstrates a priority queue.

Listing 9-14. Adding Randomly Generated Integers to a Priority Queue

```java
import java.util.PriorityQueue;
import java.util.Queue;

public class PriorityQueueDemo
{
   public static void main(String[] args)
   {
      Queue<Integer> qi = new PriorityQueue<Integer>();
      for (int i = 0; i < 15; i++)
         qi.add((int) (Math.random() * 100));
      while (!qi.isEmpty())
         System.out.print(qi.poll() + " ");
      System.out.println();
   }
}
```

After creating a priority queue, PriorityQueueDemo's main thread adds 15 randomly generated integers (ranging from 0 through 99) to this queue. It then enters a while loop that repeatedly polls the priority queue for the next element and outputs that element until the queue is empty.

When you run this application, it outputs a line of 15 integers in ascending numerical order from left to right. For example, I observed the following output from one run:

```
30 43 53 61 61 66 66 67 76 78 80 83 87 90 97
```

Because `poll()` returns null when there are no more elements, I could have coded this loop as follows:

```
Integer i;
while ((i = qi.poll()) != null)
   System.out.print(i + " ");
```

Suppose you want to reverse the order of the previous example's output so that the largest element appears on the left and the smallest element appears on the right. As Listing 9-15 demonstrates, you can achieve this task by passing a comparator to the appropriate `PriorityQueue` constructor.

Listing 9-15. Using a Comparator with a Priority Queue

```java
import java.util.Comparator;
import java.util.PriorityQueue;
import java.util.Queue;

public class PriorityQueueDemo
{
   final static int NELEM = 15; // number of elements

   public static void main(String[] args)
   {
      Comparator<Integer> cmp;
      cmp = new Comparator<Integer>()
            {
               @Override
               public int compare(Integer e1, Integer e2)
               {
                  return e2 - e1;
               }
            };
      Queue<Integer> qi = new PriorityQueue<Integer>(NELEM, cmp);
      for (int i = 0; i < NELEM; i++)
         qi.add((int) (Math.random() * 100));
      while (!qi.isEmpty())
         System.out.print(qi.poll() + " ");
      System.out.println();
   }
}
```

Listing 9-15 is similar to Listing 9-14, but there are some differences. First, I have declared a constant named NELEM so that I can easily change both the priority queue's initial capacity and the number of elements inserted into the priority queue by specifying the new value in one place.

Second, Listing 9-15 declares and instantiates an anonymous class that implements Comparator. Its compareTo() method subtracts element e2 from element e1 to achieve descending numerical order. The compiler handles the task of unboxing e2 and e1 by converting e2 - e1 to e2.intValue() - e1.intValue().

Finally, Listing 9-15 passes an initial capacity of NELEM elements and the instantiated comparator to the PriorityQueue(int initialCapacity, Comparator<? super E> comparator) constructor. The priority queue will use this comparator to order these elements.

Run this application and you will now see a single output line of 15 integers shown in descending numerical order from left to right. For example, I observed this output line:

```
97 72 70 70 67 64 56 43 36 22 9 5 3 2 1
```

Exploring Deques

A *deque* (pronounced deck) is a double-ended queue in which element insertion or removal occurs at its *head* or *tail*. Deques can be used as queues or stacks.

Deque, whose generic type is Deque<E>, extends Queue in which the inherited add(E e) method inserts e at the deque's tail. Table 9-6 describes Deque-specific methods.

Table 9-6. Deque-Specific Methods

Method	Description
void addFirst(E e)	Insert e at the head of this deque if it is possible to do so immediately without violating capacity restrictions. When using a capacity-restricted deque, it is generally preferable to use method offerFirst(). This method throws IllegalStateException when e cannot be added at this time because of capacity restrictions, ClassCastException when e's class prevents e from being added to this deque, NullPointerException when e contains the null reference and this deque doesn't permit null elements to be added, and IllegalArgumentException when some property of e prevents it from being added to this deque.
void addLast(E e)	Insert e at the tail of this deque if it is possible to do so immediately without violating capacity restrictions. When using a capacity-restricted deque, it is generally preferable to use method offerLast(). This method throws IllegalStateException when e cannot be added at this time because of capacity restrictions, ClassCastException when e's class prevents e from being added to this deque, NullPointerException when e contains the null reference and this deque doesn't permit null elements to be added, and IllegalArgumentException when some property of e prevents it from being added to this deque.
Iterator<E> descendingIterator()	Return an iterator over the elements in this deque in reverse sequential order. The elements will be returned in order from last (tail) to first (head). The inherited Iterator<E> iterator() method returns elements from the head to the tail.

(continued)

Table 9-6. (continued)

Method	Description
E element()	Retrieve but don't remove the first element of this deque (at the head). This method differs from peek() only in that it throws NoSuchElementException when this deque is empty. This method is equivalent to getFirst().
E getFirst()	Retrieve but don't remove the first element of this deque. This method differs from peekFirst() only in that it throws NoSuchElementException when this deque is empty.
E getLast()	Retrieve but don't remove the last element of this deque. This method differs from peekLast() only in that it throws NoSuchElementException when this deque is empty.
boolean offer(E e)	Insert e at the tail of this deque if it is possible to do so immediately without violating capacity restrictions, returning true on success and false when no space is currently available. When using a capacity-restricted deque, this method is generally preferable to the add() method, which can fail to insert an element only by throwing an exception. This method throws ClassCastException when e's class prevents e from being added to this deque, NullPointerException when e contains the null reference and this deque doesn't permit null elements to be added, and IllegalArgumentException when some property of e prevents it from being added to this deque. This method is equivalent to offerLast().
boolean offerFirst(E e)	Insert e at the head of this deque unless it would violate capacity restrictions. When using a capacity-restricted deque, this method is generally preferable to the addFirst() method, which can fail to insert an element only by throwing an exception. This method throws ClassCastException when e's class prevents e from being added to this deque, NullPointerException when e contains the null reference and this deque doesn't permit null elements to be added, and IllegalArgumentException when some property of e prevents it from being added to this deque.
boolean offerLast(E e)	Insert e at the tail of this deque unless it would violate capacity restrictions. When using a capacity-restricted deque, this method is generally preferable to the addLast() method, which can fail to insert an element only by throwing an exception. This method throws ClassCastException when e's class prevents e from being added to this deque, NullPointerException when e contains the null reference and this deque doesn't permit null elements to be added, and IllegalArgumentException when some property of e prevents it from being added to this deque.

(continued)

Table 9-6. (continued)

Method	Description
E peek()	Retrieve but don't remove the first element of this deque (at the head) or return null when this deque is empty. This method is equivalent to peekFirst().
E peekFirst()	Retrieve but don't remove the first element of this deque (at the head) or return null when this deque is empty.
E peekLast()	Retrieve but don't remove the last element of this deque (at the tail) or return null when this deque is empty.
E poll()	Retrieve and remove the first element of this deque (at the head) or return null when this deque is empty. This method is equivalent to pollFirst().
E pollFirst()	Retrieve and remove the first element of this deque (at the head) or return null when this deque is empty.
E pollLast()	Retrieve and remove the last element of this deque (at the tail) or return null when this deque is empty.
E pop()	Pop an element from the stack represented by this deque. In other words, remove and return the first element of this deque. This method is equivalent to removeFirst().
void push(E e)	Push e onto the stack represented by this deque (in other words, at the head of this deque) if it is possible to do so immediately without violating capacity restrictions, returning true on success and throwing IllegalStateException when no space is currently available. This method also throws ClassCastException when e's class prevents e from being added to this deque, NullPointerException when e contains the null reference and this deque doesn't permit null elements to be added, and IllegalArgumentException when some property of e prevents it from being added to this deque. This method is equivalent to addFirst().
E remove()	Retrieve and remove the first element of this deque (at the head). This method differs from poll() only in that it throws NoSuchElementException when this deque is empty. This method is equivalent to removeFirst().
E removeFirst()	Retrieve and remove the first element of this deque. This method differs from pollFirst() only in that it throws NoSuchElementException when this deque is empty.
boolean removeFirstOccurrence(Object o)	Remove the first occurrence of o from this deque. If the deque doesn't contain o, it is unchanged. Return true when this deque contained o (or equivalently, when this deque changed as a result of the call). This method throws ClassCastException when o's class prevents o from being added to this deque and NullPointerException when o contains the null reference and this deque doesn't permit null elements to be added. The inherited boolean remove(Object o) method is equivalent to this method.

(continued)

Table 9-6. (continued)

Method	Description
`E removeLast()`	Retrieve and remove the last element of this deque. This method differs from `pollLast()` only in that it throws `NoSuchElementException` when this deque is empty.
`boolean removeLastOccurrence(Object o)`	Remove the last occurrence of o from this deque. If the deque doesn't contain o, it is unchanged. Return true when this deque contained o (or equivalently, when this deque changed as a result of the call). This method throws `ClassCastException` when o's class prevents o from being added to this deque and `NullPointerException` when o contains the null reference and this deque doesn't permit null elements to be added.

As Table 9-6 reveals, `Deque` declares methods to access elements at both ends of the deque. Methods are provided to insert, remove, and examine the element. Each of these methods exists in two forms: one throws an exception when the operation fails, the other returns a special value (either null or false, depending on the operation). The latter form of the insert operation is designed specifically for use with capacity-restricted `Deque` implementations; in most implementations, insert operations cannot fail.

Figure 9-2 reveals a table from `Deque`'s Java documentation that nicely summarizes both forms of the insert, remove, and examine methods for both the head and the tail.

	First Element (Head)		Last Element (Tail)	
	Throws exception	*Special value*	*Throws exception*	*Special value*
Insert	`addFirst(e)`	`offerFirst(e)`	`addLast(e)`	`offerLast(e)`
Remove	`removeFirst()`	`pollFirst()`	`removeLast()`	`pollLast()`
Examine	`getFirst()`	`peekFirst()`	`getLast()`	`peekLast()`

Figure 9-2. *Deque declares 12 methods for inserting, removing, and examining elements at the head or tail of a deque*

When a deque is used as a queue, you observe FIFO (First-In, First-Out) behavior. Elements are added at the end of the deque and removed from the beginning. The methods inherited from the Queue interface are precisely equivalent to the Deque methods as indicated in Table 9-7.

Table 9-7. *Queue and Equivalent Deque Methods*

Queue Method	Equivalent Deque Method
`add(e)`	`addLast(e)`
`offer(e)`	`offerLast(e)`
`remove()`	`removeFirst()`
`poll()`	`pollFirst()`
`element()`	`getFirst()`
`peek()`	`peekFirst()`

Finally, deques can also be used as LIFO (Last-In, First-Out) stacks. When a deque is used as a stack, elements are pushed and popped from the beginning of the deque. Because a stack's push(e) method would be equivalent to Deque's addFirst(e) method, its pop() method would be equivalent to Deque's removeFirst() method, and its peek() method would be equivalent to Deque's peekFirst() method, Deque declares the E peek(), E pop(), and void push(E e) stack-oriented convenience methods.

ArrayDeque

The ArrayDeque class provides a resizable-array implementation of the Deque interface. It prohibits null elements from being added to a deque, and its iterator() method returns fail-fast iterators.

ArrayDeque supplies three constructors:

- ArrayDeque() creates an empty array deque with an initial capacity of 16 elements.

- ArrayDeque(Collection<? extends E> c) creates an array deque containing c's elements in the order in which they are returned by c's iterator. (The first element returned by c's iterator becomes the first element or front of the deque.) NullPointerException is thrown when c contains the null reference.

- ArrayDeque(int numElements) creates an empty array deque with an initial capacity sufficient to hold numElements elements. No exception is thrown when the argument passed to numElements is less than or equal to zero.

Listing 9-16 demonstrates an array deque.

Listing 9-16. Using an Array Deque as a Stack

```
import java.util.ArrayDeque;
import java.util.Deque;

public class ArrayDequeDemo
{
   public static void main(String[] args)
   {
      Deque<String> stack = new ArrayDeque<String>();
      String[] weekdays = { "Sunday", "Monday", "Tuesday", "Wednesday",
                            "Thursday", "Friday", "Saturday" };
      for (String weekday: weekdays)
         stack.push(weekday);
      while (stack.peek() != null)
         System.out.println(stack.pop());
   }
}
```

ArrayDequeDemo creates a deque for use as a stack and an array of weekday names. It then pushes these names on this stack and pops them, outputting the names in reverse order.

When you run this application, it generates the following output:

```
Saturday
Friday
Thursday
Wednesday
Tuesday
Monday
Sunday
```

Exploring Maps

A *map* is a group of key/value pairs (also known as *entries*). Because the *key* identifies an entry, a map cannot contain duplicate keys. Furthermore, each key can map to at most one value. Maps are described by the Map interface, which has no parent interface, and whose generic type is Map<K,V> (K is the key's type; V is the value's type).

Table 9-8 describes Map's methods.

Table 9-8. Map Methods

Method	Description
void clear()	Remove all elements from this map, leaving it empty. This method throws UnsupportedOperationException when clear() is not supported.
boolean containsKey(Object key)	Return true when this map contains an entry for the specified key; otherwise, return false. This method throws ClassCastException when key is of an inappropriate type for this map and NullPointerException when key contains the null reference and this map doesn't permit null keys.
boolean containsValue(Object value)	Return true when this map maps one or more keys to value. This method throws ClassCastException when value is of an inappropriate type for this map and NullPointerException when value contains the null reference and this map doesn't permit null values.
Set<Map.Entry<K,V>> entrySet()	Return a Set view of the entries contained in this map. Because this map backs the view, changes that are made to the map are reflected in the set and vice versa.
boolean equals(Object o)	Compare o with this map for equality. Return true when o is also a map and the two maps represent the same entries; otherwise, return false.
V get(Object key)	Return the value to which key is mapped or null when this map contains no entry for key. If this map permits null values, then a return value of null doesn't necessarily indicate that the map contains no entry for key; it is also possible that the map explicitly maps key to the null reference. The containsKey() method may be used to distinguish between these two cases. This method throws ClassCastException when key is of an inappropriate type for this map and NullPointerException when key contains the null reference and this map doesn't permit null keys.

(continued)

Table 9-8. (continued)

Method	Description
int hashCode()	Return the hash code for this map. A map's hash code is defined to be the sum of the hash codes for the entries in the map's entrySet() view.
boolean isEmpty()	Return true when this map contains no entries; otherwise, return false.
Set<K> keySet()	Return a Set view of the keys contained in this map. Because this map backs the view, changes that are made to the map are reflected in the set and vice versa.
V put(K key,V value)	Associate value with key in this map. If the map previously contained an entry for key, the old value is replaced by value. This method returns the previous value associated with key or null when there was no entry for key. (The null return value can also indicate that the map previously associated the null reference with key, if the implementation supports null values.) This method throws UnsupportedOperationException when put() is not supported, ClassCastException when key's or value's class is not appropriate for this map, IllegalArgumentException when some property of key or value prevents it from being stored in this map, and NullPointerException when key or value contains the null reference and this map doesn't permit null keys or values.
void putAll(Map<? extends K,? extends V> m)	Copy all entries from map m to this map. The effect of this call is equivalent to that of calling put(k, v) on this map once for each mapping from key k to value v in map m. This method throws UnsupportedOperationException when putAll() is not supported, ClassCastException when the class of a key or value in map m is not appropriate for this map, IllegalArgumentException when some property of a key or value in map m prevents it from being stored in this map, and NullPointerException when m contains the null reference or when m contains null keys or values and this map doesn't permit null keys or values.
V remove(Object key)	Remove key's entry from this map when it is present. This method returns the value to which this map previously associated with key or null when the map contained no mapping for key. If this map permits null values, then a return value of null doesn't necessarily indicate that the map contained no entry for key; it is also possible that the map explicitly mapped key to null. This map will not contain an entry for key once the call returns. This method throws UnsupportedOperationException when remove() is not supported, ClassCastException when the class of key is not appropriate for this map, and NullPointerException when key contains the null reference and this map doesn't permit null keys.
int size()	Return the number of key/value entries in this map. If the map contains more than Integer.MAX_VALUE entries, this method returns Integer.MAX_VALUE.
Collection<V> values()	Return a Collection view of the values contained in this map. Because this map backs the view, changes that are made to the map are reflected in the collection and vice versa.

Unlike List, Set, and Queue, Map doesn't extend Collection. However, it is possible to view a map as a Collection instance by calling Map's keySet(), values(), and entrySet() methods, which, respectively, return a Set of keys, a Collection of values, and a Set of key/value pair entries.

> **Note** The values() method returns Collection instead of Set because multiple keys can map to the same value, and values() would then return multiple copies of the same value.

The Collection views returned by these methods (recall that a Set is a Collection because Set extends Collection) provide the only means to iterate over a Map. For example, suppose you declare Listing 9-17's Color enum with its three Color constants, RED, GREEN, and BLUE.

Listing 9-17. A Colorful enum

```
enum Color
{
   RED(255, 0, 0),
   GREEN(0, 255, 0),
   BLUE(0, 0, 255);

   private int r, g, b;

   private Color(int r, int g, int b)
   {
      this.r = r;
      this.g = g;
      this.b = b;
   }

   @Override
   public String toString()
   {
      return "r = " + r + ", g = " + g + ", b = " + b;
   }
}
```

The following example declares a map of String keys and Color values, adds several entries to the map, and iterates over the keys and values:

```
Map<String, Color> colorMap = ...; // ... represents the creation of a Map implementation
colorMap.put("red", Color.RED);
colorMap.put("blue", Color.BLUE);
colorMap.put("green", Color.GREEN);
colorMap.put("RED", Color.RED);
for (String colorKey: colorMap.keySet())
   System.out.println(colorKey);
Collection<Color> colorValues = colorMap.values();
for (Iterator<Color> it = colorValues.iterator(); it.hasNext();)
   System.out.println(it.next());
```

When running this code fragment against a hashmap implementation (discussed later) of colorMap, you should observe output similar to the following:

```
red
blue
green
RED
r = 255, g = 0, b = 0
r = 0, g = 0, b = 255
r = 0, g = 255, b = 0
r = 255, g = 0, b = 0
```

The first four output lines identify the map's keys; the second four output lines identify the map's values.

The entrySet() method returns a Set of Map.Entry objects. Each of these objects describes a single entry as a key/value pair and is an instance of a class that implements the Map.Entry interface, where Entry is a nested interface of Map. Table 9-9 describes Map.Entry's methods.

Table 9-9. Map.Entry Methods

Method	Description
boolean equals(Object o)	Compare o with this entry for equality. Return true when o is also a map entry and the two entries have the same key and value.
K getKey()	Return this entry's key. This method optionally throws IllegalStateException when this entry has previously been removed from the backing map.
V getValue()	Return this entry's value. This method optionally throws IllegalStateException when this entry has previously been removed from the backing map.
int hashCode()	Return this entry's hash code.
V setValue(V value)	Replace this entry's value with value. The backing map is updated with the new value. This method throws UnsupportedOperationException when setValue() is not supported, ClassCastException when value's class prevents it from being stored in the backing map, NullPointerException when value contains the null reference and the backing map doesn't permit null, IllegalArgumentException when some property of value prevents it from being stored in the backing map, and (optionally) IllegalStateException when this entry has previously been removed from the backing map.

The following example shows you how you might iterate over the previous example's map entries:

```
for (Map.Entry<String, Color> colorEntry: colorMap.entrySet())
    System.out.println(colorEntry.getKey() + ": " + colorEntry.getValue());
```

When running this example against the previously mentioned hashmap implementation, you would observe the following output:

```
red: r = 255, g = 0, b = 0
blue: r = 0, g = 0, b = 255
green: r = 0, g = 255, b = 0
RED: r = 255, g = 0, b = 0
```

TreeMap

The TreeMap class provides a map implementation that is based on a red-black tree. As a result, entries are stored in sorted order of their keys. However, accessing these entries is somewhat slower than with the other Map implementations (which are not sorted) because links must be traversed.

> **Note**   Check out Wikipedia's "Red-black tree" entry (http://en.wikipedia.org/wiki/Red-black_tree) to learn about red-black trees.

TreeMap supplies four constructors:

- TreeMap() creates a new, empty tree map that is sorted according to the natural ordering of its keys. All keys inserted into the map must implement the Comparable interface.

- TreeMap(Comparator<? super K> comparator) creates a new, empty tree map that is sorted according to the specified comparator. Passing null to comparator implies that natural ordering will be used.

- TreeMap(Map<? extends K, ? extends V> m) creates a new tree map containing m's entries, sorted according to the natural ordering of its keys. All keys inserted into the new map must implement the Comparable interface. This constructor throws ClassCastException when m's keys don't implement Comparable or are not mutually comparable and NullPointerException when m contains the null reference.

- TreeMap(SortedMap<K, ? extends V> sm) creates a new tree map containing the same entries and using the same ordering as sm. (I discuss sorted maps later in this chapter.) This constructor throws NullPointerException when sm contains the null reference.

Listing 9-18 demonstrates a tree map.

Listing 9-18. Sorting a Map's Entries According to the Natural Ordering of Their String-Based Keys

```java
import java.util.Map;
import java.util.TreeMap;

public class TreeMapDemo
{
   public static void main(String[] args)
```

```
    {
        Map<String, Integer> msi = new TreeMap<String, Integer>();
        String[] fruits = {"apples", "pears", "grapes", "bananas", "kiwis"};
        int[] quantities = {10, 15, 8, 17, 30};
        for (int i = 0; i < fruits.length; i++)
            msi.put(fruits[i], quantities[i]);
        for (Map.Entry<String, Integer> entry: msi.entrySet())
            System.out.println(entry.getKey() + ": " + entry.getValue());
    }
}
```

TreeMapDemo creates a tree map and an array of fruit names. It then populates this map with these names and dumps the map's entries to standard output.

When you run this application, it generates the following output:

```
apples: 10
bananas: 17
grapes: 8
kiwis: 30
pears: 15
```

HashMap

The HashMap class provides a map implementation that is based on a hashtable data structure. This implementation supports all Map operations and permits null keys and null values. It makes no guarantees on the order in which entries are stored.

A hashtable maps keys to integer values with the help of a *hash function*. Java provides this function in the form of Object's hashCode() method, which classes override to provide appropriate hash codes.

A *hash code* identifies one of the hashtable's array elements, which is known as a *bucket* or *slot*. For some hashtables, the bucket may store the value that is associated with the key. Figure 9-3 illustrates this kind of hashtable.

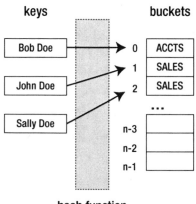

Figure 9-3. A simple hashtable maps keys to buckets that store values associated with those keys

The hash function hashes Bob Doe to 0, which identifies the first bucket. This bucket contains ACCTS, which is Bob Doe's employee type. The hash function also hashes John Doe and Sally Doe to 1 and 2 (respectively) whose buckets contain SALES.

A perfect hash function hashes each key to a unique integer value. However, this ideal is very difficult to meet. In practice, some keys will hash to the same integer value. This nonunique mapping is referred to as a *collision*.

To address collisions, most hashtables associate a linked list of entries with a bucket. Instead of containing a value, the bucket contains the address of the first node in the linked list, and each node contains one of the colliding entries. See Figure 9-4.

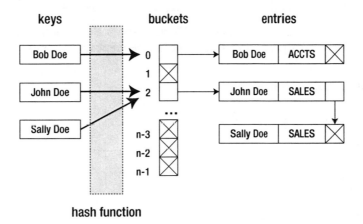

Figure 9-4. A complex hashtable maps keys to buckets that store references to linked lists whose node values are hashed from the same keys

When storing a value in a hashtable, the hashtable uses the hash function to hash the key to its hash code and then searches the appropriate linked list to see if an entry with a matching key exists. If there is an entry, its value is updated with the new value. Otherwise, a new node is created, populated with the key and value, and appended to the list.

When retrieving a value from a hashtable, the hashtable uses the hash function to hash the key to its hash code and then searches the appropriate linked list to see if an entry with a matching key exists. If there is an entry, its value is returned. Otherwise, the hashtable may return a special value to indicate that there is no entry, or it might throw an exception.

The number of buckets is known as the hashtable's *capacity*. The ratio of the number of stored entries divided by the number of buckets is known as the hashtable's *load factor*. Choosing the right load factor is important for balancing performance with memory use:

- As the load factor approaches 1, the probability of collisions and the cost of handling them (by searching lengthy linked lists) increase.

- As the load factor approaches 0, the hashtable's size in terms of number of buckets increases with little improvement in search cost.

- For many hashtables, a load factor of 0.75 is close to optimal. This value is the default for HashMap's hashtable implementation.

HashMap supplies four constructors:

- HashMap() creates a new, empty hashmap with an initial capacity of 16 and a load factor of 0.75.

- HashMap(int initialCapacity) creates a new, empty hashmap with a capacity specified by initialCapacity and a load factor of 0.75. This constructor throws IllegalArgumentException when initialCapacity's value is less than 0.

- HashMap(int initialCapacity, float loadFactor) creates a new, empty hashmap with a capacity specified by initialCapacity and a load factor specified by loadFactor. This constructor throws IllegalArgumentException when initialCapacity is less than 0 or when loadFactor is less than or equal to 0.

- HashMap(Map<? extends K, ? extends V> m) creates a new hashmap containing m's entries. This constructor throws NullPointerException when m contains the null reference.

Listing 9-19 demonstrates a hashmap.

Listing 9-19. Using a Hashmap to Count Command-Line Arguments

```java
import java.util.HashMap;
import java.util.Map;

public class HashMapDemo
{
   public static void main(String[] args)
   {
      Map<String, Integer> argMap = new HashMap<String, Integer>();
      for (String arg: args)
      {
         Integer count = argMap.get(arg);
         argMap.put(arg, (count == null) ? 1 : count + 1);
      }
      System.out.println(argMap);
      System.out.println("Number of distinct arguments = " + argMap.size());
   }
}
```

HashMapDemo creates a hashmap of String keys and Integer values. Each key is one of the command-line arguments passed to this application, and its value is the number of occurrences of that argument on the command line.

For example, java HashMapDemo how much wood could a woodchuck chuck if a woodchuck could chuck wood generates the following output:

```
{wood=2, could=2, how=1, if=1, chuck=2, a=2, woodchuck=2, much=1}
Number of distinct arguments = 8
```

Because the String class overrides equals() and hashCode(), Listing 9-19 can use String objects as keys in a hashmap. When you create a class whose instances are to be used as keys, you must ensure that you override both methods.

Listing 9-6 showed you that a class's overriding hashCode() method can call a reference field's hashCode() method and return its value, provided that the class declares a single reference field (and no primitive-type fields).

More commonly, classes declare multiple fields, and a better implementation of the hashCode() method is required. The implementation should try to generate hash codes that minimize collisions.

There is no rule on how to best implement hashCode(), and various *algorithms* (recipes for accomplishing tasks) have been created. My favorite algorithm appears in *Effective Java, Second Edition*, by Joshua Bloch (Addison-Wesley, 2008; ISBN: 0321356683).

The following algorithm, which assumes the existence of an arbitrary class that is referred to as *X*, closely follows Bloch's algorithm, but is not identical:

1. Initialize int variable hashCode (the name is arbitrary) to an arbitrary nonzero integer value, such as 19. This variable is initialized to a nonzero value to ensure that it takes into account any initial fields whose hash codes are zeros. If you initialize hashCode to 0, the final hash code will be unaffected by such fields and you run the risk of increased collisions.

2. For each field f that is also used in *X*'s equals() method, calculate f's hash code and assign it to int variable hc as follows:

    a. If f is of Boolean type, calculate hc = f ? 1 : 0.

    b. If f is of byte integer, character, integer, or short integer type, calculate hc = (int) f. The integer value is the hash code.

    c. If f is of long integer type, calculate hc = (int) (f ^ (f >>> 32)). This expression exclusive ORs the long integer's least significant 32 bits with its most significant 32 bits.

    d. If f is of type floating-point, calculate hc = Float.floatToIntBits(f). This method takes +infinity, -infinity, and NaN into account.

    e. If f is of type double precision floating-point, calculate long l = Double.doubleToLongBits(f); hc = (int) (l ^ (l >>> 32)).

    f. If f is a reference field with a null reference, calculate hc = 0.

    g. If f is a reference field with a nonnull reference, and if *X*'s equals() method compares the field by recursively calling equals() (as in Listing 9-12's Employee class), calculate hc = f.hashCode(). However, if equals() employs a more complex comparison, create a *canonical* (simplest possible) representation of the field and call hashCode() on this representation.

    h. If f is an array, treat each element as a separate field by applying this algorithm recursively and combining the hc values as shown in the next step.

3. Combine hc with hashCode as follows: hashCode = hashCode * 31 + hc. Multiplying hashCode by 31 makes the resulting hash value dependent on the order in which fields appear in the class, which improves the hash value when a class contains multiple fields that are similar (several ints, for example). I chose 31 to be consistent with the String class's hashCode() method.

4. Return hashCode from hashCode().

In Chapter 4, Listing 4-7's Point class overrode equals() but didn't override hashCode(). I later presented a small code fragment that must be appended to Point's main() method to demonstrate the problem of not overriding hashCode(). I restate this problem here:

Although objects p1 and Point(10, 20) are logically equivalent, these objects have different hash codes, resulting in each object referring to a different entry in the hashmap. If an object is not stored (via put()) in that entry, get() returns null.

Listing 9-20 modifies Listing 4-7's Point class by declaring a hashCode() method. This method uses the aforementioned algorithm to ensure that logically equivalent Point objects hash to the same entry.

Listing 9-20. Overriding hashCode() to Return Proper Hash Codes for Point Objects

```
import java.util.HashMap;
import java.util.Map;

public class Point
{
   private int x, y;

   Point(int x, int y)
   {
      this.x = x;
      this.y = y;
   }

   int getX()
   {
      return x;
   }

   int getY()
   {
      return y;
   }

   @Override
   public boolean equals(Object o)
   {
      if (!(o instanceof Point))
         return false;
      Point p = (Point) o;
      return p.x == x && p.y == y;
   }

   @Override
   public int hashCode()
   {
      int hashCode = 19;
      int hc = x;
      hashCode = hashCode * 31 + hc;
```

```
      hc = y;
      hashCode = hashCode * 31 + hc;
      return hashCode;
   }

   public static void main(String[] args)
   {
      Point p1 = new Point(10, 20);
      Point p2 = new Point(20, 30);
      Point p3 = new Point(10, 20);
      // Test reflexivity
      System.out.println(p1.equals(p1)); // Output: true
      // Test symmetry
      System.out.println(p1.equals(p2)); // Output: false
      System.out.println(p2.equals(p1)); // Output: false
      // Test transitivity
      System.out.println(p2.equals(p3)); // Output: false
      System.out.println(p1.equals(p3)); // Output: true
      // Test nullability
      System.out.println(p1.equals(null)); // Output: false
      // Extra test to further prove the instanceof operator's usefulness.
      System.out.println(p1.equals("abc")); // Output: false
      Map<Point, String> map = new HashMap<Point, String>();
      map.put(p1, "first point");
      System.out.println(map.get(p1)); // Output: first point
      System.out.println(map.get(new Point(10, 20))); // Output: null
   }
}
```

Listing 9-20's hashCode() method is a little verbose in that it assigns each of x and y to local variable hc rather than directly using these fields in the hash code calculation. However, I decided to follow this approach to more closely mirror the hash code algorithm.

When you run this application, its last two lines of output are of the most interest. Instead of presenting first point followed by null on two separate lines, the application now correctly presents first point followed by first point on these lines.

Note   LinkedHashMap is a subclass of HashMap that uses a linked list to store its entries. As a result, LinkedHashMap's iterator returns entries in the order in which they were inserted. For example, if Listing 9-19 had specified Map<String, Integer> argMap = new LinkedHashMap<String, Integer>();, the application's output for java HashMapDemo how much wood could a woodchuck chuck if a woodchuck could chuck wood would have been {how=1, much=1, wood=2, could=2, a=2, woodchuck=2, chuck=2, if=1} followed by Number of distinct arguments = 8.

IdentityHashMap

The IdentityHashMap class provides a Map implementation that uses reference equality (==) instead of object equality (equals()) when comparing keys and values. This is an intentional violation of Map's general contract, which mandates the use of equals() when comparing elements.

IdentityHashMap obtains hash codes via System's int identityHashCode(Object x) class method instead of via each key's hashCode() method. identityHashCode() returns the same hash code for x as returned by Object's hashCode() method, whether or not x's class overrides hashCode(). The hash code for the null reference is zero.

These characteristics give IdentityHashMap a performance advantage over other Map implementations. Also, IdentityHashMap supports *mutable keys* (objects used as keys and whose hash codes change when their field values change while in the map). Listing 9-21 contrasts IdentityHashMap with HashMap where mutable keys are concerned.

Listing 9-21. Contrasting IdentityHashMap with HashMap in a Mutable Key Context

```java
import java.util.IdentityHashMap;
import java.util.HashMap;
import java.util.Map;

public class IdentityHashMapDemo
{
   public static void main(String[] args)
   {
      Map<Employee, String> map1 = new IdentityHashMap<Employee, String>();
      Map<Employee, String> map2 = new HashMap<Employee, String>();
      Employee e1 = new Employee("John Doe", 28);
      map1.put(e1, "SALES");
      System.out.println(map1);
      Employee e2 = new Employee("Jane Doe", 26);
      map2.put(e2, "MGMT");
      System.out.println(map2);
      System.out.println("map1 contains key e1 = " + map1.containsKey(e1));
      System.out.println("map2 contains key e2 = " + map2.containsKey(e2));
      e1.setAge(29);
      e2.setAge(27);
      System.out.println(map1);
      System.out.println(map2);
      System.out.println("map1 contains key e1 = " + map1.containsKey(e1));
      System.out.println("map2 contains key e2 = " + map2.containsKey(e2));
   }
}

class Employee
{
   private String name;
   private int age;
```

```java
Employee(String name, int age)
{
   this.name = name;
   this.age = age;
}

@Override
public boolean equals(Object o)
{
   if (!(o instanceof Employee))
      return false;
   Employee e = (Employee) o;
   return e.name.equals(name) && e.age == age;
}

@Override
public int hashCode()
{
   int hashCode = 19;
   hashCode = hashCode * 31 + name.hashCode();
   hashCode = hashCode * 31 + age;
   return hashCode;
}

void setAge(int age)
{
   this.age = age;
}

void setName(String name)
{
   this.name = name;
}

@Override
public String toString()
{
   return name + " " + age;
}
}
```

Listing 9-21's main() method creates IdentityHashMap and HashMap instances that each store an entry consisting of an Employee key and a String value. Because Employee instances are mutable (because of setAge() and setName()), main() changes their ages while these keys are stored in their maps. These changes result in the following output:

```
{John Doe 28=SALES}
{Jane Doe 26=MGMT}
map1 contains key e1 = true
map2 contains key e2 = true
{John Doe 29=SALES}
```

```
{Jane Doe 27=MGMT}
map1 contains key e1 = true
map2 contains key e2 = false
```

The last four lines show that the changed entries remain in their maps. However, map2's containsKey() method reports that its HashMap instance no longer contains its Employee key (which should be Jane Doe 27), whereas map1's containsKey() method reports that its IdentityHashMap instance still contains its Employee key, which is now John Doe 29.

> **Note** IdentityHashMap's documentation states that "a typical use of this class is topology-preserving object graph transformations, such as serialization or deep copying." (I discuss serialization in Chapter 11.) It also states that "another typical use of this class is to maintain proxy objects." Also, stackoverflow's "Use Cases for Identity HashMap" topic (http://stackoverflow.com/questions/838528/use-cases-for-identity-hashmap)) mentions that it is much faster to use IdentityHashMap than HashMap when the keys are java.lang.Class objects.

EnumMap

The EnumMap class provides a Map implementation whose keys are the members of the same enum. Null keys are not permitted; any attempt to store a null key results in a thrown NullPointerException. Because an enum map is represented internally as an array, an enum map approaches an array in terms of performance.

EnumMap supplies the following constructors:

- EnumMap(Class<K> keyType) creates an empty enum map with the specified keyType. This constructor throws NullPointerException when keyType contains the null reference.

- EnumMap(EnumMap<K,? extends V> m) creates an enum map with the same key type as m and with m's entries. This constructor throws NullPointerException when m contains the null reference.

- EnumMap(Map<K,? extends V> m) creates an enum map initialized with m's entries. If m is an EnumMap instance, this constructor behaves like the previous constructor. Otherwise, m must contain at least one entry to determine the new enum map's key type. This constructor throws NullPointerException when m contains the null reference and IllegalArgumentException when m is not an EnumMap instance and is empty.

Listing 9-22 demonstrates EnumMap.

Listing 9-22. An Enum Map of Coin Constants

```java
import java.util.EnumMap;
import java.util.Map;

enum Coin
{
   PENNY, NICKEL, DIME, QUARTER
}

public class EnumMapDemo
{
   public static void main(String[] args)
   {
      Map<Coin, Integer> map = new EnumMap<Coin, Integer>(Coin.class);
      map.put(Coin.PENNY, 1);
      map.put(Coin.NICKEL, 5);
      map.put(Coin.DIME, 10);
      map.put(Coin.QUARTER, 25);
      System.out.println(map);
      Map<Coin,Integer> mapCopy = new EnumMap<Coin, Integer>(map);
      System.out.println(mapCopy);
   }
}
```

EnumMapDemo creates a map of Coin keys and Integer values. It then inserts several Coin instances into this map and outputs the map. Finally, it creates a copy of this map and outputs the copy.

When you run this application, it generates the following output:

```
{PENNY=1, NICKEL=5, DIME=10, QUARTER=25}
{PENNY=1, NICKEL=5, DIME=10, QUARTER=25}
```

Exploring Sorted Maps

TreeMap is an example of a *sorted map*, which is a map that maintains its entries in ascending order, sorted according to the keys' natural ordering or according to a comparator that is supplied when the sorted map is created. Sorted maps are described by the SortedMap interface.

SortedMap (whose generic type is SortedMap<K, V>) extends Map. With two exceptions, the methods it inherits from Map behave identically on sorted maps as on other maps:

- The Iterator instance returned by the iterator() method on any of the sorted map's Collection views traverses the collections in order.

- The arrays returned by the Collection views' toArray() methods contain the keys, values, or entries in order.

> **Note** Although not guaranteed, the toString() methods of the Collection views of SortedMap implementations in the Collections Framework (e.g., TreeMap) return a string containing all of the view's elements in order.

SortedMap's documentation requires that an implementation must provide the four standard constructors that I presented in my discussion of TreeMap. Furthermore, implementations of this interface must implement the methods that are described in Table 9-10.

Table 9-10. SortedMap-Specific Methods

Method	Description
Comparator<? super K> comparator()	Return the comparator used to order the keys in this map, or null when this map uses the natural ordering of its keys.
Set<Map.Entry<K,V>> entrySet()	Return a Set view of the mappings contained in this map. The set's iterator returns these entries in ascending key order. Because the view is backed by this map, changes that are made to the map are reflected in the set and vice versa.
K firstKey()	Return the first (lowest) key currently in this map, or throw a NoSuchElementException instance when this map is empty.
SortedMap<K, V> headMap(K toKey)	Return a view of that portion of this map whose keys are strictly less than toKey. Because this map backs the returned map, changes in the returned map are reflected in this map and vice versa. The returned map supports all optional map operations that this map supports. This method throws ClassCastException when toKey is not compatible with this map's comparator (or, when the map has no comparator, when toKey doesn't implement Comparable), NullPointerException when toKey is null and this map doesn't permit null keys, and IllegalArgumentException when this map has a restricted range and toKey lies outside of this range's bounds.
Set<K> keySet()	Return a Set view of the keys contained in this map. The set's iterator returns the keys in ascending order. Because the map backs the view, changes that are made to the map are reflected in the set and vice versa.
K lastKey()	Return the last (highest) key currently in this map, or throw a NoSuchElementException instance when this map is empty.
SortedMap<K, V> subMap(K fromKey, K toKey)	Return a view of the portion of this map whose keys range from fromKey, inclusive, to toKey, exclusive. (When fromKey and toKey are equal, the returned map is empty.) Because this map backs the returned map, changes in the returned map are reflected in this map and vice versa. The returned map supports all optional map operations that this map supports. This method throws ClassCastException when fromKey and toKey cannot be compared to one another using this map's comparator (or, when the map has no comparator, using natural ordering), NullPointerException when fromKey or toKey is null and this map doesn't permit null keys, and IllegalArgumentException when fromKey is greater than toKey or when this map has a restricted range and fromKey or toKey lies outside of this range's bounds.

(continued)

Table 9-10. (*continued*)

Method	Description
SortedMap<K, V> tailMap(K fromKey)	Return a view of that portion of this map whose keys are greater than or equal to fromKey. Because this map backs the returned map, changes in the returned map are reflected in this map and vice versa. The returned map supports all optional map operations that this map supports. This method throws ClassCastException when fromKey is not compatible with this map's comparator (or, when the map has no comparator, when fromKey doesn't implement Comparable), NullPointerException when fromKey is null and this map doesn't permit null elements, and IllegalArgumentException when this map has a restricted range and fromKey lies outside of the range's bounds.
Collection<V> values()	Return a Collection view of the values contained in this map. The collection's iterator returns the values in ascending order of the corresponding keys. Because the map backs the collection, changes that are made to the map are reflected in the collection and vice versa.

Listing 9-23 demonstrates a sorted map based on a tree map.

Listing 9-23. A Sorted Map of Office Supply Names and Quantities

```java
import java.util.Comparator;
import java.util.SortedMap;
import java.util.TreeMap;

public class SortedMapDemo
{
   public static void main(String[] args)
   {
      SortedMap<String, Integer> smsi = new TreeMap<String, Integer>();
      String[] officeSupplies =
      {
         "pen", "pencil", "legal pad", "CD", "paper"
      };
      int[] quantities =
      {
         20, 30, 5, 10, 20
      };
      for (int i = 0; i < officeSupplies.length; i++)
         smsi.put(officeSupplies[i], quantities[i]);
      System.out.println(smsi);
      System.out.println(smsi.headMap("pencil"));
      System.out.println(smsi.headMap("paper"));
      SortedMap<String, Integer> smsiCopy;
      Comparator<String> cmp;
      cmp = new Comparator<String>()
               {
                  @Override
                  public int compare(String key1, String key2)
```

```
                {
                    return key2.compareTo(key1); // descending order
                }
            };
        smsiCopy = new TreeMap<String, Integer>(cmp);
        smsiCopy.putAll(smsi);
        System.out.println(smsiCopy);
    }
}
```

SortedMapDemo creates a sorted map and arrays of office supply names and quantities. It then proceeds to populate the map from these arrays. After dumping out the map's contents and head views of parts of the map, it creates and outputs a copy of the map in descending order.

When you run this application, it generates the following output:

```
{CD=10, legal pad=5, paper=20, pen=20, pencil=30}
{CD=10, legal pad=5, paper=20, pen=20}
{CD=10, legal pad=5}
{pencil=30, pen=20, paper=20, legal pad=5, CD=10}
```

Exploring Navigable Maps

TreeMap is an example of a *navigable map*, which is a sorted map that can be iterated over in descending order as well as ascending order and which can report closest matches for given search targets. Navigable maps are described by the NavigableMap interface, whose generic type is NavigableMap<K,V>, which extends SortedMap and which is described in Table 9-11.

Table 9-11. NavigableMap-Specific Methods

Method	Description
Map.Entry<K,V> ceilingEntry(K key)	Return the key-value mapping associated with the least key greater than or equal to key or null when there is no such key. This method throws ClassCastException when key cannot be compared with the keys currently in the map and NullPointerException when key is null and this map doesn't permit null keys.
K ceilingKey(K key)	Return the least key greater than or equal to key or null when there is no such key. This method throws ClassCastException when key cannot be compared with the keys currently in the map and NullPointerException when key is null and this map doesn't permit null keys.
NavigableSet<K> descendingKeySet()	Return a reverse order navigable set-based view of the keys contained in this map. The set's iterator returns the keys in descending order. This map backs the set, so changes to the map are reflected in the set and vice versa. If the map is modified (except through the iterator's own remove() operation) while iterating over the set, the results of the iteration are undefined.

(continued)

Table 9-11. (*continued*)

Method	Description
NavigableMap<K,V> descendingMap()	Return a reverse order view of the mappings contained in this map. This map backs the descending map, so changes to the map are reflected in the descending map and vice versa. If either map is modified while iterating over a collection view of either map (except through the iterator's own remove() operation), the results of the iteration are undefined.
Map.Entry<K,V> firstEntry()	Return a key-value mapping associated with the least key in this map or null when the map is empty.
Map.Entry<K,V> floorEntry(K key)	Return a key-value mapping associated with the greatest key less than or equal to key or null when there is no such key. This method throws ClassCastException when key cannot be compared with the keys currently in the map and NullPointerException when key is null and this map doesn't permit null keys.
K floorKey(K key)	Return the greatest key less than or equal to key or null when there is no such key. This method throws ClassCastException when key cannot be compared with the keys currently in the map and NullPointerException when key is null and this map doesn't permit null keys.
NavigableMap<K,V> headMap(K toKey, boolean inclusive)	Return a view of the portion of this map whose keys are less than (or equal to, when inclusive is true) toKey. This map backs the returned map, so changes in the returned map are reflected in this map and vice versa. The returned map supports all optional map operations that this map supports. This method throws ClassCastException when toKey is not compatible with this map's comparator (or, when the map has no comparator, when toMap doesn't implement Comparable), NullPointerException when toKey is null and this map doesn't permit null keys, and IllegalArgumentException when this map has a restricted range and toKey lies outside of this range's bounds.
Map.Entry<K,V> higherEntry(K key)	Return a key-value mapping associated with the least key strictly greater than key or null when there is no such key. This method throws ClassCastException when key cannot be compared with the keys currently in the map and NullPointerException when key is null and this map doesn't permit null keys.
K higherKey(K key)	Return the least key strictly greater than key or null when there is no such key. This method throws ClassCastException when key cannot be compared with the keys currently in the map and NullPointerException when key is null and this map doesn't permit null keys.
Map.Entry<K,V> lastEntry()	Return a key-value mapping associated with the greatest key in this map or null when the map is empty.
Map.Entry<K,V> lowerEntry(K key)	Return a key-value mapping associated with the greatest key strictly less than key or null when there is no such key. This method throws ClassCastException when key cannot be compared with the keys currently in the map and NullPointerException when key is null and this map doesn't permit null keys.

(*continued*)

Table 9-11. (*continued*)

Method	Description
K lowerKey(K key)	Return the greatest key strictly less than key or null when there is no such key. This method throws ClassCastException when key cannot be compared with the keys currently in the map and NullPointerException when key is null and this map doesn't permit null keys.
NavigableSet<K> navigableKeySet()	Return a navigable set-based view of the keys contained in this map. The set's iterator returns the keys in ascending order. This map backs the set, so changes to the map are reflected in the set and vice versa. If the map is modified while iterating over the set (except through the iterator's own remove() operation), the results of the iteration are undefined.
Map.Entry<K,V> pollFirstEntry()	Remove and return a key-value mapping associated with the least key in this map or null when the map is empty.
Map.Entry<K,V> pollLastEntry()	Remove and return a key-value mapping associated with the greatest key in this map or null when the map is empty.
NavigableMap<K,V> subMap(K fromKey, boolean fromInclusive, K toKey, boolean toInclusive)	Return a view of the portion of this map whose keys range from fromKey to toKey. (When fromKey and toKey are equal, the returned map is empty unless fromInclusive and toInclusive are both true.) This map backs the returned map, so changes in the returned map are reflected in this map and vice versa. The returned map supports all optional map operations that this map supports. This method throws ClassCastException when fromKey and toKey cannot be compared to one another using this map's comparator (or, when the map has no comparator, using natural ordering), NullPointerException when fromKey or toKey is null and this map doesn't permit null elements, and IllegalArgumentException when fromKey is greater than toKey or when this map has a restricted range and fromKey or toKey lies outside of this range's bounds.
NavigableMap<K,V> tailMap(K fromKey, boolean inclusive)	Return a view of the portion of this map whose keys are greater than (or equal to, when inclusive is true) fromKey. This map backs the returned map, so changes in the returned map are reflected in this map and vice versa. The returned map supports all optional map operations that this map supports. This method throws ClassCastException when fromKey is not compatible with this map's comparator (or, when the map has no comparator, when fromKey doesn't implement Comparable), NullPointerException when fromKey is null and this map doesn't permit null keys, and IllegalArgumentException when this map has a restricted range and fromKey lies outside of this range's bounds.

Table 9-11's methods describe the NavigableMap equivalents of the NavigableSet methods presented in Table 9-4 and even return NavigableSet instances in two instances.

Listing 9-24 demonstrates a navigable map based on a tree map.

Listing 9-24. Navigating a Map of (Bird, Count Within A Small Acreage) Entries

```
import java.util.Iterator;
import java.util.NavigableMap;
```

```java
import java.util.NavigableSet;
import java.util.TreeMap;

public class NavigableMapDemo
{
    public static void main(String[] args)
    {
        NavigableMap<String, Integer> nm = new TreeMap<String, Integer>();
        String[] birds = { "sparrow", "bluejay", "robin" };
        int[] ints = { 83, 12, 19 };
        for (int i = 0; i < birds.length; i++)
            nm.put(birds[i], ints[i]);
        System.out.println("Map = " + nm);
        System.out.print("Ascending order of keys: ");
        NavigableSet<String> ns = nm.navigableKeySet();
        Iterator iter = ns.iterator();
        while (iter.hasNext())
            System.out.print(iter.next() + " ");
        System.out.println();
        System.out.print("Descending order of keys: ");
        ns = nm.descendingKeySet();
        iter = ns.iterator();
        while (iter.hasNext())
            System.out.print(iter.next() + " ");
        System.out.println();
        System.out.println("First entry = " + nm.firstEntry());
        System.out.println("Last entry = "  + nm.lastEntry());
        System.out.println("Entry < ostrich is " + nm.lowerEntry("ostrich"));
        System.out.println("Entry > crow is " + nm.higherEntry("crow"));
        System.out.println("Poll first entry: " + nm.pollFirstEntry());
        System.out.println("Map = " + nm);
        System.out.println("Poll last entry: " + nm.pollLastEntry());
        System.out.println("Map = " + nm);
    }
}
```

Listing 9-24's System.out.println("Map = " + nm); method calls rely on TreeMap's toString() method to obtain the contents of a navigable map.

When you run this application, you observe the following output:

```
Map = {bluejay=12, robin=19, sparrow=83}
Ascending order of keys: bluejay robin sparrow
Descending order of keys: sparrow robin bluejay
First entry = bluejay=12
Last entry = sparrow=83
Entry < ostrich is bluejay=12
Entry > crow is robin=19
Poll first entry: bluejay=12
Map = {robin=19, sparrow=83}
Poll last entry: sparrow=83
Map = {robin=19}
```

Exploring the Arrays and Collections Utility APIs

The Collections Framework would be incomplete without its Arrays and Collections utility classes. Each class supplies various class methods that implement useful algorithms in the contexts of collections and arrays.

Following is a sampling of the Arrays class's array-oriented utility methods:

- static <T> List<T> asList(T... a) returns a fixed-size list backed by array a. (Changes to the returned list "write through" to the array.) For example, List<String> birds = Arrays.asList("Robin", "Oriole", "Bluejay"); converts the three-element array of Strings (recall that a variable sequence of arguments is implemented as an array) to a List whose reference is assigned to birds.

- static int binarySearch(int[] a, int key) searches array a for entry key using the binary search algorithm (explained following this list). The array must be sorted before calling this method; otherwise, the results are undefined. This method returns the index of the search key, if it is contained in the array; otherwise (-(insertion point) - 1) is returned. The insertion point is the point at which key would be inserted into the array (the index of the first element greater than key, or a.length if all elements in the array are less than key) and guarantees that the return value will be greater than or equal to 0 if and only if key is found. For example, Arrays.binarySearch(new String[] {"Robin", "Oriole", "Bluejay"}, "Oriole") returns 1, "Oriole"'s index.

- static void fill(char[] a, char ch) stores ch in each element of the specified character array. For example, Arrays.fill(screen[i], ' '); fills the ith row of a 2D screen array with spaces.

- static void sort(long[] a) sorts the elements in the long integer array a into ascending numerical order, for example, long lArray = new long[] { 20000L, 89L, 66L, 33L}; Arrays.sort(lArray);.

- static <T> void sort(T[] a, Comparator<? super T> c) sorts the elements in array a using comparator c to order them. For example, when given Comparator<String> cmp = new Comparator<String>() { @Override public int compare(String e1, String e2) { return e2.compareTo(e1); } }; String[] innerPlanets = { "Mercury", "Venus", "Earth", "Mars" };, Arrays.sort(innerPlanets, cmp); uses cmp to help in sorting innerPlanets into descending order of its elements: Venus, Mercury, Mars, Earth is the result.

There are two common algorithms for searching an array for a specific element. *Linear search* searches the array element by element from index 0 to the index of the searched-for element or the end of the array. On average, half of the elements must be searched; larger arrays take longer to search. However, the arrays don't need to be sorted.

In contrast, *binary search* searches ordered array *a*'s *n* items for element *e* in a much faster amount of time. It works by recursively performing the following steps:

1. Set low index to 0.

2. Set high index to *n* - 1.

3. If low index > high index, then Print "Unable to find " *e*. End.

4. Set middle index to (low index + high index) / 2.

5. If *e* > a[middle index], then set low index to middle index + 1. Go to 3.

6. If *e* < a[middle index], then set high index to middle index - 1. Go to 3.

7. Print "Found " *e* "at index " middle index.

The algorithm is similar to optimally looking for a name in a phone book. Start by opening the book to the exact middle. If the name is not on that page, proceed to open the book to the exact middle of the first half or the second half, depending on which half the name occurs in. Repeat until you find the name (or not).

Applying a linear search to 4,000,000,000 elements results in approximately 2,000,000,000 comparisons (on average), which takes time. In contrast, applying binary search to 4,000,000,000 elements performs a maximum of 32 comparisons. This is why `Arrays` contains `binarySearch()` methods and not also `linearSearch()` methods.

Following is a sampling of the `Collections` class's collection-oriented class methods:

- `static <T extends Object & Comparable<? super T>> T min(Collection <? extends T> c)` returns the minimum element of collection c according to the natural ordering of its elements. For example, `System.out.println(Collections.min (Arrays.asList(10, 3, 18, 25)));` outputs 3. All of c's elements must implement the `Comparable` interface. Furthermore, all elements must be mutually comparable. This method throws `NoSuchElementException` when c is empty.

- `static void reverse(List<?> l)` reverses the order of list l's elements. For example, `List<String> birds = Arrays.asList("Robin", "Oriole", "Bluejay"); Collections.reverse(birds); System.out.println(birds);` results in `[Bluejay, Oriole, Robin]` as the output.

- `static <T> List<T> singletonList(T o)` returns an immutable list containing only object o. For example, `list.removeAll(Collections.singletonList(null));` removes all null elements from `list`.

- `static <T> Set<T> synchronizedSet(Set<T> s)` returns a synchronized (thread-safe) set backed by the specified set s, for example, `Set<String> ss = Collections.synchronizedSet(new HashSet<String>());`. To guarantee serial access, it's critical that all access to the backing set (s) is accomplished through the returned set.

■ static <K,V> Map<K,V> unmodifiableMap(Map<? extends K,? extends V> m)
returns an unmodifiable view of map m, for example, Map<String, Integer>
msi = Collections.unmodifiableMap(new HashMap<String, Integer>());.
Query operations on the returned map "read through" to the specified map; and
attempts to modify the returned map, whether direct or via its collection views,
result in an UnsupportedOperationException.

Note   For performance reasons, collections implementations are unsynchronized—unsynchronized collections have better performance than synchronized collections. To use a collection in a multithreaded context, however, you need to obtain a synchronized version of that collection. You obtain that version by calling a method such as synchronizedSet().

You might be wondering about the purpose for the various "empty" class methods in the Collections class. For example, static final <T> List<T> emptyList() returns an immutable empty list, as in List<String> ls = Collections.emptyList();. These methods are present because they offer a useful alternative to returning null (and avoiding potential NullPointerExceptions) in certain contexts. Consider Listing 9-25.

Listing 9-25. Empty and Nonempty Lists of Birds

```
import java.util.ArrayList;
import java.util.Collections;
import java.util.Iterator;
import java.util.List;

class Birds
{
   private List<String> birds;

   Birds()
   {
      birds = Collections.emptyList();
   }

   Birds(String... birdNames)
   {
      birds = new ArrayList<String>();
      for (String birdName: birdNames)
         birds.add(birdName);
   }

   @Override
   public String toString()
   {
      return birds.toString();
   }
}
```

```
class EmptyListDemo
{
   public static void main(String[] args)
   {
      Birds birds = new Birds();
      System.out.println(birds);
      birds = new Birds("Swallow", "Robin", "Bluejay", "Oriole");
      System.out.println(birds);
   }
}
```

Listing 9-25 declares a Birds class that stores the names of various birds in a list. This class provides two constructors: a noargument constructor and a constructor that takes a variable number of String arguments identifying various birds.

The noargument constructor invokes emptyList() to initialize its private birds field to an empty List of String—emptyList() is a generic method and the compiler infers its return type from its context.

If you're wondering about the need for emptyList(), look at the toString() method. Notice that this method evaluates birds.toString(). If you didn't assign a reference to an empty List<String> to birds, birds would contain null (the default value for this instance field when the object is created), and a NullPointerException instance would be thrown when attempting to evaluate birds.toString().

When you run this application (java EmptyListDemo), it generates the following output:

```
[]
[Swallow, Robin, Bluejay, Oriole]
```

The emptyList() method is implemented as follows: return (List<T>) EMPTY_LIST;. This statement returns the single List instance assigned to the EMPTY_LIST class field in the Collections class.

You might want to work with EMPTY_LIST directly, but you'll run into an unchecked warning message if you do because EMPTY_LIST is declared to be of the raw type List, and mixing raw and generic types leads to such messages. Although you could suppress the warning, you're better off using the emptyList() method.

Suppose you add a void setBirds(List<String> birds) method to Birds and pass an empty list to this method, as in birds.setBirds(Collections.emptyList());. The compiler will respond with an error message stating that it requires the argument to be of type List<String>, but instead the argument is of type List<Object>. It does so because the compiler cannot figure out the proper type from this context, and so it chooses List<Object>.

There is a way to solve this problem, which will probably look very strange. Specify birds.setBirds (Collections.<String>emptyList());, where the formal type parameter list and its actual type argument appear after the member access operator and before the method name. The compiler will now know that the proper type argument is String and that emptyList() is to return List<String>.

Exploring the Legacy Collection APIs

Java 1.2 introduced the Collections Framework. Before the framework's inclusion in Java, developers had two choices where collections were concerned: create their own frameworks, or use the Vector, Enumeration, Stack, Dictionary, Hashtable, Properties, and BitSet types, which were introduced by Java 1.0.

Vector is a concrete class that describes a growable array, much like ArrayList. Unlike an ArrayList instance, a Vector instance is synchronized. Vector has been generified and also retrofitted to support the Collections Framework, which makes statements such as List<String> list = new Vector<String>(); legal.

The Collections Framework provides Iterator for iterating over a collection's elements. In contrast, Vector's elements() method returns an instance of a class that implements the Enumeration interface for *enumerating* (iterating over and returning) a Vector instance's elements via Enumeration's hasMoreElements() and nextElement() methods.

Vector is subclassed by the concrete Stack class, which represents a LIFO data structure. Stack provides an E push(E item) method for pushing an object onto the stack, an E pop() method for popping an item off the top of the stack, and a few other methods, such as boolean empty() for determining whether or not the stack is empty.

Stack is a good example of bad API design. By inheriting from Vector, it's possible to call Vector's void add(int index, E element) method to add an element anywhere you wish and violate a Stack instance's integrity. In hindsight, Stack should have used composition in its design: use a Vector instance to store a Stack instance's elements.

Dictionary is an abstract superclass for subclasses that map keys to values. The concrete Hashtable class is Dictionary's only subclass. As with Vector, HashTable instances are synchronized, HashTable has been generified, and HashTable has been retrofitted to support the Collections Framework.

Hashtable is subclassed by Properties, a concrete class representing a persistent set of *properties* (String-based key/value pairs that identify application settings). Properties provides Object setProperty(String key, String value) for storing a property and String getProperty(String key) for returning a property's value.

> **Note**   Applications use properties for various purposes. For example, if your application has a graphical user interface, you could store the screen location and size of its main window in a file via a Properties object so that the application can restore the window's location and size when it next runs.

Properties is another good example of bad API design. By inheriting from Hashtable, you can call Hashtable's V put(K key, V value) method to store an entry with a non-String key and/or a non-String value. In hindsight, Properties should have leveraged composition: store a Properties instance's elements in a Hashtable instance.

Note   In Chapter 4 I discussed wrapper classes, which is how `Stack` and `Properties` should have been implemented.

Finally, `BitSet` is a concrete class that describes a variable-length set of bits. This class's ability to represent bitsets of arbitrary length contrasts with the previously described integer-based, fixed-length bitset that is limited to a maximum number of members: 32 members for an `int`-based bitset or 64 members for a `long`-based bitset.

`BitSet` provides a pair of constructors for initializing a `BitSet` instance: `BitSet()` initializes the instance to initially store an implementation-dependent number of bits, whereas `BitSet(int nbits)` initializes the instance to initially store `nbits` bits. `BitSet` also provides various methods, including the following:

- `void and(BitSet bs)` bitwise ANDs this bitset with `bs`. This bitset is modified such that a bit is set to 1 when it and the bit at the same position in `bs` are 1.

- `void andNot(BitSet bs)` sets all of the bits in this bitset to 0 whose corresponding bits are set to 1 in `bs`.

- `void clear()` sets all of the bits in this bitset to 0.

- `Object clone()` clones this bitset to produce a new bitset. The clone has exactly the same bits set to one as this bitset.

- `boolean get(int bitIndex)` returns the value of this bitset's bit as a Boolean true/false value (true for 1, false for 0) at the zero-based `bitIndex`. This method throws `IndexOutOfBoundsException` when `bitIndex` is less than 0.

- `int length()` returns the "logical size" of this bitset, which is the index of the highest 1 bit plus 1, or 0 if this bitset contains no 1 bits.

- `void or(BitSet bs)` bitwise inclusive ORs this bitset with `bs`. This bitset is modified such that a bit is set to 1 when it or the bit at the same position in `bs` is 1 or when both bits are 1.

- `void set(int bitIndex, boolean value)` sets the bit at the zero-based `bitIndex` to `value` (true is converted to 1; false is converted to 0). This method throws `IndexOutOfBoundsException` when `bitIndex` is less than 0.

- `int size()` returns the number of bits that are being used by this bitset to represent bit values.

- `String toString()` returns a string representation of this bitset in terms of the positions of bits that are 1, for example, `{4, 5, 9, 10}`.

- `void xor(BitSet set)` bitwise exclusive ORs this bitset with `bs`. This bitset is modified such that a bit is set to 1 when either it or the bit at the same position in `bs` (but not both) is 1.

Listing 9-26 presents an application that demonstrates some of these methods and gives you more insight into how the bitwise AND (&), bitwise inclusive OR (|), and bitwise exclusive OR (^) operators work.

Listing 9-26. Working with Variable-Length Bitsets

```java
import java.util.BitSet;

public class BitSetDemo
{
   public static void main(String[] args)
   {
      BitSet bs1 = new BitSet();
      bs1.set(4, true);
      bs1.set(5, true);
      bs1.set(9, true);
      bs1.set(10, true);
      BitSet bsTemp = (BitSet) bs1.clone();
      dumpBitset("         ", bs1);
      BitSet bs2 = new BitSet();
      bs2.set(4, true);
      bs2.set(6, true);
      bs2.set(7, true);
      bs2.set(9, true);
      dumpBitset("         ", bs2);
      bs1.and(bs2);
      dumpSeparator(Math.min(bs1.size(), 16));
      dumpBitset("AND (&) ", bs1);
      System.out.println();
      bs1 = bsTemp;
      dumpBitset("         ", bs1);
      dumpBitset("         ", bs2);
      bsTemp = (BitSet) bs1.clone();
      bs1.or(bs2);
      dumpSeparator(Math.min(bs1.size(), 16));
      dumpBitset("OR (|)  ", bs1);
      System.out.println();
      bs1 = bsTemp;
      dumpBitset("         ", bs1);
      dumpBitset("         ", bs2);
      bsTemp = (BitSet) bs1.clone();
      bs1.xor(bs2);
      dumpSeparator(Math.min(bs1.size(), 16));
      dumpBitset("XOR (^) ", bs1);
   }

   static void dumpBitset(String preamble, BitSet bs)
   {
      System.out.print(preamble);
      int size = Math.min(bs.size(), 16);
      for (int i = 0; i < size; i++)
         System.out.print(bs.get(i) ? "1" : "0");
      System.out.print("  size(" + bs.size() + "), length(" + bs.length() + ")");
      System.out.println();
   }
```

```
    static void dumpSeparator(int len)
    {
       System.out.print("           ");
       for (int i = 0; i < len; i++)
          System.out.print("-");
       System.out.println();
    }
}
```

Why did I specify `Math.min(bs.size(), 16)` in `dumpBitset()` and pass a similar expression to `dumpSeparator()`? I wanted to display exactly 16 bits and 16 dashes (for aesthetics) and needed to account for a bitset's size being less than 16. Although this doesn't happen with Oracle's and Google's `BitSet` classes, it might happen with some other variant.

When you run this application, it generates the following output:

```
         0000110001100000  size(64), length(11)
         0000101101000000  size(64), length(10)
         ----------------
AND (&)  0000100001000000  size(64), length(10)

         0000110001100000  size(64), length(11)
         0000101101000000  size(64), length(10)
         ----------------
OR (|)   0000111101100000  size(64), length(11)

         0000110001100000  size(64), length(11)
         0000101101000000  size(64), length(10)
         ----------------
XOR (^)  0000011100100000  size(64), length(11)
```

> **Caution** Unlike `Vector` and `Hashtable`, `BitSet` is not synchronized. You must externally synchronize access to this class when using `BitSet` in a multithreaded context.

The Collections Framework has made `Vector`, `Enumeration`, `Stack`, `Dictionary`, and `Hashtable` obsolete. These types continue to be part of the standard class library to support legacy code. Also, the Preferences API has made `Properties` largely obsolete. Because `BitSet` is still relevant, this class continues to be improved (as recently as Java 7).

Note   It's not surprising that `BitSet` is being improved when you realize the usefulness of variable-length bitsets. Because of their compactness and other advantages, variable-length bitsets are often used to implement an operating system's priority queues and facilitate memory page allocation. Unix-oriented file systems also use bitsets to facilitate the allocation of *inodes* (information nodes) and disk sectors. And bitsets are useful in *Huffman coding*, a data-compression algorithm for achieving lossless data compression.

EXERCISES

The following exercises are designed to test your understanding of Chapter 9's content:

1. What is a collection?

2. What is the Collections Framework?

3. The Collections Framework largely consists of what components?

4. Define comparable.

5. When would you have a class implement the `Comparable` interface?

6. What is a comparator and what is its purpose?

7. True or false: A collection uses a comparator to define the natural ordering of its elements.

8. What does the `Iterable` interface describe?

9. What does the `Collection` interface represent?

10. Identify a situation where `Collection`'s `add()` method would throw an instance of the `UnsupportedOperationException` class.

11. `Iterable`'s `iterator()` method returns an instance of a class that implements the `Iterator` interface. What methods does this interface provide?

12. What is the purpose of the enhanced for loop statement?

13. How is the enhanced for loop statement expressed?

14. True or false: The enhanced for loop works with arrays.

15. Define autoboxing.

16. Define unboxing.

17. What is a list?

18. What does a `ListIterator` instance use to navigate through a list?

19. What is a view?

20. Why would you use the `subList()` method?

21. What does the `ArrayList` class provide?

22. What does the `LinkedList` class provide?

23. Define node.

24. True or false: `ArrayList` provides faster element insertions and deletions than `LinkedList`.

25. What is a set?

26. What does the `TreeSet` class provide?

27. What does the `HashSet` class provide?

28. True or false: To avoid duplicate elements in a hashset, your own classes must correctly override `equals()` and `hashCode()`.

29. What is the difference between `HashSet` and `LinkedHashSet`?

30. What does the `EnumSet` class provide?

31. Define sorted set.

32. What is a navigable set?

33. True or false: `HashSet` is an example of a sorted set.

34. Why would a sorted set's `add()` method throw `ClassCastException` when you attempt to add an element to the sorted set?

35. What is a queue?

36. True or false: Queue's `element()` method throws `NoSuchElementException` when it is called on an empty queue.

37. What does the `PriorityQueue` class provide?

38. What is a map?

39. What does the `TreeMap` class provide?

40. What does the `HashMap` class provide?

41. What does a hashtable use to map keys to integer values?

42. Continuing from the previous question, what are the resulting integer values called and what do they accomplish?

43. What is a hashtable's capacity?

44. What is a hashtable's load factor?

45. What is the difference between `HashMap` and `LinkedHashMap`?

46. What does the `IdentityHashMap` class provide?

47. What does the `EnumMap` class provide?

48. Define sorted map.

49. What is a navigable map?

50. True or false: TreeMap is an example of a sorted map.

51. What is the purpose of the Arrays class's static <T> List<T> asList(T... array) method?

52. True or false: Binary search is slower than linear search.

53. Which Collections method would you use to return a synchronized variation of a hashset?

54. Identify the seven legacy collections-oriented types.

55. As an example of array list usefulness, create a JavaQuiz application that presents a multiple-choice-based quiz on Java features. The JavaQuiz class's main() method first populates the array list with the entries in a QuizEntry array (e.g., new QuizEntry("What was Java's original name?", new String[] { "Oak", "Duke", "J", "None of the above" }, 'A')). Each entry consists of a question, four possible answers, and the letter (A, B, C, or D) of the correct answer. main() then uses the array list's iterator() method to return an Iterator instance and this instance's hasNext() and next() methods to iterate over the list. Each of the iterations outputs the question and four possible answers and then prompts the user to enter the correct choice. After the user enters A, B, C, or D (via System.in.read()), main() outputs a message stating whether or not the user made the correct choice.

56. Why is (int) (f ^ (f >>> 32)) used instead of (int) (f ^ (f >> 32)) in the hash code generation algorithm?

57. Collections provides the static int frequency(Collection<?> c, Object o) method to return the number of collection c elements that are equal to o. Create a FrequencyDemo application that reads its command-line arguments and stores all arguments except for the last argument in a list and then calls frequency() with the list and last command-line argument as this method's arguments. It then outputs this method's return value (the number of occurrences of the last command-line argument in the previous command-line arguments). For example, java FrequencyDemo should output Number of occurrences of null = 0, and java FrequencyDemo how much wood could a woodchuck chuck if a woodchuck could chuck wood wood should output Number of occurrences of wood = 2.

Summary

A collection is a group of objects that are stored in an instance of a class designed for this purpose. To save you from having to create your own collections classes, Java provides the Collections Framework for representing and manipulating collections.

The Collections Framework largely consists of core interfaces, implementation classes, and the Arrays and Collections utility classes. The core interfaces make it possible to manipulate collections independently of their implementations.

Core interfaces include Iterable, Collection, List, Set, SortedSet, NavigableSet, Queue, Deque, Map, SortedMap, and NavigableMap. Collection extends Iterable; List, Set, and Queue each extend Collection; SortedSet extends Set; NavigableSet extends SortedSet; Deque extends Queue; SortedMap extends Map; and NavigableMap extends SortedMap.

Implementation classes include ArrayList, LinkedList, TreeSet, HashSet, LinkedHashSet, EnumSet, PriorityQueue, ArrayDeque, TreeMap, HashMap, LinkedHashMap, IdentityHashMap, WeakHashMap, and EnumMap. The name of each concrete class ends in a core interface name, identifying the core interface on which it is based.

The Collections Framework would not be complete without its Arrays and Collections utility classes. Each class supplies various class methods that implement useful algorithms in the contexts of arrays and collections. For example, Arrays lets you efficiently search and sort arrays, and Collections lets you obtain synchronized and unmodifiable collections.

Before Java 1.2's introduction of the Collections Framework, developers could create their own frameworks or use the Vector, Enumeration, Stack, Dictionary, Hashtable, Properties, and BitSet types, which were introduced by Java 1.0.

The Collections Framework has made Vector, Enumeration, Stack, Dictionary, and Hashtable obsolete. Also, the Preferences API has made Properties largely obsolete. Because BitSet is still relevant, this class continues to be improved.

In Chapter 10 I continue to explore the utility APIs by focusing on the Concurrency Utilities, the Date class, the Formatter class, the Random class, the Scanner class, and more.

Exploring Additional Utility APIs

In Chapter 10 I continue to explore Java's utility APIs by introducing Concurrency Utilities, the Date class (for representing time), the Formatter class (for formatting data items), the Random class (for generating random numbers), the Scanner class (for parsing an input stream of characters into integers, strings, and other values), and the APIs for working with ZIP and JAR files.

Exploring the Concurrency Utilities

Java 5 introduced *Concurrency Utilities* whose classes and interfaces simplify the development of *concurrent* (multithreaded) applications, and which were extended by Java 6. These types are located in the java.util.concurrent package and in its java.util.concurrent.atomic and java.util.concurrent.locks subpackages.

> **Note** Android supports all of the Java 5 and Java 6 concurrency types. It doesn't support Java 7 additions at the time of writing.

These utilities leverage the low-level Threads API (see Chapter 8) in their implementations and provide higher-level building blocks (such as locking idioms) to make it easier to create multithreaded applications. They are organized into executor, synchronizer, concurrent collection, lock, and atomic variable categories.

Executors

In Chapter 8 I introduced the Threads API, which lets you execute runnable tasks via expressions such as new java.lang.Thread(new RunnableTask()).start();. These expressions tightly couple task submission with the task's execution mechanics (run on the current thread, a new thread, or a thread arbitrarily chosen from a *pool* [group] of threads).

> **Note**   A *task* is an object whose class implements the `java.lang.Runnable` interface (a runnable task) or the `java.util.concurrent.Callable` interface (a callable task).

The concurrency-oriented utilities provide executors as a high-level alternative to low-level Threads API expressions for executing runnable tasks. An *executor* is an object whose class directly or indirectly implements the `java.util.concurrent.Executor` interface, which decouples task submission from task-execution mechanics.

> **Note**   The executor framework's use of interfaces to decouple task submission from task-execution mechanics is analogous to the Collections Framework's use of core interfaces to decouple lists, sets, queues, and maps from their implementations. Decoupling results in flexible code that is easier to maintain.

`Executor` declares a solitary void `execute(Runnable runnable)` method that executes the runnable task named `runnable` at some point in the future. `execute()` throws `java.lang.NullPointerException` when `runnable` is `null` and `java.util.concurrent.RejectedExecutionException` when it cannot execute `runnable`.

> **Note**   `RejectedExecutionException` can be thrown when an executor is shutting down and doesn't want to accept new tasks. Also, this exception can be thrown when the executor doesn't have enough room to store the task (perhaps the executor uses a bounded blocking queue to store tasks and the queue is full—I discuss blocking queues later in this chapter).

The following example presents the `Executor` equivalent of the aforementioned new `Thread` (new `RunnableTask()).start();` expression:

```
Executor executor = ...; //  ... represents some executor creation
executor.execute(new RunnableTask());
```

Although `Executor` is easy to use, this interface is limited in various ways:

- `Executor` focuses exclusively on `Runnable`. Because `Runnable`'s `run()` method doesn't return a value, there is no convenient way for a runnable task to return a value to its caller.

- `Executor` doesn't provide a way to track the progress of executing runnable tasks, cancel an executing runnable task, or determine when the runnable task finishes execution.

- Executor cannot execute a collection of runnable tasks.

- Executor doesn't provide a way for an application to shut down an executor (much less to properly shut down an executor).

These limitations are addressed by the `java.util.concurrent.ExecutorService` interface, which extends Executor and whose implementation is typically a thread pool. Table 10-1 describes ExecutorService's methods.

Table 10-1. ExecutorService Methods

Method	Description
`boolean awaitTermination` `(long timeout,` `TimeUnit unit)`	Block (wait) until all tasks have finished after a shutdown request, the timeout (measured in unit time units) expires, or the current thread is interrupted, whichever happens first. Return true when this executor has terminated and false when the timeout elapses before termination. This method throws `java.lang.InterruptedException` when interrupted.
`<T> List<Future<T>>` `invokeAll(Collection<?` `extends Callable<T>> tasks)`	Execute each callable task in the tasks collection and return a `java.util.List` of `java.util.concurrent.Future` instances that hold task statuses and results when all tasks complete—a task completes through normal termination or by throwing an exception. The List of Futures is in the same sequential order as the sequence of tasks returned by tasks' iterator. This method throws `InterruptedException` when it is interrupted while waiting, in which case unfinished tasks are canceled; `NullPointerException` when tasks or any of its elements is null; and `RejectedExecutionException` when any one of tasks' tasks cannot be scheduled for execution.
`<T> List<Future<T>>` `invokeAll(Collection<?` `extends Callable<T>> tasks,` `long timeout,` `TimeUnit unit)`	Execute each callable task in the tasks collection and return a `List` of `Future` instances that hold task statuses and results when all tasks complete—a task completes through normal termination or by throwing an exception—or the timeout (measured in unit time units) expires. Tasks that are not completed at expiry are canceled. The List of Futures is in the same sequential order as the sequence of tasks returned by tasks' iterator. This method throws `InterruptedException` when it is interrupted while waiting, in which case unfinished tasks are canceled. It also throws `NullPointerException` when tasks, any of its elements, or unit is null; and throws `RejectedExecutionException` when any one of tasks' tasks cannot be scheduled for execution.

(continued)

Table 10-1. (*continued*)

Method	Description
`<T> T invokeAny(Collection< ? extends Callable<T>> tasks)`	Execute the given `tasks`, returning the result of an arbitrary task that has completed successfully (i.e., without throwing an exception), if any does. On normal or exceptional return, tasks that have not completed are canceled. This method throws `InterruptedException` when it is interrupted while waiting, `NullPointerException` when `tasks` or any of its elements is null, `java.lang.IllegalArgumentException` when `tasks` is empty, `java.util.concurrent.ExecutionException` when no task completes successfully, and `RejectedExecutionException` when none of the tasks can be scheduled for execution.
`<T> T invokeAny(Collection<? extends Callable<T>> tasks, long timeout, TimeUnit unit)`	Execute the given `tasks`, returning the result of an arbitrary task that has completed successfully (i.e., without throwing an exception), if any does before the `timeout` (measured in unit time units) expires—tasks that are not completed at expiry are canceled. On normal or exceptional return, tasks that have not completed are canceled. This method throws `InterruptedException` when it is interrupted while waiting; `NullPointerException` when `tasks`, any of its elements, or unit is null; `IllegalArgumentException` when `tasks` is empty; `java.util.concurrent. TimeoutException` when the `timeout` elapses before any task successfully completes; `ExecutionException` when no task completes successfully; and `RejectedExecutionException` when none of the tasks can be scheduled for execution.
`boolean isShutdown()`	Return true when this executor has been shut down; otherwise, return false.
`boolean isTerminated()`	Return true when all tasks have completed following shutdown; otherwise, return false. This method will never return true prior to `shutdown()` or `shutdownNow()` being called.
`void shutdown()`	Initiate an orderly shutdown in which previously submitted tasks are executed, but no new tasks will be accepted. Calling this method has no effect after the executor has shut down. This method doesn't wait for previously submitted tasks to complete execution. Use `awaitTermination()` when waiting is necessary.
`List<Runnable> shutdownNow()`	Attempt to stop all actively executing tasks, halt the processing of waiting tasks, and return a list of the tasks that were awaiting execution. There are no guarantees beyond best-effort attempts to stop processing actively executing tasks. For example, typical implementations will cancel via `Thread.interrupt()`, so any task that fails to respond to interrupts may never terminate.

(*continued*)

Table 10-1. (*continued*)

Method	Description
`<T> Future<T> submit(Callable<T> task)`	Submit a callable task for execution and return a Future instance representing task's pending results. The Future instance's get() method returns task's result on successful completion. This method throws RejectedExecutionException when task cannot be scheduled for execution and NullPointerException when task is null. If you would like to immediately block while waiting for a task to complete, you can use constructions of the form result = exec.submit(aCallable).get();.
`Future<?> submit(Runnable task)`	Submit a runnable task for execution and return a Future instance representing task's pending results. The Future instance's get() method returns task's result on successful completion. This method throws RejectedExecutionException when task cannot be scheduled for execution and NullPointerException when task is null.
`<T> Future<T> submit(Runnable task, T result)`	Submit a runnable task for execution and return a Future instance whose get() method returns result on successful completion. This method throws RejectedExecutionException when task cannot be scheduled for execution and NullPointerException when task is null.

Table 10-1 refers to `java.util.concurrent.TimeUnit`, an enum that represents time durations at given units of granularity: DAYS, HOURS, MICROSECONDS, MILLISECONDS, MINUTES, NANOSECONDS, and SECONDS. Furthermore, `TimeUnit` declares methods for converting across units (e.g., `long toHours(long duration)`) and for performing timing and delay operations (e.g., `void sleep (long timeout)`) in these units.

Table 10-1 also refers to callable tasks, which are analogous to runnable tasks. Unlike Runnable, whose `void run()` method cannot throw checked exceptions, `Callable<V>` declares a `V call()` method that returns a value and which can throw checked exceptions because `call()` is declared with a `throws Exception` clause.

Finally, Table 10-1 refers to the `Future` interface, which represents the result of an asynchronous computation. `Future`, whose generic type is `Future<V>`, provides methods for canceling a task, for returning a task's value, and for determining whether or not the task has finished. Table 10-2 describes `Future`'s methods.

Table 10-2. Future Methods

Method	Description
`boolean cancel(boolean mayInterruptIfRunning)`	Attempt to cancel execution of this task and return true when the task was canceled; otherwise, return false (perhaps the task completed normally before this method was called).
	The cancellation attempt fails when the task has completed, has already been canceled, or could not be canceled for some other reason. If successful and this task had not started when `cancel()` was called, the task should never run. If the task has already started, then `mayInterruptIfRunning` determines whether (true) or not (false) the thread executing this task should be interrupted in an attempt to stop the task. After this method returns, subsequent calls to `isDone()` always return true. Subsequent calls to `isCancelled()` always return true when `cancel()` returns true.
`V get()`	Wait if necessary for the task to complete and then return the result. This method throws `java.util.concurrent.CancellationException` when the task was canceled prior to this method being called, `ExecutionException` when the task threw an exception, and `InterruptedException` when the current thread was interrupted while waiting.
`V get(long timeout, TimeUnit unit)`	Wait at most `timeout` units (as specified by `unit`) for the task to complete and then return the result (if available). This method throws `CancellationException` when the task was canceled prior to this method being called, `ExecutionException` when the task threw an exception, `InterruptedException` when the current thread was interrupted while waiting, and `TimeoutException` when this method's timeout value expires (the wait times out).
`boolean isCancelled()`	Return true when this task was canceled before it completed normally; otherwise, return false.
`boolean isDone()`	Return true when this task completed; otherwise, return false. Completion may be due to normal termination, an exception, or cancellation—this method returns true in all of these cases.

Suppose you intend to write an application whose graphical user interface lets the user enter a word. After the user enters the word, the application presents this word to several online dictionaries and obtains each dictionary's entry. These entries are subsequently displayed to the user.

Because online access can be slow, and because the user interface should remain responsive (perhaps the user might want to end the application), you offload the "obtain word entries" task to an executor that runs this task on a separate thread. The following example uses `ExecutorService`, `Callable`, and `Future` to accomplish this objective:

```
ExecutorService executor = ...; //  ... represents some executor creation
Future<String[]> taskFuture = executor.submit(new Callable<String[]>()
```

```
                                               {
                                                   @Override
                                                   public String[] call()
                                                   {
                                                       String[] entries = ...;
                                                       // Access online dictionaries
                                                       // with search word and populate
                                                       // entries with their resulting
                                                       // entries.
                                                       return entries;
                                                   }
                                               });
// Do stuff.
String entries = taskFuture.get();
```

After obtaining an executor in some manner (you will learn how shortly), the example's main thread submits a callable task to the executor. The `submit()` method immediately returns with a reference to a `Future` object for controlling task execution and accessing results. The main thread ultimately calls this object's `get()` method to get these results.

> **Note**   The `java.util.concurrent.ScheduledExecutorService` interface extends
> `ExecutorService` and describes an executor that lets you schedule tasks to run once or to execute
> periodically after a given delay.

Although you could create your own `Executor`, `ExecutorService`, and `ScheduledExecutorService` implementations (such as `class DirectExecutor implements Executor { @Override public void execute(Runnable r) { r.run(); } }`—run executor directly on the calling thread), there is a simpler alternative: `java.util.concurrent.Executors`.

> **Tip**   If you intend to create your own `ExecutorService` implementations, you will find it helpful to work
> with the `java.util.concurrent.AbstractExecutorService` and
> `java.util.concurrent.FutureTask` classes.

The `Executors` utility class declares several class methods that return instances of various `ExecutorService` and `ScheduledExecutorService` implementations (and other kinds of instances). This class's `static` methods accomplish the following tasks:

- Create and return an `ExecutorService` instance that is configured with commonly used configuration settings.

- Create and return a `ScheduledExecutorService` instance that is configured with commonly used configuration settings.

- Create and return a "wrapped" ExecutorService or ScheduledExecutorService instance that disables reconfiguration of the executor service by making implementation-specific methods inaccessible.

- Create and return a java.util.concurrent.ThreadFactory instance (i.e., an instance of a class that implements the ThreadFactory interface) for creating new threads.

- Create and return a Callable instance out of other closure-like forms so that it can be used in execution methods that require Callable arguments (e.g., ExecutorService's submit(Callable) method). (Check out Wikipedia's "Closure (computer science)" entry [http://en.wikipedia.org/wiki/Closure_(computer_science)] to learn about closures.)

For example, static ExecutorService newFixedThreadPool(int nThreads) creates a thread pool that reuses a fixed number of threads operating off of a shared unbounded queue. At most, nThreads threads are actively processing tasks. If additional tasks are submitted when all threads are active, they wait in the queue for an available thread.

If any thread terminates because of a failure during execution before the executor shuts down, a new thread will take its place when needed to execute subsequent tasks. The threads in the pool will exist until the executor is explicitly shut down. This method throws IllegalArgumentException when you pass zero or a negative value to nThreads.

> **Note**   Thread pools are used to eliminate the overhead from having to create a new thread for each submitted task. Thread creation is not cheap, and having to create many threads could severely impact an application's performance.

You would commonly use executors, runnables, callables, and futures in file and network input/output contexts. Performing a lengthy calculation offers another scenario where you could use these types. For example, Listing 10-1 uses an executor, a callable, and a future in a calculation context of Euler's number e (2.71828...).

Listing 10-1. Calculating Euler's Number e

```
import java.math.BigDecimal;
import java.math.MathContext;
import java.math.RoundingMode;

import java.util.concurrent.Callable;
import java.util.concurrent.ExecutionException;
import java.util.concurrent.ExecutorService;
import java.util.concurrent.Executors;
import java.util.concurrent.Future;

public class CalculateE
{
   final static int LASTITER = 17;
```

```java
public static void main(String[] args)
{
    ExecutorService executor = Executors.newFixedThreadPool(1);
    Callable<BigDecimal> callable;
    callable = new Callable<BigDecimal>()
                {
                    @Override
                    public BigDecimal call()
                    {
                        MathContext mc = new MathContext(100,
                                                    RoundingMode.HALF_UP);
                        BigDecimal result = BigDecimal.ZERO;
                        for (int i = 0; i <= LASTITER; i++)
                        {
                            BigDecimal factorial = factorial(new BigDecimal (i));
                            BigDecimal res = BigDecimal.ONE.divide(factorial, mc);
                            result = result.add(res);
                        }
                        return result;
                    }

                    public BigDecimal factorial(BigDecimal n)
                    {
                        if (n.equals(BigDecimal.ZERO))
                            return BigDecimal.ONE;
                        else
                            return n.multiply(factorial(n.subtract(BigDecimal.ONE)));
                    }
                };
    Future<BigDecimal> taskFuture = executor.submit(callable);
    try
    {
        while (!taskFuture.isDone())
            System.out.println("waiting");
        System.out.println(taskFuture.get());
    }
    catch(ExecutionException ee)
    {
        System.err.println("task threw an exception");
        System.err.println(ee);
    }
    catch(InterruptedException ie)
    {
        System.err.println("interrupted while waiting");
    }
    executor.shutdownNow();
}
}
```

The main thread that executes Listing 10-1's main() method first obtains an executor by calling Executors' newFixedThreadPool() method. It then instantiates an anonymous class that implements the Callable interface and submits this task to the executor, receiving a Future instance in response.

After submitting a task, a thread typically does some other work until it requires the task's result. I've chosen to simulate this work by having the main thread repeatedly output a waiting message until the `Future` instance's `isDone()` method returns true. (In a realistic application, I would avoid this looping.) At this point, the main thread calls the instance's `get()` method to obtain the result, which is then output.

> **Caution**   It's important to shut down the executor after it completes; otherwise, the application might not end. The executor accomplishes this task by calling `shutdownNow()`.

The callable's `call()` method calculates e by evaluating the mathematical power series e = 1 / 0! + 1 / 1! + 1 / 2! + …. This series can be evaluated by summing 1 / n!, where n ranges from 0 to infinity.

`call()` first instantiates `java.math.MathContext` to encapsulate a *precision* (number of digits) and a rounding mode. I chose 100 as an upper limit on e's precision, and I also chose `HALF_UP` as the rounding mode.

> **Tip**   Increase the precision as well as `LASTITER`'s value to converge the series to a lengthier and more accurate approximation of e.

`call()` next initializes a `java.math.BigDecimal` local variable named `result` to `BigDecimal.ZERO`. It then enters a loop that calculates a factorial, divides `BigDecimal.ONE` by the factorial, and adds the division result to `result`.

The `divide()` method takes the `MathContext` instance as its second argument to ensure that the division doesn't result in a *nonterminating decimal expansion* (the quotient result of the division cannot be represented exactly—0.3333333…, for example), which throws `java.lang.ArithmeticException` (to alert the caller to the fact that the quotient cannot be represented exactly), which the executor rethrows as `ExecutionException`.

When you run this application, you should observe output similar to the following:

```
waiting
waiting
waiting
waiting
waiting
2.718281828459045070516047795848605061178979635251032698900735004065225042504843314055887974344245
741730039454062711
```

Synchronizers

The Threads API offers synchronization primitives for synchronizing thread access to critical sections. Because it can be difficult to correctly write synchronized code that is based on these primitives, the concurrency-oriented utilities includes *synchronizers*, classes that facilitate common forms of synchronization.

Four commonly used synchronizers are countdown latches, cyclic barriers, exchangers, and semaphores:

- A *countdown latch* lets one or more threads wait at a "gate" until another thread opens this gate, at which point these other threads can continue. The java.util.concurrent.CountDownLatch class implements this synchronizer.

- A *cyclic barrier* lets a group of threads wait for each other to reach a common *barrier point*. The java.util.concurrent.CyclicBarrier class implements this synchronizer and makes use of the java.util.concurrent.BrokenBarrierException class. CyclicBarrier instances are useful in applications involving fixed size parties of threads that must occasionally wait for each other. CyclicBarrier supports an optional Runnable known as a *barrier action*, which runs once per barrier point after the last thread in the party arrives but before any threads are released. This barrier action is useful for updating shared state before any of the parties continue.

- An *exchanger* lets a pair of threads exchange objects at a synchronization point. The java.util.concurrent.Exchanger class implements this synchronizer. Each thread presents some object on entry to Exchanger's exchange() method, matches with a partner thread, and receives its partner's object on return. Exchangers may be useful in applications such as *genetic algorithms* (see http://en.wikipedia.org/wiki/Genetic_algorithm) and pipeline designs.

- A *semaphore* maintains a set of permits for restricting the number of threads that can access a limited resource. The java.util.concurrent.Semaphore class implements this synchronizer. Each call to one of Semaphore's acquire() methods blocks if necessary until a permit is available and then takes it. Each call to release() returns a permit, potentially releasing a blocking acquirer. However, no actual permit objects are used; the Semaphore instance only keeps a count of the number of available permits and acts accordingly. Semaphores are often used to restrict the number of threads that can access some (physical or logical) resource.

Consider the CountDownLatch class. Each of its instances is initialized to a nonzero count. A thread calls one of CountDownLatch's await() methods to block until the count reaches zero. Another thread calls CountDownLatch's countDown() method to decrement the count. Once the count reaches zero, the waiting threads are allowed to continue.

> **Note**   After waiting threads are released, subsequent calls to await() return immediately. Also, because the count cannot be reset, a CountDownLatch instance can be used only once. When repeated use is a requirement, use the CyclicBarrier class instead.

You can use CountDownLatch to ensure that threads start working at approximately the same time. For example, check out Listing 10-2.

Listing 10-2. Using a Countdown Latch to Trigger a Coordinated Start

```java
import java.util.concurrent.CountDownLatch;
import java.util.concurrent.ExecutorService;
import java.util.concurrent.Executors;

public class CountDownLatchDemo
{
   final static int NTHREADS = 3;

   public static void main(String[] args)
   {
      final CountDownLatch startSignal = new CountDownLatch(1);
      final CountDownLatch doneSignal = new CountDownLatch(NTHREADS);
      Runnable r = new Runnable()
                  {
                     @Override
                     public void run()
                     {
                        try
                        {
                           report("entered run()");
                           startSignal.await(); // wait until told to proceed
                           report("doing work");
                           Thread.sleep((int) (Math.random() * 1000));
                           doneSignal.countDown(); // reduce count on which
                                                   // main thread is waiting
                        }
                        catch (InterruptedException ie)
                        {
                           System.err.println(ie);
                        }
                     }

                     void report(String s)
                     {
                        System.out.println(System.currentTimeMillis() + ": " +
                                          Thread.currentThread() + ": " + s);
                     }
                  };
```

```
ExecutorService executor = Executors.newFixedThreadPool(NTHREADS);
for (int i = 0; i < NTHREADS; i++)
   executor.execute(r);
try
{
   System.out.println("main thread doing something");
   Thread.sleep(1000); // sleep for 1 second
   startSignal.countDown(); // let all threads proceed
   System.out.println("main thread doing something else");
   doneSignal.await(); // wait for all threads to finish
   executor.shutdownNow();
}
catch (InterruptedException ie)
{
   System.err.println(ie);
}
   }
}
```

Listing 10-2's main thread first creates a pair of countdown latches. The startSignal countdown latch prevents any worker thread from proceeding until the main thread is ready for them to proceed. The doneSignal countdown latch causes the main thread to wait until all worker threads have finished.

The main thread next creates a runnable whose run() method is executed by subsequently created worker threads.

The run() method first outputs an initial message and then calls startSignal's await() method to wait for this countdown latch's count to read zero before it can proceed. Once this happens, run() outputs a message that indicates work being done and sleeps for a random period of time (0 through 999 milliseconds) to simulate this work.

At this point, run() invokes doneSignal's countDown() method to decrement this latch's count. Once this count reaches zero, the main thread waiting on this signal will continue, shutting down the executor and terminating the application.

After creating the runnable, the main thread obtains an executor that's based on a thread pool of NTHREADS threads and then calls the executor's execute() method NTHREADS times, passing the runnable to each of the NTHREADS pool-based threads. This action starts the worker threads, which enter run().

Next, the main thread outputs a message and sleeps for one second to simulate doing additional work (giving all the worker threads a chance to have entered run() and invoke startSignal.await()), invokes startSignal's countDown() method to cause the worker threads to start running, outputs a message to indicate that it is doing something else, and invokes doneSignal's await() method to wait for this countdown latch's count to reach zero before it can proceed.

When you run this application, you will observe output similar to the following:

```
main thread doing something
1353265795934: Thread[pool-1-thread-3,5,main]: entered run()
1353265795934: Thread[pool-1-thread-2,5,main]: entered run()
1353265795934: Thread[pool-1-thread-1,5,main]: entered run()
```

```
main thread doing something else
1353265796948: Thread[pool-1-thread-1,5,main]: doing work
1353265796948: Thread[pool-1-thread-2,5,main]: doing work
1353265796948: Thread[pool-1-thread-3,5,main]: doing work
```

> **Note**   For brevity, I've avoided examples that demonstrate CyclicBarrier, Exchanger, and Semaphore.
> Instead, I refer you to Java documentation for these classes. Each class's documentation provides
> an example that shows you how to use the class.

Concurrent Collections

The java.util.concurrent package includes several interfaces and classes that are concurrency-oriented extensions to the Collections Framework (see Chapter 9):

- BlockingDeque is a subinterface of BlockingQueue and java.util.Deque that also supports blocking operations that wait for the deque to become nonempty before retrieving an element and wait for space to become available in the deque before storing an element. The LinkedBlockingDeque class implements this interface.

- BlockingQueue is a subinterface of java.util.Queue that also supports blocking operations that wait for the queue to become nonempty before retrieving an element and wait for space to become available in the queue before storing an element. Each of the ArrayBlockingQueue, DelayQueue, LinkedBlockingDeque, LinkedBlockingQueue, PriorityBlockingQueue, and SynchronousQueue classes implements this interface.

- ConcurrentMap is a subinterface of java.util.Map that declares additional atomic putIfAbsent(), remove(), and replace() methods. The ConcurrentHashMap class (the concurrent equivalent of java.util.HashMap) and the ConcurrentSkipListMap class implement this interface.

- ConcurrentNavigableMap is a subinterface of ConcurrentMap and java.util. NavigableMap. The ConcurrentSkipListMap class implements this interface.

- ConcurrentLinkedQueue is an unbounded, thread-safe FIFO implementation of the Queue interface.

- ConcurrentSkipListSet is a scalable concurrent NavigableSet implementation.

- CopyOnWriteArrayList is a thread-safe variant of java.util.ArrayList in which all *mutative* (nonimmutable) operations (add, set, and so on) are implemented by making a fresh copy of the underlying array.

- CopyOnWriteArraySet is a java.util.Set implementation that uses an internal CopyOnWriteArrayList instance for all its operations.

Listing 10-3 uses BlockingQueue and ArrayBlockingQueue in an alternative to Listing 8-14's producer-consumer application (PC).

Listing 10-3. The Blocking Queue Equivalent of Listing 8-14's PC Application

```java
import java.util.concurrent.ArrayBlockingQueue;
import java.util.concurrent.BlockingQueue;
import java.util.concurrent.ExecutorService;
import java.util.concurrent.Executors;

public class PC
{
   public static void main(String[] args)
   {
      final BlockingQueue<Character> bq;
      bq = new ArrayBlockingQueue<Character>(26);
      final ExecutorService executor = Executors.newFixedThreadPool(2);
      Runnable producer;
      producer = new Runnable()
                 {
                     @Override
                     public void run()
                     {
                        for (char ch = 'A'; ch <= 'Z'; ch++)
                        {
                           try
                           {
                              bq.put(ch);
                              System.out.println(ch + " produced by producer.");
                           }
                           catch (InterruptedException ie)
                           {
                              assert false;
                           }
                        }
                     }
                 };
      executor.execute(producer);
      Runnable consumer;
      consumer = new Runnable()
                 {
                     @Override
                     public void run()
                     {
                        char ch = '\0';
                        do
                        {
                           try
                           {
                              ch = bq.take();
                              System.out.println(ch + " consumed by consumer.");
                           }
```

```
                        catch (InterruptedException ie)
                        {
                            assert false;
                        }
                    }
                    while (ch != 'Z');
                    executor.shutdownNow();
                }
            };
        executor.execute(consumer);
    }
}
```

Listing 10-3 uses BlockingQueue's put() and take() methods, respectively, to put an object on the blocking queue and to remove an object from the blocking queue. put() blocks when there is no room to put an object; take() blocks when the queue is empty.

Although BlockingQueue ensures that a character is never consumed before it is produced, this application's output may indicate otherwise. For example, here is a portion of the output from one run:

```
Y consumed by consumer.
Y produced by producer.
Z consumed by consumer.
Z produced by producer.
```

Chapter 8's PC application overcame this incorrect output order by introducing an extra layer of synchronization around setSharedChar()/System.out.println() and an extra layer of synchronization around getSharedChar()/System.out.println(). In the next section I show you an alternative in the form of locks.

Locks

The java.util.concurrent.locks package provides interfaces and classes for locking and waiting for conditions in a manner that is distinct from built-in synchronization and monitors. This package's most basic lock interface is Lock, which provides more extensive locking operations than can be achieved via the synchronized reserved word. Lock also supports a wait/notification mechanism through associated Condition objects.

> **Note** The biggest advantage of Lock objects over the implicit locks that are obtained when threads enter critical sections (controlled via the synchronized reserved word) is their ability to back out of an attempt to acquire a lock. For example, the tryLock() method backs out when the lock is not available immediately or before a timeout expires (if specified). Also, the lockInterruptibly() method backs out when another thread sends an interrupt before the lock is acquired.

ReentrantLock implements Lock, describing a reentrant mutual exclusion Lock implementation with the same basic behavior and semantics as the implicit monitor lock accessed via synchronized but with extended capabilities.

Listing 10-4 demonstrates Lock and ReentrantLock in a version of Listing 10-3 that ensures that the output is never shown in incorrect order (a consumed message appearing before a produced message).

Listing 10-4. Achieving Synchronization in Terms of Locks

```java
import java.util.concurrent.ArrayBlockingQueue;
import java.util.concurrent.BlockingQueue;
import java.util.concurrent.ExecutorService;
import java.util.concurrent.Executors;

import java.util.concurrent.locks.Lock;
import java.util.concurrent.locks.ReentrantLock;

public class PC
{
   public static void main(String[] args)
   {
      final Lock lock = new ReentrantLock();
      final BlockingQueue<Character> bq;
      bq = new ArrayBlockingQueue<Character>(26);
      final ExecutorService executor = Executors.newFixedThreadPool(2);
      Runnable producer;
      producer = new Runnable()
                  {
                     @Override
                     public void run()
                     {
                        for (char ch = 'A'; ch <= 'Z'; ch++)
                        {
                           try
                           {
                              lock.lock();
                              try
                              {
                                 while (!bq.offer(ch))
                                 {
                                    lock.unlock();
                                    Thread.sleep(50);
                                    lock.lock();
                                 }
                                 System.out.println(ch + " produced by producer.");
                              }
                              catch (InterruptedException ie)
                              {
                                 assert false;
                              }
                        }
```

```
                                    finally
                                    {
                                        lock.unlock();
                                    }
                                }
                            }
                    };
            executor.execute(producer);
            Runnable consumer;
            consumer = new Runnable()
                        {
                            @Override
                            public void run()
                            {
                                char ch = '\0';
                                do
                                {
                                    try
                                    {
                                        lock.lock();
                                        try
                                        {
                                            Character c;
                                            while ((c = bq.poll()) == null)
                                            {
                                                lock.unlock();
                                                Thread.sleep(50);
                                                lock.lock();
                                            }
                                            ch = c; // unboxing behind the scenes
                                            System.out.println(ch + " consumed by consumer.");
                                        }
                                        catch (InterruptedException ie)
                                        {
                                            assert false;
                                        }
                                    }
                                    finally
                                    {
                                        lock.unlock();
                                    }
                                }
                                while (ch != 'Z');
                                executor.shutdownNow();
                            }
                    };
            executor.execute(consumer);
        }
}
```

Listing 10-4 uses Lock's `lock()` and `unlock()` methods to obtain and release a lock. When a thread calls `lock()` and the lock is unavailable, the thread is disabled (and cannot be scheduled) until the lock becomes available.

This listing also uses BlockingQueue's `offer()` method instead of `put()` to store an object in the blocking queue and its `poll()` method instead of `take()` to retrieve an object from the queue. These alternative methods are used because they don't block.

If I had used `put()` and `take()`, this application would have deadlocked in the following scenario:

1. The consumer thread acquires the lock via its `lock.lock()` call.

2. The producer thread attempts to acquire the lock via its `lock.lock()` call and is disabled because the consumer thread has already acquired the lock.

3. The consumer thread calls `take()` to obtain the next `java.lang.Character` object from the queue.

4. Because the queue is empty, the consumer thread must wait.

5. The consumer thread doesn't give up the lock that the producer thread requires before waiting, so the producer thread also continues to wait.

> **Note**   If I had access to the private lock used by BlockingQueue implementations, I would have used `put()` and `take()` and also would have called Lock's `lock()` and `unlock()` methods on that lock. The resulting application would then have been identical (from a lock perspective) to Listing 8-14's PC application, which used `synchronized` twice for each of the producer and consumer threads.

Run this application and you'll discover that, as with Listing 8-14's PC application, it never outputs a consuming message before a producing message for the same item.

Atomic Variables

The `java.util.concurrent.atomic` package provides Atomic-prefixed classes (such as `AtomicLong`) that support lock-free, thread-safe operations on single variables. Each class declares methods such as `get()` and `set()` to read and write this variable without the need for external synchronization.

Listing 8-10 declared a small utility class named ID for returning unique long integer identifiers via ID's `getNextID()` class method. Because this method wasn't synchronized, multiple threads could obtain the same identifier. Listing 10-5 fixes this problem by including reserved word `synchronized` in the method header.

Listing 10-5. Returning Unique Identifiers in a Thread-Safe Manner via synchronized

```
class ID
{
   private static long nextID = 0;
   static synchronized long getNextID()
   {
      return nextID++;
   }
}
```

Although synchronized is appropriate for this class, excessive use of this reserved word in more complex classes can lead to deadlock, starvation, or other problems. Listing 10-6 shows you how to avoid these assaults on a concurrent application's *liveness* (the ability to execute in a timely manner) by replacing synchronized with an atomic variable.

Listing 10-6. Returning Unique IDs in a Thread-Safe Manner via AtomicLong

```
import java.util.concurrent.atomic.AtomicLong;

class ID
{
   private static AtomicLong nextID = new AtomicLong(0);
   static long getNextID()
   {
      return nextID.getAndIncrement();
   }
}
```

In Listing 10-6, I've converted nextID from a long to an AtomicLong instance, initializing this object to 0. I've also refactored the getNextID() method to call AtomicLong's getAndIncrement() method, which increments the AtomicLong instance's internal long integer variable by 1 and returns the previous value in one indivisible step.

Exploring the Date Class

In Chapter 8 I introduced you to the java.lang.System class's long currentTimeMillis() class method, which returns the number of milliseconds since January 1, 1970 00:00:00 UTC. Because Unix was officially released on this date, it is forever known as the *Unix epoch*.

The java.util.Date class describes dates in terms of these long integers. Although much of this class has been deprecated, portions of Date are still useful. Table 10-3 describes the non-deprecated part of the Date class.

Table 10-3. *Date Constructors and Methods*

Method	Description
Date()	Allocate a Date object and initialize it to the current time by calling System.currentTimeMillis().
Date(long date)	Allocate a Date object and initialize it to the time represented by date milliseconds. A negative value indicates a time before the epoch, 0 indicates the epoch, and a positive value indicates a time after the epoch.
boolean after(Date date)	Return true when this date occurs after date. This method throws NullPointerException when date is null.
boolean before(Date date)	Return true when this date occurs before date. This method throws NullPointerException when date is null.
Object clone()	Return a copy of this object.
int compareTo(Date date)	Compare this date with date. Return 0 when this date equals date, a negative value when this date comes before date, and a positive value when this date comes after date. This method throws NullPointerException when date is null.
boolean equals(Object obj)	Compare this date with the Date object represented by obj. Return true if and only if obj is not null and is a Date object that represents the same point in time (to the millisecond) as this date.
long getTime()	Return the number of milliseconds that must elapse before the epoch (a negative value) or have elapsed since the epoch (a positive value).
int hashCode()	Return this date's hash code. The result is the exclusive OR of the two halves of the long integer value returned by getTime(). That is, the hash code is the value of expression (int) (this.getTime() ^ (this.getTime() >>> 32)).
void setTime(long time)	Set this date to represent the point in time specified by time milliseconds (a negative value refers to before the epoch; a positive value refers to after the epoch).
String toString()	Return a java.lang.String object containing this date's representation as dow mon dd hh:mm:ss zzz yyyy, where dow is the day of the week (Sun, Mon, Tue, Wed, Thu, Fri, Sat); mon is the month (Jan, Feb, Mar, Apr, May, Jun, Jul, Aug, Sep, Oct, Nov, Dec); dd is the two-decimal digit day of the month (01 through 31); hh is the two-decimal digit hour of the day (00 through 23); mm is the two-decimal digit minute within the hour (00 through 59); ss is the two-decimal digit second within the minute (00 through 61, where 60 and 61 account for leap seconds); zzz is the (possibly empty) time zone (and may reflect daylight saving time); and yyyy is the four-decimal digit year.

Listing 10-7 provides a small demonstration of the Date class.

Listing 10-7. Demonstrating the Date Class

```java
import java.util.Date;

public class DateDemo
{
   public static void main(String[] args)
   {
      Date now = new Date();
      System.out.println(now);
      Date later = new Date(now.getTime() + 86400);
      System.out.println(later);
      System.out.println(now.after(later));
      System.out.println(now.before(later));
   }
}
```

Listing 10-7's main() method creates a pair of Date objects (now and later) and outputs their dates, formatted according to Date's implicitly called toString() method. main() then demonstrates after() and before(), proving that now comes before later, which is in the future.

When you run this application, it generates output similar to the following:

```
Wed Nov 21 13:21:20 CST 2012
Wed Nov 21 13:22:46 CST 2012
false
true
```

Exploring the Formatter Class

The C language's standard library offers a powerful data-formatting capability via printf() and related functions. For example, printf("%05d %x", 2380, 2830); formats integer literal 2380 as a decimal character sequence and integer literal 2830 as a hexadecimal character sequence. Format specifier %05d tells printf() to fit the formatted result of 2380 into a five-character field with leading zeros for values smaller than this width. Format specifier %x tells printf() to create the hexadecimal equivalent of 2830 and use lowercase for hexadecimal digits A-F. The resulting 02380 b0e character sequence is output to the standard output device.

Java 5 introduced the java.util.Formatter class as an interpreter for printf()-style format strings. This class provides support for layout justification and alignment; common formats for numeric, string, and date/time data; and more. Commonly used Java types (e.g., byte and BigDecimal) are supported. Also, limited formatting customization for arbitrary user-defined types is provided through the associated java.util.Formattable interface and java.util.FormattableFlags class.

Formatter declares several constructors for creating Formatter objects. These constructors give you the opportunity to specify where you want formatted output to be sent. For example, the Formatter() constructor writes formatted output to an internal java.lang.StringBuilder instance, whereas Formatter(OutputStream os) writes formatted output to the specified output stream—I discuss output streams in Chapter 11. You can access the destination by calling Formatter's Appendable out() method.

> **Note**   The java.lang.Appendable interface describes an object to which char values and character sequences can be appended. Classes whose instances are to receive formatted output (via the Formatter class) implement Appendable. It declares methods such as Appendable append(char c)—append c's character to this appendable. This method throws java.io.IOException when an I/O error occurs.

After creating a Formatter object, you would call a format() method to format a varying number of values. For example, Formatter format(String format, Object...args) formats the args array according to the string of format specifiers passed to the format parameter. This method throws java.util.IllegalFormatException when a format string contains an illegal syntax, a format specifier that's incompatible with the given arguments, insufficient arguments given the format string, or other illegal conditions. It throws java.util.FormatterClosedException when this formatter has been closed by calling its void close() method. A reference to this Formatter instance is returned so that you can chain format() method calls together.

Listing 10-8 provides a simple demonstration of Formatter.

Listing 10-8. Demonstrating with the Formatter Class

```java
import java.util.Formatter;

public class FormatterDemo
{
   public static void main(String[] args)
   {
      Formatter formatter = new Formatter();
      formatter.format("%05d %x", 2380, 2830);
      System.out.println(formatter.toString()); // Output: 02380 b0e
   }
}
```

Listing 10-8's main() method first creates a Formatter object whose destination is a StringBuilder instance. It then invokes format() to format the second and third format() arguments according to the first argument and sends the formatted character sequence to the StringBuilder appendable. Finally, it invokes Formatter's String toString() method to return this appendable's content, which it subsequently outputs. (I could have specified System.out.println(formatter); instead because the System.out.print() and System.out.println() methods automatically call an object's toString() method to return a string representation of that object.)

For more information on Formatter and its supported format specifiers, I refer you to Formatter's Java documentation. You might also want to check out Oracle's documentation on the Formattable interface and FormattableFlags class to learn about customizing Formatter.

Exploring the Random Class

In Chapter 7 I formally introduced you to the java.lang.Math class's random() method. If you were to investigate this method's source code from the perspective of Java 7, you would encounter the following implementation:

```
private static Random randomNumberGenerator;

private static synchronized Random initRNG() {
   Random rnd = randomNumberGenerator;
   return (rnd == null) ? (randomNumberGenerator = new Random()) : rnd;
}

public static double random() {
   Random rnd = randomNumberGenerator;
   if (rnd == null) rnd = initRNG();
   return rnd.nextDouble();
}
```

This code excerpt shows you that Math's random() method is implemented in terms of a class named Random, which is located in the java.util package. Random instances generate sequences of random numbers and are known as *random number generators*.

> **Note**   These numbers are not truly random because they are generated from a mathematical algorithm.
> As a result, they are often referred to as *pseudorandom numbers*. However, it is often convenient
> to drop the "pseudo" prefix and refer to them as random numbers. Also, delaying object creation
> (new Random(), for example) until the first time the object is needed is known as *lazy initialization*.

Random generates its sequence of random numbers by starting with a special 48-bit value that is known as a *seed*. This value is subsequently modified by a mathematical algorithm, which is known as a *linear congruential generator*.

> **Note**   Check out Wikipedia's "Linear congruential generator" entry
> (http://en.wikipedia.org/wiki/Linear_congruential_generator) to learn about this algorithm
> for generating random numbers.

Random declares a pair of constructors:

- Random() creates a new random number generator. This constructor sets the seed of the random number generator to a value that is very likely to be distinct from any other call to this constructor.

- Random(long seed) creates a new random number generator using its seed argument. This argument is the initial value of the internal state of the random number generator, which is maintained by the protected int next(int bits) method.

Because `Random()` doesn't take a `seed` argument, the resulting random number generator always generates a different sequence of random numbers. This explains why `Math.random()` generates a different sequence each time an application starts running.

> **Tip** `Random(long seed)` gives you the opportunity to reuse the same seed value, allowing the same sequence of random numbers to be generated. You will find this capability useful when debugging a faulty application that involves random numbers.

`Random(long seed)` calls the `void setSeed(long seed)` method to set the seed to the specified value. If you call `setSeed()` after instantiating `Random`, the random number generator is reset to the state that it was in immediately after calling `Random(long seed)`.

The previous code excerpt demonstrates `Random`'s `double nextDouble()` method, which returns the next pseudorandom, uniformly distributed double precision floating-point value between 0.0 and 1.0 in this random number generator's sequence.

`Random` also declares the following methods for returning other kinds of values:

- `boolean nextBoolean()` returns the next pseudorandom, uniformly distributed Boolean value in this random number generator's sequence. Values true and false are generated with (approximately) equal probability.

- `void nextBytes(byte[] bytes)` generates pseudorandom byte integer values and stores them in the `bytes` array. The number of generated bytes is equal to the length of the `bytes` array.

- `float nextFloat()` returns the next pseudorandom, uniformly distributed floating-point value between 0.0 and 1.0 in this random number generator's sequence.

- `double nextGaussian()` returns the next pseudorandom, *Gaussian* ("normally") distributed double precision floating-point value with mean 0.0 and standard deviation 1.0 in this random number generator's sequence.

- `int nextInt()` returns the next pseudorandom, uniformly distributed integer value in this random number generator's sequence. All 4,294,967,296 possible integer values are generated with (approximately) equal probability.

- `int nextInt(int n)` returns a pseudorandom, uniformly distributed integer value between 0 (inclusive) and the specified value (exclusive) drawn from this random number generator's sequence. All n possible integer values are generated with (approximately) equal probability.

- `long nextLong()` returns the next pseudorandom, uniformly distributed long integer value in this random number generator's sequence. Because Random uses a seed with only 48 bits, this method will not return all possible 64-bit long integer values.

The java.util.Collections class declares a pair of shuffle() methods for shuffling the contents of a list. In contrast, the java.util.Arrays class doesn't declare a shuffle() method for shuffling the contents of an array. Listing 10-9 addresses this omission.

Listing 10-9. Shuffling an Array of Integers

```
import java.util.Random;

public class Shuffler
{
   public static void main(String[] args)
   {
      Random r = new Random();
      int[] array = { 0, 1, 2, 3, 4, 5, 6, 7, 8, 9 };
      for (int i = 0; i < array.length; i++)
      {
         int n = r.nextInt(array.length);
         // swap array[i] with array[n]
         int temp = array[i];
         array[i] = array[n];
         array[n] = temp;
      }
      for (int i = 0; i < array.length; i++)
         System.out.print(array[i] + " ");
      System.out.println();
   }
}
```

Listing 10-9 presents a simple recipe for shuffling an array of integers—this recipe could be generalized. For each array entry from the start of the array to the end of the array, this entry is swapped with another entry whose index is chosen by int nextInt(int n).

When you run this application, you will observe a shuffled sequence of integers that is similar to the following sequence that I observed:

```
9 0 5 6 2 3 8 4 1 7
```

Exploring the Scanner Class

The C language's standard library offers a scanf() function for parsing an input stream of characters into integers, floating-point values, and so on. Not to be outdone, Java 5 introduced the java.util.Scanner class to parse these characters into primitive types, strings, and big integers/ decimals with the help of regular expressions (discussed in Chapter 13).

Scanner declares several constructors for scanning content originating from diverse sources. For example, Scanner(InputStream source) creates a scanner for scanning the specified input stream, whereas Scanner(String source) creates a scanner for scanning the specified string.

A Scanner instance uses a *delimiter pattern*, which matches whitespace by default, to break its input into discrete values. After creating this instance, you can call one of the "hasNext" methods to verify that an anticipated character sequence is present for scanning. For example, you could call boolean hasNextDouble() to determine whether or not the next sequence of characters can be scanned into a double precision floating-point value.

When the value is present, you would call the appropriate "next" method to scan the value. For example, you would call double nextDouble() to scan this sequence and return a double containing its value.

The following example shows you how to create a scanner for scanning values from standard input and then scanning an integer followed by a double precision floating-point value:

```
Scanner sc = new Scanner(System.in);
if (sc.hasNextInt())
   i = sc.nextInt();
if (sc.hasNextDouble())
   d = sc.nextDouble();
```

Listing 10-10 presents a more realistic (menu-oriented) example.

Listing 10-10. Scanning Input in a Menu Context

```java
import java.util.Scanner;

public class ScannerDemo
{
   public static void main(String[] args)
   {
      Scanner scanner = new Scanner(System.in);
      while (true)
      {
         System.out.printf("%nMenu Options%n%n");
         System.out.println("1: Frequency Count");
         System.out.printf("2: Quit%n%n");
         System.out.print("Enter your selection (1 or 2): ");
         int selection = scanner.nextInt();
         scanner.nextLine();
         if (selection == 1)
         {
            System.out.printf("%nEnter sentence: ");
            String sentence = scanner.nextLine();
            System.out.print("Enter index: ");
            int index = scanner.nextInt();
            int count = 0;
            for (int i = 0; i < sentence.length(); i++)
               if (sentence.charAt(i) == sentence.charAt(index))
                  count++;
            System.out.printf("Count of [%c] in [%s]: %d%n",
                              sentence.charAt(index), sentence, count);
         }
```

```
            else
            if (selection == 2)
                break;
        }
    }
}
```

Listing 10-10's `main()` method creates a scanner that scans input from the standard input stream and then enters a while loop. Each of the loop iterations presents a two-option menu and prompts the user to select one of these options.

Option selection is made via a `scanner.nextInt()` method call. Because `nextInt()` doesn't consume the line terminator following the selection number, a call to Scanner's void `nextLine()` method is made to skip over the line terminator so as not to affect sentence entry (when option 1 is chosen).

If the user selected option 1, the user is prompted to enter a sentence along with the zero-based index of one of the sentence characters. The sentence is then iterated over and all occurrences of the indexed character are tallied. This count is subsequently output.

If the user selected option 2, the loop is broken and the application ends.

Compile Listing 10-10 (`javac ScannerDemo.java`) and run this application (`java ScannerDemo`). The following output reveals one run of this application:

```
Menu Options

1: Frequency Count
2: Quit

Enter your selection (1 or 2): 1

Enter sentence: This is a test.
Enter index: 2
Count of [i] in [This is a test.]: 2

Menu Options

1: Frequency Count
2: Quit

Enter your selection (1 or 2): 2
```

To learn more about Scanner, check out this class's Java documentation.

Exploring the ZIP and JAR APIs

You might need to develop an application that must create a new ZIP file and store files in that file or extract content from an existing ZIP file. Perhaps you might need to perform either task in the context of a JAR file, which you might think of as a ZIP file with a `.jar` file extension. This section introduces you to the APIs for working with ZIP and JAR files.

Exploring the ZIP API

The `java.util.zip` package provides classes for working with ZIP files, which are also known as *ZIP archives*. Each ZIP archive stores files that are typically compressed, and each stored file is known as a *ZIP entry*. You can use these classes to write ZIP entries to or read ZIP entries from a ZIP archive in the standard ZIP and GZIP (GNU ZIP) file formats, compress and decompress data via the DEFLATE compression algorithm that these formats use, and compute the CRC-32 and Adler-32 checksums of arbitrary input streams.

> **Note** See Wikipedia's "Cyclic redundancy check" (`http://en.wikipedia.org/wiki/CRC-32`) and "Adler-32" (`http://en.wikipedia.org/wiki/Adler-32`) entries to learn about CRC-32 and Adler-32.

The `ZipEntry` class represents a ZIP entry. You must instantiate this class to write new entries to a ZIP archive or read entries from an existing ZIP archive. `ZipEntry` offers two constructors:

- `ZipEntry(String name)` creates a new ZIP entry with the specified `name`. This constructor throws `NullPointerException` when `name` is null and `IllegalArgumentException` when the length of the string assigned to `name` exceeds 65,535 bytes.

- `ZipEntry(ZipEntry ze)` creates a new ZIP entry with values taken from existing ZIP entry `ze`.

Additionally, `ZipEntry` declares several methods including those presented in the following list:

- `String getComment()` returns the entry's comment string or null when there is no comment string. A *comment* provides user-specific information associated with an entry.

- `long getCompressedSize()` returns the size of the entry's compressed data or –1 when not specified. The compressed size is the same as the uncompressed size when the entry data is stored without compression.

- `long getCrc()` returns the CRC-32 checksum of the entry's uncompressed data or –1 when the checksum has not been specified.

- `int getMethod()` returns the compression method used to compress the entry's data. This value is one of `ZipEntry`'s `DEFLATED` or `STORED` (not compressed) constants or is –1 when the compression method has not been specified.

- `String getName()` returns the entry's name.

- `long getSize()` returns the uncompressed size of the entry's data or –1 when the size has not been specified.

- `boolean isDirectory()` returns true when the entry describes a directory; otherwise, this method returns false.

- void setComment(String comment) sets the entry's comment string to comment. A comment string is optional. When specified, the maximum length should be 65,535 bytes; remaining bytes are truncated.

- void setCompressedSize(long csize) sets the size (in bytes) of the entry's compressed data to csize.

- void setCrc(long crc) sets the CRC-32 checksum of the entry's uncompressed data to crc. This method throws IllegalArgumentException when crc's value is less than 0 or greater than 0xFFFFFFFF.

- void setMethod(int method) sets the compression method to method. This method throws IllegalArgumentException when any value other than ZipEntry.DEFLATED (compress data file at a specific level) or ZipEntry.STORED (don't compress) is passed to method.

- void setSize(long size) sets the uncompressed size of the entry's data to size. This method throws IllegalArgumentException when size's value is less than 0 or the value is greater than 0xFFFFFFFF when "ZIP64" (http://en.wikipedia.org/wiki/Zip_(file_format)#ZIP64) isn't supported.

You will shortly learn how to work with this class.

Writing Files to a ZIP Archive

Use the ZipOutputStream class to write ZIP entries (compressed as well as uncompressed) to a ZIP archive.

> **Note**   Use the GZIPOutputStream class to create a GZIP archive and write files to this archive in the GZIP format. For brevity, I don't discuss this class.

ZipOutputStream declares the ZipOutputStream(OutputStream out) constructor for creating a ZIP output stream. (You will learn about output streams in Chapter 11.) Although ZipEntry instances are conceptually written to this stream, it's really the data described by these instances that is written.

The following example instantiates ZipOutputStream with an underlying file output stream:

```
ZipOutputStream zos = new ZipOutputStream(new FileOutputStream("archive.zip"));
```

ZipOutputStream also declares several methods and inherits additional methods from its DeflaterOutputStream superclass. You minimally work with the following methods:

- void close() closes the ZIP output stream along with the underlying output stream.

- void closeEntry() closes the current ZIP entry and positions the stream for writing the next entry.

- void putNextEntry(ZipEntry e) begins writing a new ZIP entry and positions the stream to the start of the entry data. The current entry is closed when still active (i.e., when closeEntry() was not invoked on the previous entry).

- void write(byte[] b, int off, int len) writes len bytes starting at offset off from buffer b to the current ZIP entry. This method will block until all the bytes are written.

Each method throws IOException when a generic I/O error has occurred and ZipException (which subclasses IOException) when a ZIP-specific I/O error has occurred.

Listing 10-11 presents a ZipCreate application that shows you how to minimally use ZipOutputStream and ZipEntry to store assorted files in a new ZIP archive.

Listing 10-11. Creating a ZIP Archive and Storing Specified Files in That Archive

```java
import java.io.FileInputStream;
import java.io.FileOutputStream;
import java.io.IOException;

import java.util.zip.ZipEntry;
import java.util.zip.ZipOutputStream;

public class ZipCreate
{
   public static void main(String[] args) throws IOException
   {
      if (args.length < 2)
      {
         System.err.println("usage: java ZipCreate ZIPfile infile1 "+
                            "infile2 ...");
         return;
      }
      ZipOutputStream zos = null;
      try
      {
         zos = new ZipOutputStream(new FileOutputStream(args[0]));
         byte[] buf = new byte[1024];
         for (String filename: args)
         {
            if (filename.equals(args[0]))
               continue;
            FileInputStream fis = null;
            try
            {
               fis = new FileInputStream(filename);
               zos.putNextEntry(new ZipEntry(filename));
               int len;
               while ((len = fis.read(buf)) > 0)
                  zos.write(buf, 0, len);
            }
```

```
            catch (IOException ioe)
            {
               System.err.println("I/O error: " + ioe.getMessage());
            }
            finally
            {
               if (fis != null)
                  try
                  {
                     fis.close();
                  }
                  catch (IOException ioe)
                  {
                     assert false; // shouldn't happen in this context
                  }
            }
            zos.closeEntry();
         }
      }
      catch (IOException ioe)
      {
         System.err.println("I/O error: " + ioe.getMessage());
      }
      finally
      {
         if (zos != null)
            try
            {
               zos.close();
            }
            catch (IOException ioe)
            {
               assert false; // shouldn't happen in this context
            }
      }
   }
}
```

Listing 10-11 is fairly straightforward. It first validates the number of command-line arguments, which must be at least two: the first argument is always the name of the ZIP file to be created. If successful, this application creates a ZIP output stream with an underlying file output stream to this file and then writes the contents of those files identified by successive command-line arguments to the ZIP output stream.

The only part of this source code that might seem confusing is if (filename.equals(args[0])) continue;. This statement prevents the first command-line argument, which happens to be the name of the ZIP archive, from being added to the archive, which doesn't make sense because of its recursive nature. If this possibility was permitted, a ZipException instance containing a "duplicate entry" message would be thrown.

Compile Listing 10-11 (javac ZipCreate.java) and run this application via the following command line, which creates a ZIP archive named a.zip and stores file ZipCreate.java in this archive—the application isn't recursive (it will not recurse into directories):

```
java ZipCreate a.zip ZipCreate.java
```

You should not observe any output. Instead, you should observe a file named a.zip in the current directory. Furthermore, when you unzip a.zip, you should detect an unarchived ZipCreate.java file.

You cannot store duplicate files in an archive because that makes no sense. For example, you will observe an exception message about a duplicate entry when you execute the following command line:

```
java ZipCreate a.zip ZipCreate.java ZipCreate.java
```

ZipOutputStream offers more capabilities. For example, you can use its void setLevel(int level) method to set the compression level for successive entries. Specify an integer argument from 0 through 9, where 0 indicates no compression and 9 indicates best compression—better compression slows down performance. (Google reports these limits as –1 and 8.) Alternatively, specify one of the Deflator class's BEST_COMPRESSION, BEST_SPEED, DEFAULT_COMPRESSION (to which setLevel() defaults), and other constants as an argument.

Reading Files from a ZIP Archive

Use the ZipInputStream class to read ZIP entries (compressed as well as uncompressed) from a ZIP archive.

> **Note**   Use the GZIPInputStream class to open a GZIP archive and read files from this archive in the GZIP format. For brevity, I don't discuss this class.

ZipInputStream declares the ZipInputStream(InputStream in) constructor for creating a ZIP input stream. (You will learn about input streams in Chapter 11.) Although ZipEntry instances are conceptually read from this stream, it is really the data described by these instances that is read.

The following example instantiates ZipInputStream with an underlying file input stream:

```
ZipInputStream zis = new ZipInputStream(new FileInputStream("archive.zip"));
```

ZipInputStream also declares several methods and inherits additional methods from its InflaterInputStream superclass. You minimally work with the following methods:

- void close() closes the ZIP input stream along with the underlying input stream.
- void closeEntry() closes the current ZIP entry and positions the stream for reading the next entry.

- ZipEntry getNextEntry() reads the next ZIP entry and positions the stream to the start of the entry data. This method returns null when there are no more entries.

- int read(byte[] b, int off, int len) reads a maximum of len bytes from the current ZIP entry into buffer b starting at offset off. This method will block until all the bytes are read.

Each method throws IOException when a generic I/O error has occurred and (except for close()) ZipException when a ZIP-specific I/O error has occurred. Also, read() throws NullPointerException when b is null and java.lang.IndexOutOfBoundsException when off is negative, len is negative, or len is greater than b.length - off.

Listing 10-12 presents a ZipAccess application that shows you how to minimally use ZipInputStream and ZipEntry to extract assorted files from an existing ZIP archive.

Listing 10-12. Accessing a ZIP Archive and Extracting Specified Files from That Archive

```java
import java.io.FileInputStream;
import java.io.FileOutputStream;
import java.io.IOException;

import java.util.zip.ZipEntry;
import java.util.zip.ZipInputStream;

public class ZipAccess
{
   public static void main(String[] args) throws IOException
   {
      if (args.length != 1)
      {
         System.err.println("usage: java ZipAccess zipfile");
         return;
      }
      ZipInputStream zis = null;
      try
      {
         zis = new ZipInputStream(new FileInputStream(args[0]));
         byte[] buffer = new byte[4096];
         ZipEntry ze;
         while ((ze = zis.getNextEntry()) != null)
         {
            System.out.println("Extracting: " + ze);
            FileOutputStream fos = null;
            try
            {
               fos = new FileOutputStream(ze.getName());
               int numBytes;
               while ((numBytes = zis.read(buffer, 0, buffer.length)) != -1)
                  fos.write(buffer, 0, numBytes);
            }
```

```
            catch (IOException ioe)
            {
                System.err.println("I/O error: " + ioe.getMessage());
            }
            finally
            {
                if (fos != null)
                   try
                   {
                       fos.close();
                   }
                   catch (IOException ioe)
                   {
                       assert false; // shouldn't happen in this context
                   }
            }
            zis.closeEntry();
         }
      }
      catch (IOException ioe)
      {
         System.err.println("I/O error: " + ioe.getMessage());
      }
      finally
      {
         if (zis != null)
            try
            {
                zis.close();
            }
            catch (IOException ioe)
            {
                assert false; // shouldn't happen in this context
            }
      }
   }
}
```

Listing 10-12 is fairly straightforward. It first validates the number of command-line arguments, which must be exactly one: the name of the ZIP file to be accessed. Assuming success, it creates a ZIP input stream with an underlying file input stream to this file and then reads the contents of the various files that are stored in this archive, creating these files in the current directory.

Compile Listing 10-12 (javac ZipAccess.java) and run this application via the following command line, which accesses the previous a.zip archive and extracts file ZipCreate.java from this archive:

```
java ZipAccess a.zip
```

You should observe "Extracting: ZipCreate.java" as the single line of output, and also note the appearance of a ZipCreate.java file in the current directory.

```
┌─────────────────────────────────────────────────────────────────────────┐
│                    ZIPFILE VERSUS ZIPINPUTSTREAM                          │
└─────────────────────────────────────────────────────────────────────────┘
```

The java.util.zip package contains a ZipFile class that seems to be an alias for ZipInputStream. As with ZipInputStream, you can use ZipFile to read a ZIP file's entries. However, ZipFile has a couple of differences that make it worth considering as an alternative:

- ZipFile allows random access to ZIP entries via its ZipEntry getEntry(String name) method. Given a ZipEntry instance, you can call ZipEntry's InputStream getInputStream(ZipEntry entry) method to obtain an input stream for reading the entry's content. ZipInputStream supports sequential access to ZIP entries.

- According to the "Compressing and Decompressing Data Using Java APIs" article (www.oracle.com/technetwork/articles/java/compress-1565076.html), ZipFile internally caches ZIP entries for improved performance. ZipInputStream doesn't cache entries.

You might be curious about a ZipFile constructor that declares a mode parameter of type int. The argument passed to mode is ZipFile.OPEN_READ or ZipFile.OPEN_READ | ZipFile.OPEN_DELETE. The latter argument causes the underlying file to be deleted sometime between when it is opened and when it is closed.

This capability was introduced by Java 1.3 to solve a problem related to caching downloaded JAR files in the context of long-running server applications or Remote Method Invocation. The problem is discussed at http://docs.oracle.com/javase/7/docs/technotes/guides/lang/enhancements.html.

Exploring the JAR API

The java.util.jar package provides classes for working with JAR files. Because a JAR file is a kind of ZIP file, it isn't surprising that this package provides classes that extend their java.util.zip counterparts. For example, java.util.jar.JarEntry extends java.util.zip.ZipEntry.

The java.util.jar package also provides classes that have no java.util.zip counterparts, for example, Manifest. These classes provide access to JAR-specific capabilities. For example, Manifest lets you work with a JAR file's manifest (explained shortly).

Listing 10-13 presents a MakeRunnableJAR application that shows you how to work with some of the types in the java.util.jar package to create a runnable JAR file.

Listing 10-13. Creating a Runnable JAR File

```java
import java.io.FileInputStream;
import java.io.FileOutputStream;
import java.io.IOException;

import java.util.jar.Attributes;
import java.util.jar.JarEntry;
import java.util.jar.JarOutputStream;
import java.util.jar.Manifest;
```

```java
public class MakeRunnableJAR
{
   public static void main(String[] args) throws IOException
   {
      if (args.length < 2)
      {
         System.err.println("usage: java MakeRunnableJAR JARfile " +
                            "classfile1 classfile2 ...");
         return;
      }
      JarOutputStream jos = null;
      try
      {
         Manifest mf = new Manifest();
         Attributes attr = mf.getMainAttributes();
         attr.put(Attributes.Name.MANIFEST_VERSION, "1.0");
         attr.put(Attributes.Name.MAIN_CLASS,
                 args[1].substring(0, args[1].indexOf('.')));
         jos = new JarOutputStream(new FileOutputStream(args[0]), mf);
         byte[] buf = new byte[1024];
         for (String filename: args)
         {
            if (filename.equals(args[0]))
               continue;
            FileInputStream fis = null;
            try
            {
               fis = new FileInputStream(filename);
               jos.putNextEntry(new JarEntry(filename));
               int len;
               while ((len = fis.read(buf)) > 0)
                  jos.write(buf, 0, len);
            }
            catch (IOException ioe)
            {
               System.err.println("I/O error: " + ioe.getMessage());
            }
            finally
            {
               if (fis != null)
                  try
                  {
                     fis.close();
                  }
                  catch (IOException ioe)
                  {
                     assert false; // shouldn't happen in this context
                  }
            }
            jos.closeEntry();
         }
      }
```

```
      catch (IOException ioe)
      {
          System.err.println("I/O error: " + ioe.getMessage());
      }
      finally
      {
          if (jos != null)
              try
              {
                  jos.close();
              }
              catch (IOException ioe)
              {
                  assert false; // shouldn't happen in this context
              }
      }
   }
}
```

Because Listing 10-13 is very similar to Listing 10-11, albeit with `java.util.jar` classes replacing their `java.util.zip` counterparts, I'll focus on only that part of this application the creates the manifest. However, you first need to understand the concept of a JAR file manifest.

A *manifest* is a special file named MANIFEST.MF that stores information about the contents of the JAR file. This file is located in the JAR file's META-INF directory. For example, the manifest would look as follows for an executable `hello.jar` JAR file containing a `Hello` application class:

```
Manifest-Version: 1.0
Main-Class: Hello
```

The first line signifies the version of the manifest and must be present. The second line identifies the application class that is to run when the JAR file is executed. A `.class` file extension must not be specified. Doing so would suggest that you want to run class `class` in the `Hello` package.

Caution   You must insert an empty line after `Main-Class: Hello`. Otherwise, you will receive a "`no main manifest attribute, in hello.jar`" error message when trying to run the application.

The key part of Listing 10-13 that sets it apart from Listing 10-11 is the following code fragment:

```
Manifest mf = new Manifest();
Attributes attr = mf.getMainAttributes();
attr.put(Attributes.Name.MANIFEST_VERSION, "1.0");
attr.put(Attributes.Name.MAIN_CLASS,
         args[1].substring(0, args[1].indexOf('.')));
jos = new JarOutputStream(new FileOutputStream(args[0]), mf);
```

The Manifest class is first instantiated (via its noargument constructor) to describe the soon-to-be-created manifest. Its getMainAttributes() method is then called to return an Attributes instance for accessing existing manifest attributes or creating new manifest attributes (such as Main-Class).

Attributes is essentially a map and provides Object put(Object key, Object value) for storing an attribute name/value pair. The value passed to key must be an Attributes.Name constant such as Attributes.Name.MANIFEST_VERSION or Attributes.Name.MAIN_CLASS.

> **Caution**   You must store MANIFEST_VERSION; otherwise, you'll observe a thrown exception at runtime.

Because the .class file extension must be specified when specifying the name of a classfile as a command-line argument, expression args[1].substring(0, args[1].indexOf('.')) is used to remove this extension—you can specify multiple classfile names as command-line arguments; the first name is stored (without its .class extension) in the manifest.

Finally, JarOutputStream is instantiated in a similar manner to ZipOutputStream. However, the initialized Manifest instance is also passed to the constructor, as the second argument.

To play with this application, you minimally need a class with a public static void main (String[] args) method. For simplicity, consider Listing 10-14.

Listing 10-14. Saying Hello

```
public class Hello
{
   public static void main(String[] args)
   {
      System.out.println("Hello");
   }
}
```

Listing 10-14 isn't much of an application but is sufficient for our purpose. Compile Listings 10-13 and 10-14 and execute the following command:

```
java MakeRunnableJAR hello.jar Hello.class
```

If all goes well, you should observe a hello.jar file in the current directory. Execute the following command to run this file:

```
java -jar hello.jar
```

Assuming success, you should observe a single line of output consisting of Hello.

EXERCISES

The following exercises are designed to test your understanding of Chapter 10's content:

1. Define task.

2. Define executor.

3. Identify the `Executor` interface's limitations.

4. How are `Executor`'s limitations overcome?

5. What differences exist between `Runnable`'s `run()` method and `Callable`'s `call()` method?

6. True or false: You can throw checked and unchecked exceptions from `Runnable`'s `run()` method but can only throw unchecked exceptions from `Callable`'s `call()` method.

7. Define future.

8. Describe the `Executors` class's `newFixedThreadPool()` method.

9. Define synchronizer.

10. Identify and describe four commonly used synchronizers.

11. What concurrency-oriented extensions to the Collections Framework are provided by the Concurrency Utilities?

12. Define lock.

13. What is the biggest advantage that `Lock` objects hold over the implicit locks that are obtained when threads enter critical sections (controlled via the `synchronized` reserved word)?

14. Define atomic variable.

15. What does the `Date` class describe?

16. What is the purpose of the `Formatter` class?

17. What does the `Random` class accomplish?

18. What is the purpose of the `Scanner` class?

19. What do you do to determine if a character sequence represents an integer or some other kind of value before scanning that sequence?

20. Identify two differences between `ZipFile` and `ZipInputStream`.

21. Create a `ZipList` application that is similar to `ZipAccess` but only outputs information about the archive: It doesn't extract file contents as well. Information to be output is the name of the entry, the compressed and uncompressed sizes, and the last modification time. Use the `Date` class to convert the last modification time to a human-readable string.

Summary

Java 5 introduced Concurrency Utilities to simplify the development of concurrent applications. These utilities are organized into executor, synchronizer, concurrent collection, lock, and atomic variable categories and leverage the low-level Threads API in their implementations.

An executor decouples task submission from task-execution mechanics and is described by the Executor, ExecutorService, and ScheduledExecutorService interfaces. A synchronizer facilitates common forms of synchronization; countdown latches, cyclic barriers, exchangers, and semaphores are commonly used synchronizers.

A concurrent collection is an extension to the Collections Framework. A lock supports high-level locking and can associate with conditions in a manner that is distinct from built-in synchronization and monitors. Finally, an atomic variable encapsulates a single variable and supports lock-free, thread-safe operations on that variable.

The Date class describes dates in terms of long integer values that are relative to the Unix epoch. Although much of this class has been deprecated, portions of Date (e.g., the long getTime() method) are still useful.

Java 5 introduced the Formatter class as an interpreter for printf()-style format strings. This class provides support for layout justification and alignment; common formats for numeric, string, and date/time data; and more.

The Math class's random() method is implemented in terms of the Random class, whose instances are known as random number generators. Random generates a sequence of random numbers by starting with a special 48-bit seed. This value is subsequently modified via a mathematical algorithm that is known as a linear congruential generator.

Java 5 introduced the Scanner class for parsing an input stream of characters into primitive types, strings, and big integers/decimals with the help of regular expressions. You invoke a "hasNext" method to verify that an anticipated character sequence is present for scanning and the appropriate "next" method to scan the value.

You might need to develop an application that must create a new ZIP file and store files in that file or extract content from an existing ZIP file. The java.util.zip package provides classes for working with ZIP files, which are also known as ZIP archives. Each ZIP archive stores files that are typically compressed, and each stored file is known as a ZIP entry.

Perhaps you might need to perform either task in the context of a JAR file, which you might think of as a ZIP file with a .jar file extension. The java.util.jar package provides classes for working with JAR files. Because a JAR file is a kind of ZIP file, it isn't surprising that this package provides classes that extend their java.util.zip counterparts.

This chapter completes my tour of Java's utility APIs. In Chapter 11 I explore Java's classic I/O APIs: File, RandomAccessFile, streams, and writers/readers.

Performing Classic I/O

Applications often input data for processing and output processing results. Data is input from a file or some other source and is output to a file or some other destination. Java supports I/O via the classic I/O APIs located in the `java.io` package and the new I/O APIs located in `java.nio` and related subpackages (and `java.util.regex`). This chapter introduces you to the classic I/O APIs.

> **Note**   You've already experienced classic I/O in the context of Chapter 1's Standard I/O coverage, Chapter 8's `Process` class, and Chapter 10's ZIP and JAR APIs.

Working with the File API

Applications often interact with a *filesystem*, which is usually expressed as a hierarchy of files and directories starting from a *root directory*.

Android and other platforms on which a virtual machine runs typically support at least one filesystem. For example, a Unix/Linux (and Linux-based Android) platform combines all *mounted* (attached and prepared) disks into one virtual filesystem. In contrast, Windows associates a separate filesystem with each active disk drive.

Java offers access to the underlying platform's available filesystem(s) via its concrete `java.io.File` class. `File` declares the `File[] listRoots()` class method to return the root directories (roots) of available filesystems as an array of `File` objects.

> **Note**   The set of available filesystem roots is affected by platform-level operations, such as inserting or ejecting removable media, and disconnecting or unmounting physical or virtual disk drives.

Listing 11-1 presents a DumpRoots application that uses listRoots() to obtain an array of available filesystem roots and then outputs the array's contents.

Listing 11-1. Dumping Available Filesystem Roots to Standard Output

```
import java.io.File;

public class DumpRoots
{
   public static void main(String[] args)
   {
      File[] roots = File.listRoots();
      for (File root: roots)
         System.out.println(root);
   }
}
```

When I run this application on my Windows 7 platform, I receive the following output, which reveals four available roots:

```
C:\
D:\
E:\
F:\
```

If I happened to run DumpRoots on a Unix or Linux platform, I would receive one line of output that consists of the virtual filesystem root (/).

Apart from using listRoots(), you can obtain a File instance by calling a File constructor such as File(String pathname), which creates a File instance that stores the pathname string. The following assignment statements demonstrate this constructor:

```
File file1 = new File("/x/y");
File file2 = new File("C:\\temp\\x.dat");
```

The first statement assumes a Unix/Linux platform, starts the pathname with root directory symbol /, and continues with directory name x, separator character /, and file or directory name y. (It also works on Windows, which assumes this path begins at the root directory on the current drive.)

Note A *path* is a hierarchy of directories that must be traversed to locate a file or a directory.
A *pathname* is a string representation of a path; a platform-dependent *separator character*
(e.g., the Windows backslash [\] character) appears between consecutive names.

The second statement assumes a Windows platform, starts the pathname with drive specifier C:, and continues with root directory symbol \, directory name temp, separator character \, and filename x.dat (although x.dat might refer to a directory).

> **Caution**   Always double backslash characters that appear in a string literal, especially when specifying a pathname; otherwise, you run the risk of bugs or compiler error messages. For example, I doubled the backslash characters in the second statement to denote a backslash and not a tab (\t) and to avoid a compiler error message (\x is illegal).

Each statement's pathname is an *absolute pathname*, which is a pathname that starts with the root directory symbol; no other information is required to locate the file/directory that it denotes. In contrast, a *relative pathname* doesn't start with the root directory symbol; it's interpreted via information taken from some other pathname.

> **Note**   The `java.io` package's classes default to resolving relative pathnames against the current user (also known as working) directory, which is identified by system property `user.dir` and which is typically the directory in which the virtual machine was launched. (Chapter 8 showed you how to read system properties via `java.lang.System`'s `getProperty()` method.)

`File` instances contain abstract representations of file and directory pathnames (these files or directories may or may not exist in their filesystems) by storing *abstract pathnames*, which offer platform-independent views of hierarchical pathnames. In contrast, user interfaces and operating systems use platform-dependent *pathname strings* to name files and directories.

An abstract pathname consists of an optional platform-dependent prefix string, such as a disk drive specifier—"/" for the Unix/Linux root directory or "\\" for a Windows Universal Naming Convention (UNC) pathname—and a sequence of zero or more string names. The first name in an abstract pathname may be a directory name or, in the case of Windows UNC pathnames, a hostname. Each subsequent name denotes a directory; the last name may denote a directory or a file. The *empty abstract pathname* has no prefix and an empty name sequence.

The conversion of a pathname string to or from an abstract pathname is inherently platform dependent. When a pathname string is converted into an abstract pathname, the names within this string may be separated by the default name-separator character or by any other name-separator character that is supported by the underlying platform. When an abstract pathname is converted into a pathname string, each name is separated from the next by a single copy of the default name-separator character.

> **Note**   The *default name-separator character* is defined by the system property `file.separator` and is made available in `File`'s `public static separator` and `separatorChar` fields—the first field stores the character in a `java.lang.String` instance and the second field stores it as a `char` value.

File offers additional constructors for instantiating this class. For example, the following constructors merge parent and child pathnames into combined pathnames that are stored in File objects:

- File(String parent, String child) creates a new File instance from a parent pathname string and a child pathname string.

- File(File parent, String child) creates a new File instance from a parent pathname File instance and a child pathname string.

Each constructor's parent parameter is passed a *parent pathname*, a string that consists of all pathname components except for the last name, which is specified by child. The following statement demonstrates this concept via File(String, String):

```
File file3 = new File("prj/books/", "ljfad2");
```

The constructor merges parent pathname prj/books/ with child pathname ljfad2 into pathname prj/books/ljfad2. (If I had specified prj/books as the parent pathname, the constructor would have added the separator character after books.)

Tip   Because File(String pathname), File(String parent, String child), and File(File parent, String child) don't detect invalid pathname arguments (apart from throwing java.lang.NullPointerException when pathname or child is null), you must be careful when specifying pathnames. You should strive to only specify pathnames that are valid for all platforms on which the application will run. For example, instead of hard-coding a drive specifier (such as C:) in a pathname, use the roots that are returned from listRoots(). Even better, keep your pathnames relative to the current user/working directory (returned from the user.dir system property).

After obtaining a File object, you can interrogate it to learn about its stored abstract pathname by calling the methods that are described in Table 11-1.

Table 11-1. `File` *Methods for Learning About a Stored Abstract Pathname*

Method	Description
`File getAbsoluteFile()`	Return the absolute form of this `File` object's abstract pathname. This method is equivalent to `new File(this.getAbsolutePath())`.
`String getAbsolutePath()`	Return the absolute pathname string of this `File` object's abstract pathname. When it's already absolute, the pathname string is returned as if by calling `getPath()`. When it's the empty abstract pathname, the pathname string of the current user directory (identified via `user.dir`) is returned. Otherwise, the abstract pathname is resolved in a platform-dependent manner. On Unix/Linux platforms, a relative pathname is made absolute by resolving it against the current user directory. On Windows platforms, the pathname is made absolute by resolving it against the current directory of the drive named by the pathname, or the current user directory when there is no drive.
`File getCanonicalFile()`	Return the *canonical* (simplest possible, absolute and unique) form of this `File` object's abstract pathname. This method throws `java.io.IOException` when an I/O error occurs (creating the canonical pathname may require filesystem queries); it equates to `new File(this.getCanonicalPath())`.
`String getCanonicalPath()`	Return the canonical pathname string of this `File` object's abstract pathname. This method first converts this pathname to absolute form when necessary, as if by invoking `getAbsolutePath()`, and then maps it to its unique form in a platform-dependent way. Doing so typically involves removing redundant names such as "." and ".." from the pathname, resolving symbolic links (on Unix/Linux platforms), and converting drive letters to a standard case (on Windows platforms). This method throws `IOException` when an I/O error occurs (creating the canonical pathname may require filesystem queries).
`String getName()`	Return the filename or directory name denoted by this `File` object's abstract pathname. This name is the last in a pathname's name sequence. The empty string is returned when the pathname's name sequence is empty.
`String getParent()`	Return the parent pathname string of this `File` object's pathname, or return null when this pathname doesn't name a parent directory.
`File getParentFile()`	Return a `File` object storing this `File` object's abstract pathname's parent abstract pathname; return null when the parent pathname isn't a directory.
`String getPath()`	Convert this `File` object's abstract pathname into a pathname string where the names in the sequence are separated by the character stored in `File`'s `separator` field. Return the resulting pathname string.
`boolean isAbsolute()`	Return true when this `File` object's abstract pathname is absolute; otherwise, return false when it's relative. The definition of absolute pathname is system dependent. On Unix/Linux platforms, a pathname is absolute when its prefix is "/". On Windows platforms, a pathname is absolute when its prefix is a drive specifier followed by "\" or when its prefix is "\\".
`String toString()`	A synonym for `getPath()`.

Table 11-1 refers to IOException, which is the common exception superclass for those exception classes that describe various kinds of I/O errors such as java.io.FileNotFoundException.

Listing 11-2 instantiates File with its pathname command-line argument and calls some of the File methods described in Table 11-1 to learn about this pathname.

Listing 11-2. Obtaining Abstract Pathname Information

```java
import java.io.File;
import java.io.IOException;

public class PathnameInfo
{
   public static void main(final String[] args) throws IOException
   {
      if (args.length != 1)
      {
         System.err.println("usage: java PathnameInfo pathname");
         return;
      }
      File file = new File(args[0]);
      System.out.println("Absolute path = " + file.getAbsolutePath());
      System.out.println("Canonical path = " + file.getCanonicalPath());
      System.out.println("Name = " + file.getName());
      System.out.println("Parent = " + file.getParent());
      System.out.println("Path = " + file.getPath());
      System.out.println("Is absolute = " + file.isAbsolute());
   }
}
```

For example, when I specify java PathnameInfo . (the period represents the current directory on my Windows 7 platform), I observe the following output:

```
Absolute path = C:\prj\dev\ljfad2\ch11\code\PathnameInfo\.
Canonical path = C:\prj\dev\ljfad2\ch11\code\PathnameInfo
Name = .
Parent = null
Path = .
Is absolute = false
```

This output reveals that the canonical pathname doesn't include the period. It also shows that there is no parent pathname and that the pathname is relative.

Continuing, I now specify java PathnameInfo c:\reports\2012\..\2011\February. This time, I observe the following output:

```
Absolute path = c:\reports\2012\..\2011\February
Canonical path = C:\reports\2011\February
Name = February
Parent = c:\reports\2012\..\2011
Path = c:\reports\2012\..\2011\February
Is absolute = true
```

This output reveals that the canonical pathname doesn't include 2012. It also shows that the pathname is absolute.

For my final example, suppose I specify java PathnameInfo "" to obtain information for the empty pathname. In response, this application generates the following output:

```
Absolute path = C:\prj\dev\ljfad2\ch11\code\PathnameInfo
Canonical path = C:\prj\dev\ljfad2\ch11\code\PathnameInfo
Name =
Parent = null
Path =
Is absolute = false
```

The output reveals that getName() and getPath() return the empty string ("") because the empty pathname is empty.

You can interrogate the filesystem to learn about the file or directory represented by a File object's stored pathname by calling the methods that are described in Table 11-2.

Table 11-2. File Methods for Learning About a File or Directory

Method	Description
boolean canExecute()	Return true when this File object's abstract pathname represents an existing executable file.
boolean canRead()	Return true when this File object's abstract pathname represents an existing readable file.
boolean canWrite()	Return true when this File object's abstract pathname represents an existing file that can be modified.
boolean exists()	Return true if and only if the file or directory that's denoted by this File object's abstract pathname exists.
boolean isDirectory()	Return true when this File object's abstract pathname refers to an existing directory.
boolean isFile()	Return true when this File object's abstract pathname refers to an existing normal file. A file is *normal* when it's not a directory and satisfies other platform-dependent criteria: it's not a symbolic link or a named pipe, for example. Any nondirectory file created by a Java application is guaranteed to be a normal file.
boolean isHidden()	Return true when the file denoted by this File object's abstract pathname is hidden. The exact definition of *hidden* is platform dependent. On Unix/Linux platforms, a file is hidden when its name begins with a period character. On Windows platforms, a file is hidden when it has been marked as such in the filesystem.
long lastModified()	Return the time that the file denoted by this File object's abstract pathname was last modified, or 0 when the file doesn't exist or an I/O error occurred during this method call. The returned value is measured in milliseconds since the *Unix epoch* (00:00:00 GMT, January 1, 1970).
long length()	Return the length of the file denoted by this File object's abstract pathname. The return value is unspecified when the pathname denotes a directory and will be 0 when the file doesn't exist.

Listing 11-3 instantiates File with its pathname command-line argument, and calls all of the File methods described in Table 11-2 to learn about the pathname's file/directory.

Listing 11-3. Obtaining File/Directory Information

```java
import java.io.File;
import java.io.IOException;

import java.util.Date;

public class FileDirectoryInfo
{
   public static void main(final String[] args) throws IOException
   {
      if (args.length != 1)
      {
         System.err.println("usage: java FileDirectoryInfo pathname");
         return;
      }
      File file = new File(args[0]);
      System.out.println("About " + file + ":");
      System.out.println("Can execute = " + file.canExecute());
      System.out.println("Can read = " + file.canRead());
      System.out.println("Can write = " + file.canWrite());
      System.out.println("Exists = " + file.exists());
      System.out.println("Is directory = " + file.isDirectory());
      System.out.println("Is file = " + file.isFile());
      System.out.println("Is hidden = " + file.isHidden());
      System.out.println("Last modified = " + new Date(file.lastModified()));
      System.out.println("Length = " + file.length());
   }
}
```

For example, suppose I have a 3-byte read-only file named x.dat. When I specify java FileDirectoryInfo x.dat, I observe the following output:

```
About x.dat:
Can execute = true
Can read = true
Can write = false
Exists = true
Is directory = false
Is file = true
Is hidden = false
Last modified = Tue Nov 20 12:12:09 CST 2012
Length = 3
```

> **Note**   Java 6 added long getFreeSpace(), long getTotalSpace(), and long getUsableSpace() methods to File that return disk space information about the *partition* (a platform-specific portion of storage for a filesystem; for example, C:\) described by the File instance's pathname. Android supports these additional methods.

File declares five methods that return the names of files and directories located in the directory identified by a File object's abstract pathname. Table 11-3 describes these methods.

Table 11-3. File Methods for Obtaining Directory Content

Method	Description
String[] list()	Return a potentially empty array of strings naming the files and directories in the directory denoted by this File object's abstract pathname. If the pathname doesn't denote a directory, or if an I/O error occurs, this method returns null. Otherwise, it returns an array of strings, one string for each file or directory in the directory.
	Names denoting the directory itself and the directory's parent directory are not included in the result. Each string is a filename rather than a complete path. Also, there is no guarantee that the name strings in the resulting array will appear in alphabetical or any other order.
String[] list(FilenameFilter filter)	A convenience method for calling list() and returning only those Strings that satisfy filter.
File[] listFiles()	A convenience method for calling list(), converting its array of Strings to an array of Files, and returning the Files array.
File[] listFiles(FileFilter filter)	A convenience method for calling list(), converting its array of Strings to an array of Files, but only for those Strings that satisfy filter, and returning the Files array.
File[] listFiles(FilenameFilter filter)	A convenience method for calling list(), converting its array of Strings to an array of Files, but only for those Strings that satisfy filter, and returning the Files array.

The overloaded list() methods return arrays of Strings denoting file and directory names. The second method lets you return only those names of interest (e.g., only those names that end with extension .txt) via a java.io.FilenameFilter-based filter object.

The FilenameFilter interface declares a single boolean accept(File dir, String name) method that is called for each file/directory located in the directory identified by the File object's pathname:

- dir identifies the parent portion of the pathname (the directory path).
- name identifies the final directory name or the filename portion of the pathname.

The accept() method uses the arguments passed to these parameters to determine whether or not the file or directory satisfies its criteria for what is acceptable. It returns true when the file/directory name should be included in the returned array; otherwise, this method returns false.

Listing 11-4 presents a Dir(ectory) application that uses list(FilenameFilter) to obtain only those names that end with a specific extension.

Listing 11-4. Listing Specific Names

```java
import java.io.File;
import java.io.FilenameFilter;

public class Dir
{
   public static void main(final String[] args)
   {
      if (args.length != 2)
      {
         System.err.println("usage: java Dir dirpath ext");
         return;
      }
      File file = new File(args[0]);
      FilenameFilter fnf = new FilenameFilter()
                           {
                              @Override
                              public boolean accept(File dir, String name)
                              {
                                 return name.endsWith(args[1]);
                              }
                           };
      String[] names = file.list(fnf);
      for (String name: names)
         System.out.println(name);
   }
}
```

When I, for example, specify java Dir c:\windows exe on my Windows 7 platform, Dir outputs only those \windows directory filenames that have the .exe extension:

```
bfsvc.exe
explorer.exe
fveupdate.exe
HelpPane.exe
hh.exe
notepad.exe
regedit.exe
splwow64.exe
twunk_16.exe
twunk_32.exe
winhlp32.exe
write.exe
```

The overloaded listFiles() methods return arrays of Files. For the most part, they're symmetrical with their list() counterparts. However, listFiles(FileFilter) introduces an asymmetry.

The java.io.FileFilter interface declares a single boolean accept(String pathname) method that is called for each file/directory located in the directory identified by the File object's pathname: the argument passed to pathname identifies the complete path of the file or directory.

The accept() method uses this argument to determine whether or not the file or directory satisfies its criteria for what is acceptable. It returns true when the file/directory name should be included in the returned array; otherwise, this method returns false.

> **Note**   Because each interface's accept() method accomplishes the same task, you might be wondering which interface to use. If you prefer a path broken into its directory and name components, use FilenameFilter. However, if you prefer a complete pathname, use FileFilter; you can always call getParent() and getName() to get these components.

File also declares several methods for creating files and manipulating existing files. Table 11-4 describes these methods.

Table 11-4. File Methods for Creating Files and Manipulating Existing Files

Method	Description
boolean createNewFile()	Atomically create a new, empty file named by this File object's abstract pathname if and only if a file with this name doesn't yet exist. The check for file existence and the creation of the file when it doesn't exist are a single operation that's atomic with respect to all other filesystem activities that might affect the file. This method returns true when the named file doesn't exist and was successfully created, and returns false when the named file already exists. It throws IOException when an I/O error occurs.
static File createTempFile (String prefix, String suffix)	Create an empty file in the default temporary file directory using the given prefix and suffix to generate its name. This overloaded class method calls its three-parameter variant, passing prefix, suffix, and null to this other method, and returning the other method's return value.
static File createTempFile(String prefix, String suffix, File directory)	Create an empty file in the specified directory using the given prefix and suffix to generate its name. The name begins with the character sequence specified by prefix and ends with the character sequence specified by suffix; ".tmp" is used as the suffix when suffix is null. This method returns the created file's pathname when successful. It throws java.lang.IllegalArgumentException when prefix contains fewer than three characters and IOException when the file couldn't be created.

(continued)

Table 11-4. (continued)

Method	Description
`boolean delete()`	Delete the file or directory denoted by this `File` object's pathname. Return true when successful; otherwise, return false. If the pathname denotes a directory, the directory must be empty to be deleted.
`void deleteOnExit()`	Request that the file or directory denoted by this `File` object's abstract pathname be deleted when the virtual machine terminates. Reinvoking this method on the same `File` object has no effect. Once deletion has been requested, it's not possible to cancel the request. Therefore, this method should be used with care.
`boolean mkdir()`	Create the directory named by this `File` object's abstract pathname. Return true when successful; otherwise, return false.
`boolean mkdirs()`	Create the directory and any necessary intermediate directories named by this `File` object's abstract pathname. Return true when successful; otherwise, return false.
`boolean renameTo(File dest)`	Rename the file denoted by this `File` object's abstract pathname to `dest`. Return true when successful; otherwise, return false. This method throws `NullPointerException` when `dest` is null. Many aspects of this method's behavior are platform dependent. For example, the rename operation might not be able to move a file from one filesystem to another, the operation might not be atomic, or it might not succeed when a file with the destination pathname already exists. The return value should always be checked to make sure that the rename operation was successful.
`boolean setLastModified(long time)`	Set the last-modified time of the file or directory named by this `File` object's abstract pathname. Return true when successful; otherwise, return false. This method throws `IllegalArgumentException` when `time` is negative. All platforms support file-modification times to the nearest second, but some provide more precision. The `time` value will be truncated to fit the supported precision. If the operation succeeds and no intervening operations on the file take place, the next call to `lastModified()` will return the (possibly truncated) time value passed to this method.
`boolean setReadOnly()`	Mark the file or directory denoted by this `File` object's abstract pathname so that only read operations are allowed. After calling this method, the file or directory is guaranteed not to change until it's deleted or marked to allow write access. Whether or not a read-only file or directory can be deleted depends on the filesystem.

Suppose you're designing a text-editor application that a user will implement to open a text file and make changes to its content. Until the user explicitly saves these changes to the file, you want the text file to remain unchanged.

Because the user doesn't want to lose these changes when the application crashes or the computer loses power, you design the application to save these changes to a temporary file every few minutes. This way, the user has a backup of the changes.

You can use the overloaded createTempFile() methods to create the temporary file. If you don't specify a directory in which to store this file, it's created in the directory identified by the java.io.tmpdir system property.

You probably want to remove the temporary file after the user tells the application to save or discard the changes. The deleteOnExit() method lets you register a temporary file for deletion; it's deleted when the virtual machine ends without a crash/power loss.

Listing 11-5 presents a TempFileDemo application for experimenting with the createTempFile() and deleteOnExit() methods.

Listing 11-5. Experimenting With Temporary Files

```java
import java.io.File;
import java.io.IOException;

public class TempFileDemo
{
   public static void main(String[] args) throws IOException
   {
      System.out.println(System.getProperty("java.io.tmpdir"));
      File temp = File.createTempFile("text", ".txt");
      System.out.println(temp);
      temp.deleteOnExit();
   }
}
```

After outputting the location where temporary files are stored, TempFileDemo creates a temporary file whose name begins with text and ends with the .txt extension. TempFileDemo next outputs the temporary file's name and registers the temporary file for deletion on the successful termination of the application.

I observed the following output during one run of TempFileDemo (and the file disappeared on exit):

```
C:\Users\Owner\AppData\Local\Temp\
C:\Users\Owner\AppData\Local\Temp\text3173127870811188221.txt
```

> **Note** Java 6 added to File new boolean setExecutable(boolean executable),
> boolean setExecutable(boolean executable, boolean ownerOnly), boolean
> setReadable(boolean readable), boolean setReadable(boolean readable,
> boolean ownerOnly), boolean setWritable(boolean writable), and boolean
> setWritable(boolean writable, boolean ownerOnly) methods that let you set the owner's
> or everybody's execute, read, and write permissions for the file identified by the File object's abstract
> pathname. Android supports these additional methods.

Finally, File implements the java.lang.Comparable interface's compareTo() method and overrides equals() and hashCode(). Table 11-5 describes these miscellaneous methods.

Table 11-5. File's Miscellaneous Methods

Method	Description
int compareTo(File pathname)	Compare two pathnames lexicographically. The ordering defined by this method depends on the underlying platform. On Unix/Linux platforms, alphabetic case is significant when comparing pathnames; on Windows platforms, alphabetic case is insignificant. Return zero when pathname's abstract pathname equals this File object's abstract pathname, a negative value when this File object's abstract pathname is less than pathname, and a positive value otherwise. To accurately compare two File objects, call getCanonicalFile() on each File object and then compare the returned File objects.
boolean equals(Object obj)	Compare this File object with obj for equality. Abstract pathname equality depends on the underlying platform. On Unix/Linux platforms, alphabetic case is significant when comparing pathnames; on Windows platforms, alphabetic case is insignificant. Return true if and only if obj is not null and is a File object whose abstract pathname denotes the same file/directory as this File object's abstract pathname.
int hashCode()	Calculate and return a hash code for this pathname. This calculation depends on the underlying platform. On Unix/Linux platforms, a pathname's hash code equals the exclusive OR of its pathname string's hash code and decimal value 1234321. On Windows platforms, the hash code is the exclusive OR of the lowercased pathname string's hash code and decimal value 1234321. The current *locale* (geographical, political, or cultural region) is not taken into account when lowercasing the pathname string.

Working with the RandomAccessFile API

Files can be created and/or opened for *random access* in which a mixture of write and read operations can occur until the file is closed. Java supports this random access via its concrete java.io.RandomAccessFile class.

RandomAccessFile declares the following constructors:

- RandomAccessFile(File file, String mode) creates and opens a new file if it doesn't exist or opens an existing file. The file is identified by file's abstract pathname and is created and/or opened according to mode.

- RandomAccessFile(String pathname, String mode) creates and opens a new file if it doesn't exist or opens an existing file. The file is identified by pathname and is created and/or opened according to mode.

Either constructor's mode argument must be one of "r", "rw", "rws", or "rwd"; otherwise, the constructor throws IllegalArgumentException. These string literals have the following meanings:

- "r" informs the constructor to open an existing file for reading only. Any attempt to write to the file results in a thrown instance of the IOException class.

- "rw" informs the constructor to create and open a new file when it doesn't exist for reading and writing or open an existing file for reading and writing.

- "rwd" informs the constructor to create and open a new file when it doesn't exist for reading and writing or open an existing file for reading and writing. Furthermore, each update to the file's content must be written synchronously to the underlying storage device.

- "rws" informs the constructor to create and open a new file when it doesn't exist for reading and writing or open an existing file for reading and writing. Furthermore, each update to the file's content or metadata must be written synchronously to the underlying storage device.

> **Note** A file's *metadata* is data about the file and not actual file contents. Examples of metadata include the file's length and the time the file was last modified.

The "rwd" and "rws" modes ensure than any writes to a file located on a local storage device are written to the device, which guarantees that critical data isn't lost when the operating system crashes. No guarantee is made when the file doesn't reside on a local device.

> **Note** Operations on a random access file opened in "rwd" or "rws" mode are slower than these same operations on a random access file opened in "rw" mode.

These constructors throw FileNotFoundException when mode is "r" and the file identified by pathname cannot be opened (it might not exist or it might be a directory) or when mode is "rw" and pathname is read-only or a directory.

The following example demonstrates the second constructor by attempting to open an existing file for read access via the "r" mode string:

```
RandomAccessFile raf = new RandomAccessFile("employee.dat", "r");
```

A random access file is associated with a *file pointer*, a cursor that identifies the location of the next byte to write or read. When an existing file is opened, the file pointer is set to its first byte at offset 0. The file pointer is also set to 0 when the file is created.

Write or read operations start at the file pointer and advance it past the number of bytes written or read. Operations that write past the current end of the file cause the file to be extended. These operations continue until the file is closed.

RandomAccessFile declares a wide variety of methods. I present a representative sample of these methods in Table 11-6.

Table 11-6. RandomAccessFile Methods

Method	Description
void close()	Close the file and release any associated platform resources. Subsequent writes or reads result in IOException. Also, the file cannot be reopened with this RandomAccessFile object. This method throws IOException when an I/O error occurs.
FileDescriptor getFD()	Return the file's associated file descriptor object. This method throws IOException when an I/O error occurs.
long getFilePointer()	Return the file pointer's current zero-based byte offset into the file. This method throws IOException when an I/O error occurs.
long length()	Return the length (measured in bytes) of the file. This method throws IOException when an I/O error occurs.
int read()	Read and return (as an int in the range 0 to 255) the next byte from the file or return –1 when the end of the file is reached. This method blocks when no input is available and throws IOException when an I/O error occurs.
int read(byte[] b)	Read up to b.length bytes of data from the file into byte array b. This method blocks until at least 1 byte of input is available. It returns the number of bytes read into the array, or returns –1 when the end of the file is reached. It throws NullPointerException when b is null and IOException when an I/O error occurs.
char readChar()	Read and return a character from the file. This method reads 2 bytes from the file starting at the current file pointer. If the bytes read, in order, are b1 and b2, where 0 <= b1, b2 <= 255, the result is equal to (char) ((b1 << 8) | b2). This method blocks until the 2 bytes are read, the end of the file is detected, or an exception is thrown. It throws java.io.EOFException (a subclass of IOException) when the end of the file is reached before reading both bytes and IOException when an I/O error occurs.
int readInt()	Read and return a 32-bit integer from the file. This method reads 4 bytes from the file starting at the current file pointer. If the bytes read, in order, are b1, b2, b3, and b4, where 0 <= b1, b2, b3, b4 <= 255, the result is equal to (b1 << 24) | (b2 << 16) | (b3 << 8) | b4. This method blocks until the 4 bytes are read, the end of the file is detected, or an exception is thrown. It throws EOFException when the end of the file is reached before reading the 4 bytes and IOException when an I/O error occurs.
void seek(long pos)	Set the file pointer's current offset to pos (which is measured in bytes from the beginning of the file). If the offset is set beyond the end of the file, the file's length doesn't change. The file length will only change by writing after the offset has been set beyond the end of the file. This method throws IOException when the value in pos is negative or when an I/O error occurs.

(continued)

Table 11-6. (*continued*)

Method	Description
void setLength(long newLength)	Set the file's length. If the present length as returned by length() is greater than newLength, the file is truncated. In this case, if the file offset as returned by getFilePointer() is greater than newLength, the offset will be equal to newLength after setLength() returns. If the present length is smaller than newLength, the file is extended. In this case, the contents of the extended portion of the file are not defined. This method throws IOException when an I/O error occurs.
int skipBytes(int n)	Attempt to skip over n bytes. This method skips over a smaller number of bytes (possibly zero) when the end of file is reached before n bytes have been skipped. It doesn't throw EOFException in this situation. If n is negative, no bytes are skipped. The actual number of bytes skipped is returned. This method throws IOException when an I/O error occurs.
void write(byte[] b)	Write b.length bytes from byte array b to the file starting at the current file pointer position. This method throws IOException when an I/O error occurs.
void write(int b)	Write the lower 8 bits of b to the file at the current file pointer position. This method throws IOException when an I/O error occurs.
void writeChars(String s)	Write string s to the file as a sequence of characters starting at the current file pointer position. This method throws IOException when an I/O error occurs.
void writeInt(int i)	Write 32-bit integer i to the file starting at the current file pointer position. The 4 bytes are written with the high byte first. This method throws IOException when an I/O error occurs.

Most of Table 11-6's methods are fairly self-explanatory. However, the getFD() method requires further enlightenment.

> **Note**   RandomAccessFile's read-prefixed methods and skipBytes() originate in the
> java.io.DataInput interface, which this class implements. Furthermore, RandomAccessFile's
> write-prefixed methods originate in the java.io.DataOutput interface, which this class also implements.

When a file is opened, the underlying platform creates a platform-dependent structure to represent the file. A handle to this structure is stored in an instance of the java.io.FileDescriptor class, which getFD() returns.

> **Note**   A *handle* is an identifier that Java passes to the underlying platform to identify, in this case,
> a specific open file when it requires that the underlying platform perform a file operation.

FileDescriptor is a small class that declares three FileDescriptor constants named in, out, and err. These constants let System.in, System.out, and System.err provide access to the standard input, standard output, and standard error streams.

FileDescriptor also declares the following pair of methods:

- void sync() tells the underlying platform to *flush* (empty) the contents of the open file's output buffers to their associated local disk device. sync() returns after all modified data and attributes have been written to the relevant device. It throws java.io.SyncFailedException when the buffers cannot be flushed or because the platform cannot guarantee that all the buffers have been synchronized with physical media.

- boolean valid() determines whether or not this file descriptor object is valid. It returns true when the file descriptor object represents an open file or other active I/O connection; otherwise, it returns false.

Data that is written to an open file ends up being stored in the underlying platform's output buffers. When the buffers fill to capacity, the platform empties them to the disk. Buffers improve performance because disk access is slow.

However, when you write data to a random access file that's been opened via mode "rwd" or "rws", each write operation's data is written straight to the disk. As a result, write operations are slower than when the random access file is opened in "rw" mode.

Suppose you have a situation that combines writing data through the output buffers and writing data directly to the disk. The following example addresses this hybrid scenario by opening the file in mode "rw" and selectively calling FileDescriptor's sync() method.

```
RandomAccessFile raf = new RandomAccessFile("employee.dat", "rw");
FileDescriptor fd = raf.getFD();
// Perform a critical write operation.
raf.write(...);
// Synchronize with underlying disk by flushing platform's output buffers to disk.
fd.sync();
// Perform non-critical write operation where synchronization isn't necessary.
raf.write(...);
// Do other work.
// Close file, emptying output buffers to disk.
raf.close();
```

RandomAccessFile is useful for creating a *flat file database*, a single file organized into records and fields. A *record* stores a single entry (e.g., a part in a parts database) and a *field* stores a single attribute of the entry (e.g., a part number).

> **Note** The term *field* is also used to refer to a variable declared within a class. To avoid confusion with this overloaded terminology, think of a field variable as being analogous to a record's field attribute.

A flat file database typically organizes its content into a sequence of fixed-length records. Each record is further organized into one or more fixed-length fields. Figure 11-1 illustrates this concept in the context of a parts database.

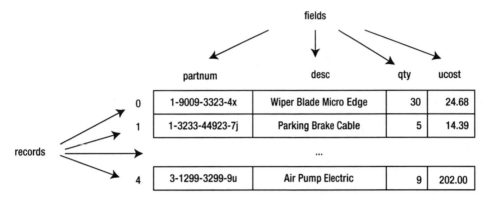

Figure 11-1. *A flat file database of automotive parts is divided into records and fields*

According to Figure 11-1, each field has a name (partnum, desc, qty, and ucost). Also, each record is assigned a number starting at 0. This example consists of five records, of which only three are shown for brevity.

To show you how to implement a flat file database in terms of `RandomAccessFile`, I've created a simple `PartsDB` class to model Figure 11-1. Check out Listing 11-6.

Listing 11-6. *Implementing the Parts Flat File Database*

```
import java.io.IOException;
import java.io.RandomAccessFile;

public class PartsDB
{
   public final static int PNUMLEN = 20;
   public final static int DESCLEN = 30;
   public final static int QUANLEN = 4;
   public final static int COSTLEN = 4;

   private final static int RECLEN = 2 * PNUMLEN + 2 * DESCLEN + QUANLEN + COSTLEN;
   private RandomAccessFile raf;

   public PartsDB(String pathname) throws IOException
   {
      raf = new RandomAccessFile(pathname, "rw");
   }

   public void append(String partnum, String partdesc, int qty, int ucost)
      throws IOException
```

```
   {
      raf.seek(raf.length());
      write(partnum, partdesc, qty, ucost);
   }

   public void close()
   {
      try
      {
         raf.close();
      }
      catch (IOException ioe)
      {
         System.err.println(ioe);
      }
   }

   public int numRecs() throws IOException
   {
      return (int) raf.length() / RECLEN;
   }

   public Part select(int recno) throws IOException
   {
      if (recno < 0 || recno >= numRecs())
         throw new IllegalArgumentException(recno + " out of range");
      raf.seek(recno * RECLEN);
      return read();
   }

   public void update(int recno, String partnum, String partdesc, int qty,
                      int ucost) throws IOException
   {
      if (recno < 0 || recno >= numRecs())
         throw new IllegalArgumentException(recno + " out of range");
      raf.seek(recno * RECLEN);
      write(partnum, partdesc, qty, ucost);
   }

   private Part read() throws IOException
   {
      StringBuffer sb = new StringBuffer();
      for (int i = 0; i < PNUMLEN; i++)
         sb.append(raf.readChar());
      String partnum = sb.toString().trim();
      sb.setLength(0);
      for (int i = 0; i < DESCLEN; i++)
         sb.append(raf.readChar());
      String partdesc = sb.toString().trim();
      int qty = raf.readInt();
      int ucost = raf.readInt();
      return new Part(partnum, partdesc, qty, ucost);
   }
```

```java
private void write(String partnum, String partdesc, int qty, int ucost)
   throws IOException
{
   StringBuffer sb = new StringBuffer(partnum);
   if (sb.length() > PNUMLEN)
      sb.setLength(PNUMLEN);
   else
   if (sb.length() < PNUMLEN)
   {
      int len = PNUMLEN - sb.length();
      for (int i = 0; i < len; i++)
         sb.append(" ");
   }
   raf.writeChars(sb.toString());
   sb = new StringBuffer(partdesc);
   if (sb.length() > DESCLEN)
      sb.setLength(DESCLEN);
   else
   if (sb.length() < DESCLEN)
   {
      int len = DESCLEN - sb.length();
      for (int i = 0; i < len; i++)
         sb.append(" ");
   }
   raf.writeChars(sb.toString());
   raf.writeInt(qty);
   raf.writeInt(ucost);
}

public static class Part
{
   private String partnum;
   private String desc;
   private int qty;
   private int ucost;

   public Part(String partnum, String desc, int qty, int ucost)
   {
      this.partnum = partnum;
      this.desc = desc;
      this.qty = qty;
      this.ucost = ucost;
   }

   String getDesc()
   {
      return desc;
   }
```

```
    String getPartnum()
    {
        return partnum;
    }

    int getQty()
    {
        return qty;
    }

    int getUnitCost()
    {
        return ucost;
    }
    }
}
```

PartsDB first declares constants that identify the lengths of the string and 32-bit integer fields. It then declares a constant that calculates the record length in terms of bytes. The calculation takes into account the fact that a character occupies 2 bytes in the file.

These constants are followed by a field named raf that is of type RandomAccessFile. This field is assigned an instance of the RandomAccessFile class in the subsequent constructor, which creates/opens a new file or opens an existing file because of "rw".

PartsDB next declares append(), close(), numRecs(), select(), and update(). These methods append a record to the file, close the file, return the number of records in the file, select and return a specific record, and update a specific record:

- The append() method first calls length() and seek(). Doing so ensures that the file pointer is positioned to the end of the file before calling the private write() method to write a record containing this method's arguments.

- RandomAccessFile's close() method can throw IOException. Because this is a rare occurrence, I chose to handle this exception in PartDB's close() method, which keeps that method's signature simple. However, I print a message when IOException occurs.

- The numRecs() method returns the number of records in the file. These records are numbered starting with 0 and ending with numRecs() - 1. Each of the select() and update() methods verifies that its recno argument lies within this range.

- The select() method calls the private read() method to return the record identified by recno as an instance of the nested Part class. Part's constructor initializes a Part object to a record's field values, and its getter methods return these values.

- The update() method is equally simple. As with select(), it first positions the file pointer to the start of the record identified by recno. As with append(), it calls write() to write out its arguments but replaces a record instead of adding one.

Records are written with the private write() method. Because fields must have exact sizes, write() pads String-based values that are shorter than a field size with spaces on the right and truncates these values to the field size when needed.

Records are read via the private read() method. read() removes the padding before saving a String-based field value in the Part object.

By itself, PartsDB is useless. You need an application that lets you experiment with this class, and Listing 11-7 fulfills this requirement.

Listing 11-7. Experimenting with the Parts Flat File Database

```java
import java.io.IOException;

public class UsePartsDB
{
   public static void main(String[] args)
   {
      PartsDB pdb = null;
      try
      {
         pdb = new PartsDB("parts.db");
         if (pdb.numRecs() == 0)
         {
            // Populate the database with records.
            pdb.append("1-9009-3323-4x", "Wiper Blade Micro Edge", 30, 2468);
            pdb.append("1-3233-44923-7j", "Parking Brake Cable", 5, 1439);
            pdb.append("2-3399-6693-2m", "Halogen Bulb H4 55/60W", 22, 813);
            pdb.append("2-599-2029-6k", "Turbo Oil Line O-Ring ", 26, 155);
            pdb.append("3-1299-3299-9u", "Air Pump Electric", 9, 20200);
         }
         dumpRecords(pdb);
         pdb.update(1, "1-3233-44923-7j", "Parking Brake Cable", 5, 1995);
         dumpRecords(pdb);
      }
      catch (IOException ioe)
      {
         System.err.println(ioe);
      }
      finally
      {
         if (pdb != null)
            pdb.close();
      }
   }

   static void dumpRecords(PartsDB pdb) throws IOException
   {
      for (int i = 0; i < pdb.numRecs(); i++)
      {
         PartsDB.Part part = pdb.select(i);
         System.out.print(format(part.getPartnum(), PartsDB.PNUMLEN, true));
         System.out.print(" | ");
```

```
            System.out.print(format(part.getDesc(), PartsDB.DESCLEN, true));
            System.out.print(" | ");
            System.out.print(format("" + part.getQty(), 10, false));
            System.out.print(" | ");
            String s = part.getUnitCost() / 100 + "." + part.getUnitCost() % 100;
            if (s.charAt(s.length() - 2) == '.') s += "0";
            System.out.println(format(s, 10, false));
         }
         System.out.println("Number of records = " + pdb.numRecs());
         System.out.println();
      }

      static String format(String value, int maxWidth, boolean leftAlign)
      {
         StringBuffer sb = new StringBuffer();
         int len = value.length();
         if (len > maxWidth)
         {
            len = maxWidth;
            value = value.substring(0, len);
         }
         if (leftAlign)
         {
            sb.append(value);
            for (int i = 0; i < maxWidth-len; i++)
               sb.append(" ");
         }
         else
         {
            for (int i = 0; i < maxWidth-len; i++)
               sb.append(" ");
            sb.append(value);
         }
         return sb.toString();
      }
   }
}
```

Listing 11-7's main() method begins by instantiating PartsDB, with parts.db as the name of the database file. When this file has no records, numRecs() returns 0 and several records are appended to the file via the append() method.

main() next dumps the five records stored in parts.db to the standard output stream, updates the unit cost in the record whose number is 1, once again dumps these records to the standard output stream to show this change, and closes the database.

Note   I store unit cost values as integer-based penny amounts. For example, I specify literal 1995 to represent 1995 pennies, or $19.95. If I were to use java.math.BigDecimal objects to store currency values, I would have to refactor PartsDB to take advantage of object serialization, and I'm not prepared to do that right now. (I discuss object serialization later in this chapter.)

main() relies on a dumpRecords() helper method to dump these records, and dumpRecords() relies on a format() helper method to format field values so that they can be presented in properly aligned columns—I could have used java.util.Formatter (see Chapter 10) instead. The following output reveals this alignment:

```
1-9009-3323-4x      | Wiper Blade Micro Edge        |      30 |     24.68
1-3233-44923-7j     | Parking Brake Cable           |       5 |     14.39
2-3399-6693-2m      | Halogen Bulb H4 55/60W        |      22 |      8.13
2-599-2029-6k       | Turbo Oil Line O-Ring         |      26 |      1.55
3-1299-3299-9u      | Air Pump Electric             |       9 |    202.00
Number of records = 5

1-9009-3323-4x      | Wiper Blade Micro Edge        |      30 |     24.68
1-3233-44923-7j     | Parking Brake Cable           |       5 |     19.95
2-3399-6693-2m      | Halogen Bulb H4 55/60W        |      22 |      8.13
2-599-2029-6k       | Turbo Oil Line O-Ring         |      26 |      1.55
3-1299-3299-9u      | Air Pump Electric             |       9 |    202.00
Number of records = 5
```

And there you have it: a simple flat file database. Despite its lack of support for advanced database features such as indexes and transaction management, a flat file database might be all that your Android application requires.

> **Note** To learn more about flat file databases, check out Wikipedia's "Flat file database" entry (http://en.wikipedia.org/wiki/Flat_file_database).

Working with Streams

Along with File and RandomAccessFile, Java uses streams to perform I/O operations. A *stream* is an ordered sequence of bytes of arbitrary length. Bytes flow over an *output stream* from an application to a destination and flow over an *input stream* from a source to an application. Figure 11-2 illustrates these flows.

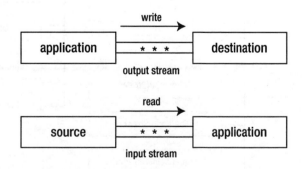

Figure 11-2. *Conceptualizing output and input streams as flows of bytes*

> **Note** Java's use of the word *stream* is analogous to "stream of water," "stream of electrons," and so on.

Java recognizes various stream destinations; for example, byte arrays, files, screens, *sockets* (network endpoints), and thread pipes. Java also recognizes various stream sources. Examples include byte arrays, files, keyboards, sockets, and thread pipes. (I will discuss sockets in Chapter 12.)

Stream Classes Overview

The java.io package provides several output stream and input stream classes that are descendents of the abstract OutputStream and InputStream classes. Figure 11-3 reveals the hierarchy of output stream classes.

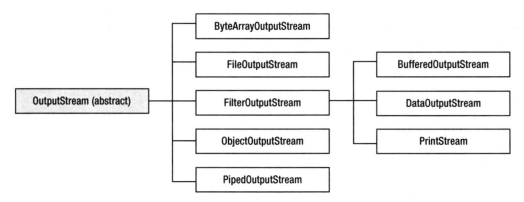

Figure 11-3. *All output stream classes except for* PrintStream *are denoted by their* OutputStream *suffixes*

Figure 11-4 reveals the hierarchy of input stream classes.

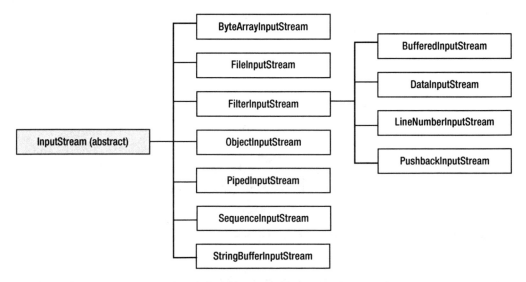

Figure 11-4. LineNumberInputStream *and* StringBufferInputStream *are deprecated*

LineNumberInputStream and StringBufferInputStream have been deprecated because they don't support different character encodings, a topic I discuss later in this chapter. LineNumberReader and StringReader are their replacements. (I discuss readers later in this chapter.)

> **Note**   PrintStream is another class that should be deprecated because it doesn't support different character encodings; PrintWriter is its replacement. However, it's doubtful that Oracle (and Google) will deprecate this class because PrintStream is the type of the java.lang.System class's out and err class fields, and too much legacy code depends on this fact.

Other Java packages provide additional output stream and input stream classes. For example, java.util.zip provides four output stream classes that compress uncompressed data into various formats and four matching input stream classes that uncompress compressed data from the same formats:

- CheckedOutputStream
- CheckedInputStream
- DeflaterOutputStream
- GZIPOutputStream
- GZIPInputStream
- InflaterInputStream
- ZipOutputStream
- ZipInputStream

Also, the java.util.jar package provides a pair of stream classes for writing content to a JAR file and for reading content from a JAR file:

- JarOutputStream
- JarInputStream

In the next several sections, I take you on a tour of most of java.io's output stream and input stream classes, beginning with OutputStream and InputStream.

OutputStream and InputStream

Java provides the OutputStream and InputStream classes for performing stream I/O. OutputStream is the superclass of all output stream subclasses. Table 11-7 describes OutputStream's methods.

Table 11-7. OutputStream Methods

Method	Description
`void close()`	Close this output stream and release any platform resources associated with the stream. This method throws `IOException` when an I/O error occurs.
`void flush()`	Flush this output stream by writing any buffered output bytes to the destination. If the intended destination of this output stream is an abstraction provided by the underlying platform (for example, a file), flushing the stream only guarantees that bytes previously written to the stream are passed to the underlying platform for writing; it doesn't guarantee that they're actually written to a physical device such as a disk drive. This method throws `IOException` when an I/O error occurs.
`void write(byte[] b)`	Write `b.length` bytes from byte array `b` to this output stream. In general, `write(b)` behaves as if you specified `write(b, 0, b.length)`. This method throws `NullPointerException` when `b` is null and `IOException` when an I/O error occurs.
`void write(byte[] b, int off, int len)`	Write `len` bytes from byte array `b` starting at offset `off` to this output stream. This method throws `NullPointerException` when `b` is null; `java.lang.IndexOutOfBoundsException` when `off` is negative, `len` is negative, or `off` + `len` is greater than `b.length`; and `IOException` when an I/O error occurs.
`void write(int b)`	Write byte `b` to this output stream. Only the 8 low-order bits are written; the 24 high-order bits are ignored. This method throws `IOException` when an I/O error occurs.

The `flush()` method is useful in a long-running application where you need to save changes every so often, for example, the previously mentioned text-editor application that saves changes to a temporary file every few minutes. Remember that `flush()` only flushes bytes to the platform; doing so doesn't necessarily result in the platform flushing these bytes to the disk.

> **Note**   The `close()` method automatically flushes the output stream. If an application ends before `close()` is called, the output stream is automatically closed and its data is flushed.

`InputStream` is the superclass of all input stream subclasses. Table 11-8 describes `InputStream`'s methods.

Table 11-8. InputStream Methods

Method	Description
int available()	Return an estimate of the number of bytes that can be read from this input stream via the next read() method call (or skipped over via skip()) without blocking the calling thread. This method throws IOException when an I/O error occurs.
	It's never correct to use this method's return value to allocate a buffer for holding all of the stream's data because a subclass might not return the total size of the stream.
void close()	Close this input stream and release any platform resources associated with the stream. This method throws IOException when an I/O error occurs.
void mark(int readlimit)	Mark the current position in this input stream. A subsequent call to reset() repositions this stream to the last marked position so that subsequent read operations re-read the same bytes. The readlimit argument tells this input stream to allow that many bytes to be read before invalidating this mark (so that the stream cannot be reset to the marked position).
boolean markSupported()	Return true when this input stream supports mark() and reset(); otherwise, return false.
int read()	Read and return (as an int in the range 0 to 255) the next byte from this input stream, or return −1 when the end of the stream is reached. This method blocks until input is available, the end of the stream is detected, or an exception is thrown. It throws IOException when an I/O error occurs.
int read(byte[] b)	Read some number of bytes from this input stream and store them in byte array b. Return the number of bytes actually read (which might be less than b's length but is never more than this length), or return −1 when the end of the stream is reached (no byte is available to read). This method blocks until input is available, the end of the stream is detected, or an exception is thrown. It throws NullPointerException when b is null and IOException when an I/O error occurs.
int read(byte[] b, int off, int len)	Read no more than len bytes from this input stream and store them in byte array b, starting at the offset specified by off. Return the number of bytes actually read (which might be less than len but is never more than len), or return −1 when the end of the stream is reached (no byte is available to read). This method blocks until input is available, the end of the stream is detected, or an exception is thrown. It throws NullPointerException when b is null; IndexOutOfBoundsException when off is negative, len is negative, or len is greater than b.length - off; and IOException when an I/O error occurs.
void reset()	Reposition this input stream to the position at the time mark() was last called. This method throws IOException when this input stream has not been marked or the mark has been invalidated.
long skip(long n)	Skip over and discard n bytes of data from this input stream. This method might skip over some smaller number of bytes (possibly zero), for example, when the end of the file is reached before n bytes have been skipped. The actual number of bytes skipped is returned. When n is negative, no bytes are skipped. This method throws IOException when this input stream doesn't support skipping or when some other I/O error occurs.

InputStream subclasses such as ByteArrayInputStream support marking the current read position in the input stream via the mark() method and later return to that position via the reset() method.

> **Caution**   Don't forget to call markSupported() to find out if the subclass supports mark() and reset().

ByteArrayOutputStream and ByteArrayInputStream

Byte arrays are often useful as stream destinations and sources. The ByteArrayOutputStream class lets you write a stream of bytes to a byte array; the ByteArrayInputStream class lets you read a stream of bytes from a byte array.

ByteArrayOutputStream declares two constructors. Each constructor creates a byte array output stream with an internal byte array; a copy of this array can be returned by calling ByteArrayOutputStream's byte[] toByteArray() method:

- ByteArrayOutputStream() creates a byte array output stream with an internal byte array whose initial size is 32 bytes. This array grows as necessary.

- ByteArrayOutputStream(int size) creates a byte array output stream with an internal byte array whose initial size is specified by size and grows as necessary. This constructor throws IllegalArgumentException when size is less than zero.

The following example uses ByteArrayOutputStream() to create a byte array output stream with an internal byte array set to the default size:

```
ByteArrayOutputStream baos = new ByteArrayOutputStream();
```

ByteArrayInputStream also declares a pair of constructors. Each constructor creates a byte array input stream based on the specified byte array and also keeps track of the next byte to read from the array and the number of bytes to read:

- ByteArrayInputStream(byte[] ba) creates a byte array input stream that uses ba as its byte array (ba is used directly; a copy isn't created). The position is set to 0 and the number of bytes to read is set to ba.length.

- ByteArrayInputStream(byte[] ba, int offset, int count) creates a byte array input stream that uses ba as its byte array (no copy is made). The position is set to offset and the number of bytes to read is set to count.

The following example uses ByteArrayInputStream(byte[]) to create a byte array input stream whose source is a copy of the previous byte array output stream's byte array:

```
ByteArrayInputStream bais = new ByteArrayInputStream(baos.toByteArray());
```

ByteArrayOutputStream and ByteArrayInputStream are useful in a scenario where you need to convert an image to an array of bytes, process these bytes in some manner, and convert the bytes back to the image.

For example, suppose you're writing an Android-based image-processing application. You decode a file containing the image into an Android-specific android.graphics.BitMap instance, compress this instance into a ByteArrayOutputStream instance, obtain a copy of the byte array output stream's array, process this array in some manner, convert this array to a ByteArrayInputStream instance, and use the byte array input stream to decode these bytes into another BitMap instance, as follows:

```
String pathname = ... ; // Assume a legitimate pathname to an image.
Bitmap bm = BitmapFactory.decodeFile(pathname);
ByteArrayOutputStream baos = new ByteArrayOutputStream();
if (bm.compress(Bitmap.CompressFormat.PNG, 100, baos))
{
   byte[] imageBytes = baos.toByteArray();
   // Do something with imageBytes.
   bm = BitMapFactory.decodeStream(new ByteArrayInputStream(imageBytes));
}
```

This example obtains an image file's pathname and then calls the concrete android.graphics.BitmapFactory class's Bitmap decodeFile(String pathname) class method. This method decodes the image file identified by pathname into a bitmap and returns a Bitmap instance that represents this bitmap.

After creating a ByteArrayOutputStream object, the example uses the returned BitMap instance to call BitMap's boolean compress(Bitmap.CompressFormat format, int quality, OutputStream stream) method to write a compressed version of the bitmap to the byte array output stream:

- format identifies the format of the compressed image. I've chosen to use the popular Portable Network Graphics (PNG) format.

- quality hints to the compressor as to how much compression is required. This value ranges from 0 through 100, where 0 means maximum compression at the expense of quality and 100 means maximum quality at the expense of compression. Formats such as PNG ignore quality because they employ lossless compression.

- stream identifies the stream on which to write the compressed image data.

When compress() returns true, which means that it successfully compressed the image onto the byte array output stream in the PNG format, the ByteArrayOutputStream object's toByteArray() method is called to create and return a byte array with the image's bytes.

Continuing, the array is processed, a ByteArrayInputStream object is created with the processed bytes serving as the source of this stream, and BitmapFactory's BitMap decodeStream(InputStream is) class method is called to convert the byte array input stream's source of bytes to a BitMap instance.

FileOutputStream and FileInputStream

Files are common stream destinations and sources. The concrete FileOutputStream class lets you write a stream of bytes to a file; the concrete FileInputStream class lets you read a stream of bytes from a file.

FileOutputStream subclasses OutputStream and declares five constructors for creating file output streams. For example, FileOutputStream(String name) creates a file output stream to the existing file identified by name. This constructor throws FileNotFoundException when the file doesn't exist and cannot be created, it is a directory rather than a normal file, or there is some other reason why the file cannot be opened for output.

The following example uses FileOutputStream(String pathname) to create a file output stream with employee.dat as its destination:

```
FileOutputStream fos = new FileOutputStream("employee.dat");
```

> **Tip** FileOutputStream(String name) overwrites an existing file. To append data instead of overwriting existing content, call a FileOutputStream constructor that includes a boolean append parameter and pass true to this parameter.

FileInputStream subclasses InputStream and declares three constructors for creating file input streams. For example, FileInputStream(String name) creates a file input stream from the existing file identified by name. This constructor throws FileNotFoundException when the file doesn't exist, it is a directory rather than a normal file, or there is some other reason why the file cannot be opened for input.

The following example uses FileInputStream(String name) to create a file input stream with employee.dat as its source:

```
FileInputStream fis = new FileInputStream("employee.dat");
```

FileOutputStream and FileInputStream are useful in a file-copying context. Listing 11-8 presents the source code to a Copy application that provides a demonstration.

Listing 11-8. Copying a Source File to a Destination File

```java
import java.io.FileInputStream;
import java.io.FileNotFoundException;
import java.io.FileOutputStream;
import java.io.IOException;

public class Copy
{
   public static void main(String[] args)
   {
      if (args.length != 2)
      {
         System.err.println("usage: java Copy srcfile dstfile");
         return;
      }
      FileInputStream fis = null;
      FileOutputStream fos = null;
      try
      {
         fis = new FileInputStream(args[0]);
         fos = new FileOutputStream(args[1]);
         int b; // I chose b instead of byte because byte is a reserved word.
         while ((b = fis.read()) != -1)
            fos.write(b);
      }
```

```
    catch (FileNotFoundException fnfe)
    {
        System.err.println(args[0] + " could not be opened for input, or " +
                            args[1] + " could not be created for output");
    }
    catch (IOException ioe)
    {
        System.err.println("I/O error: " + ioe.getMessage());
    }
    finally
    {
        if (fis != null)
            try
            {
                fis.close();
            }
            catch (IOException ioe)
            {
                assert false; // shouldn't happen in this context
            }

        if (fos != null)
            try
            {
                fos.close();
            }
            catch (IOException ioe)
            {
                assert false; // shouldn't happen in this context
            }
    }
  }
}
```

Listing 11-8's main() method first verifies that two command-line arguments, identifying the names of source and destination files, are specified. It then proceeds to instantiate FileInputStream and FileOutputStream and enter a while loop that repeatedly reads bytes from the file input stream and writes them to the file output stream.

Of course something might go wrong. Perhaps the source file doesn't exist, or perhaps the destination file cannot be created (a same-named read-only file might exist, for example). In either scenario, FileNotFoundException is thrown and must be handled. Another possibility is that an I/O error occurred during the copy operation. Such an error results in IOException.

Regardless of an exception being thrown or not, the input and output streams are closed via the finally block. In a simple application like this, I could ignore the close() method calls and let the application terminate. Although Java automatically closes open files at this point, it's good form to explicitly close files on exit.

Because close() is capable of throwing an instance of the checked IOException class, a call to this method is wrapped in a try block with an appropriate catch block that catches this exception. Notice the if statement that precedes each try block. This statement is necessary to avoid a thrown NullPointerException instance should either fis or fos contain the null reference.

PipedOutputStream and PipedInputStream

Threads must often communicate. One approach involves using shared variables. Another approach involves using piped streams via the PipedOutputStream and PipedInputStream classes. The PipedOutputStream class lets a sending thread write a stream of bytes to an instance of the PipedInputStream class, which a receiving thread uses to subsequently read those bytes.

> **Caution**   Attempting to use a PipedOutputStream object and a PipedInputStream object from a single thread is not recommended because it might deadlock the thread.

PipedOutputStream declares a pair of constructors for creating piped output streams:

- PipedOutputStream() creates a piped output stream that's not yet connected to a piped input stream. It must be connected to a piped input stream, either by the receiver or the sender, before being used.

- PipedOutputStream(PipedInputStream dest) creates a piped output stream that's connected to piped input stream dest. Bytes written to the piped output stream can be read from dest. This constructor throws IOException when an I/O error occurs.

PipedOutputStream declares a void connect(PipedInputStream dest) method that connects this piped output stream to dest. This method throws IOException when this piped output stream is already connected to another piped input stream.

PipedInputStream declares four constructors for creating piped input streams:

- PipedInputStream() creates a piped input stream that's not yet connected to a piped output stream. It must be connected to a piped output stream before being used.

- PipedInputStream(int pipeSize) creates a piped input stream that's not yet connected to a piped output stream and uses pipeSize to size the piped input stream's buffer. It must be connected to a piped output stream before being used. This constructor throws IllegalArgumentException when pipeSize is less than or equal to 0.

- PipedInputStream(PipedOutputStream src) creates a piped input stream that's connected to piped output stream src. Bytes written to src can be read from this piped input stream. This constructor throws IOException when an I/O error occurs.

- PipedInputStream(PipedOutputStream src, int pipeSize) creates a piped input stream that's connected to piped output stream src and uses pipeSize to size the piped input stream's buffer. Bytes written to src can be read from this piped input stream. This constructor throws IOException when an I/O error occurs and IllegalArgumentException when pipeSize is less than or equal to 0.

PipedInputStream declares a void connect(PipedOutputStream src) method that connects this piped input stream to src. This method throws IOException when this piped input stream is already connected to another piped output stream.

The easiest way to create a pair of piped streams is in the same thread and in either order. For example, you can first create the piped output stream:

```
PipedOutputStream pos = new PipedOutputStream();
PipedInputStream pis = new PipedInputStream(pos);
```

Alternatively, you can first create the piped input stream:

```
PipedInputStream pis = new PipedInputStream();
PipedOutputStream pos = new PipedOutputStream(pis);
```

You can leave both streams unconnected and later connect them to each other using the appropriate piped stream's connect() method, as follows:

```
PipedOutputStream pos = new PipedOutputStream();
PipedInputStream pis = new PipedInputStream();
// ...
pos.connect(pis);
```

Listing 11-9 presents a PipedStreamsDemo application whose sender thread streams a sequence of randomly generated byte integers to a receiver thread, which outputs this sequence.

Listing 11-9. Piping Randomly Generated Bytes from a Sender Thread to a Receiver Thread

```
import java.io.IOException;
import java.io.PipedInputStream;
import java.io.PipedOutputStream;

public class PipedStreamsDemo
{
   public static void main(String[] args) throws IOException
   {
      final PipedOutputStream pos = new PipedOutputStream();
      final PipedInputStream pis = new PipedInputStream(pos);
      Runnable senderTask = new Runnable()
                           {
                              final static int LIMIT = 10;

                              @Override
                              public void run()
                              {
                                 try
                                 {
                                    for (int i = 0 ; i < LIMIT; i++)
                                       pos.write((byte) (Math.random() * 256));
                                 }
                                 catch (IOException ioe)
```

```
                  {
                     ioe.printStackTrace();
                  }
                  finally
                  {
                     try
                     {
                        pos.close();
                     }
                     catch (IOException ioe)
                     {
                        ioe.printStackTrace();
                     }
                  }
               }
            };
      Runnable receiverTask = new Runnable()
                  {
                     @Override
                     public void run()
                     {
                        try
                        {
                           int b;
                           while ((b = pis.read()) != -1)
                              System.out.println(b);
                        }
                        catch (IOException ioe)
                        {
                           ioe.printStackTrace();
                        }
                        finally
                        {
                           try
                           {
                              pis.close();
                           }
                           catch (IOException ioe)
                           {
                              ioe.printStackTrace();
                           }
                        }
                     }
                  };
      Thread sender = new Thread(senderTask);
      Thread receiver = new Thread(receiverTask);
      sender.start();
      receiver.start();
   }
}
```

Listing 11-9's main() method creates piped output and piped input streams that will be used by the senderTask thread to communicate a sequence of randomly generated byte integers and by the receiverTask thread to receive this sequence.

The sender task's run() method explicitly closes its pipe stream when it finishes sending the data. If it didn't do this, an IOException instance with a "write end dead" message would be thrown when the receiver thread invoked read() for the final time (which would otherwise return −1 to indicate end of stream). For more information on this message, check out Daniel Ferber's "Whats this? IOException: Write end dead" blog post (http://techtavern.wordpress.com/2008/07/16/whats-this-ioexception-write-end-dead/).

Compile Listing 11-9 (javac PipedStreamsDemo.java) and run this application (java PipedStreamsDemo). You'll discover output similar to the following:

```
93
23
125
50
126
131
210
29
150
91
```

FilterOutputStream and FilterInputStream

Byte array, file, and piped streams pass bytes unchanged to their destinations. Java also supports *filter streams* that buffer, compress/uncompress, encrypt/decrypt, or otherwise manipulate a stream's byte sequence (which is input to the filter) before it reaches its destination.

A *filter output stream* takes the data passed to its write() methods (the input stream), filters it, and writes the filtered data to an underlying output stream, which might be another filter output stream or a destination output stream such as a file output stream.

Filter output streams are created from subclasses of the concrete FilterOutputStream class, an OutputStream subclass. FilterOutputStream declares a single FilterOutputStream(OutputStream out) constructor that creates a filter output stream built on top of out, the underlying output stream.

Listing 11-10 reveals that it's easy to subclass FilterOutputStream. At minimum, you declare a constructor that passes its OutputStream argument to FilterOutputStream's constructor and override FilterOutputStream's write(int) method.

Listing 11-10. Scrambling a Stream of Bytes

```java
import java.io.FilterOutputStream;
import java.io.IOException;
import java.io.OutputStream;

public class ScrambledOutputStream extends FilterOutputStream
{
    private int[] map;
```

```
    public ScrambledOutputStream(OutputStream out, int[] map)
    {
        super(out);
        if (map == null)
            throw new NullPointerException("map is null");
        if (map.length != 256)
            throw new IllegalArgumentException("map.length != 256");
        this.map = map;
    }

    @Override
    public void write(int b) throws IOException
    {
        out.write(map[b]);
    }
}
```

Listing 11-10 presents a ScrambledOutputStream class that performs trivial encryption on its input stream by scrambling the input stream's bytes via a remapping operation. This constructor takes a pair of arguments:

- out identifies the output stream on which to write the scrambled bytes.

- map identifies an array of 256 byte-integer values to which input stream bytes map.

The constructor first passes its out argument to the FilterOutputStream parent via a super(out); call. It then verifies its map argument's integrity (map must be nonnull and have a length of 256: a byte stream offers exactly 256 bytes to map) before saving map.

The write(int) method is trivial: it calls the underlying output stream's write(int) method with the byte to which argument b maps. FilterOutputStream declares out to be protected (for performance), which is why I can directly access this field.

> **Note**   It's only essential to override write(int) because FilterOutputStream's other two
> write() methods are implemented via this method.

Listing 11-11 presents the source code to a Scramble application for experimenting with scrambling a source file's bytes via ScrambledOutputStream and writing these scrambled bytes to a destination file.

Listing 11-11. Scrambling a File's Bytes

```
import java.io.FileInputStream;
import java.io.FileOutputStream;
import java.io.IOException;

import java.util.Random;
```

```java
public class Scramble
{
   public static void main(String[] args)
   {
      if (args.length != 2)
      {
         System.err.println("usage: java Scramble srcpath destpath");
         return;
      }
      FileInputStream fis = null;
      ScrambledOutputStream sos = null;
      try
      {
         fis = new FileInputStream(args[0]);
         FileOutputStream fos = new FileOutputStream(args[1]);
         sos = new ScrambledOutputStream(fos, makeMap());
         int b;
         while ((b = fis.read()) != -1)
            sos.write(b);
      }
      catch (IOException ioe)
      {
         ioe.printStackTrace();
      }
      finally
      {
         if (fis != null)
            try
            {
               fis.close();
            }
            catch (IOException ioe)
            {
               ioe.printStackTrace();
            }
         if (sos != null)
            try
            {
               sos.close();
            }
            catch (IOException ioe)
            {
               ioe.printStackTrace();
            }
      }
   }

   static int[] makeMap()
   {
      int[] map = new int[256];
      for (int i = 0; i < map.length; i++)
         map[i] = i;
```

```
    // Shuffle map.
    Random r = new Random(0);
    for (int i = 0; i < map.length; i++)
    {
        int n = r.nextInt(map.length);
        int temp = map[i];
        map[i] = map[n];
        map[n] = temp;
    }
    return map;
    }
}
```

Scramble's `main()` method first verifies the number of command-line arguments: the first argument identifies the source path of the file with unscrambled content; the second argument identifies the destination path of the file that stores scrambled content.

Assuming that two command-line arguments have been specified, `main()` instantiates `FileInputStream`, creating a file input stream that's connected to the file identified by `args[0]`.

Continuing, `main()` instantiates `FileOutputStream`, creating a file output stream that's connected to the file identified by `args[1]`. It then instantiates `ScrambledOutputStream` and passes the `FileOutputStream` instance to `ScrambledOutputStream`'s constructor.

> **Note**   When a stream instance is passed to another stream class's constructor, the two streams are *chained together*. For example, the scrambled output stream is chained to the file output stream.

`main()` now enters a loop, reading bytes from the file input stream and writing them to the scrambled output stream by calling `ScrambledOutputStream`'s `write(int)` method. This loop continues until `FileInputStream`'s `read()` method returns -1 (end of file).

The finally block closes the file input stream and scrambled output stream by calling their `close()` methods. It doesn't call the file output stream's `close()` method because `FilterOutputStream` automatically calls the underlying output stream's `close()` method.

The `makeMap()` method is responsible for creating the map array that's passed to `ScrambledOutputStream`'s constructor. The idea is to populate the array with all 256 byte-integer values, storing them in random order.

> **Note**   I pass 0 as the seed argument when creating the `java.util.Random` object to return a predictable sequence of random numbers. I need to use the same sequence of random numbers when creating the complementary map array in the `Unscramble` application, which I will present shortly. Unscrambling will not work without the same sequence.

Suppose you have a simple 15-byte file named hello.txt that contains "Hello, World!" (followed by a carriage return and a line feed). If you execute java Scramble hello.txt hello.out on a Windows 7 platform, you'll observe Figure 11-5's scrambled output.

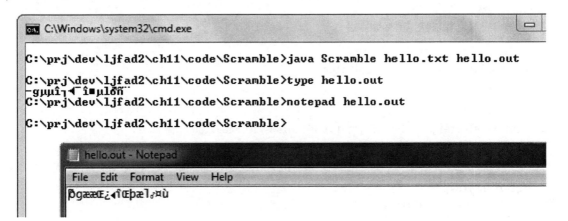

Figure 11-5. Different fonts yield different-looking scrambled output

A *filter input stream* takes the data obtained from its underlying input stream—which might be another filter input stream or a source input stream such as a file input stream—filters it, and makes this data available via its read() methods (the output stream).

Filter input streams are created from subclasses of the concrete FilterInputStream class, an InputStream subclass. FilterInputStream declares a single FilterInputStream(InputStream in) constructor that creates a filter input stream built on top of in, the underlying input stream.

Listing 11-12 shows that it's easy to subclass FilterInputStream. At minimum, declare a constructor that passes its InputStream argument to FilterInputStream's constructor and override FilterInputStream's read() and read(byte[], int, int) methods.

Listing 11-12. Unscrambling a Stream of Bytes

```java
import java.io.FilterInputStream;
import java.io.InputStream;
import java.io.IOException;

public class ScrambledInputStream extends FilterInputStream
{
    private int[] map;

    public ScrambledInputStream(InputStream in, int[] map)
    {
        super(in);
        if (map == null)
            throw new NullPointerException("map is null");
```

```
        if (map.length != 256)
            throw new IllegalArgumentException("map.length != 256");
        this.map = map;
    }

    @Override
    public int read() throws IOException
    {
        int value = in.read();
        return (value == -1) ? -1 : map[value];
    }

    @Override
    public int read(byte[] b, int off, int len) throws IOException
    {
        int nBytes = in.read(b, off, len);
        if (nBytes <= 0)
            return nBytes;
        for (int i = 0; i < nBytes; i++)
            b[off + i] = (byte) map[off + i];
        return nBytes;
    }
}
```

Listing 11-12 presents a ScrambledInputStream class that performs trivial decryption on its underlying input stream by unscrambling the underlying input stream's scrambled bytes via a remapping operation.

The read() method first reads the scrambled byte from its underlying input stream. If the returned value is −1 (end of file), this value is returned to its caller. Otherwise, the byte is mapped to its unscrambled value, which is returned.

The read(byte[], int, int) method is similar to read() but stores bytes read from the underlying input stream in a byte array, taking an offset into this array and a length (number of bytes to read) into account.

Once again, −1 might be returned from the underlying read() method call. If so, this value must be returned. Otherwise, each byte in the array is mapped to its unscrambled value, and the number of bytes read is returned.

> **Note** It's only essential to override read() and read(byte[], int, int) because
> FilterInputStream's read(byte[]) method is implemented via the latter method.

Listing 11-13 presents the source code to an Unscramble application for experimenting with ScrambledInputStream by unscrambling a source file's bytes and writing these unscrambled bytes to a destination file.

Listing 11-13. Unscrambling a File's Bytes

```java
import java.io.FileInputStream;
import java.io.FileOutputStream;
import java.io.IOException;

import java.util.Random;

public class Unscramble
{
   public static void main(String[] args)
   {
      if (args.length != 2)
      {
         System.err.println("usage: java Unscramble srcpath destpath");
         return;
      }
      ScrambledInputStream sis = null;
      FileOutputStream fos = null;
      try
      {
         FileInputStream fis = new FileInputStream(args[0]);
         sis = new ScrambledInputStream(fis, makeMap());
         fos = new FileOutputStream(args[1]);
         int b;
         while ((b = sis.read()) != -1)
            fos.write(b);
      }
      catch (IOException ioe)
      {
         ioe.printStackTrace();
      }
      finally
      {
         if (sis != null)
            try
            {
               sis.close();
            }
            catch (IOException ioe)
            {
               ioe.printStackTrace();
            }
         if (fos != null)
            try
            {
               fos.close();
            }
```

```
            catch (IOException ioe)
            {
                ioe.printStackTrace();
            }
        }
    }

    static int[] makeMap()
    {
        int[] map = new int[256];
        for (int i = 0; i < map.length; i++)
            map[i] = i;
        // Shuffle map.
        Random r = new Random(0);
        for (int i = 0; i < map.length; i++)
        {
            int n = r.nextInt(map.length);
            int temp = map[i];
            map[i] = map[n];
            map[n] = temp;
        }
        int[] temp = new int[256];
        for (int i = 0; i < temp.length; i++)
            temp[map[i]] = i;
        return temp;
    }
}
```

Unscramble's `main()` method first verifies the number of command-line arguments: the first argument identifies the source path of the file with scrambled content; the second argument identifies the destination path of the file that stores unscrambled content.

Assuming that two command-line arguments have been specified, `main()` instantiates `FileInputStream`, creating a file input stream that's connected to the file identified by `args[1]`.

Continuing, `main()` instantiates `FileInputStream`, creating a file input stream that's connected to the file identified by `args[0]`. It then instantiates `ScrambledInputStream` and passes the `FileInputStream` instance to `ScrambledInputStream`'s constructor.

Note   When a stream instance is passed to another stream class's constructor, the two streams are *chained together*. For example, the scrambled input stream is chained to the file input stream.

`main()` now enters a loop, reading bytes from the scrambled input stream and writing them to the file output stream. This loop continues until `ScrambledInputStream`'s `read()` method returns −1 (end of file).

The finally block closes the scrambled input stream and file output stream by calling their `close()` methods. It doesn't call the file input stream's `close()` method because `FilterOutputStream` automatically calls the underlying input stream's `close()` method.

The makeMap() method is responsible for creating the map array that's passed to ScrambledInputStream's constructor. The idea is to duplicate Listing 11-11's map array and then invert it so that unscrambling can be performed.

Continuing from the previous hello.txt/hello.out example, execute java Unscramble hello.out hello.bak and you'll see the same unscrambled content in hello.bak that's present in hello.txt.

> **Note**   For an additional example of a filter output stream and its complementary filter input stream, check out the "Extending Java Streams to Support Bit Streams" article (http://drdobbs.com/184410423) on the Dr. Dobb's web site. This article introduces BitStreamOutputStream and BitStreamInputStream classes that are useful for outputting and inputting bit streams. The article then demonstrates these classes in a Java implementation of the Lempel-Zif-Welch (LZW) data compression and decompression algorithm.

BufferedOutputStream and BufferedInputStream

FileOutputStream and FileInputStream have a performance problem. Each file output stream write() method call and file input stream read() method call results in a call to one of the underlying platform's native methods, and these native calls slow down I/O.

> **Note**   A *native method* is an underlying platform API function that Java connects to an application via the *Java Native Interface (JNI)*. Java supplies reserved word native to identify a native method. For example, the RandomAccessFile class declares a private native void open(String name, int mode) method. When a RandomAccessFile constructor calls this method, Java asks the underlying platform (via the JNI) to open the specified file in the specified mode on Java's behalf.

The concrete BufferedOutputStream and BufferedInputStream filter stream classes improve performance by minimizing underlying output stream write() and underlying input stream read() method calls. Instead, calls to BufferedOutputStream's write() and BufferedInputStream's read() methods take Java buffers into account:

- When a write buffer is full, write() calls the underlying output stream write() method to empty the buffer. Subsequent calls to BufferedOutputStream's write() methods store bytes in this buffer until it's once again full.

- When the read buffer is empty, read() calls the underlying input stream read() method to fill the buffer. Subsequent calls to BufferedInputStream's read() methods return bytes from this buffer until it's once again empty.

BufferedOutputStream declares the following constructors:

- BufferedOutputStream(OutputStream out) creates a buffered output stream that streams its output to out. An internal buffer is created to store bytes written to out.

- `BufferedOutputStream(OutputStream out, int size)` creates a buffered output stream that streams its output to `out`. An internal buffer of length `size` is created to store bytes written to `out`.

The following example chains a `BufferedOutputStream` instance to a `FileOutputStream` instance. Subsequent `write()` method calls on the `BufferedOutputStream` instance buffer bytes and occasionally results in internal `write()` method calls on the encapsulated `FileOutputStream` instance:

```
FileOutputStream fos = new FileOutputStream("employee.dat");
BufferedOutputStream bos = new BufferedOutputStream(fos); // Chain bos to fos.
bos.write(0); // Write to employee.dat through the buffer.
// Additional write() method calls.
bos.close(); // This method call internally calls fos's close() method.
```

`BufferedInputStream` declares the following constructors:

- `BufferedInputStream(InputStream in)` creates a buffered input stream that streams its input from `in`. An internal buffer is created to store bytes read from `in`.

- `BufferedInputStream(InputStream in, int size)` creates a buffered input stream that streams its input from `in`. An internal buffer of length `size` is created to store bytes read from `in`.

The following example chains a `BufferedInputStream` instance to a `FileInputStream` instance. Subsequent `read()` method calls on the `BufferedInputStream` instance unbuffer bytes and occasionally result in internal `read()` method calls on the encapsulated `FileInputStream` instance:

```
FileInputStream fis = new FileInputStream("employee.dat");
BufferedInputStream bis = new BufferedInputStream(fis); // Chain bis to fis.
int ch = bis.read(); // Read employee.dat through the buffer.
// Additional read() method calls.
bis.close(); // This method call internally calls fis's close() method.
```

DataOutputStream and DataInputStream

`FileOutputStream` and `FileInputStream` are useful for writing and reading bytes and arrays of bytes. However, they provide no support for writing and reading primitive type values (e.g., integers) and strings.

For this reason, Java provides the concrete `DataOutputStream` and `DataInputStream` filter stream classes. Each class overcomes this limitation by providing methods to write or read primitive type values and strings in a platform-independent way:

- Integer values are written and read in *big-endian format* (the most significant byte comes first). Check out Wikipedia's "Endianness" entry (http://en.wikipedia.org/wiki/Endianness) to learn about the concept of *endianness*.

- Floating-point and double precision floating-point values are written and read according to the IEEE 754 standard, which specifies 4 bytes per floating-point value and 8 bytes per double precision floating-point value.

■   Strings are written and read according to a modified version of *UTF-8*, a
    variable-length encoding standard for efficiently storing 2-byte Unicode characters.
    Check out Wikipedia's "UTF-8" entry (http://en.wikipedia.org/wiki/Utf-8) to
    learn more about UTF-8.

DataOutputStream declares a single DataOutputStream(OutputStream out) constructor. Because
this class implements the DataOutput interface, DataOutputStream also provides access to the
same-named write methods as provided by RandomAccessFile.

DataInputStream declares a single DataInputStream(InputStream in) constructor. Because
this class implements the DataInput interface, DataInputStream also provides access to the
same-named read methods as provided by RandomAccessFile.

Listing 11-14 presents the source code to a DataStreamsDemo application that uses a
DataOutputStream instance to write multibyte values to a FileOutputStream instance and uses a
DataInputStream instance to read multibyte values from a FileInputStream instance.

Listing 11-14. Outputting and Then Inputting a Stream of Multibyte Values

```java
import java.io.DataInputStream;
import java.io.DataOutputStream;
import java.io.FileInputStream;
import java.io.FileOutputStream;
import java.io.IOException;

public class DataStreamsDemo
{
   final static String FILENAME = "values.dat";

   public static void main(String[] args)
   {
      DataOutputStream dos = null;
      DataInputStream dis = null;
      try
      {
         FileOutputStream fos = new FileOutputStream(FILENAME);
         dos = new DataOutputStream(fos);
         dos.writeInt(1995);
         dos.writeUTF("Saving this String in modified UTF-8 format!");
         dos.writeFloat(1.0F);
         dos.close(); // Close underlying file output stream.
         // The following null assignment prevents another close attempt on
         // dos (which is now closed) should IOException be thrown from
         // subsequent method calls.
         dos = null;
         FileInputStream fis = new FileInputStream(FILENAME);
         dis = new DataInputStream(fis);
         System.out.println(dis.readInt());
         System.out.println(dis.readUTF());
         System.out.println(dis.readFloat());
      }
      catch (IOException ioe)
```

```
      {
          System.err.println("I/O error: " + ioe.getMessage());
      }
      finally
      {
          if (dos != null)
              try
              {
                  dos.close();
              }
              catch (IOException ioe2) // Cannot redeclare local variable ioe.
              {
                  assert false; // shouldn't happen in this context
              }
          if (dis != null)
              try
              {
                  dis.close();
              }
              catch (IOException ioe2) // Cannot redeclare local variable ioe.
              {
                  assert false; // shouldn't happen in this context
              }
      }
   }
}
```

DataStreamsDemo creates a file named values.dat; calls DataOutputStream methods to write an integer, a string, and a floating-point value to this file; and calls DataInputStream methods to read back these values. Unsurprisingly, it generates the following output:

```
1995
Saving this String in modified UTF-8 format!
1.0
```

Caution   When reading a file of values written by a sequence of DataOutputStream method calls, make sure to use the same method-call sequence. Otherwise, you're bound to end up with erroneous data and, in the case of the readUTF() methods, thrown instances of the java.io.UTFDataFormatException class (a subclass of IOException).

Object Serialization and Deserialization

Java provides the DataOutputStream and DataInputStream classes to stream primitive type values and String objects. However, you cannot use these classes to stream non-String objects. Instead, you must use object serialization and deserialization to stream objects of arbitrary types.

Object serialization is a virtual machine mechanism for *serializing* an object state into a stream of bytes. Its *deserialization* counterpart is a virtual machine mechanism for *deserializing* this state from a byte stream.

> **Note**   An object's state consists of instance fields that store primitive type values and/or references to other objects. When an object is serialized, the objects that are part of this state are also serialized (unless you prevent them from being serialized). Furthermore, the objects that are part of those objects' states are serialized (unless you prevent this), and so on.

Java supports default serialization and deserialization, custom serialization and deserialization, and externalization.

Default Serialization and Deserialization

Default serialization and deserialization is the easiest form to use but offers little control over how objects are serialized and deserialized. Although Java handles most of the work on your behalf, there are a couple of tasks that you must perform.

Your first task is to have the class of the object that is to be serialized implement the java.io.Serializable interface, either directly or indirectly via the class's superclass. The rationale for implementing Serializable is to avoid unlimited serialization.

> **Note**   Serializable is an empty marker interface (there are no methods to implement) that a class implements to tell the virtual machine that it's okay to serialize the class's objects. When the serialization mechanism encounters an object whose class doesn't implement Serializable, it throws an instance of the java.io.NotSerializableException class (an indirect subclass of IOException).

Unlimited serialization is the process of serializing an entire *object graph* (all objects that are reachable from a starting object). Java doesn't support unlimited serialization for the following reasons:

- *Security*: If Java automatically serialized an object containing sensitive information (e.g., a password or a credit card number), it would be easy for a hacker to discover this information and wreak havoc. It's better to give the developer a choice to prevent this from happening.

- *Performance*: Serialization leverages the Reflection API, which tends to slow down application performance. Unlimited serialization could really hurt an application's performance.

- *Objects not amenable to serialization*: Some objects exist only in the context of a running application and it's meaningless to serialize them. For example, a file stream object that's deserialized no longer represents a connection to a file.

Listing 11-15 declares an Employee class that implements the Serializable interface to tell the virtual machine that it's okay to serialize Employee objects.

Listing 11-15. Implementing `Serializable`

```
import java.io.Serializable;

public class Employee implements Serializable
{
   private String name;
   private int age;

   public Employee(String name, int age)
   {
      this.name = name;
      this.age = age;
   }

   public String getName() { return name; }

   public int getAge() { return age; }
}
```

Because `Employee` implements `Serializable`, the serialization mechanism will not throw a `NotSerializableException` instance when serializing an `Employee` object. Not only does `Employee` implement `Serializable`, the `String` class also implements this interface.

Your second task is to work with the `ObjectOutputStream` class and its `writeObject()` method to serialize an object and the `OutputInputStream` class and its `readObject()` method to deserialize the object.

> **Note**   Although `ObjectOutputStream` extends `OutputStream` instead of `FilterOutputStream`, and although `ObjectInputStream` extends `InputStream` instead of `FilterInputStream`, these classes behave as filter streams.

Java provides the concrete `ObjectOutputStream` class to initiate the serialization of an object's state to an object output stream. This class declares an `ObjectOutputStream(OutputStream out)` constructor that chains the object output stream to the output stream specified by out.

When you pass an output stream reference to out, this constructor attempts to write a serialization header to that output stream. It throws `NullPointerException` when out is null and `IOException` when an I/O error prevents it from writing this header.

`ObjectOutputStream` serializes an object via its void `writeObject(Object obj)` method. This method attempts to write information about obj's class followed by the values of obj's instance fields to the underlying output stream.

`writeObject()` doesn't serialize the contents of `static` fields. In contrast, it serializes the contents of all instance fields that are not explicitly prefixed with the `transient` reserved word. For example, consider the following field declaration:

```
public transient char[] password;
```

This declaration specifies `transient` to avoid serializing a password for some hacker to encounter. The virtual machine's serialization mechanism ignores any instance field that's marked `transient`.

`writeObject()` throws `IOException` or an instance of an `IOException` subclass when something goes wrong. For example, this method throws `NotSerializableException` when it encounters an object whose class doesn't implement `Serializable`.

> **Note**   Because `ObjectOutputStream` implements `DataOutput`, it also declares methods for writing primitive-type values and strings to an object output stream.

Java provides the concrete `ObjectInputStream` class to initiate the deserialization of an object's state from an object input stream. This class declares an `ObjectInputStream(InputStream in)` constructor that chains the object input stream to the input stream specified by `in`.

When you pass an input stream reference to `in`, this constructor attempts to read a serialization header from that input stream. It throws `NullPointerException` when `in` is null, `IOException` when an I/O error prevents it from reading this header, and `java.io.StreamCorruptedException` (an indirect subclass of `IOException`) when the stream header is incorrect.

`ObjectInputStream` deserializes an object via its `Object readObject()` method. This method attempts to read information about `obj`'s class followed by the values of `obj`'s instance fields from the underlying input stream.

`readObject()` throws `java.lang.ClassNotFoundException`, `IOException`, or an instance of an `IOException` subclass when something goes wrong. For example, this method throws `java.io.OptionalDataException` when it encounters primitive-type values instead of objects.

> **Note**   Because `ObjectInputStream` implements `DataInput`, it also declares methods for reading primitive-type values and strings from an object input stream.

Listing 11-16 presents an application that uses these classes to serialize and deserialize an instance of Listing 11-15's Employee class to and from an `employee.dat` file.

Listing 11-16. Serializing and Deserializing an Employee Object

```
import java.io.FileInputStream;
import java.io.FileOutputStream;
import java.io.IOException;
import java.io.ObjectInputStream;
import java.io.ObjectOutputStream;

public class SerializationDemo
{
   final static String FILENAME = "employee.dat";
```

```java
public static void main(String[] args)
{
   ObjectOutputStream oos = null;
   ObjectInputStream ois = null;
   try
   {
      FileOutputStream fos = new FileOutputStream(FILENAME);
      oos = new ObjectOutputStream(fos);
      Employee emp = new Employee("John Doe", 36);
      oos.writeObject(emp);
      oos.close();
      oos = null;
      FileInputStream fis = new FileInputStream(FILENAME);
      ois = new ObjectInputStream(fis);
      emp = (Employee) ois.readObject(); // (Employee) cast is necessary.
      ois.close();
      System.out.println(emp.getName());
      System.out.println(emp.getAge());
   }
   catch (ClassNotFoundException cnfe)
   {
      System.err.println(cnfe.getMessage());
   }
   catch (IOException ioe)
   {
      System.err.println(ioe.getMessage());
   }
   finally
   {
      if (oos != null)
         try
         {
            oos.close();
         }
         catch (IOException ioe)
         {
            assert false; // shouldn't happen in this context
         }

      if (ois != null)
         try
         {
            ois.close();
         }
         catch (IOException ioe)
         {
            assert false; // shouldn't happen in this context
         }
   }
}
}
```

Listing 11-16's main() method first instantiates Employee and serializes this instance via writeObject() to employee.dat. It then deserializes this instance from this file via readObject() and invokes the instance's getName() and getAge() methods. Along with employee.dat, you'll discover the following output when you run this application:

```
John Doe
36
```

There's no guarantee that the same class will exist when a serialized object is deserialized (perhaps an instance field has been deleted). During deserialization, this mechanism causes readObject() to throw java.io.InvalidClassException—an indirect subclass of the IOException class—when it detects a difference between the deserialized object and its class.

Every serialized object has an identifier. The deserialization mechanism compares the identifier of the object being deserialized with the serialized identifier of its class (all serializable classes are automatically given unique identifiers unless they explicitly specify their own identifiers) and causes InvalidClassException to be thrown when it detects a mismatch.

Perhaps you've added an instance field to a class, and you want the deserialization mechanism to set the instance field to a default value rather than have readObject() throw an InvalidClassException instance. (The next time you serialize the object, the new field's value will be written out.)

You can avoid the thrown InvalidClassException instance by adding a static final long serialVersionUID = *long integer value*; declaration to the class. The *long integer value* must be unique and is known as a *stream unique identifier (SUID)*.

During deserialization, the virtual machine will compare the deserialized object's SUID to its class's SUID. If they match, readObject() will not throw InvalidClassException when it encounters a *compatible class change* (e.g., adding an instance field). However, it will still throw this exception when it encounters an *incompatible class change* (e.g., changing an instance field's name or type).

> **Note** Whenever you change a class in some fashion, you must calculate a new SUID and assign it to serialVersionUID.

The JDK provides a serialver tool for calculating the SUID. For example, to generate an SUID for Listing 11-15's Employee class, change to the directory containing Employee.class and execute serialver Employee. In response, serialver generates the following output, which you paste (except for Employee:) into Employee.java:

```
Employee:    static final long serialVersionUID = 15173313364702470316L;
```

The Windows version of serialver also provides a graphical user interface that you might find more convenient to use. To access this interface, specify serialver -show. When the serialver window appears, enter **Employee** into the Full Class Name textfield and click the Show button, as demonstrated in Figure 11-6.

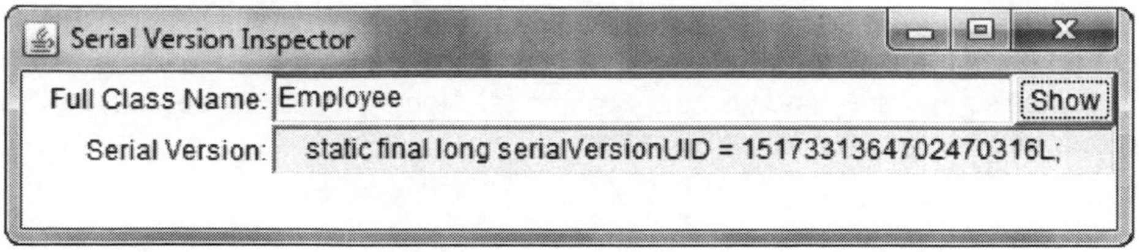

Figure 11-6. *The* serialver *user interface reveals* Employee's *SUID*

Custom Serialization and Deserialization

My previous discussion focused on default serialization and deserialization (with the exception of marking an instance field `transient` to prevent it from being included during serialization). However, situations arise in which you need to customize these tasks.

For example, suppose you want to serialize instances of a class that doesn't implement `Serializable`. As a workaround, you subclass this other class, have the subclass implement `Serializable`, and forward subclass constructor calls to the superclass.

Although this workaround lets you serialize subclass objects, you cannot deserialize these serialized objects when the superclass doesn't declare a noargument constructor, which is required by the deserialization mechanism. Listing 11-17 demonstrates this problem.

Listing 11-17. Problematic Deserialization

```java
import java.io.FileInputStream;
import java.io.FileOutputStream;
import java.io.IOException;
import java.io.ObjectInputStream;
import java.io.ObjectOutputStream;
import java.io.Serializable;

class Employee
{
   private String name;

   Employee(String name)
   {
      this.name = name;
   }

   @Override
   public String toString()
   {
      return name;
   }
}
```

```
class SerEmployee extends Employee implements Serializable
{
   SerEmployee(String name)
   {
      super(name);
   }
}

public class SerializationDemo
{
   public static void main(String[] args)
   {
      ObjectOutputStream oos = null;
      ObjectInputStream ois = null;
      try
      {
         oos = new ObjectOutputStream(new FileOutputStream("employee.dat"));
         SerEmployee se = new SerEmployee("John Doe");
         System.out.println(se);
         oos.writeObject(se);
         oos.close();
         oos = null;
         System.out.println("se object written to file");
         ois = new ObjectInputStream(new FileInputStream("employee.dat"));
         se = (SerEmployee) ois.readObject();
         System.out.println("se object read from file");
         System.out.println(se);
      }
      catch (ClassNotFoundException cnfe)
      {
         cnfe.printStackTrace();
      }
      catch (IOException ioe)
      {
         ioe.printStackTrace();
      }
      finally
      {
         if (oos != null)
            try
            {
               oos.close();
            }
            catch (IOException ioe)
            {
               assert false; // shouldn't happen in this context
            }
         if (ois != null)
            try
            {
               ois.close();
            }
```

```
            catch (IOException ioe)
            {
                assert false; // shouldn't happen in this context
            }
        }
    }
}
```

Listing 11-17's `main()` method instantiates `SerEmployee` with an employee name. This class's `SerEmployee(String)` constructor passes this argument to its `Employee` counterpart.

`main()` next calls `Employee`'s `toString()` method indirectly via `System.out.println()`, to obtain this name, which is then output.

Continuing, `main()` serializes the `SerEmployee` instance to an `employee.dat` file via `writeObject()`. It then attempts to deserialize this object via `readObject()`, and this is where the trouble occurs as revealed by the following output:

```
John Doe
se object written to file
java.io.InvalidClassException: SerEmployee; no valid constructor
        at java.io.ObjectStreamClass$ExceptionInfo.newInvalidClassException(Unknown Source)
        at java.io.ObjectStreamClass.checkDeserialize(Unknown Source)
        at java.io.ObjectInputStream.readOrdinaryObject(Unknown Source)
        at java.io.ObjectInputStream.readObject0(Unknown Source)
        at java.io.ObjectInputStream.readObject(Unknown Source)
        at SerializationDemo.main(SerializationDemo.java:48)
```

This output reveals a thrown instance of the `InvalidClassException` class. This exception object was thrown during deserialization because `Employee` doesn't possess a noargument constructor.

You can overcome this problem by taking advantage of the wrapper class pattern that I presented in Chapter 4. Furthermore, you declare a pair of private methods in the subclass that the serialization and deserialization mechanisms look for and call.

Normally, the serialization mechanism writes out a class's instance fields to the underlying output stream. However, you can prevent this from happening by declaring a private void `writeObject(ObjectOutputStream oos)` method in that class.

When the serialization mechanism discovers this method, it calls the method instead of automatically outputting instance field values. The only values that are output are those explicitly output via the method.

Conversely, the deserialization mechanism assigns values to a class's instance fields that it reads from the underlying input stream. However, you can prevent this from happening by declaring a private void `readObject(ObjectInputStream ois)` method.

When the deserialization mechanism discovers this method, it calls the method instead of automatically assigning values to instance fields. The only values that are assigned to instance fields are those explicitly assigned via the method.

Because SerEmployee doesn't introduce any fields, and because Employee doesn't offer access to its internal fields (assume you don't have the source code for this class), what would a serialized SerEmployee object include?

Although you cannot serialize Employee's internal state, you can serialize the argument(s) passed to its constructors, such as the employee name.

Listing 11-18 reveals the refactored SerEmployee and SerializationDemo classes.

Listing 11-18. Solving Problematic Deserialization

```java
import java.io.FileInputStream;
import java.io.FileOutputStream;
import java.io.IOException;
import java.io.ObjectInputStream;
import java.io.ObjectOutputStream;
import java.io.Serializable;

class Employee
{
   private String name;

   Employee(String name)
   {
      this.name = name;
   }

   @Override
   public String toString()
   {
      return name;
   }
}

class SerEmployee implements Serializable
{
   private Employee emp;
   private String name;

   SerEmployee(String name)
   {
      this.name = name;
      emp = new Employee(name);
   }

   private void writeObject(ObjectOutputStream oos) throws IOException
   {
      oos.writeUTF(name);
   }

   private void readObject(ObjectInputStream ois)
      throws ClassNotFoundException, IOException
```

```java
      {
         name = ois.readUTF();
         emp = new Employee(name);
      }

      @Override
      public String toString()
      {
         return name;
      }
   }

public class SerializationDemo
{
   public static void main(String[] args)
   {
      ObjectOutputStream oos = null;
      ObjectInputStream ois = null;
      try
      {
         oos = new ObjectOutputStream(new FileOutputStream("employee.dat"));
         SerEmployee se = new SerEmployee("John Doe");
         System.out.println(se);
         oos.writeObject(se);
         oos.close();
         oos = null;
         System.out.println("se object written to file");
         ois = new ObjectInputStream(new FileInputStream("employee.dat"));
         se = (SerEmployee) ois.readObject();
         System.out.println("se object read from file");
         System.out.println(se);
      }
      catch (ClassNotFoundException cnfe)
      {
         cnfe.printStackTrace();
      }
      catch (IOException ioe)
      {
         ioe.printStackTrace();
      }
      finally
      {
         if (oos != null)
            try
            {
               oos.close();
            }
            catch (IOException ioe)
            {
               assert false; // shouldn't happen in this context
            }
```

```
        if (ois != null)
           try
           {
              ois.close();
           }
           catch (IOException ioe)
           {
              assert false; // shouldn't happen in this context
           }
     }
   }
}
```

SerEmployee's writeObject() and readObject() methods rely on DataOutput and DataInput methods: they don't need to call writeObject() and readObject() to perform their tasks.

When you run this application, it generates the following output:

```
John Doe
se object written to file
se object read from file
John Doe
```

The writeObject() and readObject() methods can be used to serialize/deserialize data items beyond the normal state (non-transient instance fields), for example, serializing/deserializing the contents of a static field.

However, before serializing or deserializing the additional data items, you must tell the serialization and deserialization mechanisms to serialize or deserialize the object's normal state. The following methods help you accomplish this task:

* ObjectOutputStream's defaultWriteObject() method outputs the object's normal state. Your writeObject() method first calls this method to output that state and then outputs additional data items via ObjectOutputStream methods such as writeUTF().

* ObjectInputStream's defaultReadObject() method inputs the object's normal state. Your readObject() method first calls this method to input that state and then inputs additional data items via ObjectInputStream methods such as readUTF().

Externalization

Along with default serialization/deserialization and custom serialization/deserialization, Java supports externalization. Unlike default/custom serialization/deserialization, *externalization* offers complete control over the serialization and deserialization tasks.

> **Note** Externalization helps you improve the performance of the reflection-based serialization and deserialization mechanisms by giving you complete control over what fields are serialized and deserialized.

Java supports externalization via java.io.Externalizable. This interface declares the following pair of public methods:

- void writeExternal(ObjectOutput out) saves the calling object's contents by calling various methods on the out object. This method throws IOException when an I/O error occurs. (java.io.ObjectOutput is a subinterface of DataOutput and is implemented by ObjectOutputStream.)

- void readExternal(ObjectInput in) restores the calling object's contents by calling various methods on the in object. This method throws IOException when an I/O error occurs and ClassNotFoundException when the class of the object being restored cannot be found. (java.io.ObjectInput is a subinterface of DataInput and is implemented by ObjectInputStream.)

If a class implements Externalizable, its writeExternal() method is responsible for saving all field values that are to be saved. Also, its readExternal() method is responsible for restoring all saved field values and in the order they were saved.

Listing 11-19 presents a refactored version of Listing 11-15's Employee class to show you how to take advantage of externalization.

Listing 11-19. Refactoring Listing 11-15's Employee Class to Support Externalization

```
import java.io.Externalizable;
import java.io.IOException;
import java.io.ObjectInput;
import java.io.ObjectOutput;

public class Employee implements Externalizable
{
   private String name;
   private int age;

   public Employee()
   {
      System.out.println("Employee() called");
   }

   public Employee(String name, int age)
   {
      this.name = name;
      this.age = age;
   }

   public String getName() { return name; }

   public int getAge() { return age; }

   @Override
   public void writeExternal(ObjectOutput out) throws IOException
```

```
   {
      System.out.println("writeExternal() called");
      out.writeUTF(name);
      out.writeInt(age);
   }

   @Override
   public void readExternal(ObjectInput in)
      throws IOException, ClassNotFoundException
   {
      System.out.println("readExternal() called");
      name = in.readUTF();
      age = in.readInt();
   }
}
```

Employee declares a `public Employee()` constructor because each class that participates in externalization must declare a `public` noargument constructor. The deserialization mechanism calls this constructor to instantiate the object.

> **Caution** The deserialization mechanism throws `InvalidClassException` with a "no valid constructor" message when it doesn't detect a `public` noargument constructor.

Initiate externalization by instantiating `ObjectOutputStream` and calling its `writeObject(Object)` method, or by instantiating `ObjectInputStream` and calling its `readObject()` method.

> **Note** When passing an object whose class (directly/indirectly) implements `Externalizable` to `writeObject()`, the `writeObject()`-initiated serialization mechanism writes only the identity of the object's class to the object output stream.

Suppose you compiled Listing 11-16's `SerializationDemo.java` source code and Listing 11-19's `Employee.java` source code in the same directory. Now suppose you executed java `SerializationDemo`. In response, you would observe the following output:

```
writeExternal() called
Employee() called
readExternal() called
John Doe
36
```

Before serializing an object, the serialization mechanism checks the object's class to see if it implements `Externalizable`. If so, the mechanism calls `writeExternal()`. Otherwise, it looks for a private `writeObject(ObjectOutputStream)` method and calls this method when present. When this method isn't present, this mechanism performs default serialization, which includes only nontransient instance fields.

Before deserializing an object, the deserialization mechanism checks the object's class to see if it implements `Externalizable`. If so, the mechanism attempts to instantiate the class via the public noargument constructor. Assuming success, it calls `readExternal()`.

When the object's class doesn't implement `Externalizable`, the deserialization mechanism looks for a private `readObject(ObjectInputStream)` method. When this method isn't present, this mechanism performs default deserialization, which includes only non`transient` instance fields.

PrintStream

Of all the stream classes, `PrintStream` is an oddball: it should have been named `PrintOutputStream` for consistency with the naming convention. This filter output stream class writes string representations of input data items to the underlying output stream.

> **Note**   `PrintStream` uses the default character encoding to convert a string's characters to bytes. (I'll discuss character encodings when I introduce you to writers and readers in the next section.) Because `PrintStream` doesn't support different character encodings, you should use the equivalent `PrintWriter` class instead of `PrintStream`. However, you need to know about `PrintStream` when working with `System.out` and `System.err` because these class fields are of type `PrintStream`.

`PrintStream` instances are print streams whose various `print()` and `println()` methods print string representations of integers, floating-point values, and other data items to the underlying output stream. Unlike the `print()` methods, `println()` methods append a line terminator to their output.

> **Note**   The line terminator (also known as line separator) isn't necessarily the newline (also commonly referred to as line feed). Instead, to promote portability, the line separator is the sequence of characters defined by system property `line.separator`. On Windows platforms, `System.getProperty("line.separator")` returns the actual carriage return code (13), which is symbolically represented by \r, followed by the actual newline/line feed code (10), which is symbolically represented by \n. In contrast, `System.getProperty("line.separator")` returns only the actual newline/line feed code on Unix and Linux platforms.

The `println()` methods call their corresponding `print()` methods followed by the equivalent of the `void println()` method, which evenutally results in `line.separator`'s value being output. For example, `void println(int x)` outputs x's string representation and calls this method to output the line separator.

> **Caution**   Never hard-code the \n escape sequence in a string literal that you are going to output
> via a print() or println() method. Doing so isn't portable. For example, when Java executes
> System.out.print("first line\n"); followed by System.out.println("second
> line");, you will see first line on one line followed by second line on a subsequent line when
> this output is viewed at the Windows command line. In contrast, you'll see first linesecond line
> when this output is viewed in the Windows Notepad application (which requires a carriage return/line
> feed sequence to terminate lines). When you need to output a blank line, the easiest way to do this is
> to call System.out.println();, which is why you find this method call used elsewhere in my book.
> I confess that I don't always follow my own advice, so you might find instances of \n in literal strings
> being passed to System.out.print() or System.out.println() elsewhere in this book.

PrintStream offers three other features that you'll find useful:

- Unlike other output streams, a print stream never rethrows an IOException instance thrown from the underlying output stream. Instead, exceptional situations set an internal flag that can be tested by calling PrintStream's boolean checkError() method, which returns true to indicate a problem.

- PrintStream objects can be created to automatically flush their output to the underlying output stream. In other words, the flush() method is automatically called after a byte array is written, one of the println() methods is called, or a newline is written. The PrintStream instances assigned to System.out and System.err automatically flush their output to the underlying output stream.

- PrintStream declares a PrintStream format(String format, Object... args) method for achieving formatted output. Behind the scene, this method works with the Formatter class that I introduced in Chapter 10. PrintStream also declares a printf(String format, Object... args) convenience method that delegates to the format() method. For example, invoking printf() via out.printf(format, args) is identical to invoking out.format(format, args).

Working with Writers and Readers

Java's stream classes are good for streaming sequences of bytes, but they're not good for streaming sequences of characters because bytes and characters are two different things: a byte represents an 8-bit data item and a character represents a 16-bit data item. Also, Java's char and String types naturally handle characters instead of bytes.

More important, byte streams have no knowledge of *character sets* (sets of mappings between integer values, known as *code points,* and symbols, such as Unicode) and their *character encodings* (mappings between the members of a character set and sequences of bytes that encode these characters for efficiency, such as UTF-8).

If you need to stream characters, you should take advantage of Java's writer and reader classes, which were designed to support character I/O (they work with char instead of byte). Furthermore, the writer and reader classes take character encodings into account.

A BRIEF HISTORY OF CHARACTER SETS AND CHARACTER ENCODINGS

Early computers and programming languages were created mainly by English-speaking programmers in countries where English was the native language. They developed a standard mapping between code points 0 through 127 and the 128 commonly used characters in the English language (e.g., A–Z). The resulting character set/encoding was named *American Standard Code for Information Interchange (ASCII)*.

The problem with ASCII is that it's inadequate for most non-English languages. For example, ASCII doesn't support diacritical marks such as the cedilla used in the French language. Because a byte can represent a maximum of 256 different characters, developers around the world started creating different character sets/encodings that encoded the 128 ASCII characters but also encoded extra characters to meet the needs of languages such as French, Greek, or Russian. Over the years, many legacy (and still important) data files have been created whose bytes represent characters defined by specific character sets/encodings.

The International Organization for Standardization (ISO) and the International Electrotechnical Commission (IEC) have worked to standardize these 8-bit character sets/encodings under a joint umbrella standard called ISO/IEC 8859. The result is a series of substandards named ISO/IEC 8859-1, ISO/IEC 8859-2, and so on. For example, ISO/IEC 8859–1 (also known as Latin-1) defines a character set/encoding that consists of ASCII plus the characters covering most Western European countries. Also, ISO/IEC 8859-2 (also known as Latin-2) defines a similar character set/encoding covering Central and Eastern European countries.

Despite ISO's/IEC's best efforts, a plethora of character sets/encodings is still inadequate. For example, most character sets/encodings only allow you to create documents in a combination of English and one other language (or a small number of other languages). You cannot, for example, use an ISO/IEC character set/encoding to create a document using a combination of English, French, Turkish, Russian, and Greek characters.

This and other problems are being addressed by an international effort that has created and is continuing to develop *Unicode*, a single universal character set. Because Unicode characters are bigger than ISO/IEC characters, Unicode uses one of several variable-length encoding schemes known as *Unicode Transformation Format (UTF)* to encode Unicode characters for efficiency. For example, UTF-8 encodes every character in the Unicode character set in 1 to 4 bytes (and is backward compatible with ASCII).

The terms *character set* and *character encoding* are often used interchangeably. They mean the same thing in the context of ISO/IEC character sets in which a code point is the encoding. However, these terms are different in the context of Unicode in which Unicode is the character set and UTF-8 is one of several possible character encodings for Unicode characters.

Writer and Reader Classes Overview

The `java.io` package provides several writer and reader classes that are descendents of the abstract `Writer` and `Reader` classes. Figure 11-7 reveals the hierarchy of writer classes.

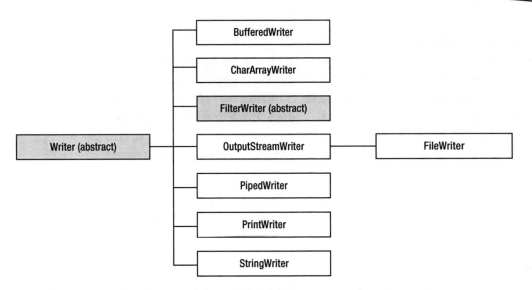

Figure 11-7. *Unlike* `FilterOutputStream,` `FilterWriter` *is abstract*

Figure 11-8 reveals the hierarchy of reader classes.

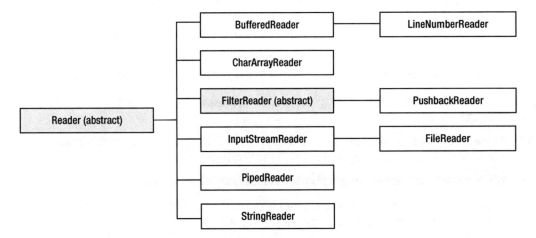

Figure 11-8. *Unlike* `FilterInputStream,` `FilterReader` *is abstract*

Although the writer and reader class hierarchies are similar to their output stream and input stream counterparts, there are differences. For example, `FilterWriter` and `FilterReader` are abstract, whereas their `FilterOutputStream` and `FilterInputStream` equivalents are not abstract. Also, `BufferedWriter` and `BufferedReader` don't extend `FilterWriter` and `FilterReader`, whereas `BufferedOutputStream` and `BufferedInputStream` extend `FilterOutputStream` and `FilterInputStream`.

The output stream and input stream classes were introduced in Java 1.0. After their release, design issues emerged. For example, `FilterOutputStream` and `FilterInputStream` should have been abstract. However, it was too late to make these changes because the classes were already being used; making these changes would have resulted in broken code. The designers of Java 1.1's writer and reader classes took the time to correct these mistakes.

> **Note**   Regarding BufferedWriter and BufferedReader directly subclassing Writer and Reader instead of FilterWriter and FilterReader, I believe that this change has to do with performance. Calls to BufferedOutputStream's write() methods and BufferedInputStream's read() methods result in calls to FilterOutputStream's write() methods and FilterInputStream's read() methods. Because a file I/O activity such as copying one file to another can involve many write()/read() method calls, you want the best performance possible. By not subclassing FilterWriter and FilterReader, BufferedWriter and BufferedReader achieve better performance.

For brevity, I focus only on the Writer, Reader, OutputStreamWriter, OutputStreamReader, FileWriter, and FileReader classes in this chapter.

Writer and Reader

Java provides the Writer and Reader classes for performing character I/O. Writer is the superclass of all writer subclasses. The following list identifies differences between Writer and OutputStream:

- Writer declares several append() methods for appending characters to this writer. These methods exist because Writer implements the java.lang.Appendable interface, which is used in partnership with the Formatter class (discussed in Chapter 10) to output formatted strings.

- Writer declares additional write() methods, including a convenient void write(String str) method for writing a String object's characters to this writer.

Reader is the superclass of all reader subclasses. The following list identifies differences between Reader and InputStream:

- Reader declares read(char[]) and read(char[], int, int) methods instead of read(byte[]) and read(byte[], int, int) methods.

- Reader doesn't declare an available() method.

- Reader declares a boolean ready() method that returns true when the next read() call is guaranteed not to block for input.

- Reader declares an int read(CharBuffer target) method for reading characters from a character buffer. (I discuss CharBuffer in Chapter 13.)

OutputStreamWriter and InputStreamReader

The concrete OutputStreamWriter class (a Writer subclass) is a bridge between an incoming sequence of characters and an outgoing stream of bytes. Characters written to this writer are encoded into bytes according to the default or specified character encoding.

> **Note**   The default character encoding is accessible via the file.encoding system property.

Each call to one of OutputStreamWriter's write() methods causes an encoder to be called on the given character(s). The resulting bytes are accumulated in a buffer before being written to the underlying output stream. The characters passed to the write() methods are not buffered.

OutputStreamWriter declares four constructors, including the following pair:

- OutputStreamWriter(OutputStream out) creates a bridge between an incoming sequence of characters (passed to OutputStreamWriter via its append() and write() methods) and the underlying output stream out. The default character encoding is used to encode characters into bytes.

- OutputStreamWriter(OutputStream out, String charsetName) creates a bridge between an incoming sequence of characters (passed to OutputStreamWriter via its append() and write() methods) and underlying output stream out. charsetName identifies the character encoding used to encode characters into bytes. This constructor throws java.io.UnsupportedEncodingException when the named character encoding isn't supported.

> **Note** OutputStreamWriter depends on the abstract java.nio.charset.Charset and java.nio.charset.CharsetEncoder classes to perform character encoding.

The following example uses the second constructor to create a bridge to an underlying file output stream so that Polish text can be written to an ISO/IEC 8859-2-encoded file.

```
FileOutputStream fos = new FileOutputStream("polish.txt");
OutputStreamWriter osw = new OutputStreamWriter(fos, "8859_2");
char ch = '\u0323'; // Accented N.
osw.write(ch);
```

The concrete InputStreamReader class (a Reader subclass) is a bridge between an incoming stream of bytes and an outgoing sequence of characters. Characters read from this reader are decoded from bytes according to the default or specified character encoding.

Each call to one of InputStreamReader's read() methods may cause one or more bytes to be read from the underlying input stream. To enable the efficient conversion of bytes to characters, more bytes may be read ahead from the underlying stream than are necessary to satisfy the current read operation.

InputStreamReader declares four constructors, including the following pair:

- InputStreamReader(InputStream in) creates a bridge between underlying input stream in and an outgoing sequence of characters (returned from InputStreamReader via its read() methods). The default character encoding is used to decode bytes into characters.

- InputStreamReader(InputStream in, String charsetName) creates a bridge between underlying input stream in and an outgoing sequence of characters (returned from InputStreamReader via its read() methods). charsetName identifies the character encoding used to decode bytes into characters. This constructor throws `UnsupportedEncodingException` when the named character encoding is not supported.

> **Note**   InputStreamReader depends on the abstract `Charset` and `java.nio.charset.`
> `CharsetDecoder` classes to perform character decoding.

The following example uses the second constructor to create a bridge to an underlying file input stream so that Polish text can be read from an ISO/IEC 8859-2-encoded file.

```
FileInputStream fis = new FileInputStream("polish.txt");
InputStreamReader isr = new InputStreamReader(fis, "8859_2");
char ch = isr.read(ch);
```

> **Note**   OutputStreamWriter and InputStreamReader declare a `String getEncoding()`
> method that returns the name of the character encoding in use. If the encoding has a historical name,
> that name is returned; otherwise, the encoding's canonical name is returned.

FileWriter and FileReader

FileWriter is a convenience class for writing characters to files. It subclasses `OutputStreamWriter`, and its constructors call `OutputStreamWriter(OutputStream)`. An instance of this class is equivalent to the following code fragment:

```
FileOutputStream fos = new FileOutputStream(pathname);
OutputStreamWriter osw;
osw = new OutputStreamWriter(fos, System.getProperty("file.encoding"));
```

In Chapter 5, I presented a logging library with a File class that didn't incorporate file-writing code. Listing 11-20 addresses this situation by presenting a revised File class that uses FileWriter to log messages to a file.

Listing 11-20. Logging Messages to an Actual File

```
package logging;

import java.io.FileWriter;
import java.io.IOException;

class File implements Logger
{
   private final static String LINE_SEPARATOR = System.getProperty("line.separator");
```

```java
   private String dstName;
   private FileWriter fw;

   File(String dstName)
   {
      this.dstName = dstName;
   }

   public boolean connect()
   {
      if (dstName == null)
         return false;
      try
      {
         fw = new FileWriter(dstName);
      }
      catch (IOException ioe)
      {
         return false;
      }
      return true;
   }

   public boolean disconnect()
   {
      if (fw == null)
         return false;
      try
      {
         fw.close();
      }
      catch (IOException ioe)
      {
         return false;
      }
      return true;
   }

   public boolean log(String msg)
   {
      if (fw == null)
          return false;
      try
      {
         fw.write(msg + LINE_SEPARATOR);
      }
      catch (IOException ioe)
      {
         return false;
      }
      return true;
   }
}
```

Listing 11-20 refactors Chapter 5's File class to support FileWriter by making changes to each of the connect(), disconnect(), and log() methods:

- connect() attempts to instantiate FileWriter, whose instance is saved in fw on success; otherwise, fw continues to store its default null reference.

- disconnect() attempts to close the file by calling FileWriter's close() method, but only when fw doesn't contain its default null reference.

- log() attempts to write its String argument to the file by calling FileWriter's void write(String str) method, but only when fw doesn't contain its default null reference.

connect()'s catch block specifies IOException instead of FileNotFoundException because FileWriter's constructors throw IOException when they cannot connect to existing normal files; FileOutputStream's constructors throw FileNotFoundException.

log()'s write(String) method appends the line.separator value (which I assigned to a constant for convenience) to the string being output instead of appending \n, which would violate portability.

FileReader is a convenience class for reading characters from files. It subclasses InputStreamReader, and its constructors call InputStreamReader(InputStream). An instance of this class is equivalent to the following code fragment:

```
FileInputStream fis = new FileInputStream(pathname);
InputStreamReader isr;
isr = new InputStreamReader(fis, System.getProperty("file.encoding"));
```

It's often necessary to search text files for occurrences of specific strings. Although regular expressions (discussed in Chapter 13) are ideal for this task, I have yet to discuss them. As a result, Listing 11-21 presents the more verbose alternative to regular expressions.

Listing 11-21. Finding All Files That Contain Content Matching a Search String

```
import java.io.BufferedReader;
import java.io.File;
import java.io.FileReader;
import java.io.IOException;

public class FindAll
{
   public static void main(String[] args)
   {
      if (args.length != 2)
      {
         System.err.println("usage: java FindAll start search-string");
         return;
      }
      if (!findAll(new File(args[0]), args[1]))
         System.err.println("not a directory");
   }
```

```java
static boolean findAll(File file, String srchText)
{
   File[] files = file.listFiles();
   if (files == null)
      return false;
   for (int i = 0; i < files.length; i++)
      if (files[i].isDirectory())
         findAll(files[i], srchText);
      else
      if (find(files[i].getPath(), srchText))
         System.out.println(files[i].getPath());
   return true;
}

static boolean find(String filename, String srchText)
{
   BufferedReader br = null;
   try
   {
      br = new BufferedReader(new FileReader(filename));
      int ch;
      outer_loop:
      do
      {
         if ((ch = br.read()) == -1)
            return false;
         if (ch == srchText.charAt(0))
         {
            for (int i = 1; i < srchText.length(); i++)
            {
               if ((ch = br.read()) == -1)
                  return false;
               if (ch != srchText.charAt(i))
                  continue outer_loop;
            }
            return true;
         }
      }
      while (true);
   }
   catch (IOException ioe)
   {
      System.err.println("I/O error: " + ioe.getMessage());
   }
   finally
   {
      if (br != null)
         try
         {
            br.close();
         }
```

```
            catch (IOException ioe)
            {
                assert false; // shouldn't happen in this context
            }
        }
        return false;
    }
}
```

Listing 11-21's FindAll class declares main(), findAll(), and find() class methods.

main() validates the number of command-line arguments, which must be two. The first argument identifies the starting location within the filesystem for the search and is used to construct a File object. The second argument specifies search text. main() then passes the File object and the search text to findAll() to perform a search for all files containing this text.

The recursive findAll() method first invokes listFiles() on the File object passed to this method to obtain the names of all files in the current directory. If listFiles() returns null, meaning that the File object doesn't refer to an existing directory, findAll() returns false and a suitable error message is output.

For each name in the returned list, findAll() either recursively invokes itself when the name represents a directory, or invokes the find() method to search the file for the text; the file's pathname string is output when the file contains this text.

The find() method first opens the file identified by its first argument via the FileReader class and then passes the FileReader instance to a BufferedReader instance to improve file-reading performance. It then enters a loop that continues to read characters from the file until the end of the file is reached.

If the currently read character matches the first character in the search text, an inner loop is entered to read subsequent characters from the file and compare them with subsequent characters in the search text. When all characters match, find() returns true. Otherwise, the labeled continue statement is used to skip the remaining iterations of the inner loop and transfer execution to the labeled outer loop. After the last character has been read and there's still no match, find() returns false.

Now that you know how FindAll works, you'll probably want to try it out. The following examples show you how I might use this application on my Windows 7 platform:

```
java FindAll \prj\dev RenderScript
```

This example searches the \prj\dev directory on my default drive (C:) for all files that contain the word RenderScript (case is significant) and generates the following output:

```
\prj\dev\ar2\appb\ar\1-4302-4614-5_Friesen_AppB_Android_Tools_Overview.doc
\prj\dev\ar2\appb\ce\1-4302-4614-5_Friesen_AppB_Android_Tools_Overview.doc
\prj\dev\ar2\ch08\1-4302-4614-5_Friesen_Ch08_Working_with_Android_NDK_and_Renderscript.doc
\prj\dev\ar2\ch08\ar\1-4302-4614-5_Friesen_Ch08_Working_with_Android_NDK_and_Renderscript.doc
\prj\dev\ar2\ch08\ce\1-4302-4614-5_Friesen_Ch08_Working_with_Android_NDK_and_Renderscript.doc
\prj\dev\ar2\ch08\code\GrayScale\GrayScale.java
\prj\dev\ar2\ch08\code\WavyImage\WavyImage.java
\prj\dev\ar2\code\ch08\GrayScale\GrayScale.java
\prj\dev\ar2\code\ch08\WavyImage\WavyImage.java
\prj\dev\ar2\xtra\ndkrs.txt
```

```
\prj\dev\EmbossImage\src\ca\tutortutor\embossimage\EmbossImage.java
\prj\dev\GrayScale\src\ca\tutortutor\grayscale\GrayScale.java
\prj\dev\WavyImage\src\ca\tutortutor\wavyimage\WavyImage.java
```

If I now specify java FindAll \prj\dev "Jelly Bean", I observe the following abbreviated output:

```
\prj\dev\ar2\ch01\1-4302-4614-5_Friesen_Ch01_Getting_Started_with_Android.doc
\prj\dev\ar2\ch01\ar\1-4302-4614-5_Friesen_Ch01_Getting_Started_with_Android.doc
\prj\dev\ar2\ch01\ce\1-4302-4614-5_Friesen_Ch01_Getting_Started_with_Android.doc
```

EXERCISES

The following exercises are designed to test your understanding of Chapter 11's content:

1. What is the purpose of the File class?

2. What do instances of the File class contain?

3. What does File's listRoots() method accomplish?

4. What is a path and what is a pathname?

5. What is the difference between an absolute pathname and a relative pathname?

6. How do you obtain the current user (also known as working) directory?

7. Define parent pathname.

8. File's constructors normalize their pathname arguments. What does normalize mean?

9. How do you obtain the default name-separator character?

10. What is a canonical pathname?

11. What is the difference between File's getParent() and getName() methods?

12. True or false: File's exists() method only determines whether or not a file exists.

13. What is a normal file?

14. What does File's lastModified() method return?

15. True or false: File's list() method returns an array of Strings in which each entry is a filename rather than a complete path.

16. What is the difference between the FilenameFilter and FileFilter interfaces?

17. True or false: File's createNewFile() method doesn't check for file existence and creates the file when it doesn't exist in a single operation that's atomic with respect to all other filesystem activities that might affect the file.

18. File's createTempFile(String, String) method creates a temporary file in the default temporary directory. How can you locate this directory?

19. Temporary files should be removed when no longer needed after an application exits (to avoid cluttering the filesystem). How do you ensure that a temporary file is removed when the virtual machine ends normally (it doesn't crash and the power isn't lost)?

20. How would you accurately compare two File objects?

21. What is the purpose of the RandomAccessFile class?

22. What is the purpose of the "rwd" and "rws" mode arguments?

23. What is a file pointer?

24. True or false: When you call RandomAccessFile's seek(long) method to set the file pointer's value, and when this value is greater than the length of the file, the file's length changes.

25. Define flat file database.

26. What is a stream?

27. What is the purpose of OutputStream's flush() method?

28. True or false: OutputStream's close() method automatically flushes the output stream.

29. What is the purpose of InputStream's mark(int) and reset() methods?

30. How would you access a copy of a ByteArrayOutputStream instance's internal byte array?

31. True or false: FileOutputStream and FileInputStream provide internal buffers to improve the performance of write and read operations.

32. Why would you use PipedOutputStream and PipedInputStream?

33. Define filter stream.

34. What does it mean for two streams to be chained together?

35. How do you improve the performance of a file output stream or a file input stream?

36. How do DataOutputStream and DataInputStream support FileOutputStream and FileInputStream?

37. What is object serialization and deserialization?

38. What three forms of serialization and deserialization does Java support?

39. What is the purpose of the Serializable interface?

40. What does the serialization mechanism do when it encounters an object whose class doesn't implement Serializable?

41. Identify the three stated reasons for Java not supporting unlimited serialization.

42. How do you initiate serialization? How do you initiate deserialization?

43. True or false: Class fields are automatically serialized.

44. What is the purpose of the transient reserved word?

45. What does the deserialization mechanism do when it attempts to deserialize an object whose class has changed?

46. How does the deserialization mechanism detect that a serialized object's class has changed?

47. How can you add an instance field to a class and avoid trouble when deserializing an object that was serialized before the instance field was added? What JDK tool can you use to help with this task?

48. How do you customize the default serialization and deserialization mechanisms without using externalization?

49. How do you tell the serialization and deserialization mechanisms to serialize or deserialize the object's normal state before serializing or deserializing additional data items?

50. How does externalization differ from default and custom serialization and deserialization?

51. How does a class indicate that it supports externalization?

52. True or false: During externalization, the deserialization mechanism throws `InvalidClassException` with a "no valid constructor" message when it doesn't detect a `public` noargument constructor.

53. What is the difference between `PrintStream`'s `print()` and `println()` methods?

54. What does `PrintStream`'s noargument `void println()` method accomplish?

55. Why are Java's stream classes not good at streaming characters?

56. What does Java provide as the preferred alternative to stream classes when it comes to character I/O?

57. True or false: `Reader` declares an `available()` method.

58. What is the purpose of the `OutputStreamWriter` class? What is the purpose of the `InputStreamReader` class?

59. How do you identify the default character encoding?

60. What is the purpose of the `FileWriter` class? What is the purpose of the `FileReader` class?

61. Create a Java application named Touch for setting a file's or directory's timestamp to the current time. This application has the following usage syntax: `java Touch` *pathname*.

62. Improve Listing 11-8's Copy application (performance wise) by using `BufferedInputStream` and `BufferedOutputStream`. Copy should read the bytes to be copied from the buffered input stream and write these bytes to the buffered output stream.

63. Create a Java application named Split for splitting a large file into a number of smaller part*x* files (where *x* starts at 0 and increments; for example, part0, part1, part2, and so on). Each part*x* file (except possibly the last part*x* file, which holds the remaining bytes) will have the same size. This application has the following usage syntax: `java Split` *pathname*. Furthermore, your implementation must use the `BufferedInputStream`, `BufferedOutputStream`, `File`, `FileInputStream`, and `FileOutputStream` classes.

64. It's often convenient to read lines of text from standard input, and the `InputStreamReader` and `BufferedReader` classes make this task possible. Create a Java application named `CircleInfo` that, after obtaining a `BufferedReader` instance that is chained to standard input, presents a loop that prompts the user to enter a radius, parses the entered radius into a `double` value, and outputs a pair of messages that report the circle's circumference and area based on this radius.

Summary

Applications often input data for processing and output processing results. Data is input from a file or some other source and is output to a file or some other destination. Java supports I/O via the classic I/O APIs located in the `java.io` package.

File I/O activities often interact with a filesystem. Java offers access to the underlying platform's available filesystem(s) via its concrete `File` class. `File` instances contain the pathnames of files and directories that may or may not exist in their filesystems.

Files can be opened for random access in which a mixture of write and read operations can occur until the file is closed. Java supports this random access by providing the concrete `RandomAccessFile` class.

Java uses streams to perform I/O operations. A stream is an ordered sequence of bytes of arbitrary length. Bytes flow over an output stream from an application to a destination and flow over an input stream from a source to an application.

The `java.io` package provides several output stream and input stream classes that are descendents of the abstract `OutputStream` and `InputStream` classes. `BufferedOutputStream` and `FileInputStream` are examples.

Java's stream classes are good for streaming sequences of bytes but are not good for streaming sequences of characters because bytes and characters are two different things, and because byte streams have no knowledge of character sets and encodings.

If you need to stream characters, you should take advantage of Java's writer and reader classes, which were designed to support character I/O (they work with `char` instead of `byte`). Furthermore, the writer and reader classes take character encodings into account.

The `java.io` package provides several writer and reader classes that are descendents of the abstract `Writer` and `Reader` classes. `FileWriter` and `FileReader` are examples. These convenience classes are based on file output/input streams and `OutputStreamWriter`/`InputStreamReader`.

This chapter focused on I/O in the context of a filesystem. However, you can also perform I/O in the context of a network. Chapter 12 introduces you to several of Java's network-oriented APIs.

Chapter 12

Accessing Networks

Applications often need to access networks to acquire resources (e.g., images) or to communicate with remote executable entities (e.g., web services). A *network* is a group of interconnected *nodes* (computing devices such as tablets and peripherals such as scanners or laser printers) that can be shared among the network's users.

> **Note** An intranet is a network located within an organization and an internet is a network connecting organizations to each other. The Internet is the global network of networks.
>
> Intranets and internets often use *TCP/IP* (http://en.wikipedia.org/wiki/TCP/IP_model) to communicate between nodes. TCP/IP includes *Transmission Control Protocol (TCP)*, which is a connection-oriented protocol; *User Datagram Protocol (UDP)*, which is a connectionless protocol; and *Internet Protocol (IP)*, which is the basic protocol over which TCP and UDP perform their tasks.

The java.net package provides types that support TCP/IP between *processes* (executing applications) running on the same or different *hosts* (computer-based TCP/IP nodes). In this chapter, I first present the types for performing socket-based and URL-based communication. I then present the low-level network interface and interface address types and cookie-oriented types.

> **Note** Android apps must have permission to access the network. Permission can be obtained by including <uses-permission android:name="android.permission.INTERNET" /> in the manifest file.
>
> Network-oriented applications often have to deal with the topic of *endianness* (http://en.wikipedia.org/wiki/Endianness), which refers to the ordering of individually addressable subcomponents within the representation of a larger data item. For example, given a 16-bit short integer, do you first transmit the most significant byte or the least significant byte?

Accessing Networks via Sockets

Two processes communicate by way of *sockets*, which are endpoints in a communications link between these processes. Each endpoint is identified by an *IP address* that identifies the host and by a *port number* that identifies the process running on that host.

IP ADDRESSES AND PORT NUMBERS

An *IP address* is a 32-bit or 128-bit unsigned integer that uniquely identifies a network host or some other network node (e.g., a router).

It is common to specify a 32-bit IP address as four 8-bit integer components in a period-separated decimal notation, where each component is a decimal integer ranging from 0 through 255 and is separated from the next component via a period (e.g., 127.0.0.1). A 32-bit IP address is often referred to as an *Internet Protocol Version 4 (IPv4) address* (see http://en.wikipedia.org/wiki/IPv4).

It's common to specify a 128-bit IP address as eight 16-bit integer components in colon-separated hexadecimal notation, where each component is a hexadecimal integer ranging from 0 through FFFF and is separated from the next component via a colon (e.g., 1080:0:0:0:8:800:200C:417A). A 128-bit IP address is often referred to as an *Internet Protocol Version 6 (IPv6) address* (see http://en.wikipedia.org/wiki/IPv6).

A *port number* is a 16-bit integer that uniquely identifies a process, which is the ultimate source or recipient of a message. Port numbers that are less than 1024 are reserved for standard processes. For example, port number 25 has traditionally identified the Simple Mail Transfer Protocol (SMTP) process for sending email, although port number 587 has largely obsoleted this older port number (see http://en.wikipedia.org/wiki/Smtp).

One process writes a *message* (a sequence of bytes) to its socket. The network management software portion of the underlying platform breaks the message into a sequence of *packets* (addressable message chunks that are often referred to as *IP datagrams*), and forwards them to the other process's socket where they are recombined into the original message for processing.

Figure 12-1 shows how two sockets communicate in a TCP/IP context.

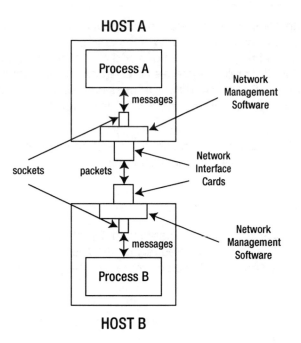

HOST A

HOST B

Figure 12-1. Two processes use sockets to communicate

In the context of Figure 12-1, suppose that Process A wants to send a message to Process B. Process A sends that message to its socket with the destination socket address of Process B. Host A's network management software (often referred to as a *protocol stack*) obtains this message and reduces it to a sequence of packets, with each packet including the destination host's IP address and port number. The network management software then sends these packets through Host A's Network Interface Card (NIC) to Host B.

> **Note**   The NIC's various *network interfaces* are connections between a computer and a network.

Host B's protocol stack receives packets through the NIC and reassembles them into the original message (packets may be received out of order), which it then makes available to Process B via its socket. This scenario reverses when Process B communicates with Process A.

The network management software uses TCP to create an ongoing conversation between two hosts in which messages are sent back and forth. Before this conversation occurs, a connection is established between these hosts. After the connection has been established, TCP enters a pattern where it sends message packets and waits for a reply that they arrived correctly (or for a timeout to expire when the reply doesn't arrive because of some network problem). This pattern repeats and guarantees a reliable connection. For detailed information on this pattern, check out http://en.wikipedia.org/wiki/Tcp_receive_window#Flow_control.

Because it can take time to establish a connection, and it also takes time to send packets (as it is necessary to receive reply acknowledgments and also because of timeouts), TCP is slow. On the other hand, UDP, which doesn't require connections and packet acknowledgment, is much faster. The downside is that UDP isn't as reliable (there's no guarantee of packet delivery, ordering, or protection against duplicate packets, although UDP uses checksums to verify that data is correct) because there's no acknowledgment. Furthermore, UDP is limited to single-packet conversations.

The java.net package provides Socket, ServerSocket, and other Socket-suffixed classes for performing TCP-based or UDP-based communications. Before investigating these classes, you need to understand socket addresses and socket options.

Socket Addresses

An instance of a Socket-suffixed class is associated with a *socket address* comprised of an IP address and a port number. These classes often rely on the InetAddress class to represent the IPv4 or IPv6 address portion of the socket address and represent the port number separately.

Note   InetAddress relies on its Inet4Address subclass to represent an IPv4 address and on its Inet6Address subclass to represent an IPv6 address.

InetAddress declares several class methods for obtaining an InetAddress instance. These methods include the following:

- InetAddress[] getAllByName(String host) returns an array of InetAddresses that store the IP addresses associated with host. You can pass either a domain name (e.g., "tutortutor.ca") or an IP address (e.g., "70.33.247.10") argument to this parameter. (To learn about domain names, check out Wikipedia's "Domain name" entry [http://en.wikipedia.org/wiki/Domain_name]). Pass null to obtain an InetAddress instance that stores the IP address of the *loopback interface* (a software-based network interface where outgoing data loops back as incoming data). This method throws UnknownHostException when no IP address for the specified host can be found or when a scope identifier is specified for a global IPv6 address.

- InetAddress getByAddress(byte[] addr) returns an InetAddress object for the given raw IP address. The argument passed to addr is in *network byte order* (most significant byte comes first), where the highest order byte is stored in addr[0]. The addr array's length must be 4 bytes for an IPv4 address and 16 bytes for an IPv6 address. This method throws UnknownHostException when the array has another length.

- InetAddress getByAddress(String hostName, byte[] ipAddress) returns an InetAddress instance based on the host name and IP address arguments. This method throws UnknownHostException when the array's length is neither 4 nor 16.

- InetAddress getByName(String host) returns an InetAddress instance based on the host argument, which can be a machine name (e.g., "tutortutor.ca") or a textual representation of its IP address. Passing null to host results in an InetAddress instance representing an address of the loopback interface being returned.

- InetAddress getLocalHost() returns the address of the *local host* (the current host), which is represented by hostname localhost or by an IP address that's commonly expressed as 127.0.0.1 (IPv4) or ::1 (IPv6). This method throws UnknownHostException when the local host couldn't be resolved into an address.

After you obtain an InetAddress instance, you can interrogate it by invoking instance methods such as byte[] getAddress(), which returns the raw IP address (in network byte order) of this InetAddress object, and boolean isLoopbackAddress(), which determines whether or not this InetAddress instance represents a loopback address.

Java 1.4 introduced the abstract SocketAddress class to represent a socket address "with no protocol attachment." (This class's creator might have anticipated that Java would eventually support low-level communication protocols other than the widely popular Internet Protocol.)

SocketAddress is subclassed by the concrete InetSocketAddress class, which represents a socket address as an IP address and a port number. It can also represent a hostname and a port number and will make an attempt to resolve the hostname.

InetSocketAddress instances are created by invoking InetSocketAddress(InetAddress addr, int port) and other constructors. After an instance has been created, you can call methods such as InetAddress getAddress() and int getPort() to return socket address components.

Socket Options

An instance of a Socket-suffixed class shares the concept of *socket options*, which are parameters for configuring socket behavior. Socket options are described by constants that are declared in the SocketOptions interface:

- IP_MULTICAST_IF: Specify the outgoing network interface for multicast packets (on *multihomed* [multiple NIC] hosts). This option isn't implemented by Android.

- IP_MULTICAST_IF2: Specify the outgoing network interface for multicast packets using an interface index.

- IP_MULTICAST_LOOP: Enable or disable local loopback of multicast datagrams.

- IP_TOS: Set the type-of-service (IPv4) or traffic class (IPv6) field in the IP header for a TCP or UDP socket.

- SO_BINDADDR: Fetch the socket's local address binding. This option isn't implemented by Android.

- SO_BROADCAST: Enable a socket to send broadcast messages.

- SO_KEEPALIVE: Turn on socket keepalive.

- SO_LINGER: Specify the number of seconds to wait when closing a socket when there is still some buffered data to be sent.

- SO_OOBINLINE: Enable inline reception of TCP urgent data.

- ▨ SO_RCVBUF: Set or get the maximum socket receive buffer size (in bytes).

- ▨ SO_REUSEADDR: Enable a socket's reuse address.

- ▨ SO_SNDBUF: Set or get the maximum socket send buffer size (in bytes).

- ▨ SO_TIMEOUT: Specify a timeout (in milliseconds) on blocking accept or read/receive (but not write/send) socket operations. (Don't block forever!)

- ▨ TCP_NODELAY: Disable Nagle's algorithm (http://en.wikipedia.org/wiki/Nagle's_algorithm). In other words, this option lets you send data immediately (but perhaps as efficiently) on this socket.

SocketOptions also declares the following methods for setting and getting these options:

- ▨ void setOption(int optID, Object value)

- ▨ Object getOption(int optID)

optID is one of the aforementioned constants and value is an object of a suitable class (e.g., java.lang.Boolean).

SocketOptions is implemented by the abstract SocketImpl and DatagramSocketImpl classes. Concrete instances of these classes are wrapped by the various Socket-suffixed classes. As a result, you cannot invoke these methods. Instead, you work with the type-safe setter and getter methods provided by the Socket-suffixed classes for setting and getting these options.

For example, Socket declares void setKeepAlive(boolean keepAlive) for setting the SO_KEEPALIVE option, and ServerSocket declares void setSoTimeout(int timeout) for setting the SO_TIMEOUT option. Check the documentation on the Socket-suffixed classes to learn about these and other socket option methods.

> **Note**   Socket option methods that apply to DatagramSocket also apply to its MulticastSocket subclass.

Socket and ServerSocket

The Socket and ServerSocket classes support TCP-based communications between client processes (e.g., an application running on a tablet) and server processes (e.g., an application running on one of your Internet Service Provider's computers that provides access to the World Wide Web). Because Socket is associated with the java.io.InputStream and java.io.OutputStream classes, sockets based on the Socket class are commonly referred to as *stream sockets*.

Socket supports the creation of client-side sockets. It declares several constructors for this purpose, including the following pair:

- ▨ Socket(InetAddress dstAddress, int dstPort) creates a stream socket and connects it to the specified port number (described by dstPort) at the specified IP address (described by dstAddress). This constructor throws java.io.IOException when an I/O error occurs while creating the socket; java.lang.IllegalArgumentException when the argument passed to dstPort is outside the valid range of port values, which is 0 through 65535; and java.lang.NullPointerException when dstAddress is null.

▪ Socket(String dstName, int dstPort) creates a stream socket and connects it to the port identified by dstPort on the host identified by dstName. When dstName is null, this constructor is equivalent to invoking Socket(InetAddress.getByName(null), port). It throws the same IOException and IllegalArgumentException instances as the previous constructor. However, instead of throwing NullPointerException, it throws UnknownHostException when the host's IP address cannot be determined.

After a Socket instance is created via these constructors, it's bound to an arbitrary local host socket address before a connection is made to the remote host socket address. *Binding* makes a client socket address available to a server socket so that a server process can communicate with the client process via the server socket.

Socket offers additional constructors. For example, Socket() and Socket(Proxy proxy) create unbound and unconnected sockets. Before using these sockets, they must be bound to local socket addresses by calling void bind(SocketAddress localAddr), and then connections must be made by calling Socket's connect() methods (e.g., void connect(SocketAddress remoteAddr)).

> **Note**   A *proxy* is a host that sits between an intranet and the Internet for security purposes. Proxy settings are represented via instances of the Proxy class and help sockets communicate through proxies.

Another constructor is Socket(InetAddress dstAddress, int dstPort, InetAddress localAddr, int localPort), which lets you specify your own local host socket address via localAddr and localPort. This constructor automatically binds to the local socket address and then attempts a connection to the remote dstPort on dstAddress.

After creating a Socket instance, and possibly invoking bind() and connect() on that instance, an application invokes Socket's InputStream getInputStream() and OutputStream getOutputStream() methods to acquire an input stream for reading bytes from the socket and an output stream for writing bytes to the socket. Also, the application often calls Socket's void close() method to close the socket when no longer needed for I/O.

The following example demonstrates how to create a socket that's bound to port number 9999 on the local host and then access its input and output streams—exceptions are ignored for brevity:

```
Socket socket = new Socket("localhost", 9999);
InputStream is = socket.getInputStream();
OutputStream os = socket.getOutputStream();
// Do some work with the socket.
socket.close();
```

ServerSocket supports the creation of server-side sockets. It declares the following four constructors for this purpose:

- ServerSocket() creates an unbound server socket. You can bind this socket to a specific socket address (to which client sockets communicate) by invoking either of ServerSocket's two bind() methods. *Binding* makes the server socket address available to a client socket so that a client process can communicate with the server process via the client socket. This constructor throws IOException when an I/O error occurs while attempting to open the socket.

- ServerSocket(int port) creates a server socket bound to the specified port value and an IP address associated with one of the host's NICs. When you pass 0 to port, an arbitrary port number is chosen. The port number can be retrieved by calling int getLocalPort(). The maximum queue length for incoming connection requests from clients is set to 50. If a connection request arrives when the queue is full, the connection is refused. This constructor throws IOException when an I/O error occurs while attempting to open the socket and IllegalArgumentException when port's value lies outside the specified range of valid port values, which is between 0 and 65535, inclusive.

- ServerSocket(int port, int backlog) is equivalent to the previous constructor, but it also lets you specify the maximum queue length for incoming connections by passing a positive integer to backlog.

- ServerSocket(int port, int backlog, InetAddress localAddress) is equivalent to the previous constructor, but it also lets you specify a different IP address to which the server socket binds. (Any address is chosen when null is passed.) This constructor is useful for machines that have multiple NICs and you want to listen for connection requests on a specific NIC.

After a server socket is created via these constructors, a server application enters a loop that first invokes ServerSocket's Socket accept() method to listen for a connection request and return a Socket instance that lets it communicate with the associated client socket. It then communicates with the client socket to perform some kind of processing. When processing finishes, the server socket calls the client socket's close() method to terminate its connection with the client.

> **Note** ServerSocket declares a void close() method for closing a server socket before terminating the server application. An unclosed socket is automatically closed when an application terminates.

The following example demonstrates how to create a server socket that's bound to port 9999 on the current host, listen for incoming connection requests, return their sockets, perform work on those sockets, and close the sockets—exceptions are ignored for brevity:

```
ServerSocket ss = new ServerSocket(9999);
while (true)
{
   Socket socket = ss.accept();
```

```
        // obtain socket input/output streams and communicate with socket
        socket.close();
}
```

The accept() method call blocks until a connection request is available and then returns a Socket object so that the server application can communicate with its associated client. The socket is closed after this communication takes place. The server socket is automatically closed when the application exits.

This example assumes that socket communication takes place on the server application's main thread, which is a problem when processing takes time to perform because server response time to incoming connection requests decreases. To speed up response time, it's often necessary to communicate with the socket on a worker thread, as demonstrated in the following example:

```
ServerSocket ss = new ServerSocket(9999);
while (true)
{
    final Socket s = ss.accept();
    new Thread(new Runnable()
            {
                @Override
                public void run()
                {
                    // obtain socket input/output streams and communicate with socket
                    try { s.close(); } catch (IOException ioe) {}
                }
            }).start();
}
```

Each time a connection request arrives, accept() returns a Socket instance, and then a java.lang.Thread object is created whose runnable accesses that socket for communicating with the socket on a worker thread.

> **Tip**   Although this example uses the Thread class, you could use an executor (see Chapter 10) instead.

I've created EchoClient and EchoServer applications that demonstrate Socket and ServerSocket. Listing 12-1 presents EchoClient's source code.

Listing 12-1. Echoing Data to and Receiving It Back from a Server

```
import java.io.BufferedReader;
import java.io.InputStream;
import java.io.InputStreamReader;
import java.io.IOException;
import java.io.OutputStream;
import java.io.OutputStreamWriter;
import java.io.PrintWriter;
```

```java
import java.net.Socket;
import java.net.UnknownHostException;

public class EchoClient
{
   public static void main(String[] args)
   {
      if (args.length != 1)
      {
         System.err.println("usage  : java EchoClient message");
         System.err.println("example: java EchoClient \"This is a test.\"");
         return;
      }
      try
      {
         Socket socket = new Socket("localhost", 9999);
         OutputStream os = socket.getOutputStream();
         OutputStreamWriter osw = new OutputStreamWriter(os);
         PrintWriter pw = new PrintWriter(osw);
         pw.println(args[0]);
         pw.flush();
         InputStream is = socket.getInputStream();
         InputStreamReader isr = new InputStreamReader(is);
         BufferedReader br = new BufferedReader(isr);
         System.out.println(br.readLine());
      }
      catch (UnknownHostException uhe)
      {
         System.err.println("unknown host: " + uhe.getMessage());
      }
      catch (IOException ioe)
      {
         System.err.println("I/O error: " + ioe.getMessage());
      }
   }
}
```

EchoClient first verifies that it has received a single command-line argument and then creates a socket that will connect to a process running on port 9999 of the local host.

After creating the socket, EchoClient obtains an output stream for writing a string to the socket. Because the output stream can only handle a sequence of bytes, the java.io.OutputStreamWriter and java.io.PrintWriter classes (see Chapter 11) are used to connect the writer that outputs characters to the byte-oriented output stream.

After instantiating PrintWriter, EchoClient invokes its void println(String str) method to write the string followed by a newline character. The void flush() method is subsequently called to ensure that all pending data is written to the server.

EchoClient now obtains an input stream for reading the string as a sequence of bytes. It then connects the reader (that inputs characters) to the byte-oriented input stream by instantiating java.io.InputStreamReader and java.io.BufferedReader (see Chapter 11).

Finally, EchoClient invokes BufferedReader's String readLine() method to read the characters followed by a newline from the socket. (readLine() doesn't include the newline character in the returned string.) These characters followed by a newline are then written to standard output.

> **Note**   In a long-running application, you would explicitly close the socket instance by invoking its void close() method when the socket is no longer needed. For brevity, I've chosen not to do so in this and most of the remaining Socket-suffixed class examples.

Listing 12-2 presents EchoServer's source code.

Listing 12-2.   Receiving Data from and Echoing It Back to a Client

```java
import java.io.BufferedReader;
import java.io.InputStream;
import java.io.InputStreamReader;
import java.io.IOException;
import java.io.OutputStream;
import java.io.OutputStreamWriter;
import java.io.PrintWriter;

import java.net.ServerSocket;
import java.net.Socket;

public class EchoServer
{
   public static void main(String[] args) throws IOException
   {
      System.out.println("Starting echo server...");
      ServerSocket ss = new ServerSocket(9999);
      while (true)
      {
         Socket s = ss.accept();
         try
         {
            InputStream is = s.getInputStream();
            InputStreamReader isr = new InputStreamReader(is);
            BufferedReader br = new BufferedReader(isr);
            String msg = br.readLine();
            System.out.println(msg);
            OutputStream os = s.getOutputStream();
            OutputStreamWriter osw = new OutputStreamWriter(os);
            PrintWriter pw = new PrintWriter(osw);
            pw.println(msg);
            pw.flush();
         }
         catch (IOException ioe)
         {
            System.err.println("I/O error: " + ioe.getMessage());
         }
```

```
      finally
      {
         try
         {
            s.close();
         }
         catch (IOException ioe)
         {
            assert false; // shouldn't happen in this context
         }
      }
    }
  }
}
```

EchoServer first outputs an introductory message to standard output and then creates a server socket that listens for connections on port 9999. It then enters an infinite loop, where each iteration invokes ServerSocket's Socket accept() method to block until a connection is received and then return a Socket object representing this connection.

After obtaining the socket, EchoServer obtains an input stream for reading from the socket. Because the input stream can only handle a sequence of bytes, the InputStreamReader and BufferedReader classes are used to connect the reader that inputs characters to the byte-oriented input stream.

EchoServer now obtains an output stream for writing the string as a sequence of bytes. It then connects the writer that outputs characters to the byte-oriented output stream by instantiating OutputStreamWriter and PrintWriter.

After outputting the message to standard output, EchoServer calls flush() to flush the output to the client. The client socket is then closed.

To experiment with these applications, copy EchoClient.java and EchoServer.java to the same directory and open two console windows with this directory being current. Compile each source file and execute java EchoServer in one window—you should observe an introductory message, although you might first need to enable port 9999 on the *firewall* (http://en.wikipedia.org/wiki/Firewall_(computing)). Having started the server, echo the following command to echo text to both windows:

java EchoClient "This is a test."

You should observe "This is a test." in both windows.

DatagramSocket and MulticastSocket

The DatagramSocket and MulticastSocket classes let you perform UDP-based communications between a pair of hosts (DatagramSocket) or between many hosts (MulticastSocket). With either class, you communicate one-way messages via *datagram packets*, which are arrays of bytes associated with instances of the DatagramPacket class.

> **Note** Although you might think that Socket and ServerSocket are all that you need, DatagramSocket (and its MulticastSocket subclass) have their uses. For example, consider a scenario in which a group of machines need to occasionally tell a server that they're alive. It shouldn't matter when the occasional message is lost or even when the message doesn't arrive on time. Another example is a low-priority stock ticker that periodically broadcasts stock prices. When a packet doesn't arrive, odds are that the next packet will arrive and you'll then receive notification of the latest prices. Timely rather than reliable or orderly delivery is more important in realtime applications.

DatagramPacket declares several constructors with DatagramPacket(byte[] buf, int length) being the simplest. This constructor requires you to pass byte array and integer arguments to buf and length, where buf is a data buffer that stores data to be sent or received, and length (which must be less than or equal to buf.length) specifies the number of bytes (starting at buf[0]) to send/receive.

The following example demonstrates this constructor:

```
byte[] buffer = new byte[100];
DatagramPacket dgp = new DatagramPacket(buffer, buffer.length);
```

> **Note** Additional constructors let you specify an offset into buf that identifies the storage location of the first outgoing or incoming byte and/or let you specify a destination socket address.

DatagramSocket describes a socket for the client or server side of the UDP-communication link. Although this class declares several constructors, I find it convenient in this chapter to use the DatagramSocket() constructor for the client side and the DatagramSocket(int port) constructor for the server side. Either constructor throws SocketException when it cannot create the datagram socket or bind the datagram socket to a local port.

After an application instantiates DatagramSocket, it calls void send(DatagramPacket dgp) and void receive(DatagramPacket dgp) to send and receive datagram packets.

Listing 12-3 demonstrates DatagramPacket and DatagramSocket in a server context.

Listing 12-3. Receiving Datagram Packets from and Echoing Them Back to Clients

```java
import java.io.IOException;

import java.net.DatagramPacket;
import java.net.DatagramSocket;
import java.net.SocketException;

public class DGServer
{
    final static int PORT = 10000;
```

```
public static void main(String[] args) throws SocketException
{
    System.out.println("Server is starting");
    DatagramSocket dgs = new DatagramSocket(PORT);
    try
    {
        System.out.println("Send buffer size = " + dgs.getSendBufferSize());
        System.out.println("Receive buffer size = " +
                            dgs.getReceiveBufferSize());
        byte[] data = new byte[100];
        DatagramPacket dgp = new DatagramPacket(data, data.length);
        while (true)
        {
            dgs.receive(dgp);
            System.out.println(new String(data));
            dgs.send(dgp);
        }
    }
    catch (IOException ioe)
    {
        System.err.println("I/O error: " + ioe.getMessage());
    }
}
}
```

Listing 12-3's main() method first creates a DatagramSocket object and binds the socket to port 10000 on the local host. It then invokes DatagramSocket's int getSendBufferSize() and int getReceiveBufferSize() methods to get the values of the SO_SNDBUF and SO_RCVBUF socket options, which are then output.

> **Note**   Sockets are associated with underlying platform send and receive buffers, and their sizes are accessed by calling getSendBufferSize() and getReceiveBufferSize(). Similarly, their sizes can be set by calling DatagramSocket's void setReceiveBufferSize(int size) and void setSendBufferSize(int size) methods. Although you can adjust these buffer sizes to improve performance, there's a practical limit with regard to UDP. The maximum size of a UDP packet that can be sent or received is 65,507 bytes under IPv4—it's derived from subtracting the 8-byte UDP header and 20-byte IP header values from 65,535. Although you can specify a send/receive buffer with a greater value, doing so is wasteful because the largest packet is restricted to 65,507 bytes. Also, attempting to send or receive a packet with a buffer length that exceeds 65,507 bytes results in IOException.

main() next instantiates DatagramPacket in preparation for receiving a datagram packet from a client and then echoing the packet back to the client. It assumes that packets will be 100 bytes or less in size.

Finally, main() enters an infinite loop that receives a packet, outputs packet content, and sends the packet back to the client—the client's addressing information is stored in DatagramPacket.

Compile Listing 12-3 (javac DGServer.java) and run the application (java DGServer). You should observe output that's the same as or similar to that shown following:

```
Server is starting
Send buffer size = 8192
Receive buffer size = 8192
```

Listing 12-4 demonstrates DatagramPacket and DatagramSocket in a client context.

Listing 12-4. Sending a Datagram Packet to and Receiving It Back from a Server

```java
import java.io.IOException;

import java.net.DatagramPacket;
import java.net.DatagramSocket;
import java.net.InetAddress;
import java.net.SocketException;

public class DGClient
{
   final static int PORT = 10000;
   final static String ADDR = "localhost";

   public static void main(String[] args) throws SocketException
   {
      System.out.println("client is starting");
      DatagramSocket dgs = new DatagramSocket();
      try
      {
         byte[] buffer;
         buffer = "Send me a datagram".getBytes();
         InetAddress ia = InetAddress.getByName(ADDR);
         DatagramPacket dgp = new DatagramPacket(buffer, buffer.length, ia,
                                                 PORT);
         dgs.send(dgp);
         byte[] buffer2 = new byte[100];
         dgp = new DatagramPacket(buffer2, buffer.length, ia, PORT);
         dgs.receive(dgp);
         System.out.println(new String(dgp.getData()));
      }
      catch (IOException ioe)
      {
         System.err.println("I/O error: " + ioe.getMessage());
      }
   }
}
```

Listing 12-4 is similar to Listing 12-3, but there's one big difference. I use the DatagramPacket(byte[] buf, int length, InetAddress address, int port) constructor to specify the server's destination, which happens to be port 10000 on the local host, in the datagram packet. The send() method call routes the packet to this destination.

Compile Listing 12-4 (javac DGClient.java) and run the application (java DGClient). Assuming that DGServer is also running, you should observe the following output in DGClient's command window (and the last line of this output in DGServer's command window):

```
client is starting
Send me a datagram
```

MulticastSocket describes a socket for the client or server side of a UDP-based multicasting session. Two commonly used constructors are MulticastSocket() (create a multicast socket not bound to a port) and MulticastSocket(int port) (create a multicast socket bound to the specified port). Either constructor throws IOException when an I/O error occurs.

WHAT IS MULTICASTING?

Previous examples have demonstrated *unicasting*, which occurs when a server sends a message to a single client. However, it's also possible to broadcast the same message to multiple clients (e.g., transmit a "school closed due to bad weather" announcement to all members of a group of parents who have registered with an online program to receive this announcement); this activity is known as *multicasting*.

A server multicasts by sending a sequence of datagram packets to a special IP address, which is known as a *multicast group address*, and a specific port (as specified by a port number). Clients wanting to receive those datagram packets create a multicast socket that uses that port number. They request to join the group through a *join group operation* that specifies the special IP address. At this point, the client can receive datagram packets sent to the group and can even send datagram packets to other group members. After the client has read all datagram packets that it wants to read, it removes itself from the group by applying a *leave group operation* that specifies the special IP address.

IPv4 addresses 224.0.0.1 to 239.255.255.255 (inclusive) are reserved for use as multicast group addresses.

Listing 12-5 presents a multicasting server.

Listing 12-5. Multicasting Datagram Packets

```java
import java.io.IOException;

import java.net.DatagramPacket;
import java.net.InetAddress;
import java.net.MulticastSocket;

public class MCServer
{
   final static int PORT = 10000;

   public static void main(String[] args)
   {
      try
      {
         MulticastSocket mcs = new MulticastSocket();
         InetAddress group = InetAddress.getByName("231.0.0.1");
         byte[] dummy = new byte[0];
```

```
            DatagramPacket dgp = new DatagramPacket(dummy, 0, group, PORT);
            int i = 0;
            while (true)
            {
               byte[] buffer = ("line " + i).getBytes();
               dgp.setData(buffer);
               dgp.setLength(buffer.length);
               mcs.send(dgp);
               i++;
            }
         }
         catch (IOException ioe)
         {
            System.err.println("I/O error: " + ioe.getMessage());
         }
      }
   }
}
```

Listing 12-5's main() method first creates a MulticastSocket instance via the MulticastSocket() constructor. The multicast socket doesn't need to bind to a port number because the port number is specified along with the multicast group's IP address (231.0.0.1) as part of the DatagramPacket instance that's subsequently created. (The dummy array is present to prevent a NullPointerException object from being thrown from the DatagramPacket constructor—this array isn't used to store data to be broadcasted.)

At this point, main() enters an infinite loop that first creates an array of bytes from a java.lang.String instance and uses the platform's default character encoding (see Chapter 11) to convert from Unicode characters to bytes. (Although extraneous java.lang.StringBuilder and String objects are created via expression "line" + i in each loop iteration, I'm not worried about their impact on garbage collection in this short throwaway application.)

This data buffer is subsequently assigned to the DatagramPacket instance by calling its void setData(byte[] buf) method, and then the datagram packet is broadcast to all members of the group associated with port 10000 and multicast IP address 231.0.0.1.

Compile Listing 12-5 (javac MCServer.java) and run this application (java MCServer). You shouldn't observe any output.

Listing 12-6 presents a multicasting client.

Listing 12-6. Receiving Multicasted Datagram Packets

```
import java.io.IOException;

import java.net.DatagramPacket;
import java.net.InetAddress;
import java.net.MulticastSocket;

public class MCClient
{
   final static int PORT = 10000;
```

```
public static void main(String[] args)
{
    try
    {
        MulticastSocket mcs = new MulticastSocket(PORT);
        InetAddress group = InetAddress.getByName("231.0.0.1");
        mcs.joinGroup(group);
        for (int i = 0; i < 10; i++)
        {
            byte[] buffer = new byte[256];
            DatagramPacket dgp = new DatagramPacket(buffer, buffer.length);
            mcs.receive(dgp);
            byte[] buffer2 = new byte[dgp.getLength()];
            System.arraycopy(dgp.getData(), 0, buffer2, 0, dgp.getLength());
            System.out.println(new String(buffer2));
        }
        mcs.leaveGroup(group);
    }
    catch (IOException ioe)
    {
        System.err.println("I/O error: " + ioe.getMessage());
    }
}
}
```

Listing 12-6's main() method first creates a MulticastSocket instance bound to port 10000 via the MulticastSocket(int port) constructor.

It then obtains an InetAddress object that contains multicast group IP address 231.0.0.1 and uses this object to join the group at this address by calling MulticastSocket's void joinGroup(InetAddress mcastaddr) method.

main() next receives 10 datagram packets, prints their contents, and leaves the group by calling MulticastSocket's void leaveGroup(InetAddress mcastaddr) method with the same multicast IP address as its argument.

> **Note** joinGroup() and leaveGroup() throw IOException when an I/O error occurs while attempting to join or leave the group or when the IP address is not a multicast IP address.

Because the client doesn't know exactly how long the arrays of bytes will be, it assumes 256 bytes to ensure that the data buffer will hold the entire array. If it tried to print out the returned array, you would see a lot of empty space after the actual data had been printed.

To eliminate this space, the client invokes DatagramPacket's int getLength() method to obtain the actual length of the array, creates a second byte array (buffer2) with this length, and uses System.arraycopy()—discussed in Chapter 8—to copy this many bytes to buffer2. After converting this byte array to a String object (via the String(byte[] bytes) constructor, which uses the platform's default character set—see Chapter 11 to learn about character sets), it prints the resulting characters to the standard output stream.

Compile Listing 12-6 (javac MCClient.java) and run this application (java MCClient). You should observe output similar to the following:

```
line 462615
line 462616
line 462617
line 462618
line 462619
line 462620
line 462621
line 462622
line 462623
line 462624
```

Accessing Networks via URLs

A *Uniform Resource Locator (URL)* is a character string that specifies where a resource (e.g., a web page) is located on a TCP/IP-based network (e.g., the Internet). Also, it provides the means to retrieve that resource. For example, http://tutortutor.ca is a URL that locates my web site's main page. The http:// prefix specifies that *HyperText Transfer Protocol (HTTP)*, which is a high-level protocol on top of TCP/IP for locating HTTP resources (e.g., web pages), must be used to retrieve the web page located at tutortutor.ca.

URNS AND URIS

A *Uniform Resource Name (URN)* is a character string that names a resource and doesn't provide a way to access that resource (the resource might not be available). For example, urn:isbn:9781430231561 identifies an Apress book named *Learn Java for Android Development* and that's all.

URNs and URLs are examples of *Uniform Resource Identifiers (URIs)*, which are character strings for identifying names (URNs) and resources (URLs). Every URN and URL is also a URI.

The java.net package provides URL and URLConnection classes for accessing URL-based resources. It also provides URLEncoder and URLDecoder classes for encoding and decoding URLs as well as the URI class for performing URI-based operations (e.g., relativization) and returning URL instances containing the results. For brevity, I don't discuss URI in this chapter.

URL and URLConnection

The URL class represents URLs and provides access to the resources to which they refer. Each URL instance unambiguously identifies an Internet resource.

URL declares several constructors with URL(String s) being the simplest. This constructor creates a URL instance from the String argument passed to s and is demonstrated as follows:

```
try
{
   URL url = new URL("http://tutortutor.ca");
}
```

```
catch (MalformedURLException murle)
{
    // handle the exception
}
```

This example creates a URL object that uses HTTP to access the web page at http://tutortutor.ca. If I specified an illegal URL (e.g., foo) the constructor would throw MalformedURLException (an IOException subclass).

Although you'll commonly specify http:// as the protocol prefix, this isn't your only choice. For example, you can also specify file:/// when the resource is located on the local host. Furthermore, you can prepend jar: to either http:// or file:/// when the resource is stored in a JAR file, as demonstrated here:

```
jar:file:///C:./rt.jar!/java/util/Timer.class
```

The jar: prefix indicates that you want to access a JAR file resource (e.g., a stored classfile). The file:/// prefix identifies the local host's resource location, which happens to be rt.jar (Java 5's runtime JAR file) in the current directory on the Windows C: hard drive in this example.

The path to the JAR file is followed by an exclamation mark (!) to separate the JAR file path from the JAR resource path, which happens to be the /java/util/Timer.class classfile entry in this JAR file (the leading / character is required).

> **Note**   The URL class in Oracle's Java reference implementation supports additional protocols, including ftp.

After creating a URL object, you can invoke various URL methods to access portions of the URL. For example, String getProtocol() returns the protocol portion of the URL (e.g., http). You can also retrieve the resource by calling the InputStream openStream() method.

openStream() creates a connection to the resource and returns an InputStream instance for reading resource data from that connection, as demonstrated here:

```
InputStream is = url.openStream();
int ch;
while ((ch = is.read()) != -1)
    System.out.print((char) ch);
```

> **Note**   For an HTTP connection, an internal socket is created that connects to HTTP port 80 on the server identified via the URL's domain name/IP address, unless you append a different port number to the domain name/IP address (e.g., http://tutortutor.ca:8080).

I've created a ListResource application that demonstrates URL by using this class to fetch a resource and list its contents. Listing 12-7 presents ListResource's source code.

Listing 12-7. Listing the Contents of the Resource Identified via a URL Command-Line Argument

```java
import java.io.InputStream;
import java.io.IOException;

import java.net.MalformedURLException;
import java.net.URL;

public class ListResource
{
   public static void main(String[] args)
   {
      if (args.length != 1)
      {
         System.err.println("usage: java ListResource url");
         return;
      }
      try
      {
         URL url = new URL(args[0]);
         InputStream is = url.openStream();
         try
         {
            int ch;
            while ((ch = is.read()) != -1)
               System.out.print((char) ch);
         }
         catch (IOException ioe)
         {
            is.close();
         }
      }
      catch (MalformedURLException murle)
      {
         System.err.println("invalid URL");
      }
      catch (IOException ioe)
      {
         System.err.println("I/O error: " + ioe.getMessage());
      }
   }
}
```

ListResource first verifies that it has received a single command-line argument and then attempts to instantiate URL with this argument. Assuming that the URL is valid, which means that MalformedURLException isn't thrown, ListResource calls openStream() on the URL instance and proceeds to list the resource contents to standard output.

Compile this source code (javac ListResource.java) and execute java ListResource
http://tutortutor.ca. The following output presents a short prefix of the returned web page:

```
<!DOCTYPE html PUBLIC "-//W3C//DTD HTML 4.01//EN" "http://www.w3.org/TR/html4/strict.dtd">

<html>
  <head>
    <title>
      TutorTutor -- /main
    </title>

    <link rel="stylesheet" href="/shared/styles.css" media="screen">
...
```

openStream() is a convenience method for invoking openConnection().getInputStream(). Each of
URL's URLConnection openConnection() and URLConnection openConnection(Proxy proxy) methods
returns an instance of the URLConnection class, which represents a communications link between the
application and a URL.

URLConnection gives you additional control over client/server communication. For example, you can
use this class to output content to various resources that accept content. In contrast, URL only lets
you input content via openStream().

URLConnection declares various methods, including the following:

- InputStream getInputStream() returns an input stream that reads from this
  open connection.

- OutputStream getOutputStream() returns an output stream that writes to this
  open connection.

- void setDoInput(boolean doInput) specifies that this URLConnection object
  supports (pass true to doInput) or doesn't support (pass false to doInput)
  input. Because true is the default, you would only pass true to this method to
  document your intention to perform input.

- void setDoOutput(boolean doOutput) specifies that this URLConnection object
  supports (pass true to doOutput) or doesn't support (pass false to doOutput)
  output. Because false is the default, you must call this method before you can
  perform output.

- void setRequestProperty(String field, String newValue) sets a request
  property (such as HTTP's accept property). When a field already exists, its value
  is overwritten with the specified value.

The following example shows you how to obtain an URLConnection object from a URL object
referenced by the precreated url variable, enable its dooutput property, and obtain an output stream
for writing to the resource:

```
URLConnection urlc = url.openConnection();
urlc.setDoOutput(true);
OutputStream os = urlc.getOutputStream();
```

URLConnection is subclassed by HttpURLConnection and JarURLConnection. These classes declare constants and/or methods that are specific to working with the HTTP protocol or interacting with JAR-based resources.

> **Note**   For brevity, I refer you to the Java documentation on URLConnection, HttpURLConnection, and JarURLConnection to learn more about these classes.

URLEncoder and URLDecoder

HyperText Markup Language (HTML) lets you introduce forms into web pages that solicit information from page visitors. After filling out a form's fields, the visitor clicks the form's Submit button (which may specify something other than Submit) and the form content (field names and values) is sent to a server program. Before sending the form content, a web browser encodes this data by replacing spaces and other URL-illegal characters, and sets the content's Internet media type (also known as Multipurpose Internet Mail Extensions [MIME] type) to application/x-www-form-urlencoded.

> **Note**   The data is encoded for HTTP POST and HTTP GET operations. Unlike POST, GET requires a *query string* (a ?-prefixed string containing the encoded content) to be appended to the server program's URL.

The java.net package provides URLEncoder and URLDecoder classes to assist you with the tasks of encoding and decoding form content.

URLEncoder applies the following encoding rules:

- Alphanumeric characters "a" through "z", "A" through "Z", and "0" through "9" remain the same.

- Special characters ".", "-", "*", and "_" remain the same.

- The space character " " is converted into a plus sign "+".

- All other characters are unsafe and are first converted into 1 or more bytes using some encoding scheme. Each byte is then represented by the three-character string %*xy*, where *xy* is the 2-digit hexadecimal representation of that byte. The recommended encoding scheme to use is UTF-8. However, for compatibility reasons, the platform's default encoding is used when an encoding isn't specified.

For example, using UTF-8 as the encoding scheme, the string "string ü@foo-bar" is converted to "string+%C3%BC%40foo-bar". In UTF-8, character ü is encoded as 2 bytes C3 (hex) and BC (hex); and character @ is encoded as 1 byte 40 (hex).

URLEncoder declares the following class method for encoding a string:

```
String encode(String s, String enc)
```

This method translates the `String` argument passed to s into `application/x-www-form-urlencoded` format using the encoding scheme specified by enc. It uses the supplied encoding scheme to obtain the bytes for unsafe characters, and throws `java.io.UnsupportedEncodingException` when enc's value isn't supported.

`URLDecoder` applies the following decoding rules:

- Alphanumeric characters "a" through "z", "A" through "Z", and "0" through "9" remain the same.

- Special characters ".", "-", "*", and "_" remain the same.

- The plus sign "+" is converted into a space character " ".

- A sequence of the form %*xy* will be treated as representing a byte, where *xy* is the 2-digit hexadecimal representation of the 8 bits. Then, all substrings containing one or more of these byte sequences consecutively will be replaced by the character(s) whose encoding would result in those consecutive bytes. The encoding scheme used to decode these characters may be specified; when unspecified, the platform's default encoding is used.

`URLDecoder` declares the following class method for decoding an encoded string:

```
String decode(String s, String enc)
```

This method decodes an `application/x-www-form-urlencoded` string using the encoding scheme specified by enc. The supplied encoding is used to determine what characters are represented by any consecutive sequences of the form %*xy*. `UnsupportedEncodingException` is thrown when enc's value isn't supported.

There are two possible ways in which the decoder could deal with illegally encoded strings. It could either leave illegal characters alone or it could throw `IllegalArgumentException`. Which approach the decoder takes is left to the implementation.

> **Note**   The World Wide Web Consortium recommends
> (`www.w3.org/TR/html40/appendix/notes.html#non-ascii-chars`) that UTF-8 be used as the
> encoding scheme for `encode()` and `decode()`. Not doing so may introduce incompatibilities.

I've created an ED (Encode/Decode) application that demonstrates `URLEncoder` and `URLDecoder` in the context of the previous "`string ü@foo-bar`" and "`string+%C3%BC%40foo-bar`" example. Listing 12-8 presents the application's source code.

Listing 12-8. Encoding and Decoding an Encoded String

```
import java.io.UnsupportedEncodingException;

import java.net.URLDecoder;
import java.net.URLEncoder;
```

```
public class ED
{
    public static void main(String[] args) throws UnsupportedEncodingException
    {
        String encodedData = URLEncoder.encode("string ü@foo-bar", "UTF-8");
        System.out.println(encodedData);
        System.out.println(URLDecoder.decode(encodedData, "UTF-8"));
    }
}
```

When you run this application, it generates the following output:

```
string+%C3%BC%40foo-bar
string ü@foo-bar
```

> **Note**   Check out Wikipedia's "Percent-encoding" topic (http://en.wikipedia.org/wiki/
> Percent-encoding) to learn more about URL encoding (and the more accurate percent-encoding term).

Accessing Network Interfaces and Interface Addresses

The NetworkInterface class represents a network interface in terms of a name (e.g., le0) and a list of IP addresses assigned to this interface. Although a network interface is often implemented on a physical NIC, it also can be implemented in software; for example, the *loopback interface* (which is useful for testing a client).

Table 12-1 presents NetworkInterface's methods.

Table 12-1. NetworkInterface Methods

Method	Description
boolean equals(Object obj)	Compare this NetworkInterface object with obj. The result is true if and only if obj isn't null and represents the same network interface as this object. (Two NetworkInterface objects represent the same network interface when their names and addresses are the same.)
static NetworkInterface getByInetAddress(InetAddress address)	Return the NetworkInterface corresponding to the given address or null when no interface has this address. This method throws SocketException when an I/O error occurs and NullPointerException when address is null.
static NetworkInterface getByName(String interfaceName)	Return the NetworkInterface with the specified name, or return null when there's no such network interface. This method throws SocketException on an I/O error and NullPointerException when interfaceName is null.

(continued)

Table 12-1. (*continued*)

Method	Description
`String getDisplayName()`	Return this network interface's *display name* (a human-readable string describing the network device). On Android, this is the same string as returned by `getName()`.
`byte[] getHardwareAddress()`	Return an array of bytes containing this network interface's hardware address, which is often referred to as the *media access control (MAC)* address. When the interface doesn't have a MAC address, or when the address cannot be accessed (perhaps the user doesn't have sufficient privileges), the method returns null. This method throws `SocketException` when an I/O error occurs.
`Enumeration<InetAddress> getInetAddresses()`	Return an *enumeration* (the results of an iteration) with all or a subset of the addresses bound to this network interface.
`List<InterfaceAddress> getInterfaceAddresses()`	Return a `java.util.List` containing this network interface's `InterfaceAddresses`.
`int getMTU()`	Return this network interface's *maximum transmission unit (MTU)*. This method throws `SocketException` when an I/O error occurs.
`String getName()`	Return this network interface's name (e.g., `eth0` or `lo`).
`static Enumeration<NetworkInterface> getNetworkInterfaces()`	Return all of the network interfaces on this machine, or return null when no network interfaces could be found. This method throws `SocketException` when an I/O error occurs.
`NetworkInterface getParent()`	Return this network interface's parent `NetworkInterface` when this network interface is a subinterface. When this network interface has no parent, or when it's a physical (nonvirtual) interface, this method returns null. (A physical network interface can be logically divided into multiple *virtual subinterfaces*, which are commonly used in routing and switching. These subinterfaces can be organized into a hierarchy where the physical network interface serves as the root.)
`Enumeration<NetworkInterface> getSubInterfaces()`	Return an enumeration containing the virtual subinterfaces that are attached to this network interface. For example, `eth0:1` is a subinterface of `eth0`.
`int hashCode()`	This method is overridden because `equals()` is overridden.
`boolean isLoopback()`	Return true when this network interface reflects outgoing data back to itself as incoming data. This method throws `SocketException` when an I/O error occurs.
`boolean isPointToPoint()`	Return true when this network interface is point-to-point (e.g., a PPP connection through a modem). This method throws `SocketException` when an I/O error occurs.

(continued)

Table 12-1. (*continued*)

Method	Description
boolean isUp()	Return true when this network interface is *up* (routing entries have been established) and *running* (platform resources have been allocated). This method throws SocketException when an I/O error occurs.
boolean isVirtual()	Return true when this network interface is a virtual subinterface. On some platforms, virtual subinterfaces are network interfaces created as children of a physical network interface and given different settings (e.g., address or MTU). Usually, the name of the interface will be the name of the parent followed by a colon (:) and a number identifying the child because there can be several virtual subinterfaces attached to a single physical network interface.
boolean supportsMulticast()	Return true when this network interface supports *multicasting*. This method throws SocketException when an I/O error occurs.
String toString()	Return a string representation of this network interface.

You can use these methods to gather useful information about your platform's network interfaces. For example, Listing 12-9 presents an application that iterates over all network interfaces, invoking the methods listed in Table 12-1 that obtain the network interface's name and display name, determine if the network interface is a loopback interface, determine if the network interface is up and running, obtain the MTU, determine if the network interface supports multicasting, and enumerate all of the network interface's virtual subinterfaces.

Listing 12-9. Enumerating All Network Interfaces

```
import java.net.NetworkInterface;
import java.net.SocketException;

import java.util.Collections;
import java.util.Enumeration;

public class NetInfo
{
   public static void main(String[] args) throws SocketException
   {
      Enumeration<NetworkInterface> eni;
      eni = NetworkInterface.getNetworkInterfaces();
      for (NetworkInterface ni: Collections.list(eni))
      {
         System.out.println("Name = " + ni.getName());
         System.out.println("Display Name = " + ni.getDisplayName());
         System.out.println("Loopback = " + ni.isLoopback());
         System.out.println("Up and running = " + ni.isUp());
```

```
            System.out.println("MTU = " + ni.getMTU());
            System.out.println("Supports multicast = " + ni.supportsMulticast());
            System.out.println("Sub-interfaces");
            Enumeration<NetworkInterface> eni2;
            eni2 = ni.getSubInterfaces();
            for (NetworkInterface ni2: Collections.list(eni2))
                System.out.println("   " + ni2);
            System.out.println();
        }
    }
}
```

> **Tip** The java.util.Collections class's ArrayList<T> list(Enumeration<T>
> enumeration) method is useful for converting a legacy enumeration to a modern array list.

Compile Listing 12-9 (javac NetInfo.java) and execute this application (java NetInfo). When I run NetInfo on my Windows 7 platform, I observe information that begins with the following output:

```
Name = lo
Display Name = Software Loopback Interface 1
Loopback = true
Up and running = true
MTU = -1
Supports multicast = true
Sub-interfaces

Name = net0
Display Name = WAN Miniport (SSTP)
Loopback = false
Up and running = false
MTU = -1
Supports multicast = true
Sub-interfaces
```

The complete output reveals a different MTU size for a few network interfaces. Each size represents the maximum length of a message that can fit into an *IP datagram* without needing to fragment the message into multiple IP datagrams. This fragmentation has performance implications, especially in the context of networked games. For this reason alone, the getMTU() method is a valuable member of NetworkInterface.

The getInterfaceAddresses() method returns a list of InterfaceAddress objects, with each object containing a network interface's IP address along with broadcast address and subnet mask (IPv4) or network prefix length (IPv6).

Table 12-2 presents InterfaceAddress's methods.

Table 12-2. InterfaceAddress Methods

Method	Description
`boolean equals(Object obj)`	Compare this `InterfaceAddress` object with obj. Return true when obj is also an `InterfaceAddress` and when both objects contain the same `InetAddress`, the same subnet masks/network prefix lengths (depending on IPv4 or IPv6), and the same broadcast addresses.
`InetAddress getAddress()`	Return this `InterfaceAddress`'s IP address, as an `InetAddress` object.
`InetAddress getBroadcast()`	Return this `InterfaceAddress`'s broadcast address (IPv4) or null (IPv6); IPv6 doesn't support broadcast addresses.
`short getNetworkPrefixLength()`	Return this `InterfaceAddress`'s network prefix length (IPv6) or subnet mask (IPv4). Oracle's Java documentation shows 128 (::1/128) and 10 (fe80::203:baff:fe27:1243/10) as typical IPv6 values. Typical IPv4 values are 8 (255.0.0.0), 16 (255.255.0.0), and 24 (255.255.255.0).
`int hashCode()`	Return this `InterfaceAddress`'s hash code. The hash code is a combination of the `InetAddress`'s hash code, the broadcast address (when present) hash code, and the network prefix length.
`String toString()`	Return a string representation of this `InterfaceAddress`. This representation has the form *InetAddress / network prefix length [broadcast address]*.

Listing 12-10, which extends Listing 12-9 (with a few lines removed), enumerates all network interfaces, outputting their display names, and enumerates each network interface's interface addresses, outputting interface address information.

Listing 12-10. Enumerating All Network Interfaces and Interface Addresses

```java
import java.net.InterfaceAddress;
import java.net.NetworkInterface;
import java.net.SocketException;

import java.util.Collections;
import java.util.Enumeration;
import java.util.Iterator;
import java.util.List;

public class NetInfo
{
    public static void main(String[] args) throws SocketException
    {
        Enumeration<NetworkInterface> eni;
        eni = NetworkInterface.getNetworkInterfaces();
        for (NetworkInterface ni: Collections.list(eni))
        {
            System.out.println("Name = " + ni.getName());
            List<InterfaceAddress> ias = ni.getInterfaceAddresses();
            Iterator<InterfaceAddress> iter = ias.iterator();
```

```
        while (iter.hasNext())
            System.out.println(iter.next());
        System.out.println();
    }
  }
}
```

Compile Listing 12-10 (javac NetInfo.java) and execute this application (java NetInfo). When I run NetInfo on my Windows 7 platform, I observe the following information:

```
Name = lo
/127.0.0.1/8 [/127.255.255.255]
/0:0:0:0:0:0:0:1/128 [null]

Name = net0

Name = net1

Name = net2

Name = ppp0

Name = eth0

Name = eth1

Name = eth2

Name = ppp1

Name = net3

Name = eth3
/192.xxx.xxx.xxx/xx [/192.xxx.xxx.xxx]
/fe80:0:0:0:xxxx:xxxx:xxxx:xxxx%xx/xx [null]

Name = net4
/fe80:0:0:0:0:xxxx:xxxx:xxxx%xx/xxx [null]

Name = net5
/2001:0:xxxx:xxxx:xxxx:xxxx:xxxx:xxxx/x [null]
/fe80:0:0:0:xxxx:xxxx:xxxx:xxxx%xx/xx [null]

Name = eth4

Name = eth5

Name = eth6

Name = eth7

Name = eth8
```

Managing Cookies

Server applications commonly use *HTTP cookies* (state objects)—*cookies* for short—to persist small amounts of information on clients. For example, the identifiers of currently selected items in a shopping cart can be stored as cookies. It's preferable to store cookies on the client rather than on the server because of the potential for millions of cookies (depending on a web site's popularity). In that case, not only would a server require a massive amount of storage just for cookies, but also searching for and maintaining cookies would be time consuming.

> **Note**   Check out Wikipedia's "HTTP cookie" entry (http://en.wikipedia.org/wiki/HTTP_cookie) for a quick refresher on cookies.

A server application sends a cookie to a client as part of an HTTP response. A client (e.g., a web browser) sends a cookie to the server as part of an HTTP request. Before Java 5, applications worked with the URLConnection class (and its HttpURLConnection subclass) to get an HTTP response's cookies and to set an HTTP request's cookies. The String getHeaderFieldKey(int n) and String getHeaderField(int n) methods were used to access a response's Set-Cookie headers, and the void setRequestProperty(String key, String value) method was used to create a request's Cookie header.

> **Note**   RFC 2109: HTTP State Management Mechanism (www.ietf.org/rfc/rfc2109.txt) describes the Set-Cookie and Cookie headers.

Java 5 introduced the abstract CookieHandler class as a callback mechanism that connects HTTP state management to an HTTP protocol handler (think concrete HttpURLConnection subclass). An application installs a concrete CookieHandler subclass as the system-wide cookie handler via the CookieHandler class's void setDefault(CookieHandler cHandler) class method. A companion CookieHandler getDefault() class method returns this cookie handler, which is null when a system-wide cookie handler hasn't been installed.

An HTTP protocol handler accesses response and request headers. This handler invokes the system-wide cookie handler's void put(URI uri, Map<String, List<String>> responseHeaders) method to store response cookies in a cookie cache and invokes the Map<String, List<String>> get(URI uri, Map<String, List<String>> requestHeaders) method to fetch request cookies from this cache. Unlike Java 5, Java 6 introduced a concrete implementation of CookieHandler so that HTTP protocol handlers and applications can work with cookies.

The concrete CookieManager class extends CookieHandler to manage cookies. A CookieManager object is initialized as follows:

- With a *cookie store* for storing cookies. The cookie store is based on the CookieStore interface.

- With a *cookie policy* for determining which cookies to accept for storage. The cookie policy is based on the CookiePolicy interface.

Create a cookie manager by calling either the CookieManager() constructor or the CookieManager(CookieStore store, CookiePolicy policy) constructor. The CookieManager() constructor invokes the latter constructor with null arguments, using the default in-memory cookie store and the default accept-cookies-from-the-original-server-only cookie policy. Unless you plan to create your own CookieStore and CookiePolicy implementations, you'll most likely work with the default constructor. The following example creates and establishes a new CookieManager object as the system-wide cookie handler:

```
CookieHandler.setDefault(new CookieManager());
```

Along with the aforementioned constructors, CookieManager declares the following methods:

- Map<String, List<String>> get(URI uri, Map<String, List<String>> requestHeaders) returns an immutable map of Cookie and Cookie2 request headers for cookies obtained from the cookie store whose path matches uri's path. Although requestHeaders isn't used by the default implementation of this method, it can be used by subclasses. IOException is thrown when an I/O error occurs.

- CookieStore getCookieStore() returns the cookie manager's cookie store.

- void put(URI uri, Map<String, List<String>> responseHeaders) stores all applicable cookies whose Set-Cookie and Set-Cookie2 response headers were retrieved from the specified uri value and placed (with all other response headers) in the immutable responseHeaders map in the cookie store. IOException is thrown when an I/O error occurs.

- void setCookiePolicy(CookiePolicy cookiePolicy) sets the cookie manager's cookie policy to one of CookiePolicy.ACCEPT_ALL (accept all cookies), CookiePolicy.ACCEPT_NONE (accept no cookies), or CookiePolicy.ACCEPT_ORIGINAL_SERVER (accept cookies from original server only—this is the default). Passing null to this method has no effect on the current policy.

In contrast to the get() and put() methods, which are called by HTTP protocol handlers, an application works with the getCookieStore() and setCookiePolicy() methods. Consider Listing 12-11.

Listing 12-11. Listing All Cookies for a Specific Domain

```
import java.io.IOException;

import java.net.CookieHandler;
import java.net.CookieManager;
import java.net.CookiePolicy;
```

```
import java.net.HttpCookie;
import java.net.URL;

import java.util.List;

public class ListAllCookies
{
    public static void main(String[] args) throws IOException
    {
        if (args.length != 1)
        {
            System.err.println("usage: java ListAllCookies url");
            return;
        }
        CookieManager cm = new CookieManager();
        cm.setCookiePolicy(CookiePolicy.ACCEPT_ALL);
        CookieHandler.setDefault(cm);
        new URL(args[0]).openConnection().getContent();
        List<HttpCookie> cookies = cm.getCookieStore().getCookies();
        for (HttpCookie cookie: cookies)
        {
            System.out.println("Name = " + cookie.getName());
            System.out.println("Value = " + cookie.getValue());
            System.out.println("Lifetime (seconds) = " + cookie.getMaxAge());
            System.out.println("Path = " + cookie.getPath());
            System.out.println();
        }
    }
}
```

Listing 12-11 describes a command-line application that obtains and lists all cookies from its single domain name argument.

After creating a cookie manager and invoking setCookiePolicy() to set the cookie manager's policy to accept all cookies, ListAllCookies installs the cookie manager as the system-wide cookie handler. It next connects to the domain identified by the command-line argument and reads the content (via URL's Object getContent() method).

The cookie store is obtained via getCookieStore() and used to retrieve all nonexpired cookies via its List<HttpCookie> getCookies() method. For each of these HttpCookies, String getName(), String getValue(), and other HttpCookie methods are invoked to return cookie-specific information.

The following output resulted from invoking java ListAllCookies http://java.net:

```
Name = SESSe2db433431725a35762565c526a602d3
Value = 29va73kqorof3k2tmchn1fka11
Lifetime (seconds) = 3971
Path = /
```

> **Note** For more information about cookie management, including examples that show you how to create your own CookiePolicy and CookieStore implementations, check out *The Java Tutorial*'s "Working With Cookies" lesson (http://docs.oracle.com/javase/tutorial/networking/cookies/index.html).

EXERCISES

The following exercises are designed to test your understanding of Chapter 12's content:

1. Define network.

2. What is an intranet and what is an internet?

3. What do intranets and internets often use to communicate between nodes?

4. Define host.

5. What is a socket?

6. How is a socket identified?

7. Define IP address.

8. What is a packet?

9. A socket address is comprised of what elements?

10. Identify the InetAddress subclasses that are used to represent IPv4 and IPv6 addresses.

11. What is the loopback interface?

12. True or false: In network byte order, the least significant byte comes first.

13. How is the local host represented?

14. Define socket option.

15. How are socket options described?

16. True or false: You set a socket option by calling the void setOption(int optID, Object value) method.

17. Why are sockets based on the Socket class commonly referred to as stream sockets?

18. What does binding accomplish in the context of a Socket instance?

19. Define proxy. How does Java represent proxy settings?

20. True or false: The ServerSocket() constructor creates a bound sever socket.

21. What is the difference between the DatagramSocket and MulticastSocket classes?

22. What is a datagram packet?

23. What is the difference between unicasting and multicasting?

24.   What is a URL?

25.   What is a URN?

26.   True or false: URLs and URNs are also URIs.

27.   What does the URL(String s) constructor do when you pass null to s?

28.   What is the equivalent of openStream()?

29.   True or false: You need to invoke URLConnection's void setDoInput(boolean doInput) method with true as the argument before you can input content from a web resource.

30.   What does URLEncoder do when it encounters a space character?

31.   What does the NetworkInterface class accomplish?

32.   What is a MAC address?

33.   What does MTU stand for and what is its purpose?

34.   True or false: NetworkInterface's getName() method returns a human-readable name.

35.   What does InterfaceAddress's getNetworkPrefixLength() method return under IPv4?

36.   Define HTTP Cookie.

37.   Why is it preferable to store cookies on the client rather than on the server?

38.   Identify the four java.net types that are used to work with cookies.

39.   Modify Listing 12-1's EchoClient source code to explicitly close the socket.

40.   Modify Listing 12-2's EchoServer source code to exit the while loop and explicitly close the server socket when a file named kill appears in the directory from which the server was started. After this file appears, the server will probably not die immediately because it's most likely waiting (via the accept() call) for an incoming client connection. However, it should die after servicing the next incoming connection.

Summary

A network is a group of interconnected nodes that can be shared among the network's users. An intranet is a network located within an organization and an internet is a network connecting organizations to each other. The Internet is the global network of networks.

The java.net package provides types that support TCP/IP between processes running on the same or different hosts. Two processes communicate by way of sockets, which are endpoints in a communications link between these processes. Each endpoint is identified by an IP address that identifies a host and by a port number that identifies the process running on that host.

One process writes a message to its socket, the network management software portion of the underlying operating system breaks the message into a sequence of packets that it forwards to the other process's socket, and the other process recombines received packets into the original message for its own processing.

The network management software uses TCP to create an ongoing conversation between two hosts in which messages are sent back and forth. Before this conversation occurs, a connection is established between these hosts. After the connection has been established, TCP enters a pattern where it sends message packets and waits for a reply that they arrived correctly (or for a timeout to expire when the reply doesn't arrive because of some network problem). This pattern repeats and guarantees a reliable connection.

Because it can take time to establish a connection, and it also takes time to send packets (as it is necessary to receive reply acknowledgments and also because of timeouts), TCP is slow. On the other hand, UDP, which doesn't require connections and packet acknowledgment, is much faster. The downside is that UDP isn't as reliable (there's no guarantee of packet delivery, ordering, or protection against duplicate packets, although UDP uses checksums to verify that data is correct) because there's no acknowledgment. Furthermore, UDP is limited to single-packet conversations.

An instance of a Socket-suffixed class is associated with a socket address comprised of an IP address and a port number. These classes often rely on the InetAddress class to represent the IPv4 or IPv6 address portion of the socket address and represent the port number separately.

An instance of a Socket-suffixed class shares the concept of socket options, which are parameters for configuring socket behavior. Socket options are described by constants that are declared in the SocketOptions interface.

The Socket and ServerSocket classes support TCP-based communications between client processes and server processes. Socket supports the creation of client-side sockets, whereas ServerSocket supports the creation of server-side sockets.

The DatagramSocket and MulticastSocket classes let you perform UDP-based communications between a pair of hosts (DatagramSocket) or between as many hosts as necessary (MulticastSocket). With either class, you communicate one-way messages via datagram packets.

Two processes communicating via sockets demonstrate low-level network access. Java also supports high-level access via URLs that identify resources and specify where they are located on TCP/IP-based networks.

URLs are represented by the URL class, which provides access to the resources to which they refer. URLConnection gives you additional control over client/server communication. For example, you can use this class to output content to various resources that accept content. In contrast, URL only lets you input content via openStream().

HTML lets you introduce forms into web pages that solicit information from page visitors. The java.net package provides URLEncoder and URLDecoder classes to assist you with the tasks of encoding and decoding form content.

The NetworkInterface class represents a network interface in terms of a name (e.g., le0) and a list of IP addresses assigned to this interface. NetworkInterface's getInterfaceAddresses() method returns a list of InterfaceAddress objects, with each object containing a network interface's IP address along with broadcast address and subnet mask (IPv4) or network prefix length (IPv6).

Server applications commonly use HTTP cookies (state objects)—cookies for short—to persist small amounts of information on clients. Java provides the CookieHandler and CookieManager classes and the CookiePolicy and CookieStore interfaces for working with cookies.

This chapter focused on I/O in a network context. New I/O lets you perform file-based and network-based I/O in a more performant manner. Chapter 13 introduces you to Java's New I/O APIs.

Migrating to New I/O

Chapters 11 and 12 introduced you to Java's classic I/O APIs. Chapter 11 presented classic I/O in terms of the `java.io.RandomAccessFile` class, streams, and writers/readers. Chapter 12 presented classic I/O in terms of sockets and URLs.

Modern operating systems offer powerful I/O features that are not supported by Java's classic I/O APIs. Features include *memory-mapped file I/O* (the ability to map part of a process's *virtual memory* [see http://en.wikipedia.org/wiki/Virtual_memory] to some portion of a file so that writes to or reads from that portion of the process's memory space actually write/read the associated portion of the file), *readiness selection* (a step above nonblocking I/O that offloads to the operating system the work involved in checking for I/O stream readiness to perform write and read operations), and *file locking* (the ability for one process to prevent other processes from accessing a file or to limit the access in some way).

Java 1.4 introduced a more powerful I/O architecture that supports memory-mapped file I/O, readiness selection, file locking, and more. This architecture consists of buffers, channels, selectors, regular expressions, and charsets and is commonly known as New I/O (NIO).

> **Note** Regular expressions were included as part of NIO (see JSR 51—http://jcp.org/en/jsr/detail?id=51) because NIO is all about performance, and regular expressions are useful for scanning text (read from an I/O source) in a highly performant manner. (A simple `printf`-style formatting facility based on the `java.util.Formatter` class [see Chapter 10] was also included in NIO.)

Chapter 13 introduces you to NIO in terms of buffers, channels, and regular expressions. (I don't discuss selectors and charsets for brevity.)

> **Note** NIO is a huge architecture; a comprehensive discussion could occupy an entire book. For brevity, I omit many details in this chapter.

Working with Buffers

NIO is based on buffers. A *buffer* is an object that stores a fixed amount of data to be sent to or received from an *I/O service* (a means for performing input/output). It sits between an application and a *channel* that writes the buffered data to the service or reads the data from the service and deposits it into the buffer.

Buffers possess four properties:

- *Capacity*: The total number of data items that can be stored in the buffer. The capacity is specified when the buffer is created and cannot be changed later.

- *Limit*: The number of "live" data items in the buffer. No items starting from the zero-based limit should be written or read.

- *Position*: The zero-based index of the next data item that can be read or the location where the data item can be written.

- *Mark*: A zero-based position that can be recalled. The mark is initially undefined.

These four properties are related as follows: 0 <= mark <= position <= limit <= capacity.

Figure 13-1 reveals a newly created and byte-oriented buffer.

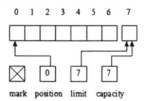

Figure 13-1. *The logical layout of a byte-oriented buffer includes an undefined mark, a current position, a limit, and a capacity*

Figure 13-1's buffer can store a maximum of seven elements. The mark is initially undefined, the position is initially set to 0, and the limit is initially set to the capacity, which specifies the maximum number of bytes that can be stored in the buffer. You can only access positions 0 through 6.

Buffer and Its Children

Buffers are implemented by classes that derive from the abstract `java.nio.Buffer` class. Table 13-1 describes `Buffer`'s methods.

Table 13-1. `Buffer Methods`

Method	Description
`Object array()`	Return the array that backs this buffer. This method is intended to allow array-backed buffers to be passed to *native code* more efficiently. Concrete subclasses override this method and provide more strongly typed return values via covariant return types (discussed in Chapter 4). This method throws `java.nio.ReadOnlyBufferException` when this buffer is backed by an array but is read only and throws `java.lang.UnsupportedOperationException` when this buffer isn't backed by an accessible array.
`int arrayOffset()`	Return the offset of the first buffer element within this buffer's backing array. When this buffer is backed by an array, buffer position p corresponds to array index p + `arrayOffset()`. Invoke `hasArray()` before invoking this method to ensure that this buffer has an accessible backing array. This method throws `ReadOnlyBufferException` when this buffer is backed by an array but is read only and throws `UnsupportedOperationException` when this buffer isn't backed by an accessible array.
`int capacity()`	Return this buffer's capacity.
`Buffer clear()`	Clear this buffer. The position is set to zero, the limit is set to the capacity, and the mark is discarded. This method doesn't erase the data in the buffer but is named as if it did because it will most often be used in situations in which that might as well be the case.
`Buffer flip()`	Flip this buffer. The limit is set to the current position and then the position is set to zero. When the mark is defined, it's discarded.
`boolean hasArray()`	Return true when this buffer is backed by an array and isn't read-only; otherwise, return false. When this method returns true, `array()` and `arrayOffset()` may be invoked safely.
`boolean hasRemaining()`	Return true when at least one element remains in this buffer (i.e., between the current position and the limit); otherwise, return false.
`boolean isDirect()`	Return true when this buffer is a direct byte buffer (discussed later in this section); otherwise, return false.
`boolean isReadOnly()`	Return true when this buffer is read-only; otherwise, return false.
`int limit()`	Return this buffer's limit.
`Buffer limit(int newLimit)`	Set this buffer's limit to newLimit. When the position is larger than newLimit, the position is set to newLimit. When the mark is defined and is larger than newLimit, the mark is discarded. This method throws `java.lang.IllegalArgumentException` when newLimit is negative or larger than this buffer's capacity; otherwise, it returns this buffer.
`Buffer mark()`	Set this buffer's mark at its position and return this buffer.
`int position()`	Return this buffer's position.

(continued)

Table 13-1. (continued)

Method	Description
Buffer position (int newPosition)	Set this buffer's position to newPosition. When the mark is defined and is larger than newPosition, the mark is discarded. This method throws IllegalArgumentException when newPosition is negative or larger than this buffer's current limit; otherwise, it returns this buffer.
int remaining()	Return the number of elements between the current position and the limit.
Buffer reset()	Reset this buffer's position to the previously marked position. Invoking this method neither changes nor discards the mark's value. This method throws java.nio.InvalidMarkException when the mark hasn't been set; otherwise, it returns this buffer.
Buffer rewind()	Rewind and then return this buffer. The position is set to zero and the mark is discarded.

Table 13-1 shows that many of Buffer's methods return Buffer references so that you can chain instance method calls together (Chapter 3 discusses method call chaining). For example, instead of specifying the following three lines.

```
buf.mark();
buf.position(2);
buf.reset();
```

you can more conveniently specify the following line:

```
buf.mark().position(2).reset();
```

Table 13-1 also shows that all buffers can be read, but not all buffers can be written—for example, a buffer backed by a memory-mapped file that's read-only. You must not write to a read-only buffer; otherwise, ReadOnlyBufferException is thrown. Call isReadOnly() when you're unsure that a buffer is writable before attempting to write to that buffer.

Note   Buffers are not thread safe. You must employ synchronization when you want to access a buffer from multiple threads.

The java.nio package includes several abstract classes that extend Buffer, one for each primitive type except for Boolean: ByteBuffer, CharBuffer, DoubleBuffer, FloatBuffer, IntBuffer, LongBuffer, and ShortBuffer. Furthermore, this package includes MappedByteBuffer as an abstract ByteBuffer subclass.

> **Note**   Operating systems perform byte-oriented I/O and you use `ByteBuffer` to create byte-oriented buffers that store the bytes to write to a destination or that are read from a source. The other primitive-type buffer classes let you create multibyte view buffers (discussed later) so that you can conceptually perform I/O in terms of characters, double precision floating-point values, 32-bit integers, and so on. However, the I/O operation is really being carried out as a flow of bytes.

Listing 13-1 demonstrates the `Buffer` class in terms of `ByteBuffer`, capacity, limit, position, and remaining elements.

Listing 13-1. Demonstrating a Byte-Oriented Buffer

```
import java.nio.Buffer;
import java.nio.ByteBuffer;

public class BufferDemo
{
   public static void main(String[] args)
   {
      Buffer buffer = ByteBuffer.allocate(7);
      System.out.println("Capacity: " + buffer.capacity());
      System.out.println("Limit: " + buffer.limit());
      System.out.println("Position: " + buffer.position());
      System.out.println("Remaining: " + buffer.remaining());
      System.out.println("Changing buffer limit to 5");
      buffer.limit(5);
      System.out.println("Limit: " + buffer.limit());
      System.out.println("Position: " + buffer.position());
      System.out.println("Remaining: " + buffer.remaining());
      System.out.println("Changing buffer position to 3");
      buffer.position(3);
      System.out.println("Position: " + buffer.position());
      System.out.println("Remaining: " + buffer.remaining());
      System.out.println(buffer);
   }
}
```

Listing 13-1's `main()` method first needs to obtain a buffer. It cannot instantiate the `Buffer` class because that class is abstract. Instead, it uses the `ByteBuffer` class and its `allocate()` class method to allocate the 7-byte buffer shown in Figure 13-1. `main()` then calls assorted `Buffer` methods to demonstrate capacity, limit, position, and remaining elements.

Compile Listing 13-1 (`javac BufferDemo.java`) and run this application (`java BufferDemo`). You should observe the following output:

```
Capacity: 7
Limit: 7
Position: 0
Remaining: 7
```

```
Changing buffer limit to 5
Limit: 5
Position: 0
Remaining: 5
Changing buffer position to 3
Position: 3
Remaining: 2
java.nio.HeapByteBuffer[pos=3 lim=5 cap=7]
```

The final output line reveals that the ByteBuffer instance assigned to buffer is actually an instance of the package-private java.nio.HeapByteBuffer class.

Buffers in Depth

The previous discussion of the Buffer class has given you some insight into NIO buffers. However, there is much more to explore. This section takes you deeper into buffers by exploring buffer creation, writing and reading buffers, buffer flipping, buffer marking, Buffer subclass operations, byte ordering, and direct buffers.

> **Note**   Although the primitive-type buffer classes have similar capabilities, ByteBuffer is the largest and most versatile. After all, bytes are the basic unit used by operating systems to transfer data items. I'll therefore use ByteBuffer to demonstrate most buffer operations. I'll also use CharBuffer to add variety.

Buffer Creation

ByteBuffer and the other primitive-type buffer classes declare various class methods for creating a buffer of that type. For example, ByteBuffer declares the following class methods for creating ByteBuffer instances:

- ByteBuffer allocate(int capacity) allocates a new byte buffer with the specified capacity value. Its position is 0, its limit is its capacity, its mark is undefined, and each element is initialized to 0. It has a backing array, and its array offset is 0. This method throws IllegalArgumentException when capacity is negative.

- ByteBuffer allocateDirect(int capacity) allocates a new direct byte buffer with the specified capacity value. Its position is 0, its limit is its capacity, its mark is undefined, and each element is initialized to 0. Whether or not it has a backing array is unspecified. This method throws IllegalArgumentException when capacity is negative.

- ByteBuffer wrap(byte[] array) wraps a byte array into a buffer. The new buffer is backed by array; that is, modifications to the buffer will cause the array to be modified and vice versa. The new buffer's capacity and limit are set to array.length, its position is set to 0, and its mark is undefined. Its array offset is 0.

- ▪ ByteBuffer wrap(byte[] array, int offset, int length) wraps a byte array into a buffer. The new buffer is backed by array. The new buffer's capacity is set to array.length, its position is set to offset, its limit is set to offset + length, and its mark is undefined. Its array offset is 0. This method throws java.lang. IndexOutOfBoundsException when offset is negative or greater than array. length or when length is negative or greater than array.length - offset.

These methods show two ways to create a byte buffer: create the ByteBuffer object and allocate an internal array that stores capacity bytes or create the ByteBuffer object and use the specified array to store these bytes. Consider these examples:

```
ByteBuffer buffer = ByteBuffer.allocate(10);
byte[] bytes = new byte[200];
ByteBuffer buffer2 = ByteBuffer.wrap(bytes);
```

The first line creates a byte buffer with an internal byte array that stores a maximum of 10 bytes, and the second and third lines create a byte array and a byte buffer that uses this array to store a maximum of 200 bytes.

Now, consider the following example, which extends the previous example:

```
buffer = ByteBuffer.wrap(bytes, 10, 50);
```

This example creates a byte buffer with a position of 10, a limit of 50, and a capacity of bytes.length (which happens to be 200). Although it appears that the buffer can only access a subrange of this array, it actually has access to the entire array: the values of 10 and 50 are only the starting values for the position and limit.

ByteBuffers (and other primitive type buffers) created via allocate() or wrap() are nondirect byte buffers—you'll learn about direct byte buffers later. Nondirect byte buffers have backing arrays, and you can access these backing arrays via the array() method (which happens to be declared as byte[] array() in the ByteArray class) as long as hasArray() returns true. (When hasArray() returns true, you'll need to call arrayOffset() to obtain the location of the first data item in the array.)

Listing 13-2 demonstrates buffer allocation and wrapping.

Listing 13-2. Creating Byte-Oriented Buffers via Allocation and Wrapping

```
import java.nio.ByteBuffer;

public class BufferDemo
{
   public static void main(String[] args)
   {
      ByteBuffer buffer1 = ByteBuffer.allocate(10);
      if (buffer1.hasArray())
      {
         System.out.println("buffer1 array: " + buffer1.array());
         System.out.println("Buffer1 array offset: " + buffer1.arrayOffset());
         System.out.println("Capacity: " + buffer1.capacity());
```

```
                System.out.println("Limit: " + buffer1.limit());
                System.out.println("Position: " + buffer1.position());
                System.out.println("Remaining: " + buffer1.remaining());
                System.out.println();
        }

        byte[] bytes = new byte[200];
        ByteBuffer buffer2 = ByteBuffer.wrap(bytes);
        buffer2 = ByteBuffer.wrap(bytes, 10, 50);
        if (buffer2.hasArray())
        {
            System.out.println("buffer2 array: " + buffer2.array());
            System.out.println("Buffer2 array offset: " + buffer2.arrayOffset());
            System.out.println("Capacity: " + buffer2.capacity());
            System.out.println("Limit: " + buffer2.limit());
            System.out.println("Position: " + buffer2.position());
            System.out.println("Remaining: " + buffer2.remaining());
        }
    }
}
```

Compile Listing 13-2 (javac BufferDemo.java) and run this application (java BufferDemo).
You should observe the following output:

```
buffer1 array: [B@15e565bd
Buffer1 array offset: 0
Capacity: 10
Limit: 10
Position: 0
Remaining: 10

buffer2 array: [B@77a6686
Buffer2 array offset: 0
Capacity: 200
Limit: 60
Position: 10
Remaining: 50
```

As well as managing data elements stored in external arrays (via the wrap() methods), buffers can
manage data stored in other buffers. When you create a buffer that manages another buffer's data,
the created buffer is known as a *view buffer*. Changes made in either buffer are reflected in the other.

View buffers are created by calling a Buffer subclass's duplicate() method. The resulting view
buffer is equivalent to the original buffer; both buffers share the same data items and have equivalent
capacities. However, each buffer has its own position, limit, and mark. When the buffer being
duplicated is read-only or direct, the view buffer is also read-only or direct.

Consider the following example:

```
ByteBuffer buffer = ByteBuffer.allocate(10);
ByteBuffer bufferView = buffer.duplicate();
```

The ByteBuffer instance identified by bufferView shares the same internal array of 10 elements as buffer. At the moment, these buffers have the same position, limit, and (undefined) mark. However, these properties in one buffer can be changed independently of the properties in the other buffer.

View buffers are also created by calling one of ByteBuffer's as*x*Buffer() methods. For example, LongBuffer asLongBuffer() returns a view buffer that conceptualizes the byte buffer as a buffer of long integers.

> **Note**   Read-only view buffers can be created by calling a method such as ByteBuffer asReadOnlyBuffer(). Any attempt to change a read-only view buffer's content results in ReadOnlyBufferException. However, the original buffer content (provided that it isn't read-only) can be changed, and the read-only view buffer will reflect these changes.

Writing and Reading Buffers

ByteBuffer and the other primitive-type buffer classes declare several overloaded put() and get() methods for writing data items to and reading data items from a buffer. These methods are absolute when they require an index argument or relative when they don't require an index.

For example, ByteBuffer declares the absolute ByteBuffer put(int index, byte b) method to store byte b in the buffer at the index value and the absolute byte get(int index) method to fetch the byte located at position index. This class also declares the relative ByteBuffer put(byte b) method to store byte b in the buffer at the current position and then increment the current position, and the relative byte get() method to fetch the byte located at the buffer's current position and increment the current position.

The absolute put() and get() methods throw IndexOutOfBoundsException when index is negative or greater than or equal to the buffer's limit. The relative put() method throws java.nio.BufferOverflowException when the current position is greater than or equal to the limit, and the relative get() method throws java.nio.BufferUnderflowException when the current position is greater than or equal to the limit. Furthermore, the absolute and relative put() methods throw ReadOnlyBufferException when the buffer is read-only.

Listing 13-3 demonstrates the relative put() method and the absolute get() method.

Listing 13-3. Writing Bytes to and Reading Them From a Buffer

```
import java.nio.ByteBuffer;

public class BufferDemo
{
   public static void main(String[] args)
   {
      ByteBuffer buffer = ByteBuffer.allocate(7);
      System.out.println("Capacity = " + buffer.capacity());
      System.out.println("Limit = " + buffer.limit());
      System.out.println("Position = " + buffer.position());
      System.out.println("Remaining = " + buffer.remaining());
```

```
buffer.put((byte) 10).put((byte) 20).put((byte) 30);

System.out.println("Capacity = " + buffer.capacity());
System.out.println("Limit = " + buffer.limit());
System.out.println("Position = " + buffer.position());
System.out.println("Remaining = " + buffer.remaining());

for (int i = 0; i < buffer.position(); i++)
   System.out.println(buffer.get(i));
   }
}
```

Compile Listing 13-3 (javac BufferDemo.java) and run this application (java BufferDemo).
You should observe the following output:

```
Capacity = 7
Limit = 7
Position = 0
Remaining = 7
Capacity = 7
Limit = 7
Position = 3
Remaining = 4
10
20
30
```

> **Tip**   For maximum efficiency, you can perform bulk data transfers by using the ByteBuffer
> put(byte[] src), ByteBuffer put(byte[] src, int offset, int length), ByteBuffer
> get(byte[] dst), and ByteBuffer get(byte[] dst, int offset, int length) methods
> to write and read an array of bytes.

Flipping Buffers

After filling a buffer, you must prepare it for draining by a channel. When you pass the buffer as is, the channel accesses undefined data beyond the current position.

To solve this problem, you could reset the position to 0, but how would the channel know when the end of the inserted data had been reached? The solution is to work with the limit property, which indicates the end of the active portion of the buffer. Basically, you set the limit to the current position and then reset the current position to 0.

You could accomplish this task by executing the following code, which also clears any defined mark:

```
buffer.limit(buffer.position()).position(0);
```

However, there's an easier way to accomplish the same task, as shown here:

```
buffer.flip();
```

In either case, the buffer is ready to be drained.

Listing 13-4 demonstrates buffer flipping in the context of a character buffer.

Listing 13-4. Writing Characters to and Reading Them From a Character Buffer

```
import java.nio.CharBuffer;

public class BufferDemo
{
   public static void main(String[] args)
   {
      String[] poem =
      {
         "Roses are red",
         "Violets are blue",
         "Sugar is sweet",
         "And so are you."
      };

      CharBuffer buffer = CharBuffer.allocate(50);

      for (int i = 0; i < poem.length; i++)
      {
         // Fill the buffer.
         for (int j = 0; j < poem[i].length(); j++)
            buffer.put(poem[i].charAt(j));

         // Flip the buffer so that its contents can be read.
         buffer.flip();

         // Drain the buffer.
         while (buffer.hasRemaining())
            System.out.print(buffer.get());

         // Empty the buffer to prevent BufferOverflowException.
         buffer.clear();

         System.out.println();
      }
   }
}
```

Compile Listing 13-4 (javac BufferDemo.java) and run this application (java BufferDemo). You should observe the following output:

```
Roses are red
Violets are blue
Sugar is sweet
And so are you.
```

> **Note**   rewind() is similar to flip() but ignores the limit. Also, calling flip() twice doesn't return you to the original state. Instead, the buffer has a zero size. Calling a put() method results in BufferOverflowException, and calling a get() method results in BufferUnderflowException or (in the case of get(int)), IndexOutOfBoundsException.

Marking Buffers

You can mark a buffer by invoking the mark() method and later return to the marked position by invoking reset(). For example, suppose you've executed ByteBuffer buffer = ByteBuffer. allocate(7);, followed by buffer.put((byte) 10).put((byte) 20).put((byte) 30).put((byte) 40);, followed by buffer.limit(4);. The current position and limit are set to 4.

Continuing, suppose you execute buffer.position(1).mark().position(3);. If you sent this buffer to a channel, byte 40 would be sent (the current position is 3 because of position(3)) and the position would advance to 4. If you subsequently executed buffer.reset(); and sent this buffer to the channel, the position would be set to the mark (1); and bytes 20, 30, and 40 (all bytes from the current position to one position below the limit) would be sent to the channel (and in that order).

Listing 13-5 demonstrates this mark/reset scenario.

Listing 13-5. Marking the Current Buffer Position and Resetting the Current Position to the Marked Position

```java
import java.nio.ByteBuffer;

public class BufferDemo
{
   public static void main(String[] args)
   {
      ByteBuffer buffer = ByteBuffer.allocate(7);
      buffer.put((byte) 10).put((byte) 20).put((byte) 30).put((byte) 40);
      buffer.limit(4);
      buffer.position(1).mark().position(3);
      System.out.println(buffer.get());
      System.out.println();
      buffer.reset();
      while (buffer.hasRemaining())
         System.out.println(buffer.get());
   }
}
```

Compile Listing 13-5 (javac BufferDemo.java) and run this application (java BufferDemo).
You should observe the following output:

```
40

20
30
40
```

> **Caution**   Don't confuse reset() with clear(). The clear() method marks a buffer as empty,
> whereas reset() changes the buffer's current position to the previously set mark, or throws
> InvalidMarkException when there's no previously set mark.

Buffer Subclass Operations

ByteBuffer and the other primitive-type buffer classes declare a compact() method that's useful for
compacting a buffer by copying all bytes between the current position and the limit to the beginning
of the buffer. The byte at index p = position() is copied to index 0, the byte at index p + 1 is
copied to index 1, and so on until the byte at index limit() - 1 is copied to index n = limit() - 1 - p.
The buffer's current position is then set to n + 1, and its limit is set to its capacity. The mark, when
defined, is discarded.

You invoke compact() after writing data from a buffer to handle situations where not all of the buffer's
content is written. Consider the following example that copies content from an in channel to an out
channel via buffer buf:

```
buf.clear(); // Prepare buffer for use
while (in.read(buf) != -1)
{
    buf.flip(); // Prepare buffer for draining.
    out.write(buf); // Write the buffer.
    buf.compact(); // Do this in case of a partial write.
}
```

The compact() method call moves unwritten buffer data to the beginning of the buffer so that the
next read() method call appends read data to the buffer's data instead of overwriting that data when
compact() isn't specified.

You may occasionally need to compare buffers for equality or order. All Buffer subclasses except for
ByteBuffer's MappedByteBuffer subclass override the equals() and compareTo() methods to perform
these comparisons—MappedByteBuffer inherits these methods from its ByteBuffer superclass.
The following example shows you how to compare byte buffers bytBuf1 and bytBuf2 for equality
and ordering:

```
System.out.println(bytBuf1.equals(bytBuf2));
System.out.println(bytBuf1.compareTo(bytBuf2));
```

The equals() contract for ByteBuffer states that 2 byte buffers are equal if and only if they have the same element type; they have the same number of remaining elements; and the two sequences of remaining elements, considered independently of their starting positions, are individually equal. This contract is the same for the other Buffer subclasses.

The compareTo() method for ByteBuffer states that 2 byte buffers are compared for order by comparing their sequences of remaining elements lexicographically, without regard to the starting position of each sequence within its corresponding buffer. Pairs of byte elements are compared as if by invoking Byte.compare(byte, byte). Similar descriptions apply to the other Buffer subclasses.

Byte Ordering

Nonbyte primitive types except for Boolean (which might be represented by a bit or by a byte) are composed of several bytes: a character or a short integer occupies 2 bytes, a 32-bit integer or a floating-point value occupies 4 bytes, and a long integer or a double precision floating-point value occupies 8 bytes. Each value of one of these multibyte types is stored in a sequence of contiguous memory locations. However, the order of these bytes can differ from platform to platform.

For example, consider 32-bit long integer 0x10203040. This value's 4 bytes could be stored in memory (from low address to high address) as 10, 20, 30, 40; this arrangement is known as *big-endian order* (the most significant byte, the "big" end, is stored at the lowest address). Alternatively, these bytes could be stored as 40, 30, 20, 10; this arrangement is known as *little-endian order* (the least significant byte, the "little" end, is stored at the lowest address).

Java provides the java.nio.ByteOrder class to help you deal with byte-order issues when writing/reading multibyte values to/from a multibyte buffer. ByteOrder declares a ByteOrder nativeOrder() method that returns the platform's byte order as a ByteOrder instance. Because this instance is one of ByteOrder's BIG_ENDIAN and LITTLE_ENDIAN constants, and because no other ByteOrder instances can be created, you can compare nativeOrder()'s return value to one of these constants via the == or != operator.

Also, each multibyte class (e.g., FloatBuffer) declares a ByteOrder order() method that returns the byte order of that buffer. This method returns ByteOrder.BIG_ENDIAN or ByteOrder.LITTLE_ENDIAN.

The ByteOrder value returned from order() can take on a different value based on how the buffer was created. If a multibyte buffer (e.g., a float buffer) was created by allocation or by wrapping an existing array, the buffer's byte order is the native order of the underlying platform. However, if a multibyte buffer was created as a view of a byte buffer, the view buffer's byte order is that of the byte buffer when the view was created. The view buffer's byte order cannot be subsequently changed.

ByteBuffer differs from the multibyte classes when it comes to byte order. Its default byte order is always big endian, even when the underlying platform's byte order is little endian. ByteBuffer defaults to big endian because Java's default byte order is also big endian, which lets classfiles and serialized objects store data consistently across virtual machines.

Because this big endian default can impact performance on little-endian platforms, ByteBuffer also declares a ByteBuffer order(ByteOrder bo) method to change the byte buffer's byte order.

Although it may seem unusual to change the byte order of a byte buffer (where only single-byte data items are accessed), this method is useful because ByteBuffer also declares several convenience methods for writing and reading multibyte values (e.g., ByteBuffer putInt(int value) and int getInt()). These convenience methods write these values according to the byte buffer's current byte order. Furthermore, you can subsequently call ByteBuffer's LongBuffer asLongBuffer() or another asxBuffer() method to return a view buffer whose order will reflect the byte buffer's changed byte order.

Direct Byte Buffers

Unlike multibyte buffers, byte buffers can serve as the sources and/or targets of channel-based I/O. This shouldn't come as a surprise because operating systems perform I/O on memory areas that are contiguous sequences of 8-bit bytes (not floating-point values, not 32-bit integers, and so on).

Operating systems can directly access the address space of a process. For example, an operating system could directly access a virtual machine process's address space to perform a data transfer operation based on a byte array. However, a virtual machine might not store the array of bytes contiguously or its garbage collector might move the byte array to another location. Because of these limitations, direct byte buffers were created.

A *direct byte buffer* is a byte buffer that interacts with channels and native code to perform I/O. The direct byte buffer attempts to store byte elements in a memory area that a channel uses to perform *direct* (raw) access via native code that tells the operating system to drain or fill the memory area directly.

Direct byte buffers are the most efficient means for performing I/O on the virtual machine. Although you can also pass nondirect byte buffers to channels, a performance problem might arise because nondirect byte buffers are not always able to serve as the target of native I/O operations.

When a channel is passed a nondirect byte buffer, the channel might have to create a temporary direct byte buffer, copy the nondirect byte buffer's content to the direct byte buffer, perform the I/O operation on the temporary direct byte buffer, and copy the temporary direct byte buffer's content to the nondirect byte buffer. The temporary direct byte buffer will then be subject to garbage collection.

Although optimal for I/O, a direct byte buffer can be expensive to create because memory extraneous to the virtual machine's heap will need to be allocated by the operating system, and setting up and/or tearing down this memory might take longer than when the buffer was located within the heap. After your code is working and should you want to experiment with performance optimization, you can easily obtain a direct byte buffer by invoking ByteBuffer's allocateDirect() method, which I discussed earlier.

Working with Channels

Channels partner with buffers to achieve high-performance I/O. A *channel* is an object that represents an open connection to a hardware device, a file, a network socket, an application component, or another entity that's capable of performing write, read, and other I/O operations. Channels efficiently transfer data between byte buffers and I/O service sources or destinations.

> **Note** Channels are the gateways through which native I/O services are accessed. Channels use byte buffers as the endpoints for sending and receiving data.

There often exists a one-to-one correspondence between an operating system file handle or file descriptor and a channel. When you work with channels in a file context, the channel will often be connected to an open file descriptor. Despite channels being more abstract than file descriptors, they are still capable of modeling an operating system's native I/O facilities.

Channel and Its Children

Java supports channels via its `java.nio.channels` and `java.nio.channels.spi` packages. Applications interact with the types located in the former package; developers who are defining new selector providers work with the latter package.

All channels are instances of classes that ultimately implement the `java.nio.channels.Channel` interface. `Channel` declares the following methods:

- `void close()`: Close this channel. When this channel is already closed, invoking `close()` has no effect. When another thread has already invoked `close()`, a new `close()` invocation blocks until the first invocation finishes, after which `close()` returns without effect. This method throws `IOException` when an I/O error occurs. After the channel is closed, any further attempts to invoke I/O operations on it result in `java.nio.channels.ClosedChannelException` being thrown.

- `boolean isOpen()`: Return this channel's open status. This method returns true when the channel is open; otherwise, it returns false.

These methods indicate that only two operations are common to all channels: close the channel and determine whether the channel is open or closed. To support I/O, `Channel` is extended by the `java.nio.channels.WritableByteChannel` and `java.nio.channels.ReadableByteChannel` interfaces:

- `WritableByteChannel` declares an abstract `int write(ByteBuffer buffer)` method that writes a sequence of bytes from `buffer` to the current channel. This method returns the number of bytes actually written. It throws `java.nio.channels.NonWritableChannelException` when the channel was not opened for writing, `java.nio.channels.ClosedChannelException` when the channel is closed, `java.nio.channels.AsynchronousCloseException` when another thread closes the channel during the write, `java.nio.channels.ClosedByInterruptException` when another thread interrupts the current thread while the write operation is in progress (thereby closing the channel and setting the current thread's interrupt status), and `java.io.IOException` when some other I/O error occurs.

- `ReadableByteChannel` declares an abstract `int read(ByteBuffer buffer)` method that reads bytes from the current channel into `buffer`. This method returns the number of bytes actually read (or −1 when there are no more bytes to read). It throws `java.nio.channels.NonReadableChannelException` when the channel was not opened for reading; `ClosedChannelException` when the channel is closed; `AsynchronousCloseException` when another thread closes the channel during the read; `ClosedByInterruptException` when another thread interrupts the current thread while the write operation is in progress, thereby closing the channel and setting the current thread's interrupt status; and `IOException` when some other I/O error occurs.

> **Note**   A channel whose class implements only `WritableByteChannel` or `ReadableByteChannel` is *unidirectional*. Attempting to read from a writable byte channel or write to a readable byte channel results in a thrown exception.
>
> You can use the `instanceof` operator to determine if a channel instance implements either interface. Because it's somewhat awkward to test for both interfaces, Java supplies the `java.nio.channels.ByteChannel` interface, which is an empty marker interface that subtypes `WritableByteChannel` and `ReadableByteChannel`. When you need to learn whether or not a channel is *bidirectional*, it's more convenient to specify an expression such as `channel instanceof ByteChannel`.

Along with `WritableByteChannel` and `ReadableByteChannel`, `InterruptibleChannel` directly extends `Channel`. `InterruptibleChannel` describes a channel that can be asynchronously closed and interrupted. This interface overrides its `Channel` superinterface's `close()` method header, presenting the following additional stipulation to `Channel`'s contract for this method: Any thread currently blocked in an I/O operation on this channel will receive `AsynchronousCloseException` (an `IOException` descendent).

A channel that implements this interface is asynchronously *closeable*: When a thread is blocked in an I/O operation on an interruptible channel, another thread may invoke the channel's `close()` method. This causes the blocked thread to receive a thrown `AsynchronousCloseException` instance.

A channel that implements this interface is also *interruptible*: When a thread is blocked in an I/O operation on an interruptible channel, another thread may invoke the blocked thread's `interrupt()` method. Doing this causes the channel to be closed, the blocked thread to receive a thrown `ClosedByInterruptException` instance, and the blocked thread to have its interrupt status set. (When a thread's interrupt status is already set and it invokes a blocking I/O operation on a channel, the channel is closed and the thread will immediately receive a thrown `ClosedByInterruptException` instance; its interrupt status will remain set.)

NIO's designers chose to shut down a channel when a blocked thread is interrupted because they couldn't find a way to reliably handle interrupted I/O operations in the same manner across platforms. The only way to guarantee deterministic behavior was to shut down the channel.

> **Tip**   You can determine whether or not a channel supports asynchronous closing and interruption by using the `instanceof` operator in an expression such as `channel instanceof InterruptibleChannel`.

You previously learned that you must call a class method on a Buffer subclass to obtain a buffer. Regarding channels, there are two ways to obtain a channel:

- The java.nio.channels package provides a Channels utility class that offers two methods for obtaining channels from streams—for each of the following methods, the underlying stream is closed when the channel is closed, and the channel isn't buffered:

  - WritableByteChannel newChannel(OutputStream outputStream) returns a writable byte channel for the given outputStream.

  - ReadableByteChannel newChannel(InputStream inputStream) returns a readable byte channel for the given inputStream.

- Various classic I/O classes have been retrofitted to support channel creation. For example, RandomAccessFile declares a FileChannel getChannel() method for returning a file channel instance, and java.net.Socket declares a SocketChannel getChannel() method for returning a socket channel.

Listing 13-6 uses the Channels class to obtain channels for the standard input and output streams and then uses these channels to copy bytes from the input channel to the output channel.

Listing 13-6. Copying Bytes From an Input Channel to an Output Channel

```
import java.io.IOException;

import java.nio.ByteBuffer;

import java.nio.channels.Channels;
import java.nio.channels.ReadableByteChannel;
import java.nio.channels.WritableByteChannel;

public class ChannelDemo
{
   public static void main(String[] args)
   {
      ReadableByteChannel src = Channels.newChannel(System.in);
      WritableByteChannel dest = Channels.newChannel(System.out);

      try
      {
         copy(src, dest); // or copyAlt(src, dest);
      }
      catch (IOException ioe)
      {
         System.err.println("I/O error: " + ioe.getMessage());
      }
      finally
      {
```

```
      try
      {
         src.close();
         dest.close();
      }
      catch (IOException ioe)
      {
         ioe.printStackTrace();
      }
   }
}

static void copy(ReadableByteChannel src, WritableByteChannel dest)
   throws IOException
{
   ByteBuffer buffer = ByteBuffer.allocateDirect(2048);
   while (src.read(buffer) != -1)
   {
      buffer.flip();
      dest.write(buffer);
      buffer.compact();
   }
   buffer.flip();
   while (buffer.hasRemaining())
      dest.write(buffer);
}

static void copyAlt(ReadableByteChannel src, WritableByteChannel dest)
   throws IOException
{
   ByteBuffer buffer = ByteBuffer.allocateDirect(2048);
   while (src.read(buffer) != -1)
   {
      buffer.flip();
      while (buffer.hasRemaining())
         dest.write(buffer);
      buffer.clear();
   }
}
}
```

Listing 13-6 presents two approaches to copying bytes from the standard input stream to the standard output stream. In the first approach, which is exemplified by the copy() method, the goal is to minimize native I/O calls (via the write() method calls), although more data may end up being copied as a result of the compact() method calls. In the second approach, as demonstrated by copyAlt(), the goal is to eliminate data copying, although more native I/O calls might occur.

Each of copy() and copyAlt() first allocates a direct byte buffer (recall that a direct byte buffer is the most efficient means for performing I/O on the virtual machine) and enters a while loop that continually reads bytes from the source channel until end-of-input (read() returns –1). Following the read, the buffer is flipped so that it can be drained. Here is where the methods diverge.

- The copy() method while loop makes a single call to write(). Because write() might not completely drain the buffer, compact() is called to compact the buffer prior to the next read. Compaction ensures that unwritten buffer content isn't overwritten during the next read operation. Following the while loop, copy() flips the buffer in preparation for draining any remaining content, and then works with hasRemaining() and write() to completely drain the buffer.

- The copyAlt() method while loop contains a nested while loop that works with hasRemaining() and write() to continue draining the buffer until the buffer is empty. This is followed by a clear() method call that empties the buffer so that it can be filled on the next read() call.

> **Note**   It's important to realize that a single write() method call may not output the entire content of a buffer. Similarly, a single read() call may not completely fill a buffer.

Compile Listing 13-6 (javac ChannelDemo.java) and run this application (java ChannelDemo and java ChannelDemo <ChannelDemo.java >ChannelDemo.bak are examples) to verify that standard input is copied to standard output. After testing the copy() method, replace copy(src, dest); with copyAlt(src, dest); and repeat.

Channels in Depth

The previous discussion of the Channel interface and its direct descendents has given you some insight into NIO channels. However, there is much more to explore. This section takes you deeper into channels by exploring scatter/gather I/O and file channels. Unfortunately, the need for brevity restrains me from also exploring socket channels.

Scatter/Gather I/O

Channels provide the ability to perform a single I/O operation across multiple buffers. This capability is known as *scatter/gather I/O* (and is also known as *vectored I/O*).

In the context of a write operation, the contents of several buffers are *gathered* (drained) in sequence and then sent through the channel to a destination—these buffers are not required to have identical capacities. In the context of a read operation, the contents of a channel are *scattered* (filled) to multiple buffers in sequence; each buffer is filled to its limit until the channel is empty or total buffer space is used up.

> **Note**   Modern operating systems provide APIs that support vectored I/O to eliminate (or at least reduce) system calls or buffer copies and hence improve performance. For example, the Win32/Win64 APIs provide ReadFileScatter() and WriteFileGather() functions for this purpose.

Java provides the java.nio.channels.ScatteringByteChannel interface to support scattering and the java.nio.channels.GatheringByteChannel interface to support gathering.

ScatteringByteChannel offers the following methods:

- long read(ByteBuffer[] buffers, int offset, int length)
- long read(ByteBuffer[] buffers)

GatheringByteChannel offers the following methods:

- long write(ByteBuffer[] buffers, int offset, int length)
- long write(ByteBuffer[] buffers)

The first read() method and the first write() method let you identify the first buffer to read/write by passing a zero-based offset to offset and the number of buffers to read/write by passing a value to length. The second read() method and the second write() method read/write all buffers in sequence.

Listing 13-7 Demonstrates read(ByteBuffer[] buffers) and write(ByteBuffer[] buffers).

Listing 13-7. Demonstrating Scatter/Gather

```java
import java.io.FileInputStream;
import java.io.FileOutputStream;
import java.io.IOException;

import java.nio.ByteBuffer;

import java.nio.channels.Channels;
import java.nio.channels.GatheringByteChannel;
import java.nio.channels.ReadableByteChannel;
import java.nio.channels.ScatteringByteChannel;

public class ChannelDemo
{
   public static void main(String[] args) throws IOException
   {
      ScatteringByteChannel src;
      src = (ScatteringByteChannel) Channels.newChannel(new FileInputStream("x.dat"));
      ByteBuffer buffer1 = ByteBuffer.allocateDirect(5);
      ByteBuffer buffer2 = ByteBuffer.allocateDirect(3);
      ByteBuffer[] buffers = { buffer1, buffer2 };
      src.read(buffers);
      buffer1.flip();
      while (buffer1.hasRemaining())
         System.out.printf("%c%n", buffer1.get());
      System.out.println();
      buffer2.flip();
      while (buffer2.hasRemaining())
         System.out.printf("%c%n", buffer2.get());
      buffer1.rewind();
      buffer2.rewind();
```

```
        GatheringByteChannel dest;
        dest = (GatheringByteChannel) Channels.newChannel(new FileOutputStream("y.dat"));
        buffers[0] = buffer2;
        buffers[1] = buffer1;
        dest.write(buffers);
    }
}
```

Listing 13-7's main() method first obtains a scattering byte channel by instantiating java.io.FileInputStream and passing this instance to the Channels class's ReadableByteChannel newChannel(InputStream inputStream) method. The returned ReadableByteChannel instance is cast to ScatteringByteChannel because this instance is actually a file channel (discussed later) that implements ScatteringByteChannel.

Next, main() creates a couple of direct byte buffers; the first buffer has a capacity of 5 bytes and the second buffer has a capacity of 3 bytes. These buffers are subsequently stored in an array and this array is passed to read(ByteBuffer[]) to fill them.

After filling the buffers, main() flips them so that it can output their contents to standard output. After these contents have been output, the buffers are rewound in preparation for being drained via a gather operation.

main() now obtains a gathering byte channel by instantiating java.io.FileOutputStream and passing this instance to the Channels class's WritableByteChannel newChannel(OutputStream outputStream) method. The returned WritableByteChannel instance is cast to GatheringByteChannel because this instance is actually a file channel (discussed later) that implements GatheringByteChannel.

Finally, main() assigns these buffers to the buffers array in reverse order to how they were originally assigned and then passes this array to write(ByteBuffer[]) to drain them.

> **Note**   The %n format specifier in the System.out.printf() method calls is a portable way to specify the *line terminator* (a 1-or-2-character sequence designating the end of the line). It's not a good idea to specify \n because some platforms require \r\n as the line terminator, whereas other platforms require \r.

Create a file named x.dat and store the following text in this file:

12345abcdefg

Now compile Listing 13-7 (javac ChannelDemo.java) and run this application (java ChannelDemo). You should observe the following output:

```
1
2
3
4
5
```

a
b
c

Additionally, you should observe a newly created y.dat file with the following content:

abc12345

File Channels

I previously mentioned that RandomAccessFile declares a FileChannel getChannel() method for returning a file channel instance. It turns out that FileInputStream and FileOutputStream also provide the same method. In contrast, FileReader and FileWriter don't offer a way to obtain a file channel.

> **Caution**   The file channel returned from FileInputStream's getChannel() method is read-only, and the file channel returned from FileOutputStream's getChannel() method is write-only. Attempting to write to a read-only file channel or read from a write-only file channel results in an exception.

The abstract java.nio.channels.FileChannel class describes a file channel. Because this class extends the abstract java.nio.channels.spi.AbstractInterruptibleChannel class, which implements the InterruptibleChannel interface, file channels are interruptible. Because this class implements the ByteChannel, GatheringByteChannel, and ScatteringByteChannel interfaces, you can write to, read from, and perform scattering I/O on underlying files. However, there's more.

> **Note**   Unlike buffers, which are not thread-safe, file channels are thread-safe.

A file channel maintains a virtual pointer into the file, which is known as the *file pointer*, and FileChannel lets you obtain and change the file pointer value. It also lets you obtain the size of the file underlying the channel, attempt to lock the entire file or just a region of the file, perform memory-mapped file I/O, request that cached data be forced to the disk, and transfer data directly to another channel in a manner that has the potential to be optimized by the platform.

Table 13-2 describes a few of FileChannel's methods.

Table 13-2. `FileChannel Methods`

Method	Description
`void force(boolean metadata)`	Request that all updates to this file channel be committed to the storage device. When this method returns, all modifications made to the platform file underlying this channel have been committed when the file resides on a local storage device. However, when the file isn't hosted locally (e.g., it's on a networked file system), applications cannot be certain that the modifications have been committed. (No assurances are given that changes made to the file using methods defined elsewhere will be committed. For example, changes made via a mapped byte buffer may not be committed.)
	The `metadata` value indicates whether the update should include the file's metadata (e.g., last modification time and last access time), when `true` is passed, or not include the file's metadata, when `false` is passed. Passing `true` may invoke an underlying write to the operating system (if the platform is maintaining metadata, such as last access time), even when the channel is opened as a read-only channel.
	This method throws `ClosedChannelException` when the channel is already closed and throws `IOException` when any other I/O error occurs.
`FileLock lock()`	Obtain an exclusive lock on this file channel's underlying file. This convenience method is equivalent to executing `fileChannel.lock(0L, Long.MAX_VALUE, false);`, where `fileChannel` references a file channel.
	This method returns a `java.nio.channels.FileLock` object representing the locked area. It throws `ClosedChannelException` when the file channel is closed; `NonWritableChannelException` when the channel isn't open for writing; `java.nio.channels.OverlappingFileLockException` when either a lock is already held that overlaps this lock request or another thread is waiting to acquire a lock that will overlap with this request; `java.nio.channels.FileLockInterruptionException` when the calling thread was interrupted while waiting to acquire the lock; `AsynchronousCloseException` when the channel was closed while the calling thread was waiting to acquire the lock; and `IOException` when another I/O error occurs while obtaining the requested lock.

(continued)

Table 13-2. (*continued*)

Method	Description
MappedByteBuffer map (FileChannel.MapMode mode, long position, long size)	Map a region of this file channel's file directly into memory according to one of three modes:
	*read-only: any attempt to modify the resulting buffer will cause ReadOnlyBufferException to be thrown (MapMode.READ_ONLY)
	*read/write: changes made to the resulting buffer will eventually be propagated to the file; they may or may not be made visible to other programs that have mapped the same file (MapMode.READ_WRITE)
	*private: changes made to the resulting buffer will not be propagated to the file and will not be visible to other programs that have mapped the same file; instead, they will cause private copies of the modified portions of the buffer to be created (MapMode.PRIVATE)
	For a read-only mapping, this channel must have been opened for reading; for a read/write or private mapping, this channel must have been opened for both reading and writing.
	The value passed to position identifies the position within the file at which the mapped region is to start. The value passed to size identifies the length of the mapped region.
	When successful, this method returns the mapped byte buffer. The returned mapped byte buffer will have a position of zero and a limit and capacity of size; its mark will be undefined. The buffer and the mapping that it represents will remain valid until the buffer itself is garbage-collected.
	When unsuccessful, this method throws an exception. It throws NonReadableChannelException when mode is READ_ONLY, but this channel wasn't opened for reading; NonWritableChannelException when mode is READ_WRITE or PRIVATE, but this channel wasn't opened for both reading and writing; IllegalArgumentException when mode isn't one of the constants defined by the FileChannel.MapMode class, a negative value is passed to position, or the value passed to size is negative or greater than java.lang.Integer.MAX_VALUE; and IOException when any other I/O error occurs.
	Once established, a mapping isn't dependent on the file channel that was used to create it. In particular, closing the channel has no effect on the mapping's validity.
	Many of the details of memory-mapped files are inherently dependent on the underlying operating system and are therefore unspecified. The behavior of this method when the requested region is not completely contained within this channel's file is unspecified. Whether changes made to the content or size of the underlying file, by this or another application, are propagated to the buffer is unspecified. The rate at which changes to the buffer are propagated to the file is unspecified.
	For most operating systems, mapping a file into memory is more expensive than reading or writing a few tens of kilobytes of data via the usual read/write methods. From a performance perspective, it's generally only worth mapping relatively large files into memory.

Table 13-2. (*continued*)

Method	Description
`long position()`	Return the current value of this file channel's file pointer, which is relative to zero. This method throws `ClosedChannelException` when the file channel is closed and `IOException` when another I/O error occurs.
`FileChannel position (long offset)`	Set this file channel's file pointer to `offset`. The argument is the number of bytes counted from the start of the file. The position cannot be set to a value that is negative. The new position can be set beyond the current file size. If set beyond the current file size, attempts to read will return end of file. Write operations will succeed, but they will fill the bytes between the current end of file and the new position with the required number of (unspecified) byte values. This method throws `IllegalArgumentException` when `offset` is negative, `ClosedChannelException` when the file channel is closed, and `IOException` when another I/O error occurs.
`int read (ByteBuffer buffer)`	Read bytes from this file channel into the given buffer. The maximum number of bytes that will be read is the remaining number of bytes in the buffer when the method is invoked. The bytes will be copied into the buffer starting at the buffer's current position. The call may block when other threads are also attempting to read from this channel. On completion, the buffer's position is set to the end of the bytes that have been read. The buffer's limit isn't changed. This method returns the number of bytes actually read and throws the same exceptions as previously discussed regarding `ReadableByteChannel`.
`long size()`	Return the size (in bytes) of the file underlying this file channel. This method throws `ClosedChannelException` when the file channel is closed and `IOException` when another I/O error occurs.
`FileChannel truncate (long size)`	Truncate the file underlying this file channel to `size`. Any bytes beyond the given `size` are removed from the file. When there are no bytes beyond the given size, the file contents are unmodified. When the file pointer is currently greater than the given size, it's set to the new size.
`FileLock tryLock()`	Attempt to obtain an exclusive lock on this file channel's underlying file without blocking. This convenience method is equivalent to executing `fileChannel.tryLock(0L, Long.MAX_VALUE, false);` where `fileChannel` references a file channel.
	This method returns a `FileLock` object representing the locked area or null when the lock would overlap with an existing exclusive lock in another operating system process. It throws `ClosedChannelException` when the file channel is closed; `OverlappingFileLockException` when a lock that overlaps the requested region is already held by this virtual machine, or when another thread is already blocked in this method and is attempting to lock an overlapping region; and `IOException` when another I/O error occurs while obtaining the requested lock.

(continued)

Table 13-2. (continued)

Method	Description
int write (ByteBuffer buffer)	Write a sequence of bytes to this file channel from the given buffer. Bytes are written starting at the channel's current file position unless the channel is in append mode, in which case the position is first advanced to the end of the file. The file is grown (when necessary) to accommodate the written bytes, and then the file position is updated with the number of bytes actually written. Otherwise this method behaves exactly as specified by the WritableByteChannel interface. This method returns the number of bytes actually written and throws the same exceptions as previously discussed regarding WritableByteChannel.

Table 13-2 provides a lot of material to understand. To help you gain this knowledge, Listing 13-8 demonstrates several of these methods

Listing 13-8. Demonstrating a File Channel

```java
import java.io.FileInputStream;
import java.io.FileOutputStream;
import java.io.IOException;

import java.nio.ByteBuffer;
import java.nio.MappedByteBuffer;

import java.nio.channels.FileChannel;

public class ChannelDemo
{
   public static void main(String[] args) throws IOException
   {
      if (args.length != 1)
      {
         System.out.println("usage: java ChannelDemo newfilespec");
         return;
      }
      FileOutputStream fos = new FileOutputStream(args[0]);
      FileChannel fc = fos.getChannel();
      System.out.println("position: " + fc.position());
      System.out.println("size: " + fc.size());
      String msg = "This is a test message.";
      ByteBuffer buffer = ByteBuffer.allocateDirect(msg.length() * 2);
      buffer.asCharBuffer().put(msg);
      fc.write(buffer);
      System.out.println("position: " + fc.position());
      System.out.println("size: " + fc.size());
      fc.truncate(24L);
      fc.close();
      FileInputStream fis = new FileInputStream(args[0]);
      fc = fis.getChannel();
```

```
        System.out.println("size: " + fc.size());
        buffer.clear();
        fc.read(buffer);
        buffer.flip();
        while (buffer.hasRemaining())
            System.out.print(buffer.getChar());
        System.out.println();
        System.out.println(buffer.getChar(0));
        System.out.println(buffer.getChar(1));
        System.out.println(buffer.getChar(2));
        MappedByteBuffer mbb = fc.map(FileChannel.MapMode.READ_ONLY, 0, 4);
        System.out.println(mbb.getChar(0));
        System.out.println(mbb.getChar(2));
        System.out.println(mbb.getChar(4));
        fc.close();
    }
}
```

Listing 13-8's main() method first verifies that you've specified a single command-line argument, which is the name of a file that's to be created and overwritten. It then creates a file output stream, obtains a file channel for this stream, outputs some information about the channel, outputs some content to the file, once again outputs channel information, truncates the file, and closes the file.

main() next creates a file input stream, obtains a file channel for this stream, outputs channel information, reads file content into a buffer, and outputs buffer contents. Finally, a mapped byte buffer (which provides a memory-mapped region of the file) is obtained and content is output.

Compile Listing 13-8 (javac ChannelDemo.java) and run this application (e.g., java ChannelDemo x.dat). You should observe the following output:

```
position: 0
size: 0
position: 46
size: 46
size: 24
This is a te
T
?
h
T
H
Exception in thread "main"
java.lang.IndexOutOfBoundsException
                at java.nio.Buffer.checkIndex(Unknown Source)
                at java.nio.DirectByteBuffer.getChar(Unknown Source)
                at ChannelDemo.main(ChannelDemo.java:46)
```

There are two interesting items in this output: the question mark (?) and the exception. The question mark arises from outputting an undisplayable Unicode character via System.out.println(buffer.getChar(1));, where buffer.getChar(1) returns the second half of the 2-byte Unicode character starting at byte index 0 and the first half of the 2-byte Unicode character starting at byte index 2.

The exception arises from `mbb.getChar(4)`'s attempt to access the Unicode character at byte indexes 4 and 5. However, the only valid byte indexes in the mapped byte buffer are indexes 0 through 3.

Working With Regular Expressions

Text-processing applications often need to match text against *patterns* (character strings that concisely describe sets of strings that are considered to be matches). For example, an application might need to locate all occurrences of a specific word pattern in a text file so that it can replace those occurrences with another word. The NIO JSR includes regular expressions to help text-processing applications perform pattern matching with high performance.

Pattern, PatternSyntaxException, and Matcher

A *regular expression* (also known as a *regex* or *regexp*) is a string-based pattern that represents the set of strings that match this pattern. The pattern consists of literal characters and *metacharacters*, which are characters with special meanings instead of literal meanings.

The Regular Expressions API provides the `java.util.regex.Pattern` class to represent patterns via compiled regexes. Regexes are compiled for performance reasons; pattern matching via compiled regexes is much faster than if the regexes were not compiled. Table 13-3 describes `Pattern`'s methods.

Table 13-3. Pattern Methods

Method	Description
`static Pattern compile(String regex)`	Compile regex and return its `Pattern` object. This method throws `java.util.regex.PatternSyntaxException` when regex's syntax is invalid.
`static Pattern compile(String regex,int flags)`	Compile regex according to the given flags (a bitset consisting of some combination of `Pattern`'s `CANON_EQ`, `CASE_INSENSITIVE`, `COMMENTS`, `DOTALL`, `LITERAL`, `MULTILINE`, `UNICODE_CASE`, and `UNIX_LINES` constants) and return its `Pattern` object. This method throws `PatternSyntaxException` when regex's syntax is invalid, and throws `IllegalArgumentException` when bit values other than those corresponding to the defined match flags are set in flags.
`int flags()`	Return this `Pattern` object's match flags. This method returns 0 for `Pattern` instances created via `compile(String)` and the bitset of flags for `Pattern` instances created via `compile(String, int)`.
`Matcher matcher(CharSequence input)`	Return a `Matcher` that will match input against this `Pattern`'s compiled regex.

(continued)

Table 13-3. (*continued*)

Method	Description
static boolean matches(String regex, CharSequence input)	Compile regex and attempt to match input against the compiled regex. Return true when there is a match; otherwise, return false. This convenience method is equivalent to Pattern.compile(regex).matcher(input).matches() and throws PatternSyntaxException when regex's syntax is invalid.
String pattern()	Return this Pattern's uncompiled regex.
static String quote(String s)	Quote s using "\Q" and "\E" so that all other metacharacters lose their special meaning. When the returned java.lang.String object is later compiled into a Pattern instance, it only can be matched literally.
String[] split(CharSequence input)	Split input around matches of this Pattern's compiled regex and return an array containing the matches.
String[] split(CharSequence input, int limit)	Split input around matches of this Pattern's compiled regex; limit controls the number of times the compiled regex is applied and thus affects the length of the resulting array.
String toString()	Return this Pattern's uncompiled regex.

Table 13-3 reveals the java.lang.CharSequence interface, which describes a readable and immutable sequence of char values—the underlying implementation may be mutable. Instances of any class that implements this interface (e.g., String, java.lang.StringBuffer, and java.lang.StringBuilder) can be passed to Pattern methods that take CharSequence arguments (e.g., split(CharSequence)).

Table 13-3 also reveals that each of Pattern's compile() methods and its matches() method (which calls the compile(String) method) throws PatternSyntaxException when a syntax error is encountered while compiling the pattern argument. Table 13-4 describes PatternSyntaxException's methods.

Table 13-4. *PatternSyntaxException Methods*

Method	Description
String getDescription()	Return a description of the syntax error.
int getIndex()	Return the approximate index of where the syntax error occurred in the pattern or −1 when the index isn't known.
String getMessage()	Return a multiline string containing the description of the syntax error and its index, the erroneous pattern, and a visual indication of the error index within the pattern.
String getPattern()	Return the erroneous pattern.

Finally, Table 13-4's `Matcher matcher(CharSequence input)` method reveals that the Regular Expressions API also provides the `java.util.regex.Matcher` class, whose *matchers* attempt to match compiled regexes against `input` text. `Matcher` declares the following methods to perform matching operations:

- `boolean matches()` attempts to match the entire region against the pattern. When the match succeeds, more information can be obtained by calling `Matcher`'s `start()`, `end()`, and `group()` methods. For example, `int start()` returns the start index of the previous match, `int end()` returns the offset of the first character following the previous match, and `String group()` returns the input subsequence matched by the previous match. Each method throws `java.lang.IllegalStateException` when a match has not yet been attempted or the previous match attempt failed.

- `boolean lookingAt()` attempts to match the input sequence, starting at the beginning of the region, against the pattern. As with `matches()`, this method always starts at the beginning of the region. Unlike `matches()`, `lookingAt()` doesn't require that the entire region be matched. When the match succeeds, more information can be obtained by calling `Matcher`'s `start()`, `end()`, and `group()` methods.

- `boolean find()` attempts to find the next subsequence of the input sequence that matches the pattern. It starts at the beginning of this matcher's region, or, if a previous call to this method was successful and the matcher hasn't since been reset (by calling `Matcher`'s `Matcher reset()` or `Matcher reset(CharSequence input)` method), at the first character not matched by the previous match. When the match succeeds, more information can be obtained by calling `Matcher`'s `start()`, `end()`, and `group()` methods.

> **Note**   A matcher finds matches in a subset of its input called the *region*. By default, the region contains all of the matcher's input. The region can be modified by calling `Matcher`'s `Matcher region(int start, int end)` method (set the limits of this matcher's region) and queried by calling `Matcher`'s `int regionStart()` and `int regionEnd()` methods.

I've created a simple application that demonstrates `Pattern`, `PatternSyntaxException`, and `Matcher`. Listing 13-9 presents this application's source code.

Listing 13-9. Playing With Regular Expressions

```
import java.util.regex.Matcher;
import java.util.regex.Pattern;
import java.util.regex.PatternSyntaxException;

public class RegExDemo
{
   public static void main(String[] args)
   {
```

```
    if (args.length != 2)
    {
        System.err.println("usage: java RegExDemo regex input");
        return;
    }
    try
    {
        System.out.println("regex = " + args[0]);
        System.out.println("input = " + args[1]);
        Pattern p = Pattern.compile(args[0]);
        Matcher m = p.matcher(args[1]);
        while (m.find())
            System.out.println("Located [" + m.group() + "] starting at "
                                + m.start() + " and ending at " + (m.end() - 1));
    }
    catch (PatternSyntaxException pse)
    {
        System.err.println("Bad regex: " + pse.getMessage());
        System.err.println("Description: " + pse.getDescription());
        System.err.println("Index: " + pse.getIndex());
        System.err.println("Incorrect pattern: " + pse.getPattern());
    }
    }
}
```

Compile Listing 13-9 (javac RegExDemo.java) and run this application via java RegExDemo ox ox. You'll discover the following output:

```
regex = ox
input = ox
Located [ox] starting at 0 and ending at 1
```

find() searches for a match by comparing regex characters with the input characters in left-to-right order and returns true because o equals o and x equals x.

Continuing, execute java RegExDemo box ox. This time, you'll discover the following output:

```
regex = box
input = ox
```

find() first compares regex character b with input character o. Because these characters are not equal and because there are not enough characters in the input to continue the search, find() doesn't output a "Located" message to indicate a match. However, if you execute java RegExDemo ox box, you'll discover a match:

```
regex = ox
input = box
Located [ox] starting at 1 and ending at 2
```

The ox regex consists of literal characters. More sophisticated regexes combine literal characters with metacharacters (e.g., the period [.]) and other regex constructs.

> **Tip**   To specify a metacharacter as a literal character, precede the metacharacter with a backslash character (as in \.) or place the metacharacter between \Q and \E (as in \Q.\E). In either case, make sure to double the backslash character when the escaped metacharacter appears in a string literal; for example, "\\." or "\\Q.\\E".

The period metacharacter matches all characters except for the line terminator. For example, each of java RegExDemo .ox box and java RegExDemo .ox fox report a match because the period matches the b in box and the f in fox.

> **Note**   Pattern recognizes the following line terminators: carriage return (\r), newline (line feed) (\n), carriage return immediately followed by newline (\r\n), next line (\u0085), line separator (\u2028), and paragraph separator (\u2029). The period metacharacter can be made to also match these line terminators by specifying the Pattern.DOTALL flag when calling Pattern.compile(String, int).

Character Classes

A *character class* is a set of characters appearing between [and]. There are six kinds of character classes:

- A *simple character class* consists of literal characters placed side by side and matches only these characters. For example, [abc] consists of characters a, b, and c. Also, java RegExDemo t[aiou]ck tack reports a match because a is a member of [aiou]. It also reports a match when the input is tick, tock, or tuck because i, o, and u are members.

- A *negation character class* consists of a circumflex metacharacter (^), followed by literal characters placed side by side, and matches all characters except for the characters in the class. For example, [^abc] consists of all characters except for a, b, and c. Also, java RegExDemo "[^b]ox" box doesn't report a match because b isn't a member of [^b], whereas java RegExDemo "[^b]ox" fox reports a match because f is a member. (The double quotes surrounding [^b]ox are necessary on my Windows 7 platform because ^ is treated specially at the command line.)

- A *range character class* consists of successive literal characters expressed as a starting literal character, followed by the hyphen metacharacter (–), followed by an ending literal character, and matches all characters in this range. For example, [a-z] consists of all characters from a through z. Also, java RegExDemo [h-l]ouse house reports a match because h is a member of the class, whereas java RegExDemo [h-l]ouse mouse doesn't report a match because m lies outside of the range and is therefore not part of the class. You can combine multiple ranges within the same range character class by placing them side by side; for example, [A-Za-z] consists of all uppercase and lowercase Latin letters.

- A *union character class* consists of multiple nested character classes and matches all characters that belong to the resulting union. For example, [abc[u-z]] consists of characters a, b, c, u, v, w, x, y, and z. Also, java RegExDemo [[0-9][A-F][a-f]] e reports a match because e is a hexadecimal character. (I could have alternatively expressed this character class as [0-9A-Fa-f] by combining multiple ranges.)

- An *intersection character class* consists of multiple &&–separated nested character classes and matches all characters that are common to these nested character classes. For example, [a-c&&[c-f]] consists of character c, which is the only character common to [a-c] and [c-f]. Also, java RegExDemo "[aeiouy&&[y]]" y reports a match because y is common to classes [aeiouy] and [y].

- A *subtraction character class* consists of multiple &&-separated nested character classes, where at least one nested character class is a negation character class, and matches all characters except for those indicated by the negation character class/classes. For example, [a-z&&[^x-z]] consists of characters a through w. (The square brackets surrounding ^x-z are necessary; otherwise, ^ is ignored and the resulting class consists of only x, y, and z.) Also, java RegExDemo "[a-z&&[^aeiou]]" g reports a match because g is a consonant and only consonants belong to this class. (I'm ignoring y, which is sometimes regarded as a consonant and sometimes regarded as a vowel.)

A *predefined character class* is a regex construct for a commonly specified character class. Table 13-5 identifies Pattern's predefined character classes.

Table 13-5. Predefined Character Classes

Predefined Character Class	Description
\d	Match any digit character. \d is equivalent to [0-9].
\D	Match any nondigit character. \D is equivalent to [^\d].
\s	Match any whitespace character. \s is equivalent to [\t\n\x0B\f\r].
\S	Match any nonwhitespace character. \S is equivalent to [^\s].
\w	Match any word character. \w is equivalent to [a-zA-Z0-9].
\W	Match any nonword character. \W is equivalent to [^\w].

For example, java RegExDemo \wbc abc reports a match because \w matches the word character a in abc.

Capturing Groups

A *capturing group* saves a match's characters for later recall during pattern matching and is expressed as a character sequence surrounded by parentheses metacharacters (and). All characters within a capturing group are treated as a unit. For example, the (Android) capturing group combines A, n, d, r, o, i, and d into a unit. It matches the Android pattern against all occurrences of Android in the input. Each match replaces the previous match's saved Android characters with the next match's Android characters.

Capturing groups can appear inside other capturing groups. For example, capturing groups (A) and (B(C)) appear inside capturing group ((A)(B(C))), and capturing group (C) appears inside capturing group (B(C)). Each nested or nonnested capturing group receives its own number, numbering starts at 1, and capturing groups are numbered from left to right. For example, ((A)(B(C))) is assigned 1, (A) is assigned 2, (B(C)) is assigned 3, and (C) is assigned 4.

A capturing group saves its match for later recall via a *back reference*, which is a backslash character followed by a digit character denoting a capturing group number. The back reference causes the matcher to use the back reference's capturing group number to recall the capturing group's saved match and then use that match's characters to attempt a further match. The following example uses a back reference to determine if the input consists of two consecutive Android patterns:

```
java RegExDemo "(Android) \1" "Android Android"
```

RegExDemo reports a match because the matcher detects Android, followed by a space, followed by Android in the input.

Boundary Matchers and Zero-Length Matches

A *boundary matcher* is a regex construct for identifying the beginning of a line, a word boundary, the end of text, and other commonly occurring boundaries. See Table 13-6.

Table 13-6. Boundary Matchers

Boundary Matcher	Description
^	Match beginning of line.
$	Match end of line.
\b	Match word boundary.
\B	Match nonword boundary.
\A	Match beginning of text.
\G	Match end of previous match.
\Z	Match end of text except for line terminator (when present).
\z	Match end of text.

For example, java RegExDemo \b\b "I think" reports several matches, as revealed in the following output:

```
regex = \b\b
input = I think
Located [] starting at 0 and ending at -1
Located [] starting at 1 and ending at 0
Located [] starting at 2 and ending at 1
Located [] starting at 7 and ending at 6
```

This output reveals several *zero-length matches*. When a zero-length match occurs, the starting and ending indexes are equal, although the output shows the ending index to be one less than the starting index because I specified end() - 1 in Listing 13-9 (so that a match's end index identifies a non-zero-length match's last character, not the character following the non-zero-length match's last character).

> **Note**   A zero-length match occurs in empty input text, at the beginning of input text, after the last character of input text, or between any two characters of that text. Zero-length matches are easy to identify because they always start and end at the same index position.

Quantifiers

The final regex construct I present is the *quantifier*, a numeric value implicitly or explicitly bound to a pattern. Quantifiers are categorized as greedy, reluctant, or possessive:

- A *greedy quantifier* (?, *, or +) attempts to find the longest match. Specify X? to find one or no occurrences of X, X* to find zero or more occurrences of X, X+ to find one or more occurrences of X, $X\{n\}$ to find n occurrences of X, $X\{n,\}$ to find at least n (and possibly more) occurrences of X, and $X\{n,m\}$ to find at least n but no more than m occurrences of X.

- A *reluctant quantifier* (??, *?, or +?) attempts to find the shortest match. Specify X?? to find one or no occurrences of X, X*? to find zero or more occurrences of X, X+? to find one or more occurrences of X, $X\{n\}$? to find n occurrences of X, $X\{n,\}$? to find at least n (and possibly more) occurrences of X, and $X\{n,m\}$? to find at least n but no more than m occurrences of X.

- A *possessive quantifier* (?+, *+, or ++) is similar to a greedy quantifier except that a possessive quantifier only makes one attempt to find the longest match, whereas a greedy quantifier can make multiple attempts. Specify X?+ to find one or no occurrences of X, X*+ to find zero or more occurrences of X, X++ to find one or more occurrences of X, $X\{n\}$+ to find n occurrences of X, $X\{n,\}$+ to find at least n (and possibly more) occurrences of X, and $X\{n,m\}$+ to find at least n but no more than m occurrences of X.

For an example of a greedy quantifier, execute java RegExDemo .*end "wend rend end". You'll discover the following output:

```
regex = .*end
input = wend rend end
Located [wend rend end] starting at 0 and ending at 12
```

The greedy quantifier (.*) matches the longest sequence of characters that terminates in end. It starts by consuming all of the input text and then is forced to back off until it discovers that the input text terminates with these characters.

For an example of a reluctant quantifier, execute java RegExDemo .*?end "wend rend end". You'll discover the following output:

```
regex = .*?end
input = wend rend end
Located [wend] starting at 0 and ending at 3
Located [ rend] starting at 4 and ending at 8
Located [ end] starting at 9 and ending at 12
```

The reluctant quantifier (.*?) matches the shortest sequence of characters that terminates in end. It begins by consuming nothing and then slowly consumes characters until it finds a match. It then continues until it exhausts the input text.

For an example of a possessive quantifier, execute java RegExDemo .*+end "wend rend end". You'll discover the following output:

```
regex = .*+end
input = wend rend end
```

The possessive quantifier (.*+) doesn't detect a match because it consumes the entire input text, leaving nothing left over to match end at the end of the regex. Unlike a greedy quantifier, a possessive quantifier doesn't back off.

While working with quantifiers, you'll probably encounter zero-length matches. For example, execute java RegExDemo 1? 101101:

```
regex = 1?
input = 101101
Located [1] starting at 0 and ending at 0
Located [] starting at 1 and ending at 0
Located [1] starting at 2 and ending at 2
Located [1] starting at 3 and ending at 3
Located [] starting at 4 and ending at 3
Located [1] starting at 5 and ending at 5
Located [] starting at 6 and ending at 5
```

The result of this greedy quantifier is that 1 is detected at locations 0, 2, 3, and 5 in the input text and that nothing is detected (a zero-length match) at locations 1, 4, and 6.

This time, execute java RegExDemo 1?? 101101:

```
regex = 1??
input = 101101
Located [] starting at 0 and ending at -1
Located [] starting at 1 and ending at 0
Located [] starting at 2 and ending at 1
Located [] starting at 3 and ending at 2
Located [] starting at 4 and ending at 3
Located [] starting at 5 and ending at 4
Located [] starting at 6 and ending at 5
```

This output might look surprising, but remember that a reluctant quantifier looks for the shortest match, which (in this case) is no match at all.

Finally, execute java RegExDemo 1+? 101101:

```
regex = 1+?
input = 101101
Located [1] starting at 0 and ending at 0
Located [1] starting at 2 and ending at 2
Located [1] starting at 3 and ending at 3
Located [1] starting at 5 and ending at 5
```

This possessive quantifier only matches the locations where 1 is detected in the input text. It doesn't perform zero-length matches.

> **Note**   Check out the Java documentation on the Pattern class to learn about additional regex constructs.

Practical Regular Expressions

Most of the previous regex examples haven't been practical, except to help you grasp how to use the various regex constructs. In contrast, the following examples reveal a regex that matches phone numbers of the form (ddd) ddd-dddd or ddd-dddd. A single space appears between (ddd) and ddd; there's no space on either side of the hyphen.

```
java RegExDemo "(\(\d{3}\))?\s*\d{3}-\d{4}" "(800) 555-1212"
regex = (\(\d{3}\))?\s*\d{3}-\d{4}
input = (800) 555-1212
Located [(800) 555-1212] starting at 0 and ending at 13

java RegExDemo "(\(\d{3}\))?\s*\d{3}-\d{4}" 555-1212
regex = (\(\d{3}\))?\s*\d{3}-\d{4}
input = 555-1212
Located [555-1212] starting at 0 and ending at 7
```

> **Note** To learn more about regular expressions, check out "Lesson: Regular Expressions"
> (http://download.oracle.com/javase/tutorial/essential/regex/index.html) in
> *The Java Tutorials*.

EXERCISES

The following exercises are designed to test your understanding of Chapter 13's content:

1. Define New I/O.

2. What is a buffer?

3. Identify a buffer's four properties.

4. What happens when you invoke Buffer's array() method on a buffer backed by a read-only array?

5. What happens when you invoke Buffer's flip() method on a buffer?

6. What happens when you invoke Buffer's reset() method on a buffer where a mark has not been set?

7. True or False: Buffers are thread-safe.

8. Identify the classes that extend the abstract Buffer class.

9. How do you create a byte buffer?

10. Define view buffer.

11. How is a view buffer created?

12. How do you create a read-only view buffer?

13. Identify ByteBuffer's methods for storing a single byte in a byte buffer and fetching a single byte from a byte buffer.

14. What causes BufferOverflowException or BufferUnderflowException to occur?

15. What is the equivalent of executing buffer.flip();?

16. True or false: Calling flip() twice returns you to the original state.

17. What is the difference between Buffer's clear() and reset() methods?

18. What does ByteBuffer's compact() method accomplish?

19. What is the purpose of the ByteOrder class?

20. Define direct byte buffer.

21. How do you obtain a direct byte buffer?

22. What is a channel?

23. What capabilities does the Channel interface provide?

24. Identify the three interfaces that directly extend `Channel`.

25. True or false: A channel that implements `InterruptibleChannel` is asynchronously closeable.

26. Identify the two ways to obtain a channel.

27. Define scatter/gather I/O.

28. What interfaces are provided for achieving scatter/gather I/O?

29. Define file channel.

30. True or false: File channels don't support scatter/gather I/O.

31. What method does `FileChannel` provide for mapping a region of a file into memory?

32. What is the fundamental difference between `FileChannel`'s `lock()` and `tryLock()` methods?

33. Define regular expression.

34. What does the `Pattern` class accomplish?

35. What do `Pattern`'s `compile()` methods do when they discover illegal syntax in their regular expression arguments?

36. What does the `Matcher` class accomplish?

37. What is the difference between `Matcher`'s `matches()` and `lookingAt()` methods?

38. Define character class.

39. Identify the various kinds of character classes.

40. Define capturing group.

41. What is a zero-length match?

42. Define quantifier.

43. What is the difference between a greedy quantifier and a reluctant quantifier?

44. How do possessive and greedy quantifiers differ?

45. Refactor Listing 11-8 (Chapter 11's Copy application) to use the `ByteBuffer` and `FileChannel` classes in partnership with `FileInputStream` and `FileOutputStream`.

46. Create a `ReplaceText` application that takes input text, a pattern that specifies text to replace, and replacement text command-line arguments, and uses `Matcher`'s `String replaceAll(String replacement)` method to replace all matches of the pattern with the replacement text (passed to `replacement`). For example, `java ReplaceText "too many embedded spaces" "\s+" " "` should output too many embedded spaces with only a single space character between successive words.

Summary

Java 1.4 introduced a more powerful I/O architecture that supports memory-mapped file I/O, readiness selection, file locking, and more. This architecture consists of buffers, channels, selectors, regular expressions, and charsets and is commonly known as New I/O (NIO).

A buffer is an object that stores a fixed amount of data to be sent to or received from an I/O service or that has been received from an I/O service. It sits between an application and a channel that writes buffered data to the service or reads the data from the service and deposits it into the buffer.

A channel is an object that represents an open connection to a hardware device, a file, a network socket, an application component, or another entity that's capable of performing write, read, and other I/O operations. Channels transfer data between a buffer and this other entity.

A regular expression (also known as a regex or regexp) is a string-based pattern that represents the set of strings that match this pattern. The pattern consists of literal characters and metacharacters, which are characters with special meanings instead of literal meanings.

Chapter 14 focuses on database access. You first encounter the Java DB and SQLite database products and then learn how to use the JDBC API to create/access their databases.

Accessing Databases

Applications often need to access databases to store and retrieve various kinds of data. A *database* (http://en.wikipedia.org/wiki/Database) is an organized collection of data. Although there are many kinds of databases (e.g., hierarchical, object oriented, and relational), *relational databases*, which organize data into tables that can be related to each other, are common.

> **Note**   In a relational database, each row stores a single item (e.g., an employee) and each column stores a single item attribute (e.g., an employee's name).

Except for the most trivial of databases (e.g., Chapter 11's flat file database based on a single data file), databases are created and managed through a *database management system (DBMS)*—see http://en.wikipedia.org/wiki/Database_management_system. Relational DBMSs (RDBMSs) support *Structured Query Language (SQL)* for working with tables and more.

> **Note**   For brevity, I assume that you're familiar with SQL. If not, you might want to check out Wikipedia's "SQL" entry (http://en.wikipedia.org/wiki/SQL) for an introduction.

Java supports database access and creation (and more) via its relational database-oriented JDBC (Java DataBase Connectivity) API. Because you need an RDBMS before you can explore JDBC, this chapter first introduces you to Java DB, which is included with the JDK, followed by SQLite (http://en.wikipedia.org/wiki/Sqlite). Chapter 14 then focuses on JDBC.

> **Note**   Android offers an alternative to JDBC via its `android.database` and
> `android.database.sqlite` packages, which are the preferred means for accessing databases from
> an Android application. Although Android supports JDBC by including this API and an undocumented JDBC
> driver (discussed later in this chapter), you should focus on using Android's database access alternative
> when developing an Android application that requires database access. Because you still might find JDBC
> useful, especially when creating a non-Android application, I present JDBC in this chapter.

Introducing Java DB

First introduced by Sun Microsystems as part of JDK 6 (and not included in the JRE) to give
developers an RDBMS to test their JDBC code, *Java DB* is a distribution of Apache's open-source
Derby product, which is based on IBM's Cloudscape RDBMS code base. This pure-Java RDBMS
is also bundled with JDK 7 (but not in the JRE). It's secure, supports JDBC and SQL (including
transactions, stored procedures, and concurrency), and has a small footprint—its core engine and
JDBC driver occupy approximately 2 MB.

> **Note**   A *JDBC driver* is a classfile plug-in for communicating with a database. I'll have more to say
> about JDBC drivers when I introduce JDBC later in this chapter.

Java DB is capable of running in an embedded environment or in a client/server environment.
In an embedded environment, where an application accesses the database engine via Java
DB's *embedded driver*, the database engine runs in the same virtual machine as the application.
Figure 14-1 illustrates the embedded environment architecture, where the database engine is
embedded in the application.

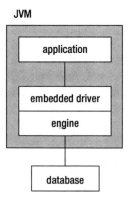

Figure 14-1. No separate processes are required to start up or shut down an embedded database engine

In a client/server environment, client applications and the database engine run in separate virtual machines. A client application accesses the network server through Java DB's *client driver*. The network server, which runs in the same virtual machine as the database engine, accesses the database engine through the embedded driver. Figure 14-2 illustrates this architecture.

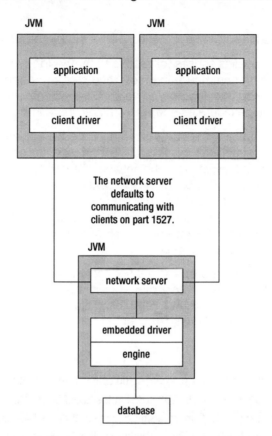

Figure 14-2. Multiple clients communicate with the same database engine through the network server

Java DB implements the database portion of the architectures shown in Figures 14-1 and 14-2 as a directory with the same name as the database. Within this directory, Java DB creates a log directory to store transaction logs, a seg0 directory to store the data files, and a service.properties file to store configuration parameters.

> **Note**   Java DB doesn't provide an SQL command to *drop* (destroy) a database. Destroying a database requires that you manually delete its directory structure.

Java DB Installation and Configuration

When you install JDK 7 with the default settings, the bundled Java DB is installed into %JAVA_HOME%\db on Windows platforms or into the db subdirectory in the equivalent location on Unix/Linux platforms. (For convenience, I adopt the Windows convention when presenting environment variable paths.)

> **Note** I focus on Java DB 10.8.2.2 in this chapter because it's included with JDK 7 build 1.7.0_06-b24, which is the Java build on which this book is based.

The db directory contains five files and the following pair of subdirectories:

- The bin directory contains scripts for setting up embedded and client/server environments, running command-line tools, and starting/stopping the network server. You should add this directory to your PATH environment variable so that you can conveniently execute its scripts from anywhere in the filesystem.

- The lib directory contains various JAR files that house the engine library (derby.jar), the command-line tools libraries (derbytools.jar and derbyrun.jar), the network server library (derbynet.jar), the network client library (derbyclient.jar), and various locale libraries. This directory also contains derby.war, which is used to register the network *servlet* (see http://en.wikipedia.org/wiki/Java_Servlet) at the /derbynet relative path—it's also possible to manage the Java DB network server remotely via the servlet interface (see http://db.apache.org/derby/docs/10.8/adminguide/cadminservlet98430.html).

Before you can run the tools and start/stop the network server, you must set the DERBY_HOME environment variable. Set this variable for Windows via set DERBY_HOME=%JAVA_HOME%\db, and for Unix (Korn shell) via export DERBY_HOME=$JAVA_HOME/db. (This setting will not persist past the current command shell session unless you make it permanent.)

> **Note** The embedded and client/server environment setup scripts refer to a DERBY_INSTALL environment variable. According to the "Re: DERBY_INSTALL and DERBY_HOME" mail item (www.mail-archive.com/derby-dev@db.apache.org/msg22098.html), DERBY_HOME is equivalent to and replaces DERBY_INSTALL for consistency with other Apache projects.

You must also set the CLASSPATH environment variable. The easiest way to set this environment variable is to run a script file included with Java DB. Windows and Unix/Linux versions of various "set***xxx***CP" script files (which extend the current classpath) are located in the %JAVA_HOME%\db\bin directory. The script file(s) to run will depend on whether you work with the embedded or client/server environment:

- For the embedded environment, invoke setEmbeddedCP to add derby.jar and derbytools.jar to the classpath.

- For the client/server environment, invoke setNetworkServerCP to add derbynet.jar and derbytools.jar to the classpath. In a separate command window, invoke setNetworkClientCP to add derbyclient.jar and derbytools.jar to the classpath.

Java DB Demos

For JDK 7, the Java DB demos are included with other Java demos in a separate distribution file—see www.oracle.com/technetwork/java/javase/downloads/index-jsp-138363.html. After downloading and unarchiving the distribution file, you can move it to %JAVA_HOME%. If you're running Windows 7, you'll also need to ensure that Java DB can write files to subdirectories of C:\Program Files (64-bit JDK) or C:\Program Files (x86) (32-bit JDK). Otherwise, you'll encounter "access denied" errors.

The %JAVA_HOME%\demo\db\programs directory contains HTML documentation that describes the demos included with Java DB; the demo.html file is the entry point into this documentation. These demos include a simple JDBC application for working with Java DB, a network server sample program, and sample programs that are introduced in the *Working with Derby* manual.

> **Note** The *Working with Derby* manual underscores Java DB's Derby heritage. You can download this manual and other Derby manuals from the documentation section (http://db.apache.org/derby/manuals/index.html) of Apache's Derby project site (http://db.apache.org/derby/index.html).

For brevity, I'll focus only on the simple JDBC application that's located in the programs directory's simple subdirectory. This application runs in either the default embedded environment or the client/server environment. It creates and connects to a derbyDB database, introduces a table into this database, performs SQL insert/update/select operations on this table, *drops* (removes) the table, and disconnects from the database.

To run this application in the embedded environment, open a command window and make sure that the DERBY_HOME and CLASSPATH environment variables have been set properly; invoke setEmbeddedCP to set the classpath. Assuming that simple is the current directory, invoke java SimpleApp or java SimpleApp embedded to run this application. You should observe the following output:

```
SimpleApp starting in embedded mode
Loaded the appropriate driver
Connected to and created database derbyDB
Created table location
Inserted 1956 Webster
Inserted 1910 Union
Updated 1956 Webster to 180 Grand
Updated 180 Grand to 300 Lakeshore
Verified the rows
Dropped table location
Committed the transaction
Derby shut down normally
SimpleApp finished
```

This output reveals that an application running in the embedded environment shuts down the database engine before exiting. This is done to perform a checkpoint and release resources. When this shutdown doesn't occur, Java DB notes the absence of the checkpoint, assumes a crash, and causes recovery code to run before the next database connection (which takes longer to complete).

> **Tip** When running SimpleApp (or any other Java DB application) in the embedded environment,
> you can determine where the database directory will be created by setting the derby.system.home
> property. For example, java -Dderby.system.home=c:\temp SimpleApp causes derbyDB to be
> created in the temp subdirectory of the root directory of the C: drive on the Windows 7 platform.

To run this application in the client/server environment, you need to start the network server and run the application in separate command windows.

In one command window, set DERBY_HOME. Start the network server via the startNetworkServer script (located in %JAVA_HOME%\db\bin), which takes care of setting the classpath. You should see output similar to this:

```
Sun Nov 25 16:01:23 CST 2012 : Security manager installed using the Basic server security policy.
Sun Nov 25 16:01:24 CST 2012 : Apache Derby Network Server - 10.8.2.2 - (1181258) started and ready
to accept connections on port 1527
```

In the other command window, set DERBY_HOME followed by CLASSPATH (via setNetworkClientCP). Assuming that the simple directory is current, execute the java SimpleApp derbyClient command line to run this application. This time, you should observe the following output:

```
SimpleApp starting in derbyclient mode
Loaded the appropriate driver
Connected to and created database derbyDB
Created table location
Inserted 1956 Webster
Inserted 1910 Union
Updated 1956 Webster to 180 Grand
Updated 180 Grand to 300 Lakeshore
Verified the rows
Dropped table location
Committed the transaction
SimpleApp finished
```

Notice that the database engine is not shut down in the client/server environment. Although not indicated in the output, there's a second difference between running SimpleApp in the embedded and client/server environments. In the embedded environment, the derbyDB database directory is created in the simple directory. In the client/server environment, this database directory is created in the directory that was current when you executed startNetworkServer.

When you're finished playing with SimpleApp in the client/server environment, you should shut down the network server and database engine. Accomplish this task by invoking the stopNetworkServer script (located in %JAVA_HOME%\db\bin). You can also shut down (or start and otherwise control) the network server by running the NetworkServerControl script (also located in %JAVA_HOME%\db\bin). For example, NetworkServerControl shutdown shuts down the network server and database engine.

Java DB Command-Line Tools

The %JAVA_HOME%\db\bin directory contains sysinfo, ij, and dblook Windows and Unix/Linux script files for launching command-line tools:

- Run sysinfo to view the Java environment/Java DB configuration.

- Run ij to run scripts that execute ad hoc SQL commands and perform repetitive tasks.

- Run dblook to view all or part of a database's Data Definition Language (DDL).

If you experience trouble with Java DB (e.g., not being able to connect to a database), you can run sysinfo to find out if the problem is configuration related. This tool reports various settings under the Java Information, Derby Information, and Locale Information headings. It outputs the following information on my platform:

```
------------------ Java Information ------------------
Java Version:    1.7.0_06
Java Vendor:     Oracle Corporation
Java home:       C:\Program Files\Java\jdk1.7.0_06\jre
Java classpath:  C:\PROGRA~1\Java\JDK17~2.0_0\db\lib\derbyclient.jar;C:\PROGRA~1\Java\JDK17~2.0_0\
db\lib\derbytools.jar;.;C:\Program Files (x86)\QuickTime\QTSystem\QTJava.zip;C:\PROGRA~1\Java\
JDK17~2.0_0\db/lib/derby.jar;C:\PROGRA~1\Java\JDK17~2.0_0\db/lib/derbynet.jar;C:\PROGRA~1\Java\
JDK17~2.0_0\db/lib/derbyclient.jar;C:\PROGRA~1\Java\JDK17~2.0_0\db/lib/derbytools.jar
OS name:         Windows 7
OS architecture: amd64
OS version:      6.1
Java user name:  Owner
Java user home:  C:\Users\Owner
Java user dir:   C:\PROGRA~1\Java\jdk1.7.0_06\db\bin
java.specification.name: Java Platform API Specification
java.specification.version: 1.7
java.runtime.version: 1.7.0_06-b24
--------- Derby Information --------
JRE - JDBC: Java SE 7 - JDBC 4.0
[C:\Program Files\Java\jdk1.7.0_06\db\lib\derby.jar] 10.8.2.2 - (1181258)
[C:\Program Files\Java\jdk1.7.0_06\db\lib\derbytools.jar] 10.8.2.2 - (1181258)
[C:\Program Files\Java\jdk1.7.0_06\db\lib\derbynet.jar] 10.8.2.2 - (1181258)
[C:\Program Files\Java\jdk1.7.0_06\db\lib\derbyclient.jar] 10.8.2.2 - (1181258)
------------------------------------------------------
------------------ Locale Information ------------------
Current Locale :  [English/Canada [en_CA]]
Found support for locale: [cs]
                 version: 10.8.2.2 - (1181258)
Found support for locale: [de_DE]
                 version: 10.8.2.2 - (1181258)
Found support for locale: [es]
                 version: 10.8.2.2 - (1181258)
Found support for locale: [fr]
                 version: 10.8.2.2 - (1181258)
Found support for locale: [hu]
                 version: 10.8.2.2 - (1181258)
```

```
Found support for locale: [it]
                version: 10.8.2.2 - (1181258)
Found support for locale: [ja_JP]
                version: 10.8.2.2 - (1181258)
Found support for locale: [ko_KR]
                version: 10.8.2.2 - (1181258)
Found support for locale: [pl]
                version: 10.8.2.2 - (1181258)
Found support for locale: [pt_BR]
                version: 10.8.2.2 - (1181258)
Found support for locale: [ru]
                version: 10.8.2.2 - (1181258)
Found support for locale: [zh_CN]
                version: 10.8.2.2 - (1181258)
Found support for locale: [zh_TW]
                version: 10.8.2.2 - (1181258)
---------------------------------------------------------
```

The ij script is useful for creating a database and initializing a user's *schema* (a namespace that logically organizes tables and other database objects) by running a script file that specifies the appropriate DDL statements. For example, you've created an EMPLOYEES table with its NAME and PHOTO columns and have created a create_emp_schema.sql script file in the current directory that contains the following line:

```
CREATE TABLE EMPLOYEES(NAME VARCHAR(30), PHOTO BLOB);
```

The following embedded ij script session creates the employees database and EMPLOYEES table:

```
C:\db>ij
ij version 10.8
ij> connect 'jdbc:derby:employees;create=true';
ij> run 'create_emp_schema.sql';
ij> CREATE TABLE EMPLOYEES(NAME VARCHAR(30), PHOTO BLOB);
0 rows inserted/updated/deleted
ij> disconnect;
ij> exit;
C:>\db>
```

The connect command causes the employees database to be created—I'll have more to say about this command's syntax when I introduce JDBC later in this chapter. The run command causes create_emp_schema.sql to execute, and the subsequent pair of lines is generated as a result.

The CREATE TABLE EMPLOYEES(NAME VARCHAR(30), PHOTO BLOB); line is an SQL statement for creating a table named EMPLOYEES with NAME and PHOTO columns. Data items entered into the NAME column are of SQL type VARCHAR (a varying number of characters—a string) with a maximum of 30 characters, and data items entered into the PHOTO column are of SQL type BLOB (a binary large object, such as an image).

After run 'create_emp_schema.sql' finishes, the specified EMPLOYEES table is added to the newly created employees database. To verify the table's existence, run dblook against the employees directory, as the following session demonstrates.

```
C:\db>dblook -d jdbc:derby:employees
-- Timestamp: 2012-11-25 16:13:42.693
-- Source database is: employees
-- Connection URL is: jdbc:derby:employees
-- appendLogs: false


-- ----------------------------------------------
-- DDL Statements for tables
-- ----------------------------------------------

CREATE TABLE "APP"."EMPLOYEES" ("NAME" VARCHAR(30), "PHOTO" BLOB(2147483647));

C:\db>
```

All database objects (e.g., tables and indexes) are assigned to user and system schemas, which logically organize these objects in the same way that packages logically organize classes. When a user creates or accesses a database, Java DB uses the specified username as the namespace name for newly added database objects. In the absence of a username, Java DB chooses APP, as the preceding session output shows.

Introducing SQLite

SQLite (http://sqlite.org/) is a very simple and popular RDBMS. Basically, it implements a self-contained, serverless, zero-configuration, transactional SQL database engine; and is considered to be the most widely deployed database engine in the world. For example, SQLite is found in Mozilla Firefox, Google Chrome, and other web browsers. It's also found in Google Android, Apple iOS, and other mobile operating systems.

Note   To learn what sets SQLite apart from other RDBMs, visit the "Distinctive Features of SQLite" page at **http://sqlite.org/different.html**. As well as learning about features such as the aforementioned zero-configuration, you'll learn about features such as *manifest typing*, in which you can store any value of any data type into any column regardless of the declared type of that column.

To introduce yourself to SQLite, visit the SQLite home page at http://sqlite.org/. You can explore online documentation (http://sqlite.org/docs.html), download SQLite software (http://sqlite.org/download.html), and so on. Regarding downloads, you can download source code, documentation, and precompiled binaries for the Linux, Mac OS X (x86), and Windows platforms.

I downloaded the `sqlite-shell-win32-x86-3071401.zip` distribution file for my Windows 7 platform. This archive contains a single `sqlite3` executable, which offers a command-line shell for accessing and modifying SQLite databases. According to the SQLite downloads page, this program is compatible with all versions of SQLite through version 3.7.14.1 (and beyond). (The Android SDK for Windows also includes `sqlite3.exe` but not necessarily the same version.)

You can specify `sqlite3` with a database filename argument (e.g., `sqlite3 employees`) to create the database file (e.g., employees) when it doesn't exist (you must create a table at least) or open the existing file and enter this tool's shell from where you can execute `sqlite3`-specific dot-prefixed commands and SQL statements. As Figure 14-3 shows, you can also specify `sqlite3` without an argument and enter the shell.

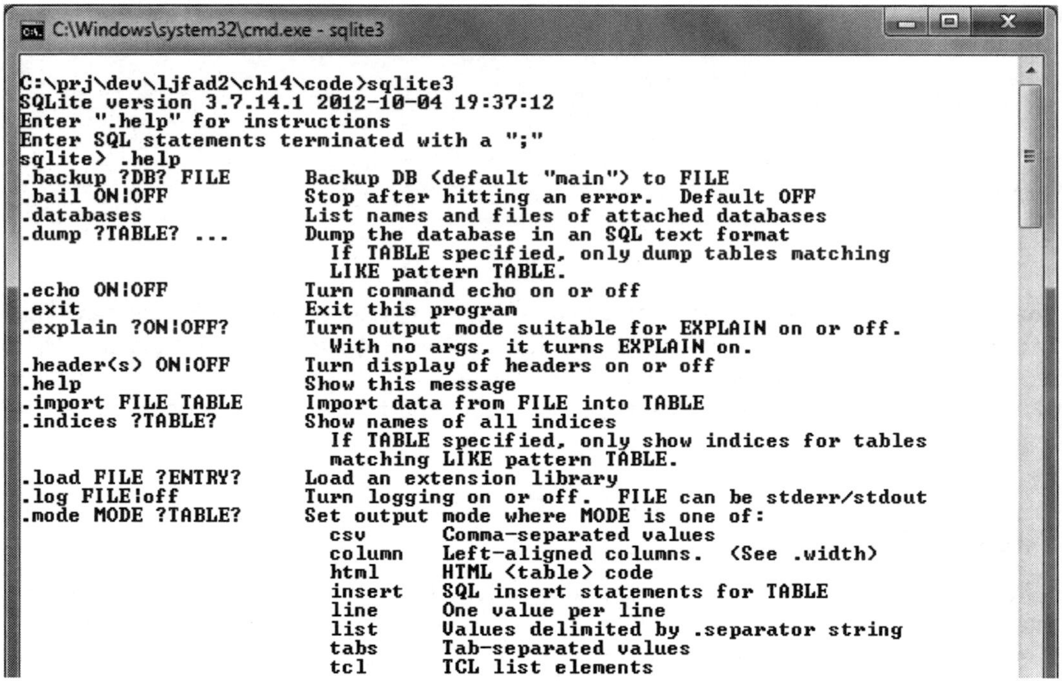

Figure 14-3. `sqlite3` *is invoked without a database filename argument*

Figure 14-3 reveals the prologue that greets you after entering the `sqlite3` shell, which is indicated by the `sqlite>` prompt from where you enter commands. It also reveals part of the help text that's presented when you type the `sqlite3`-specific ".help" command.

Tip   You can create a database after specifying `sqlite3` without an argument by entering the appropriate SQL statements to create and populate desired tables (and possibly create indexes) and then invoking `.backup` *filename* (where *filename* identifies the file that stores the database) before exiting `sqlite3`.

While discussing Java DB command-line tools, I presented a small employee-oriented database example consisting of an `employees` database and a `create_emp_schema.sql` script file that contains the following SQL statement for creating an EMPLOYEES table (consisting of names and photos):

```
CREATE TABLE EMPLOYEES(NAME VARCHAR(30), PHOTO BLOB);
```

Let's find out how to create this database and table with `sqlite3`.

At the command-line, execute `sqlite3 employees`. At the resulting `sqlite>` command prompt, execute the aforementioned SQL statement, and then execute `.quit` to quit `sqlite3`. You should now observe an `employees` file in the same directory as `sqlite3`.

Re-execute `sqlite3 employees`. At the `sqlite>` command prompt, execute `.tables`. You should observe a single output line consisting of EMPLOYEES. Now execute `.schema employees` (case isn't significant) and you should see the aforementioned `CREATE TABLE` statement.

You can continue to play with `sqlite3` and the `employees` database/EMPLOYEES table. For example, you could insert a single row of data into the EMPLOYEES table via the following INSERT statement and then select/output this row via the following SELECT statement:

```
INSERT INTO EMPLOYEES VALUES('Duke', null);
SELECT * FROM EMPLOYEES;
```

You should observe the following line as the result—nothing appears for the photo because of its `null` value:

```
DUKE|
```

Accessing Databases via JDBC

JDBC is an API (associated with the `java.sql` and `javax.sql` packages—I mainly focus on `java.sql` in this chapter) for communicating with RDBMSs in an RDBMS-independent manner. You can use JDBC to perform various database operations, such as submitting SQL statements that tell the RDBMS to create a table and to update or query tabular data.

Data Sources, Drivers, and Connections

Although JDBC is typically used to communicate with RDBMSs, it also can be used to communicate with a flat file database. For this reason, JDBC uses the term *data source* (a data-storage facility ranging from a simple file to a complex relational database managed by an RDBMS) to abstract the source of data.

Because data sources are accessed in different ways (e.g., Chapter 11's flat file database is accessed via methods of the `java.io.RandomAccessFile` class, whereas Java DB and SQLite databases are accessed via SQL statements), JDBC uses *drivers* (classfile plug-ins) to abstract over their implementations. This abstraction lets you write an application that can be adapted to an arbitrary data source without having to change a single line of code (in most cases). Drivers are implementations of the `java.sql.Driver` interface.

JDBC recognizes four types of drivers:

- *Type 1 drivers* implement JDBC as a mapping to another data-access API (e.g., Open Database Connectivity, or ODBC—see http://en.wikipedia.org/wiki/ODBC). The driver converts JDBC method calls into function calls on the other library. The JDBC-ODBC Bridge Driver is an example and isn't supported by Oracle. It was commonly used in the early days of JDBC when other kinds of drivers were uncommon.

- *Type 2 drivers* are written partly in Java and partly in native code. They interact with a data source-specific native client library and are not portable for this reason. Oracle's OCI (Oracle Call Interface) client-side driver is an example.

- *Type 3 drivers* don't depend on native code and communicate with a *middleware server* (a server that sits between the application client and the data source) via an RDBMS-independent protocol. The middleware server then communicates the client's requests to the data source.

- *Type 4 drivers* don't depend on native code and implement the network protocol for a specific data source. The client connects directly to the data source instead of going through a middleware server.

Before you can communicate with a data source, you need to establish a connection. JDBC provides the `java.sql.DriverManager` class and the `javax.sql.DataSource` interface for this purpose:

- `DriverManager` lets an application connect to a data source by specifying a URL. When this class first attempts to establish a connection, it automatically loads any JDBC 4.*x* drivers located via the classpath. (Pre-JDBC 4.*x* drivers must be loaded manually.)

- `DataSource` hides connection details from the application to promote data source portability and is preferred over `DriverManager` for this reason. Because a discussion of `DataSource` is somewhat involved (and is typically used in a Java EE context), I focus on `DriverManager` in this chapter.

Before letting you obtain a data source connection, early JDBC versions required you to explicitly load a suitable driver by specifying `Class.forName()` with the name of the class that implements the `Driver` interface. For example, the JDBC-ODBC Bridge driver was loaded via `Class.forName("sun.jdbc.odbc.JdbcOdbcDriver");`. Later JDBC versions relaxed this requirement by letting you specify a list of drivers to load via the `jdbc.drivers` system property. `DriverManager` would attempt to load all of these drivers during its initialization.

Under Java 7, `DriverManager` first loads all drivers identified by the `jdbc.drivers` system property. It then uses the `java.util.ServiceLoader`-based service provider mechanism to load all drivers from accessible driver JAR files so that you don't have to explicitly load drivers. This mechanism requires a driver to be packaged into a JAR file that includes `META-INF/services/java.sql.Driver`. The `java.sql.Driver` text file must contain a single line that names the driver's implementation of the `Driver` interface.

Each loaded driver instantiates and registers itself with `DriverManager` via `DriverManager`'s void `registerDriver(Driver driver)` class method. When invoked, a `getConnection()` method walks through registered drivers, returning an implementation of the `java.sql.Connection` interface from the first driver that recognizes getConnection()'s JDBC URL. (You might want to check out DriverManager's source code to see how this is done.)

> **Note**   To maintain data source-independence, much of JDBC consists of interfaces. Each driver provides implementations of the various interfaces.

To connect to a data source and obtain a Connection instance, call one of DriverManager's Connection getConnection(String url), Connection getConnection(String url, Properties info), or Connection getConnection(String url, String user, String password) methods. With either method, the url argument specifies a string-based URL that starts with the jdbc: prefix and continues with data source-specific syntax.

Consider Java DB. The URL syntax varies depending on the driver. For the embedded driver (when you want to access a local database), this syntax is as follows:

jdbc:derby:*databaseName;URLAttributes*

For the client driver (when you want to access a remote database, although you can also access a local database with this driver), this syntax is as follows:

jdbc:derby://*host:port/databaseName;URLAttributes*

With either syntax, *URLAttributes* is an optional sequence of semicolon-delimited *name=value* pairs. For example, create=true tells Java DB to create a new database.

The following example demonstrates the first syntax by telling JDBC to load the Java DB embedded driver and create the database named testdb on the local host:

```
Connection con = DriverManager.getConnection("jdbc:derby:testdb;create=true");
```

The following example demonstrates the second syntax by telling JDBC to load the Java DB client driver and create the database named testdb on port 8500 of the xyz host:

```
Connection con;
con = DriverManager.getConnection("jdbc:derby://xyz:8500/testdb;create=true");
```

Consider SQLite. The Xerial project (www.xerial.org/trac/Xerial) provides the SQLite JDBC driver (www.xerial.org/trac/Xerial/wiki/SQLiteJDBC) for testing JDBC with SQLite. Point your browser to www.xerial.org/maven/repository/artifact/org/xerial/sqlite-jdbc/, navigate to the appropriate directory (e.g., 3.7.2), and download an appropriate driver JAR file (e.g., sqlite-jdbc-3.7.2.jar).

For creating an actual file in which to store the database, the URL syntax for the Xerial SQLite driver is as follows:

jdbc:sqlite:*databaseName*

The following examples demonstrate this syntax for connecting to a database file (which is created when it doesn't exist) named `sample.db`:

```
Connection con1 = DriverManager.getConnection("jdbc:sqlite:sample.db");
Connection con2 = DriverManager.getConnection("jdbc:sqlite:C:/temp/sample.db ");
```

The first example obtains a connection to the current directory's `sample.db` file; the second example obtains a connection to a `sample.db` file in the `C:\temp` directory.

SQLite also supports in-memory database management, which doesn't create any database files. The following example shows you how to connect to an existing in-memory database:

```
Connection con = DriverManager.getConnection("jdbc:sqlite::memory:");
```

The following example shows you how to create and obtain a connection to an in-memory database:

```
Connection con = DriverManager.getConnection("jdbc:sqlite:");
```

> **Note**   For the most part, this chapter's applications can be used with either the Java DB embedded driver connection syntax or the non-in-memory SQLite driver connection syntax.

Exceptions

`DriverManager`'s `getConnection()` methods (and other JDBC methods in the various JDBC interfaces) throw `java.sql.SQLException` or one of its subclasses when something goes wrong. Along with the methods it inherits from `java.lang.Throwable` (e.g., `String getMessage()`), `SQLException` declares various constructors (not discussed for brevity) and the following methods:

- `int getErrorCode()` returns a vendor-specific integer error code. Normally this value will be the actual error code returned by the underlying data source.

- `SQLException getNextException()` returns the `SQLException` instance chained to this `SQLException` object (via a call to `setNextException(SQLException ex)`) or null when there isn't a chained exception.

- `String getSQLState()` returns a "SQLstate" string that provides an X/Open or SQL:1999 (see http://en.wikipedia.org/wiki/SQL:1999) error code identifying the exception.

- `Iterator<Throwable> iterator()` returns an iterator over the chained `SQLExceptions` and their causes in proper order. The iterator will be used to iterate over each `SQLException` and its underlying cause (if any). You would normally not call this method but would instead use the enhanced for statement (discussed in Chapter 9), which calls `iterator()` when you need to iterate over the chain of `SQLExceptions`. (The Android documentation at the current time of writing reports this method to be obsolete.)

■ void setNextException(SQLException sqlex) appends sqlex to the end of the chain. (The Android documentation at the current time of writing reports this method to be obsolete.)

One or more SQLExceptions might occur while processing a request, and the code that throws these exceptions can add them to a *chain* of SQLExceptions by invoking setNextException(). Also, an SQLException instance might be thrown as a result of a different exception (e.g., java.io.IOException), which is known as that exception's *cause* (see Chapter 5).

SQL state error codes are defined by the ISO/ANSI and Open Group (X/Open) SQL standards. The error code is a five-character string consisting of a two-character class value followed by a three-character subclass value. Class value "00" indicates success, class value "01" indicates a warning, and other class values normally indicate an exception. Examples of SQL state error codes are 00000 (success) and 08001 (unable to connect to the data source).

Listing 14-1 presents a framework for structuring a JDBC application that connects to a JDBC or SQLite data source, perform some work, and respond to a thrown SQLException instance.

Listing 14-1. Architecting a Basic JDBC Application

```
import java.sql.Connection;
import java.sql.DriverManager;
import java.sql.SQLException;

public class JDBCDemo
{
   final static String URL1 = "jdbc:derby:employee;create=true";
   final static String URL2 = "jdbc:sqlite:employee";

   public static void main(String[] args)
   {
      String url = null;
      if (args.length != 1)
      {
         System.err.println("usage 1: java JDBCDemo javadb");
         System.err.println("usage 2: java JDBCDemo sqlite");
         return;
      }
      if (args[0].equals("javadb"))
         url = URL1;
      else
      if (args[0].equals("sqlite"))
         url = URL2;
      else
      {
         System.err.println("invalid command-line argument");
         return;
      }
      Connection con = null;
```

```
        try
        {
            if (args[0].equals("sqlite"))
                Class.forName("org.sqlite.JDBC");
            con = DriverManager.getConnection(url);
            // Perform useful work. The following throw statement simulates a
            // JDBC method throwing SQLException.
            throw new SQLException("Unable to access database table",
                                    new java.io.IOException("File I/O problem"));
        }
        catch (ClassNotFoundException cnfe)
        {
            System.err.println("unable to load sqlite driver");
        }
        catch (SQLException sqlex)
        {
            while (sqlex != null)
            {
                System.err.println("SQL error : " + sqlex.getMessage());
                System.err.println("SQL state : " + sqlex.getSQLState());
                System.err.println("Error code: " + sqlex.getErrorCode());
                System.err.println("Cause: " + sqlex.getCause());
                sqlex = sqlex.getNextException();
            }
        }
        finally
        {
            if (con != null)
                try
                {
                    con.close();
                }
                catch (SQLException sqle)
                {
                    sqle.printStackTrace();
                }
        }
    }
}
```

Listing 14-1 requires that you run this application with the javadb or sqlite command-line argument. This argument determines which JDBC driver to use. If you specify sqlite as the argument, Xerial requires that the SQLite driver classfile be explicitly loaded, and this task is accomplished via the Class.forName("org.sqlite.JDBC") method call.

Next, a connection to the data source is obtained. When successful, IOException and SQLException objects are created, and the IOException instance is wrapped inside the SQLException instance (as its cause), which is subsequently thrown. The catch block that handles the SQL exception uses a while loop to demonstrate outputting the SQL exception and all chained exceptions.

Connections must be closed when no longer needed. Connection declares a void close() method for this purpose. This method is documented to throw SQLException.

Compile Listing 14-1 via the following command line:

```
javac JDBCDemo.java
```

Run this application via the following command line:

```
java JDBCDemo javadb
```

Assuming that Java DB hasn't been configured (by setting the `DERBY_HOME` and `CLASSPATH` environment variables), you should expect the following output:

```
SQL error : No suitable driver found for jdbc:derby:employee;create=true
SQL state : 08001
Error code: 0
Cause: null
```

Set the `DERBY_HOME` environment variable, and then execute `setEmbeddedCP` to install Java DB's embedded driver. Then re-execute `java JDBCDemo javadb`. This time, you should observe the following correct output:

```
SQL error : Unable to access database table
SQL state : null
Error code: 0
Cause: java.io.IOException: File I/O problem
```

Furthermore, an `employee` directory containing the database and a `derby.log` file should appear in the current directory.

Now, run this application via the following command:

```
java JDBCDemo sqlite
```

Assuming that SQLite hasn't been configured, you should observe the following output:

```
unable to load sqlite driver
```

This error message results from the thrown `java.lang.ClassNotFoundException` instance. This exception was thrown from the `Class.forName("org.sqlite.JDBC")` method call that attempted to load a nonexistent driver classfile.

You need to add the Xerial SQLite driver to the classpath when running `JDBCDemo`. Accomplish this task via the following command line:

```
java -cp sqlite-jdbc-3.7.2.jar;. JDBCDemo sqlite
```

Because of the previously created `employee` directory, you should observe the following output:

```
SQL error : [SQLITE_CANTOPEN]  Unable to open the database file (out of memory)
SQL state : null
Error code: 0
Cause: null
```

Remove the employee directory (and derby.log for neatness) and re-execute the aforementioned command line. This time, you should observe the following correct output:

```
SQL error : Unable to access database table
SQL state : null
Error code: 0
Cause: java.io.IOException: File I/O problem
```

SQLException declares several subclasses (e.g., java.sql.BatchUpdateException—an error has occurred during a batch update operation). Many of these subclasses are categorized under java.sql.SQLNonTransientException- and java.sql.SQLTransientException-rooted class hierarchies in which SQLNonTransientException describes failed operations that cannot be retried without changing application source code or some aspect of the data source, and SQLTransientException describes failed operations that can be retried immediately.

Statements

After obtaining a connection to a data source, an application interacts with the data source by issuing SQL statements (e.g., CREATE TABLE, INSERT, SELECT, UPDATE, DELETE, and DROP TABLE). JDBC supports SQL statements via the java.sql.Statement, java.sql.PreparedStatement, and java.sql.CallableStatement interfaces. Furthermore, Connection declares various createStatement(), prepareStatement, and prepareCall() methods that return Statement, PreparedStatement, or CallableStatement implementation instances, respectively.

Statement and ResultSet

Statement is the easiest-to-use interface, and Connection's Statement createStatement() method is the easiest-to-use method for obtaining a Statement instance. After calling this method, you can execute various SQL statements by invoking Statement methods such as the following:

- ResultSet executeQuery(String sql) executes a SELECT statement and (assuming no exception is thrown) provides access to its results via a java.sql.ResultSet instance.

- int executeUpdate(String sql) executes a CREATE TABLE, INSERT, UPDATE, DELETE, or DROP TABLE statement and (assuming no exception is thrown) typically returns the number of table rows affected by this statement.

I've created a second JDBCDemo application that demonstrates these methods. Listing 14-2 presents its source code.

Listing 14-2. Creating, Inserting Values into, Querying, and Dropping an EMPLOYEES Table

```
import java.sql.Connection;
import java.sql.DriverManager;
import java.sql.ResultSet;
import java.sql.SQLException;
import java.sql.Statement;
```

```java
public class JDBCDemo
{
    final static String URL1 = "jdbc:derby:employee;create=true";
    final static String URL2 = "jdbc:sqlite:employee";

    public static void main(String[] args)
    {
        String url = null;
        if (args.length != 1)
        {
            System.err.println("usage 1: java JDBCDemo javadb");
            System.err.println("usage 2: java JDBCDemo sqlite");
            return;
        }
        if (args[0].equals("javadb"))
            url = URL1;
        else
        if (args[0].equals("sqlite"))
            url = URL2;
        else
        {
            System.err.println("invalid command-line argument");
            return;
        }
        Connection con = null;
        try
        {
            if (args[0].equals("sqlite"))
                Class.forName("org.sqlite.JDBC");
            con = DriverManager.getConnection(url);
            Statement stmt = null;
            try
            {
                stmt = con.createStatement();
                String sql = "CREATE TABLE EMPLOYEES(ID INTEGER, NAME VARCHAR(30))";
                stmt.executeUpdate(sql);
                sql = "INSERT INTO EMPLOYEES VALUES(1, 'John Doe')";
                stmt.executeUpdate(sql);
                sql = "INSERT INTO EMPLOYEES VALUES(2, 'Sally Smith')";
                stmt.executeUpdate(sql);
                ResultSet rs = stmt.executeQuery("SELECT * FROM EMPLOYEES");
                while (rs.next())
                    System.out.println(rs.getInt("ID") + " " + rs.getString("NAME"));
                stmt.executeUpdate("DROP TABLE EMPLOYEES");
            }
            catch (SQLException sqlex)
            {
                while (sqlex != null)
                {
                    System.err.println("SQL error : " + sqlex.getMessage());
                    System.err.println("SQL state : " + sqlex.getSQLState());
                    System.err.println("Error code: " + sqlex.getErrorCode());
```

```java
                  System.err.println("Cause: " + sqlex.getCause());
                  sqlex = sqlex.getNextException();
               }
         }
         finally
         {
            if (stmt != null)
               try
               {
                  stmt.close();
               }
               catch (SQLException sqle)
               {
                  sqle.printStackTrace();
               }
         }
      }
      catch (ClassNotFoundException cnfe)
      {
         System.err.println("unable to load sqlite driver");
      }
      catch (SQLException sqlex)
      {
         while (sqlex != null)
         {
            System.err.println("SQL error : " + sqlex.getMessage());
            System.err.println("SQL state : " + sqlex.getSQLState());
            System.err.println("Error code: " + sqlex.getErrorCode());
            System.err.println("Cause: " + sqlex.getCause());
            sqlex = sqlex.getNextException();
         }
      }
      finally
      {
         if (con != null)
            try
            {
               con.close();
            }
            catch (SQLException sqle)
            {
               sqle.printStackTrace();
            }
      }
   }
}
```

Listing 14-2 presents a similar architecture to Listing 14-1. For brevity, I won't repeat the same instructions and examples that I presented while discussing SQL exceptions. Instead, I prefer to focus on new aspects of JDBC.

After successfully establishing a connection to the `employee` data source, `main()` creates a statement and uses it to execute SQL statements for creating, inserting values into, querying, and dropping an EMPLOYEES table.

The `executeQuery()` method returns a `ResultSet` object that provides access to a query's tabular results. Each result set is associated with a *cursor* that provides access to a specific row of data. The cursor initially points before the first row; call `ResultSet`'s boolean `next()` method to advance the cursor to the next row. As long as there's a next row, this method returns true; it returns false when there are no more rows to examine.

`ResultSet` also declares various methods for returning the current row's column values based on their types. For example, `int getInt(String columnLabel)` returns the integer value corresponding to the INTEGER-based column identified by `columnLabel`. Similarly, `String getString(String columnLabel)` returns the string value corresponding to the VARCHAR-based column identified by `columnLabel`.

> **Tip** If you don't have column names but have zero-based column indexes, call `ResultSet` methods such as `int getInt(int columnIndex)` and `String getString(int columnIndex)`. However, best practice is to call `int getInt(String columnLabel)`.

Compile Listing 14-2 and run this application as previously discussed—you will want to first delete the employee directory/file left behind by the previous application. You should observe the following output:

```
1 John Doe
2 Sally Smith
```

SQL's INTEGER and VARCHAR types map to Java's int and String types. Table 14-1 presents a more complete list of type mappings.

Table 14-1. SQL Type/Java Type Mappings

SQL Type	Java Type
ARRAY	java.sql.Array
BIGINT	long
BINARY	byte[]
BIT	boolean
BLOB	java.sql.Blob
BOOLEAN	boolean
CHAR	java.lang.String
CLOB	java.sql.Clob

(continued)

Table 14-1. (*continued*)

SQL Type	Java Type
DATE	java.sql.Date
DECIMAL	java.math.BigDecimal
DOUBLE	double
FLOAT	double
INTEGER	int
LONGVARBINARY	byte[]
LONGVARCHAR	java.lang.String
NUMERIC	java.math.BigDecimal
REAL	Float
REF	java.sql.Ref
SMALLINT	Short
STRUCT	java.sql.Struct
TIME	java.sql.Time
TIMESTAMP	java.sql.Timestamp
TINYINT	Byte
VARBINARY	byte[]
VARCHAR	java.lang.String

Check out http://docs.oracle.com/javase/1.5.0/docs/guide/jdbc/getstart/mapping.html for more information on type mappings.

PreparedStatement

PreparedStatement is the next easiest-to-use interface, and Connection's PreparedStatement prepareStatement() method is the easiest-to-use method for obtaining a PreparedStatement instance—PreparedStatement is a subinterface of Statement.

Unlike a regular statement, a *prepared statement* represents a precompiled SQL statement. The SQL statement is compiled to improve performance and prevent *SQL injection* (see http://en.wikipedia.org/wiki/SQL_injection), and the compiled result is stored in a PreparedStatement implementation instance.

You typically obtain this instance when you want to execute the same prepared statement multiple times (e.g., you want to execute an SQL INSERT statement multiple times to populate a database table). Consider Listing 14-3.

Listing 14-3. Creating, Inserting Values via a Prepared Statement into, Querying, and Dropping an EMPLOYEES Table

```java
import java.sql.Connection;
import java.sql.DriverManager;
import java.sql.PreparedStatement;
import java.sql.ResultSet;
import java.sql.SQLException;
import java.sql.Statement;

public class JDBCDemo
{
   final static String URL1 = "jdbc:derby:employee;create=true";
   final static String URL2 = "jdbc:sqlite:employee";

   public static void main(String[] args)
   {
      String url = null;
      if (args.length != 1)
      {
         System.err.println("usage 1: java JDBCDemo javadb");
         System.err.println("usage 2: java JDBCDemo sqlite");
         return;
      }
      if (args[0].equals("javadb"))
         url = URL1;
      else
      if (args[0].equals("sqlite"))
         url = URL2;
      else
      {
         System.err.println("invalid command-line argument");
         return;
      }
      Connection con = null;
      try
      {
         if (args[0].equals("sqlite"))
            Class.forName("org.sqlite.JDBC");
         con = DriverManager.getConnection(url);
         Statement stmt = null;
         try
         {
            stmt = con.createStatement();
            String sql = "CREATE TABLE EMPLOYEES(ID INTEGER, NAME VARCHAR(30))";
            stmt.executeUpdate(sql);
            PreparedStatement pstmt = null;
            try
            {
               pstmt = con.prepareStatement("INSERT INTO EMPLOYEES VALUES(?, ?)");
               String[] empNames = { "John Doe", "Sally Smith" };
               for (int i = 0; i < empNames.length; i++)
```

```
        {
           pstmt.setInt(1, i+1);
           pstmt.setString(2, empNames[i]);
           pstmt.executeUpdate();
        }
        ResultSet rs = stmt.executeQuery("SELECT * FROM EMPLOYEES");
        while (rs.next())
           System.out.println(rs.getInt("ID") + " " + rs.getString("NAME"));
        stmt.executeUpdate("DROP TABLE EMPLOYEES");
     }
     catch (SQLException sqlex)
     {
        while (sqlex != null)
        {
           System.err.println("SQL error : " + sqlex.getMessage());
           System.err.println("SQL state : " + sqlex.getSQLState());
           System.err.println("Error code: " + sqlex.getErrorCode());
           System.err.println("Cause: " + sqlex.getCause());
           sqlex = sqlex.getNextException();
        }
     }
     finally
     {
        if (pstmt != null)
           try
           {
              pstmt.close();
           }
           catch (SQLException sqle)
           {
              sqle.printStackTrace();
           }
     }
  }
  catch (SQLException sqlex)
  {
     while (sqlex != null)
     {
        System.err.println("SQL error : " + sqlex.getMessage());
        System.err.println("SQL state : " + sqlex.getSQLState());
        System.err.println("Error code: " + sqlex.getErrorCode());
        System.err.println("Cause: " + sqlex.getCause());
        sqlex = sqlex.getNextException();
     }
  }
  finally
  {
     if (stmt != null)
        try
        {
           stmt.close();
        }
        catch (SQLException sqle
```

```
               {
                  sqle.printStackTrace();
               }
         }
      }
      catch (ClassNotFoundException cnfe)
      {
         System.err.println("unable to load sqlite driver");
      }
      catch (SQLException sqlex)
      {
         while (sqlex != null)
         {
            System.err.println("SQL error : " + sqlex.getMessage());
            System.err.println("SQL state : " + sqlex.getSQLState());
            System.err.println("Error code: " + sqlex.getErrorCode());
            System.err.println("Cause: " + sqlex.getCause());
            sqlex = sqlex.getNextException();
         }
      }
      finally
      {
         if (con != null)
            try
            {
               con.close();
            }
            catch (SQLException sqle)
            {
               sqle.printStackTrace();
            }
      }
   }
}
```

Listing 14-3 creates a String object that specifies an SQL INSERT statement. Each "?" character serves as a placeholder for a value that's specified before the statement is executed.

After the PreparedStatement implementation instance has been obtained, this interface's void setInt(int parameterIndex, int x) and void setString(int parameterIndex, String x) methods are called on this instance to provide these values (the first argument passed to each method is a 1-based integer column index into the table associated with the statement—1 corresponds to the leftmost column), and then PreparedStatement's int executeUpdate() method is called to execute this SQL statement. The end result is that a pair of rows containing John Doe, Sally Smith, and their respective identifiers is added to the EMPLOYEES table.

CallableStatement

CallableStatement is the most specialized of the statement interfaces; it extends PreparedStatement. You use this interface to execute SQL stored procedures in which a *stored procedure* is a list of SQL statements that perform a specific task (e.g., fire an employee). Java DB differs from other RDBMSs in that a stored procedure's body is implemented as a `public static` Java method. Furthermore, the class in which this method is declared must be `public`.

Note   SQLite doesn't support stored procedures.

You create a stored procedure by executing an SQL statement that typically begins with `CREATE PROCEDURE` and then continues with RDBMS-specific syntax. For example, the Java DB syntax for creating a stored procedure, as specified on the web page at `http://db.apache.org/derby/docs/10.8/ref/rrefcreateprocedurestatement.html`, is as follows:

```
CREATE PROCEDURE procedure-name ([ procedure-parameter [, procedure-parameter ] ]*)
[ procedure-element ]*
```

procedure-name is expressed as

```
[ schemaName .] SQL92Identifier
```

procedure-parameter is expressed as

```
[{ IN | OUT | INOUT }] [ parameter-Name ] DataType
```

procedure-element is expressed as

```
{
| [ DYNAMIC ] RESULT SETS INTEGER
| LANGUAGE { JAVA }
| DeterministicCharacteristic
| EXTERNAL NAME string
| PARAMETER STYLE JAVA
| EXTERNAL SECURITY { DEFINER | INVOKER }
| { NO SQL | MODIFIES SQL DATA | CONTAINS SQL | READS SQL DATA }
}
```

Anything between [ ] is optional, the * to the right of [ ] indicates that anything between these metacharacters can appear zero or more times, the {} metacharacters surround a list of items, and | separates possible items—only one of these items can be specified.

For example, `CREATE PROCEDURE FIRE(IN ID INTEGER) PARAMETER STYLE JAVA LANGUAGE JAVA DYNAMIC RESULT SETS 0 EXTERNAL NAME 'JDBCDemo.fire'` creates a stored procedure named FIRE. This procedure specifies an input parameter named ID and is associated with a `public static` method named `fire` in a `public` class named JDBCDemo.

After creating the stored procedure, you need to obtain a `CallableStatement` implementation instance to call that procedure, and you do so by invoking one of `Connection`'s `prepareCall()` methods, for example, `CallableStatement prepareCall(String sql)`.

The string passed to `prepareCall()` is an *escape clause* (RDBMS-independent syntax) consisting of an open {, followed by the word `call`, followed by a space, followed by the name of the stored procedure, followed by a parameter list with "?" placeholder characters for the arguments that will be passed, followed by a closing }.

> **Note** Escape clauses are JDBC's way of smoothing out some of the differences in how different RDBMS vendors implement SQL. When a JDBC driver detects escape syntax, it converts it into the code that the particular RDBMS understands. This makes escape syntax RDBMS independent.

Once you have a `CallableStatement` reference, you pass arguments to these parameters in the same way as with `PreparedStatement`. The following example demonstrates:

```
CallableStatement cstmt = null;
try
{
   cstmt = con.prepareCall("{ call FIRE(?)}"))
   cstmt.setInt(1, 2);
   cstmt.execute();
}
catch (SQLException sqle)
{
   // handle the exception
}
finally
{
   // close the callable statement
}
```

The `cstmt.setInt(1, 2)` method call assigns 2 to the leftmost stored procedure parameter—parameter index 1 corresponds to the leftmost parameter (or to a single parameter when there's only one). The `cstmt.execute()` method call executes the stored procedure, which results in a callback to the application's `public static void fire(int id)` method.

I've created another version of the `JDBCDemo` application that demonstrates this callable statement in a Java DB context only. Listing 14-4 presents its source code.

Listing 14-4. Firing an Employee via a Stored Procedure

```
import java.sql.CallableStatement;
import java.sql.Connection;
import java.sql.DriverManager;
import java.sql.ResultSet;
import java.sql.SQLException;
import java.sql.Statement;

public class JDBCDemo
{
   public static void main(String[] args)
   {
      String url = "jdbc:derby:employee;create=true";
```

```
Connection con = null;
try
{
   con = DriverManager.getConnection(url);
   Statement stmt = null;
   try
   {
      stmt = con.createStatement();
      String sql = "CREATE PROCEDURE FIRE(IN ID INTEGER)" +
                   "   PARAMETER STYLE JAVA" +
                   "   LANGUAGE JAVA" +
                   "   DYNAMIC RESULT SETS 0" +
                   "   EXTERNAL NAME 'JDBCDemo.fire'";
      stmt.executeUpdate(sql);
      sql = "CREATE TABLE EMPLOYEES(ID INTEGER, NAME VARCHAR(30), " +
            "FIRED BOOLEAN)";
      stmt.executeUpdate(sql);
      sql = "INSERT INTO EMPLOYEES VALUES(1, 'John Doe', false)";
      stmt.executeUpdate(sql);
      sql = "INSERT INTO EMPLOYEES VALUES(2, 'Sally Smith', false)";
      stmt.executeUpdate(sql);
      dump(stmt.executeQuery("SELECT * FROM EMPLOYEES"));
      CallableStatement cstmt = null;
      try
      {
         cstmt = con.prepareCall("{ call FIRE(?)}");
         cstmt.setInt(1, 2);
         cstmt.execute();
         dump(stmt.executeQuery("SELECT * FROM EMPLOYEES"));
         stmt.executeUpdate("DROP TABLE EMPLOYEES");
         stmt.executeUpdate("DROP PROCEDURE FIRE");
      }
      catch (SQLException sqlex)
      {
         while (sqlex != null)
         {
            System.err.println("SQL error : " + sqlex.getMessage());
            System.err.println("SQL state : " + sqlex.getSQLState());
            System.err.println("Error code: " + sqlex.getErrorCode());
            System.err.println("Cause: " + sqlex.getCause());
            sqlex = sqlex.getNextException();
         }
      }
      finally
      {
         if (cstmt != null)
            try
            {
               cstmt.close();
            }
            catch (SQLException sqle)
```

```java
                     {
                        sqle.printStackTrace();
                     }
                  }
               }
               catch (SQLException sqlex)
               {
                  while (sqlex != null)
                  {
                     System.err.println("SQL error : " + sqlex.getMessage());
                     System.err.println("SQL state : " + sqlex.getSQLState());
                     System.err.println("Error code: " + sqlex.getErrorCode());
                     System.err.println("Cause: " + sqlex.getCause());
                     sqlex = sqlex.getNextException();
                  }
               }
               finally
               {
                  if (stmt != null)
                     try
                     {
                        stmt.close();
                     }
                     catch (SQLException sqle)
                     {
                        sqle.printStackTrace();
                     }
               }
            }
            catch (SQLException sqlex)
            {
               while (sqlex != null)
               {
                  System.err.println("SQL error : " + sqlex.getMessage());
                  System.err.println("SQL state : " + sqlex.getSQLState());
                  System.err.println("Error code: " + sqlex.getErrorCode());
                  System.err.println("Cause: " + sqlex.getCause());
                  sqlex = sqlex.getNextException();
               }
            }
            finally
            {
               if (con != null)
                  try
                  {
                     con.close();
                  }
                  catch (SQLException sqle)
                  {
                     sqle.printStackTrace();
                  }
            }
         }
      }
```

```
static void dump(ResultSet rs) throws SQLException
{
    StringBuilder sb = new StringBuilder();
    while (rs.next())
    {
        sb.append(rs.getInt("ID"));
        sb.append(' ');
        sb.append(rs.getString("NAME"));
        sb.append(' ');
        sb.append(rs.getBoolean("FIRED"));
        System.out.println(sb);
        sb.setLength(0);
    }
    System.out.println();
}

public static void fire(int id) throws SQLException
{
    Connection con = DriverManager.getConnection("jdbc:default:connection");
    String sql = "UPDATE EMPLOYEES SET FIRED=TRUE WHERE ID=" + id;
    Statement stmt = null;
    try
    {
        stmt = con.createStatement();
        stmt.executeUpdate(sql);
    }
    finally
    {
        if (stmt != null)
            try
            {
                stmt.close();
            }
            catch (SQLException sqle)
            {
                sqle.printStackTrace();
            }
    }
}
}
```

Much of Listing 14-4 should be fairly understandable, so I'll only discuss the fire() method. As previously stated, this method is invoked as a result of the callable statement invocation.

fire() is called with the integer identifier of the employee to fire. It first accesses the current Connection object by invoking getConnection() with the jdbc.default:connection argument, which is supported by Oracle virtual machines through a special internal driver.

After creating an SQL UPDATE statement string to set the FIRED column to true in the EMPLOYEES table row where its ID field equals the value in id, fired() invokes executeUpdate() to update the table appropriately.

Compile Listing 14-4 (javac JDBCDemo.java) and run this application (java JDBCDemo). You should observe the following output:

```
1 John Doe false
2 Sally Smith false

1 John Doe false
2 Sally Smith true
```

Metadata

A data source is typically associated with *metadata* (data about data) that describes the data source. When the data source is an RDBMS, this data is typically stored in a collection of tables.

Metadata includes a list of *catalogs* (RDBMS databases whose tables describe RDBMS objects such as *base tables* [tables that physically exist], *views* [virtual tables], and *indexes* [files that improve the speed of data retrieval operations]), *schemas* (namespaces that partition database objects), and additional information (e.g., version numbers, identification strings, and limits).

To access a data source's metadata, invoke Connection's DatabaseMetaData getMetaData() method. This method returns an implementation instance of the java.sql.DatabaseMetaData interface.

I've created yet another JDBCDemo application that demonstrates getMetaData() and various DatabaseMetaData methods in the context of Java DB. Listing 14-5 presents MetaData's source code.

Listing 14-5. Obtaining Metadata from an Employee Data Source

```java
import java.sql.Connection;
import java.sql.DatabaseMetaData;
import java.sql.DriverManager;
import java.sql.ResultSet;
import java.sql.SQLException;
import java.sql.Statement;

public class JDBCDemo
{
   public static void main(String[] args)
   {
      String url = "jdbc:derby:employee;create=true";
      Connection con = null;
      try
      {
         con = DriverManager.getConnection(url);
         dump(con.getMetaData());
      }
      catch (SQLException sqlex)
      {
         while (sqlex != null)
         {
            System.err.println("SQL error : " + sqlex.getMessage());
            System.err.println("SQL state : " + sqlex.getSQLState());
```

```
                System.err.println("Error code: " + sqlex.getErrorCode());
                System.err.println("Cause: " + sqlex.getCause());
                sqlex = sqlex.getNextException();
            }
        }
    }
    finally
    {
        if (con != null)
            try
            {
                con.close();
            }
            catch (SQLException sqle)
            {
                sqle.printStackTrace();
            }
    }
}

static void dump(DatabaseMetaData dbmd) throws SQLException
{
    System.out.println("DB Major Version = " + dbmd.getDatabaseMajorVersion());
    System.out.println("DB Minor Version = " + dbmd.getDatabaseMinorVersion());
    System.out.println("DB Product = " + dbmd.getDatabaseProductName());
    System.out.println("Driver Name = " + dbmd.getDriverName());
    System.out.println("Numeric function names for escape clause = " +
                        dbmd.getNumericFunctions());
    System.out.println("String function names for escape clause = " +
                        dbmd.getStringFunctions());
    System.out.println("System function names for escape clause = " +
                        dbmd.getSystemFunctions());
    System.out.println("Time/date function names for escape clause = " +
                        dbmd.getTimeDateFunctions());
    System.out.println("Catalog term: " + dbmd.getCatalogTerm());
    System.out.println("Schema term: " + dbmd.getSchemaTerm());
    System.out.println();
    System.out.println("Catalogs");
    System.out.println("--------");
    ResultSet rsCat = dbmd.getCatalogs();
    while (rsCat.next())
        System.out.println(rsCat.getString("TABLE_CAT"));
    System.out.println();
    System.out.println("Schemas");
    System.out.println("-------");
    ResultSet rsSchem = dbmd.getSchemas();
    while (rsSchem.next())
        System.out.println(rsSchem.getString("TABLE_SCHEM"));
    System.out.println();
    System.out.println("Schema/Table");
    System.out.println("------------");
    rsSchem = dbmd.getSchemas();
    while (rsSchem.next())
```

```
      {
         String schem = rsSchem.getString("TABLE_SCHEM");
         ResultSet rsTab = dbmd.getTables(null, schem, "%", null);
         while (rsTab.next())
            System.out.println(schem + " " + rsTab.getString("TABLE_NAME"));
      }
   }
}
```

Listing 14-5's dump() method invokes various methods on its dbmd argument to output assorted metadata.

The int getDatabaseMajorVersion() and int getDatabaseMinorVersion() methods return the major (e.g., 10) and minor (e.g., 8) parts of Java DB's version number. Similarly, String getDatabaseProductName() returns the name of this product (e.g., Apache Derby), and String getDriverName() returns the name of the driver (e.g., Apache Derby Embedded JDBC Driver).

SQL defines various functions that can be invoked as part of SELECT and other statements. For example, you can specify SELECT COUNT(*) AS TOTAL FROM EMPLOYEES to return a one-row-by-one-column result set with the column named TOTAL and the row value containing the number of rows in the EMPLOYEES table.

Because not all RDMSs adopt the same syntax for specifying function calls, JDBC uses a *function escape clause*, consisting of { fn *functionname*(*arguments*) }, to abstract over differences. For example, SELECT {fn UCASE(NAME)} FROM EMPLOYEES selects all NAME column values from EMPLOYEES and uppercases their values in the result set.

The String getNumericFunctions(), String getStringFunctions(), String getSystemFunctions(), and String getTimeDateFunctions() methods return lists of function names that can appear in function escape clauses. For example, getNumericFunctions() returns ABS,ACOS,ASIN,ATAN,ATAN2, CEILING,COS,COT,DEGREES,EXP,FLOOR,LOG,LOG10,MOD,PI,RADIANS,RAND,SIGN,SIN,SQRT,TAN for Java DB 10.8.

Not all vendors use the same terminology for catalog and schema. For this reason, the String getCatalogTerm() and String getSchemaTerm() methods are present to return the vendor-specific terms, which happen to be CATALOG and SCHEMA for Java DB 10.8.

The ResultSet getCatalogs() method returns a result set of catalog names, which are accessible via the result set's TABLE_CAT column. This result set is empty for Java DB 10.8, which divides a single default catalog into various schemas.

The ResultSet getSchemas() method returns a result set of schema names, which are accessible via the result set's TABLE_SCHEM column. This column contains APP, NULLID, SQLJ, SYS, SYSCAT, SYSCS_DIAG, SYSCS_UTIL, SYSFUN, SYSIBM, SYSPROC, and SYSSTAT values for Java DB 10.8. APP is the default schema in which a user's database objects are stored.

The ResultSet getTables(String catalog, String schemaPattern, String tableNamePattern, String[] types) method returns a result set containing table names (in the TABLE_NAME column) and other table-oriented metadata that match the specified catalog, schemaPattern, tableNamePattern, and types. To obtain a result set of all tables for a specific schema, pass null to catalog and types, the schema name to schemaPattern, and the % wildcard to tableNamePattern.

For example, the SYS schema stores SYSALIASES, SYSCHECKS, SYSCOLPERMS, SYSCOLUMNS, SYSCONGLOMERATES, SYSCONSTRAINTS, SYSDEPENDS, SYSFILES, SYSFOREIGNKEYS, SYSKEYS, SYSPERMS, SYSROLES, SYSROUTINEPERMS, SYSSCHEMAS, SYSSEQUENCES, SYSSTATEMENTS, SYSSTATISTICS, SYSTABLEPERMS, SYSTABLES, SYSTRIGGERS, and SYSVIEWS tables.

Listings 14-2 through 14-4 suffer from an architectural problem. After creating the EMPLOYEES table, suppose that SQLException is thrown before the table is dropped. The next time the JDBCDemo application runs (under Java DB), SQLException is thrown when the application attempts to recreate EMPLOYEES because this table already exists. You have to manually delete the employee directory before you can re-run JDBCDemo.

It would be nice to call an isExist() function before creating EMPLOYEES, but that function doesn't exist. However, you can create a same-named method with help from getTables(), and Listing 14-6 shows you how to accomplish this task.

Listing 14-6. Determining the Existence of Employee Before Creating This Table

```java
import java.sql.Connection;
import java.sql.DatabaseMetaData;
import java.sql.DriverManager;
import java.sql.ResultSet;
import java.sql.SQLException;
import java.sql.Statement;

public class JDBCDemo
{
   public static void main(String[] args)
   {
      String url = "jdbc:derby:employee;create=true";
      Connection con = null;
      try
      {
         con = DriverManager.getConnection(url);
         Statement stmt = null;
         try
         {
            stmt = con.createStatement();
            String sql;
            if (!isExist(con, "EMPLOYEES"))
            {
               System.out.println("EMPLOYEES doesn't exist");
               sql = "CREATE TABLE EMPLOYEES(ID INTEGER, NAME VARCHAR(30))";
               stmt.executeUpdate(sql);
            }
            else
               System.out.println("EMPLOYEES already exists");
            sql = "INSERT INTO EMPLOYEES VALUES(1, 'John Doe')";
            stmt.executeUpdate(sql);
            sql = "INSERT INTO EMPLOYEES VALUES(2, 'Sally Smith')";
            stmt.executeUpdate(sql);
            ResultSet rs = stmt.executeQuery("SELECT * FROM EMPLOYEES");
            while (rs.next())
```

```java
            System.out.println(rs.getInt("ID") + " " + rs.getString("NAME"));
            stmt.executeUpdate("DROP TABLE EMPLOYEES");
        }
        catch (SQLException sqlex)
        {
            while (sqlex != null)
            {
                System.err.println("SQL error : " + sqlex.getMessage());
                System.err.println("SQL state : " + sqlex.getSQLState());
                System.err.println("Error code: " + sqlex.getErrorCode());
                System.err.println("Cause: " + sqlex.getCause());
                sqlex = sqlex.getNextException();
            }
        }
        finally
        {
            if (stmt != null)
                try
                {
                    stmt.close();
                }
                catch (SQLException sqle)
                {
                    sqle.printStackTrace();
                }
        }
    }
    catch (SQLException sqlex)
    {
        while (sqlex != null)
        {
            System.err.println("SQL error : " + sqlex.getMessage());
            System.err.println("SQL state : " + sqlex.getSQLState());
            System.err.println("Error code: " + sqlex.getErrorCode());
            System.err.println("Cause: " + sqlex.getCause());
            sqlex = sqlex.getNextException();
        }
    }
    finally
    {
        if (con != null)
            try
            {
                con.close();
            }
            catch (SQLException sqle)
            {
                sqle.printStackTrace();
            }
    }
}
```

```
static boolean isExist(Connection con, String tableName) throws SQLException
{
   DatabaseMetaData dbmd = con.getMetaData();
   ResultSet rs = dbmd.getTables(null, "APP", tableName, null);
   return rs.next();
}
}
```

Listing 14-6 refactors Listing 14-2 (from a Java DB perspective only) by introducing a boolean isExist(Connection con, String tableName) class method, which returns true when tableName exists, and using this method to determine the existence of EMPLOYEES before creating this table.

When the specified table exists, a ResultSet object containing one row is returned, and ResultSet's next() method returns true. Otherwise, the result set contains no rows and next() returns false.

> **Caution**   isExist() assumes the default APP schema, which might not be the case when usernames are involved (each user's database objects are stored in a schema corresponding to the user's name).

EXERCISES

The following exercises are designed to test your understanding of Chapter 14's content:

1.   Define database.

2.   What is a relational database?

3.   Identify two other database categories.

4.   Define database management system.

5.   What is Java DB?

6.   True or false: Java DB's client driver causes the database engine to run in the same virtual machine as the application.

7.   What does setEmbeddedCP accomplish?

8.   True or false: You run Java DB's dblook command-line tool to view the Java environment/Java DB configuration.

9.   What is SQLite?

10.   Define manifest typing.

11.   What tool does SQLite provide for accessing and modifying SQLite databases?

12.   What is JDBC?

13.   Define data source.

14.   A JDBC driver implements what interface?

15. True or false: There are three kinds of JDBC drivers.

16. Describe a Type 3 JDBC driver.

17. What types does JDBC provide for communicating with a data source?

18. How do you obtain a connection to a Java DB data source via the embedded driver?

19. True or false: `String getSQLState()` returns a vendor-specific error code.

20. What is a SQL state error code?

21. What is the difference between `SQLNonTransientException` and `SQLTransientException`?

22. Identify JDBC's three statement types.

23. Which `Statement` method do you call to execute an SQL `SELECT` statement?

24. What does a result set's cursor accomplish?

25. To which Java type does the SQL `FLOAT` type map?

26. What does a prepared statement represent?

27. True or false: `CallableStatement` extends `PreparedStatement`.

28. Define stored procedure.

29. How do you call a stored procedure?

30. What is an escape clause?

31. Define metadata.

32. What does metadata include?

33. Refactor Listing 14-5 to output metadata for the SQLite driver as well as for the Java DB embedded driver.

Summary

A database is an organized collection of data. Although there are many kinds of databases (e.g., hierarchical, object oriented, and relational), relational databases, which organize data into tables that can be related to each other, are common.

Except for the most trivial of databases (e.g., Chapter 11's flat file database based on a single data file), databases are created and managed through a database management system. Relational DBMSs support SQL for working with tables and more.

First introduced by Sun Microsystems as part of JDK 6 (and not included in the JRE) to give developers an RDBMS to test their JDBC code, Java DB is a distribution of Apache's open-source Derby product, which is based on IBM's Cloudscape RDBMS code base.

Java DB is capable of running in an embedded environment or in a client/server environment. In an embedded environment, where an application accesses the database engine via Java DB's embedded driver, the database engine runs in the same virtual machine as the application.

In a client/server environment, client applications and the database engine run in separate virtual machines. A client application accesses the network server through Java DB's client driver. The network server, which runs in the same virtual machine as the database engine, accesses the database engine through the embedded driver.

SQLite is a self-contained, serverless, zero-configuration, transactional SQL database engine and is considered to be the most widely deployed database engine in the world. For example, SQLite is found in Mozilla Firefox, Google Chrome, and other web browsers. It's also found in Google Android, Apple iOS, and other mobile operating systems.

The sqlite3 executable offers a command-line shell for accessing and modifying SQLite databases. You can specify sqlite3 with a database filename argument to create the database file when it doesn't exist (you must create a table at least) or open the existing file and enter this tool's shell from where you can execute sqlite3-specific, dot-prefixed commands and SQL statements.

JDBC is an API for performing various database operations, such as submitting SQL statements that tell the RDBMS to create a table and to update or query tabular data. Although JDBC is typically used to communicate with RDBMSs, it also can be used to communicate with a flat file database. For this reason, JDBC uses the term data source to abstract the source of data.

Because data sources are accessed in different ways, JDBC uses drivers to abstract over their implementations. This abstraction lets you write an application that can be adapted to an arbitrary data source without having to change a single line of code (in most cases). Drivers are implementations of the java.sql.Driver interface. JDBC recognizes four types of drivers.

To connect to a data source and obtain a Connection instance, call one of DriverManager's getConnection() methods. With either method, the url argument specifies a string-based URL that starts with the jdbc: prefix and continues with data source-specific syntax.

DriverManager's getConnection() methods (and other JDBC methods in the various JDBC interfaces) throw SQLException or one of its subclasses when something goes wrong. Instances of this class provide vendor codes, SQL state strings, and other kinds of information.

After obtaining a connection to a data source, an application interacts with the data source by issuing SQL statements. JDBC supports SQL statements via the Statement, PreparedStatement, and CallableStatement interfaces.

The executeQuery() methods return a ResultSet object that provides access to a query's tabular results. Each result set is associated with a cursor that provides access to a specific row of data. The cursor initially points before the first row.

ResultSet also declares various methods for returning the current row's column values based on their types. For example, int getInt(String columnLabel) returns the integer value corresponding to the INTEGER-based column identified by columnLabel.

A prepared statement represents a precompiled SQL statement. The SQL statement is compiled to improve performance and prevent SQL injection, and the compiled result is stored in a PreparedStatement implementation instance.

A callable statement is a special kind of prepared statement for executing SQL stored procedures in which a stored procedure is a list of SQL statements that perform a specific task. The argument passed to a callable statement's prepareCall() method is specified using escape syntax.

A data source is typically associated with metadata that describes the data source. When the data source is an RDBMS, this data is typically stored in a collection of tables. Metadata includes a list of catalogs, base tables, views, indexes, schemas, and additional information.

Now that you've reached the end of this chapter, check out Appendixes A and B, which offer solutions to all exercises in Chapters 1 through 14 and introduce you to a card game application.

Solutions to Exercises

Each of Chapters 1 through 14 closes with an "Exercises" section that tests your understanding of the chapter's material. Solutions to these exercises are presented in this appendix.

Chapter 1: Getting Started with Java

1. Java is a language and a platform. The language is partly patterned after the C and C++ languages to shorten the learning curve for C/C++ developers. The platform consists of a virtual machine and associated execution environment.

2. A virtual machine is a software-based processor that presents its own instruction set.

3. The purpose of the Java compiler is to translate source code into instructions (and associated data) that are executed by the virtual machine.

4. The answer is true: a classfile's instructions are commonly referred to as bytecode.

5. When the virtual machine's interpreter learns that a sequence of bytecode instructions is being executed repeatedly, it informs the virtual machine's Just In Time (JIT) compiler to compile these instructions into native code.

6. The Java platform promotes portability by providing an abstraction over the underlying platform. As a result, the same bytecode runs unchanged on Windows-based, Linux-based, Mac OS X–based, and other platforms.

7. The Java platform promotes security by providing a secure environment in which code executes. It accomplishes this task in part by using a bytecode verifier to make sure that the classfile's bytecode is valid.

8. The answer is false: Java SE is the platform for developing applications and applets.

9. The JRE implements the Java SE platform and makes it possible to run Java programs.

10. The difference between the public and private JREs is that the public JRE exists apart from the JDK, whereas the private JRE is a component of the JDK that makes it possible to run Java programs independently of whether or not the public JRE is installed.

11. The JDK provides development tools (including a compiler) for developing Java programs. It also provides a private JRE for running these programs.

12. The JDK's `javac` tool is used to compile Java source code.

13. The JDK's `java` tool is used to run Java applications.

14. Standard I/O is a mechanism consisting of Standard Input, Standard Output, and Standard Error that makes it possible to read text from different sources (keyboard or file), write nonerror text to different destinations (screen or file), and write error text to different destinations (screen or file).

15. You specify the `main()` method's header as `public static void main(String[] args)`.

16. An IDE is a development framework consisting of a project manager for managing a project's files, a text editor for entering and editing source code, a debugger for locating bugs, and other features. The IDE that Google supports for developing Android apps is Eclipse.

Chapter 2: Learning Language Fundamentals

1. Unicode is a computing industry standard for consistently encoding, representing, and handling text that's expressed in most of the world's writing systems.

2. A comment is a language feature for embedding documentation in source code.

3. The three kinds of comments that Java supports are single-line, multiline, and Javadoc.

4. An identifier is a language feature that consists of letters (A–Z, a–z, or equivalent uppercase/lowercase letters in other human alphabets), digits (0–9 or equivalent digits in other human alphabets), connecting punctuation characters (e.g., the underscore), and currency symbols (e.g., the dollar sign $). This name must begin with a letter, a currency symbol, or a connecting punctuation character; and its length cannot exceed the line in which it appears.

5. The answer is false: Java is a case-sensitive language.

6. A type is a language feature that identifies a set of values (and their representation in memory) and a set of operations that transform these values into other values of that set.

7. A primitive type is a type that's defined by the language and whose values are not objects.

8. Java supports the Boolean, character, byte integer, short integer, integer, long integer, floating-point, and double precision floating-point primitive types.

9. A user-defined type is a type that's defined by the developer using a class, an interface, an enum, or an annotation type and whose values are objects.

10. An array type is a special reference type that signifies an array, a region of memory that stores values in equal-size and contiguous slots, which are commonly referred to as elements.

11. A variable is a named memory location that stores some type of value.

12. An expression is a combination of literals, variable names, method calls, and operators. At runtime, it evaluates to a value whose type is referred to as the expression's type.

13. The two expression categories are simple expression and compound expression.

14. A literal is a value specified verbatim.

15. String literal `"The quick brown fox \jumps\ over the lazy dog."` is illegal because, unlike `\"`, `\j` and `\` (a backslash followed by a space character) are not valid escape sequences. To make this string literal legal, you must escape these backslashes, as in `"The quick brown fox \\jumps\\ over the lazy dog."`.

16. An operator is a sequence of instructions symbolically represented in source code.

17. The difference between a prefix operator and a postfix operator is that a prefix operator precedes its operand and a postfix operator trails its operand.

18. The purpose of the cast operator is to convert from one type to another type. For example, you can use this operator to convert from floating-point type to 32-bit integer type.

19. Precedence refers to an operator's level of importance.

20. The answer is true: most of Java's operators are left-to-right associative.

21. A statement is a language feature that assigns a value to a variable, controls a program's flow by making a decision and/or repeatedly executing another statement, or performs another task.

22. The while statement evaluates its Boolean expression at the top of the loop, whereas the do-while statement evaluates its Boolean expression at the bottom of the loop. As a result, while executes zero or more times, whereas do-while executes one or more times.

23. The difference between the break and continue statements is that break transfers execution to the first statement following a switch statement or a loop, whereas continue skips the remainder of the current loop iteration, reevaluates the loop's Boolean expression, and performs another iteration (when true) or terminates the loop (when false).

24. Listing A-1 presents an OutputGradeLetter application (the class is named OutputGradeLetter) whose main() method executes the grade letter code sequence presented while discussing the if-else statement.

Listing A-1. Classifying a Grade

```
public class OutputGradeLetter
{
   public static void main(String[] args)
   {
      char gradeLetter = 'u'; // unknown
      int testMark = 100;

      if (testMark >= 90)
      {
         gradeLetter = 'A';
         System.out.println("You aced the test.");
      }
      else
      if (testMark >= 80)
      {
         gradeLetter = 'B';
         System.out.println("You did very well on this test.");
      }
      else
      if (testMark >= 70)
      {
         gradeLetter = 'C';
         System.out.println("Not bad, but you need to study more for future tests.");
      }
      else
      if (testMark >= 60)
      {
         gradeLetter = 'D';
         System.out.println("Your test result suggests that you need a tutor.");
      }
```

```
        else
        {
            gradeLetter = 'F';
            System.out.println("Your test result is pathetic; you need summer school.");
        }
    }
}
```

25. Listing A-2 presents a `Triangle` application whose `main()` method uses a pair of nested for statements along with `System.out.print()` to output a 10-row triangle of asterisks, where each row contains an odd number of asterisks (1, 3, 5, 7, and so on).

Listing A-2. Printing a Triangle of Asterisks

```
public class Triangle
{
    public static void main(String[] args)
    {
        for (int row = 1; row < 20; row += 2)
        {
            for (int col = 0; col < 19 - row / 2; col++)
                System.out.print(" ");
            for (int col = 0; col < row; col++)
                System.out.print("*");
            System.out.print('\n');
        }
    }
}
```

Chapter 3: Discovering Classes and Objects

1. A class is a template for manufacturing objects.

2. You declare a class by providing a header followed by a body. The header minimally consists of reserved word `class` followed by an identifier. The body consists of a sequence of declarations placed between a pair of brace characters.

3. An object is a named aggregate of code and data.

4. You instantiate an object by using the `new` operator followed by a constructor.

5. A constructor is a block of code for constructing an object by initializing it in some manner.

6. The answer is true: Java creates a default noargument constructor when a class declares no constructors.

7. A parameter list is a round bracket-delimited and comma-separated list of zero or more parameter declarations. A parameter is a constructor or method variable that receives an expression value passed to the constructor or method when it is called.

8. An argument list is a round bracket-delimited and comma-separated list of zero or more expressions. An argument is one of these expressions whose value is passed to the corresponding parameter when a constructor or method variable is called.

9. The answer is false: you invoke another constructor by specifying this followed by an argument list.

10. Arity is the number of arguments passed to a constructor or method or the number of operator operands.

11. A local variable is a variable that is declared in a constructor or method and is not a member of the constructor or method parameter list.

12. Lifetime is a property of a variable that determines how long the variable exists. For example, local variables and parameters come into existence when a constructor or method is called and are destroyed when the constructor or method finishes. Similarly, an instance field comes into existence when an object is created and is destroyed when the object is garbage collected.

13. Scope is a property of a variable that determines how accessible the variable is to code. For example, a parameter can be accessed only by the code within the constructor or method in which the parameter is declared.

14. Encapsulation refers to the merging of state and behaviors into a single source code entity. Instead of separating state and behaviors, which is done in structured programs, state and behaviors are combined into classes and objects, which are the focus of object-based programs. For example, whereas a structured program makes you think in terms of separate balance state and deposit/withdraw behaviors, an object-based program makes you think in terms of bank accounts, which unite balance state with deposit/withdraw behaviors through encapsulation.

15. A field is a variable declared within a class body.

16. The difference between an instance field and a class field is that an instance field describes some attribute of the real-world entity that an object is modeling and is unique to each object, and a class field identifies some data item that is shared by all objects.

17. A blank final is a read-only instance field. It differs from a true constant in that there are multiple copies of blank finals (one per object) and only one true constant (one per class).

18. You prevent a field from being shadowed by changing the name of a same-named local variable or parameter or by qualifying the local variable's name or parameter's name with `this` or the class name followed by the member access operator.

19. A method is a named block of code declared within a class body.

20. The difference between an instance method and a class method is that an instance method describes some behavior of the real-world entity that an object is modeling and can access a specific object's state, and a class method identifies some behavior that is common to all objects and cannot access a specific object's state.

21. Recursion is the act of a method invoking itself.

22. You overload a method by introducing a method with the same name as an existing method but with a different parameter list into the same class.

23. A class initializer is a `static`-prefixed block that is introduced into a class body. An instance initializer is a block that is introduced into a class body as opposed to being introduced as the body of a method or a constructor.

24. A garbage collector is code that runs in the background and occasionally checks for unreferenced objects.

25. The answer is false: `String[] letters = new String[2] { "A", "B" };` is incorrect syntax. Remove the 2 from between the square brackets to make it correct.

26. A ragged array is a two-dimensional array in which each row can have a different number of columns.

27. Calculating the greatest common divisor of two positive integers, which is the greatest positive integer that divides evenly into both positive integers, provides another example of tail recursion. Listing A-3 presents the source code.

Listing A-3. Recursively Calculating the Greatest Common Divisor

```
public static int gcd(int a, int b)
{
    // The greatest common divisor is the largest positive integer that
    // divides evenly into two positive integers a and b. For example,
    // GCD(12, 18) is 6.

    if (b == 0) // Base problem
        return a;
    else
        return gcd(b, a % b);
}
```

28. Listing A-4 presents the source code to a Book class with name, author, and
International Standard Book Number (ISBN) fields and a suitable constructor
and getter methods that return field values. Furthermore, a main() method
is present that creates an array of Book objects and iterates over this array
outputting each book's name, author, and ISBN.

Listing A-4. Building a Library of Books

```
public class Book
{
   private String name;
   private String author;
   private String isbn;

   public Book(String name, String author, String isbn)
   {
      this.name = name;
      this.author = author;
      this.isbn = isbn;
   }

   public String getName()
   {
      return name;
   }

   public String getAuthor()
   {
      return author;
   }

   public String getISBN()
   {
      return isbn;
   }

   public static void main(String[] args)
   {
      Book[] books = new Book[]
                   {
                       new Book("Jane Eyre",
                               "Charlotte Brontë",
                               "0895772000"),
                       new Book("A Kick in the Seat of the Pants",
                               "Roger von Oech",
                               "0060155280"),
                       new Book("The Prince and the Pilgrim",
                               "Mary Stewart",
                               "0340649925")
                   };
```

```
        for (int i = 0; i < books.length; i++)
            System.out.println(books[i].getName() + " - " +
                                    books[i].getAuthor() + " - " +
                                    books[i].getISBN());
    }
}
```

Chapter 4: Discovering Inheritance, Polymorphism, and Interfaces

1. Implementation inheritance is inheritance through class extension.

2. Java supports implementation inheritance by providing reserved word extends.

3. A subclass can have only one superclass because Java doesn't support multiple implementation inheritance.

4. You prevent a class from being subclassed by declaring the class final.

5. The answer is false: the super() call can only appear in a constructor.

6. If a superclass declares a constructor with one or more parameters, and if a subclass constructor doesn't use super() to call that constructor, the compiler reports an error because the subclass constructor attempts to call a nonexistent noargument constructor in the superclass. (When a class doesn't declare any constructors, the compiler creates a constructor with no parameters [a noargument constructor] for that class. Therefore, if the superclass didn't declare any constructors, a noargument constructor would be created for the superclass. Continuing, if the subclass constructor didn't use super() to call the superclass constructor, the compiler would insert the call and there would be no error.)

7. An immutable class is a class whose instances cannot be modified.

8. The answer is false: a class cannot inherit constructors.

9. Overriding a method means to replace an inherited method with another method that provides the same signature and the same return type but provides a new implementation.

10. To call a superclass method from its overriding subclass method, prefix the superclass method name with reserved word super and the member access operator in the method call.

11. You prevent a method from being overridden by declaring the method final.

12. You cannot make an overriding subclass method less accessible than the superclass method it is overriding because subtype polymorphism would not work properly if subclass methods could be made less accessible. Suppose you upcast a subclass instance to superclass type by assigning the instance's reference to a variable of superclass type. Now suppose you specify a superclass method call on the variable. If this method is overridden by the subclass, the subclass version of the method is called. However, if access to the subclass's overriding method's access could be made private, calling this method would break encapsulation—private methods cannot be called directly from outside of their class.

13. You tell the compiler that a method overrides another method by prefixing the overriding method's header with the @Override annotation.

14. Java doesn't support multiple implementation inheritance because this form of inheritance can lead to ambiguities.

15. The name of Java's ultimate superclass is `Object`. This class is located in the `java.lang` package.

16. The purpose of the `clone()` method is to duplicate an object without calling a constructor.

17. `Object`'s `clone()` method throws `CloneNotSupportedException` when the class whose instance is to be shallowly cloned doesn't implement the `Cloneable` interface.

18. The difference between shallow copying and deep copying is that shallow copying copies each primitive or reference field's value to its counterpart in the clone, whereas deep copying creates, for each reference field, a new object and assigns its reference to the field. This deep copying process continues recursively for these newly created objects.

19. The `==` operator cannot be used to determine if two objects are logically equivalent because this operator only compares object references and not the contents of these objects.

20. `Object`'s `equals()` method compares the current object's `this` reference to the reference passed as an argument to this method. (When I refer to `Object`'s `equals()` method, I am referring to the `equals()` method in the `Object` class.)

21. Expression `"abc" == "a" + "bc"` returns true. It does so because the `String` class contains special support that allows literal strings and string-valued constant expressions to be compared via `==`.

22. You can optimize a time-consuming `equals()` method by first using `==` to determine if this method's reference argument identifies the current object (which is represented in source code via reserved word `this`).

23. The purpose of the `finalize()` method is to provide a safety net for calling an object's cleanup method in case that method is not called.

24. You should not rely on `finalize()` for closing open files because file descriptors are a limited resource and an application might not be able to open additional files until `finalize()` is called, and this method might be called infrequently (or perhaps not at all).

25. A hash code is a small value that results from applying a mathematical function to a potentially large amount of data.

26. The answer is true: you should override the `hashCode()` method whenever you override the `equals()` method.

27. `Object`'s `toString()` method returns a string representation of the current object that consists of the object's class name, followed by the @ symbol, followed by a hexadecimal representation of the object's hash code. (When I refer to `Object`'s `toString()` method, I am referring to the `toString()` method in the `Object` class.)

28. You should override `toString()` to provide a concise but meaningful description of the object to facilitate debugging via `System.out.println()` method calls. It is more informative for `toString()` to reveal object state than to reveal a class name, followed by the @ symbol, followed by a hexadecimal representation of the object's hash code.

29. Composition is a way to reuse code by composing classes out of other classes based on a "has-a" relationship between them.

30. The answer is false: composition is used to describe "has-a" relationships and implementation inheritance is used to describe "is-a" relationships.

31. The fundamental problem of implementation inheritance is that it breaks encapsulation. You fix this problem by ensuring that you have control over the superclass as well as its subclasses by ensuring that the superclass is designed and documented for extension or by using a wrapper class in lieu of a subclass when you would otherwise extend the superclass.

32. Subtype polymorphism is a kind of polymorphism where a subtype instance appears in a supertype context, and executing a supertype operation on the subtype instance results in the subtype's version of that operation executing.

33. Subtype polymorphism is accomplished by upcasting the subtype instance to its supertype; by assigning the instance's reference to a variable of that type; and, via this variable, calling a superclass method that has been overridden in the subclass.

34. You would use abstract classes and abstract methods to describe generic concepts (e.g., shape, animal, or vehicle) and generic operations (e.g., drawing a generic shape). Abstract classes cannot be instantiated and abstract methods cannot be called because they have no code bodies.

35. An abstract class can contain concrete methods.

36. The purpose of downcasting is to access subtype features. For example, you would downcast a `Point` variable that contains a `Circle` instance reference to the `Circle` type so that you can call `Circle`'s `getRadius()` method on the instance.

37. Two forms of RTTI are the virtual machine verifying that a cast is legal and using the `instanceof` operator to determine whether or not an instance is a member of a type.

38. A covariant return type is a method return type that, in the superclass's method declaration, is the supertype of the return type in the subclass's overriding method declaration.

39. You formally declare an interface by specifying at least reserved word `interface`, followed by a name, followed by a brace-delimited body of constants and/or method headers.

40. The answer is true: you can precede an interface declaration with the `abstract` reserved word. However, doing so is redundant.

41. A marker interface is an interface that declares no members.

42. Interface inheritance is inheritance through interface implementation or interface extension.

43. You implement an interface by appending an implements clause, consisting of reserved word `implements` followed by the interface's name, to a class header and by overriding the interface's method headers in the class.

44. You might encounter one or more name collisions when you implement multiple interfaces.

45. You form a hierarchy of interfaces by appending reserved word `extends` followed by an interface name to an interface header.

46. Java's interfaces feature is so important because it gives developers the utmost flexibility in designing their applications.

47. Interfaces and abstract classes describe abstract types.

48. Interfaces and abstract classes differ in that interfaces can only declare abstract methods and constants and can be implemented by any class in any class hierarchy. In contrast, abstract classes can declare constants and nonconstant fields; can declare abstract and concrete methods; and can only appear in the upper levels of class hierarchies, where they are used to describe abstract concepts and behaviors.

49. Listings A-5 through A-11 declare the Animal, Bird, Fish, AmericanRobin, DomesticCanary, RainbowTrout, and SockeyeSalmon classes that were called for in Chapter 4.

Listing A-5. The Animal Class Abstracting Over Birds and Fish (and Other Organisms)

```java
public abstract class Animal
{
   private String kind;
   private String appearance;

   public Animal(String kind, String appearance)
   {
      this.kind = kind;
      this.appearance = appearance;
   }

   public abstract void eat();

   public abstract void move();

   @Override
   public final String toString()
   {
      return kind + " -- " + appearance;
   }
}
```

Listing A-6. The Bird Class Abstracting Over American Robins, Domestic Canaries, and Other Kinds of Birds

```java
public abstract class Bird extends Animal
{
   public Bird(String kind, String appearance)
   {
      super(kind, appearance);
   }

   @Override
   public final void eat()
   {
      System.out.println("eats seeds and insects");
   }

   @Override
   public final void move()
   {
      System.out.println("flies through the air");
   }
}
```

Listing A-7. The Fish Class Abstracting Over Rainbow Trout, Sockeye Salmon, and Other Kinds of Fish

```java
public abstract class Fish extends Animal
{
   public Fish(String kind, String appearance)
   {
      super(kind, appearance);
   }

   @Override
   public final void eat()
   {
      System.out.println("eats krill, algae, and insects");
   }

   @Override
   public final void move()
   {
      System.out.println("swims through the water");
   }
}
```

Listing A-8. The AmericanRobin Class Denoting a Bird with a Red Breast

```java
public final class AmericanRobin extends Bird
{
   public AmericanRobin()
   {
      super("americanrobin", "red breast");
   }
}
```

Listing A-9. The DomesticCanary Class Denoting a Bird of Various Colors

```java
public final class DomesticCanary extends Bird
{
   public DomesticCanary()
   {
      super("domestic canary", "yellow, orange, black, brown, white, red");
   }
}
```

Listing A-10. The RainbowTrout Class Denoting a Rainbow-Colored Fish

```java
public final class RainbowTrout extends Fish
{
   public RainbowTrout()
   {
      super("rainbowtrout", "bands of brilliant speckled multicolored " +
            "stripes running nearly the whole length of its body");
   }
}
```

Listing A-11. The SockeyeSalmon Class Denoting a Red-and-Green Fish

```
public final class SockeyeSalmon extends Fish
{
   public SockeyeSalmon()
   {
      super("sockeyesalmon", "bright red with a green head");
   }
}
```

Animal's toString() method is declared final because it doesn't make sense to override this method, which is complete in this example. Also, each of Bird's and Fish's overriding eat() and move() methods is declared final because it doesn't make sense to override these methods in this example, which assumes that all birds eat seeds and insects; all fish eat krill, algae, and insects; all birds fly through the air; and all fish swim through the water.

The AmericanRobin, DomesticCanary, RainbowTrout, and SockeyeSalmon classes are declared final because they represent the bottom of the Bird and Fish class hierarchies, and it doesn't make sense to subclass them.

50. Listing A-12 declares the Animals class that was called for in Chapter 4.

Listing A-12. The Animals Class Letting Animals Eat and Move

```
public class Animals
{
   public static void main(String[] args)
   {
      Animal[] animals = { new AmericanRobin(), new RainbowTrout(),
                           new DomesticCanary(), new SockeyeSalmon() };
      for (int i = 0; i < animals.length; i++)
      {
         System.out.println(animals[i]);
         animals[i].eat();
         animals[i].move();
         System.out.println();
      }
   }
}
```

51. Listings A-13 through A-15 declare the Countable interface, the modified Animal class, and the modified Animals class that were called for in Chapter 4.

Listing A-13. The Countable Interface for Use in Taking a Census of Animals

```
public interface Countable
{
   String getID();
}
```

Listing A-14. The Refactored Animal Class for Help in Census Taking

```java
public abstract class Animal implements Countable
{
   private String kind;
   private String appearance;

   public Animal(String kind, String appearance)
   {
      this.kind = kind;
      this.appearance = appearance;
   }

   public abstract void eat();

   public abstract void move();

   @Override
   public final String toString()
   {
      return kind + " -- " + appearance;
   }

   @Override
   public final String getID()
   {
      return kind;
   }
}
```

Listing A-15. The Modified Animals Class for Carrying Out the Census

```java
public class Animals
{
   public static void main(String[] args)
   {
      Animal[] animals = { new AmericanRobin(), new RainbowTrout(),
                           new DomesticCanary(), new SockeyeSalmon(),
                           new RainbowTrout(), new AmericanRobin() };
      for (int i = 0; i < animals.length; i++)
      {
         System.out.println(animals[i]);
         animals[i].eat();
         animals[i].move();
         System.out.println();
      }

      Census census = new Census();
      Countable[] countables = (Countable[]) animals;
      for (int i = 0; i < countables.length; i++)
         census.update(countables[i].getID());
```

```
            for (int i = 0; i < Census.SIZE; i++)
                System.out.println(census.get(i));
        }
    }
```

Chapter 5: Mastering Advanced Language Features Part 1

1. A nested class is a class that is declared as a member of another class or scope.

2. The four kinds of nested classes are static member classes, nonstatic member classes, anonymous classes, and local classes.

3. Nonstatic member classes, anonymous classes, and local classes are also known as inner classes.

4. The answer is false: a static member class doesn't have an enclosing instance.

5. You instantiate a nonstatic member class from beyond its enclosing class by first instantiating the enclosing class and then prefixing the new operator with the enclosing class instance as you instantiate the enclosed class. Example: new EnclosingClass().new EnclosedClass().

6. It's necessary to declare local variables and parameters final when they are being accessed by an instance of an anonymous class or a local class.

7. The answer is true: an interface can be declared within a class or within another interface.

8. A package is a unique namespace that can contain a combination of top-level classes, other top-level types, and subpackages.

9. You ensure that package names are unique by specifying your reversed Internet domain name as the top-level package name.

10. A package statement is a statement that identifies the package in which a source file's types are located.

11. The answer is false: you cannot specify multiple package statements in a source file.

12. An import statement is a statement that imports types from a package by telling the compiler where to look for unqualified type names during compilation.

13. You indicate that you want to import multiple types via a single import statement by specifying the wildcard character (*).

14. During a runtime search, the virtual machine reports a "no class definition found" error when it cannot find a classfile.

15. You specify the user classpath to the virtual machine via the `-classpath` option used to start the virtual machine or, when not present, the `CLASSPATH` environment variable.

16. A constant interface is an interface that only exports constants.

17. Constant interfaces are used to avoid having to qualify their names with their classes.

18. Constant interfaces are bad because their constants are nothing more than an implementation detail that should not be allowed to leak into the class's exported interface because they might confuse the class's users (what is the purpose of these constants?). Also, they represent a future commitment: even when the class no longer uses these constants, the interface must remain to ensure binary compatibility.

19. A static import statement is a version of the import statement that lets you import a class's static members so that you don't have to qualify them with their class names.

20. You specify a static import statement as `import`, followed by `static`, followed by a member access operator–separated list of package and subpackage names, followed by the member access operator, followed by a class's name, followed by the member access operator, followed by a single static member name or the asterisk wildcard, for example, `import static java.lang.Math.cos;` (import the `cos()` static method from the `Math` class).

21. An exception is a divergence from an application's normal behavior.

22. Objects are superior to error codes for representing exceptions because error code Boolean or integer values are less meaningful than object names and because objects can contain information about what led to the exception. These details can be helpful to a suitable workaround. Furthermore, error codes are easy to ignore.

23. A throwable is an instance of `Throwable` or one of its subclasses.

24. The `getCause()` method returns an exception that is wrapped inside another exception.

25. `Exception` describes exceptions that result from external factors (e.g., not being able to open a file) and from flawed code (e.g., passing an illegal argument to a method). `Error` describes virtual machine-oriented exceptions such as running out of memory or being unable to load a classfile.

26. A checked exception is an exception that represents a problem with the possibility of recovery and for which the developer must provide a workaround.

27. A runtime exception is an exception that represents a coding mistake.

28. You would introduce your own exception class when no existing exception class in the standard class library meets your needs.

29. The answer is false: you use a throws clause to identify exceptions that are thrown from a method by appending this clause to a method's header.

30. The purpose of a try statement is to provide a scope (via its brace-delimited body) in which to present code that can throw exceptions. The purpose of a catch block is to receive a thrown exception and provide code (via its brace-delimited body) that handles that exception by providing a workaround.

31. The purpose of a finally block is to provide cleanup code that is executed whether an exception is thrown or not.

32. Listing A-16 presents the G2D class that was called for in Chapter 5.

Listing A-16. The G2D Class with Its Matrix Nonstatic Member Class

```
public class G2D
{
   private Matrix xform;

   public G2D()
   {
      xform = new Matrix();
      xform.a = 1.0;
      xform.e = 1.0;
      xform.i = 1.0;
   }

   private class Matrix
   {
      double a, b, c;
      double d, e, f;
      double g, h, i;
   }
}
```

33. To extend the logging package (presented in Chapter 5's discussion of packages) to support a null device in which messages are thrown away, first introduce Listing A-17's NullDevice package-private class.

Listing A-17. Implementing the Proverbial "Bit Bucket" Class

```
package logging;

class NullDevice implements Logger
{
   private String dstName;
```

```
            NullDevice(String dstName)
            {
            }

            public boolean connect()
            {
               return true;
            }

            public boolean disconnect()
            {
               return true;
            }

            public boolean log(String msg)
            {
               return true;
            }
        }
```

Continue by introducing, into the LoggerFactory class, a NULLDEVICE constant and code that instantiates NullDevice with a null argument—a destination name is not required—when newLogger()'s dstType parameter contains this constant's value. Check out Listing A-18.

Listing A-18. A Refactored LoggerFactory Class

```
package logging;

public abstract class LoggerFactory
{
   public final static int CONSOLE = 0;
   public final static int FILE = 1;
   public final static int NULLDEVICE = 2;

   public static Logger newLogger(int dstType, String...dstName)
   {
      switch (dstType)
      {
         case CONSOLE   : return new Console(dstName.length == 0 ? null
                                                                 : dstName[0]);
         case FILE      : return new File(dstName.length == 0 ? null
                                                              : dstName[0]);
         case NULLDEVICE: return new NullDevice(null);
         default        : return null;
      }
   }
}
```

34. Modifying the `logging` package (presented in Chapter 5's discussion of packages) so that `Logger`'s `connect()` method throws a `CannotConnectException` instance when it cannot connect to its logging destination, and the other two methods each throw a `NotConnectedException` instance when `connect()` was not called or when it threw a `CannotConnectException` instance, results in Listing A-19's `Logger` interface.

Listing A-19. A Logger Interface Whose Methods Throw Exceptions

```
package logging;

public interface Logger
{
    void connect() throws CannotConnectException;
    void disconnect() throws NotConnectedException;
    void log(String msg) throws NotConnectedException;
}
```

Listing A-20 presents the `CannotConnectException` class.

Listing A-20. An Uncomplicated CannotConnectException Class

```
package logging;

public class CannotConnectException extends Exception
{
}
```

The `NotConnectedException` class has the same structure but with a different name.

Listing A-21 presents the `Console` class.

Listing A-21. The Console Class Satisfying Logger's Contract Without Throwing Exceptions

```
package logging;

class Console implements Logger
{
    private String dstName;

    Console(String dstName)
    {
        this.dstName = dstName;
    }

    public void connect() throws CannotConnectException
    {
    }

    public void disconnect() throws NotConnectedException
    {
    }
```

```java
    public void log(String msg) throws NotConnectedException
    {
        System.out.println(msg);
    }
}
```

Listing A-22 presents the File class.

Listing A-22. The File Class Satisfying Logger's Contract by Throwing Exceptions As Necessary

```java
package logging;

class File implements Logger
{
    private String dstName;

    File(String dstName)
    {
        this.dstName = dstName;
    }

    public void connect() throws CannotConnectException
    {
        if (dstName == null)
            throw new CannotConnectException();
    }

    public void disconnect() throws NotConnectedException
    {
        if (dstName == null)
            throw new NotConnectedException();
    }

    public void log(String msg) throws NotConnectedException
    {
        if (dstName == null)
            throw new NotConnectedException();
        System.out.println("writing " + msg + " to file " + dstName);
    }
}
```

35. When you modify TestLogger to respond appropriately to thrown
    CannotConnectException and NotConnectedException objects, you end up
    with something similar to Listing A-23.

    Listing A-23. A TestLogger Class That Handles Thrown Exceptions

```java
import logging.*;

public class TestLogger
{
    public static void main(String[] args)
```

```
    {
        try
        {
            Logger logger = LoggerFactory.newLogger(LoggerFactory.CONSOLE);
            logger.connect();
            logger.log("test message #1");
            logger.disconnect();
        }
        catch (CannotConnectException cce)
        {
            System.err.println("cannot connect to console-based logger");
        }
        catch (NotConnectedException nce)
        {
            System.err.println("not connected to console-based logger");
        }

        try
        {
            Logger logger = LoggerFactory.newLogger(LoggerFactory.FILE, "x.txt");
            logger.connect();
            logger.log("test message #2");
            logger.disconnect();
        }
        catch (CannotConnectException cce)
        {
            System.err.println("cannot connect to file-based logger");
        }
        catch (NotConnectedException nce)
        {
            System.err.println("not connected to file-based logger");
        }

        try
        {
            Logger logger = LoggerFactory.newLogger(LoggerFactory.FILE);
            logger.connect();
            logger.log("test message #3");
            logger.disconnect();
        }
        catch (CannotConnectException cce)
        {
            System.err.println("cannot connect to file-based logger");
        }
        catch (NotConnectedException nce)
        {
            System.err.println("not connected to file-based logger");
        }
    }
}
```

Chapter 6: Mastering Advanced Language Features Part 2

1. An assertion is a statement that lets you express an assumption of program correctness via a Boolean expression.

2. You would use assertions to validate internal invariants, control-flow invariants, preconditions, postconditions, and class invariants.

3. The answer is false: specifying the -ea command-line option with no argument enables all assertions except for system assertions.

4. An annotation is an instance of an annotation type and associates metadata with an application element. It's expressed in source code by prefixing the type name with the @ symbol.

5. Constructors, fields, local variables, methods, packages, parameters, and types (annotation, class, enum, and interface) can be annotated.

6. The three compiler-supported annotation types are Override, Deprecated, and SuppressWarnings.

7. You declare an annotation type by specifying the @ symbol, immediately followed by reserved word interface, followed by the type's name, followed by a body.

8. A marker annotation is an instance of an annotation type that supplies no data apart from its name—the type's body is empty.

9. An element is a method header that appears in the annotation type's body. It cannot have parameters or a throws clause. Its return type must be primitive (e.g., int), String, Class, an enum type, an annotation type, or an array of the preceding types. It can have a default value.

10. You assign a default value to an element by specifying default followed by the value, whose type must match the element's return type. For example, String developer() default "unassigned";.

11. A meta-annotation is an annotation that annotates an annotation type.

12. Java's four meta-annotation types are Target, Retention, Documented, and Inherited.

13. Generics can be defined as a suite of language features for declaring and using type-agnostic classes and interfaces.

14. You would use generics to ensure that your code is typesafe by avoiding thrown ClassCastExceptions.

15. The difference between a generic type and a parameterized type is that a generic type is a class or interface that introduces a family of parameterized types by declaring a formal type parameter list, and a parameterized type is an instance of a generic type.

16. Anonymous classes cannot be generic because they have no names.

17. The five kinds of actual type arguments are concrete types, concrete parameterized types, array types, type parameters, and wildcards.

18. The answer is true: you cannot specify a primitive-type name (e.g., `double` or `int`) as an actual type argument.

19. A raw type is a generic type without its type parameters.

20. The compiler reports an unchecked warning message when it detects an explicit cast that involves a type parameter. The compiler is concerned that downcasting to whatever type is passed to the type parameter might result in a violation of type safety.

21. You suppress an unchecked warning message by prefixing the constructor or method that contains the unchecked code with the `@SuppressWarnings("unchecked")` annotation.

22. The answer is true: `List<E>`'s `E` type parameter is unbounded.

23. You specify a single upper bound via reserved word `extends` followed by a type name.

24. A recursive type bound is a type parameter bound that includes the type parameter.

25. Wildcard type arguments are necessary because by accepting any actual type argument, they provide a typesafe workaround to the problem of polymorphic behavior not applying to multiple parameterized types that differ only in regard to one type parameter being a subtype of another type parameter. For example, because `List<String>` is not a kind of `List<Object>`, you cannot pass an object whose type is `List<String>` to a method parameter whose type is `List<Object>`. However, you can pass a `List<String>` object to `List<?>` provided that you are not going to add the `List<String>` object to the `List<?>`.

26. A generic method is a class or instance method with a type-generalized implementation.

27. Although you might think otherwise, Listing 6-36's `methodCaller()` generic method calls `someOverloadedMethod(Object o)`. This method, instead of `someOverloadedMethod(Date d)`, is called because overload resolution happens at compile time, when the generic method is translated to its unique bytecode representation, and erasure (which takes care of that mapping) causes type parameters to be replaced by their leftmost bound or `Object` (when there is no bound). After erasure, you are left with Listing A-24's nongeneric `methodCaller()` method.

Listing A-24. The Nongeneric methodCaller() Method That Results from Erasure

```
public static void methodCaller(Object t)
{
    someOverloadedMethod(t);
}
```

28. Reification is representing the abstract as if it was concrete.

29. The answer is false: type parameters are not reified.

30. Erasure is the throwing away of type parameters following compilation so that they are not available at runtime. Erasure also involves replacing uses of other type variables by the upper bound of the type variable (e.g., Object) and inserting casts to the appropriate type when the resulting code is not type correct.

31. An enumerated type is a type that specifies a named sequence of related constants as its legal values.

32. Three problems that can arise when you use enumerated types whose constants are int-based are lack of compile-time type safety, brittle applications, and the inability to translate int constants into meaningful string-based descriptions.

33. An enum is an enumerated type that is expressed via reserved word enum.

34. You use a switch statement with an enum by specifying an enum constant as the statement's selector expression and constant names as case values.

35. You can enhance an enum by adding fields, constructors, and methods— you can even have the enum implement interfaces. Also, you can override toString() to provide a more useful description of a constant's value and subclass constants to assign different behaviors.

36. The purpose of the abstract Enum class is to serve as the common base class of all Java language-based enumeration types.

37. The difference between Enum's name() and toString() methods is that name() always returns a constant's name, but toString() can be overridden to return a more meaningful description instead of the constant's name.

38. The answer is true: Enum's generic type is Enum<E extends Enum<E>>.

39. Listing A-25 presents a ToDo marker annotation type that annotates only type elements and that also uses the default retention policy.

Listing A-25. The ToDo Annotation Type for Marking Types That Need to Be Completed

```
import java.lang.annotation.ElementType;
import java.lang.annotation.Target;
```

```
@Target(ElementType.TYPE)
public @interface ToDo
{
}
```

40. Listing A-26 presents a rewritten StubFinder application that works with Listing 6-13's Stub annotation type (with appropriate @Target and @Retention annotations) and Listing 6-14's Deck class.

Listing A-26. Reporting a Stub's ID, Due Date, and Developer via a New Version of StubFinder

```
import java.lang.reflect.Method;

public class StubFinder
{
   public static void main(String[] args) throws Exception
   {
      if (args.length != 1)
      {
         System.err.println("usage: java StubFinder classfile");
         return;
      }
      Method[] methods = Class.forName(args[0]).getMethods();
      for (int i = 0; i < methods.length; i++)
         if (methods[i].isAnnotationPresent(Stub.class))
         {
            Stub stub = methods[i].getAnnotation(Stub.class);
            System.out.println("Stub ID = " + stub.id());
            System.out.println("Stub Date = " + stub.dueDate());
            System.out.println("Stub Developer = " + stub.developer());
            System.out.println();
         }
   }
}
```

41. Listing A-27 presents the generic Stack class and the StackEmptyException and StackFullException helper classes that were called for in Chapter 6.

Listing A-27. Stack and Its StackEmptyException and StackFullException Helper Classes Proving That Not All Helper Classes Need to Be Nested

```
public class Stack<E>
{
   private E[] elements;
   private int top;

   @SuppressWarnings("unchecked")
   Stack(int size)
   {
      if (size < 2)
         throw new IllegalArgumentException("" + size);
```

```java
        elements = (E[]) new Object[size];
        top = -1;
    }

    void push(E element) throws StackFullException
    {
        if (top == elements.length - 1)
            throw new StackFullException();
        elements[++top] = element;
    }

    E pop() throws StackEmptyException
    {
        if (isEmpty())
            throw new StackEmptyException();
        return elements[top--];
    }

    boolean isEmpty()
    {
        return top == -1;
    }

    public static void main(String[] args)
        throws StackFullException, StackEmptyException
    {
        Stack<String> stack = new Stack<String>(5);
        assert stack.isEmpty();
        stack.push("A");
        stack.push("B");
        stack.push("C");
        stack.push("D");
        stack.push("E");
        // Uncomment the following line to generate a StackFullException.
        //stack.push("F");
        while (!stack.isEmpty())
            System.out.println(stack.pop());
        // Uncomment the following line to generate a StackEmptyException.
        //stack.pop();
        assert stack.isEmpty();
    }
}

class StackEmptyException extends Exception
{
}

class StackFullException extends Exception
{
}
```

42.   Listing A-28 presents the Compass enum that was called for in Chapter 6.

Listing A-28. A Compass Enum with Four Direction Constants

```
enum Compass
{
   NORTH, SOUTH, EAST, WEST
}
```

Listing A-29 presents the UseCompass class that was called for in Chapter 6.

Listing A-29. Using the Compass Enum to Keep from Getting Lost

```
public class UseCompass
{
   public static void main(String[] args)
   {
      int i = (int) (Math.random() * 4);
      Compass[] dir = { Compass.NORTH, Compass.EAST, Compass.SOUTH,
                        Compass.WEST };
      switch(dir[i])
      {
         case NORTH: System.out.println("heading north"); break;
         case EAST : System.out.println("heading east"); break;
         case SOUTH: System.out.println("heading south"); break;
         case WEST : System.out.println("heading west"); break;
         default   : assert false; // Should never be reached.
      }
   }
}
```

Chapter 7: Exploring the Basic APIs Part 1

1.   Math declares double constants E and PI that represent, respectively, the natural logarithm base value (2.71828. . .) and the ratio of a circle's circumference to its diameter (3.14159. . .). E is initialized to 2.718281828459045 and PI is initialized to 3.141592653589793.

2.   Math.abs(Integer.MIN_VALUE) equals Integer.MIN_VALUE because there doesn't exist a positive 32-bit integer equivalent of MIN_VALUE. (Integer.MIN_VALUE equals -2147483648 and Integer.MAX_VALUE equals 2147483647.)

3.   Math's random() method returns a pseudorandom number between 0.0 (inclusive) and 1.0 (exclusive). Expression (int) Math.random() * limit is incorrect because this expression always returns 0. The (int) cast operator has higher precedence than *, which means that the cast is performed before multiplication. random() returns a fractional value and the cast converts this value to 0, which is then multiplied by limit's value, resulting in an overall value of 0.

4. The five special values that can arise during floating-point calculations are +infinity, –infinity, NaN, +0.0, and –0.0.

5. Math and StrictMath differ in the following ways:

    ■   StrictMath's methods return exactly the same results on all platforms. In contrast, some of Math's methods might return values that vary ever so slightly from platform to platform.

    ■   Because StrictMath cannot utilize platform-specific features such as an extended-precision math coprocessor, an implementation of StrictMath might be less efficient than an implementation of Math.

6. The purpose of strictfp is to restrict floating-point calculations to ensure portability. This reserved word accomplishes portability in the context of intermediate floating-point representations and overflows/underflows (generating a value too large or small to fit a representation). Furthermore, it can be applied at the method level or at the class level.

7. BigDecimal is an immutable class that represents a signed decimal number (e.g., 23.653) of arbitrary precision (number of digits) with an associated scale (an integer that specifies the number of digits after the decimal point). You might use this class to accurately store floating-point values that represent monetary values and properly round the result of each monetary calculation.

8. The RoundingMode constant that describes the form of rounding commonly taught at school is HALF_UP.

9. BigInteger is an immutable class that represents a signed integer of arbitrary precision. It stores its value in two's complement format (all bits are flipped—1s to 0s and 0s to 1s—and 1 has been added to the result to be compatible with the two's complement format used by Java's byte integer, short integer, integer, and long integer types).

10. The answer is true: a string literal is a String object.

11. The purpose of String's intern() method is to store a unique copy of a String object in an internal table of String objects. intern() makes it possible to compare strings via their references and == or !=. These operators are the fastest way to compare strings, which is especially valuable when sorting a huge number of strings.

12. String and StringBuffer differ in that String objects contain immutable sequences of characters, whereas StringBuffer objects contain mutable sequences of characters.

13. StringBuffer and StringBuilder differ in that StringBuffer methods are synchronized, whereas StringBuilder's equivalent methods are not synchronized. As a result, you would use the thread-safe but slower StringBuffer class in multithreaded situations and the nonthread-safe but faster StringBuilder class in single-threaded situations.

14. The purpose of Package's isSealed() method is to indicate whether or not a package is sealed (all classes that are part of the package are archived in the same JAR file). This method returns true when the package is sealed.

15. The answer is true: getPackage() requires at least one classfile to be loaded from the package before it returns a Package object describing that package.

16. Listing A-30 presents the PrimeNumberTest application that was called for in Chapter 7.

    Listing A-30. Checking a Positive Integer Argument to Discover If It Is Prime

```java
public class PrimeNumberTest
{
   public static void main(String[] args)
   {
      if (args.length != 1)
      {
         System.err.println("usage: java PrimeNumberTest integer");
         System.err.println("integer must be 2 or higher");
         return;
      }
      try
      {
         int n = Integer.parseInt(args[0]);
         if (n < 2)
         {
            System.err.println(n + " is invalid because it is less than 2");
            return;
         }
         for (int i = 2; i <= Math.sqrt(n); i++)
            if (n % i == 0)
            {
               System.out.println (n + " is not prime");
               return;
            }
         System.out.println(n + " is prime");
      }
      catch (NumberFormatException nfe)
      {
         System.err.println("unable to parse " + args[0] + " into an int");
      }
   }
}
```

17. The following loop uses StringBuffer to minimize object creation:

```java
String[] imageNames = new String[NUM_IMAGES];
StringBuffer sb = new StringBuffer();
for (int i = 0; i < imageNames.length; i++)
```

```
      {
         sb.append("image");
         sb.append(i);
         sb.append(".png");
         imageNames[i] = sb.toString();
         sb.setLength(0); // Erase previous StringBuffer contents.
      }
```

18. Listing A-31 presents the DigitsToWords application that was called for in
     Chapter 7.

Listing A-31. Converting an Integer Value to Its Textual Representation

```
public class DigitsToWords
{
   public static void main(String[] args)
   {
      if (args.length != 1)
      {
         System.err.println("usage: java DigitsToWords integer");
         return;
      }
      System.out.println(convertDigitsToWords(Integer.parseInt(args[0])));
   }

   static String convertDigitsToWords(int integer)
   {
      if (integer < 0 || integer > 9999)
         throw new IllegalArgumentException("Out of range: " + integer);
      if (integer == 0)
         return "zero";
      String[] group1 =
      {
         "one",
         "two",
         "three",
         "four",
         "five",
         "six",
         "seven",
         "eight",
         "nine"
      };
      String[] group2 =
      {
         "ten",
         "eleven",
         "twelve",
         "thirteen",
         "fourteen",
         "fifteen",
         "sixteen",
```

```java
        "seventeen",
        "eighteen",
        "nineteen"
    };
    String[] group3 =
    {
        "twenty",
        "thirty",
        "fourty",
        "fifty",
        "sixty",
        "seventy",
        "eighty",
        "ninety"
    };
    StringBuffer result = new StringBuffer();
    if (integer >= 1000)
    {
        int tmp = integer / 1000;
        result.append(group1[tmp - 1] + " thousand");
        integer -= tmp * 1000;
        if (integer == 0)
            return result.toString();
        result.append(" ");
    }
    if (integer >= 100)
    {
        int tmp = integer / 100;
        result.append(group1[tmp - 1] + " hundred");
        integer -= tmp * 100;
        if (integer == 0)
            return result.toString();
        result.append(" and ");
    }
    if (integer >= 10 && integer <= 19)
    {
        result.append(group2[integer - 10]);
        return result.toString();
    }
    if (integer >= 20)
    {
        int tmp = integer / 10;
        result.append(group3[tmp - 2]);
        integer -= tmp * 10;
        if (integer == 0)
            return result.toString();
        result.append("-");
    }
    result.append(group1[integer - 1]);
    return result.toString();
    }
}
```

Chapter 8: Exploring the Basic APIs Part 2

1. A primitive type wrapper class is a class whose instances wrap themselves around values of primitive types.

2. Java's primitive type wrapper classes include `Boolean`, `Byte`, `Character`, `Double`, `Float`, `Integer`, `Long`, and `Short`.

3. Java provides primitive type wrapper classes so that primitive-type values can be stored in collections and to provide a good place to associate useful constants and class methods with primitive types.

4. The answer is false: `Boolean` is the smallest of the primitive type wrapper classes.

5. You should use `Character` class methods instead of expressions such as `ch >= '0' && ch <= '9'` to determine whether or not a character is a digit, a letter, and so on because it's too easy to introduce a bug into the expression, expressions are not very descriptive of what they are testing, and the expressions are biased toward Latin digits (0–9) and letters (A–Z and a–z).

6. You determine whether or not `double` variable d contains +infinity or −infinity by passing this variable as an argument to Double's boolean `isInfinite(double d)` class method, which returns true when this argument is +infinity or −infinity.

7. `Number` is the superclass of `Byte`, `Character`, and the other primitive type wrapper classes.

8. A thread is an independent path of execution through an application's code.

9. The purpose of the `Runnable` interface is to identify those objects that supply code for threads to execute via this interface's solitary `void run()` method.

10. The purpose of the `Thread` class is to provide a consistent interface to the underlying operating system's threading architecture. It provides methods that make it possible to associate code with threads as well as to start and manage those threads.

11. The answer is false: a `Thread` object associates with a single thread.

12. A race condition is a scenario in which multiple threads update the same object at the same time or nearly at the same time. Part of the object stores values written to it by one thread, and another part of the object stores values written to it by another thread.

13. Thread synchronization is the act of allowing only one thread at a time to execute code within a method or a block.

14. Synchronization is implemented in terms of monitors and locks.

15. Synchronization works by requiring that a thread that wants to enter a monitor-controlled critical section first acquire a lock. The lock is released automatically when the thread exits the critical section.

16. The answer is true: variables of type `long` or `double` are not atomic on 32-bit virtual machines.

17. The purpose of reserved word `volatile` is to let threads running on multiprocessor or multicore machines access a single copy of an instance field or class field. Without `volatile`, each thread might access its cached copy of the field and will not see modifications made by other threads to their copies.

18. The answer is false: `Object`'s `wait()` methods cannot be called from outside of a synchronized method or block.

19. Deadlock is a situation in which locks are acquired by multiple threads, neither thread holds its own lock but holds the lock needed by some other thread, and neither thread can enter and later exit its critical section to release its held lock because some other thread holds the lock to that critical section.

20. The purpose of the `ThreadLocal` class is to associate per-thread data (e.g., a user ID) with a thread.

21. `InheritableThreadLocal` differs from `ThreadLocal` in that the former class lets a child thread inherit a thread-local value from its parent thread.

22. The four `java.lang` package system classes discussed in Chapter 8 are `System`, `Runtime`, `Process`, and `ProcessBuilder`.

23. You invoke `System.arraycopy()` to copy an array to another array.

24. The `exec(String program)` method executes the program named `program` in a separate native process. The new process inherits the environment of the method's caller, and a `Process` object is returned to allow communication with the new process. `IOException` is thrown when an I/O error occurs.

25. `Process`'s `getInputStream()` method returns an `InputStream` reference for reading bytes that the new process writes to its output stream.

26. Listing A-32 presents the `MultiPrint` application that was called for in Chapter 8.

Listing A-32. Printing a Line of Text Multiple Times

```
public class MultiPrint
{
    public static void main(String[] args)
    {
        if (args.length != 2)
```

```
        {
            System.err.println("usage: java MultiPrint text count");
            return;
        }
        String text = args[0];
        int count = Integer.parseInt(args[1]);
        for (int i = 0; i < count; i++)
            System.out.println(text);
    }
}
```

27. Listing A-33 presents the revised CountingThreads application that was called for in Chapter 8.

Listing A-33. Counting via Daemon Threads

```
public class CountingThreads
{
    public static void main(String[] args)
    {
        Runnable r = new Runnable()
                     {
                         @Override
                         public void run()
                         {
                             String name = Thread.currentThread().getName();
                             int count = 0;
                             while (true)
                                 System.out.println(name + ": " + count++);
                         }
                     };
        Thread thdA = new Thread(r);
        thdA.setDaemon(true);
        Thread thdB = new Thread(r);
        thdB.setDaemon(true);
        thdA.start();
        thdB.start();
    }
}
```

When you run this application, the two daemon threads start executing and you will probably see some output. However, the application will end as soon as the default main thread leaves the main() method and dies.

28. Listing A-34 presents the StopCountingThreads application that was called for in Chapter 8.

Listing A-34. Stopping the Counting Threads When Return/Enter Is Pressed

```java
import java.io.IOException;

public class StopCountingThreads
{
   private static volatile boolean stopped = false;

   public static void main(String[] args)
   {
      Runnable r = new Runnable()
                   {
                       @Override
                       public void run()
                       {
                           String name = Thread.currentThread().getName();
                           int count = 0;
                           while (!stopped)
                               System.out.println(name + ": " + count++);
                       }
                   };
      Thread thdA = new Thread(r);
      Thread thdB = new Thread(r);
      thdA.start();
      thdB.start();
      try { System.in.read(); } catch (IOException ioe) {}
      stopped = true;
   }
}
```

29. Listing A-35 presents the EVDump application that was called for in Chapter 8.

Listing A-35. Dumping All Environment Variables to Standard Output

```java
public class EVDump
{
   public static void main(String[] args)
   {
      System.out.println(System.getenv()); // System.out.println() calls toString()
                                           // on its object argument and outputs this
                                           // string
   }
}
```

Chapter 9: Exploring the Collections Framework

1. A collection is a group of objects that are stored in an instance of a class designed for this purpose.

2. The Collections Framework is a group of types that offers a standard architecture for representing and manipulating collections.

3. The Collections Framework largely consists of core interfaces, implementation classes, and utility classes.

4. A comparable is an object whose class implements the `Comparable` interface.

5. You would have a class implement the `Comparable` interface when you want objects to be compared according to their natural ordering.

6. A comparator is an object whose class implements the `Comparator` interface. Its purpose is to allow objects to be compared according to an order that is different from their natural ordering.

7. The answer is false: a collection uses a comparable (an object whose class implements the `Comparable` interface) to define the natural ordering of its elements.

8. The `Iterable` interface describes any object that can return its contained objects in some sequence.

9. The `Collection` interface represents a collection of objects that are known as elements.

10. A situation where `Collection`'s `add()` method would throw an instance of the `UnsupportedOperationException` class is an attempt to add an element to an unmodifiable collection.

11. `Iterable`'s `iterator()` method returns an instance of a class that implements the `Iterator` interface. This interface provides a `hasNext()` method to determine if the end of the iteration has been reached, a `next()` method to return a collection's next element, and a `remove()` method to remove the last element returned by `next()` from the collection.

12. The purpose of the enhanced for loop statement is to simplify collection or array iteration.

13. The enhanced for loop statement is expressed as `for` (*type id*: *collection*) or `for` (*type id*: *array*) and reads "for each *type* object in *collection*, assign this object to *id* at the start of the loop iteration"; or "for each *type* object in *array*, assign this object to *id* at the start of the loop iteration."

14. The answer is true: the enhanced for loop works with arrays. For example, `int[] x = { 1, 2, 3 }; for (int i: x) System.out.println(i);` declares array x and outputs all of its `int`-based elements.

15. Autoboxing is the act of wrapping a primitive-type value in an object of a primitive type wrapper class whenever a primitive type is specified but a reference is required. This feature saves the developer from having to explicitly instantiate a wrapper class when storing the primitive value in a collection.

16. Unboxing is the act of unwrapping a primitive-type value from its wrapper object whenever a reference is specified but a primitive type is required. This feature saves the developer from having to explicitly call a method on the object (e.g., `intValue()`) to retrieve the wrapped value.

17. A list is an ordered collection, which is also known as a sequence. Elements can be stored in and accessed from specific locations via integer indexes.

18. A `ListIterator` instance uses a cursor to navigate through a list.

19. A view is a list that is backed by another list. Changes that are made to the view are reflected in this backing list.

20. You would use the `subList()` method to perform range-view operations over a collection in a compact manner. For example, `list.subList(fromIndex, toIndex).clear();` removes a range of elements from `list`, where the first element is located at `fromIndex` and the last element is located at `toIndex - 1`.

21. The `ArrayList` class provides a list implementation that is based on an internal array.

22. The `LinkedList` class provides a list implementation that is based on linked nodes.

23. A node is a fixed sequence of value and link memory locations (i.e., an arrangement of a specific number of values and links, such as one value location followed by one link location). From an object-oriented perspective, it's an object whose fields store values and references to other node objects. These references are also known as links.

24. The answer is false: `ArrayList` provides slower element insertions and deletions than `LinkedList`.

25. A set is a collection that contains no duplicate elements.

26. The `TreeSet` class provides a set implementation that is based on a tree data structure. As a result, elements are stored in sorted order.

27. The `HashSet` class provides a set implementation that is backed by a hashtable data structure.

28. The answer is true: to avoid duplicate elements in a hashset, your own classes must correctly override `equals()` and `hashCode()`.

29. The difference between `HashSet` and `LinkedHashSet` is that `LinkedHashSet` uses a linked list to store its elements, resulting in its iterator returning elements in the order in which they were inserted.

30. The `EnumSet` class provides a `Set` implementation that is based on a bitset.

31. A sorted set is a set that maintains its elements in ascending order, sorted according to their natural ordering or according to a comparator that is supplied when the sorted set is created. Furthermore, the set's implementation class must implement the `SortedSet` interface.

32. A navigable set is a sorted set that can be iterated over in descending order as well as ascending order and which can report closest matches for given search targets.

33. The answer is false: `HashSet` is not an example of a sorted set. However, `TreeSet` is an example of a sorted set.

34. A sorted set's `add()` method would throw `ClassCastException` when you attempt to add an element to the sorted set because the element's class doesn't implement `Comparable`.

35. A queue is a collection in which elements are stored and retrieved in a specific order. Most queues are categorized as "first-in, first out," "last-in, first-out," or priority.

36. The answer is true: Queue's `element()` method throws `NoSuchElementException` when it's called on an empty queue.

37. The `PriorityQueue` class provides an implementation of a priority queue, which is a queue that orders its elements according to their natural ordering or by a comparator provided when the queue is instantiated.

38. A map is a group of key/value pairs (also known as entries).

39. The `TreeMap` class provides a map implementation that is based on a red-black tree. As a result, entries are stored in sorted order of their keys.

40. The `HashMap` class provides a map implementation that is based on a hashtable data structure.

41. A hashtable uses a hash function to map keys to integer values.

42. Continuing from the previous exercise, the resulting integer values are known as hash codes; they identify hashtable array elements, which are known as buckets or slots.

43. A hashtable's capacity refers to the number of buckets.

44. A hashtable's load factor refers to the ratio of the number of stored entries divided by the number of buckets.

45. The difference between `HashMap` and `LinkedHashMap` is that `LinkedHashMap` uses a linked list to store its entries, resulting in its iterator returning entries in the order in which they were inserted.

46. The `IdentityHashMap` class provides a `Map` implementation that uses reference equality (`==`) instead of object equality (`equals()`) when comparing keys and values.

47. The `EnumMap` class provides a `Map` implementation whose keys are the members of the same enum.

48. A sorted map is a map that maintains its entries in ascending order, sorted according to the keys' natural ordering or according to a comparator that is supplied when the sorted map is created. Furthermore, the map's implementation class must implement the `SortedMap` interface.

49. A navigable map is a sorted map that can be iterated over in descending order as well as ascending order and which can report closest matches for given search targets.

50. The answer is true: `TreeMap` is an example of a sorted map.

51. The purpose of the `Arrays` class's `static <T> List<T> asList(T... array)` method is to return a fixed-size list backed by the specified `array`. (Changes to the returned list "write through" to the `array`.)

52. The answer is false: binary search is faster than linear search.

53. You would use `Collections`' `static <T> Set<T> synchronizedSet(Set<T> s)` method to return a synchronized variation of a hashset.

54. The seven legacy collections-oriented types are `Vector`, `Enumeration`, `Stack`, `Dictionary`, `Hashtable`, `Properties`, and `BitSet`.

55. Listing A-36 presents the `JavaQuiz` application that was called for in Chapter 9.

Listing A-36. How Much Do You Know About Java? Take the Quiz and Find Out!

```java
import java.util.ArrayList;
import java.util.Iterator;
import java.util.List;

public class JavaQuiz
{
   private static class QuizEntry
   {
      private String question;
      private String[] choices;
      private char answer;

      QuizEntry(String question, String[] choices, char answer)
      {
         this.question = question;
         this.choices = choices;
         this.answer = answer;
      }
```

```java
    String[] getChoices()
    {
        // Demonstrate returning a copy of the choices array to prevent clients
        // from directly manipulating (and possibly screwing up) the internal
        // choices array.
        String[] temp = new String[choices.length];
        System.arraycopy(choices, 0, temp, 0, choices.length);
        return temp;
    }

    String getQuestion()
    {
        return question;
    }

    char getAnswer()
    {
        return answer;
    }
}

static QuizEntry[] quizEntries =
{
    new QuizEntry("What was Java's original name?",
                  new String[] { "Oak", "Duke", "J", "None of the above" },
                  'A'),
    new QuizEntry("Which of the following reserved words is also a literal?",
                  new String[] { "for", "long", "true", "enum" },
                  'C'),
    new QuizEntry("The conditional operator (?:) resembles which statement?",
                  new String[] { "switch", "if-else", "if", "while" },
                  'B')
};

public static void main(String[] args)
{
    // Populate the quiz list.
    List<QuizEntry> quiz = new ArrayList<QuizEntry>();
    for (QuizEntry entry: quizEntries)
        quiz.add(entry);
    // Perform the quiz.
    System.out.println("Java Quiz");
    System.out.println("---------\n");
    Iterator<QuizEntry> iter = quiz.iterator();
    while (iter.hasNext())
    {
        QuizEntry qe = iter.next();
        System.out.println(qe.getQuestion());
        String[] choices = qe.getChoices();
        for (int i = 0; i < choices.length; i++)
            System.out.println("   " + (char) ('A' + i) + ": " + choices[i]);
        int choice = -1;
```

```
            while (choice < 'A' || choice > 'A' + choices.length)
            {
                System.out.print("Enter choice letter: ");
                try
                {
                    choice = System.in.read();
                    // Remove trailing characters up to and including the newline
                    // to avoid having these characters automatically returned in
                    // subsequent System.in.read() method calls.
                    while (System.in.read() != '\n');
                    choice = Character.toUpperCase((char) choice);
                }
                catch (java.io.IOException ioe)
                {
                }
            }
            if (choice == qe.getAnswer())
                System.out.println("You are correct!\n");
            else
                System.out.println("You are not correct!\n");
        }
    }
}
```

56. `(int) (f ^ (f >>> 32))` is used instead of `(int) (f ^ (f >> 32))` in the hash code generation algorithm because `>>>` always shifts a 0 to the right, which doesn't affect the hash code, whereas `>>` shifts a 0 or a 1 to the right (whatever value is in the sign bit), which affects the hash code when a 1 is shifted.

57. Listing A-37 presents the `FrequencyDemo` application that was called for in Chapter 9.

Listing A-37. Reporting the Frequency of Last Command-Line Argument Occurrences in the Previous Command-Line Arguments

```
import java.util.Collections;
import java.util.LinkedList;
import java.util.List;

public class FrequencyDemo
{
    public static void main(String[] args)
    {
        List<String> listOfArgs = new LinkedList<String>();
        String lastArg = (args.length == 0) ? null : args[args.length - 1];
        for (int i = 0; i < args.length - 1; i++)
            listOfArgs.add(args[i]);
        System.out.println("Number of occurrences of " + lastArg + " = " +
                            Collections.frequency(listOfArgs, lastArg));
    }
}
```

Chapter 10: Exploring Additional Utility APIs

1. A task is an object whose class implements the Runnable interface (a runnable task) or the Callable interface (a callable task).

2. An executor is an object whose class directly or indirectly implements the Executor interface, which decouples task submission from task-execution mechanics.

3. The Executor interface focuses exclusively on Runnable, which means that there is no convenient way for a runnable task to return a value to its caller (because Runnable's run() method doesn't return a value); Executor doesn't provide a way to track the progress of executing runnable tasks, cancel an executing runnable task, or determine when the runnable task finishes execution; Executor cannot execute a collection of runnable tasks; and Executor doesn't provide a way for an application to shut down an executor (much less to properly shut down an executor).

4. Executor's limitations are overcome by providing the ExecutorService interface.

5. The differences existing between Runnable's run() method and Callable's call() method are as follows: run() cannot return a value, whereas call() can return a value; and run() cannot throw checked exceptions, whereas call() can throw checked exceptions.

6. The answer is false: you can throw checked and unchecked exceptions from Callable's call() method but can only throw unchecked exceptions from Runnable's run() method.

7. A future is an object whose class implements the Future interface. It represents an asynchronous computation and provides methods for canceling a task, for returning a task's value, and for determining whether or not the task has finished.

8. The Executors class's newFixedThreadPool() method creates a thread pool that reuses a fixed number of threads operating off of a shared unbounded queue. At most, nThreads threads are actively processing tasks. If additional tasks are submitted when all threads are active, they wait in the queue for an available thread. If any thread terminates because of a failure during execution before the executor shuts down, a new thread will take its place when needed to execute subsequent tasks. The threads in the pool will exist until the executor is explicitly shut down.

9. A synchronizer is a class that facilitates a common form of synchronization.

10. Four commonly used synchronizers are countdown latches, cyclic barriers, exchangers, and semaphores. A countdown latch lets one or more threads wait at a "gate" until another thread opens this gate, at which point these other threads can continue. A cyclic barrier lets a group of threads wait for each other to reach a common barrier point. An exchanger lets a pair of threads exchange objects at a synchronization point. A semaphore maintains a set of permits for restricting the number of threads that can access a limited resource.

11. The concurrency-oriented extensions to the Collections Framework provided by the Concurrency Utilities are ArrayBlockingQueue, BlockingDeque, BlockingQueue, ConcurrentHashMap, ConcurrentMap, ConcurrentNavigableMap, ConcurrentLinkedQueue, ConcurrentSkipListMap, ConcurrentSkipListSet, CopyOnWriteArrayList, CopyOnWriteArraySet, DelayQueue, LinkedBlockingDeque, LinkedBlockingQueue, PriorityBlockingQueue, and SynchronousQueue.

12. A lock is an instance of a class that implements the Lock interface, which provides more extensive locking operations than can be achieved via the synchronized reserved word. Lock also supports a wait/notification mechanism through associated Condition objects.

13. The biggest advantage that Lock objects hold over the implicit locks that are obtained when threads enter critical sections (controlled via the synchronized reserved word) is their ability to back out of an attempt to acquire a lock.

14. An atomic variable is an instance of a class that encapsulates a single variable and supports lock-free, thread-safe operations on that variable, for example, AtomicInteger.

15. The Date class describes a date in terms of a long integer that is relative to the Unix epoch.

16. The Formatter class is an interpreter for printf()-style format strings. This class provides support for layout justification and alignment; common formats for numeric, string, and date/time data; and more. Commonly used Java types (e.g., byte and BigDecimal) are supported.

17. Instances of the Random class generate sequences of random numbers by starting with a special 48-bit value that is known as a seed. This value is subsequently modified by a mathematical algorithm, which is known as a linear congruential generator.

18. The Scanner class parses an input stream of characters into primitive types, strings, and big integers/decimals under the control of regular expressions.

19. You call one of Scanner's "hasNext" methods to determine if a character sequence represents an integer or some other kind of value before scanning that sequence.

20. Two differences between `ZipFile` and `ZipInputStream` are `ZipFile` allows random access to ZIP entries, whereas `ZipInputStream` allows sequential access; and `ZipFile` internally caches ZIP entries for improved performance, whereas `ZipInputStream` doesn't cache entries.

21. Listing A-38 presents the `ZipList` application that was called for in Chapter 10.

Listing A-38. Listing Archive Contents

```java
import java.io.FileInputStream;
import java.io.IOException;

import java.util.Date;

import java.util.zip.ZipEntry;
import java.util.zip.ZipInputStream;

public class ZipList
{
   public static void main(String[] args) throws IOException
   {
      if (args.length != 1)
      {
         System.err.println("usage: java ZipList zipfile");
         return;
      }
      ZipInputStream zis = null;
      try
      {
         zis = new ZipInputStream(new FileInputStream(args[0]));
         ZipEntry ze;
         while ((ze = zis.getNextEntry()) != null)
         {
            System.out.println(ze.getName());
            System.out.println("   Compressed Size: " + ze.getCompressedSize());
            System.out.println("   Uncompressed Size: " + ze.getSize());
            if (ze.getTime() != -1)
               System.out.println("   Modification Time: " + new Date(ze.getTime()));
            System.out.println();
            zis.closeEntry();
         }
      }
      catch (IOException ioe)
      {
         System.err.println("I/O error: " + ioe.getMessage());
      }
      finally
      {
         if (zis != null)
            try
```

```
            {
                zis.close();
            }
            catch (IOException ioe)
            {
                assert false; // shouldn't happen in this context
            }
        }
    }
}
```

Chapter 11: Performing Classic I/O

1. The purpose of the File class is to offer access to the underlying platform's available filesystem(s).

2. Instances of the File class contain the pathnames of files and directories that may or may not exist in their filesystems.

3. File's listRoots() method returns an array of File objects denoting the root directories (roots) of available filesystems.

4. A path is a hierarchy of directories that must be traversed to locate a file or a directory. A pathname is a string representation of a path; a platform-dependent separator character (e.g., the Windows backslash [\] character) appears between consecutive names.

5. The difference between an absolute pathname and a relative pathname is as follows: an absolute pathname is a pathname that starts with the root directory symbol, whereas a relative pathname is a pathname that doesn't start with the root directory symbol; it's interpreted via information taken from some other pathname.

6. You obtain the current user (also known as working) directory by specifying System.getProperty("user.dir").

7. A parent pathname is a string that consists of all pathname components except for the last name.

8. Normalize means to replace separator characters with the default name-separator character so that the pathname is compliant with the underlying filesystem.

9. You obtain the default name-separator character by accessing File's separator and separatorChar class fields. The first field stores the character as a char and the second field stores it as a String.

10. A canonical pathname is a pathname that's absolute and unique and is formatted the same way every time.

11. The difference between File's getParent() and getName() methods is that getParent() returns the parent pathname and getName() returns the last name in the pathname's name sequence.

12. The answer is false: File's exists() method determines whether or not a file or directory exists.

13. A normal file is a file that's not a directory and satisfies other platform-dependent criteria: it's not a symbolic link or named pipe, for example. Any nondirectory file created by a Java application is guaranteed to be a normal file.

14. File's lastModified() method returns the time that the file denoted by this File object's pathname was last modified or 0 when the file doesn't exist or an I/O error occurred during this method call. The returned value is measured in milliseconds since the Unix epoch (00:00:00 GMT, January 1, 1970).

15. The answer is true: File's list() method returns an array of Strings where each entry is a filename rather than a complete path.

16. The difference between the FilenameFilter and FileFilter interfaces is as follows: FilenameFilter declares a single boolean accept(File dir, String name) method, whereas FileFilter declares a single boolean accept(String pathname) method. Either method accomplishes the same task of accepting (by returning true) or rejecting (by returning false) the inclusion of the file or directory identified by the argument(s) in a directory listing.

17. The answer is false: File's createNewFile() method checks for file existence and creates the file when it doesn't exist in a single operation that's atomic with respect to all other filesystem activities that might affect the file.

18. The default temporary directory where File's createTempFile(String, String) method creates temporary files can be located by reading the java.io.tmpdir system property.

19. You ensure that a temporary file is removed when the virtual machine ends normally (it doesn't crash and the power isn't lost) by registering the temporary file for deletion through a call to File's deleteOnExit() method.

20. You would accurately compare two File objects by first calling File's getCanonicalFile() method on each File object and then comparing the returned File objects.

21. The purpose of the RandomAccessFile class is to create and/or open files for random access in which a mixture of write and read operations can occur until the file is closed.

22. The purpose of the "rwd" and "rws" mode arguments is to ensure than any writes to a file located on a local storage device are written to the device, which guarantees that critical data isn't lost when the system crashes. No guarantee is made when the file doesn't reside on a local device.

23. A file pointer is a cursor that identifies the location of the next byte to write or read. When an existing file is opened, the file pointer is set to its first byte at offset 0. The file pointer is also set to 0 when the file is created.

24. The answer is false: when you call RandomAccessFile's seek(long) method to set the file pointer's value, and if this value is greater than the length of the file, the file's length doesn't change. The file length will only change by writing after the offset has been set beyond the end of the file.

25. A flat file database is a single file organized into records and fields. A record stores a single entry (e.g., a part in a parts database) and a field stores a single attribute of the entry (e.g., a part number).

26. A stream is an ordered sequence of bytes of arbitrary length. Bytes flow over an output stream from an application to a destination and flow over an input stream from a source to an application.

27. The purpose of OutputStream's flush() method is to write any buffered output bytes to the destination. If the intended destination of this output stream is an abstraction provided by the underlying platform (e.g., a file), flushing the stream only guarantees that bytes previously written to the stream are passed to the underlying platform for writing; it doesn't guarantee that they're actually written to a physical device such as a disk drive.

28. The answer is true: OutputStream's close() method automatically flushes the output stream. If an application ends before close() is called, the output stream is automatically closed and its data is flushed.

29. The purpose of InputStream's mark(int) and reset() methods is to reread a portion of a stream. mark(int) marks the current position in this input stream. A subsequent call to reset() repositions this stream to the last marked position so that subsequent read operations reread the same bytes. Don't forget to call markSupported() to find out if the subclass supports mark() and reset().

30. You would access a copy of a ByteArrayOutputStream instance's internal byte array by calling ByteArrayOutputStream's toByteArray() method.

31. The answer is false: FileOutputStream and FileInputStream don't provide internal buffers to improve the performance of write and read operations.

32. You would use PipedOutputStream and PipedInputStream to communicate data between a pair of executing threads.

33. A filter stream is a stream that buffers, compresses/uncompresses, encrypts/decrypts, or otherwise manipulates an input stream's byte sequence before it reaches its destination.

34. Two streams are chained together when a stream instance is passed to another stream class's constructor.

35. You improve the performance of a file output stream by chaining a `BufferedOutputStream` instance to a `FileOutputStream` instance and calling the `BufferedOutputStream` instance's `write()` methods so that data is buffered before flowing to the file output stream. You improve the performance of a file input stream by chaining a `BufferedInputStream` instance to a `FileInputStream` instance so that data flowing from a file input stream is buffered before being returned from the `BufferedInputStream` instance by calling this instance's `read()` methods.

36. `DataOutputStream` and `DataInputStream` support `FileOutputStream` and `FileInputStream` by providing methods to write and read primitive-type values and strings in a platform-independent way. In contrast, `FileOutputStream` and `FileInputStream` provide methods for writing/reading bytes and arrays of bytes only.

37. Object serialization is a virtual machine mechanism for serializing object state into a stream of bytes. Its deserialization counterpart is a virtual machine mechanism for deserializing this state from a byte stream.

38. The three forms of serialization and deserialization that Java supports are default serialization and deserialization, custom serialization and deserialization, and externalization.

39. The purpose of the `Serializable` interface is to tell the virtual machine that it's okay to serialize objects of the implementing class.

40. When the serialization mechanism encounters an object whose class doesn't implement `Serializable`, it throws an instance of the `NotSerializableException` class.

41. The three stated reasons for Java not supporting unlimited serialization are as follows: security, performance, and objects not amenable to serialization.

42. You initiate serialization by creating an `ObjectOutputStream` instance and calling its `writeObject()` method. You initialize deserialization by creating an `ObjectInputStream` instance and calling its `readObject()` method.

43. The answer is false: class fields are not automatically serialized.

44. The purpose of the `transient` reserved word is to mark instance fields that don't participate in default serialization and default deserialization.

45. The deserialization mechanism causes `readObject()` to throw an instance of the `InvalidClassException` class when it attempts to deserialize an object whose class has changed.

46. The deserialization mechanism detects that a serialized object's class has changed as follows: Every serialized object has an identifier. The deserialization mechanism compares the identifier of the object being deserialized with the serialized identifier of its class (all serializable classes are automatically given unique identifiers unless they explicitly specify their own identifiers) and causes `InvalidClassException` to be thrown when it detects a mismatch.

47. You can add an instance field to a class and avoid trouble when deserializing an object that was serialized before the instance field was added by introducing a `long serialVersionUID` = *long integer value*; declaration into the class. The *long integer value* must be unique and is known as a stream unique identifier (SUID). You can use the JDK's `serialver` tool to help with this task.

48. You customize the default serialization and deserialization mechanisms without using externalization by declaring private void `writeObject(ObjectOutputStream)` and void `readObject(ObjectInputStream)` methods in the class.

49. You tell the serialization and deserialization mechanisms to serialize or deserialize the object's normal state before serializing or deserializing additional data items by first calling `ObjectOutputStream`'s `defaultWriteObject()` method in `writeObject(ObjectOutputStream)` and by first calling `ObjectInputStream`'s `defaultReadObject()` method in `readObject(ObjectInputStream)`.

50. Externalization differs from default and custom serialization and deserialization in that it offers complete control over the serialization and deserialization tasks.

51. A class indicates that it supports externalization by implementing the `Externalizable` interface instead of `Serializable` and by declaring void `writeExternal(ObjectOutput)` and void `readExternal(ObjectInput in)` methods instead of void `writeObject(ObjectOutputStream)` and void `readObject(ObjectInputStream)` methods.

52. The answer is true: during externalization, the deserialization mechanism throws `InvalidClassException` with a "no valid constructor" message when it doesn't detect a `public` noargument constructor.

53. The difference between `PrintStream`'s `print()` and `println()` methods is that the `print()` methods don't append a line terminator to their output, whereas the `println()` methods append a line terminator.

54. `PrintStream`'s noargument void `println()` method outputs the `line.separator` system property's value to ensure that lines are terminated in a portable manner (e.g., a carriage return followed by a newline/line feed on Windows or only a newline/line feed on Unix/Linux).

55. Java's stream classes are not good at streaming characters because bytes and characters are two different things: a byte represents an 8-bit data item and a character represents a 16-bit data item. Also, byte streams have no knowledge of character sets and their character encodings.

56. Java provides writer and reader classes as the preferred alternative to stream classes when it comes to character I/O.

57. The answer is false: `Reader` doesn't declare an `available()` method.

58. The purpose of the `OutputStreamWriter` class is to serve as a bridge between an incoming sequence of characters and an outgoing stream of bytes. Characters written to this writer are encoded into bytes according to the default or specified character encoding. The purpose of the `InputStreamReader` class is to serve as a bridge between an incoming stream of bytes and an outgoing sequence of characters. Characters read from this reader are decoded from bytes according to the default or specified character encoding.

59. You identify the default character encoding by reading the value of the `file.encoding` system property.

60. The purpose of the `FileWriter` class is to conveniently connect to the underlying file output stream using the default character encoding. The purpose of the `FileReader` class is to conveniently connect to the underlying file input stream using the default character encoding.

61. Listing A-39 presents the Touch application that was called for in Chapter 11.

Listing A-39. Setting a File or Directory's Timestamp to the Current Time

```java
import java.io.File;

import java.util.Date;

public class Touch
{
   public static void main(String[] args)
   {
      if (args.length != 1)
      {
         System.err.println("usage: java Touch pathname");
         return;
      }
      new File(args[0]).setLastModified(new Date().getTime());
   }
}
```

62. Listing A-40 presents the Copy application that was called for in Chapter 11.

Listing A-40. Copying a Source File to a Destination File with Buffered I/O

```java
import java.io.BufferedInputStream;
import java.io.BufferedOutputStream;
import java.io.FileInputStream;
import java.io.FileNotFoundException;
import java.io.FileOutputStream;
import java.io.IOException;

public class Copy
{
   public static void main(String[] args)
   {
      if (args.length != 2)
      {
         System.err.println("usage: java Copy srcfile dstfile");
         return;
      }
      BufferedInputStream bis = null;
      BufferedOutputStream bos = null;
      try
      {
         FileInputStream fis = new FileInputStream(args[0]);
         bis = new BufferedInputStream(fis);
         FileOutputStream fos = new FileOutputStream(args[1]);
         bos = new BufferedOutputStream(fos);
         int b; // I chose b instead of byte because byte is a reserved word.
         while ((b = bis.read()) != -1)
            bos.write(b);
      }
      catch (FileNotFoundException fnfe)
      {
         System.err.println(args[0] + " could not be opened for input, or " +
                            args[1] + " could not be created for output");
      }
      catch (IOException ioe)
      {
         System.err.println("I/O error: " + ioe.getMessage());
      }
      finally
      {
         if (bis != null)
            try
            {
               bis.close();
            }
            catch (IOException ioe)
            {
               assert false; // shouldn't happen in this context
            }
```

```
                  if (bos != null)
                      try
                      {
                          bos.close();
                      }
                      catch (IOException ioe)
                      {
                          assert false; // shouldn't happen in this context
                      }
              }
          }
      }
```

63. Listing A-41 presents the Split application that was called for in Chapter 11.

Listing A-41. Splitting a Large File into Numerous Smaller Part Files

```java
import java.io.BufferedInputStream;
import java.io.BufferedOutputStream;
import java.io.File;
import java.io.FileInputStream;
import java.io.FileOutputStream;
import java.io.IOException;

public class Split
{
    static final int FILESIZE = 1400000;
    static byte[] buffer = new byte[FILESIZE];

    public static void main(String[] args)
    {
        if (args.length != 1)
        {
            System.err.println("usage: java Split pathname");
            return;
        }
        File file = new File(args[0]);
        long length = file.length();
        int nWholeParts = (int) (length / FILESIZE);
        int remainder = (int) (length % FILESIZE);
        System.out.printf("Splitting %s into %d parts%n", args[0],
                          (remainder == 0) ? nWholeParts : nWholeParts + 1);
        BufferedInputStream bis = null;
        BufferedOutputStream bos = null;
        try
        {
            FileInputStream fis = new FileInputStream(args[0]);
            bis = new BufferedInputStream(fis);
            for (int i = 0; i < nWholeParts; i++)
            {
                bis.read(buffer);
                System.out.println("Writing part " + i);
```

```java
            FileOutputStream fos = new FileOutputStream("part" + i);
            bos = new BufferedOutputStream(fos);
            bos.write(buffer);
            bos.close();
            bos = null;
         }
         if (remainder != 0)
         {
            int br = bis.read(buffer);
            if (br != remainder)
            {
               System.err.println("Last part mismatch: expected " + remainder
                                  + " bytes");
               System.exit(0);
            }
            System.out.println("Writing part " + nWholeParts);
            FileOutputStream fos = new FileOutputStream("part" + nWholeParts);
            bos = new BufferedOutputStream(fos);
            bos.write(buffer, 0, remainder);
         }
      }
      catch (IOException ioe)
      {
         ioe.printStackTrace();
      }
      finally
      {
         if (bis != null)
            try
            {
               bis.close();
            }
            catch (IOException ioe)
            {
               assert false; // shouldn't happen in this context
            }
         if (bos != null)
            try
            {
               bos.close();
            }
            catch (IOException ioe)
            {
               assert false; // shouldn't happen in this context
            }
      }
   }
}
```

64. Listing A-42 presents the `CircleInfo` application that was called for in
     Chapter 11.

*Listing A-42. Reading Lines of Text from Standard Input That Represent Circle Radii and Outputting
Circumference and Area Based on the Current Radius*

```java
import java.io.BufferedReader;
import java.io.InputStreamReader;
import java.io.IOException;

public class CircleInfo
{
    public static void main(String[] args) throws IOException
    {
        InputStreamReader isr = new InputStreamReader(System.in);
        BufferedReader br = new BufferedReader(isr);
        while (true)
        {
            System.out.print("Enter circle's radius: ");
            String str = br.readLine();
            double radius;
            try
            {
                radius = Double.valueOf(str).doubleValue();
                if (radius <= 0)
                    System.err.println("radius must not be 0 or negative");
                else
                {
                    System.out.println("Circumference: " + Math.PI * 2.0 * radius);
                    System.out.println("Area: " + Math.PI * radius * radius);
                    System.out.println();
                }
            }
            catch (NumberFormatException nfe)
            {
                System.err.println("not a number: " + nfe.getMessage());
            }
        }
    }
}
```

Chapter 12: Accessing Networks

1. A network is a group of interconnected nodes that can be shared among the
    network's users.

2. An intranet is a network located within an organization, and an internet is a
    network connecting organizations to each other.

3. Intranets and internets often use TCP/IP to communicate between nodes. Transmission Control Protocol (TCP) is a connection-oriented protocol, User Datagram Protocol (UDP) is a connectionless protocol, and Internet Protocol (IP) is the basic protocol over which TCP and UDP perform their tasks.

4. A host is a computer-based TCP/IP node.

5. A socket is an endpoint in a communications link between two processes.

6. A socket is identified by an IP address that identifies the host and by a port number that identifies the process running on that host.

7. An IP address is a 32-bit or 128-bit unsigned integer that uniquely identifies a network host or some other network node.

8. A packet is an addressable message chunk. Packets are often referred to as IP datagrams.

9. A socket address is comprised of an IP address and a port number.

10. The InetAddress subclasses that are used to represent IPv4 and IPv6 addresses are Inet4Address and Inet6Address.

11. The loopback interface is a software-based network interface where outgoing data loops back as incoming data.

12. The answer is false: in network byte order, the most significant byte comes first.

13. The local host is represented by hostname localhost or by an IP address that's commonly expressed as 127.0.0.1 (IPv4) or ::1 (IPv6).

14. A socket option is a parameter for configuring socket behavior.

15. Socket options are described by constants that are declared in the SocketOptions interface.

16. The answer is false: you don't set a socket option by calling the void setOption(int optID, Object value) method. Instead, you call one of the type-safe socket option methods that are declared in a Socket-suffixed class.

17. Sockets based on the Socket class are commonly referred to as stream sockets because Socket is associated with the InputStream and OutputStream classes.

18. In the context of a Socket instance, binding makes a client socket address available to a server socket so that a server process can communicate with the client process via the server socket.

19. A proxy is a host that sits between an intranet and the Internet for security purposes. Java represents proxy settings via instances of the java.net.Proxy class.

20. The answer is false: the ServerSocket() constructor creates an unbound server socket.

21. The difference between the DatagramSocket and MulticastSocket classes is as follows: DatagramSocket lets you perform UDP-based communications between a pair of hosts, whereas MulticastSocket lets you perform UDP-based communications between many hosts.

22. A datagram packet is an array of bytes associated with an instance of the DatagramPacket class.

23. The difference between unicasting and multicasting is as follows: unicasting is the act of a server sending a message to a single client, whereas multicasting is the act of a server sending a message to multiple clients.

24. A URL is a character string that specifies where a resource (e.g., a web page) is located on a TCP/IP-based network (e.g., the Internet). Also, it provides the means to retrieve that resource.

25. A URN is a character string that names a resource and doesn't provide a way to access that resource (the resource might not be available).

26. The answer is true: URLs and URNs are also URIs.

27. The URL(String s) constructor throws MalformedURLException when you pass null to s.

28. The equivalent of openStream() is to execute openConnection().getInputStream().

29. The answer is false: you don't need to invoke URLConnection's void setDoInput(boolean doInput) method with true as the argument before you can input content from a web resource. The default setting is true.

30. When it encounters a space character, URLEncoder converts it to a plus sign.

31. The NetworkInterface class represents a network interface as a name and a list of IP addresses assigned to this interface. Furthermore, it's used to identify the local interface on which a multicast group is joined.

32. A MAC address is an array of bytes containing a network interface's hardware address.

33. MTU stands for Maximum Transmission Unit. This size represents the maximum length of a message that can fit into an IP datagram without needing to fragment the message into multiple IP datagrams.

34. The answer is false: NetworkInterface's getName() method returns a network interface's name (e.g., eth0 or lo), not a human-readable display name.

35. InterfaceAddress's getNetworkPrefixLength() method returns the subnet mask under IPv4.

36. HTTP cookie (cookie for short) is a state object.

37. It's preferable to store cookies on the client rather than on the server because of the potential for millions of cookies (depending on a website's popularity).

38. The four java.net types that are used to work with cookies are CookieHandler, CookieManager, CookiePolicy, and CookieStore.

39. Listing A-43 presents the enhanced EchoClient application that was called for in Chapter 12.

Listing A-43. Echoing Data to and Receiving It Back from a Server and Explicitly Closing the Socket

```java
import java.io.BufferedReader;
import java.io.InputStream;
import java.io.InputStreamReader;
import java.io.IOException;
import java.io.OutputStream;
import java.io.OutputStreamWriter;
import java.io.PrintWriter;

import java.net.Socket;
import java.net.UnknownHostException;

public class EchoClient
{
   public static void main(String[] args)
   {
      if (args.length != 1)
      {
         System.err.println("usage  : java EchoClient message");
         System.err.println("example: java EchoClient \"This is a test.\"");
         return;
      }
      Socket socket = null;
      try
      {
         socket = new Socket("localhost", 9999);
         OutputStream os = socket.getOutputStream();
         OutputStreamWriter osw = new OutputStreamWriter(os);
         PrintWriter pw = new PrintWriter(osw);
         pw.println(args[0]);
         pw.flush();
         InputStream is = socket.getInputStream();
         InputStreamReader isr = new InputStreamReader(is);
         BufferedReader br = new BufferedReader(isr);
         System.out.println(br.readLine());
      }
      catch (UnknownHostException uhe)
      {
         System.err.println("unknown host: " + uhe.getMessage());
      }
```

```
            catch (IOException ioe)
            {
               System.err.println("I/O error: " + ioe.getMessage());
            }
            finally
            {
               if (socket != null)
                  try
                  {
                     socket.close();
                  }
                  catch (IOException ioe)
                  {
                     assert false; // shouldn't happen in this context
                  }
            }
         }
      }
   }
```

40. Listing A-44 presents the enhanced EchoServer application that was called for in
     Chapter 12.

*Listing A-44. Receiving Data from and Echoing It Back to a Client and Explicitly Closing the Socket
After a Kill File Appears*

```
import java.io.BufferedReader;
import java.io.File;
import java.io.InputStream;
import java.io.InputStreamReader;
import java.io.IOException;
import java.io.OutputStream;
import java.io.OutputStreamWriter;
import java.io.PrintWriter;

import java.net.ServerSocket;
import java.net.Socket;

public class EchoServer
{
   public static void main(String[] args)
   {
      System.out.println("Starting echo server...");
      ServerSocket ss = null;
      try
      {
         ss = new ServerSocket(9999);
         File file = new File("kill");
         while (!file.exists())
         {
            Socket s = ss.accept(); // waiting for client request
            try
```

```
        {
            InputStream is = s.getInputStream();
            InputStreamReader isr = new InputStreamReader(is);
            BufferedReader br = new BufferedReader(isr);
            String msg = br.readLine();
            System.out.println(msg);
            OutputStream os = s.getOutputStream();
            OutputStreamWriter osw = new OutputStreamWriter(os);
            PrintWriter pw = new PrintWriter(osw);
            pw.println(msg);
            pw.flush();
        }
        catch (IOException ioe)
        {
            System.err.println("I/O error: " + ioe.getMessage());
        }
        finally
        {
            try
            {
                s.close();
            }
            catch (IOException ioe)
            {
                assert false; // shouldn't happen in this context
            }
        }
    }
}
catch (IOException ioe)
{
    System.err.println("I/O error: " + ioe.getMessage());
}
finally
{
    if (ss != null)
        try
        {
            ss.close();
        }
        catch (IOException ioe)
        {
            assert false; // shouldn't happen in this context
        }
}
    }
}
```

Chapter 13: Migrating to New I/O

1. New I/O is an architecture that supports memory-mapped file I/O, readiness selection, file locking, and more. This architecture consists of buffers, channels, selectors, regular expressions, and charsets.

2. A buffer is an object that stores a fixed amount of data to be sent to or received from an I/O service (a means for performing input/output).

3. A buffer's four properties are capacity, limit, position, and mark.

4. When you invoke Buffer's `array()` method on a buffer backed by a read-only array, this method throws `ReadOnlyBufferException`.

5. When you invoke Buffer's `flip()` method on a buffer, the limit is set to the current position and then the position is set to zero. When the mark is defined, it's discarded. The buffer is now ready to be drained.

6. When you invoke Buffer's `reset()` method on a buffer where a mark has not been set, this method throws `InvalidMarkException`.

7. The answer is false: buffers are not thread-safe.

8. The classes that extend the abstract `Buffer` class are `ByteBuffer`, `CharBuffer`, `DoubleBuffer`, `FloatBuffer`, `IntBuffer`, `LongBuffer`, and `ShortBuffer`. Furthermore, this package includes `MappedByteBuffer` as an abstract `ByteBuffer` subclass.

9. You create a byte buffer by invoking one of its `allocate()`, `allocateDirect()`, or `wrap()` class methods.

10. A view buffer is a buffer that manages another buffer's data.

11. A view buffer is created by calling a `Buffer` subclass's `duplicate()` method.

12. You create a read-only view buffer by calling a `Buffer` subclass method such as `ByteBuffer asReadOnlyBuffer()` or `CharBuffer asReadOnlyBuffer()`.

13. ByteBuffer's methods for storing a single byte in a byte buffer are `ByteBuffer put(int index, byte b)` and `ByteBuffer put(byte b)`. ByteBuffer's methods for fetching a single byte from a byte buffer are `byte get(int index)` method and `byte get()`.

14. Attempting to use the relative `put()` method or the relative `get()` method when the current position is greater than or equal to the limit causes `BufferOverflowException` or `BufferUnderflowException` to occur.

15. The equivalent of executing `buffer.flip();` is to execute `buffer.limit(buffer.position()).position(0);`.

16. The answer is false: calling `flip()` twice doesn't return you to the original state. Instead, the buffer has a zero size.

17. The difference between Buffer's clear() and reset() methods is as follows: the clear() method marks a buffer as empty, whereas reset() changes the buffer's current position to the previously set mark or throws InvalidMarkException when there's no previously set mark.

18. ByteBuffer's compact() method copies all bytes between the current position and the limit to the beginning of the buffer. The byte at index p = position() is copied to index 0, the byte at index p + 1 is copied to index 1, and so on until the byte at index limit() - 1 is copied to index n = limit() - 1 - p. The buffer's current position is then set to n + 1 and its limit is set to its capacity. The mark, when defined, is discarded.

19. The purpose of the ByteOrder class is to help you deal with byte-order issues when writing/reading multibyte values to/from a multibyte buffer.

20. A direct byte buffer is a byte buffer that interacts with channels and native code to perform I/O. The direct byte buffer attempts to store byte elements in a memory area that a channel uses to perform direct (raw) access via native code that tells the operating system to drain or fill the memory area directly.

21. You obtain a direct byte buffer by invoking ByteBuffer's allocateDirect() method.

22. A channel is an object that represents an open connection to a hardware device, a file, a network socket, an application component, or another entity that's capable of performing write, read, and other I/O operations. Channels efficiently transfer data between byte buffers and I/O service sources or destinations.

23. The capabilities that the Channel interface provides are closing a channel (via the close() method) and determining whether or not a channel is open (via the isOpen()) method.

24. The three interfaces that directly extend Channel are WritableByteChannel, ReadableByteChannel, and InterruptibleChannel.

25. The answer is true: a channel that implements InterruptibleChannel is asynchronously closeable.

26. The two ways to obtain a channel are to invoke a Channels class method, such as WritableByteChannel newChannel(OutputStream outputStream), and to invoke a channel method on a classic I/O class, such as RandomAccessFile 's FileChannel getChannel() method.

27. Scatter/gather I/O is the ability to perform a single I/O operation across multiple buffers.

28. The ScatteringByteChannel and GatheringByteChannel interfaces are provided for achieving scatter/gather I/O.

29. A file channel is a channel to an underlying file.

30. The answer is false: file channels support scatter/gather I/O.

31. `FileChannel` provides the `MappedByteBuffer map(FileChannel.MapMode mode, long position, long size)` method for mapping a region of a file into memory.

32. The fundamental difference between `FileChannel`'s `lock()` and `tryLock()` methods is that the `lock()` methods can block and the `tryLock()` methods never block.

33. A regular expression (also known as a regex or regexp) is a string-based pattern that represents the set of strings that match this pattern.

34. Instances of the `Pattern` class represent patterns via compiled regexes. Regexes are compiled for performance reasons; pattern matching via compiled regexes is much faster than if the regexes were not compiled.

35. `Pattern`'s `compile()` methods throw instances of the `PatternSyntaxException` class when they discover illegal syntax in their regular expression arguments.

36. Instances of the `Matcher` class attempt to match compiled regexes against input text.

37. The difference between `Matcher`'s `matches()` and `lookingAt()` methods is that unlike `matches()`, `lookingAt()` doesn't require the entire region to be matched.

38. A character class is a set of characters appearing between [and].

39. There are six kinds of character classes: simple, negation, range, union, intersection, and subtraction.

40. A capturing group saves a match's characters for later recall during pattern matching.

41. A zero-length match is a match of zero length in which the start and end indexes are equal.

42. A quantifier is a numeric value implicitly or explicitly bound to a pattern. Quantifiers are categorized as greedy, reluctant, or possessive.

43. The difference between a greedy quantifier and a reluctant quantifier is that a greedy quantifier attempts to find the longest match, whereas a reluctant quantifier attempts to find the shortest match.

44. Possessive and greedy quantifiers differ in that a possessive quantifier only makes one attempt to find the longest match, whereas a greedy quantifier can make multiple attempts.

45. Listing A-45 presents the enhanced Copy application that was called for in Chapter 13.

Listing A-45. Copying a File via a Byte Buffer and a File Channel

```java
import java.io.FileInputStream;
import java.io.FileNotFoundException;
import java.io.FileOutputStream;
import java.io.IOException;

import java.nio.ByteBuffer;

import java.nio.channels.FileChannel;

public class Copy
{
   public static void main(String[] args)
   {
      if (args.length != 2)
      {
         System.err.println("usage: java Copy srcfile dstfile");
         return;
      }
      FileChannel fcSrc = null;
      FileChannel fcDest = null;
      try
      {
         FileInputStream fis = new FileInputStream(args[0]);
         fcSrc = fis.getChannel();
         FileOutputStream fos = new FileOutputStream(args[1]);
         fcDest = fos.getChannel();
         ByteBuffer buffer = ByteBuffer.allocateDirect(2048);
         while ((fcSrc.read(buffer)) != -1)
         {
            buffer.flip();
            while (buffer.hasRemaining())
               fcDest.write(buffer);
            buffer.clear();
         }
      }
      catch (FileNotFoundException fnfe)
      {
         System.err.println(args[0] + " could not be opened for input, or " +
                            args[1] + " could not be created for output");
      }
      catch (IOException ioe)
      {
         System.err.println("I/O error: " + ioe.getMessage());
      }
      finally
      {
         if (fcSrc != null)
            try
```

```
                  {
                      fcSrc.close();
                  }
                  catch (IOException ioe)
                  {
                      assert false; // shouldn't happen in this context
                  }

              if (fcDest != null)
                  try
                  {
                      fcDest.close();
                  }
                  catch (IOException ioe)
                  {
                      assert false; // shouldn't happen in this context
                  }
          }
      }
   }
```

46. Listing A-46 presents the ReplaceText application that was called for in Chapter 13.

Listing A-46. Replacing All Matches of the Pattern with Replacement Text

```java
import java.util.regex.Matcher;
import java.util.regex.Pattern;
import java.util.regex.PatternSyntaxException;

public class ReplaceText
{
   public static void main(String[] args)
   {
      if (args.length != 3)
      {
         System.err.println("usage: java ReplaceText text oldText newText");
         return;
      }
      try
      {
         Pattern p = Pattern.compile(args[1]);
         Matcher m = p.matcher(args[0]);
         String result = m.replaceAll(args[2]);
         System.out.println(result);
      }
      catch (PatternSyntaxException pse)
      {
         System.err.println(pse);
      }
   }
}
```

Chapter 14: Accessing Databases

1. A database is an organized collection of data.

2. A relational database is a database that organizes data into tables that can be related to each other.

3. Two other database categories are hierarchical databases and object-oriented databases.

4. A database management system is a set of programs that enables you to store, modify, and extract information from a database. It also provides users with tools to add, delete, access, modify, and analyze data stored in one location.

5. Java DB is a distribution of Apache's open-source Derby product, which is based on IBM's Cloudscape RDBMS code base.

6. The answer is false: Java DB's embedded driver causes the database engine to run in the same virtual machine as the application.

7. `setEmbeddedCP` adds `derby.jar` and `derbytools.jar` to the classpath so that you can access Java DB's embedded driver from your application.

8. The answer is false: you run Java DB's `sysinfo` command-line tool to view the Java environment/Java DB configuration.

9. SQLite is a very simple and popular RDBMS that implements a self-contained, serverless, zero-configuration, transactional SQL database engine and is considered to be the most widely deployed database engine in the world.

10. Manifest typing is the ability to store any value of any data type into any column regardless of the declared type of that column.

11. SQLite provides the `sqlite3` tool for accessing and modifying SQLite databases.

12. JDBC is an API for communicating with RDBMSs in an RDBMS-independent manner.

13. A data source is a data-storage facility ranging from a simple file to a complex relational database managed by an RDBMS.

14. A JDBC driver implements the `java.sql.Driver` interface.

15. The answer is false: there are four kinds of JDBC drivers.

16. A type three JDBC driver doesn't depend on native code and communicates with a middleware server via an RDBMS-independent protocol. The middleware server then communicates the client's requests to the data source.

17. JDBC provides the `java.sql.DriverManager` class and the `javax.sql.DataSource` interface for communicating with a data source.

18. You obtain a connection to a Java DB data source via the embedded driver by passing a URL of the form `jdbc:derby:`*`databaseName`*`;`*`URLAttributes`* to one of `DriverManager`'s `getConnection()` methods.

19. The answer is false: int getErrorCode() returns a vendor-specific error code.

20. A SQL state error code is a five-character string consisting of a two-character class value followed by a three-character subclass value.

21. The difference between SQLNonTransientException and SQLTransientException is as follows: SQLNonTransientException describes failed operations that cannot be retried without changing application source code or some aspect of the data source, and SQLTransientException describes failed operations that can be retried immediately.

22. JDBC's three statement types are Statement, PreparedStatement, and CallableStatement.

23. The Statement method that you call to execute an SQL SELECT statement is ResultSet executeQuery(String sql).

24. A result set's cursor provides access to a specific row of data.

25. The SQL FLOAT type maps to Java's double type.

26. A prepared statement represents a precompiled SQL statement.

27. The answer is true: CallableStatement extends PreparedStatement.

28. A stored procedure is a list of SQL statements that perform a specific task.

29. You call a stored procedure by first obtaining a CallableStatement implementation instance (via one of Connection's prepareCall() methods) that's associated with an escape clause, by next executing CallableStatement methods such as void setInt(String parameterName, int x) to pass arguments to escape clause parameters, and by finally invoking the boolean execute() method that CallableStatement inherits from its PreparedStatement superinterface.

30. An escape clause is RDBMS-independent syntax.

31. Metadata is data about data.

32. Metadata includes a list of catalogs, base tables, views, indexes, schemas, and additional information.

33. Listing A-47 presents the enhanced JDBCDemo application that was called for in Chapter 14.

Listing A-47. Outputting Database Metadata for the SQLite or Java DB Embedded Driver

```
import java.sql.Connection;
import java.sql.DatabaseMetaData;
import java.sql.DriverManager;
import java.sql.ResultSet;
import java.sql.SQLException;
import java.sql.Statement;
```

```java
public class JDBCDemo
{
    final static String URL1 = "jdbc:derby:employee;create=true";
    final static String URL2 = "jdbc:sqlite:employee";

    public static void main(String[] args)
    {
        String url = null;
        if (args.length != 1)
        {
            System.err.println("usage 1: java JDBCDemo javadb");
            System.err.println("usage 2: java JDBCDemo sqlite");
            return;
        }
        if (args[0].equals("javadb"))
            url = URL1;
        else
        if (args[0].equals("sqlite"))
            url = URL2;
        else
        {
            System.err.println("invalid command-line argument");
            return;
        }
        Connection con = null;
        try
        {
            if (args[0].equals("sqlite"))
                Class.forName("org.sqlite.JDBC");
            con = DriverManager.getConnection(url);
            dump(con.getMetaData());
        }
        catch (ClassNotFoundException cnfe)
        {
            System.err.println("unable to load sqlite driver");
        }
        catch (SQLException sqlex)
        {
            while (sqlex != null)
            {
                System.err.println("SQL error : " + sqlex.getMessage());
                System.err.println("SQL state : " + sqlex.getSQLState());
                System.err.println("Error code: " + sqlex.getErrorCode());
                System.err.println("Cause: " + sqlex.getCause());
                sqlex = sqlex.getNextException();
            }
        }
        finally
        {
            if (con != null)
                try
```

```
            {
               con.close();
            }
            catch (SQLException sqle)
            {
               sqle.printStackTrace();
            }
         }
      }

      static void dump(DatabaseMetaData dbmd) throws SQLException
      {
         System.out.println("DB Major Version = " + dbmd.getDatabaseMajorVersion());
         System.out.println("DB Minor Version = " + dbmd.getDatabaseMinorVersion());
         System.out.println("DB Product = " + dbmd.getDatabaseProductName());
         System.out.println("Driver Name = " + dbmd.getDriverName());
         System.out.println("Numeric function names for escape clause = " +
                            dbmd.getNumericFunctions());
         System.out.println("String function names for escape clause = " +
                            dbmd.getStringFunctions());
         System.out.println("System function names for escape clause = " +
                            dbmd.getSystemFunctions());
         System.out.println("Time/date function names for escape clause = " +
                            dbmd.getTimeDateFunctions());
         System.out.println("Catalog term: " + dbmd.getCatalogTerm());
         System.out.println("Schema term: " + dbmd.getSchemaTerm());
         System.out.println();
         System.out.println("Catalogs");
         System.out.println("--------");
         ResultSet rsCat = dbmd.getCatalogs();
         while (rsCat.next())
            System.out.println(rsCat.getString("TABLE_CAT"));
         System.out.println();
         System.out.println("Schemas");
         System.out.println("-------");
         ResultSet rsSchem = dbmd.getSchemas();
         while (rsSchem.next())
            System.out.println(rsSchem.getString("TABLE_SCHEM"));
         System.out.println();
         System.out.println("Schema/Table");
         System.out.println("------------");
         rsSchem = dbmd.getSchemas();
         while (rsSchem.next())
         {
            String schem = rsSchem.getString("TABLE_SCHEM");
            ResultSet rsTab = dbmd.getTables(null, schem, "%", null);
            while (rsTab.next())
               System.out.println(schem + " " + rsTab.getString("TABLE_NAME"));
         }
      }
   }
```

Four of a Kind

Application development isn't an easy task. If you don't plan carefully before you develop an application, you'll probably waste your time and money as you endeavor to create it, and waste your users' time and money when it doesn't meet their needs.

> **Caution** It's extremely important to test your software carefully. You could face a lawsuit if malfunctioning software causes financial harm to its users.

In this appendix, I present one technique for developing applications efficiently. I present this technique in the context of a Java application that lets you play a simple card game called *Four of a Kind* against the computer.

Understanding Four of a Kind

Before sitting down at the computer and writing code, you need to fully understand the problem domain that you are trying to model via that code. In this case, the problem domain is *Four of a Kind*, and you want to understand how this card game works.

Two to four players play *Four of a Kind* with a standard 52-card deck. The object of the game is to be the first player to put down four cards that have the same rank (four aces, for example), which wins the game.

The game begins by shuffling the deck and placing it face down. Each player takes a card from the top of the deck. The player with the highest ranked card (king is highest) deals four cards to each player, starting with the player to the dealer's left. The dealer then starts its turn.

The player examines its cards to determine which cards are optimal for achieving four of a kind. The player then throws away the least helpful card on a discard pile and picks up another card from the top of the deck. (If each card has a different rank, the player randomly selects a card to throw away.) If the player has four of a kind, the player puts down these cards (face up) and wins the game.

Modeling Four of a Kind in Pseudocode

Now that you understand how *Four of a Kind* works, you can begin to model this game. You will not model the game in Java source code because you would get bogged down in too many details. Instead, you will use pseudocode for this task.

Pseudocode is a compact and informal high-level description of the problem domain. Unlike the previous description of *Four of a Kind*, the pseudocode equivalent is a step-by-step recipe for solving the problem. Check out Listing B-1.

Listing B-1. Four of a Kind Pseudocode for Two Players (Human and Computer)

1. Create a deck of cards and shuffle the deck.
2. Create empty discard pile.
3. Have each of the human and computer players take a card from the top of the deck.
4. Designate the player with the highest ranked card as the current player.
5. Return both cards to the bottom of the deck.
6. The current player deals four cards to each of the two players in alternating fashion, with the first card being dealt to the other player.
7. The current player examines its current cards to see which cards are optimal for achieving four of a kind. The current player throws the least helpful card onto the top of the discard pile.
8. The current player picks up the deck's top card. If the current player has four of a kind, it puts down its cards and wins the game.
9. Designate the other player as the current player.
10. If the deck has no more cards, empty the discard pile to the deck and shuffle the deck.
11. Repeat at step 7.

Deriving Listing B-1's pseudocode from the previous description is the first step in achieving an application that implements *Four of a Kind*. This pseudocode performs various tasks including decision making and repetition.

Despite being a more useful guide to understanding how *Four of a Kind* works, Listing B-1 is too high level for translation to Java. Therefore, you must refine this pseudocode to facilitate the translation process. Listing B-2 presents this refinement.

Listing B-2. Refined Four of a Kind Pseudocode for Two Players (Human and Computer)

```
1. deck = new Deck()
2. deck.shuffle()
3. discardPile = new DiscardPile()
4. hCard = deck.deal()
5. cCard = deck.deal()
6. if hCard.rank() == cCard.rank()
   6.1. deck.putBack(hCard)
   6.2. deck.putBack(cCard)
   6.3. deck.shuffle()
   6.4. Repeat at step 4
7. curPlayer = HUMAN
   7.1. if cCard.rank() > hCard.rank()
        7.1.1. curPlayer = COMPUTER
8. deck.putBack(hCard)
```

```
 9. deck.putBack(cCard)
10. if curPlayer == HUMAN
    10.1. for i = 0 to 3
          10.1.1. cCards[i] = deck.deal()
          10.1.2. hCards[i] = deck.deal()
    else
    10.2. for i = 0 to 3
          10.2.1. hCards[i] = deck.deal()
          10.2.2. cCards[i] = deck.deal()
11. if curPlayer == HUMAN
    11.01. output(hCards)
    11.02. choice = prompt("Identify card to throw away")
    11.03. discardPile.setTopCard(hCards[choice])
    11.04. hCards[choice] = deck.deal()
    11.05. if isFourOfAKind(hCards)
           11.05.1. output("Human wins!")
           11.05.2. putDown(hCards)
           11.05.3. output("Computer's cards:")
           11.05.4. putDown(cCards)
           11.05.5. End game
    11.06. curPlayer = COMPUTER
    else
    11.07. choice = leastDesirableCard(cCards)
    11.08. discardPile.setTopCard(cCards[choice])
    11.09. cCards[choice] = deck.deal()
    11.10. if isFourOfAKind(cCards)
           11.10.1. output("Computer wins!")
           11.10.2. putDown(cCards)
           11.10.3. End game
    11.11. curPlayer = HUMAN
12. if deck.isEmpty()
    12.1. if discardPile.topCard() != null
          12.1.1. deck.putBack(discardPile.getTopCard())
          12.1.2. Repeat at step 12.1.
    12.2. deck.shuffle()
13. Repeat at step 11.
```

In addition to being longer than Listing B-1, Listing B-2 shows the refined pseudocode becoming more like Java. For example, Listing B-2 reveals Java expressions (such as new Deck(), to create a Deck object), operators (such as ==, to compare two values for equality), and method calls (such as deck.isEmpty(), to call deck's isEmpty() method to return a Boolean value indicating whether [true] or not [false] the deck identified by deck is empty of cards).

Converting Pseudocode to Java Code

Now that you've had a chance to absorb Listing B-2's Java-like pseudocode, you're ready to examine the process of converting that pseudocode to Java source code. This process consists of a couple of steps.

The first step in converting Listing B-2's pseudocode to Java involves identifying important components of the game's structure and implementing these components as classes, which I formally introduced in Chapter 3.

Apart from the computer player (which is implemented via game logic), the important components are card, deck, and discard pile. I represent these components via Card, Deck, and DiscardPile classes. Listing B-3 presents Card.

Listing B-3. Merging Suits and Ranks into Cards

```
/**
 *  Simulating a playing card.
 *
 *  @author Jeff Friesen
 */

public enum Card
{
    ACE_OF_CLUBS(Suit.CLUBS, Rank.ACE),
    TWO_OF_CLUBS(Suit.CLUBS, Rank.TWO),
    THREE_OF_CLUBS(Suit.CLUBS, Rank.THREE),
    FOUR_OF_CLUBS(Suit.CLUBS, Rank.FOUR),
    FIVE_OF_CLUBS(Suit.CLUBS, Rank.FIVE),
    SIX_OF_CLUBS(Suit.CLUBS, Rank.SIX),
    SEVEN_OF_CLUBS(Suit.CLUBS, Rank.SEVEN),
    EIGHT_OF_CLUBS(Suit.CLUBS, Rank.EIGHT),
    NINE_OF_CLUBS(Suit.CLUBS, Rank.NINE),
    TEN_OF_CLUBS(Suit.CLUBS, Rank.TEN),
    JACK_OF_CLUBS(Suit.CLUBS, Rank.JACK),
    QUEEN_OF_CLUBS(Suit.CLUBS, Rank.QUEEN),
    KING_OF_CLUBS(Suit.CLUBS, Rank.KING),
    ACE_OF_DIAMONDS(Suit.DIAMONDS, Rank.ACE),
    TWO_OF_DIAMONDS(Suit.DIAMONDS, Rank.TWO),
    THREE_OF_DIAMONDS(Suit.DIAMONDS, Rank.THREE),
    FOUR_OF_DIAMONDS(Suit.DIAMONDS, Rank.FOUR),
    FIVE_OF_DIAMONDS(Suit.DIAMONDS, Rank.FIVE),
    SIX_OF_DIAMONDS(Suit.DIAMONDS, Rank.SIX),
    SEVEN_OF_DIAMONDS(Suit.DIAMONDS, Rank.SEVEN),
    EIGHT_OF_DIAMONDS(Suit.DIAMONDS, Rank.EIGHT),
    NINE_OF_DIAMONDS(Suit.DIAMONDS, Rank.NINE),
    TEN_OF_DIAMONDS(Suit.DIAMONDS, Rank.TEN),
    JACK_OF_DIAMONDS(Suit.DIAMONDS, Rank.JACK),
    QUEEN_OF_DIAMONDS(Suit.DIAMONDS, Rank.QUEEN),
    KING_OF_DIAMONDS(Suit.DIAMONDS, Rank.KING),
    ACE_OF_HEARTS(Suit.HEARTS, Rank.ACE),
    TWO_OF_HEARTS(Suit.HEARTS, Rank.TWO),
    THREE_OF_HEARTS(Suit.HEARTS, Rank.THREE),
    FOUR_OF_HEARTS(Suit.HEARTS, Rank.FOUR),
    FIVE_OF_HEARTS(Suit.HEARTS, Rank.FIVE),
    SIX_OF_HEARTS(Suit.HEARTS, Rank.SIX),
    SEVEN_OF_HEARTS(Suit.HEARTS, Rank.SEVEN),
    EIGHT_OF_HEARTS(Suit.HEARTS, Rank.EIGHT),
```

```
  NINE_OF_HEARTS(Suit.HEARTS, Rank.NINE),
  TEN_OF_HEARTS(Suit.HEARTS, Rank.TEN),
  JACK_OF_HEARTS(Suit.HEARTS, Rank.JACK),
  QUEEN_OF_HEARTS(Suit.HEARTS, Rank.QUEEN),
  KING_OF_HEARTS(Suit.HEARTS, Rank.KING),
  ACE_OF_SPADES(Suit.SPADES, Rank.ACE),
  TWO_OF_SPADES(Suit.SPADES, Rank.TWO),
  THREE_OF_SPADES(Suit.SPADES, Rank.THREE),
  FOUR_OF_SPADES(Suit.SPADES, Rank.FOUR),
  FIVE_OF_SPADES(Suit.SPADES, Rank.FIVE),
  SIX_OF_SPADES(Suit.SPADES, Rank.SIX),
  SEVEN_OF_SPADES(Suit.SPADES, Rank.SEVEN),
  EIGHT_OF_SPADES(Suit.SPADES, Rank.EIGHT),
  NINE_OF_SPADES(Suit.SPADES, Rank.NINE),
  TEN_OF_SPADES(Suit.SPADES, Rank.TEN),
  JACK_OF_SPADES(Suit.SPADES, Rank.JACK),
  QUEEN_OF_SPADES(Suit.SPADES, Rank.QUEEN),
  KING_OF_SPADES(Suit.SPADES, Rank.KING);

  private Suit suit;

  /**
   *  Return <code>Card</code>'s suit.
   *
   *  @return <code>CLUBS</code>, <code>DIAMONDS</code>, <code>HEARTS</code>,
   *  or <code>SPADES</code>
   */

  public Suit suit()
  {
     return suit;
  }

  private Rank rank;

  /**
   *  Return <code>Card</code>'s rank.
   *
   *  @return <code>ACE</code>, <code>TWO</code>, <code>THREE</code>,
   *  <code>FOUR</code>, <code>FIVE</code>, <code>SIX</code>,
   *  <code>SEVEN</code>, <code>EIGHT</code>, <code>NINE</code>,
   *  <code>TEN</code>, <code>JACK</code>, <code>QUEEN</code>,
   *  <code>KING</code>.
   */

  public Rank rank()
  {
     return rank;
  }
```

```java
Card(Suit suit, Rank rank)
{
   this.suit = suit;
   this.rank = rank;
}

/**
 *  A card's suit is its membership.
 *
 *  @author Jeff Friesen
 */

public enum Suit
{
   CLUBS, DIAMONDS, HEARTS, SPADES
}

/**
 *  A card's rank is its integer value.
 *
 *  @author Jeff Friesen
 */

public enum Rank
{
   ACE, TWO, THREE, FOUR, FIVE, SIX, SEVEN, EIGHT, NINE, TEN, JACK, QUEEN,
   KING
}
}
```

Listing B-3 begins with a Javadoc comment that's used to briefly describe the subsequently declared Card class and identify this class's author. (I briefly introduced Javadoc comments in Chapter 2.)

> **Note**   One feature of Javadoc comments is the ability to embed HTML tags. These tags specify different kinds of formatting for sections of text within these comments. For example, `<code>` and `</code>` specify that their enclosed text is to be formatted as a code listing. Later in this appendix, you'll learn how to convert these comments into HTML documentation.

Card is an example of an *enum*, which is a special kind of class that I discussed in Chapter 6. If you haven't read that chapter, think of Card as a place to create and store Card objects that identify all 52 cards that make up a standard deck.

Card declares a nested Suit enum. (I discussed nesting in Chapter 5.) A card's suit denotes its membership. The only legal Suit values are CLUBS, DIAMONDS, HEARTS, and SPADES.

Card also declares a nested Rank enum. A card's rank denotes its value: ACE, TWO, THREE, FOUR, FIVE, SIX, SEVEN, EIGHT, NINE, TEN, JACK, QUEEN, and KING are the only legal Rank values.

A Card object is created when Suit and Rank objects are passed to its constructor. (I discussed constructors in Chapter 3.) For example, KING_OF_HEARTS(Suit.HEARTS, Rank.KING) combines Suit.HEARTS and Rank.KING into KING_OF_HEARTS.

Card provides a rank() method for returning a Card's Rank object. Similarly, Card provides a suit() method for returning a Card's Suit object. For example, KING_OF_HEARTS.rank() returns Rank.KING, and KING_OF_HEARTS.suit() returns Suit.HEARTS.

Listing B-4 presents the Java source code to the Deck class, which implements a deck of 52 cards.

Listing B-4. Pick a Card, Any Card

```java
import java.util.ArrayList;
import java.util.Collections;
import java.util.List;

/**
 *  Simulate a deck of cards.
 *
 *  @author Jeff Friesen
 */

public class Deck
{
   private Card[] cards = new Card[]
   {
      Card.ACE_OF_CLUBS,
      Card.TWO_OF_CLUBS,
      Card.THREE_OF_CLUBS,
      Card.FOUR_OF_CLUBS,
      Card.FIVE_OF_CLUBS,
      Card.SIX_OF_CLUBS,
      Card.SEVEN_OF_CLUBS,
      Card.EIGHT_OF_CLUBS,
      Card.NINE_OF_CLUBS,
      Card.TEN_OF_CLUBS,
      Card.JACK_OF_CLUBS,
      Card.QUEEN_OF_CLUBS,
      Card.KING_OF_CLUBS,
      Card.ACE_OF_DIAMONDS,
      Card.TWO_OF_DIAMONDS,
      Card.THREE_OF_DIAMONDS,
      Card.FOUR_OF_DIAMONDS,
      Card.FIVE_OF_DIAMONDS,
      Card.SIX_OF_DIAMONDS,
      Card.SEVEN_OF_DIAMONDS,
      Card.EIGHT_OF_DIAMONDS,
      Card.NINE_OF_DIAMONDS,
      Card.TEN_OF_DIAMONDS,
      Card.JACK_OF_DIAMONDS,
      Card.QUEEN_OF_DIAMONDS,
      Card.KING_OF_DIAMONDS,
```

```java
            Card.ACE_OF_HEARTS,
            Card.TWO_OF_HEARTS,
            Card.THREE_OF_HEARTS,
            Card.FOUR_OF_HEARTS,
            Card.FIVE_OF_HEARTS,
            Card.SIX_OF_HEARTS,
            Card.SEVEN_OF_HEARTS,
            Card.EIGHT_OF_HEARTS,
            Card.NINE_OF_HEARTS,
            Card.TEN_OF_HEARTS,
            Card.JACK_OF_HEARTS,
            Card.QUEEN_OF_HEARTS,
            Card.KING_OF_HEARTS,
            Card.ACE_OF_SPADES,
            Card.TWO_OF_SPADES,
            Card.THREE_OF_SPADES,
            Card.FOUR_OF_SPADES,
            Card.FIVE_OF_SPADES,
            Card.SIX_OF_SPADES,
            Card.SEVEN_OF_SPADES,
            Card.EIGHT_OF_SPADES,
            Card.NINE_OF_SPADES,
            Card.TEN_OF_SPADES,
            Card.JACK_OF_SPADES,
            Card.QUEEN_OF_SPADES,
            Card.KING_OF_SPADES
    };

    private List<Card> deck;

    /**
     * Create a <code>Deck</code> of 52 <code>Card</code> objects. Shuffle
     * these objects.
     */

    public Deck()
    {
        deck = new ArrayList<Card>();
        for (int i = 0; i < cards.length; i++)
        {
            deck.add(cards[i]);
            cards[i] = null;
        }
        Collections.shuffle(deck);
    }

    /**
     * Deal the <code>Deck</code>'s top <code>Card</code> object.
     *
     * @return the <code>Card</code> object at the top of the
     * <code>Deck</code>
     */
```

```java
    public Card deal()
    {
        return deck.remove(0);
    }

    /**
     *  Return an indicator of whether or not the <code>Deck</code> is empty.
     *
     *  @return true if the <code>Deck</code> contains no <code>Card</code>
     *  objects; otherwise, false
     */

    public boolean isEmpty()
    {
        return deck.isEmpty();
    }

    /**
     *  Put back a <code>Card</code> at the bottom of the <code>Deck</code>.
     *
     *  @param card <code>Card</code> object being put back
     */

    public void putBack(Card card)
    {
        deck.add(card);
    }

    /**
     *  Shuffle the <code>Deck</code>.
     */

    public void shuffle()
    {
        Collections.shuffle(deck);
    }
}
```

Deck initializes a private cards array to all 52 Card objects. Because it's easier to implement Deck via a list that stores these objects, Deck's constructor creates this list and adds each Card object to the list. (I discussed List and ArrayList in Chapter 9.)

Deck also provides deal(), isEmpty(), putBack(), and shuffle() methods to deal a single Card from the Deck (the Card is physically removed from the Deck), determine whether or not the Deck is empty, put a Card back into the Deck, and shuffle the Deck's Cards.

Listing B-5 presents the source code to the DiscardPile class, which implements a discard pile on which players can throw away a maximum of 52 cards.

Listing B-5. A Garbage Dump for Cards

```java
import java.util.ArrayList;
import java.util.List;

/**
 *  Simulate a pile of discarded cards.
 *
 *  @author Jeff Friesen
 */

public class DiscardPile
{
   private Card[] cards;
   private int top;

   /**
    *  Create a <code>DiscardPile</code> that can accommodate a maximum of 52
    *  <code>Card</code>s. The <code>DiscardPile</code> is initially empty.
    */

   public DiscardPile()
   {
      cards = new Card[52]; // Room for entire deck on discard pile (should
                            // never happen).
      top = -1;
   }

   /**
    *  Return the <code>Card</code> at the top of the <code>DiscardPile</code>.
    *
    *  @return <code>Card</code> object at top of <code>DiscardPile</code> or
    *  null if <code>DiscardPile</code> is empty
    */

   public Card getTopCard()
   {
      if (top == -1)
         return null;
      Card card = cards[top];
      cards[top--] = null;
      return card;
   }

   /**
    *  Set the <code>DiscardPile</code>'s top card to the specified
    *  <code>Card</code> object.
    *
    *  @param card <code>Card</code> object being thrown on top of the
    *  <code>DiscardPile</code>
    */
```

```
    public void setTopCard(Card card)
    {
        cards[++top] = card;
    }

    /**
     *  Identify the top <code>Card</code> on the <code>DiscardPile</code>
     *  without removing this <code>Card</code>.
     *
     *  @return top <code>Card</code>, or null if <code>DiscardPile</code> is
     *  empty
     */

    public Card topCard()
    {
        return (top == -1) ? null : cards[top];
    }
}
```

DiscardPile implements a discard pile on which to throw Card objects. It implements the discard pile via a stack metaphor: the last Card object thrown on the pile sits at the top of the pile and is the first Card object to be removed from the pile.

This class stores its stack of Card objects in a private cards array. I found it convenient to specify 52 as this array's storage limit because the maximum number of Cards is 52. (Game play will never result in all Cards being stored in the array.)

Along with its constructor, DiscardPile provides getTopCard(), setTopCard(), and topCard() methods to remove and return the stack's top Card, store a new Card object on the stack as its top Card, and return the top Card without removing it from the stack.

The constructor demonstrates a single-line comment, which starts with the // character sequence. This comment documents that the cards array has room to store the entire Deck of Cards. I formally introduced single-line comments in Chapter 2.

The second step in converting Listing B-2's pseudocode to Java involves introducing a FourOfAKind class whose main() method contains the Java code equivalent of this pseudocode. Listing B-6 presents FourOfAKind.

Listing B-6. FourOfAKind Application Source Code

```
/**
 *  <code>FourOfAKind</code> implements a card game that is played between two
 *  players: one human player and the computer. You play this game with a
 *  standard 52-card deck and attempt to beat the computer by being the first
 *  player to put down four cards that have the same rank (four aces, for
 *  example), and win.
 *
 *  <p>
 *  The game begins by shuffling the deck and placing it face down. Each
 *  player takes a card from the top of the deck. The player with the highest
 *  ranked card (king is highest) deals four cards to each player starting
```

```
 *   with the other player. The dealer then starts its turn.
 *
 *   <p>
 *   The player examines its cards to determine which cards are optimal for
 *   achieving four of a kind. The player then throws away one card on a
 *   discard pile and picks up another card from the top of the deck. If the
 *   player has four of a kind, the player puts down these cards (face up) and
 *   wins the game.
 *
 *   @author Jeff Friesen
 *   @version 1.0
 */

public class FourOfAKind
{
   /**
    *  Human player
    */

   final static int HUMAN = 0;

   /**
    *  Computer player
    */

   final static int COMPUTER = 1;

   /**
    *  Application entry point.
    *
    *  @param args array of command-line arguments passed to this method
    */

   public static void main(String[] args)
   {
      System.out.println("Welcome to Four of a Kind!");
      Deck deck = new Deck(); // Deck automatically shuffled
      DiscardPile discardPile = new DiscardPile();
      Card hCard;
      Card cCard;
      while (true)
      {
         hCard = deck.deal();
         cCard = deck.deal();
         if (hCard.rank() != cCard.rank())
            break;
         deck.putBack(hCard);
         deck.putBack(cCard);
         deck.shuffle(); // prevent pathological case where every successive
      }                  // pair of cards have the same rank
      int curPlayer = HUMAN;
      if (cCard.rank().ordinal() > hCard.rank().ordinal())
```

```
      curPlayer = COMPUTER;
deck.putBack(hCard);
hCard = null;
deck.putBack(cCard);
cCard = null;
Card[] hCards = new Card[4];
Card[] cCards = new Card[4];
if (curPlayer == HUMAN)
   for (int i = 0; i < 4; i++)
   {
      cCards[i] = deck.deal();
      hCards[i] = deck.deal();
   }
else
   for (int i = 0; i < 4; i++)
   {
      hCards[i] = deck.deal();
      cCards[i] = deck.deal();
   }
while (true)
{
   if (curPlayer == HUMAN)
   {
      showHeldCards(hCards);
      int choice = 0;
      while (choice < 'A' || choice > 'D')
      {
         choice = prompt("Which card do you want to throw away (A, B, " +
                         "C, D)? ");
         switch (choice)
         {
            case 'a': choice = 'A'; break;
            case 'b': choice = 'B'; break;
            case 'c': choice = 'C'; break;
            case 'd': choice = 'D';
         }
      }
      discardPile.setTopCard(hCards[choice - 'A']);
      hCards[choice - 'A'] = deck.deal();
      if (isFourOfAKind(hCards))
      {
         System.out.println();
         System.out.println("Human wins!");
         System.out.println();
         putDown("Human's cards:", hCards);
         System.out.println();
         putDown("Computer's cards:", cCards);
         return; // Exit application by returning from main()
      }
      curPlayer = COMPUTER;
   }
```

```
        else
        {
            int choice = leastDesirableCard(cCards);
            discardPile.setTopCard(cCards[choice]);
            cCards[choice] = deck.deal();
            if (isFourOfAKind(cCards))
            {
                System.out.println();
                System.out.println("Computer wins!");
                System.out.println();
                putDown("Computer's cards:", cCards);
                return; // Exit application by returning from main()
            }
            curPlayer = HUMAN;
        }
        if (deck.isEmpty())
        {
            while (discardPile.topCard() != null)
                deck.putBack(discardPile.getTopCard());
            deck.shuffle();
        }
    }
}

/**
 *  Determine if the <code>Card</code> objects passed to this method all
 *  have the same rank.
 *
 *  @param cards array of <code>Card</code> objects passed to this method
 *
 *  @return true if all <code>Card</code> objects have the same rank;
 *  otherwise, false
 */

static boolean isFourOfAKind(Card[] cards)
{
    for (int i = 1; i < cards.length; i++)
        if (cards[i].rank() != cards[0].rank())
            return false;
    return true;
}

/**
 *  Identify one of the <code>Card</code> objects that is passed to this
 *  method as the least desirable <code>Card</code> object to hold onto.
 *
 *  @param cards array of <code>Card</code> objects passed to this method
 *
 *  @return 0-based rank (ace is 0, king is 13) of least desirable card
 */
```

```java
static int leastDesirableCard(Card[] cards)
{
    int[] rankCounts = new int[13];
    for (int i = 0; i < cards.length; i++)
        rankCounts[cards[i].rank().ordinal()]++;
    int minCount = Integer.MAX_VALUE;
    int minIndex = -1;
    for (int i = 0; i < rankCounts.length; i++)
        if (rankCounts[i] < minCount && rankCounts[i] != 0)
        {
            minCount = rankCounts[i];
            minIndex = i;
        }
    for (int i = 0; i < cards.length; i++)
        if (cards[i].rank().ordinal() == minIndex)
            return i;
    return 0; // Needed to satisfy compiler (should never be executed)
}

/**
 *  Prompt the human player to enter a character.
 *
 *  @param msg message to be displayed to human player
 *
 *  @return integer value of character entered by user.
 */

static int prompt(String msg)
{
    System.out.print(msg);
    try
    {
        int ch = System.in.read();
        // Erase all subsequent characters including terminating \n newline
        // so that they do not affect a subsequent call to prompt().
        while (System.in.read() != '\n');
        return ch;
    }
    catch (java.io.IOException ioe)
    {
    }
    return 0;
}

/**
 *  Display a message followed by all cards held by player. This output
 *  simulates putting down held cards.
 *
 *  @param msg message to be displayed to human player
 *  @param cards array of <code>Card</code> objects to be identified
 */
```

```
static void putDown(String msg, Card[] cards)
{
    System.out.println(msg);
    for (int i = 0; i < cards.length; i++)
        System.out.println(cards[i]);
}

/**
 *  Identify the cards being held via their <code>Card</code> objects on
 *  separate lines. Prefix each line with an uppercase letter starting with
 *  <code>A</code>.
 *
 *  @param cards array of <code>Card</code> objects to be identified
 */

static void showHeldCards(Card[] cards)
{
    System.out.println();
    System.out.println("Held cards:");
    for (int i = 0; i < cards.length; i++)
        if (cards[i] != null)
            System.out.println((char) ('A' + i) + ". " + cards[i]);
    System.out.println();
}
}
```

Listing B-6 follows the steps outlined by and expands on Listing B-2's pseudocode. Because of the various comments, I don't have much to say about this listing. However, there are a couple of items that deserve mention:

■ Card's nested Rank enum stores a sequence of 13 Rank objects beginning with ACE and ending with KING. These objects cannot be compared directly via > to determine which object has the greater rank. However, their integer-based ordinal (positional) values can be compared by calling the Rank object's ordinal() method. For example, Card.ACE_OF_SPADES.rank().ordinal() returns 0 because ACE is located at position 0 within Rank's list of Rank objects, and Card.KING_OF_CLUBS.rank().ordinal() returns 12 because KING is located at the last position in this list.

■ The leastDesirableCard() method counts the ranks of the Cards in the array of four Card objects passed to this method and stores these counts in a rankCounts array. For example, given two of clubs, ace of spades, three of clubs, and ace of diamonds in the array passed to this method, rankCounts identifies one two, two aces, and one three. This method then searches rankCounts from smallest index (representing ace) to largest index (representing king) for the first smallest nonzero count (there might be a tie, as in one two and one three)—a zero count represents no Cards having that rank in the array of Card objects. Finally, the method searches the array of Card objects to identify the object whose rank ordinal matches the index of the smallest nonzero count and returns the index of this Card object. This behavior implies that the least desirable card is always the smallest ranked card. For example, given two of spades, three of diamonds, five of spades, and nine of clubs, two of spades is least desirable because it has the smallest rank.

Also, when there are multiple cards of the same rank, and when this rank is smaller than the rank of any other card in the array, this method will choose the first (in a left-to-right manner) of the multiple cards having the same rank as the least desirable card. For example, given (in this order) two of spades, two of hearts, three of diamonds, and jack of hearts, two of spades is least desirable because it's the first card with the smallest rank. However, when the rank of the multiple cards isn't the smallest, another card with the smallest rank is chosen as least desirable.

The JDK provides a `javadoc` tool that extracts all Javadoc comments from one or more source files and generates a set of HTML files containing this documentation in an easy-to-read format. These files serve as the program's documentation.

For example, suppose that the current directory contains `Card.java`, `Deck.java`, `DiscardPile.java`, and `FourOfAKind.java`. To extract all of the Javadoc comments that appear in these files, specify the following command:

```
javadoc *.java
```

The `javadoc` tool responds by outputting the following messages:

```
Loading source file Card.java...
Loading source file Deck.java...
Loading source file DiscardPile.java...
Loading source file FourOfAKind.java...
Constructing Javadoc information...
Standard Doclet version 1.7.0_06
Building tree for all the packages and classes...
Generating \Card.html...
Generating \Card.Rank.html...
Generating \Card.Suit.html...
Generating \Deck.html...
Generating \DiscardPile.html...
Generating \FourOfAKind.html...
Generating \package-frame.html...
Generating \package-summary.html...
Generating \package-tree.html...
Generating \constant-values.html...
Building index for all the packages and classes...
Generating \overview-tree.html...
Generating \index-all.html...
Generating \deprecated-list.html...
Building index for all classes...
Generating \allclasses-frame.html...
Generating \allclasses-noframe.html...
Generating \index.html...
Generating \help-doc.html...
```

Furthermore, it generates a series of files, including the `index.html` entry-point file. If you point your web browser to this file, you should see a page that is similar to the page shown in Figure B-1.

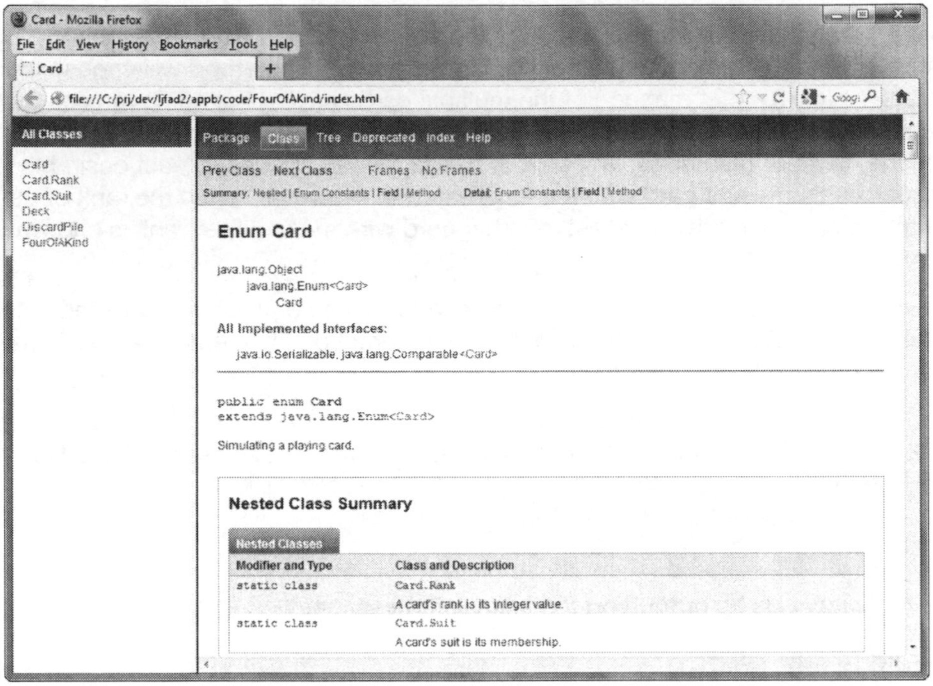

Figure B-1. Viewing the entry-point page in the generated Javadoc for FourOfAKind and supporting classes

javadoc defaults to generating HTML-based documentation for public classes and public/protected members of classes. You learned about public classes and public/protected members of classes in Chapter 3.

For this reason, FourOfAKind's documentation reveals only the public `main()` method. It doesn't reveal `isFourOfAKind()` and the other package-private methods. If you want to include these methods in the documentation, you must specify `-package` with `javadoc`:

```
javadoc -package *.java
```

Note The standard class library's documentation from Oracle was also generated by `javadoc` and adheres to the same format.

Compiling, Running, and Distributing FourOfAKind

Unlike Chapter 1's DumpArgs and EchoText applications, which each consist of one source file, FourOfAKind consists of Card.java, Deck.java, DiscardPile.java, and FourOfAKind.java. You can compile all four source files via the following command line:

```
javac FourOfAKind.java
```

The javac tool launches the Java compiler, which recursively compiles the source files of the various classes it encounters during compilation. Assuming successful compilation, you should end up with six classfiles in the current directory.

> **Tip**   You can compile all Java source files in the current directory by specifying javac *.java.

After successfully compiling FourOfAKind.java and the other three source files, specify the following command line to run this application:

```
java FourOfAKind
```

In response, you see an introductory message and the four cards that you are holding. The following output reveals a single session:

```
Welcome to Four of a Kind!

Held cards:
A. SIX_OF_CLUBS
B. QUEEN_OF_DIAMONDS
C. SIX_OF_HEARTS
D. SIX_OF_SPADES

Which card do you want to throw away (A, B, C, D)? B

Held cards:
A. SIX_OF_CLUBS
B. NINE_OF_HEARTS
C. SIX_OF_HEARTS
D. SIX_OF_SPADES

Which card do you want to throw away (A, B, C, D)? B

Held cards:
A. SIX_OF_CLUBS
B. FOUR_OF_DIAMONDS
C. SIX_OF_HEARTS
D. SIX_OF_SPADES
```

Which card do you want to throw away (A, B, C, D)? B

Held cards:
A. SIX_OF_CLUBS
B. KING_OF_HEARTS
C. SIX_OF_HEARTS
D. SIX_OF_SPADES

Which card do you want to throw away (A, B, C, D)? B

Held cards:
A. SIX_OF_CLUBS
B. QUEEN_OF_CLUBS
C. SIX_OF_HEARTS
D. SIX_OF_SPADES

Which card do you want to throw away (A, B, C, D)? B

Held cards:
A. SIX_OF_CLUBS
B. KING_OF_DIAMONDS
C. SIX_OF_HEARTS
D. SIX_OF_SPADES

Which card do you want to throw away (A, B, C, D)? B

Held cards:
A. SIX_OF_CLUBS
B. TWO_OF_HEARTS
C. SIX_OF_HEARTS
D. SIX_OF_SPADES

Which card do you want to throw away (A, B, C, D)? B

Held cards:
A. SIX_OF_CLUBS
B. FIVE_OF_DIAMONDS
C. SIX_OF_HEARTS
D. SIX_OF_SPADES

Which card do you want to throw away (A, B, C, D)? B

Held cards:
A. SIX_OF_CLUBS
B. JACK_OF_CLUBS
C. SIX_OF_HEARTS
D. SIX_OF_SPADES

Which card do you want to throw away (A, B, C, D)? B

Held cards:
A. SIX_OF_CLUBS
B. TWO_OF_SPADES
C. SIX_OF_HEARTS
D. SIX_OF_SPADES

Which card do you want to throw away (A, B, C, D)? B

Human wins!

Human's cards:
SIX_OF_CLUBS
SIX_OF_DIAMONDS
SIX_OF_HEARTS
SIX_OF_SPADES

Computer's cards:
SEVEN_OF_HEARTS
TEN_OF_HEARTS
SEVEN_OF_CLUBS
SEVEN_OF_DIAMONDS

Although *Four of a Kind* isn't much of a card game, you might decide to share the FourOfAKind application with a friend. However, if you forget to include even one of the application's five supporting classfiles, your friend will not be able to run the application.

You can overcome this problem by bundling FourOfAKind's six classfiles into a single *JAR* (Java ARchive) file, which is a ZIP file that contains a special directory and the .jar file extension. You can then distribute this single JAR file to your friend.

The JDK provides the jar tool for working with JAR files. To bundle all six classfiles into a JAR file named FourOfAKind.jar, you could specify the following command line, where c tells jar to create a JAR file and f identifies the JAR file's name:

```
jar cf FourOfAKind.jar *.class
```

After creating the JAR file, try to run the application via the following command line:

```
java -jar FourOfAKind.jar
```

Instead of the application running, you'll receive an error message having to do with the java application launcher tool not knowing which of the JAR file's six classfiles is the *main classfile* (the file whose class's main() method executes first).

You can provide this knowledge via a text file that's merged into the JAR file's *manifest*, a special file named MANIFEST.MF that stores information about the contents of a JAR file and is stored in the JAR file's META-INF directory. Consider Listing B-7.

Listing B-7. Identifying the Application's Main Class

```
Main-Class: FourOfAKind
```

Listing B-7 tells java which of the JAR's classfiles is the main classfile. (You must leave a blank line after `Main-Class: FourOfAKind`.)

The following command line, which creates `FourOfAKind.jar`, includes m and the name of the text field providing manifest content:

```
jar cfm FourOfAKind.jar manifest *.class
```

This time, java `-jar FourOfAKind.jar` succeeds and the application runs because java is able to identify `FourOfAKind` as the main classfile.

> **Note**   Now that you've finished this book, you're ready to dig into Android app development. Check out Apress's *Beginning Android* and *Android Recipes* books for guidance. After you've learned some app development basics, perhaps you might consider transforming *Four of a Kind* into an Android app.

Index

◼ D

E